P9-CPY-349

#64467-1

NEW READINGS IN THE VERCELLI BOOK

New Readings
in the Vercelli Book

Edited by Samantha Zacher
and Andy Orchard

UNIVERSITY OF TORONTO PRESS
Toronto Buffalo London

© University of Toronto Press Incorporated 2009
Toronto Buffalo London
www.utppublishing.com
Printed in Canada

ISBN 978-0-8020-9869-6 (cloth)

Printed on acid-free, 100% post-consumer recycled paper with vegetable-based inks

---

Library and Archives Canada Cataloguing in Publication

New readings in the Vercelli book / edited by Samantha Zacher and
Andy Orchard.

(Toronto Anglo-Saxon series)
Includes bibliographical references and index.
ISBN 978-0-8020-9869-6

1. English literature – Old English, ca. 450–1100 – Criticism, Textual.
2. Vercelli book.   I. Zacher, Samantha, 1973–   II. Orchard, Andy
III. Series: Toronto Anglo-Saxon series

PR1495.N49 2009   829.09   C2009-903614-2

University of Toronto Press gratefully acknowledges the financial assistance
of the Centre for Medieval Studies, University of Toronto in the publication
of this book.

University of Toronto Press acknowledges the financial assistance to its publishing program of the Canada Council for the Arts and the Ontario Arts Council.

 Canada Council   Conseil des Arts   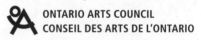 ONTARIO ARTS COUNCIL
for the Arts   du Canada   CONSEIL DES ARTS DE L'ONTARIO

University of Toronto Press acknowledges the financial support for its publishing activities of the Government of Canada through the Book Publishing
Industry Development Program (BPIDP).

Contents

Abbreviations

ACMRS	Arizona Center for Medieval and Renaissance Studies
ANQ	(formerly) *American Notes and Queries*
ASE	*Anglo-Saxon England*
ASMMF	Anglo-Saxon Manuscripts in Microfiche Facsimile
ASNSL	*Archiv für das Studium der neueren Sprachen und Literaturen*
ASPR	G.P. Krapp and E.V.K. Dobbie, eds., The Anglo-Saxon Poetic Records, 6 vols. (New York: Columbia UP, 1931–42)
BCLL	Michael Lapidge and Richard Sharpe, eds., *A Bibliography of Celtic-Latin Literature 400–1200* (Dublin: RIA, 1985)
BGDSL	*Beiträge zur Geschichte der deutschen Sprache und Literatur*
BH	*The Blickling Homilies*, ed. R. Morris, EETS o.s. 58, 63, and 73 (Oxford: OUP, repr. 1967)
BJRL	*Bulletin of the John Rylands Library*
BL	British Library
CCCC	Cambridge, Corpus Christi College
CCCM	Corpus Christianorum, Continuatio Medievalis
CCSL	Corpus Christianorum, Series Latina
CH	*Ælfric's 'Catholic Homilies*,' ed. Peter Clemoes and Malcolm Godden, 3 vols., EETS s.s. 5, 17–18 (Oxford: OUP, 1979–2000). Vol. 1: *The First Series. Text*, ed. Clemoes, 1997. Vol. 2: *The Second Series. Text*, ed. Godden, 1979. Vol. 3: *Introduction, Commentary, and Glossary*, ed. Godden, 2000.

CPG	*Clavis Patrum Graecorum: Supplementum*, ed. M. Geerard and J. Noret (Turnhout: Brepols, 1998)
CSASE	Cambridge Studies in Anglo-Saxon England
CSEL	Corpus Scriptorum Ecclesiasticorum Latinorum
CUL	Cambridge, University Library
CUP	Cambridge University Press
DIAS	Dublin Institute for Advanced Studies
DOE	*Dictionary of Old English: A to G* online, ed. Angus Cameron, Ashley Crandell Amos, Antonette diPaolo Healey et al. (Toronto: Dictionary of Old English Project, 2007)
EEMF	Early English Manuscripts in Facsimile
EETS	Early English Text Society
o.s.	old series
s.s.	supplementary series
ELN	*English Language Notes*
EME	*Early Medieval Europe*
ES	*English Studies*
Gneuss, Handlist	Helmut Gneuss, *Handlist of Anglo-Saxon Manuscripts: A List of Manuscripts and Manuscripts Fragments Written or Owned in England up to 1100* (Tempe: ACMRS, 2001)
JEGP	(formerly) *Journal of English and Germanic Philology*
JMLat	*Journal of Medieval Latin*
JTS	*Journal of Theological Studies*
Ker, *Catalogue*	N.R. Ker, *Catalogue of Manuscripts Containing Anglo-Saxon* (Oxford: Clarendon, 1990)
LS	*Ælfric's Lives of Saints*, ed. W.W. Skeat, EETS o.s. 76, 82, 94, and 114, 2 vols. (Oxford: OUP, 1881–1900; repr. 1966)
LSE	*Leeds Studies in English and Kindred Languages*
MÆ	*Medium Ævum*
MGH	Monumenta Germaniae Historica
AA	Auctores Antiquissimi
Ep.	Epistulae Carolini Aevi
ES	Epistolae Selectae
SRG	Scriptores Rerum Germanicarum
SRM	Scriptores Rerum Merovinigicarum
MLN	*Modern Language Notes*
MLR	*Modern Language Review*

MP	*Modern Philology*
MRTS	Medieval and Renaissance Texts and Studies
NM	*Neuphilologische Mitteilungen*
NPNF	*Nicene and Post-Nicene Fathers*, Series II, ed. Philip Schaff (Peabody, MA: Hendrickson Publishers, 1994)
NQ	*Notes and Queries*
OEN	*Old English Newsletter*
OUP	Oxford University Press
PBA	*Proceedings of the British Acaemy*
PG	Patrologia Graeca, ed., J.P. Migne, 162 vols. (Paris, 1857–66)
PIMS	Pontifical Institute for Mediaeval Studies
PL	Patrologia Latina, ed., J.P. Migne, 221 vols. (Paris, 1844–64)
PLL	*Papers on Language and Literature*
PMLA	*Publications of the Modern Language Association*
PQ	*Philological Quarterly*
RES	*Review of English Studies*
SN	*Studia Neophilologica*
SUNY	State University of New York
TASS	Toronto Anglo-Saxon Studies
TOES	Toronto Old English Series
UTP	University of Toronto Press
VH	*The Vercelli Homilies and Related Texts*, ed. D.G. Scragg, EETS o.s. 300 (Oxford: OUP, 1992)
WH	*The Homilies of Wulfstan*, ed. Dorothy Bethurum (Oxford: The Clarendon Press, 1957)
YWES	*Year's Work in English Studies*

NEW READINGS IN THE VERCELLI BOOK

Introduction

SAMANTHA ZACHER AND ANDY ORCHARD

The Cathedral Library of Vercelli in Northern Italy contains a rather plain codex (Vercelli, Biblioteca Capitolare CXVII), of a size slightly narrower and longer than modern A4 paper, and which in its current state comprises only 135 folios of the original fine thin parchment. The so-called Vercelli Book, written in a bold, firm hand, apparently by a single Anglo-Saxon scribe at some time during the middle of the second half of the tenth century, is in a very good state of preservation, and seems to have been little read, at least in its current location; if a single scribble attests that the book was in Italy by the twelfth century, the nineteenth-century calf binding that currently covers the medieval boards nonetheless features a rather depressing title: 'HOMILIARUM LIBER IGNOTI IDIOMATIS' ('A BOOK OF HOMILIES IN AN UNKNOWN IDIOM'). The 'unknown idiom' is of course Old English, and the book itself contains not only homilies, but texts on a range of topics in both prose and verse (and indeed in a mixture of both prose and verse), mostly either unattested elsewhere, or in those cases where there is some degree of overlap with existing texts, in for the most part significantly variant versions.

The texts themselves comprise some six poems and twenty-three so-called homilies, although other genres are also witnessed; it is unfortunate that the prose and verse texts (as so designated) have been edited and largely treated separately by modern scholars, so obscuring the clearly conscious juxtaposition of the two within the Vercelli Book itself (a mix this collection seeks to emulate). Despite its relatively early date of composition, the Vercelli Book was the latest of the four major Old English poetic codices to be brought to the attention of modern readers, and by comparison with the damaged or incomplete state of the other three main poetic codices (the *Beowulf*-manuscript has been harmed by fire, the Exeter

Book by fire and blade, and the Junius manuscript has blank spaces where illustrations should be) seems to have had the most tranquil transmission to modern times. Indeed, the most serious damage, apart from a loss of individual folios, seems to have been the result of misplaced modern zeal, when a corrosive reagent was applied to parts of the manuscript ostensibly to aid legibility, and has had the opposite effect today.

The fact that the book left Anglo-Saxon England certainly seems to have aided its survival, as well as fuelling speculation as to how the book might have reached its current home. Since Vercelli was throughout the early Middle Ages a major staging-post on the pilgrim route to Rome, the simplest explanation seems to be that the book was left behind (either as a gift or as a relic) by some presumably wealthy Anglo-Saxon en route to or from Rome, although other views persist. The original purpose of the compiler (if the single scribe can be so called) has again escaped scholarly consensus, with sharply differing views on the extent to which the collection as a whole can be viewed as having been planned, and on its purpose as a book for public performance or private devotion.

Certainly, however, given the extensive overlap in broad terms that has been detected between the contents of the Vercelli Book and other existing texts and collections that have survived from the period, it does seem that the manuscript can be regarded as a kind of florilegium or collection of more-or-less popular selected items. Modern research has identified more than two dozen manuscripts which contain texts or parts of texts with material in common with the twenty-three so-called *Vercelli Homilies*, even if none of those manuscripts can be shown to derive directly from the Vercelli Book itself. Likewise, all but one of the six poems in the Vercelli Book can be connected to a greater or lesser extent with other Old English verse preserved elsewhere:[1] the two signed poems by Cynewulf in the Vercelli Book (*Fates of the Apostles* and *Elene*) can be matched by two further signed poems by Cynewulf (*Christ II* and *Juliana*) in the Exeter Book, a manuscript that also contains in the form of *Soul and Body II* a variant version of the Vercelli Book's *Soul and Body I*; the many parallels of form and formula that connect *Andreas* not only to the signed poems of Cynewulf but also to the text of *Beowulf* have been amply documented;[2]

---

1 The exception is *Homiletic Fragment I*, on which see Jonathan Randle's paper below, 185–224.
2 See especially Alison M. Powell, 'Verbal Parallels in *Andreas* and Its Relationship to *Beowulf* and Cynewulf' (unpub. PhD diss., Univ. of Cambridge, 2002).

and the parallels that connect *The Dream of the Rood* to a range of Anglo-Saxon texts and monuments is examined within this collection.[3]

Clearly then, the cultural and physical isolation of the Vercelli Book from its homeland for some seven centuries is not reflected in its eclectic contents, which exhibits a range of literary connections beyond the manuscript itself that would otherwise have been lost or obscured. Indeed, the twin value of the Vercelli Book lies in the fact that it is one of the earliest manuscripts to contain substantial amounts of Old English verse, and that it bears crucial witness to the state of vernacular preaching before its later flowering under Ælfric and Wulfstan.[4] Moreover, recent studies have outlined the ways in which later preachers and poets seem to have drawn on that same wellspring of an earlier vernacular tradition from which the Vercelli Book so clearly derives.[5] As a manuscript that crosses and has crossed a number of temporal, generic, and literary boundaries, the Vercelli Book seems ripe for reading anew.

The essays in this volume, which generally shadow the interleaved order of prose and verse in the Vercelli Book itself, are offered here not only to demonstrate the kinds of new readings in the Vercelli Book that recent scholarship has made possible, but also to stimulate further research. Despite its long-term physical separation from Anglo-Saxon England, and its often unique readings and texts, the book can be situated securely within the wider context of Anglo-Saxon literature and learning, and it is these connections, both within and beyond the Vercelli Book, that the papers presented here seek to explore.

Paul Szarmach offers a magisterial overview of the homiletic styles witnessed in the Vercelli Book. As well as providing a summary of the main styles in the collection, Szarmach underscores the still inadequate vocabulary available for describing Old English prose, as opposed to the rich language at hand for the parallel poetic tradition. Revisiting the classical

---

3 See the paper by Andy Orchard below, 225–53.

4 For a concise discussion of the importance of the Vercelli Book in Anglo-Saxon studies, see Donald G. Scragg, 'The Significance of the Vercelli Book among Anglo-Saxon Vernacular Writings,' in *Vercelli tra Oriente ed Occidente tra Tarda Antichita e Medioevo*, ed. Vittoria Dolcetti Corazza (Vercelli: Edizioni dell'Orso, 1997), 35–43.

5 For the prose, see Donald Scragg, *Dating and Style in Old English Composite Homilies*, H.M. Chadwick Memorial Lectures 9 (Cambridge: Department of Anglo-Saxon, Norse, and Celtic, 1998); for the verse, see Andy Orchard, *The Poetic Craft of Cynewulf*, CSASE (Cambridge: CUP, forthcoming); for the influence of the vernacular poetic tradition on the *Vercelli Homilies*, see Samantha Zacher, *Preaching the Converted: Anglo-Saxon Style and Rhetoric in the Vercelli Homilies*, TASS (Toronto: UTP, 2009).

distinction between 'Asian' and 'attic' styles, Szarmach asks us to think beyond the bland and reductive classifications of exegetical and catechetical prose that have become ensconced in the scholar's vocabulary. Szarmach likewise ponders the scant history dedicated to the literary study of the Vercelli homilies on their own terms. Though it is often presumed that the Vercelli homilies are a primitive cousin to the skilful prose stylings of Ælfric and Wulfstan, Szarmach powerfully lays to rest this prejudice, showing the extent to which these and later homilists drew from the structure, rhythm, and themes of the early anonymous collections. And though Szarmach points out that many such details are surely absorbed and developed from Latin sources, he demonstrates that 'not all vernacular prose is a mere palimpsest of Latin.' Szarmach concludes that 'as a collection, the Vercelli prose is a summary of the options for prose style.'

Donald Scragg draws on the conclusions he reached in his monumental edition of the Vercelli homilies to offer some new thoughts about the language of the homilies in the Vercelli Book and that of their later copyists. Beginning with the contention that we still know little about the differences between the early and late West-Saxon dialects, Scragg attempts to close this gap by surveying the relatively small number of manuscripts that contain copies of the Vercelli homilies. Scragg's project is helped by the fact that in every case the Vercelli Book presents the earliest extant witness, and also by the fact that most of the copy-texts appear to originate in Kent. While the Vercelli scribe tended to follow the language of his exemplars, making analysis of the scribe's own identity somewhat complex, Scragg looks at examples in later copies where the language is normalized to suit the spelling and sometimes the dialect of the scribe. Scragg leaves us with a potent recommendation that we stop trusting in the analysis of dialect as the only measure for 'distinguishing between the writing habits of different areas or different scribes.'

Thomas N. Hall's essay takes on the vexed question of the relationship between the sometimes overlapping catalogues of portents for Christ's birth, as shown in the Christmas homilies Vercelli V and VI, as well of versions of the same portents found in the so-called *Catechesis celtica* (which served as a 'medium for the transition of material known to the author of Vercelli V'), and a host of other newly discovered analogues in medieval sermons and biblical commentaries. Hall's meticulous survey of these parallels offers a fresh account of the development of these catalogues up through the Anglo-Saxon period, and in some cases offers compelling theories concerning the direction of transmission. Though Hall is careful to avoid talking about 'sources' for the Vercelli homilies, he offers a persuasive nexus that links the

Vercelli homilies once again (however inexactly) to both the relevant materials in the St Père homiliary, most fully witnessed in Cambridge, Pembroke 25 (which James E. Cross and Donald G. Scragg have shown to serve as a source for several of the Vercelli homilies) and to the *Catechesis celtica*, which underlies parts of the St Père homiliary. Hall's findings reinforce the perception that the Vercelli homilies drew widely from a range of ultimate sources that far exceed the expectation of scholars who first worked on the collection.

Samantha Zacher establishes the hitherto unknown source for Vercelli Homily VII, namely, a sixth-century Latin translation of a Greek homily by John Chrysostom. This discovery helps both to suggest new emendations to the text and to highlight the choices, changes, and additions introduced by the Anglo-Saxon author. The analysis not only provides the fullest evidence to date for Chrysostom's influence on the Old English homiletic tradition, but also presents wider implications for the, in this case, likely indirect study of Greek patristic writings in Anglo-Saxon England, so supplementing the work of such scholars as Bernhard Bischoff and Michael Lapidge on those Greek texts imported by Archbishop Theodore into Anglo-Saxon England at the end of the seventh century. In the context of the Vercelli Book itself, the finding also presents a new spin on the question of the 'audience' of the homilies. While the focus to date has rested largely on the supposed religious context for which the collection may have been used (with the latest suggestion by Wright being a secular clerical audience), Vercelli VII's address to women further vexes the question: either we may suppose that the address implies a 'live' female audience, or else it may present a fossilization of an exhortation aimed originally at women in fourth-century Alexandria.

Charles D. Wright offers a much anticipated sequel to his previous study that isolates three main versions of the *Apocalypse of Thomas*, and newly identifies 'six previously unknown or neglected Latin texts' of the same. In the present essay, Wright examines the connection between Vercelli XV, the earliest extant Old English witness to the *Apocalypse*, and the various known Latin versions. Wright is able to isolate the version upon which the Vercelli texts depends, giving us a far more sharp picture of the types of sources consulted by the homilist. Additionally, by focusing on the changes likely made by the homilist himself to the Latin material he consulted, Wright is able to speculate boldly about what these changes can tell us about the political and religious climate in which the homily was written, and (though more cautiously here) by virtue of the text's inclusion in the Vercelli Book, about the collection as a whole. Wright's work (here and elsewhere) on the question of audience is suggestive in challenging us to see the Vercelli Book as a response (not as has sometimes been thought, as a precursor) to the Benedictine Reform.

Jonathan Randle, echoing Szarmach, turns to an analysis of the style and rhetoric of *Homiletic Fragment I*, easily the least studied of the Vercelli Book poems. Although, as the title suggests, the poem has been classified loosely as being 'homiletic,' Randle tests this nomenclature by investigating the poem's diction, themes, use of exhortation, and metre. Though the structure of this 'fragment' has often proved to be elusive to editors and scholars, Randle's in-depth reading of the poem's expressed themes of (for example) deceit, repentance, and death, together with his attention to patristic analogues for the poet's central metaphor of the bees, shows a unity of subject and rhetorical structure. By drawing on the wisdom poems of the Exeter Book, and also other prose homilies in a variety of corpora (including notably the Blickling homilies and the works of Ælfric and Wulfstan), Randle argues that the poem *Homiletic Fragment I* is perhaps best seen to straddle these discourses.

Andy Orchard explores a range of analogues for *The Dream of the Rood* both within and beyond the Vercelli Book, in order to illuminate further the disparate themes and rhetorical devices of the poem. Orchard begins by showing verbal and thematic parallels between *The Dream of the Rood* and the Old English and Latin riddle tradition, showing how the poet's use of prosopopoeia serves to align homiletic and secular poetic influences in the text. Orchard builds from here by comparing *The Dream of the Rood* with the variant portions of parallel text on the Ruthwell Cross, highlighting the way in which the Vercelli poet collapses point of view to allow association between the experiences of the dreamer, the cross, and Christ himself. The analysis then moves outward to a consideration of analogues in the wider corpus of Old English, suggesting closer verbal parallels with such poems as *Daniel, Elene,* and *Andreas* than have been previously noted. These parallels allow Orchard to speculate with greater authority than has hitherto been possible on some potential directions of borrowing between these poems. Orchard's panoply of resonances builds towards a view of the cross that seems on the one hand distinctly Anglo-Saxon, and on the other deeply appreciative of the individual artistry of the poet.

Michael Fox turns to the second series of Rogationtide homilies in the Vercelli Book in *Vercelli Homilies* XIX–XXI. Building on the previous work of Szarmach and Cross, who demonstrated thematic connections between the homilies (and several others outside the Vercelli collection), and that of Scragg, who argued for common authorship for the three homilies, Fox pushes still further the question of shared themes and messages of exhortation in all three Vercelli homilies. Using Virginia Day's notion of the catechetical *narratio* as derived from Augustine's *De catechizandis rudibus*, Fox applies this idea of the wide-sweeping creation narrative as a principle of design that unites all three homilies in progression. Fox takes this notion of influence one step further, showing that although there is scant evidence for knowledge of Augustine's text in Anglo-Saxon authors, other intermediary authors like Martin of Braga and Pirmin are perhaps more directly responsible for the popularization of this literary model in Anglo-Saxon England. Fox's work helps us to reorient the influences of not just the Vercelli homilies in question but also several works by Ælfric and Wulfstan.

Manish Sharma revisits the commonplace view that *Elene* is a poem chiefly about change and conversion as enacted through a series of unilateral movements from darkness to lightness, from ignorance to knowledge, and from otherness outside the Christian community to conversion within it. Sharma shows that the same trajectory has been argued for the poem's hermeneutic identification of the Jews with the 'letter' of the text and the Christians with its 'spirit,' whereby the poem has been seen to urge the abandonment of the literal in favour of the spiritual. By focusing with a fresh eye upon the 'metaphorical vectors' of the poem (and in particular those moments where Cynewulf breaks away from his known sources), Sharma goes against the grain by arguing that the image of the reburied cross in fact disrupts these perceived teleological (and typological) movements from concealment to revelation or disclosure. In so doing, Sharma asks us to recognize in the poem a far more complicated paradigm that does not necessarily abandon the literal as it embraces the spiritual, but rather treats it as a foundational component. By letting go of this either/or proposition, Sharma shows that the project of finding the true cross appropriately shifts from being a strictly literal exercise to one that finds spiritual meaning in the so-called apocalyptic ending of the poem.

Patrick McBrine provides an analysis of words depicting journeys in all six of the Vercelli Book poems, showing that there is a unity of theme across the texts in their shared expression of woe in the present life and the hope for bliss in the hereafter. McBrine begins poignantly by exploring Cynewulf's self-admitted mode of composing *siðgeomor*, which McBrine translates as 'travel-weary' in *Fates of the Apostles*, ostensibly aligning Cynewulf's own fate with that of the martyred apostles. McBrine shows how the repetition of *geomor* at the end of the poem (thus creating a giant envelope pattern) effectively serves to transform this world-weariness into the greatest of hopes for heaven. McBrine suggests a similar trajectory in Cynewulf's other poems, including *Elene*, also in the Vercelli collection. Moving from the poems attributed to this poet, McBrine gauges the use of similar sentiments in the form of authorial rumination, exhortation, and gnomic statement. McBrine concludes that despite the continual iteration of the *contemptus mundi* theme throughout the poetry, the overall sentiment is forward-thinking, and ultimately one of hope.

Finally, Paul Remley provides an extraordinarily full and detailed bibliography on the Vercelli Book, and graphically records the changing range of scholarly perspectives on the manuscript across nearly two hundred years. The superb *Bibliography* by Greenfield and Robinson that Remley's work seeks ultimately to supplement and supersede records publications up to the end of 1972,[6] and offers a rough index against which to measure the explosion of interest in the Vercelli Book in the subsequent decades. Raw totals can be misleading, but it is surely significant that by Remley's tally more than three times as many items relating to the Vercelli Book have been published since 1972 as before that date. As often in Anglo-Saxon studies, it is the poems that have garnered most critical attention, with more items produced on *The Dream of the Rood* alone than on all the *Vercelli Homilies* put together; and yet it is the increasing focus on the *Vercelli Homilies* that is the most striking result to be gleaned from a reading of the bibliographical data. In fact, comparatively little work had been done on the *Vercelli Homilies* prior to 1972, and for good reason: the splendid and learned facsimile edition by Celia Sisam was yet to appear, and the fine editions to modern standards by Paul Szarmach (for *Vercelli Homilies IX–XXIII*) and especially Donald Scragg (for all of the *Vercelli Homilies*) were still some way off; likewise, the highly influential doctoral dissertation by Éamonn Ó Carragáin was still in production.[7] These four tomes alone can be credited in large measure with the massive increase in publications on the *Vercelli Homilies* in the past few decades, with more than fifteen times as many items appearing after 1972 as were recorded previously.

---

6 Stanley B. Greenfield and Fred C. Robinson, *A Bibliography of Publications on Old English Literature up to the End of 1972* (Toronto: UTP, 1980).
7 Celia Sisam, ed., *The Vercelli Book: A Late Tenth-Century Manuscript Containing Prose and Verse, Vercelli Biblioteca Capitolare CXVII*, EEMF 19 (Copenhagen: Rosenkilde and Bagger, 1976); Paul E. Szarmach, ed., *Vercelli Homilies IX–XXIII*, TOES 5 (Toronto: UTP, 1981); D.G. Scragg, ed., *The Vercelli Homilies and Related Texts*, EETS o.s. 300 (Oxford: OUP, 1992); Éamonn Ó Carragáin, 'The Vercelli Book as an Ascetic Florilegium' (unpub. PhD diss., Queen's Univ., Belfast, 1975).

Nor does this flood of publications look to be ceasing any time soon. In prospect is a digitized version of the manuscript,[8] while more recent work, including in this very volume,[9] has demonstrated how source studies thoughtfully applied can revolutionize our understanding of the readings that underlie the texts inscribed into the Vercelli Book itself, even when those texts are unattested elsewhere. Moreover, while a detailed study on the poetry of the Vercelli Book alone is perhaps hard to envisage, given the intimate connections that seem to link those poems with others recorded elsewhere,[10] there will soon appear the first dedicated study of the style and rhetoric of the *Vercelli Homilies*.[11] In short, though there is much useful work being done, much remains before we can understand more fully such key questions as the place of the Vercelli Book within Anglo-Saxon literary culture, not to mention its place in Vercelli today.

The rather plain tome that now remains in the Cathedral Library in Vercelli has survived most of the past thousand years without close scrutiny, but has quite rightly been increasingly the object of serious scholarly study. It is hoped that the essays that follow, produced by a range of academics at every stage of their respective careers, will at once serve to indicate a continuing engagement and an engaging commitment with what by any measure is rightly to be regarded as one of the finest literary relics to remain from Anglo-Saxon England. These new readings in the Vercelli Book are offered in the firm conviction that still newer readings can and will emerge; what they share with future scholarship is the enduring sense that the Vercelli Book amply repays closer examination, and that it is a treasured artefact from a long-gone age that for all serious students of Anglo-Saxon England still remains required reading today.

---

8 The project is under the direction of Roberto Rosselli Del Turco; see further the project's website at http://islp.di.unipi.it/bifrost/vbd/dvb.html.

9 See especially the paper by Samantha Zacher below, 98–149.

10 The closest such study is by Jonathan Randle, 'The Homiletic Context of the Vercelli Book Poems' (unpub. PhD diss., Univ. of Cambridge, 1999); see too Orchard, *The Poetic Craft of Cynewulf*, which contains discussions of *Andreas*, *Fates of the Apostles*, *The Dream of the Rood*, and *Elene*.

11 See now Zacher, *Preaching the Converted*.

The Vercelli Prose and Anglo-Saxon Literary History

PAUL E. SZARMACH

However grudging the observation or uncomfortable for the scholar making it, no one has – for the last decade and more – disputed the importance of the Vercelli Book for the history of Anglo-Saxon literature. If anyone needs a quick refresher on the matter, Donald Scragg's concise treatment for the celebratory occasion in Vercelli may serve to recall most of the major points.[1] The fundamental ground for the importance of the Vercelli Book is its relative chronological priority in the history of Old English prose, which if disputed as a likely and murky tie with the Blickling homilies – both manuscripts imply earlier origins – gets resolved in Vercelli's favour because of Vercelli's variety, which really means that Vercelli has poetry and Blickling not. Blickling has a disadvantage in that there is no critical edition that meets contemporary standards, and thus it has no possible champion for its cause (nor is there any prospect soon for such a champion).[2] Yet there is a deep disconnect within literary history between the observation of Vercelli's chronological priority and the significance of that priority to the development of Old English prose and literature more generally. The main argument here is that the Vercelli homilies offer the literary historian a book of styles that for later literary history has a double effect: the twenty-three prose pieces offer a baseline for what the later period will produce in direct development and for what the later period will create on its own. The Vercelli prose is the *fons et origo* not precisely

---

1 Donald G. Scragg, 'The Significance of the Vercelli Book among Anglo-Saxon Vernacular Writings,' in *Vercelli tra Oriente ed Occidente tra Tarda Antichita e Medioevo*, ed. Vittoria Dolcetti Corazza (Vercelli: Edizioni dell'Orso, 1997), 35–43.
2 See the new edition by Richard J. Kelly, *The Blickling Homilies: Edition and Translation* (London: Continuum, 2003). In general, the reviews of this edition have not been laudatory; see, for example, Samantha Zacher, *NQ* 251.2 [n.s. 53] (2006): 216–18, and Milton McC. Gatch, *Church History* (December 2004): 847–9.

in a source relation but rather as a set of potential directions and paths for later prose writers. Literary history did not always follow the Vercelli directions, and in choosing others may have offered implied judgments. The final view here must encompass and rely on collateral points about shifting cultural contexts, editing texts, recent literary theory, and translation theory, among other large topics. There are, however, some theoretical issues for consideration, which may, if not *must*, form a prolegomenon to a discussion of the Vercelli prose. These issues concern literary history itself and its position in the study of Anglo-Saxon literature.[3]

David Perkins distinguishes between two kinds of literary history: narrative literary history and encyclopedic literary history.[4] The first type contains a master narrative, 'a story,' that has a beginning, a middle, and an end. As all narratives it has characters (figures), major themes, and likely tropes such as 'rise and decline.' Narrative literary history features emphases of one kind or another, which often become principles of exclusion that eliminate consideration of parts of the historical record, thus expunging 'minor' authors or 'minor genres' from a 'major' discussion. Narrative history can be a function of another phenomenon altogether, be it broadly cultural, historical, or even sociological, such as the time-honoured rise of the ever-rising middle class. Historical context is often adduced to explain literary phenomena. Narrative history seeks to explain a literary state of affairs and, guided by a teleology, seeks to reduce the complexity of the past. The second type of literary history makes no claims for any large continuities as it seeks to include within its compass all that it reasonably can. It is an arrangement, or a compilation, or a survey wherein incompleteness or discontinuity is not avoided, but rather embraced. It is a free form that allows for the diversity and variety of the past, the multiplicity of views thereon, and of the conclusions to be drawn. There may be a chronological flow of the subject matter, but the concept of 'period' dissolves. The encyclopedia characteristically requires several experts to achieve the intended coverage.

The reigning (literary) history in the subject, Greenfield and Calder's *A New Critical History of Old English Literature*,[5] is more encyclopedia

---

3 The choice of 'Anglo-Saxon' here rather than 'Old English' is quite deliberate, for it means that the true subject at hand is both Latin and vernacular.

4 *Is Literary History Possible?* (Baltimore and London: Johns Hopkins Univ. Press, 1992). For a full discussion of 'Narrative Literary History' see 29–51; for 'The Postmodern Encyclopedia,' 53–60. This paragraph severely compresses Perkins's discussion.

5 New York and London: New York Univ. Press, 1986. The first edition was Stanley B. Greenfield, *A Critical History of Old English Literature* (New York: New York Univ. Press, 1965).

than narrative. The co-authors describe their volume thus: 'The book is three things: a synopsis, a critical reading of texts, and a history of criticism.'[6] The important word 'critical' perhaps had more impact then than it does now, for Greenfield will probably remain the 'close reader' par excellence in the history of the subject, having encountered (particularly) patristic scholarship, in many a bout on how to read Old English literature.[7] Relative to the first edition of the *Critical History*, Greenfield and Calder expand the treatment of Old English prose, which they say 'has far too long been the step-child of Old English literary studies.'[8] In inviting Michael Lapidge to join the team with his authoritative presentation of Anglo-Latin literature, Greenfield and Calder further conform to the collaborative nature of the encyclopedic form. While there are particular explanations for one literary feature or another, Greenfield and Calder produce no master narrative of the subject, celebrating instead the Anglo-Saxons, 'who triumphed in almost every genre.'[9] The Vercelli prose receives not quite two full pages of critical analysis, which offer generalized comments about 'a harsh and strident tone' among the pieces.[10] The analysis takes place in the chapter 'Ælfric, Wulfstan, and Other Late Prose,' which begins with a consideration of the Benedictine Revival.[11]

While a complete survey of the several literary histories of Anglo-Saxon England with special reference to Vercelli would have no point here, two further twentieth-century works from different generations might be illustrative and somewhat contrastive. George K. Anderson produces a literary history encyclopedic in style in *The Literature of the Anglo-Saxons*.[12] In his view he seeks to answer two questions of importance:

---

6 Stanley B. Greenfield and Daniel Calder, with Michael Lapidge *A New Critical History* (New York: New York Univ. Press, 1986), 3. There is now R.D. Fulk and Christopher Cain, with Rachel S. Anderson, *A History of Old English Literature* (Oxford: Blackwell, 2003), which is encyclopedic in nature. Daniel Donoghue, *Old English Literature: A Short Introduction* (Oxford: Blackwell, 2004) organizes five 'figures,' viz., the vow, the hall, the miracle, the pulpit, and the scholar, in a self-described 'idiosyncratic' approach to introduce the field to students and general readers.

7 In one of his last pieces Greenfield turned to the four-fold method, delivered, self-referentially, almost tongue-in-cheek for those who remember the oral version of the paper.

8 *A New Critical History*, 2–3.

9 Ibid., 1.

10 Ibid., 74–5. Contrast Greenfield's *A Critical History of Old English Literature*, 59–60, essentially fifteen lines on contents, suggesting a 'haphazard' arrangement.

11 *A New Critical History*, 68–106.

12 Rev. ed. (Princeton: Princeton Univ. Press, 1966), which is considered here; the original edition was published in 1949.

'What has survived from those distant times? Where can one look beyond in order to know more than the general outlines of this literature?'[13] Neither question suggests that a narrative is to come but rather that some kind of reference function is the aim. Anderson further states that he is undertaking to present the entire canon 'without undue emphasis upon the alleged major works of the period ... already ... studied perhaps too much.'[14] The intention to achieve breadth or comprehensiveness apparently comes with a strong editorial attitude, which on the surface seems to be in the service of the entire corpus. This strategy might be behind Anderson's treatment of the Vercelli homilies, for he gives a sentence summary (sometimes more) for each of the twenty-three pieces. Anderson is clearly unhappy over the 'helter-skelter order of the pieces,' and the numbering of the homilies confuses him, yet he says it is 'not too difficult to follow the process going on in the mind of the scribe or scribes.'[15] Anderson's work appeared before the breakthrough on the compilation of the Vercelli Book demonstrated by Donald Scragg and now widely accepted.[16] Vercelli appears with Blickling in a section on early prose, but there is no story or narrative that links them together beyond their chronological priority to Ælfric and Wulfstan. By contrast, J.J. Jusserand offers a take on Old English literature that approaches narrative literary history.[17] Jusserand offers a broad cultural view along national lines in four chapters devoted to Anglo-Saxon, with a touch of mysticism: 'Let us therefore take this literature as a whole, and confess that the divisions here adopted, of national and worldly and of religious literature, is arbitrary, and is merely used for the sake of convenience. Religious and worldly, northern and southern literature overlap; but they most decidedly belong to the same Anglo-Saxon whole.'[18] Perhaps one can see an incipient postmodernism here in offering a framework and then undercutting it. Jusserand has nothing to say about Vercelli directly. Still, one can admire his comment, made generally about Anglo-Saxon sermon writers, whose audiences were 'rude, uneducated people': 'The authors of these homilies purposely write prose

---

13 Ibid., v.
14 Ibid., vi.
15 Ibid., 345–8.
16 D.G. Scragg, 'The Compilation of the Vercelli Book,' *Anglo-Saxon England* 2 (1973): 189–207.
17 *A Literary History of the English People: From the Origins to the Civil War* (1895; repr. London: T. Fisher Unwin, Ltd, 1925).
18 Ibid., 40.

which comes near the tone and forms of poetry.'[19] Literary history itself would seem to present problematical intellectual situations, and the Vercelli homilies necessarily share them.

Anglo-Saxon literary history certainly suffers from two conditions that do not generally affect post-medieval literature: we do not know who, for example, wrote any of the Vercelli homilies, and we are mostly uncertain about specific dates, almost always working without the assurance that a Register of Copyrights generally gives. There are as well discontinuities, overt and implied. The Grand Discontinuity, of course, is the Norman Conquest, a process that features a convenient political and military event to serve as a chronological boundary for the period and for those who need or want one. The literary-cultural boundary of 1066 is more fuzzy, as two classic 'continuity studies' have argued and as, for example, recent research into hagiography has established.[20] The Viking invasions as such may also serve as an example of another grand discontinuity, especially leading up to the Alfredian revival.[21] The general absence of supporting records of any sort provide the continuing discontinuities, so to speak, for the circumstances of Anglo-Saxon literary history. The encyclopedic literary history is thus the perfect mode for Anglo-Saxon literature and for the Vercelli homilies, which float along the pages as a set of particulars without direct links to any other particulars except chronological priority. Oddly enough, this situation is an ironic or inverse connection with contemporary literature: whereas post-modern scholarship may embrace discontinuity in the face of libraries bulging with books and journals full of contrarious view points, discontinuity stalks most Anglo-Saxonists against their will, ready to give a Beowulfian

---

19 Ibid., 88–93, and esp. 91. *En passant*, one may note another vatic or mystical statement by Jusserand: 'Anglo-Saxon poetry is like the river Saone; one doubts which way it flows' (39).

20 R.W. Chambers, *On the Continuity of English Prose from Alfred to More and His School*, EETS o.s. 186 (London: H. Milford, 1932); C.L. Wrenn pursues 'the threads of differing kinds' in 'On the Continuity of Old English Poetry,' in *The Study of Old English Literature* (London and Toronto: Harrap, 1967), 17–34; and Susan J. Ridyard, *The Royal Saints of Anglo-Saxon England: A Study of West Saxon and East Anglian Cults* (Cambridge: CUP, 1988), considers the continuity of Anglo-Saxon saints and their Norman reception. For a study focusing on one exemplary saint see Barbara Abou El-Haj, 'Saint Cuthbert: The Post-Conquest Appropriation of an Anglo-Saxon Cult,' in *Holy Men and Holy Women*, ed. Paul E. Szarmach (Albany: SUNY Press, 1996), 177–206.

21 Kemp Malone, 'The Old English Period to 1100,' in A.C. Baugh, *A Literary History of England* (New York and London: Appleton-Century-Crofts, 1948), 105, offers a florid metaphor citing Alfred as the first gardener of Old English prose and Ælfric as a continuator, whose works and workers the Normans destroyed.

bear hug. In fact, the absence of authors, and maybe even the absence of dates too, fulfills the prior condition that Foucault sought when he wrote against authors and for a discursive system of texts.[22] Anglo-Saxon literature is postmodern, after all. Unfortunately, Foucault and others do not describe a practical criticism, as the New Critics did, to assist the formation of a framework of understanding outside of authors and all that authors bring with them. Interpretive literary methods, at least in Anglo-Saxon studies, originally mortgaged to close reading at best, perhaps now move towards ideological approaches, wherein literary texts serve as proof-texts for some form of socio-political idea or cultural idea (that is, constructed relations based on power considerations). Ideological approaches could create a literary history, however satisfactory one might find it to be, but no treatment has thus far come forward. At this time it would seem possible to write a women's literary history of Anglo-Saxon England.

Two other conditions need emphasis here: aestheticism and mediation. While Greenfield and Calder have rightly beat the drum for the integration of prose into the Anglo-Saxon family, no one has successfully maintained a comprehensive argument for prose on aesthetic grounds and no one, it would seem, has ever used the word 'beautiful' in connection with Old English prose. There may be compensating positive diction here and there such as 'effective' or 'well-designed' or 'skilful' or 'balanced.' George Clark's outright declaration that 'the claim that some of the prose is good is a snare' exemplifies the standard view.[23] Narrative literary history, as Perkins reminds us, is typically literary history of 'good' literature.[24] The overwhelming emphasis on poetry in teaching and in literary criticism, especially of *Beowulf*, stands in major measure behind the 'stepchild' status of prose. The priority of poetry is at least a nineteenth-century phenomenon in Anglo-Saxon studies, ultimately rooted in classical studies. This priority of status has meant that methodology in poetry is in a similarly advanced state well beyond the comparatively primitive tools available to study non-fiction prose. It seems pretty clear that there is no future for prose studies, especially Vercelli, along aesthetic grounds.[25] The general field will not and

---

22 For a discussion of Foucault and the problem of authors see my 'Ælfric Revises: The Lives of Martin and the Idea of the Author,' in *Unlocking the Wordhord: Anglo-Saxon Studies in Memory of Edward B. Irving, Jr.*, ed. Mark C. Amodio and Katherine O'Brien O'Keeffe (Toronto, Buffalo, and London: UTP, 2003), 38–61.

23 George Clark offers this response to 'The Teaching of Introductory Old English in the U.S. and Canada: Some Comments on the 1972 Survey,' *OEN* 6.2 (1973): 25.

24 Perkins, *Is Literary History Possible?* 5–6.

25 However, see now Samantha Zacher, *Preaching the Converted: Anglo-Saxon Style and Rhetoric in the Vercelli Homilies*, TASS (Toronto: UTP, 2009).

cannot accept the proposition that prose has aesthetic value, it would not be able to follow any such arguments if one were to be somehow successfully made, and if it could follow the argument, it would not choose the conclusion. Rather, prose and Vercelli have other ways to overcome aestheticism. New theory, in broad alliance with cultural studies, needs prose, Vercelli included, to give shape and substance to its insights and findings. It needs content, and prose in the aggregate can provide content, particularly early medieval Christian thought, so necessary as a point of reference.

Mediation is a double problem in that there are mediators in Anglo-Saxon England as well as in North Atlantic scholarship. The latter are editors, but the former are even more mysterious. Who gave us the Vercelli Book as we have it is a puzzle. Milton McC. Gatch refers to the human agent(s) who produced the codex as 'redactor,' '(the) Vercelli editor,' '(the) compiler,' '(a/the) collector.'[26] Éamonn Ó Carragáin gives us 'one man,' '(the Vercelli) collector,' ' a compiler,' 'a cleric,' 'a monk.'[27] Both Gatch and Ó Carragáin are interested in defining the central intelligence behind the collection, not necessarily the sole scribe, and certainly not the evident several authors who composed the prose pieces. Both are interested in the content of the collection as reflective of this central intelligence. Ó Carragáin, who has the advantage of Scragg's pamphlet theory, suggests that the sole scribe may or may not have put the three pamphlets together when he was alive, and if not, 'the compiler' did.[28] In other contexts Ó Carragáin seems to merge the function of writing with the function of collecting. There could be two mediators because there are two functions, namely, 'setting down' and 'compiling,' or one person could have performed both functions. The various possible scenarios, as we hold on to the idea of the sole scribe, begin to multiply slowly as we move beyond the clear evidence. Did more than one person direct the scribe or otherwise co-produce the volume? Perhaps the only other clear point to emerge is that all scholars would agree that there should have been a proofreader or copy-editor for the Vercelli Book.

As to North Atlantic editors, I have to admit to a certain intellectual bind. Max Förster, whose selective edition of 1913 began editorial mediation,

---

26 Milton McC. Gatch, 'Eschatology in the Anonymous Old English Homilies,' *Traditio* 21 (1965): 117–65, particularly 136–60.
27 Éamonn Ó Carragáin, 'How Did the Vercelli Collector Interpret *The Dream of the Rood?*' in *Studies in English Language and Early English Literature in Honour of Paul Christophersen*, ed. P.M. Tilling, Occasional Papers in Lang. and Lang. Learning 8 (Coleraine: New Univ. of Ulster, 1981), 63–104, passim.
28 Ibid., 65.

should receive sympathy and understanding for the loss of his complete edition, already typeset, when his publisher died and the Nazis arrived.[29] No doubt his edition would have assisted research on Vercelli, and equally no doubt that by century's end the progress of knowledge would have required its replacement. My own published edition to complement Förster and thus to complete his work was meant to assist the Dictionary of Old English by establishing a text for reference. The apparatus I developed for my dissertation would have meant a large and complicated volume beyond the budget and scope envisioned for a *DOE* project at that time. Except for confessing that my original impulse to work on Vercelli came out of a literary interest where prose as prose, sources, and the history of ideas come into play, I shall say no more of my own circumscribed work for *nemo iudex in sua causa*. Donald Scragg's edition of course comes closest to the standard of a full-service edition that John Pope established in his two volumes on Ælfric, and accordingly will assist future generations for some time. Like my edition, the Scragg volume does not offer a literary assessment as such. This paper may serve as such an assessment, perhaps. I shall say no more about the Scragg edition, for reticence must always accompany the honour of a dedication. All three editors, however, must brace themselves for a general attack by the lobby that sees editors as a stripe of those translators who are traitors (*traduttori, traditori*). The attack on editorial assumptions could come from those who might have a quarrel with tenth-century Christianity.

Having thus suggested how and why narrative literary history offers many problematics and similarly how and why in encyclopedic literary history the Vercelli homilies has not and will not rise beyond the notice of chronological priority, I would like to take a risk and reverse field to argue for an outline of a literary history that begins with the Vercelli homilies and carries through in a lively fashion for about a half-century on either side of the millennium (with homage to Ker for his dating scheme). The literary history of later Old English prose has a *nachleben*, but this 'mini-master' narrative, while not quite about 'rising and falling,' will describe the development of vernacular prose style from Vercelli to Ælfric and Wulfstan. This attempt is about the options for style that Vercelli provides and defines and how those options developed. The absence of so many implied authors is the absence of an encumbrance, forcing the discussion to focus on texts, and all the 'helter-skelter' nature of the Vercelli homilies

---

29 Reported by Rudolph Willard in his review of Förster's *Die Vercelli Homilien*, *Speculum* 9 (1934): 225–31.

is an aid to the enterprise, for it presents varied and diverse options as
such. The Latin tradition is crucial because it presents to vernacular writers issues to consider and problems to confront or resolve. Translation is a
'carrying over,' and, as Bede notes in his discussion of Cædmon's *Hymn*,
rendering one language into another is not a simple task, particularly in
the matter of syntax.[30] The Alfredian formula, 'word for word' and/or
'sense for sense,' found in the *Preface* to the *Pastoral Care* and in the
Preface to Boethius, is happily 'text-based,' but translation involves authors and audiences too, and much more. Developments in Latin furthermore have secondary effects in the vernacular, which on its part is hardly
without its own resources to engage the task at hand, whatever it might be.
Latin may be the dominant intellectual language, but the vernacular, however subordinate as the 'receiver language,' asserts its independence as a
language system with its own resources and history. But not all vernacular
prose is a mere palimpsest of Latin, and the independence of these pieces
is an equal subject in the literary history. Let us describe how the Vercelli
homilies contribute to the master narrative of later vernacular prose by
looking at several pieces in the collection.

In his translation of Sulpicius Severus's *Vita Martini* and the *Epistola
tertia ad Bassulam* for November 11 (Martinmas) the translator-adaptor
would seem to have an unparalleled opportunity to render one of the classics of Western spirituality. The brief opening announces the occasion and
its solemnity, while the concluding paragraph reiterates Martin's moral example, his worldwide reputation, and his potential intercessory role for
the audience. The translator knows the importance of the saint and his
feast, but he does not let on that he is following Sulpicius (unlike Ælfric in
a similar endeavour) and that his is not a 'free composition.' There is no
evident anxiety over the authority to speak. Presumably the Latin exemplar and/or the weight of the tradition of the *Vita* would have given the
translator a Latin attribution. Sulpicius Severus on Martin appears in some
versions of the Roman Homiliary and also in the Cotton-Corpus legendary, not to mention the circulation of *Martiniana*.[31] It is a difficult step to

---

30 Bertram Colgrave and R.A.B. Mynors, eds., *Bede's Ecclesiastical History of the English
People* (Oxford: Clarendon Press, 1979), IV.24, 416, trans. 417.
31 In the 'Roman Homiliary' Réginald Grégoire finds three pieces of Martiniana (nos. 76,
77, 78), the first two of which are from Sulpicius (*Vita* 2–4 and *ep. ad Bassulam*), and
the last from Gregory of Tours, *Historia Francorum* 48. See Grégoire's *Homéliaires
Liturgiques Médiévaux* (Spoleto: Centro Italiano di Studi sull'Alto Medioevo, 1980).
These pieces are also in the Homiliary of Eginon of Verona, nos. 179, 180, 181; see
Grégoire, 217. For Old English connections see Patrick Zettel, 'Saints' Lives in Old
English: Latin Manuscripts and Vernacular Accounts,' *Peritia* 1 (1982): 17–37, with

turn the praise of Martin found in the opening and closing to a knowledge of the Latin tradition. The translator makes no apology for his free abbreviation of Sulpicius, excising whole chapters (the prologue, chapters 1, 4, 6, 9, 11–13, 18–19, 21–5) and shaping the narrative away from Gallic ecclesiastical politics towards the depiction of a *vir Dei*, and thus through abbreviation, presumably necessary for the occasion, altering radically the structure of the narrative in Old English. The well-worn topos that there is more to say than any man can is no admission of abbreviation.[32] The summary chapter 27 in the *Vita*, which relates Martin's virtues and comes before the narrative of his death, remains in the Old English as in the Latin. Might the translator have understood that this placement in the *Vita* is a structural move derived from Sallust, and that Sulpicius Severus, as Fontaine puts it, merits 'le surnom hyperbolique ... Salluste chrétien?'[33] It is pretty to think so, but there is no evidence to prove or disprove the point except for the preponderance of evidence regarding how the translator otherwise treats the Latin. If abbreviation is the major strategy, then chapter 27 need not have a place in the Old English, for the summary of virtues is accomplished to some measure by the concluding paragraph and the overall narrative itself.[34] Did the translator further understand that Sulpicius's prose, as scholars have celebrated, is very classical in its observance of the intricacies of Latin clausulae?[35] It is difficult to see any particular rhythmical effects beyond parallelisms and the multiplication of independent clauses here and there. One could be ready to see the use of major rhythmical patterns as a kind of aesthetic offset for Sulpicius's

---

special reference to Martiniana. See Peter Jackson and Michael Lapidge, 'The Contents of the Cotton-Corpus Legendary,' in *Holy Men and Holy Women*, ed. Paul E. Szarmach (Albany: SUNY Press, 1996), 131–46, for an update and review of Zettel's work. Clare Stanliffe, *St. Martin and His Hagiographer* (Oxford: Clarendon Press, 1983) is a necessary background study. See Raymond Van Dam, *Saints and Their Miracles in Late Antique Gaul* (Princeton: Princeton Univ. Press 1993), appendix 3, 308–17, on relevant texts that attach themselves to the cult of Martin.

32 Cf. *VH* XVIII.44–6, 293.

33 Jacques Fontaine, quoting Caspar Barthius, in his magisterial introduction to his edition, *Vie de Saint Martin*, 3 vols., Sources Chrétiennes 133–5 (Paris: Éditions du Cerf, 1967, 1968, 1969), 1: 99. See Fontaine's treatment of the literary value, 1: 97–124.

34 Stancliffe, *St. Martin and His Hagiographer*, 89–90, citing the initial insight of F. Kemper, sees Sulpicius following a Suetonian pattern where chap. 27 is the last of three chapters describing Martin's private life. The place of this chapter has led many, including this author, to conclude that the *vita* was written when Martin was alive, when in fact the rhetorical and moral summary is simply Suetonian patterning.

35 Per Hyltén, *Studien zu Sulpicius Severus* (Lund: H. Ohlssons boktryckeri, 1940), esp. 33–48, documents Sulpicius's stylistic observances with special reference to the Martiniana.

clausulae, but the long and hard look has produced no results. When the homilist relies on the adverbial *swylces* ['item'] as a connective to string along paragraphs 8 and 11–14 out of the eighteen in Scragg's paragraphing, the evidence seems to imply an uninspired response to the Latin. In short, the Old English, though showing structural independence through abbreviation, generally reflects the Latin in its prose tactics.

Chapters 4–5 from the Old English translation of Felix's *Vita Guthlaci*, equivalent to chapters 28–32 of the Latin, constitute Homily XXIII, the only other prose *vita* in the Vercelli Book.[36] The piece is brief in length but long in problems: transmission, history, possible dialect problems, dating issues, form or genre or simply 'shape.'[37] Whenever the complete, original translation came to be, it and its Vercelli out-take represent one of the earlier vernacular responses to the hermeneutic [formerly 'Hisperic'] style.[38] One can easily infer that the vernacular response is negative. Colgrave's sketch of Felix's style sees him standing at a mid-point between Aldhelm and Bede, with a tendency to show Aldhelm's influence earlier and then Bede's later in the work, when Bede's prose life of Cuthbert becomes the model.[39] The Vercelli sections, which relate Guthlac's life in the barrow, his interactions with Satan, how unclean spirits took him to the gates of hell, and how St Bartholomew rescued him, come under the Aldhelmian brush. For these passages Colgrave gives these words as unique to Felix: [chap. 28] *vestimine, poculamento*, [chap. 29] *venenifluam*, [chap. 30] *zabulaticum*, [chap. 31] *clangisonis, sparginibus, favillantium, falsivomis*; and these as borrowed from Aldhelm: [chap. 29] *caelicolae*, [chap. 30] *strofus*, [chap. 31] *buccula, flammivomo, raucisonis*.[40] Some of the inventions are modelled on Aldhelm

---

36 Bertram Colgrave, ed., *Felix's Life of Saint Guthlac* (Cambridge: CUP, 1956; repr. 1985) is the standard edition. Paul Gonser, ed., *Das angelsäsische Prose-Leben des hl. Guthlac*, Anglistische Forschungen 27 (Heidelberg: C. Winter, 1909) gives the complete life from the eleventh-century manuscript British Library, Cotton Vespasian D.xxi as well as the Vercelli extract.

37 Jane Roberts, 'The Old English Prose Translation of Felix's *Vita sancti Guthlaci*,' in *Studies in Earlier Old English Prose*, ed. Paul E. Szarmach (Albany: State Univ. of New York Press, 1986), 363–79, offers a fairly comprehensive treatment of the issues.

38 The key modern article on this stylistic phenomenon is Michael Lapidge, 'The Hermeneutic Style in Tenth-Century Anglo-Latin Literature,' *ASE* 4 (1975): 67–111, which is also available in the collection of Lapidge's work, *Anglo-Latin Literature, 900–1066* (London and Rio Grande, OH: Hambledon Press, 1996), 105–49.

39 See now Sarah Downey, 'Intertextuality in the Lives of St. Guthlac' (unpub. PhD diss., Univ. of Toronto, 2004).

40 I abstract relevant information from the wider range that Colgrave gives in his treatment of Felix's style, 17–18. See also Gonser for an exhaustive treatment of

(*flammivomus, clangisonis*), and the Grecisms are particularly a hermeneutic touch: [chap.30] *plasma, pseudosodalitate*. Guthlac's encounter with the netherworld and its denizens makes excellent narrative, full of descriptive possibilities that can dazzle (which is to say, terrify) an audience with an assault of diction, and so Felix pulls out the stops in his depiction of the hellish spirits as 'aspectu truces, forma terribiles.' The passage is an equal possibility for the Old English translator who takes an option only so far. As Colgrave, who sees the Old English prose *Guthlac* as an important piece in the development of translation technique, puts it, the Old English is a simplification of Felix characterized by the judicious omissions of difficult words and phrases.[41] One can see judgmental simplification in the Vercelli extract from *Vita*, cap. xxxi when Felix runs through a string of phrases, either adjectives plus nouns, or nouns plus nouns, to pile up the cumulative effects of horrors in describing the arrival of the devils at Guthlac's barrow. Transmission difficulties aside, the Old English translator tries to keep up with the Latin, showing that he knows the game, but stumbles or gives up, rendering *gutture flammivomo* [trans. Colgrave, 'throats vomiting flame'] more bland with *wæron þa hracan lige afylled* ['their throats were filled with flame'] and giving *ondrysenlice muðas* for *ore foetide* and *ondrysenlice on stefne* for *vocibus horrisonis*. The idea here has to be that variation is necessary for effect, and a double *ondrysenlice* is too ordinary and unvaried. The danger of keeping pace with the Latin is apparent in the rendering for *clamoribus rauciosiones* [trans. Colgrave, 'raucous cries'], which is Vercelli *hashrymedon on heora clypunge* and in the Vespasian version *hasrunigendum stefnum*; the result is a textual difficulty.[42] This translator follows his Latin source in the structural mainline, but departs from it on the level of diction. There is enough to suggest that the translator recognized the problems involved in translating Felix's 'bombast.' His overall strategy to simplify rather than to seek to use the compounding resources of Old English implies by and large a rejection of hermeneutic Latin, about which more later.

The two *vitae*, which describe vernacular reactions to Latin models that by their form and narrative authority tend to control vernacular responses, share the Latin burden with several *homiliae* proper. Vercelli XVI and XVII are examples of a type of homily known as the continuous (or running) gloss, where a passage from the Bible receives a verse-by-verse explanation.

---

translation technique, 52–96, with conclusions on 94–6. Gonser sees the translation less positively (95): 'ziemlich primitive.'

41 Colgrave, *Felix's Life of Saint Guthlac*, 19.
42 *VH*, note to XXIII.98, 394.

Within the explanation of a verse the exposition can become very intricate if the verse under consideration is full of either special meaning or mystery or some other complication such as an apparent contradiction. At first glance, the concept of the form seems very simple: the Latin text provides the foundation, and the structure provides a shell. The origin in biblical commentary seems transparent, and someone such as Bede who did both exegesis and homiletics could move between the two expressions easily.[43] The form is abstract or mechanical in theory, but in practice (and here is where the interest lies) a homilist could expand or contract exegesis within verses or find themes or ideas across the verses, thus presenting a unified idea of the Bible and a unified effect for his own piece. All really begins with the text for discussion, for a very brief reading for the day might give too little to say, an extended reading too much or a simple parable just enough, a double parable too many complications. The homilist must make the selection from among many possible options. But the liturgical reading is the *donné*. Vercelli XVI gives an excellent Epiphany reading, Mt. 3:13–17, The Baptism of the Christ, which in its short compass gives two characters, direct discourse, dramatic conflict, and heavenly intervention in the narrative, and much to explain about major doctrines such as the Incarnation and the Trinity. When a prefabricated form gives so much to a writer, the only restraint is a lack of imagination or of improvisation. Despite the loss of a leaf after fol. 85 in the Vercelli Book and other textual problems, the comparatively free response of the homilist is manifest. It is not quite clear how the biblical text from Matthew is to be presented. Scragg's second paragraph, affected by the lost leaf, seems to suggest a passage alternating Latin verse and Old English translation, which puts the Latin closer to the Old English in specifics rather than the other standard mode, where a complete translation of the passage starts the homily. The verse-by-verse exposition follows by a general adherence to the narrative flow and not by rubric or heading with repeated biblical verse. No single specific source serves as a model for this homily, though a section derives from Gregory the Great for certain and there are other source relations for

---

43 David Hurst, ed., *Bedae Venerabilis Opera*, Pars III, CCSL 122 (Turnhout: Brepols, 1955), whose notes show this movement; see also Dom Hurst's translation with Lawrence Martin, *Homilies on the Gospels*, 2 vols. (Kalamazoo: Cistercian Publications, 1991), and particularly Martin's observation, 1: xv: 'Whatever the specific use for which Bede prepared his *Homilies on the Gospel*, he undoubtedly sees his work as a continuation of the patristic tradition of exegetical preaching represented by works like Augustine's *Sermons* and *Tractates on the Gospel of St John*, and especially, by Gregory the Great's *Homilies on the Gospel*.'

particular points.[44] The homilist stays close to the account with a particular compositional move, namely, paraphrase, yet with that move he can establish his own interpretation. Thus, when the dove descends on Christ, the homilist can allegorize the meaning of the *culfre*, and transfer those meanings to a speech by John the Baptist, imagined but without any biblical precedent. Less boldly the homilist can translate literally the heavenly voice, 'Þis is min se leofa sunu in þam me wel licade,' and offer 'Efne swa he cwæde: Þis me is gecyndelic sunu.' The paraphrase is a doctrinal statement of the (divine) nature of the Son, which leads to an exposition of Trinitarian doctrine. These various compositional moves, however sharp and successful, may not finally prove so startling as the voice one can hear. The voice is double: the voice of a moral teacher is there, less strident than one may hear elsewhere in the Vercelli Book, and something like a personal voice. Augustine had such a voice, and so did Gregory, each establishing his through an embedded link to the audience.[45] The Vercelli homilist does similarly when he explains the Trinity in terms of the ternary of fire. The homely comparison comes with a rhetorical question put into the collective mouth of the audience when the homilist asks a question as if he were an unlearned man puzzling over the idea of the Trinity: 'Hu mæg ic þæt ongitan be ðære halgan Þrynnesse þæt syndon þreo hadas 7 hwæðre an God is 7 an godcund sped?'[46] and the mention of a fire at hand in XVI.155–9. The moral voice is a personal and present voice too. All these fine rhetorical gestures and moves within the topics of the occasion and beyond them suggest a confidence in composition. The running gloss was alive and well by the time of the Vercelli homilies.

Vercelli XVII exemplifies comparable strengths. The presentation of a complete translation of the pericope after a brief opening is a different presentation from XVI, as is the opening itself. While the opening of Vercelli XVI reads 'Men þa leofestan, sceolon we nu hwylcumhwegu wordum secgan'

---

44 Scragg cites Gregory the Great, *Homilia X in Evangelia* (PL 76: 1110–14) [=XVI.69–93], *VH*, 267, but finds my suggestion of Quodvultdeus for XVI.142–67 not cogent; cf. my edition, *Vercelli Homilies IX–XXIII*, TOES 5 (1981), XVI.109–29, 46. Thomas N. Hall, 'The Reversal of the Jordan in Vercelli Homily 16 and in Old English Literature,' *Traditio* 45 (1990): 53–86, is a wide-ranging study focusing on the Jordan and its reversal in the context of other, similar motifs.

45 F. Van Der Meer describes Augustine's immediacy in *Augustine the Bishop*, trans. Brian Battershaw and G.H. Lamb (London and New York: Sheed and Ward, 1961), 412–32. Among the strategies that Gregory uses to convey personal immediacy is mention of his ill health and indisposition. See, e.g., *Homilia XXII*, PL 76: 1174.

46 *VH* XVI.144–6, 272.

('Dearest men, we should now say a few words'), Vercelli XVII reads 'Men þa leofestan, sægeð us 7 myngaþ' ('Dearest men, [the holy gospel] says to us and reminds us'). Although no one has done a detailed analysis of the problem, different openings may mean different traditions. The biblical passage on the Purification is longer than that on the Baptism of Christ, requiring more selectivity to accomplish a manageable homily. The homilist uses paraphrase, as found in XVI, most significantly in repeating the *Nunc dimittis*, and unlike XVI invokes *men ða leofestan* five times within the body of the homily (at ll. 28, 47, 59, 93, 129) and *broðor mine* twice (ll. 64 and 139), citing the homiletic motif word *nydþearf* twice (at ll. 73 and 129).[47] While the occasion is a very significant liturgical feast, requiring explanation of Jewish law and practice, yet from the markers of direct address there is a strong hortatory theme throughout. If XVI can serve as an exemplary homily, XVII is a variation in blending exposition and exhortation.[48] Here I have stressed XVII's differences from XVI. The common descent of XVI and XVII in Group B2d, joining at some point in their common past, has obvious codicological importance and a somewhat murkier importance for literary history. Language and layout willing, XVI and XVII could be by the same author, who varies his presentation for whichever of many possible reasons. Authorship issues, however, do not matter for this literary history. Two texts in some positive correlation with each other give together and severally ample evidence for the development of the homily form.

Vercelli XVI and XVII are perfect homilies for Anglo-Saxon literary history because they are part of the apparent discontinuity of the subject. Each is a sole text with no apparent origin or subsequent direct influence. Homily I, by contrast, is grist for the mill of continuity because of its complex textual relations that may actually stretch over some 150 years or so from Vercelli through CCCC 303 by way of Bodley 340, CCCC 198, CCCC 162, and Cotton Tiberius A.iii, which is a hybrid blend containing interpolations from *De Parasceve* inserted into a version of Ælfric's *Dominica Palmarum de Passione Domini* (*Catholic Homilies, Second Series*).[49] Whoever put the Tiberius version together had no evident difficulty joining the anonymous

---

47 In XVII the scribe writes 'M*en*,' which Scragg expands to 'M*en þa leofestan*' (likewise the opening to XV–XVIII). This particular abbreviation would seem to define particular scribal practice.

48 See now Samantha Zacher, 'Re-reading the Style and Rhetoric of the Vercelli Homilies,' in *The Old English Homily: Precedent, Practice, and Appropriation*, ed. Aaron Kleist (Turnhout: Brepols, 2007), 173–207, who concentrates upon the use of verbal and structural repetition in Vercelli XVII.

49 *VH*, 1–5 for relationships; cf. also *CH II*, 381–90 for a composite homily related to Vercelli I.

writer with the monk of Eynsham. Thanks in major part to his adherence to the idea that Holy Thursday, Good Friday, and Holy Saturday are *swigdagas* ('days of silence'), Ælfric wrote no homilies for those days, with the result that collectors who, though following Ælfric in the main, did not share his liturgical views went to another writer (or tradition) to round out their collections.[50] *De Parasceve* was apparently a southeastern hit. The significance for the purpose at hand is not so much the popularity of Vercelli Homily I, but rather its exemplary nature. It is a very ambitious piece, serving as a biblical translation, a biblical harmony, a narrative in its own right, an example of exegesis, and an exhortation.[51] In relating the events of one of the most solemn days of the liturgical year, daunting in the complexity of the biblical narrative and in the meaning of that narrative, the homily is much more than a continuous gloss, far exceeding the generic boundaries as found in Homilies XVI and XVII. The Vercelli version, as a textual witness, stands apart from the other four, its language suggesting an earlier date, and the four later versions exhibiting modernization, expansion (perhaps), and revision.[52] These textual characteristics suggest its value to a later anonymous tradition that sought to make the piece current and in turn imply that the homily was well crafted to admit of more substantive adjustments beyond language modernization. The difficulties in textual transmission, particularly the bungling Latin, help occlude some of these strong features. When all is said and done, however, the homily with all its narrative explanations and its reconciliation of biblical features can be seen as a rewriting of the biblical narrative that at its root constitutes exegesis as well as the tendency of all biblical interpretation or presentation to 'fill in' the biblical record.[53] This latter tendency is just what the apocrypha did as well. From a contemporary perspective there is a kind of daring or confidence in the Anglo-Saxon writer to attempt what he did. Yet there are no invocations of the modesty topos at any point.

50 For *swigdagas* see Joyce Hill, 'Ælfric's "Silent Days,"' in *Sources and Relations: Studies in Honour of J.E.Cross*, ed. Marie Collins, Jocelyn Price, and Andrew Hamer, Leeds Studies in English n.s. 16 (1985): 118–31; Roberta Frank, 'A Note on Old English *Swidagas* "Silent Days,"' *Studies in Honour of René Derolez*, ed. A.M. Simon-Vandenbergen (Ghent: Seminarie voor Engelse en Oud-Germaanse Taalkunde, R.U.G., 1987), 180–9; C.A. Jones, *Ælfric's Letter to the Monks of Eynsham*, Cambridge Studies in Anglo-Saxon England 24 (Cambridge: CUP 1998), 185–6.

51 Paul E. Szarmach, 'The Earlier Homily: *De Parasceve*,' in *Studies in Earlier Old English Prose*, ed. Szarmach), 383.

52 *VH*, 1.

53 B. Harris Cowper, trans., *The Apocryphal Gospels and Other Documents Relating to the History of Christ* (London and Edinburgh: Williams and Norgate, 1867).

Homilies XVIII and XXIII, as *vitae*, and I, XVI, and XVII, as more properly varieties of *homiliae*, present the early evidence, as the Vercelli homilies must, for a way of looking at the Latin tradition. In considering the *vitae* the label 'translation' is almost too easy, but how ought one to construe the relation between the vernacular homilies and the Latin tradition when that label is not a good match? Clearly one can make the term 'translation' very elastic or one can offer another term that can cover more cases, specifically those cases that defy the customary denotation of 'translation' and in the process, I would suggest, help clarify issues in Anglo-Saxon literary history. That umbrella term is 'imitation,' that is, literary imitation and not Aristotelian *mimesis* or the 'imitation of reality.'[54] If we can understand the literary history of later Anglo-Saxon prose as a reflex of *imitatio*, the various developments in prose style, Latin and vernacular, take on a coherence that establishes bilingual and temporal links. A major problem in this potential overview is the currency of the term or the idea itself in the later tenth century. As it turns out, Quintilian and Dryden bracket the Anglo-Saxon period with their views of the process of imitation not so much as those who gave to or received influence from the Anglo-Saxon period, but rather as commentators within the problem of *imitatio* who consider the theoretical dimensions of the issues. Their role in my discussion here is formal or systemic, not historical. Quintilian, who does not make the Gneuss list of books written or owned in the Anglo-Saxon period and who gets vague notice from Ogilvy, considers the imitation of authors in *Institutio oratoria* X.2 after having given a review of Greek and Latin authors in X.1.[55] Observing in a commonsensical sort of way that imitation is how we learn, for after all musicians take the voices of their teachers, painters the works of their predecessors, and peasants the practices of agriculture as models, Quintilian sees past authors as the source for current writers: 'Neque enim dubitari potest, quin artis pars

---

54 A standard distinction; cf. M.H. Abrams, *Glossary of Literary Terms* 3rd ed. (New York: Holt, Rinehart, and Winston, 1971), s.v.

55 Helmut Gneuss, *Handlist of Anglo-Saxon Manuscripts*, Medieval and Renaissance Texts and Studies 241 (Tempe: Arizona Center for Medieval and Renaissance Studies, 2001). See also J.D.A. Ogilvy, *Books Known to the Anglo-Saxons* (Cambridge, MA: Medieval Academy of America, 1967), 233. Michael Winterbottom, 'Quintilian,' in *Texts and Transmission*, ed. L.D. Reynolds (Oxford: Clarendon Press, 1986), 332–4, describes the textual tradition of *Institutio oratoria* and entertains fleetingly the possibility that York furnished a copy to what became the French tradition. The most accessible edition of *Institutio* is in the Loeb Library: H.E. Butler, ed. and trans., *Institutio Oratoria*, 4 vols. (Cambridge, MA: Harvard Univ. Press, 1958). Book X.2 is in vol. 4, 74–91. See now Michael Lapidge, *The Anglo-Saxon Library* (Oxford: OUP, 2006), 19, 66, 68, and 129.

magna contineatur imitatione' and 'Atque omnis vitae ratio sic constat, ut quae probamus in aliis facere ipsi velimus.'[56] Yet Quintilian is very much aware of the dead hand of imitation, mere copying or slavish imitation as we might call it, arguing ultimately for a dynamic rather than a static view of the artistic process: 'Ac si omnia precenseas, nulla mansit ars, qualis inventa est, nec intra initium stetit ... Nihil autem crescit sola imitatione.'[57] There are some recognizable steps for the student of oratory to follow. The student must know what he is to imitate and why it is good; the student must know his own strengths (vires) and his talent (ingenium); the student must know the special rules (lex) and nature (decor) of the respective genres; the student must match style to the occasion. In short: 'Imitatio autem (nam saepius idem dicam) non sit tantum in verbis.'[58] Quintilian's interest in forensic oratory has no application to the Anglo-Saxon scene, nor does his treatment and description of classical authors. The problem of who were great writers was in the main solved by the tenth century, which had inherited the great patristic authors as its canon. Most importantly, Quintilian establishes the idea of imitation primarily within the Latin tradition and not across languages or, to put it another way, he has no interest in the problem of translation.

It is Dryden, whom T.R. Steiner calls 'the first major English theorist of translation,'[59] who links translation and imitation in his Preface to *Ovid's Epistles*:

> All translations, I suppose, may be reduced to these three heads. First, that of metaphrase, or turning an author word by word, and line by line, from one language into another ... The second way is that of paraphrase, or translation with latitude, where the author is kept in view by the translator, so as never to be lost, but his words are not so strictly followed as his sense ... The third

---

56 Ed. Butler, 74 with trans., 75: 'For there can be no doubt that in art no small portion of our task lies in imitation ... And it is a universal rule of life that we should wish to copy what we approve in others.'

57 Ed. Butler, 78 with trans., 79: 'Cast your eyes over the whole of history: you will find that no art has remained just as when it was discovered nor come to a standstill at its very birth ... No development is possible for those who restrict themselves to imitation.'

58 Ed. Butler, 88 and trans. 89: 'But imitation (for I must repeat this point again and again) should not be confined merely to words.'

59 T.R. Steiner, *English Translation Theory 1650–1800* (Assen, Amsterdam: Van Gorcum, 1975), Approaches to Translation Studies 2 (1975), 68. Robert Stanton, *The Culture of Translation in Anglo-Saxon England* (Cambridge: D.S. Brewer, 2002) offers a 'cultural history' of translation with special reference to glosses, biblical translation, Alfred, and Ælfric.

way is that of imitation, where the translator (if now he has not lost that name) assumes the liberty, not only to vary from the words and sense, but to forsake them both as he sees occasion; and taking only some general hints from the original, to run division on the groundwork, as he pleases.[60]

It is easy to see Alfred's 'word for word' and 'sense for sense' in Dryden's first two ways, and on the 'word' level particularly one can see these two ways operating in the *vitae* of the Vercelli homilies. The third way offers a framework that allows for the Anglo-Saxon homilists to participate in the idea of translation. The Anglo-Saxon homilists are aware of the Latin tradition as general or specific source for what they do and they take their models from it, not in a slavish way particularly. They show freedom and the flexibility in selecting and adapting the many aspects of the Latin tradition. Alfred may have been proposing or describing a straightjacket by his comments in the preface to *Pastoral Care*, but, as is well known, not even he followed the apparent prescriptions in his translations.[61] One might discern a similar practical flexibility in Bede's comment on his own translation of Cædmon: 'Hic est sensus, non autem ordo ipse verborum, quae [Cædmon] dormiens ille canebat; neque enim possunt carmina, quamuis optime conposita, ex alia in aliam linguam ad uerbum sine detrimento sui decoris ac dignitatis transferri.'[62] The practice of translation at least led to empirical principles of composition, whatever theory of translation might have been current in the early medieval period.

On the whole one would prefer to find a nice, tight equivalent for *imitatio* in the Old English lexicon, particularly instances in glossed texts, so that all appearances would be saved. *A Thesaurus of Old English* gives several leads under sections 03.06.01.01, 'Imitation,' and 09.04.03.01, 'A

---

60 Cited from Steiner, *English Translation Theory*, 68. Dryden discusses translation in the context of practice in his present day, contrasting and variously judging peers and predecessors. Of his own work he states rather forthrightly: 'For my own part, I am ready to acknowledge that I have transgressed the rules which I have given; and taken more liberty than a just translation will allow' (in Steiner, 72).

61 See my observation that Alfred translated the text as known when he translated Boethius, i.e., the commentary tradition influenced his take on Nero; 'Alfred's Nero,' in *Source of Wisdom: Old English and Early Medieval Latin Studies in Honour of Thomas D. Hill*, ed. Charles D. Wright, Frederick M. Biggs, and Thomas N. Hall (Toronto: UTP, 2007), 147–67.

62 *Bede's Ecclesiastical History*, ed. Colgrave and Mynors, 416, trans. 417: 'This is the sense but not the order of the words which he sang as he slept. For it is not possible to translate verse, however well composed, literally from one language to another without some loss of beauty and dignity.'

translation.'[63] The first category seems rather to concern words for personal behaviour or moral conduct rather than literary imitation, though the root *bisen-* augurs well. Bosworth-Toller defines *licettung* as 'feigning, pretence, false representation' among several possibilities and *gelicbisen* as 'in a personal sense, an imitator.' One must note in passing *geefenlæcestre* for *imitatrix* or 'female imitator.' For 'A translation' and the subheading 'To translate' the verb *awendan* is the major lexical item. The *DOE* 'A' volume offers nine occurrences, seven in the works of Ælfric, one in Alfred's *Preface* to the *Pastoral Care*, and one in Byrhtferth's *Enchiridion* [cited as Byrhtferth's *Manual*]. In his *Grammar* (B1.9.1) Ælfric writes: 'Ic Ælfric wolde þas lytlan boc awendan to Engliscum gereorde of ðam stæf-cræfte, þe is gehaten *Grammatica*,' where the meaning has got to be 'to translate,' as the Latin equivalent demands, 'ad vestram linguam transferre.'[64] Although what Ælfric did to the Latin has not been the subject of major research, any other rendering by me would be special pleading. Ælfric presumably was a grammarian here, trying to use terminology accurately, and we all understand him to seek no worse than paraphrase, and indeed metaphrase if he can, until someone comes along to argue otherwise. Ælfric has a bout of scruples, probably both intellectual and moral, when he considers translation in the *Preface* to Genesis (B8.1.7.1).[65] Three times he invokes *awendan* to describe his operations. The first and third occurrences concern his moral or spiritual qualms, nervousness if you like, over the burden of *awendan*, culminating in his fervent plea not to be asked to translate from Latin into English again. The second occurrence is more revealing because it talks about the two languages as languages. Granting that Genesis is 'on manegum stowum swyðe nearolice gesett' ['in many places strictly to be construed'], deep in spiritual understanding, *geendebyrd* ['disposed'] as God himself dictated it to Moses, Ælfric observes that one dare not write more in English than the Latin has (which means what, exactly?), nor translate *endebyrdnysse* except in one particular, namely, that Latin and English do not have *ane wisan* ['idiom' as per Wilcox]. The translator or the teacher finds the English has its own *wisan*,

---

63 Jane Roberts and Christian Kay, with Lynne Grundy, comp., *A Thesaurus of Old English* (London: King's College London, Centre for Late Antique and Medieval Studies, 1995), 180–1 and 474–5 respectively. The *Thesauraus* is now available online at http://libra.englang.arts.gla.ac.uk/oethesaurus/.

64 Now edited by Jonathan Wilcox, *Ælfric's Prefaces*, Durham Medieval Texts 9 (Durham: Durham Medieval Texts, 1994), texts 3a and b, 114–16, with notes on 151–3.

65 *DOE Corpus*, *awendan* for 'ÆGenPref B8.1.7.1; ed. Wilcox, 116–19, with notes on 153–5.

making it *swyðe gedwolsum* ['erroneous'] for those who do not recognize *ðæs Ledenes wise*. Ælfric is perhaps echoing Bede here about language difference. He is certainly thinking of paraphrase, which in practical terms places him on the road to imitation, thus compounding whatever moral and spiritual anxieties he has.

The response to the Latin tradition in Vercelli shows a certain suppleness that runs from closer word-to-word rendering through broader imitative composition. Significantly, the Vercelli response also shows rejection of the Latin tradition. The translator of Felix, as we have seen, avoids any attempt to render the difficult language of his Latin precursor. On the level of word formation Old English certainly has the resources to offer compounding or kenning-formation to match the extravagances of the Latin. The full ramifications of this early rejection have only recently begun to become clear. Mechthild Gretsch has argued cogently for an active bilingualism in the Benedictine Revival and the role of Æthelwold in promoting Aldhelm and his hermeneutic prose and vocabulary.[66] In her overall argument the corpus of Old English glosses play a major part in the development of English as a medium for scholarly discourse. One can readily grant the rise of a neo-Aldhelmian hermeneutical style in the face of such strong evidence, but just as the Benedictine Revival was not an all-encompassing success, the rebirth of Aldhelm could not be expected to be uniformly successful. Further, more extensive, bilingual analysis could and should prove that prose style was more of a contested ground than hitherto thought. Here I can only offer this suggestion: Vercelli Homily XXII can serve for now as perhaps the earliest example of self-conscious dissent from the new hermeneuticism.[67]

The Latin tradition sometimes casts light, sometimes shadow, on vernacular prose, and the emphasis thus far on Latin connections overshadows the several *Kompilationspredigten* that round out the importance of the Vercelli homilies for vernacular prose style. Homilies II–IV, VIII–X, and XIX–XXI show the distinctive marks of this sub-genre of religious prose, whose many examples in this collection and throughout the Old English corpus bear witness to the form. It was L.G. Whitbread who was, it would appear, the first to describe the genre as 'scissors and paste' productions,

---

66 Mechthild Gretsch, *The Intellectual Foundations of the English Benedictine Revival*, CSASE 25 (Cambridge: CUP, 1999). See my review in *Speculum* 77 (2002): 537–9.

67 It would be a perverse aestheticism to criticize Felix's 'bombast' and then criticize in turn the OE translator's rejection of it or to consider his option for a simpler style as a mere failure of ability to render the 'bombast.'

but a more positive description might consider these pieces anticipating 'word processing,' such as we all do now, in the movement and rearrange-ment of motifs and paragraph-like constructions.[68] With the discovery of the importance of Cambridge, Pembroke College 25 to the anonymous tradition, certain compositional issues concerning source work and ques-tions of independent composition have come to relative closure.[69] Whatever structural skill one might find in XX, for example, comes substantially from the Latin tradition, where Alcuin's *Liber de Virtutibus et Vitiis* had already been metamorphosed into three homilies, with some attempt to adapt them for oral delivery in the mid-ninth century, as Pembroke College 25 arts. 93–5 helps substantiate.[70] Likewise, Homily XIX derives its Rogation narratives from several items in the St Père homiliary tradition as repre-sented by Pembroke College 25, most notably art. 36 with its account of Jonah and art. 40 with its Gallic history of Rogationtide.[71] But the use of Latin here is in a different style, perhaps because of the more 'modern' late Old English, but certainly in the apparently easy familiarity in the incor-poration of elements, or the generally freer treatment.

But Homilies II and XXI make the most instructive pair for Anglo-Saxon literary history. Scragg suggests that since as yet no identifiable source has been found for II, it 'was probably freely composed in English.'[72] The piece was very popular, as the several later and related versions of the homily bear witness. The textual relations are so complex that Scragg must print Homily II and Cambridge, Corpus Christi College 419, the closest parallel in the use of anonymous material (outside of XXI), in order to as-sert better control over the textual variance.[73] This eschatological homily seeks to stir emotions by vibrant and violent imagery invoking a fear of the Last Days and through rhythmical prose of varying sorts. E.G. Stanley offers the most comprehensive treatment of the various kinds of prose

---

68 L.G. Whitbread, 'Wulfstan Homilies XXIX, XXX, and Some Related Texts,' *Anglia* 81 (1963): 36.

69 J.E. Cross, *Cambridge, Pembroke College MS 25: A Carolingian Sermonary Used by Anglo-Saxon Preachers*, King's College London Medieval Studies 1 (London: King's College, 1987).

70 See now my 'Pembroke College, arts. 93–95,' in *Via Crucis: Essays on Early Medieval Sources and Ideas in Memory of J.E. Cross*, ed. Thomas N. Hall with assistance from Thomas D. Hill and Charles D. Wright (Morgantown: West Virginia Univ. Press, 2002), 295–325.

71 Cross, *Pembroke 25*.

72 *VH*, xxxviii.

73 Scragg describes the textual situation in his introduction to Homily II, *VH*, 48–51.

rhythms in this complex of texts and lays out a set of issues relevant to the main arguments of this paper.[74] As Stanley so lucidly describes the evidence, the marked rhythms in Homily II challenge the boundaries of verse and prose and, by implication, asks the reader to adjust his reception of these rhythms. Stanley's capacious view of what constitutes Old English prose rhythms allows for parallelism and balance, the sort we would expect from good prose of our day, and he even reaches into the nature of English itself to describe effects. The passage that constitutes the moment of truth for any editor is the longish description of the day of wrath. Förster prints the section as verse (II.47–72), as does Stanley in his presentation (p. 372), but Scragg prints it as prose (II.39–51), observing that the passage is at best doggerel and dubious Sievers Type B verses.[75] It is not easy to determine whether this passage is intercalated verse, imported into a prose text from an otherwise free-standing poem, or a reflex of the original writer, who tried to heighten his own prose with an attempt at verse that goes perhaps beyond his typical sallies into prose rhythms. Aesthetics and editing aside, the point for literary history is clear: Homily II is a benchmark text for the attempt to elevate expository prose with poetic effects. The explanation for this move may lie in the antecedent history or prehistory of expository prose. So far as one can tell, with the exception of laws and perhaps 'oral' documents such as land boundary definitions, there was no tradition of expository prose in the vernacular.[76] Discussions of unlettered literature invariably concern poetry, whose oral nature seems well beyond dispute. To draw on the vernacular poetic tradition would seem to be a logical move for a prose writer to appeal to the aural expectations of his audience. Latin gives evidence for prosimetrum forms, best exemplified by Boethius's *De consolatione Philosophiae*, and sermon literature may give evidence for the use of *cursus*, but the intercalation of poetry into early Latin sermons or a 'break-out' into verse by a prose

---

74 E.G. Stanley, '*The Judgment of the Damned* (from Cambridge, Corpus Christi College 201 and Other Manuscripts), and the Definition of Old English Verse,' in *Learning and Literature in Anglo-Saxon England*, ed. Michael Lapidge and Helmut Gneuss (Cambridge: CUP, 1985), 363–91.

75 Max Förster, ed., *Die Vercelli-Homilien,* Bibliothek der Angelsächsischen Prosa 12 (Hamburg: Henri Grand, 1932), 47–9; Scragg, *VH,* 67 n. to 39–51. Had I edited Homily II, I would have done what I did in Homily XXI, viz., considered the passage as verse, warts and all.

76 Dorothy Bethurum, 'Stylistic Features of the Old English Laws,' *MLR* 27 (1932): 263–79.

writer seems uncharted territory at this time.[77] An Anglo-Saxonist's explanation seems easy enough: an ecclesiastical genre took advantage of a vernacular tradition the audience knew. In the process, vernacular sermons with marked rhythms became a tradition.

Homily XXI shows how this tradition could grow. As is well known, one can read XXI and II as collateral descendants of a common exemplar in that substantial part of XXI common to both. The Vercelli scribe was not therefore enterprising enough to merge two antecedent texts in a merely scribal way. The comparative unity in Group B4a, specifically similar layout and design, the uniformity of later language forms, and the treatment of material all support the notion of one ruling, authorial consciousness that composed XXI as it did XIX and XX. The high number of corrections in XXI, noted by Scragg,[78] further implies a degree of freshness to the presence of this unique homily in the Vercelli Book. If one can infer a 'B4a-author,' this author shows his skill at adapting Latin texts from the St Père Homiliary and in incorporating vernacular rhythms. The method of composition exemplifies how a *Kompilationspredigt* comes to be. Latin texts stand behind roughly the first half of the homily, which marshals penitential themes in more or less unadorned or bald or straightforward language. By stark rhetorical contrast, the simple effects of parallelism, repetition, balance, listing of elements (*þa twelf mægenu*) become heightened as the content of that rhetoric concerns the fear and terror of the Last Days. In the first half the homilist can quote the Beatitudes (for example, Mt. 5:7, 'Eadige beoð þa mildheortan') and in the second half he produces the same chilling verse-like picture found in Homily II. One connecting motif throughout the whole is the repetition of the exhortation *Men þa leofestan*. Each of the first six paragraphs in the Scragg edition begin with this direct address, as do the eighth and ninth. The audience can expect the repetition, and it is the presence of the voice that is a unifying element in the entire oral performance, but the ninth repetition introduces the visionary world of Homily II. All in all, this move is a kind of rhetorical 'bait-and-switch.' The bridge between the two halves is the passage XXI.128–55, constituting the eighth paragraph. There the alliteration becomes more prominent. Lines 149–55 have their echo in *An Exhortation to*

---

77 See Jan Ziolkowski, 'The Prosimetrum in the Classical Tradition,' in *Prosimetrum: Crosscultural Perspectives on Narrative in Prose and Verse*, ed. Joseph Harris and Karl Reichl (Woodbridge and Rochester, NY: D.S. Brewer, 1997), 45–65, who gives a review of prosimetrical forms in the Middle Ages.

78 *VH*, 350.

Christian Living 2–15, and lines 128–41 may echo a now lost poem.[79] In another aural way the audience begins to anticipate the rhythms that will eventually dominate the moral imagination. Source work and formalist methodologies combine to show how a skilful author composes an effective moral discourse. From another perspective the Latin origins are indeed 'translated' into the vernacular in a comparatively seamless way. It is the Old English author who chooses and orders the themes from various places. The hearer/reader may notice the structure of a theme, most simply exemplified by *þa twelf mægnu*, but the Latin origins of a theme are neither presented outright, say by the invocation of *wordwriteras*, nor recognized.

Vercelli Homily X is an earlier version of the genre, in direct contrast to XXI. If XXI shows how a *Kompilationspredigt* is put together, X shows in its textual history how a vernacular homily can be reworked and adapted. The tradition treats this text, otherwise known as Napier XLIX, much like certain Latin works in mining it for various material; again Alcuin's *Liber de uirtutibus et uitiis* comes to mind as an example of a kind of epitome and adaptation. Altogether there are nine copies: three complete and one apparently intended to be, two forming an abstractive version, two joining with other texts, and one masking its original state because of a loss of leaves.[80] There is a pre-history, one might be ready to infer, and the witnesses extend from Vercelli through Bodley 343, dateable to the second half of the twelfth century. The long popularity of Vercelli X is not without reasonable warrant, for if the title 'Vercelli Master' is to be accorded to the writer of any of the twenty-three pieces, the author of Vercelli X is surely the odds-on favourite. There is so much to praise here, and much of the praise has already appeared in print, that there need be here only two ideas relevant to the main themes of this sketched literary history. The homilist has a flare for poetic and dramatic effects, all artfully joined. He employs the *ubi sunt* theme, for instance, to great effect when he presents the mutability theme (X.233ff.). The repetitive balance of the question

---

79 See *VH*, 348. Angus McIntosh, *Wulfstan's Prose*, PBA 35 (1949): 109–42; also issued separately and repaginated, which is the version followed here, at 33 n. 29. McIntosh comments on the Vercelli passage and its relation to *An Exhortation* in connection with a more extended discussion of Napier XXX. See also Charles D. Wright, 'More Old English Poetry in Vercelli Homily XXI,' in *Early Medieval Texts and Interpretations: Studies Presented to Donald G. Scragg*, ed. E. Treharne and S. Rosser, MRTS (Tempe: ACMRS, 2003), 245–62.

80 *VH*, 191–5 for general discussion and 195 for a proposed stemma. This homily and XVIII have their witnesses in the *Blickling Homilies* [= B], which Scragg (*VH*, xxv–xxvi) sees as part of a different tradition.

Hwær sindon/Hwær com is no less effective here than it is in *The Wanderer* (ll. 92–3). For Anglo-Saxonists who read the passage the prose passage is very textural and echoic, as it must have been for the Anglo-Saxons who heard it. Here is virtually a pure example of prose-verse crossover. The theme of mutability ends with a natural image of transitoriness: the excessive love of the riches of the earth passes like a rain shower. The image is telescoped or embedded because after the rain shower there is bright sun and fair weather. The homilist could have stopped the image at the passing of the rain, but rather he makes the daring move to go beyond the terms of the comparison to the *status post hoc*, where the implied turmoil of the pursuit of earth's riches is over. Even the citation of Matthew 25:41, 'Discedite a me, maledicti, in ignem aeternum,' receives a poetic rendering in six lines of 'classical verse.'[81] The dramatic scenes of Homily X are as memorable as the terrible day of wrath in Homily II. The homilist takes from Paulinus of Aquileia, *Liber exhortationis ad Henricum comitem*, and portrays a remarkable conceit: at the Last Judgment the devil appears as a litigant seeking justice from the just Judge because the sinning souls are his. The devil describes the devil's due by relating the sins that the souls commit, which make them his. The moral inversion of the scene is considerably more effective than any direct diatribe against sins and sinners. The audience knows what it means to be 'the devil's man' from the devil's own voice. The successor scene is the Lord's just judgment of a proud and rich man. Here the rhetoric is the direct verbal attack that one associates with the anonymous tradition. The Lord asks question after question of the mute and inglorious sinner, while declarative statements and commands further render the sinner helpless before the severe Judge. As Christ says, 'Þin sawl on þisse ilcan niht bið be minre hæse of ðinum lichoman alæded' (X.192–3). The homilist has the range to offer frontal attack as well as poetic imagery.

The various Vercelli homilies chosen here suggest the kinds of issues that obtain at the outset of the literary history of later Anglo-Saxon prose in the ecclesiastical genres of saints' lives, homilies as such, and sermons as such. The clear and present reality for this prose is the extant Latin tradition and its influence. There is anxiety of influence here, but not the sort

---

81 Joseph B. Trahern, Jr, 'An Old English Verse Paraphrase of Matthew 25:41,' *Mediaevalia* 1 (1975): 109–41. For a further discussion of the poetry embedded in this homily, see Samantha Zacher, 'Sin, Syntax, and Synonyms: Rhetorical Structure and Style in Vercelli Homily X,' *JEGP* 103 (2004): 53–76.

we might associate with modern authors and their relations with the past.[82] The anxiety is the hope to replicate the Latin prose somehow in a language medium that has its own system and to 'carry over' the doctrinal content to the vernacular. The vernacular response is varied and autonomous, already before Vercelli itself gets set down. The Vercelli prose writers show a freedom in adaptation, especially in responding to structural features found in the Latin genres, and the rejection of the hermeneutic in the Guthlac rendition is telling. The move towards 'bombastic' diction is not apparent in the homilies, but the move towards rhythmical effects most certainly is. The attempt to adapt poetry to prose and to seek other marked rhythmical expressions demonstrates perhaps the most characteristic features of the Vercelli prose. Here is where Jusserand has 'builded better than he knew' in his comment on prose with the 'tone and forms of poetry.' To incorporate poetic or near-poetic forms is to seek to capitalize on the achievements of vernacular oral poetry or at the least to find some way to meet the oral expectations of an audience. The Vercelli Book shows the range of stylistic possibilities. Here one might try to revive the classical distinction between Asian and Attic prose, applying it to the Anglo-Saxon vernacular.[83] The homilies featuring marked rhythm are most definitely 'Asian' in their self-conscious use of rhythmical adornment; those that avoid such rhythmical adornment are, by contrast, 'Attic.' The citation of this classical typology, well developed in classical rhetoric, is analogical here, representing the potential of any language system to go 'fancy' or 'plain.'

The Vercelli homilies point towards Ælfric and Wulfstan in some special ways. Ælfric may very well have learned the flexible way to present the exegesis of a pericope from true homilies such as XVI and XVII. The straightforward presentation of teaching may have been another lesson Ælfric may have learned from his predecessors. Homily XVI presents a recognizable teaching voice that I would tentatively suggest is not like Ælfric's. It is off-balanced to portray one example against many, but I would not characterize Ælfric's voice as characteristically ingratiating and forthcoming. Ælfric is the serious teacher, sober and scrupulous, and though, for example, Gregory the Great shows the latter quality too, he communicates a warm teaching voice, often by references to himself and

---

82 The phrase is, of course, Harold Bloom's. See especially his *The Anxiety of Influence: A Theory of Poetry* (Oxford: OUP, 1973).

83 R. Derolez, 'Anglo-Saxon Literature: "Attic" or "Asiatic"? Old English Poetry and Its Latin Background,' in *English Studies Today*, ed. G.A. Bonnard (Bern: Francke Verlag, 1961), 93–105. My thanks to Katherine O'Brien O'Keeffe for this reference.

to his personal health. What Ælfric most assuredly did not get from the Vercelli homilies is the light alliterative, rhythmical style seen in Lives of Saints. Vercelli, however, may create the context for the development of this style. Vercelli offers the impassioned Asian style and the unadorned Attic style. When Ælfric considered the options available to him to heighten the effects of his prose, the marked rhythms found in Vercellese prose could not have appealed to his cooler *mentalité*. He rejected this option much as he rejected hermeneutical prose in his Latin. For his rhythmical prose Ælfric incorporated alliteration, rhythm less than classical, and no heightened diction.[84] In reaction to the literature of vocabulary, be it poetic or Aldhelmian, and in the avoidance of impassioned marked rhythm, whether intercalated verse or not, Ælfric finds another form to imitate elevated discourse. Ælfric saw no fit between the overall direction of his style and any Asian option.

The evidence indicates that Wulfstan chose the other main Vercellese path. The struggles by Napier, Jost, Bethurum, and McIntosh to differentiate his rhythms from those found in antecedent and contemporary texts make for a substantial body of scholarship as they seek to establish the *echt* and the *unecht* in the corpus. As McIntosh says, 'It is almost certain that Wulfstan was brought up in familiarity with the traditions which Vercelli represents.'[85] The vagaries of dating, Vercelli itself excepted, help conjure up a school or 'those cloudy figures, the Wulfstan imitators.'[86] The *Sermo Lupi* is the well-known signature piece that could, arguably, represent the tradition found in the Vercelli Book as its highpoint. But here is where aestheticism occludes judgment. Though Vercelli homilies offer vernacular marked rhythm and show, pre-Wulfstan, skill and flare, this prose tradition has never had many advocates because of its 'strained' effects. Yet the indisputable evidence from Vercelli is that this rhythmical style and exhortation on behalf of penitential themes was indeed an option. Wulfstan, who tried his hand at poetry in the Chronicle poems on the accession and death of Edgar,[87] and by implication could find himself ready to compose poetry, chose the impassioned vernacular prose style from the options available for his role as homilist and lawgiver. Most of

---

84 The classic description of the form is in John C. Pope, ed., *Homilies of Ælfric: A Supplementary Collection*, vol. 1, EETS o.s. 259 (1967): 105–36.
85 McIntosh, *Wulfstan's Prose*, 17.
86 Ibid., 18.
87 See F. Jost, 'Wulfstan und die angelsächsische Chronik,' *Anglia* 47 (1943): 105–23 and accepted by Bethurum, *WH*, 47.

the analysis that documents this tradition concentrates on the two-stress phrase and its technical manipulation. A larger sense of style and the options can make Wulfstan appear in higher relief and make him a more positive figure in the later history of Anglo-Saxon prose. Those who like to see native traditions triumph over imported Latin ones will miss the meaning here intended: the grand choice is between Asian and Attic. Wulfstan chose vernacular Asian for its apparent positive features that allow him to exhort and move his audience to obey Christian and secular law. The precise development of Wulfstan's style from the Vercelli option needs updating.

In this chapter I have tried to argue for a more narrative form of literary history in the later Anglo-Saxon period. Problems of literary history and literary approaches notwithstanding, the Vercelli prose offers a baseline for the development of Anglo-Saxon prose in the ecclesiastical genres. As a collection, the Vercelli prose is a summary of the options for prose style. These options, sometimes more sometimes less, reflect possibilities for various kinds of imitation of the Latin tradition. Here I have primarily concentrated on the Vercelli prose to describe the varieties within the collection and to suggest how these varieties may have related to each other and to select subsequent developments. McIntosh distinguishes five types of writing, 'from the rhythmical point of view': 'classical' Old English verse, 'debased' Old English verse, the rhythmical style used by Ælfric in *Lives of Saints*, Wulfstan's prose, and ordinary prose, with open acknowledgment that there may be more types.[88] The Latin context and its own stylistic developments cast another light on the vernacular that amplifies McIntosh's typology and begins the process of considering the period under discussion as a bi-lingual whole, whose issues of style 'carry over' from one language system to another. The rivalry between the Asian and the Attic, as we might choose to call them unhistorically and as embedded in any language system, appear in the tenth century in Latin and in Old English. Vercelli shows the range, while later Ælfric finds another register and Wulfstan extends Vercelli's potential.[89]

---

88 Ibid., 2–4.
89 In the collection *The Old English Homily and Its Backgrounds* (Albany, NY: State Univ. of New York Press, 1978), which I co-edited with Bernard F. Huppé, I contributed 'The Vercelli Homilies: Style and Structure,' at 241–67, which described Homilies IX–XXII on more or less formalist, i.e., 'new critical,' grounds.

Studies in the Language of Copyists
of the Vercelli Homilies

DONALD G. SCRAGG

The introduction to my edition of the Vercelli homilies[1] contains a long section on the language of the prose items in the Vercelli Book which concludes (with certain abbreviations silently expanded):

> Two important linguistic conclusions can be drawn from the evidence. First, the language of [the Vercelli Book] is a valuable witness to the variety of linguistic forms that a late-tenth-century scribe was faced with, and to his tolerance of them. Second (and related to this) is the information [the Vercelli Book] offers for the spread of late West-Saxon in the tenth century. The terms early West-Saxon, late West-Saxon, Kentish and Mercian are themselves very inexact, and they relate more to scriptorium traditions than to spoken dialects or to geographical areas. The distinction between early West-Saxon and late West-Saxon may itself be less one of date than of scriptorium tradition. We still lack a comprehensive analysis of late Old English comparable with that which exists for early West-Saxon and the major non-West-Saxon dialects. Understanding of the development of the late Anglo-Saxon scriptorium machine will not be advanced without further comprehensive studies of late Old English manuscripts.[2]

What I wrote twenty years ago seems to me still to hold: we still lack a comprehensive analysis of the language of the fullest recorded period of Old English, that is, the period from the copying of the Vercelli Book itself (middle of the second half of the tenth century) to the Norman Conquest, and we still need more studies of the language of late Old English scribes

1 *VH*, xix–lxxxii.
2 *VH*, lxxi.

and their manuscripts. By looking at the language of copies of Vercelli homilies other than those in the Vercelli Book, I intend in this essay to begin to fill some part of both of those gaps in our knowledge, and to indicate a way forward for further research. Ultimately, perhaps, examination of the language of the separate manuscripts when coupled with the information on the Vercelli Book that I published in my edition might show us something of the language of the homilies as they existed in the tenth century, and of their dissemination subsequently.

If there is one feature of my edition that I regret it is that I was not able to print a full set of variants in the apparatus. To provide a selection of substantive variants only from the base text is Early English Text Society policy for their editions, and while that makes perfect sense for Middle English texts, where many copies survive, it makes no sense at all for Old English, where multiple copies are relatively rare, and, when they do occur, are interesting for all of their forms, not just for those which an editor at the time of editing judges to be significant in the establishment of the text. In any case, choosing a base text when multiple copies survive is in itself a dangerous practice, although it may be deemed a necessary one for practical purposes. One scholar's focus of interest, the 'earliest' recorded version which is usually the choice for an editor in Old English (and was the obvious choice in the case of the Vercelli homilies), is not another's, who may reasonably wish to see how a text was used subsequent to its composition. Furthermore, the earliest manuscript copy of a text may not be the most reliable witness to the authorial version, as reference to the Latin source shows to be the case in some of the Vercelli Book readings. Since an editor has to make full collation of all available manuscripts before editing a text, it is a pity that those collations should be lost. Even the variant readings that an editor includes in the apparatus have not always reached a wide audience (for example, compilers of Old English grammars), especially when they are not included in the glossary.

Fortunately we now have available in electronic form a variety of research tools which assists those who seek information on variant readings, both those which are cited in the standard editions and those which have been suppressed. Primary place must go to the *Dictionary of Old English* corpus of Old English and its offshoots, together with the *Dictionary*'s CD-ROM, but even these magnificent tools do not have references to full spelling variants, because they exclude those which scholars have traditionally regarded as 'permissable' within the late Old English spelling system. At the time of publication of my edition, I drew attention in a different publication to the need for a comprehensive inventory of spelling variants in the eleventh century,[3] and during the last few years I have been at work at Manchester with a team of assistants in compiling such a resource. This essay will use the materials of the resulting database of eleventh-century spellings to show some features of the language of copies of the Vercelli homilies recorded in manuscripts other than the Vercelli Book, and by that means will attempt to distinguish features of the language of the originals from that of later copyists.

The Manchester database[4] has four main elements. The first is a conspectus of all eleventh-century manuscripts with texts in English,[5] detailing scribal stints and a list of items, both delineated by page and line. The second is a comprehensive analysis of the script of each hand in each manuscript, amounting in all to over five hundred scribes writing English during the eleventh century (not including more than that number again who made interlinear and marginal additions), and including, in very many cases, images of the salient palaeographic features, a part of the database which is clearly a major electronic resource in itself, as well as being an admirable teaching tool. This section also has a full bibliography of facsimiles and published works on script. Third, the database lists all copies of every English text within the manuscripts (almost two thousand) together with their generally accepted titles, Cameron numbers, and bibliographical references. Finally, and most importantly for the purposes of the present essay, it has an analysis of all the spellings that the currently uploaded texts contain, arranged by lemma so that variant spellings of the same or related words are listed together. There is also a substitutions button, which allows the user to access alternative spellings across a range of words, e.g., *-eald-* and *-ald-* spellings (e.g., *wealdend, waldend*, 'ruler'), or *-ch-* alternating with *-c-* (e.g., *tæchð, tæcð*, 'teaches'). Each of these four elements is searchable in a variety of ways and the architecture of the database allows spellings to be linked to manuscripts, texts, and scribes, and vice versa. Although much of the palaeographic data is based on existing

---

3 See my 'Spelling Variation in Eleventh-Century English,' in *England in the Eleventh Century*, ed. Carola Hicks, Harlaxton Medieval Studies 2 (Stamford: Paul Watkins, 1992), 347–54.

4 The database, entitled 'An Inventory of Script and Spellings in Eleventh-Century English,' is available at http://www.arts.manchester.ac.uk/mancass/C11database/. New material is being added regularly.

5 Excluded are manuscripts with discontinuous glosses only.

published information which can presently be found in Ker[6] and Sawyer,[7] there are additional tools such as lists of texts written by the same hand, and the material is more up-to-date than Ker. At the time of writing this essay, the manuscript versions as written by the original scribes (free from later accretions or alterations) of more than half the items in the listed manuscripts have been uploaded, giving searchable access to the work of a very large number of individual scribes and to the variety of spellings used for individual words.[8]

It is in the last function that the database offers a considerable advance not only on the *DOE* materials but on individual editions (such as my *Vercelli Homilies*) as well, because each individual word of an uploaded text can be seen within the sense-unit context of the Toronto corpus of texts, together with the sense-unit number. By clicking on the number, the user can access a complete collation of all versions of that text which the database contains. In other words, for a homily such as one of Ælfric's First Series items, which may survive in up to thirteen eleventh-century copies, clicking on a word from the Royal manuscript, Clemoes's base text,[9] will give full collation of all copies of the sense unit, with both substantive and minor spelling variants.[10] This is in addition to the principal purpose of the linguistic element of the database, which is to show the word in the context of every other spelling of the same word in eleventh-century texts, and in comparison with the rest of the work of the scribe who wrote it. The chronological span of the database is 980–1099, which means that the Vercelli Book is excluded by a generation.[11] But using my edition with the database gives access to variants that I excluded because of EETS policy.[12]

---

6 Ker, *Catalogue*.

7 P.H. Sawyer, *Anglo-Saxon Charters: An Annotated List and Bibliography* (London: Royal Historical Society, 1968). A more up-to-date version, constantly in course of revision, is available on the web at http://www.trin.cam.ac.uk/chartwww/.

8 Over a million words have been entered, representing the work of the majority of known scribes.

9 *CH* I; Clemoes's base text is British Library, Royal 7 C. XII. All references to the First Series homilies are to this edition.

10 At the time of writing, full collation of all versions of most of *Catholic Homilies I* has been entered into the database.

11 Ker (*Catalogue*, 460) dates it as X², i.e., third quarter of the tenth century, roughly 975.

12 Because the database is concerned with spellings used by principal scribes, it has no details of the work of correctors and annotators. However, thanks to new funding obtained in 2007, lists of annotations and alterations in many manuscripts may now be accessed via an annotations button.

The linguistic information is not confined to spelling, although that is the principal upon which the database was constructed. Spelling can be a guide to accidence too, insofar as differences in accidence often come down to differences in spelling. Use of wild cards (% in the database means any letter or group of letters, or no letter) can enable the end-user to see the use of a specific inflection (e.g., *-et* for *-eð*). Also the collation can show substitution of words or changes in syntax. However, the collation button works only when more than one copy of a text has the same Cameron number in the *DOE*. In the case of Vercelli II, for example, the parallel text in Vercelli XXI has a different Cameron number and will not show up in collation, and nor will Napier XL, even though much of that item parallels Vercelli II. On the other hand, copies of Napier XL are collated with each other because they have the same Cameron number. In Vercelli IX, the variant in Oxford, Bodleian Library, Hatton 115 (my L) again has a different Cameron number and is not collated. Finally, as regards the present essay, the database is concerned with eleventh-century spelling, and therefore copies of Vercelli homilies that survive in twelfth-century manuscripts, such as three of the surviving versions of Vercelli X, are excluded.

Work on the database has involved reading in manuscript a vast range of unpublished texts (unpublished in the sense that they are multiple copies of a text printed from another manuscript), and this has thrown up many details which can be easily overlooked in the printed editions. I offer just one example, which came to my attention while reading manuscripts of the *Catholic Homilies*. Vercelli V, line 37,[13] has a translation of the Gospel text *pax in hominibus bonae uoluntatis* (Lk 2:14; 'peace to men of good will') as *sybb ... þam mannum þe godes willan sien wyrcende* ('peace to those men who are working God's will'), a reading which appears in all three surviving copies, the Vercelli Book, Oxford, Bodleian Library, Bodley 340/342, and Cambridge, Corpus Christi College 198, although in Bodley 340 (where the piece is heavily emended) *wyrcende* has been erased. This is an obvious instance of an early copyist's misunderstanding of *godes willan* as 'God's will' rather than 'good will.' Interestingly, the same reading has been added twice to the earliest surviving copy of Ælfric's *CH* I.2 (which like Vercelli V is a Nativity homily), once interlinearly (l. 31) and once in the margin (l. 129).[14] Clemoes cites the additions in his variants,

---

13 All references to the Vercelli homilies are to my *VH*.
14 The additions can be seen in *Ælfric's First Series of Catholic Homilies: British Museum Royal 7 C. XII, fols. 4–218*, ed. Norman Eliason and Peter Clemoes, EEMF 13 (Copenhagen: Rosenkilde and Bagger, 1966), fols. 10r and 12v.

but apart from signalling them as written by a later hand, makes no further comment. Reference to the manuscript shows that the scribe is eleventh-century (the Manchester database catalogue of letter images shows the large number of manuscripts with the distinctive high *d* with curled ascender in combination with the dotted, straight-sided *y*). Clearly it was not just an early copyist of Vercelli V and the scribes in the transmission of it that made this error, one that shows a failure to understand in Latin a familiar Gospel reading. The point underscores Kenneth Sisam's statement made in reference to another of the poetic codices: 'A few years ago, when turning over the Beowulf MS., I was surprised to observe that certain facts had escaped notice or attention.'[15] The two instances of *wyrcende* in the Royal manuscript had certainly not escaped Clemoes's attention, but no one has hitherto brought them together with the Vercelli instance, as far as I am aware.

To turn now to the main thrust of the argument in this essay, my procedure will be to consider in turn each manuscript which contains one or more copies of the homilies, taking them in rough chronological order, and looking for details of their language, and for any information that they might provide about the language of the homilies before they were copied into surviving manuscripts. Manuscripts which are dated after the middle of the eleventh century will largely be ignored, since the linguistic evidence they provide is increasingly unrepresentative of that of the earlier period, and thus they are less likely to provide evidence of the language of the homilies when they were composed, and consideration of the development of written English after the Norman Conquest is beyond the scope of this essay. I begin with a series of related Kentish manuscripts, two already mentioned, Bodley 340/342 and CCCC 198, plus Cambridge, Corpus Christi College 162. These three manuscripts contain copies of Vercelli I and III, Bodley 340/342 and CCCC 198 also have copies of V and VIII, and Bodley alone has a copy of IX. In addition, CCCC 162 has copies of XIX and XX. The three are important witnesses to the transmission of Vercelli items because they are all closely related textually, and can be localized with reasonable precision. They all derive their Ælfric *CH* I and II items from the copy sent by the author to Archbishop Sigeric of Canterbury, a set which was integrated into a single chronological sequence (presumably at the archbishop's orders), as allowed by Ælfric's

---

15 Kenneth Sisam, 'The *Beowulf*-Manuscript,' in *Studies in the History of Old English Literature* (Oxford: Clarendon Press, 1953), 61; repr. from *MLR* in 1916.

own preface.[16] Three quarters of a century ago Kenneth Sisam showed the importance for students of Ælfric of Bodley 340/342 and the relationship of that manuscript with CCCC 198.[17] His study provided the foundation for Clemoes's edition of the First Series. The organization of CCCC 162 is different,[18] for it excludes pieces for saints' days and includes items written by Ælfric subsequent to the publication of *CH* I and II. Nonetheless, where they overlap, all three manuscripts are drawn from the same archetype, with the two Cambridge manuscripts, despite their different principle of selection, being textually closer to each other than either is to Bodley.[19] All three bear witness to the existence in south-eastern England at the end of the tenth century of a library containing copies of many Vercelli items.[20]

Bodley 340/342 was the subject of an unpublished dissertation by Neil Ker, who notes the perfection of use by the single scribe of the manuscript of the marked written space: 'To ensure the correct amount of space was used the scribe uses word division, abbreviations, special letter forms, extended end strokes ... an excellent example of the care taken by an Anglo-Saxon scribe to perfect his work.'[21] A similar care seems to extend to language, something which is not found in either of the Cambridge manuscripts or in the Vercelli Book, and it is worth examining this in some detail. Bodley 340/342 is a Kentish manuscript which was certainly in Rochester at some time during the eleventh century,[22] but which, as I have noted, derives from a Canterbury archetype, and which was probably itself written in Canterbury, according to Ker at the very end of the tenth

---

16 See *Ælfric's Prefaces*, ed. Jonathan Wilcox, Durham Medieval Texts 9 (Durham: Durham Medieval Texts, 1994). For details of the Canterbury homiliary from which these three manuscripts derive, see Clemoes, *First Series*, 68 and references there.

17 For the relationship of Bodley 340/342 and CCCC 198, see Kenneth Sisam, 'MSS. Bodley 340 and 342: Ælfric's *Catholic Homilies*,' in *Studies*, 148–98.

18 See *Homilies of Ælfric: A Supplementary Collection*, ed. John C. Pope, EETS o.s. 259–60 (London: OUP, 1967–8), 22; and D.G. Scragg, 'Cambridge, Corpus Christi College 162,' in *Anglo-Saxon Manuscripts and Their Heritage*, ed. Phillip Pulsiano and Elaine M. Treharne (Aldershot: Ashgate, 1998), 71–83.

19 See *CH II*, xxxiii, and my *VH*, 3 and 71.

20 See my 'The Vercelli Homilies and Kent,' in *Intertexts: Studies in Anglo-Saxon Culture Presented to Paul E. Szarmach*, ed. Virginia Blanton and Helene Scheck (Turnhout: ACMRS, 2008), 369–80.

21 N.R. Ker, 'A Study of the Additions and Alterations in Mss. Bodley 340 and 342' (unpubl. BLitt. dissertation, Oxford, 1933), 33–4.

22 Ker, *Catalogue*, 367.

century or the beginning of the eleventh.[23] Yet it has few of the spellings traditionally associated with the Kentish dialect.[24] Its original seventy-four items (a few more were added slightly later)[25] are all written by a single hand. In many cases, where the late Old English standard appears to give scribes a choice of spellings, the scribe of Bodley regularly writes a single form. It is possible to check this both when the archetype is an Ælfric manuscript and when he is copying anonymous material. A simple example is *sceolon/sculon* 'shall, must.' Whereas the Vercelli Book shows a preference for the latter form and most Ælfric manuscripts for the former, Bodley invariably has *sceolon*, in anonymous and Ælfric items alike.[26] The Cambridge manuscripts show a preference for *sceolon*, but *sculon* forms occur regularly, again including in their Ælfric items. If the distribution in the Vercelli Book reflects the scribe copying mechanically (for the most part) from his copy-text, as the evidence suggests,[27] and that copy-text represents what was available to the compiler of the Canterbury homiliary, then writing *eo* almost certainly represents deliberate choice on the part of the Bodley scribe or a predecessor. Although Ælfric's scribes write *sceolon* usually, all occasionally have *u*-spellings, even the earliest, BL, Royal 7 C.XII, which is annotated by Ælfric himself.[28] It may be noted in passing that the more careful of the main scribes of Royal 7 C.XII (Ker's Scribe 1) at least once first wrote *sculon* and then altered it to *sceolon* (fol. 58v4, *CH* I.XI.72).[29] More work needs to be done on the spread of the two forms in the eleventh century (and in the twelfth century as well) before any firm conclusions can be drawn, in particular because the apparent evidence that the *u*-spellings become more popular as the century advances may be skewed by the frequency with which Ælfric texts (with *eo*-spellings) are copied in the first half of the century. Such an investigation,

---

23 Ibid., 361–7.

24 See A. Campbell, *Old English Grammar* (Oxford: OUP, 1959), §§288–92 on Kentish vowels.

25 Ker, *Catalogue*, 366.

26 At the time of writing, nineteen Ælfric items from the First Series have been uploaded and three anonymous items. Sample checks elsewhere in the manuscript suggest that *sceolon* is invariable.

27 In the prose, fifty-seven examples of *scul-*, thirty of *sceol-*. Most of the examples of the latter (twenty-one) occur in homilies XIX–XXII, where only three of *scul-* occur.

28 Eliason and Clemoes, *Royal 7 C. XII*, 19. This is the pattern in both of the manuscripts which Clemoes associates with Ælfric's own scriptorium, Royal 7 C.XII and CUL Gg. 3.28 (for the association, see Clemoes, *The First Series*, 160–1).

29 The scribe also altered *scolon* to *sceolon* by the addition of *e* above the line on a number of occasions, e.g., 74r17, 75v22, 76r6.

for the eleventh century at least, will be possible when data for the Manchester database is complete. But the significant point here is that the evidence so far points to systematic use by the Bodley scribe in a feature where most of his contemporaries are far from consistent.

Invariable use of *sceolon* by the Bodley scribe is unusual, but the form itself is obviously not. It is worth noting some of the other preferences shown by this scribe in common words. Like most Ælfric scribes, he writes *heora* for 'their,' but unlike them he never writes *hira* or *hyra* in either Ælfric texts or anonymous ones, whereas many of them (including CCCC 162 and CCCC 198, which are otherwise very close to Bodley textually) use the shorter forms occasionally even in Ælfric texts, where they are unlikely to have been used by the author. As with *sceolon*, the Bodley scribe (or a predecessor in the transmission of the text) has normalized the anonymous items. On the other hand, there are some instances where normalization has not occurred. The scribe accepts the archaic adjective/pronoun *nænig* 'no' regularly (although not quite always) and the Kentish *ermð-* 'suffering' in anonymous items, and the variant *eallinga* 'always' in Vercelli VIII (l. 70), alongside *nan, yrmð-*, and *eallunga* in Ælfric texts. As against his preference for the Ælfrician *sceolon*, he reproduces the earlier *ðysse* (*ðisse*) in anonymous items for the feminine genitive and dative demonstrative 'this,' even though this is unlikely ever to have occurred in the Ælfrician texts that occupy the main body of his manuscript. There are also some words where he shows no desire to regularize, as, for example, with other parts of the word for 'this' which appear not only with one *s* or two and *i* or *y* but are occasionally also spelled with *eo*, as in *ðeosne, ðeoses, ðeossere/ðeosse* (feminine dative singular), all in both Ælfrician and anonymous items (apart from the last which are the forms of this manuscript in Ælfric and non-Ælfric texts respectively). More difficult to determine is the significance of present tense *(ge)ðænc-* forms for 'seem,' and *mænnisc-* 'human' which the Bodley scribe uses rarely in both Ælfric items and anonymous ones. It may be a south-eastern feature (in the broadest sense, including Essex),[30] but the Manchester database suggests that late Old English examples are not confined to south-eastern manuscripts in this and comparable words. My conclusion is that the

---

30 See Campbell, *Old English Grammar*, §193d, but on the Midddle English evidence, see Helmut Gneuss, 'The Origin of Standard Old English,' *ASE* 1 (1972): 72. There is a fuller bibliography in *The Old English Vision of St Paul*, ed. Antonette diPaolo Healey, Speculum Anniversary Monographs 2 (Cambridge, MA: Mediaeval Academy of America, 1978), 33.

language of the scribe of this large manuscript which is both dated and (unusually for the period) localized is worthy of a very detailed linguistic examination, something which it has hitherto not been subjected to, presumably because almost all the items which it contains survive in earlier copies and have been published from them.[31]

The Bodley manuscript is also useful in allowing us to track a series of changes in the language at the end of the Old English period, as it has many interlinear alterations and glosses by eleventh-century scribes. Ker in his dissertation lists the work of eight correctors and annotators, the most persistent being the hand that added the opening of a homily on St Augustine of Canterbury at the end of the manuscript that states that Paulinus, the first bishop of Rochester, is buried 'here,' an addition which must have been made when the manuscript was in Rochester and which therefore helps localize both the manuscript in the eleventh century and its principal corrector.[32] The changes which the correctors made include many in Vercelli items whereby the language is brought into line with Ælfrician usage, and this helps identify what the eleventh-century scribes saw as archaisms. Among them are the regular addition above the line of *re* after *þisse* (which is also found with *y*), presumably by analogy with the definite demonstrative *þære*. The Vercelli Book has no example of *þissere*. The form first appears in Old English at the end of the tenth century, and becomes increasingly common in the eleventh.[33] It is arguably the form

---

31 A doctoral student, Joanna Clatworthy, began such an examination under my direction when work for the Manchester script and spelling project began in 2000, but unfortunately she abandoned her studies before they had progressed as far as I have shown possible here. Ker himself, in his own dissertation, included some information on language, but his work does not obviate the need for a more detailed study, especially as the publication of definitive editions of both the *Catholic Homilies* and of anonymous items since his day has made a fuller study of the archetypes possible. But many of his observations are pertinent. In particular, he showed one way in which the scribe took care over the production of his finished manuscript, and in doing so he illustrated an aspect of the scribe's attitude to language: 'At 342.108 it seems that the scribe wrote *hi fæstende fæstende*, and noticing his error, emended the first *fæstende* to the correct reading *forlæte*. Since this word is one letter shorter than *fæstende*, a gap remained between *hi* and *forlæte*, which the scribe filled by altering *hi* to *heo*' (p. 34). ·

32 Ker, *Catalogue*, 367.

33 A single example of *þissere* occurs in the 'Mercian' gloss to the Rushworth Gospels (Oxford, Bodleian Library, Auct. D. 2. 19) in Mt 21:21. Dating this text is problematic, since both the 'Mercian' and the 'Northumbrian' glosses may have been influenced by the gloss to the Lindisfarne Gospels (London, British Library, Cotton Nero D. iv), which itself is of the middle of the second half of the tenth century (Ker dates it as X², *Catalogue*, 215; see also 352). Alteration of *þisse* to *þissere* is found in other eleventh-century

used by Ælfric himself,[34] and it is certainly the one (together with *þisre*, which is perhaps the earlier form) preferred by his scribes.[35] But the main scribe of Bodley 340 was happy to copy *þisse* from the archetype throughout his anonymous items, only to have it altered at a later date, perhaps indeed sometimes altering it himself after he had copied a great many Ælfric pieces.[36]

I turn next to CCCC 162, which, like Bodley 340/342, was written by a single scribe at the very end of the tenth century.[37] Linguistically this scribe shows no tendency to use any particular spelling consistently for common words such as *sceolon*, and, as with the Bodley scribe, there are some discrepancies between the language of the anonymous pieces in his collection and Ælfrician ones (for example, he preserves *nænig* in anonymous items). Superficially, then, it would appear that he is less concerned with uniformity in his language. As with the Bodley scribe, there are very few features of his language which might be regarded as Kentish, even though the Corpus manuscript was certainly drawing on a Kentish exemplar for his Ælfric pieces and was most likely written in the south-east, probably at Canterbury itself.[38] A notable exception is the scribe's use of *eam* for *eom*

---

manuscripts. Unusual, perhaps, is the change by a late-eleventh-century scribe of *þisse* to *þiossere* in the Invention of the Cross homily in Oxford, Bodleian Library, Auct. F. 4. 32, fol. 10v7.

34 See Eliason and Clemoes, *Royal 7 C. XII*, 19–20, n. 8. Eliason accepts as Ælfric's the hand that wrote the addendum slip with f. 164v which includes the word *þyssere*, but Clemoes does not. For reasons that I will advance elsewhere, I am inclined to go with Clemoes.

35 Malcolm Godden's glossary (*CH* III) shows that the older form *þysse* is used only once in the base texts in the whole of both series of the *Catholic Homilies* (the two manuscripts used for the base texts both stemming from Ælfric's own scriptorium at Cerne Abbas, see n. 20, above). Pope, whose manuscripts are not supervised by Ælfric, has four instances of the older form (*Homilies of Ælfric*, 259–60). On *þisre* as the earlier form, see A. Campbell, *Old English Grammar* (Oxford, 1959), 292: '*þissere* ... developed by parasiting from *þisre*,' but compare Karl Brunner, *Altenglische Grammatik nach der angelsächsischen Grammatik von Eduard Sievers*, 3rd ed. (Tübingen: Max Niemeyer Verlag, 1965), §338, Anm. 2, who states the opposite: that *þisre* is a syncopated form (and, by implication, later). The database shows clearly that Campbell is right.

36 It is not always easy to distinguish the hands in interlinear alterations. Ker notes many of the alterations but far from all, and he himself admits that some are hard to identify with particular scribes.

37 Vercelli homilies XIX and XX were published from this manuscript, with full details of all manuscript readings and alterations, in *Eleven Old English Rogationtide Homilies*, ed. Joyce Bazire and James E. Cross (Toronto: UTP, 1982), as their items 1 and 2. They also printed as their third item the following piece in CCCC 162, which is also anonymous.

38 There is slight indication that the manuscript may have been written at St Augustine's; see Ker, *Catalogue*, 56.

'am' (Vercelli I.95 and 102, E-version), but on this see the comments on CCCC 198 in the next paragraph. For the most part, the scribe writes standard late Old English, e.g., *yrmð*- where both Bodley and CCCC 198 have *ermð*-. CCCC 198 is significant here because, although all three manuscripts are textually close in both anonymous and Ælfrician items, the two Cambridge ones are closer to each other than either is to Bodley. In other words, it appears that the spelling with *e* comes from the common exemplar of all three, but the scribe of CCCC 162 has normalized to *y*. Similarly, where Bodley has *þysse* (later changed to *þyssere*), CCCC 162 and 198 both have *þyssere*. So although the CCCC 162 scribe has modernized his work in some respects, he is far from consistent, and is probably less reliable in allowing us to determine an earlier form of the language of pre-Ælfrician items than is the scribe of Bodley 340.

Bodley 340/342 and CCCC 162 are both manuscripts dating from the very end of the tenth century (or at the latest early in the eleventh) and hence contain copies of Vercelli homilies earlier than those in any manuscript except the Vercelli Book itself[39] and the Blickling manuscript.[40] CCCC 198, on the other hand, is a slightly later manuscript, with those of its contents which parallel ones in Bodley 340/342 having been written some twenty-five years later. Here four scribes are involved,[41] all copying Ælfric items, and three of them anonymous ones. Ker's scribe 1 copied Vercelli V, scribe 2 copied Vercelli VIII and in a later stint Vercelli I, and scribe 3 copied Vercelli III. Because scribes 2 and 3 copied alternate stints, it is clear that they were working at the same time in the same scriptorium, and that makes linguistic analysis potentially more interesting. To take only the instances of words already considered in relation to Bodley 340/342, and concentrating first on the anonymous items, scribe 1 retains *nænig* where Bodley has this altered to *nan*, and writes *æ* before a nasal consonant with even greater frequency than the scribe of Bodley (cf. *sænde his cæmpan*, Vercelli V.80), where Bodley has *e* in both words. Scribe 2 also has *æ* plus nasal in both stints, but examples do not necessarily coincide with those in Bodley, and this scribe regularly has *e* before a nasal in

---

39 Where homily II is, of course, partly repeated in homily XXI.

40 All the items of Blickling have been subject to a thorough linguistic examination in a German dissertation: Ashley K. Hardy, *Die Sprache der 'Blickling Homilien'* (Leipzig, 1899), and I shall not repeat information to be found there.

41 Details may be found in my 'The Homilies of the Blickling Manuscript,' in *Learning and Literature in Anglo-Saxon England: Studies Presented to Peter Clemoes*, ed. Michael Lapidge and Helmut Gneuss (Cambridge: CUP, 1985), 299–316.

etymologically long vowels (*clensian* 'cleanse,' *menan* 'mean'), which suggests a wider falling together of the vowel symbols than is apparent in Bodley, where the confusion affects only short vowels. Scribe 2 also uses *nænig* and has both of the instances of Kentish *eam* 'am' in Vercelli I also found in CCCC 162, indicating that in both manuscripts the form is copied from the exemplar. There is also a single instance of *e* for *y* (*senna* 'sins') but generally this south-eastern feature is absent. Scribe 3 is for the most part closer to the late Old English standard than is either of the other scribes or that of Bodley, but there is a single example of *nænig* where the Bodley scribe wrote *nan*. In Ælfric items all three scribes wrote *æ* before a nasal occasionally in words where the author would not have done so, e.g., *ænde* and *mænnisc-*, and in contexts where other Kentish manuscripts such as Bodley 340/342 do not. This then appears to be a feature of their common language. To continue in this vein would be otiose in this essay, but enough has been said to show that much can still be learnt about the spelling habits of scribes working alongside each other in the early eleventh century.

I turn next to archaic features in two copies of Vercelli homilies in other manuscripts: the copy of Vercelli IX in Oxford, Bodleian Library, Hatton 115, and that of Vercelli IV in Cambridge, Corpus Christi College 41. Vercelli IX in Hatton 115 is on a single quire written in the middle of the eleventh century which was added to a slightly later manuscript some time after it had existed separately as an unbound booklet. Its origin is unknown. Vercelli IV is one of a number of homiletic and other pieces added in the margins of an early-eleventh-century copy of the Old English Bede. Again the source of the copyist's text is unknown, as is the place at which he or she was working, although the manuscript was bequeathed to Exeter by Leofric. These two relatively late copies of Vercelli pieces have some interesting linguistic features in common. Most obviously, they both have instances of the first-person plural possessive *uss-* (*usse, ussa, ussum*), which is rare and probably regarded as archaic by the eleventh century. As part of the proof that it is seen as archaic is the fact that *usse* occurs six times in the Vercelli scribe's copy of homily V (as well as twenty-two times elsewhere in the codex), but is in all instances written *ure* in Bodley 340/342 and CCCC 198, whose scribes, as has been shown, did not always modernize the language of the text they were copying but seem to have done so here. The opening sentence of Hatton's copy of Vercelli IX begins with two examples of *usse* and there is one of *ussum* at line 172,[42] despite the

---

42 Neither sentence is paralleled in the Vercelli Book version.

relative lateness of the manuscript,[43] while the CCCC 41 version of Vercelli IV has *usse* at line 58 where the Vercelli scribe wrote *ure*. For other eleventh-century examples of *uss-* forms of the possessive outside these manuscripts, we have to go to the *Letter of Alexander to Aristotle* in the *Beowulf*-manuscript, a text which we may reasonably assume is again a copy from a tenth-century original, or to the copy of the Old English Bede in Oxford, Corpus Christi College 279, which is certainly from an early copy-text.[44]

Among other linguistic archaisms in Hatton 115 are instances of *nænig* (L-version, ll. 37 and 42), and many examples of *o* before a nasal consonant (e.g., *mon(n)-* 'man' (91), *noma* 'name' (68, 78), alongside rather more *a* examples), and one instance of *waldend-* 'ruler' (ll. 37). CCCC 41 also has *o* + nasal, but elsewhere eleventh-century examples are almost entirely confined to copies of earlier texts (e.g., the D version of the Anglo-Saxon Chronicle, the Old English Bede, prose and verse texts in the *Beowulf*-manuscript). The Hatton scribe also wrote the dative form of the demonstrative as *þæm*, never *þam*. Although the scribe is far from unique in this, of the many hundreds of examples recorded in the Manchester database, it is clear that the majority form a pattern. A few are scattered among other spellings in manuscripts such as the Ælfrician Royal 7 C.XII, but most are the work of a very few late Old English scribes, e.g., the Blickling copyists, the scribe who wrote the prose items in the *Beowulf*-manuscript, and the scribe of the D Chronicle. The spread of these spellings deserves further investigation, something which again will be a relatively easy task once the database is complete. The CCCC 41 copy of Vercelli IV has a number of idiosyncratic linguistic features (including frequent omission of letters), but most are probably the result of the scribe having to write in a confined space, as is, presumably, the frequent abbreviation of parts of *dryhten* to *dne* for *domine*. Others which are worth mentioning are confusion of *t* and *ð* in verb inflections (*bit, beþohtesð, meahtesð*) – and occasionally elsewhere (*mosðe*)[45] – and alternation of *h* and *g* in positions which, even for late Old English, are unusual (*monihra*). As far as linguistic features which might determine something of the history of the text of Vercelli IV is concerned,

---

43 There is an example of *ussum* at Vercelli IX in Hatton 115 line 172, again in a section not paralleled in the Vercelli Book. Cf. also *usra* at Vercelli IX in Hatton 115 line 124.

44 Instances of *uss-* in the earliest complete copy in Tanner are numerous, see Grant, *The B Text of the Old English Bede: A Linguistic Commentary*, Costerus n.s. 73 (Amsterdam: Rodopi, 1989), 37.

45 See also Dobbie, ASPR 6 (*Solomon and Saturn*, l. 36).

the difficulty lies in distinguishing between forms which the latest scribe may have introduced and those copied from the examplar(s). The additional items in the margins in CCCC 41 are not written continuously, but are in different parts of the manuscript, which suggests that they were copied at different times, although by the same scribe.[46] The Vercelli item is followed immediately by three other pieces added in margins, a homily for the Assumption of the Virgin, an Apocalypse of Thomas, and a 'Harrowing of Hell' homily. Two other pieces occur separately later in the manuscript, a St Michael homily and a Palm Sunday item.[47] (I ignore a number of short metrical items for the sake of simplicity.) An obvious approach to investigating the language of the Vercelli piece is to compare the language of the three pieces that follow it with that of the scribe's copy of Vercelli IV, and then to see if these contrast with the two homilies added later. The language of a number of these homilies has been analysed by their respective editors,[48] but no one has viewed the language of the additional items as a whole. My own cursory examination suggests slight similarity between the items immediately following Vercelli IV (e.g., *usses* at the opening of the Assumption homily, a number of *uss-* examples in the Thomas Apocalypse,[49] and two in the Harrowing piece, instances of *o* + nasal, and use of non–Late West Saxon words such as *nænig and nymðe*), but these in all probability have more to do with the age of the pieces than their linguistic affinity.[50] (The Michael piece, for instance, also has *nymðe*, although *nan* rather than

---

46 Ker, *Catalogue*, 45.

47 For editions of the Assumption and St Michael pieces, see *Vier altenglische Predigt aus der heterodoxen Tradition, mit Kommentar, Übersetzung und Glossar sowie drei weiteren Texten im Anhang*, ed. Hildegard L.C. Tristram (Freiburg im Breisgau: n.p., 1970); for the Harrowing of Hell homily, see William H. Hulme, 'The Old English Gospel of Nicodemus,' *Modern Philology* 1 (1904): 579–614; for the Palm Sunday piece, see K.G. Schaefer, 'An Edition of Five Old English Homilies for Palm Sunday, Holy Saturday, and Easter Sunday' (unpub. PhD diss., Columbia Univ., 1972). The Thomas Apocalypse item has been published in part by R. Willard, *Two Apocrypha in Old English Homilies* (Leipzig: B. Tauchnitz, 1935) and in part by Max Förster, 'A New Version of the Apocalypse of Thomas in Old English,' *Anglia* 73 (1955): 6–36, but the last paragraph of the item still remains unpublished.

48 Especially by Tristram and Förster (see above, n. 47), but Hulme also has occasional comments.

49 Sense units 17, 24, 70, and 74. In the case of these three items, I quote the *DOE* sense units since published editions are either hard to find (Tristram's Assumption edition is a German doctoral dissertation) or unreliable (Hulme's edition has many errors).

50 See the cross-references to 'Anglian' originals and the word choices listed for these items in Walter Hofstetter, *Winchester und der spätaltenglische Sprachgebrauch* (Munich: W. Fink, 1987), nos. 71 (238), 74 (242), and 84 (253).

nænig.) The Assumption and Thomas both have two instances of *þuruh* for *þurh* each, while the prefix *for-* is written *fer-* once in Vercelli and once in the Harrowing piece. All three pieces following Vercelli IV have instances of Kentish *io* (with *yo* frequent in the Harrowing item), but the Vercelli item has *eo*. What I deduce from all of this is that although in general the scribe copied earlier forms faithfully, which explains the *uss-* examples and other early features, occasionally we may find his or her own usage, as in *þuruh*. Thus, although the CCCC 41 copy of Vercelli IV was copied relatively late, its textual closeness to the copy in the Vercelli Book may easily be explained.[51]

Oxford, Bodleian Library, Junius 85/86 is a manuscript of the middle of the eleventh century which has been artificially split into two volumes in the modern period. According to Ker it is written by two scribes,[52] although the writing of each varies a good deal, in part because the size of writing changes (the small page size – only 160mm x 115mm in Junius 85, slightly smaller still in Junius 86 – coupled with the number of lines to a page, just 14 in some quires and up to 17 in others, make the writing either cramped on some leaves or unusually large for the line length on others). But there are also palaeographic differences, the most distinctive being that Scribe 2 regularly uses caroline *r*, while Scribe 1 has the regular insular form of the letter. Scribe 1 (if there are indeed two scribes and not one who added different material at different times in this much altered manuscript) wrote two Vercelli parallels: the opening page of Junius 85 contains the last few lines of Vercelli X (the rest lost by the loss of a quire or quires), and the last item in Junius 86 is a copy of Vercelli XVIII, which is also found in the Blickling manuscript. That the two scribes were working together in the same scriptorium at the same time is shown by the interweaving of their work, Scribe 1 beginning and ending the book and even taking over from Scribe 2 in the middle of Ker's item 6.[53] The language of the two varies somewhat, which supports the idea that there are indeed two scribes, but has some interesting points of correlation for two individuals, even two working in the same place at the same time – and this is what makes

---

51 See my *VH*, 87.
52 Ker, *Catalogue*, 411.
53 The item has been edited as no. 1 in *Nuove omelie anglosassoni della rinascenza benedettina*, ed. A. M. Luiselli Fadda (Florence: F. Le Monnier, 1977). The change of hand occurs at the beginning of Luiselli Fadda's section 36, where there is a change of subject matter and a new beginning with *mæn ða leofestan*. It is at least arguable that the rest of the homily was added from a different source at a later date, and that it is this which explains the change in appearance of the writing.

this manuscript particularly valuable for the study of eleventh-century language. Scribe 2 has many south-eastern features such as *eam* 'am,' *an* 'on,' *þem* rather than *þam*, *þæm*, and frequent instances of the digraph *yo* (e.g., *hyort-* 'heart,' *ðyostr-* 'darkness,' *lyoma-* 'light'), less frequently *io*, a number of instances of *y* for *e/æ*, e.g., *adwysced* 'cleansed,' and very frequent *æ* before a nasal (*mænn-*, *þenc-*). Among the scribe's particularly unusual spellings is *halchan* for *halgan* 'holy,' repeated in a number of items, and *codcund-* for *godcund-*, which I have written about elsewhere.[54] The language of Scribe 1 also has south-eastern features, especially in the use of *y* for earlier digraph spellings (e.g., *fyrh* 'life,' *ydig-* 'blessed,' *hyrtan* 'heart'), and *æ* for etymologically long *ea* (*gær* 'year,' *ongæton* '[they] perceived'), as well as *æ* before nasals, but in general this scribe seems to adhere more closely to the late Old English standard. What particularly links the two scribes is that both occasionally spell 'world' as *wyrold-* (the form occurs four times in the copy of Vercelli XVIII, by Scribe 1, and again in the *Visio Pauli* copied by Scribe 2).[55] To my knowledge – and according to the Manchester database – *wyrold* is unique to this manuscript. The manuscript as a whole deserves an exhaustive linguistic examination, and I hope to provide one in due course. Such an analysis might show more about the language of the copy of Vercelli XVIII that it contains (the brief extract from Vercelli X is too short to be of interest), and thence more about the transmission history of that piece.

Studies of the language of a number of other eleventh-century manuscripts containing copies of Vercelli homilies have been published already,[56] and these manuscripts are therefore ignored here. I have also chosen – as I noted near the beginning of this essay – to ignore copies of Vercelli homilies in manuscripts of the second half of the eleventh century. This is because the two most significant items involve a much wider survey than is possible in a small compass. The first of these is the composite homily known as Napier XXX, which draws on four Vercelli homilies in conjunction with extracts from Wulfstan and which now survives in a unique copy

---

54 'Spelling Variation,' 352.
55 Vercelli homily XVIII, ll. 7, 14, 16, 264, and Healey, *Old English Vision of St Paul*, l. 173.
56 For the Blickling manuscript, see Hardy, *Die Sprache der 'Blickling Homilien'*; for Cambridge, Corpus Christi College 419/421 see Jonathan Wilcox, 'The Compilation of Old English Homilies in MSS Cambridge, Corpus Christi College, 419 and 421' (unpub. PhD diss., Cambridge, 1987); for the relevant scribe of BL, Cotton Tiberius A iii, see my 'Cotton Tiberius A. iii Scribe 3 and Canterbury Libraries,' in *Anglo-Saxon Books and Their Readers*, ed. Thomas N. Hall and Donald Scragg (Kalamazoo, MI: Western Michigan University Medieval Institute, 2008), 22–30.

in Oxford, Bodleian Library, Hatton 113. I considered the composition of this item in detail many years ago.[57] The scribe involved was working at Worcester in the middle of the second half of the eleventh century, and he compiled a large collection of ecclesiastical material in what survive now as three volumes: Oxford, Bodleian Library, Junius 121, which consists largely of ecclesiastical institutes, and the double volumes of Oxford, Bodleian Library, Hatton 113 and 114, which have mainly homilies, most of them by Ælfric and Wulfstan. This carefully assembled collection was no doubt derived, by the last scribe or a predecessor, from a variety of different copy-texts, and it would not be surprising therefore to find linguistic variation between them. I showed in my earlier essay on the composite piece that there is linguistic variation even within it,[58] but the survival of such a large body of work by a single scribe offers the potential for a wide-ranging study of the language both of the latest scribe (and of the forms which he was willing to accept by his training) and of the forms carried over from the copy-texts, which, in the case of the Ælfric and Wulfstan texts and of the composite Napier XXX, can be ascertained with reasonable certainty. The second copy of a Vercelli piece surviving in a copy of the second half of the eleventh century is that of Vercelli XIX in London, British Library, Cotton Cleopatra B. xiii, which also has a copy of Napier XL which draws, in part, on Vercelli II. Cleopatra B. xiii is one of a group of manuscripts associated with the Exeter scriptorium in the third quarter of the eleventh century.[59] Again, this offers an opportunity to review the work of a substantial body of material which is connected, but not connected this time by being written by a single scribe but by a group of scribes working at the same place at the same time and presumably – since they were trained to write in a way that enables them to be linked together today – were imbued by their training with similar attitudes to the language of the material that they copied.

This essay has been exploratory rather than definitive. Necessarily, it is as yet an incomplete study, exploring ways of investigating scribes and their language, and the transmission of texts, rather than coming to firm conclusions. Today, our knowledge of eleventh-century manuscripts and

---

57 'Napier's "Wulfstan" Homily XXX: Its Sources, Its Relationship to the Vercelli Book and Its Style,' *ASE* 6 (1977): 197–211.

58 The object of *gehelpan* is both in the genitive case and the dative within the same sentence, because, as I assume, two parts of the sentences have been lifted unthinkingly by the compiler from different sources; see 'Napier's "Wulfstan" Homily XXX,' 203.

59 Ker, *Catalogue*, 184.

their scribes is very full thanks to the work of Ker and his successors. But up to now, details of the language of many of these manuscripts and scribes was relatively unknown. They have not been studied by editors who all too often confine any linguistic examination to particular texts,[60] or by doctoral students, even though there is an obvious opening here for work at doctoral level. A great many eleventh-century texts are late copies of items known to have been composed earlier, and recorded in earlier manuscripts (for example, the Alfredian translations and the works of Ælfric and Wulfstan). They have been accepted as written in the late Old English standard written dialect, which undoubtedly is broadly true. With the help of the Manchester database, the language of the eleventh century can now be more easily and fully analysed. We can search the forms of closely related manuscripts such as Bodley 340/342, CCCC 198, and CCCC 162 which derive from a common ancestor made at Canterbury, the first and the last of these being closely related in time as well as place of copying. We can search the work of very large manuscripts copied by a single scribe, such as Bodley 340/342 or Hatton 113/114 plus Junius 121.[61] We can search the work of a group of scribes whose writing suggests common training at a particular point in time, such as the scribes of the earliest part of CCCC 198 or the Exeter scribes of the third quarter of the eleventh century. And in all cases we may discover more about the education and training of eleventh-century scribes, and of their attitudes to their copy-texts. What the preliminary studies of this essay suggest is that late Old English, often now called 'Standard Old English,'[62] is not quite the uniform language that is implied in that designation. Kenneth Sisam famously stated that 'the early eleventh century was the period in which West Saxon was recognized all over England as the official and literary language,'[63] citing additions to the York Gospels from York in the first half of the eleventh century and glosses to prayers in British Library, Arundel 155 from Christ Church, Canterbury. Both exhibit what Sisam sees as 'normal West Saxon.' He further adds: 'Dialect does break through, the more frequently as the

---

60 A notable exception is John Pope, who noted unusual forms in the review of manuscripts prefacing his edition (Pope, *Homilies of Ælfric*, 14–91). Ker, *Catalogue* also occasionally remarks on 'dialect' spellings. Some other linguistic analyses of individual texts have been noted above.

61 See above, 47–50 and 58.

62 For the term and its use, see Mechthild Gretsch, 'Winchester Vocabulary and Standard Old English: The Vernacular in Late Anglo-Saxon England,' The Toller Memorial Lecture 2000, *BJRL* 83 (2001): 41–87.

63 Sisam, *Studies*, 153.

eleventh century advances; but good West Saxon may be written anywhere in its first half.' Against Sisam, we should note that in his review of so-called dialects in the Introduction to his *Old English Grammar*, Alistair Campbell observes: 'Even when West-Saxon had become a well-established literary dialect, and was used as something of a standard written language, many manuscripts display a considerable non-West-Saxon element in their orthography and inflexions,'[64] although sadly he gives precious few examples. In the last half-century, our terminology has changed (for Late West Saxon read late Old English), and our ability to track the more unusual elements in late Old English texts has improved, especially thanks to the Manchester database (again, it is preferable to speak of variations within the late Old English uniform writing system rather than non–West Saxon elements).

Sisam is no doubt right about 'good West Saxon' being written throughout England in the first half of the eleventh century insofar as the traditional written dialect criteria in spelling such as the falling together of front vowels in the south-east and *-ald* rather than *-eald* in Anglian areas are largely absent. But what I have been at pains to show here is that there may be other ways of determining the education patterns of scribes and their attitudes to the material copied which are either chronological or regional in the early eleventh century, and we now have a resource to base such studies on. In the past I have used spelling variation within the work of the Vercelli scribe to help identify points at which he may have changed from one copy-text to another, assuming that he is a mechanical copyist (as the evidence suggests). But because we have in the Vercelli Book itself some indication of the earliest form of prose items, later copies (especially when those copies are textually close to each other as in the case of the Canterbury manuscripts discussed above) can show much about variation within late Old English. What I have tried to show in this essay is that there may be further ways in which we can explore both the Vercelli scribe's use of language and that of others copying the same material at a later date. Each can show us more about the origin of the earliest surviving homilies in English. By comparing eleventh-century copies of tenth-century texts, we can see which older linguistic forms were acceptable (and acceptable to which scribes, or even – if the evidence is sufficiently full – in which scriptoria), and which were uniformly modernized. And by examination of copies of anonymous homilies by scribes who were mainly copying Ælfric texts, we can detect sometimes the same, sometimes different attitudes to the material copied – some scribes

---

64   Campbell, *Old English Grammar*, 9.

allowing Ælfrician forms to affect their copying of older material, some doing the reverse, some copying them both apparently independently. We can probably go further and investigate more fully eleventh-century scribal attitudes to Alfredian texts, to early-tenth-century texts such as the Old English Gospels, and to texts produced in the first wave of the Benedictine Reform such as the Benedictine Rule. Such examples as I have given above undoubtedly can be taken further, an obvious example being the study of *þisse / þissere* extended to the genitive plural forms *þissa / þissera*.

There are yet other possibilities. Forms in manuscripts can be compared with those in documents, which may be important because the latter can often be dated precisely. Since the documents may also be localized, it is theoretically possible that we might move into regional studies in the eleventh century, but here we would need to take account of the peripatetic nature of scribes writing documents, just as we need always to be conscious of the fact that monastic scribes might be trained at one centre and then move to another. To conclude, this study of some minor byways of late Old English language is far from exhaustive, because its purpose is simply to draw attention to a number of possible further lines of inquiry which might indicate the sorts of information that close study of even apparently minor spelling differences can elicit. It is now possible to document more fully Sisam's view that close adherence to the late Old English standard begins to disappear around the time of the Norman Conquest. I would posit that we must get away from the belief that use of traditional dialect criteria is the only way of distinguishing between the writing habits of different areas or different scribes. Most importantly, the idea that spellings which have traditionally been regarded as simply 'permissible' variants within the late Old English standard are not worth recording for that reason is one that we should abandon forthwith.

The Portents at Christ's Birth in Vercelli Homilies V and VI: Some Analogues from Medieval Sermons and Biblical Commentaries

THOMAS N. HALL

Vercelli homilies V and VI are two Christmas homilies in the Vercelli Book, the first an exegetical reading of the nativity story from Luke, the second a translation from the apocryphal *Gospel of Pseudo-Matthew* prefaced by a short account of the marvels that took place in anticipation of Christ's birth. These homilies are separated from one another in the manuscript by the Old English poems *Andreas* and *Fates of the Apostles*, and Donald Scragg has made the case that they must have come to the Vercelli compiler from different exemplars, both going back to the early tenth century but representing different lines of transmission and certainly different methods of composition.[1] Their parallel designations for Christmas aside, the one conspicuous feature which these two homilies have in common is a shared interest in recounting the wondrous events that announced Christ's advent. The relevant passage from Vercelli V reads as follows (with the individual *wundor* enumerated for ease of reference):

Manegu wundor gelumpon in Agustes rice. Þurh þa wundor wæs getacnod Cristes cyme on middangeard. (1) Þæt wæs sum þara wundra þa se casere com to Rome mid sigefæste gefean 7 mid blisse, ða æt þære ðriddan tide þæs dæges, þæt wæs æt underne, þa wæs mannum on heofonum gesine gyldnes hringes onlicnes ymbutan þa sunnan. 7 on þam hringe wæs getacnod þæt on his rice acenned wolde bion se æðeling se is rihtlice nemned soðfæstnesse sunna, þæt is þonne ure hælend Crist, þæt he mid his fægernesse gewlitgode þa sunnan þe us nu dæghwamlice lyhteð 7 hie gescop 7 mid his mihte ealne middangeard receð 7 styreð. (2) Þæt gelomp swa ilce þæt se casere on his rice forgeaf ealle scylda Romwara folce. Þa wæs on þan getacnod þæt on his rice

---

1 D.G. Scragg, 'The Compilation of the Vercelli Book,' *ASE* 2 (1973): 205.

wolde cuman on middangeard se ðe mancynne forgifan wolde ealle hira
synna 7 uncysta þurh rihtne geleafan 7 þurh soðe hreowe. (3) Ond on þæs
caseres dagum wæron genydde to rihtum þeowdome 7 to rihtre hyrnesse
ealle þa esnas þe fram hira hlaforde ær gewiton 7 him hyran noldon; 7 swa
hwylce swa ne woldon hlafordas habban, ða wæron þurh rode deaðe gewit-
node. 7 on þam wæs þa getacnod þæt þurh Cristes lare mancynn sceolde
bion underþeoded anes Godes hyrnesse 7 anes Godes willan wyrcean, 7 swa
þa þe ne willað rihtum geleafan onfon, þa bioð geniðrade in helle tintrego.
(4) 7 in Agustes dagum wearð swa mycel sybb geworden on middangearde
þæt men wæpn ne wægon, for þam þe he in sybbe wel gesette middangeardes
rice, 7 mid wisdomes cræfte sio sibb wæs geseted geond ealne middangeard.
7 he eac sende his cempan wide geond manega mægða þætte yfle men ne
dorston nanwyht to teonan don for hyra egsan. In þære myclan sybbe wæs
getacnod þære soðan sybbe cyme in middangeard, þæt wæs ure hælend Crist
þe us gesybbode wið englum 7 us geþingode wið Godfæder 7 us to sybbe
geladode, 7 he swa cwæð: 'Beati pacifici quoniam filii Dei uocabuntur. Eadige
bioð þa sybsuman men for þan þe hie bioð Godes bearn genemnde.' (5)
Ðrim wisum ungelice wæron mannum beboden on þæs caseres dagum, þæt
is þonne þæt æghwylc man sceolde gaful gildan, 7 ealle men sceoldon hit
gildan ge rice ge heane, 7 ðam gafole mon ne onfeng æt ænegum men butan
in his swæsum eðle. On þan wæs getacnod þæt we sculon in þrim wisum
Gode rihtes geleafan gaful agildan, þæt is on wordum 7 on geþohtum 7 on
dædum, 7 God þam gafole ne onfehð butan on ussum swæsum eðle þæt is
gehwæðer ge in þam inneran ge in þam utteran, þæt we mid inneweardre
heortan 7 mid eaðmodre in God gelyfen, 7 þone geleafan mid godum
weorcum gefyllen 7 mid muþe ondettan.[2]

[Many wonders occurred in the reign of Augustus. These wonders signified
Christ's coming. (1) One of these wonders was that when the emperor came
to Rome with triumphant joy and with bliss, the likeness of a golden ring
around the sun in the heavens was visible to men at the third hour of the day,
which was in the morning, and that ring signified that during his reign the
prince would be born who is rightly called the sun of justice, that is our saviour Christ, since with his beauty he beautified the sun that shines on us each
day and created it and with his power governs and guides the entire world. (2)
It also happened in his reign that the emperor forgave the sins of all the
Roman people. This signified that during his reign he would come into the
world who would forgive mankind of all their sins and vices through true
faith and through true repentance. (3) And in the days of that emperor all the

---

2 VH, 114–16, ll. 57–96.

slaves were forced back into rightful servitude who had left their masters and would not obey them; and whichever ones did not want to have masters, they were punished by death on the cross, and this signified that through Christ's teachings mankind must be subjected through obedience to one God and must do the will of one God, and thus those who will not accept the true faith, they shall be cast down into the torment of hell. (4) And in the days of Augustus there was such a great peace on earth that men carried no weapons, because he rightly founded his earthly kingdom in peace, and with the might of his wisdom this peace was established throughout the entire world. And he also sent his soldiers far and wide among many nations so that wicked men dared do nothing wrong for fear of them. This great peace signified the coming of that true peace into the world that was our saviour Christ, who made peace between us and the angels and interceded for us with God the Father and he thus said: '*Beati pacifici quoniam filii Dei uocabuntur*. Blessed be the peaceful men, for they shall be called the children of God.' (5) In three different ways were men commanded in the days of that emperor, that is that each man had to pay tribute, and all men had to pay it whether rich or poor, and this tribute could not be received from any man except in his native country. This signified that we must pay the tribute of true faith to God in three ways – that is in words and thoughts and deeds – and God does not accept that tribute except in our native country, that is both in the inward and in the outward, so that with our inward and with our humble heart we may believe in God and may fulfil that belief through good deeds and confess it with our mouth.]

The homilist emphasizes the fact that these signs all took place during the reign of the emperor Augustus, and it was in fact Augustus's arrival in Rome that precipitated this series of events, each of which is assigned by the homilist a particular symbolic significance associated with Christ. Four of these five signs (all but the ring around the sun) are not miracles as we would normally define them,[3] but rather historical or political events

---

3 For present purposes I accept as a working definition of 'miracle' an extraordinary and wondrous event that defies the laws of nature and is presumed to be divinely instigated. The texts under discussion here make no attempt to define miracles, nor do they distinguish between miracles and portents as I will here. All the phenomena in these sermons and commentaries that are said to mark the birth of Christ, whether miraculous or not, can be classed as portents, since their main function is to signal another event of greater significance, in this case the birth of Christ. I therefore take miracles in the present context to be a subset of portents (so, for instance, Augustus's arrival in Rome in a chariot on Christmas day is a non-miraculous portent, whereas the appearance of a golden ring

that have been given Christian meanings, and all are grounded within the framework of the imperial reign of Augustus, who is implicitly promoted as a type of Christ.

The signs in Vercelli VI, by contrast, are all unusual miraculous phenomena that defy the laws of nature and have only a single direct connection to Augustus:

Mitte þe hit þa þære eadegan tide nealæhte þætte dryhten lichomlice wolde wesan geboren, swiðe cyneþrymlica tacen him beforan samod siðedon: (1) Ærest geeode to þam dæge þe he on geboren wæs þæt nænige men mid wæpnum gefeohtan ne meahton, ac hraðe þæs hie mid wæpnum feohtan woldon, hiora earmas agaledon, 7 hira handa him gelugon, 7 hie sylfe wæron to sybbe geliðe wacede 7 gefeohtan ne meahton. (2) Swylce þæt eac geeode þætte siofon nihtum ær Crist geboren wære, þæt sio sunne æt midre nihte ongan scinan swa swa on sumera þonne hio hattost 7 beorhtost scinð. Þæt tacnode þæt he þas eorðlican sunnan nihtes scinende him to gisle beforan sende. (3) Swylce þæt eac geeode unmanegum nihtum ær Crist geboren wæs, onsprungon þry wyllas, 7 of þara anra gehwylcum ele fleow fram ærmergen oð æfen … (4) Ða þæt geeode þy sylfan dæge þe gyrsandæg wæs, þæs ðe dryhten on niht geboren wæs ær morgensteorra upeode, ðæt se casere ferde mid ealle his manþrymme to Bethlem þære byrig þe dryhten on geboren wæs. Mitte þe hit þa wæs sio þridde tid þæs dæges þe gyrsandæg wæs, he ða beseah on þa lyft ongean þa sunnan, 7 he geseah, mid ealle his werede þe mid him wæs, þæt sio sunne beorhtor scan þonne hio æfre ær scine, 7 hio wæs eall utan ymbworpenu mid þryfealde gyldene hringe.[4]

[When the blessed time approached that the Lord would be bodily born, very majestic signs travelled together before him. (1) It first happened on the day he was born that no men were able to fight with weapons, but as soon as they wished to fight with weapons, their arms went limp and their hands failed them and they were themselves weakened and were unable to fight. (2)

---

around the sun is a miraculous portent), and I will refer to both rather loosely as signs or wonders or marvels. It does not seem to matter in these texts that some portents chronologically precede and anticipate the birth of Christ, while others occur simultaneously with it. The scholarly literature on ancient and medieval concepts of the miraculous is of course extensive; for one recent approach to the topic, see Arnold Angenendt, 'The Miracle: A Religious-Historical and Christian Perspective,' in *Miracles and the Miraculous in Medieval Germanic and Latin Literature*, ed. K.E. Olsen, A. Harbus, and T. Hofstra, Medievalia Groningana n.s. 6, Germania Latina 5 (Leuven: Peeters, 2004), 13–34.

4   *VH*, 128–9, ll. 16–40.

Likewise, it also happened that seven nights before Christ was born the sun began to shine at midnight just as in the summer when it shines hottest and brightest. This signified that he sent before him the earthly sun shining at night as a token of good faith. (3) Likewise, it also happened not many nights before Christ was born that three wells sprang up, and oil flowed from each from morning till evening ... (4) Then it happened on the very day that was yesterday, when the Lord was born, at night before the morning star rose, that the emperor journeyed with all his entourage to Bethlehem, the city in which the Lord was born. When it was the third hour of the day that was yesterday, he beheld with all his company who were with him that the sun was shining brighter than it had ever shone before, and it was entirely surrounded by a threefold golden ring.]

In Vercelli VI the miracles are not all systematically assigned symbolic meanings as are the events in Vercelli V, and their sensational quality is generally at variance with the more mundane nature of the signs in Vercelli V, but there are still enough details in common (such as the encircled sun) to invite speculation about whether the two sets of signs are somehow related.

The suggestive points of contact between these two passages have been remarked by readers of the Vercelli homilies at least since the days of Rudolph Willard, who in his 1934 review of Max Förster's edition of the homilies identified close parallels for several of the Vercelli signs in the Pseudo-Alcuin *De divinis officiis* and the Hiberno-Latin compilation known as the *Catechesis Celtica*.[5] The *De divinis officiis*, now regarded as an anonymous Frankish text of the late ninth or early tenth century based in part on works by Amalarius of Metz and Remigius of Auxerre,[6] situates the birth of Christ within the reign of Augustus, which it says was characterized by universal peace, and it then announces four portents of Christ's birth that were witnessed during Augustus's reign: an arc or rainbow around the sun, the restoration of escaped slaves to their masters, the remission of all debts, and a fountain of oil that flowed throughout the day.[7]

---

5 Rudolph Willard, review of Max Förster, ed., *Die Vercelli-Homilien zum ersten male herausgegeben*, Bibliothek der angelsächsischen Prosa 12 (Hamburg: H. Grand, 1932) in *Speculum* 9 (1934): 225–31.

6 Marie-Hélène Jullien and Françoise Perelman, *Clavis Scriptorum Latinorum Medii Aevi. Auctores Galliae 735–987. II: Alcuin* (Turnhout: Brepols, 1999), 133–4. Richard Sharpe, *A Handlist of the Latin Writers of Great Britain and Ireland before 1540*, Publications of the Journal of Medieval Latin 1 (Turnhout: Brepols, 1997), 45, attributes the work to Remigius.

7 Pseudo-Alcuin, *De divinis officiis* (PL 101.1174–5).

All four of these portents, as well as the universal peace, appear in either Vercelli V or Vercelli VI or both. A more elaborate list of signs appears in the *Catechesis Celtica*, a florilegium-type collection of homiletic and exegetical materials with many ties to early Irish and Anglo-Saxon literature that was copied in its extant form in Brittany in the late tenth century.[8] The *Catechesis Celtica* enumerates ten *mirabilia* that accompanied Christ's birth. These are a golden circle about the sun, a fountain of oil in Rome, Augustus's command to close the gates of Janus, his remission of all debts, the rising of the sun at night, an abundance of bread that eliminated famine, an earthquake, the return of slaves to their masters, an end to the carrying of weapons, and an end to all wars.[9] Following these ten enumerated signs, the *Catechesis* then adds that at this time Augustus called for a census of the entire world and commanded everyone to render him tribute whether he be rich or poor,[10] a detail that recalls the mandated rendering of tribute to the emperor in Vercelli V.

Willard, however, had no room in his review of Förster to pursue the implications of these parallels between the *De divinis officiis*, the *Catechesis Celtica*, and the two Vercelli homilies, and it was left to J.E. Cross to try to work out the connections in a 1973 article on the portents at Christ's birth

---

8 The tenth-century Breton origin of the manuscript (Vatican, Bibliotheca Apostolica Vaticana, Reg. lat. 49) is most thoroughly established by Jean Rittmueller, ed., *Liber Questionum in Evangeliis*, CCSL 108F, Scriptores Celtigenae 5 (Turnhout: Brepols, 2003), 67*–79*. On the *Catechesis Celtica* and its ties to early Irish and Anglo-Saxon literature, see *BCLL*, no. 974; Charles D. Wright, 'Catachesis celtica,' in *Sources of Anglo-Saxon Literary Culture: A Trial Version*, ed. Frederick M. Biggs, Thomas D. Hill, and Paul E. Szarmach, MRTS 74 (Binghamton, NY: Center for Medieval and Early Renaissance Studies, 1990), 117–18; Wright, *The Irish Tradition in Old English Literature*, CSASE 6 (Cambridge: CUP, 1993), 58–9, 66, 80, 85, 96–9, 103, 114n42, 222, 227n60, 236–7, 247; Jean Rittmueller, 'MS Vat. Reg. 49 Reviewed,' *Sacris Erudiri* 33 (1992–3), 259–305; Martin McNamara, 'Sources and Affiliations of the *Catechesis Celtica* (MS Vat. Reg. lat. 49),' *Sacris Erudiri* 34 (1994): 185–237; and McNamara, 'The Affiliations and Origins of the *Catechesis Celtica*: An Ongoing Quest,' in *The Scriptures and Early Medieval Ireland: Proceedings of the 1993 Conference of the Society for Hiberno-Latin Studies on Early Irish Exegesis and Homiletics*, ed. Thomas O'Loughlin (Turnhout: Brepols, 1999), 179–203.

9 *Catechesis Celtica*, ed. André Wilmart, *Analecta Reginensia: Extraits des manuscrits latins de la reine Christine conservés au Vatican*, Studi e testi 59 (Vatican City: Biblioteca Apostolica Vaticana, 1933), 99–100, ll. 17–56. The Christmas portents in the *Catechesis Celtica* are also edited, translated, and discussed by Martin McNamara in *Apocrypha Hiberniae I. Evangelia Infantia*, ed. McNamara et al., Corpus Christianorum Series Apocryphorum 14 (Turnhout: Brepols, 2001), 518–20 and 534–7.

10 *Catechesis Celtica*, ed. Wilmart, 100, ll. 58–9; McNamara, *Apocrypha Hiberniae I*, 536–7.

in Vercelli V and VI and the *Old English Martyrology*.[11] In that article Cross clarified the relationship between Vercelli V and the *Catechesis Celtica*, which continues to provide some of the closest analogues for several features of Vercelli V (especially the golden ring around the sun and the return of slaves to their masters). Cross showed that several of the portents in the *Catechesis Celtica* and *De divinis officiis* are ultimately taken from Book VI of Orosius's *Historiae adversum paganos*, which mentions a number of the signs that occurred during the reign of Augustus. In addition, Cross also drew attention to a largely independent tradition concerning the portents at Christ's birth as represented in two Insular texts, the ninth-century *Old English Martyrology* and Patrick of Dublin's eleventh-century Latin poem on the marvels of Ireland, *De mirabilibus Hiberniae*.[12] Both report signs or miracles that are again parallelled in Orosius, and a few seem to go back beyond Orosius to Jerome's version of Eusebius's *Chronicon* and to the *Liber prodigiorum* compiled by the late Roman author Julius Obsequens from the lost books of Livy.[13] Cross's essay thus drew together a range of early witnesses to the medieval Christmas *mirabilia* tradition, which could now be understood to have roots in Roman historiography oriented to the reign of Caesar Augustus, but Cross's rather imprecise conclusion that the portents in Vercelli V were 'conflated and reworded from various sources' and that those in Vercelli VI were written 'very freely from memory' surprisingly left the question of where and how the two Vercelli homilies got their information about the portents at Christ's birth unresolved.

Meanwhile, an article that Cross seems not to have known about that uncovers still more analogues to the Vercelli portents was published in 1966 by the Norwegian scholar Mattias Tveitane, focusing on a Christmas sermon in the Old Norwegian Homily Book.[14] Tveitane had learned of

---

11   J.E. Cross, 'Portents and Events at Christ's Birth: Comments on Vercelli V and VI and the Old English Martyrology,' *ASE* 2 (1973): 209–20.

12   On the latter, see J.E. Cross, '"De Signis et Prodigiis" in *Versus Sancti Patricii Episcopi de Mirabilibus Hiberniae*,' *Proceedings of the Royal Irish Academy* 71C (1971): 247–54.

13   *Eusebii Pamphili Chronici Canones, Latine vertit, adauxit, ad sua tempora produixit S. Eusebius Hieronymus*, ed. J.K. Fotheringham (London: Humphrey Milford, 1923), 240; Julius Obsequens, *Liber prodigiorum*, ed. and trans. A.C. Schlesinger, in *Livy*, Loeb Classical Library (London: Loeb Classical Library, 1919–59), XIV: 237–319.

14   Mattias Tveitane, 'Irish Apocrypha in Norse Tradition? On the Sources of Some Medieval Homilies,' *Arv: Journal of Scandinavian Folklore* 22 (1966): 111–35. Tveitane's insistence that the Christmas portents (along with other apocryphal motifs) in the Old Norwegian Christmas homily are of Irish derivation received a sturdy rebuttal from James W. Marchand, 'The Old Norwegian Christmas Homily and the Question of Irish Influence,' *Arv: Journal of Scandinavian Folklore* 31 (1975): 23–34, who went to the

the parallels between the Vercelli homilies, Orosius, the *Catechesis Celtica*, and the *De divinis officiis* from Willard's review of Förster,[15] and he was able to augment this family of analogues by identifying two new sets of portents in a pair of Christmas sermons in the Old Norwegian and Old Icelandic Homily Books, which date to the end of the twelfth or beginning of the thirteenth century.[16] The guiding premise of Tveitane's essay was that the nature and distribution of these various portents (and of several other 'apocryphal motives' in the Old Norse and Old English homilies as well) can best be explained if the portents originated in Ireland, whence they were gradually transmitted to England, Scandinavia, and the rest of Europe on a floodtide of popular religious folklore. Tveitane, however, did little to substantiate this hypothesis of Irish origins, nor did he seek to reconcile it with his own observations that certain details in these homilies can be traced unerringly to Orosius, Virgil, and the Bible, and that the Old English and Old Norse homiletic corpora both depend in part 'on the important Frankish homiliaries from Carolingian time.'[17] How Ireland fits into this genealogy is a little hard to make out unless Orosius, Virgil, the Bible, and the Frankish homiliaries were all somehow mediated through Ireland to the whole of medieval Europe. Tveitane's argument thus seems to collapse under the weight of its own evidence, but at least it has the merit of adding the Old Norse examples of the Nativity portents to the ones already known in Latin and Old English, thereby demonstrating a broader geographical distribution of the tradition.

The labours of Willard, Cross, and Tveitane have thus enlarged our understanding of the literary history to which the Vercelli passages belong, and in particular they have highlighted the importance of the *Catechesis Celtica* as a medium for the transmission of material known to the author of Vercelli V. But the story turns out to be more complicated than any of these scholars were aware, and I would like to take these discussions a step further by drawing attention to several additional sets of Nativity portents that provide close parallels for the passages in Vercelli V and VI, all taken from medieval sermons and biblical commentaries. The

---

other extreme to claim that these are all 'simply patristic topoi' that are so widespread and commonplace throughout patristic and medieval literature that they have no discernible history and cannot be sourced.

15 See Tveitane, 'Irish Apocrypha in Norse Tradition?' 125n2.
16 On the dates and contents of these two collections, see Thomas N. Hall, 'Old Norse-Icelandic Sermons,' in *The Sermon*, ed. Beverly Mayne Kienzle, Typologie des sources du moyen âge occidental 81–3 (Turnhout: Brepols, 2000), 692–7.
17 Tveitane, 'Irish Apocrypha in Norse Tradition?' 112.

texts in question are the seventh-century Pseudo-Jerome *Expositio quatuor evangeliorum*; the eighth-century commentary on Matthew known as the *Liber quaestionum in evangeliis*; the eighth-century Vienna *Commentary on Luke*; the eighth-century Irish *Reference Bible*; a Christmas sermon from the late-eighth- or early-ninth-century Verona homiliary; a sermon on the seven signs of Christ's nativity attributed (by Migne) to Hrabanus Maurus; a text on the same topic in a ninth-century manuscript, Munich, Bayerische Staatsbibliothek, Clm 5257; a Christmas sermon from the eleventh-century Pembroke 25 homiliary; and a Christmas sermon in Salisbury, Cathedral Library 9, from the first quarter of the twelfth century.[18] As we will see, introducing these additional analogues into the discussion reshapes the picture considerably, and I begin by offering a few brief comments on each of these new analogues before turning to a revised account of the development of the Christmas portents tradition.

To take these analogues in their probable chronological order, the first recension of the Gospel commentary known as the Pseudo-Jerome *Expositio quatuor evangelorium* is a work probably of the late seventh century that is thought to come possibly from Ireland or from an Irish foundation on the continent.[19] The question of what constitutes an Irish-authored or Hiberno-Latin text at this period is of course a notoriously problematic scholarly hornet's nest, and no two authorities are in precise agreement on the pedigree of the Pseudo-Jerome *Expositio*, although it is worth observing that the biblical readings quoted within this commentary are in close agreement with the Irish 'mixed' Gospel text, and several of the commentary's manuscripts exhibit Irish and Insular features.[20] Regardless

---

18 The Christmas portents in four of these texts (the *Expositio quatuor evangeliorum*, the Vienna *Commentary on Luke*, the *Liber questionum in evangeliis*, and the Irish *Reference Bible*) as well as in the *Catechesis Celtica* are printed and discussed by McNamara, *Apocrypha Hiberniae I*, 517–37, who sees them as representing a distinctively Irish tradition of commentary going back to the seventh century.

19 See *BCLL*, no. 341; Joseph F. Kelly, 'A Catalogue of Early Medieval Hiberno-Latin Biblical Commentaries (II),' *Traditio* 45 (1989–90), 397–8 (no. 56A); and A.K. Kavanaugh, 'The Ps.-Jerome's *Expositio IV Euangeliorum*,' in *The Scriptures and Early Medieval Ireland*, ed. Thomas O'Loughlin, Instrumenta Patristica 31 (Steenbrugge: In abbatia s. Petri; Turnhout: Brepols, 1999), 124–31. On the knowledge of this work by Anglo-Saxon authors, see Charles D. Wright, 'Hiberno-Latin and Irish-Influenced Biblical Commentaries, Florilegia, and Homily Collections,' in *Sources of Anglo-Saxon Literary Culture*, 100–1.

20 The evidence is summarized by Charles D. Wright, 'Bischoff's Theory of Irish Exegesis and the Genesis Commentary in Munich Clm 6302: A Critique of a Critique,' *Journal of Medieval Latin* 10 (2000): 136–7.

of where it comes from, however, it is most relevant for our purposes that in the process of explicating the first chapter of Luke, the Pseudo-Jerome *Expositio* describes in a somewhat garbled manner three portents that anticipated or accompanied Christ's birth: Augustus's arrival in Rome in a chariot, a golden ring around the sun, and a fountain of oil that flowed from an inn:

(1) In tempore Augusti et Tiberii tempus Christi completur baptismum suum: quia xv anno de regno Augusti venerunt in uno curro ad civitatem suam Augustus et filius ejus Tiberius. Post quam adseuerunt agnum mundi, ostendit quod in regno ejus nasceretur ipse, qui regnaret in universo mundo, et pater unitatem filii sui voluntatem. (2) Ipso tempore apparuit circulus æreus erga solem, ostendit quod nascitur in tempore ejus, cujus potestas et pulchritudo, et lux, et sapientia circumdedisset omnem potentiam: primam pulchritudinem, lucem et sapientiam. (3) Ipso tempore fluxit fons oleum a taberna meritoria tota die, usque ad vesperum: ostendit quod nascitur in tempore ejus, a quo fluxisset fons olei, id est, spiritalis unctio per totum Evangelium usque in finem mundi.[21]

[(1) In the days of Augustus and Tiberius, the time of Christ is fulfilled [through] his baptism, for in the fifteenth year of the reign of Augustus, Augustus and his son Tiberius came to his city in one chariot. After that they declared [him] the lamb of the world, [this] indicates that in his reign he himself would be born who would rule the whole world, and the father [shows] the unity [and] will of his own son. (2) At that time a brazen ring appeared around the sun, which showed that in his time the one was born whose power and beauty and light and wisdom would encompass all power – the foremost beauty, light, and wisdom. (3) At that time a fountain of oil flowed from a small inn all day until evening; this shows that in his days the one was born from whom a fountain of oil would flow, that is a spiritual anointing through the entire Gospel until the end of the world.]

All three portents are interpreted allegorically, and the second and third are loosely parallelled in Vercelli VI.

Another early witness to the same tradition appears in the expansive Hiberno-Latin commentary on Matthew known as the *Liber questionum in evangeliis*, which Jean Rittmueller has convincingly argued was composed

---

21 Pseudo-Jerome, *Expositio quatuor evangeliorum* (PL 30.569); also printed and translated by McNamara, *Apocrypha Hiberniae I*, 522–3.

in Ireland, possibly at Bangor, in the early eighth century.[22] In its discussion of Matthew 2.1, the *Liber questionum in evangeliis* cites seven portents, all parallelled in the *Catechesis Celtica*, and all accompanied by succinct allegorical interpretations:

> Hic sciendum quod XLII anno Nini natus est Abraham et XLII Augusti in fine secundi ille <et> in tertio nascitur anno ut Creator et Creatura natus est Christus. (1) Sed solutis a rege debitis, peccatorum Solutor nascitur. (2) Fame inruente, Panis uitae uidetur. (3) Terrae motu facto, Architectus aduenit. (4) Seruis restitutis ad dominos proprios, uerus Dominus ad seruos uenit. (5) Crucifixis seruis quorum domini non inuenti sunt, omnis qui non seruit Domino mortem meretur. (6) Oleo de taberna meritoria fluente, gratia fidei in ecclesia lucescit. (7) Circulo praeclaro solem ambiente, Lux uera omnes potestates circumambit, reliqua.[23]
> [Here it is to be made known that Abraham was born in the forty-second year of Ninus, and in the forty-second year of Augustus, at the end of the second and in the third year Christ himself was born as Creator and Creature. (1) Now, debts having been forgiven by the king, the Forgiver of sins is born. (2) As hunger is raging, the Bread of life is seen. (3) An earthquake having occurred, the Architect arrives. (4) Slaves having been restored to their rightful masters, the true Lord comes to [his] servants. (5) The slaves whose masters were not found having been crucified, everyone who does not serve the Lord deserves death. (6) Oil flowing from a small inn [shows that] the grace of faith begins to shine in the Church. (7) A bright ring encircling the sun [shows that] the true Light surrounds all powers.]

All these portents are parallelled in the *Catechesis Celtica*, including portents 4 and 5, which evidently correspond to what Orosius and the *Catechesis Celtica* both present as a single event, namely, that on the day of Christ's birth all runaway slaves were either restored to their masters or put to death.

A more elaborate inventory of Christmas portents appears in the Hiberno-Latin commentary that has come to be known as the Irish *Reference Bible*.

---

22 On the date and place of composition of this work, see Rittmueller, *Liber questionum in evangeliis*, 11*–36*, who demonstrates unequivocally the pronounced Irish affiliations of the *LQE* through the presence of Irish words and phrases, its use of Hiberno-Latin sources, its reliance on distinctively Irish Bible readings, and an Irish palaeographical feature known as *cenn fó eitte* ('head under wing').

23 *Liber questionum in evangeliis*, ed. Rittmueller, 40–1; cf. McNamara, *Apocrypha Hiberniae I*, 526–9.

This sprawling work, still largely unpublished, consists of a series of questions or 'problems' on nearly every book of the Old and New Testaments and is generally dated to the mid or late eighth century.[24] In this case the Orosian background of at least one of the portents is impossible to miss since it is attributed to Orosius by name:

(1) Item quando Christus natus est Caesar Agustus constituit censum super totum mundum .iii. denarios de aere in figura Christi qui postulat ab omnibus hominibus cogitationem et uerbum et opus. Ideo de aere quod plus sonat omnibus metallis ut unusquisque quod in cogitatione et uerbo et opere Deo oferat ore aliis praedicet. (2) Item .iii. habuit hic census, quod omnis homo in toto mundo reddidit eum, et quod eiusdem ponderis siue diues, siue pauper, et quod a nullo accipitur nisi in sua patria. Quia regis potentia demonstratur qui omnes sibi subdidit et iustitia qua neminem priuauit patria, et habundantia in regno eius qua unusquisque habuit unde redderet censum. (3) OROSIUS: Item iste Caesar in cuius regno Christus natus est, ille initio regni sui uenit in uno curru cum Tiberio filio ad Romam postquam adsumpsit regnum Orientis. Quod significat quia in regno eius nasceretur ille qui totum mundum regeret cum Patre in unitate uoluntatis. (4) Item in eius tempore circulus aureus circa solem apparuit quod significat quod in eius tempore nasceretur ipse cuius potestas et pulchritudo et lux et sapientia circumdaret omnem potestatem et pulchritudinem et lucem et sapientiam. (5) Item in eius tempore fluxit fons olei in Roma de taberna meritoria per totam diem usque ad uesperum; quod

---

24 The *Reference Bible* is dated 's. viii' by Lapidge and Sharpe, *BCLL*, no. 762; 'ca. 750' by Martin McNamara, 'Plan and Source Analysis of *Das Bibelwerk*, Old Testament,' in *Irland und die Christenheit: Bibelstudien und Mission*, ed. Proínseás Ní Chatháin and Michael Richter (Stuttgart: Klett-Cotta, 1987), 86; 'late eighth century' by Joseph F. Kelly, 'A Catalogue of Early Medieval Hiberno-Latin Biblical Commentaries (I),' *Traditio* 44 (1988): 552; to 'the end of the eighth century' by Michael W. Herren, 'Irish Biblical Commentaries before 800,' in *Roma, magistra mundi. Itineraria culturae medievalis: Mélanges offerts au Père L.E. Boyle à l'occasion de son 75e anniversaire* (Louvain-la-Neuve: Fédération Internationale des Instituts d'Études Médiévales, 1998), 405; and ca. 800 by Dáibhí Ó Cróinín, 'Hiberno-Latin Literatùre to 1169,' in *A New History of Ireland. I: Prehistoric and Early Ireland*, ed. Ó Cróinín (Oxford: OUP, 2005), 394. Gerard MacGinty, whose recent partial edition of the *Reference Bible* covers only the section dealing with the Pentateuch, believes it was written no later than the middle of the eighth century and that two different recensions were in existence by ca. 800: see MacGinty, 'The Pentateuch of the *Reference Bible*: The Problem concerning Its Sources,' in *The Scriptures and Early Medieval Ireland*, ed. O'Loughlin, 163–77; and MacGinty, ed., *The Reference Bible / Das Bibelwerk: Inter pauca problesmata de enigmatibus ex tomis canonicis*, CCCM 173 (Turnhout: Brepols, 2000), x.

significat quia in eius tempore nasceretur ipse a quo redundaret fons olei spiritalis et unctionis per totum tempus noui testamenti usque ad iudicium. (6)
Item in eius tempore facta pace cum Parthis, Iani portae clusae sunt; quod
significat gentilitatem sub Christi fide esse cludendam. (7) Item in eius tempore debita soluta sunt omnibus a rege; quod significat quia in eius tempore
Saluator nasceretur qui peccata et debita omnibus per penitentiam indulgeret.
(8) Item in suo tempore terrae motus factus est magnus; quod significat quia
in eius tempore nasceretur ille qui elementa in die iudicii mouebit, ut dicitur:
Stellae cadent de caelo, et reliqua. (9) Item in eius tempore serui ad dominos
suis redacti sunt; quod significat quia in eius tempore nascitur cui omnes homines seruiunt, ut dicitur: *Cui omne genu flectetur caelestium,* et reliqua.

[Likewise: (1) When Christ was born Caesar Augustus enacted a census over
the whole world: three bronze denarii as a figure of Christ who requires from
everyone thought, word, and deed. It was of bronze, which is more resonant
than all metals, so that each one might preach by word of mouth to others
what he offers to God in thought, word, and deed. (2) Likewise: This census
had three things special about it: that every person in the whole world paid it;
and that it was of the same weight whether paid by rich or poor; and that it
was accepted from nobody except in his own homeland. For thereby is shown
the power of the king, who subjects everyone to himself; and justice, which
deprives no one of his homeland; and abundance in his kingdom, whereby
everyone had the wherewithal to pay the census. (3) OROSIUS. Likewise:
This Caesar, in whose reign Christ was born, at the beginning of his reign
came to Rome in one chariot with Tiberius his son, after he had taken over
the eastern Kingdom. This signifies that in his reign there would be born the
one who would rule the whole world with the Father in unity of will. (4)
Likewise: In his time a golden orb appeared about the sun. This signifies that
in his time there would be born the one whose power, beauty, light and wisdom would encompass all power, beauty, light and wisdom. (5) Likewise in
his time a spring of oil flowed in Rome from a commercial inn throughout the
whole day until evening. This means that in his time there would be born the one
from whom would pour out a spring of spiritual oil and anointing for the whole
time of the New Testament until judgment. (6) Likewise in his time peace was
made with the Parthians, the Gates of Janus were shut. This signifies that the
gentile world was to be enclosed under the faith of Christ. (7) Likewise in his
time debts were remitted to everybody by the king. This signifies that in his
time a Saviour would be born who through repentance would forgive sins
and debts to everyone. (8) Likewise in his time a great earthquake occurred.
This signifies that in his time there would be born the one who will shake the
elements in the day of judgment, as it is said: *Stars will fall from heaven,* etc.

(9) Likewise in his time slaves were returned to their masters. This signifies that in his time is born the one whom all people serve, as it is said: *To whom every knee shall bow, in heaven*, etc.][25]

As Charles D. Wright has pointed out, the *Reference Bible*'s threefold interpretation of the Caesarian tax under portent 2 – which states that 'this census had three things special about it: that every person in the whole world paid it; and that it was of the same weight whether paid by rich or poor; and that it was accepted from nobody except in his own homeland' – finds a suspiciously close parallel in Vercelli Homily V, which similarly interprets this portent in a threefold manner: 'Ðrim wisum ungelice wæron mannum beboden on þæs caseres dagum, þæt is þonne þæt æghwylc man sceolde gaful gildan, 7 ealle men sceoldon hit gildan ge rice ge heane, 7 ðam gafole mon ne onfeng æt ænegum men butan in his swæsum eðle' ('In three different ways were men commanded in the days of that emperor, that is that each man had to pay tribute, and all men had to pay it whether rich or poor, and this tribute could not be received from any man except in his native country').[26] Moreover, this same portent in Vercelli V is immediately followed by an explanatory sentence that invokes the triadic 'thought, word, and deed' formula embedded in the first portent of the *Reference Bible*: 'On þan wæs getacnod þæt we sculon in þrim wisum Gode rihtes geleafan gaful agildan, þæt is on wordum 7 on geþohtum 7 on dædum' ('This signified that we must pay the tribute of true faith to God in three ways – that is, in words and thoughts and deeds'). On these particular details, the *Reference Bible* comes closer to Vercelli V than does the *Catechesis Celtica*. At the same time, the third portent in the *Reference Bible* (the one that cites Orosius) may help clarify a problematic line in the *Expositio quatuor evangeliorum* since the *Reference Bible*'s statement that Augustus's arrival in Rome 'signifies that in his reign there would be born the one who would rule the whole world with the Father in unity of will' offers a corrective to the *Expositio*'s ungrammatical comment that Augustus's arrival in Rome 'ostendit quod in regno ejus nasceretur ipse, qui regnaret in universo mundo, et pater unitatem filii sui voluntatem' ('indicates that in his reign the one would be born who would rule the whole world, and the father [shows] the unity [and] will of his own son'). Somehow the author of the *Expositio* has evidently misconstrued a phrase that must have read 'in unitate filii sui uoluntatis,' which links the *Reference Bible* and the *Expositio* in a common line of textual inheritance.

---

25 Text and translation by McNamara, *Apocrypha Hiberniae I*, 530–3.
26 See Wright, *The Irish Tradition in Old English Literature*, 80–1.

The earliest sermon or homily I am aware of that makes use of the Nativity portents is a Christmas sermon from the Verona homiliary, a collection of eleven sermons written in the early ninth century, possibly in northern Italy, probably going back to an eighth-century exemplar.[27] These sermons exhibit several of the tell-tale 'symptoms' characteristic of Irish-Latin texts of the seventh, eighth, and ninth centuries,[28] including a *locus*, *tempus*, *persona* rhetorical triad which Irish exegetes often employed when commenting on a biblical verse.[29] The Christmas sermon, which is the first sermon in the collection, reports seven *miracula*: a rainbow encircling the sun, the restoration of slaves to their masters, the forgiveness of debts, a fountain of oil bursting forth at an inn, Caesar's rejection of the title of 'lord,' world peace, and three suns in the sky over Rome.[30] In this case all seven portents can be traced back to Orosius, and in places the language of the sermon is in fact quite close to Orosius, as indicated by the italicized

---

27 Lawrence T. Martin, 'The *Catechesis Veronensis*,' in *The Scriptures and Early Medieval Ireland*, ed. O'Loughlin, 151–61.

28 The Hiberno-Latin symptoms of the Verona homilies were first remarked in passing (but without elaboration) by Bernhard Bischoff, 'Wendepunkte in der Geschichte der lateinischen Exegese im Frühmittelalter,' *Sacris Erudiri* 6 (1954): 189–279, repr. with revisions in his *Mittelalterliche Studien: Ausgewählte Aufsätze zur Schriftkunde und Literaturgeschichte*, 3 vols. (Stuttgart: Hiersemann, 1966–81), I: 229, trans. Colm O'Grady, 'Turning-Points in the History of Latin Exegesis in the Early Irish Church: A.D. 650–800,' in *Biblical Studies: The Medieval Irish Contribution*, ed. Martin McNamara, Proceedings of the Irish Biblical Association 1 (Dublin: Dominican Publications, 1976), 95. The homilies are dated 's. viii/ix' by Lapidge and Sharpe, *BCLL*, no. 804.

29 The sermon's opening sentence quotes from Lk. 2:1, *exiit edictum a Cesare Augusto ut censum profiterentur omnes per uniuersum orbem terrae* ('there went out an edict from Caesar Augustus that everyone in the entire world would register themselves in a public census'), which agrees not with the standard Vulgate reading of this verse (*ut describeretur uniuersus orbis*, 'that the whole world should be enrolled') but with a form of this verse most closely parallelled in the Book of Kells, the Codex Usserianus Secundus (s. viii/ix), and the Gospels of St Gatien (copied probably in Brittany, Cornwall, or Wales s. viii/ix from an Irish exemplar): see the analysis by L.T. Martin, ed., *Homiliarum Veronense*, CCCM 186, Scriptores Celtigenae 4 (Turnhout: Brepols, 2000), xv and 1. Other biblical lemmata within the Verona homilies (mainly from Luke) that are in agreement with Irish bibles in contrast to the dominant Vulgate readings are identified by Martin, 'The *Catechesis Veronensis*,' 154–5.

30 Some of these Orosian *mirabilia*, as might be expected, were also picked up by medieval chroniclers. At Cambrai in the year 922, according to Flodoard of Reims, 'it seemed that three suns appeared, or that the sun had three orbs equally distant from each other': *The Annals of Flodoard of Reims, 919–966*, ed. and trans. Steven Fanning and Bernard S. Bachrach (Peterborough, ON: Broadview Press, 2004), 7.

passages below, which are all quotations from Orosius's *Historia* VI.xx.5–7 and xxii.4–6:[31]

Videamus ergo illa miracula que in diebus Cesaris, inminente Saluatoris aduentu, facta sunt. (1) *Cum primo* Iulio *Cessare interfecto, ex Apollonia rediens urbem ingrediretur, hora circiter tertia, repente liquido ac puro sereno circulus ad speciem celestis arcus orbem solis ambit, <quasi> eum unum ac potentissimum in hoc mundo solumque clarissimum in orbem monstraret, cuius tempore uenturus esset, qui ipsum solem solus mundumque totum et fecisset et regeret.* (2) Et cum *ouans urbem ingrederetur,* et *XXX milia seruorum dominis restituisset,* V milia quorum domini non exstabant in crucem egisset, (3) *et XLIIII legiones solus imperio suo ad tutamen orbis terrarum distribuisset,* ac *superiora omnia populi Romani debita donanda, literarum etiam monimentis abolitis, censuisset.* (4) *In diebus ipsis fons olei* sponte *<de taberna> meritoria* Rome terra prorupit fluxitque tota die sine intermisione, significans Christi gratiam ex gentibus. Quibus signis, *quid euidentius quam in diebus Cessaris toto orbe regnantis futura Christi natiuitas declarata est? Per totum* enim *diem, hoc est per omne Romani imperii tempus, Christum et ex eo Christianos, id est, unctum* et *ex eo unctos, de taberna meritoria, hoc est, de hospita largaque ecclesia, affluenter* et *incessabiliter processuros restituendosque per Cessarem omnes seruos, qui* tunc *cognoscerent dominum suum; caeteros, qui sine domino inuenirentur, morti supli-cioque dedendos, remitendaque sub Caessare debita peccatorum in ea urbe in qua spontaneum fluxit oleum.* . . . (5) Eodem quoque tempore quo Christus natus est, Caesar *appelationem domini ut homo declinauit.* Nam cum diceretur dominus bonus et iustus, prohibuit *dominumque se post hec apellari, ne a liberis quidem* et *nepotibus suis uel <serio uel> ioco passus est; immo non ausus, quo* tempore *uerus Dominus totius generis humani inter homines natus est.* (6) *Eodemque anno* per uniuersum orbem terrarum pax facta est in quo natus est ille qui euangelizauit pacem his qui longe et his qui prope, qui dixit: 'Pacem meam do uobis, pacem relinquo uobis': *in cuius ortu audientibus hominibus angeli cecinerunt: 'Gloria in excelsis Deo, et in terra pax hominibus bonae uoluntatis.'* (7) Sed etiam ante aliquot annos, Romae signum in celo uisum, tres soles exorti in eandem orbem, colerunt quis postea futura esset predicatio, quae tres quidem personas in una diuinitatis substantia predicaret. Hec sunt signa ac prodigia quae gentilibus inter cetera de natiuitate Domini demonstrata sunt.[32]

---

31 *Paulus Orosius, Historiarum aduersus paganos libri VII*, ed. Karl Zangemeister, CSEL 5 (Vienna: Tempsky, 1882), 419–20.

32 *Homiliarum Veronense*, ed. Martin, 4–5, ll. 95–142, with some slight adjustments to punctuation and capitalization.

[Let us see those miracles that took place in the days of Caesar in anticipation of the Saviour's coming. (1) When at first Julius Caesar was killed, [Caesar Augustus], returning from Apollonia, entered the city at about the third hour, and all of a sudden in the clear and calm and serene [sky] a ring in the appearance of a rainbow encircled the disk of the sun, as if to point him out as the one and most powerful man in this world and the most famous person on earth, in whose time he was to come who alone had made the sun itself and the whole world and was ruling them. (2) And when he entered the city in triumph and had restored thirty thousand slaves to their masters and had put to death on the cross five thousand whose masters were not to be found, (3) and after he alone had distributed forty-four legions in his empire for the protection of the world, and had decreed that all the former debts of the Roman people should be forgiven and the records of account books should be wiped clean, (4) in those very days a fountain of oil spontaneously burst forth from a small inn in the land of Rome and flowed all day long without interruption, signifying the grace of Christ among the people. What is more evident than that by these signs the future nativity of Christ was declared in the days when Caesar was ruling the whole world? For throughout an entire day, which is to say throughout the entire age of the Roman Empire, Christ and from him Christians – that is, the anointed one and from him the anointed ones – would come forth in abundance and without ceasing from an inn, from the hospitable and bountiful church, and all slaves who acknowledged their master would be restored by Caesar, and the others who were found without a master would be given over to death and punishment, and the debts of sins would be remitted under Caesar in that city in which oil flowed spontaneously ... (5) And at the same time that Christ was born, Caesar as a man rejected the title of 'lord.' For when it was said that he was a good and just lord, he forbade anyone from calling him lord ever again, even his children and grandchildren, whether in earnest or in jest, and indeed no one dared, [for] at that time the true Lord of the entire human race was born among men. (6) And in that same year over all the earth a peace reigned in which he was born who preached peace to those who were far and near, who said 'My peace I give to you; my peace I leave with you,' at whose birth as men listened the angels sang: 'Glory to God in the highest, and on earth peace to men of good will.' (7) But also before too many years a sign was seen in the sky at Rome: three suns arising in the same orbit. Those who witnessed this later [realized that] it was a future prophecy which in fact foretold three persons in one essence of the divinity. These are the signs and prodigies (among others) that were revealed to the pagans concerning the nativity of the Lord.]

Another early biblical commentary that shows at least passing familiarity with the Christmas portents is the Vienna *Commentary on Luke*. In contrast to the Pseudo-Jerome *Expositio quatuor evangeliorum*, which survives in over thirty manuscripts, this Lucan commentary is known only from a single manuscript, now in Vienna, which was in Salzburg in the late Middle Ages, a fact that led the commentary's editor, Joseph Kelly, to surmise that the text was composed within the eighth-century circle of Virgilius of Salzburg.[33] In its discussion of the first chapter of Luke, this commentary offers in rapid summary a narrative digest of five Nativity portents: a ring rising above the light of the sun, oil coming forth at an inn, the flooding of the Tiber, the restoration of slaves to their masters, and an end to war:

> *In diebus illis*: Adfuerunt magna miracula in aduentu saluatoris: (1) circulus lucem solis supereminens, (2) oleum in taberna meritoria promens, (3) in terra flumen Tiberis prorumpens in ciuitatem ueniens, (4) serui in potestatem dominorum redacti. Id, qui dominos agnouerunt non cognoscentes puniti erant, (5) et bella cessauerunt secundum historiam ut dicitur: *Auferens bella usque ad finem terrae* (Psalm 45:10).[34]
>
> [*In those days*: Great miracles occurred at the Saviour's coming: (1) a ring rising above the light of the sun, (2) oil coming forth at a small inn, (3) the river Tiber bursting out onto the land [and] coming into the city, (4) slaves restored to the power of their lords. That is, those who recognized their lords but did not acknowledge them were punished, (5) and wars ceased according to the literal level [of Scripture], as it is said: *Making wars to cease even to the end of the earth*.]

All of these portents originated in Orosius, except for the flooding of the Tiber, which sounds suspiciously like a misreading of the more commonly reported miracle of the stream of oil that flowed across the Tiber, two examples of which we will encounter momentarily.

A more perplexing case is presented by a sermon that figures at the very end of a homiliary compiled by Hrabanus Maurus in 854 or 855 for the

---

33 Lapidge and Sharpe, *BCLL*, no. 773; Kelly, 'A Catalogue of Early Medieval Hiberno-Latin Biblical Commentaries (II),' 418 (no. 92); Wright, 'Hiberno-Latin and Irish-Influenced Biblical Commentaries,' 107 (no. 31); McNamara, *Apocrypha Hiberniae I*, 517–18 and 524–5.

34 Pseudo-Jerome, *Expositio quatuor evangeliorum*, *In Lucam* 2 (PL 30.587C–D).

Frankish emperor Lothar I (847–55), who had commissioned Hrabanus to produce a book of homilies on the Gospels and Epistles that he could read for his own private edification.[35] This homiliary had a severely restricted, almost non-existent transmission history and seems not to have been copied or distributed at large, so there is very little chance that it ever had a significant impact on other writers either on the continent or in Britain. Only a single incomplete manuscript witness to about a third of this collection survives, and the edition by Migne in PL 110 is taken from a 1626 Cologne edition whose source manuscript has gone missing. This absence of even a single complete manuscript copy complicates the situation with this particular passage, since it makes it difficult to determine this text's relationship to the preceding homily. In PL 110 this passage is set off from the rest of the homily with its own separate rubric, *De septem signis nativitatis Domini* ('On the Seven Signs of the Nativity of the Lord'), and because it comes at the end of the very last homily in the collection, it has the appearance of a short independent text that was tacked on at the back of the manuscript and was then printed by Migne as an appendix to sermon 163. In the only published study of Hrabanus's homiliary, Raymond Étaix has in fact declared both sermon 163 and this little appendix inauthentic,[36] so this is probably not a text by Hrabanus after all, and we actually have no idea where it comes from or how it came to be inserted at the back of a now-lost manuscript of Hrabanus's homiliary. But if we can ignore all these complications for the moment and dwell instead on the contents of this passage, we can see that it is worth including in a discussion of the Vercelli portents since it obviously draws from a similar tradition. This passage affixed to the Pseudo-Hrabanus sermon enumerates seven signs of Christ's nativity, and the number seven is itself significant because it is interpreted at the end of the passage as a symbol of the seven gifts of the Holy Spirit. The seven signs are a single prince who rules the world, universal peace, the return of freed slaves to their masters and the payment of tribute to the emperor, a thousand and thirty slaves who decided they did not want to go back to their masters after all, a new star in the East, a golden ring around the sun, and a stream of oil that flowed across the Tiber:

---

35 Hrabanus Maurus, *Homiliae in Evangelia et epistolas* (PL 110.135–467). The collection is briefly discussed by Rosamond McKitterick, *The Frankish Church and the Carolingian Reforms, 789–895* (London: Royal Historical Society, 1977), 97–102, and is more fully described by Raymond Étaix, 'L'homéliaire composé par Raban Maur pour l'empereur Lothaire,' *Recherches Augustiniennes* 19 (1984): 211–40.

36 Étaix, 'L'homéliaire composé par Raban Maur,' 230–1.

De septem signis nativitatis Domini. Multa signa Dominus ante nativitatem suam praefiguratione sui adventus in mundum praemisit. Multa etiam in ipsa nativitate ostendit, de quibus: (1) Primum signum erat quod princeps unus per omnem orbem regnabat, quod nunquam antea fuerat; unum totius creaturae Dominum Christum praenuntians venturum. (2) Secundum autem signum erat pax admirabilis super omnem terram, qualis nec ante nec postea unquam fuerat; veram mundi pacem designans, quae est Christus ille, qui fecit pacem inter Deum et homines. (3) Tertium signum fuit quod, Caesare concedente, captivis absolutis, in quacunque fuissent captivitate, possessio propria reddebatur, et censum singuli reddere Caesari profitebantur, qui trium denariorum habentes pensionem, drachmae nomine censebantur; hoc praesignans quod genus humanum a captivitate et dominio diaboli esset per Christum liberandum et ad patriam paradisi, si fidem sanctae Trinitatis profiteatur, reducendum. (4) Quartum signum erat quod una die mille et triginta fuere servi qui ad proprios redire dominos noluerunt post captivitatem laxatam: hoc praenuntians quod qui a vitiis ad Christum redire noluerit, aeternaliter peribit. (5) Quintum signum fuit stella nova in Oriente orta, cujus ducatu Magi ad Christum pervenerunt; cujus mira supra omnes stellas claritas Dei gratiam significat: per quam non solum ex Judaeis, sed et multo plures ex gentibus ad vitam, qui Christus est, perducuntur. (6) Sextum signum est circulus magnus aureo splendens fulgore circa solem tota illa die nativitatis Christi, significans eum cujus ambitu excellentissimae etiam naturae continentur. (7) Septimum signum erat quod ipsa die tota rivulus olei in urbe Roma trans Tiberim large effluebat: significans gratuitam misericordiam Dei, qua genus humanum Christus venit quaerere et salvare quod perierat. Haec etiam septem signa, septem dona Spiritus sancti significant.[37]

[On the seven signs of the nativity of the Lord. Before his birth the Lord sent many signs into the world as a prefiguration of his coming. He also revealed many things in that same nativity, among which: (1) The first sign was that one prince was ruling over the entire world, which had never happened before, presaging the coming of the one Lord Christ over every creature. (2) And the second sign was that there was a wonderful peace over all the earth such as had never existed before nor ever since, denoting the true peace of the world, which is Christ himself, who made peace between God and men. (3) The third sign was that in deference to Caesar's wishes, after slaves had been freed, rightful possession [of them] was restored in whatever [form of] servitude they had been [in]; and they conducted a public census to render unto Caesar [whereby] those with a net worth of three denarii were assessed at the rate of one drachma.

---

37 PL 110.466–8, with some slight repunctuation.

This foretold that the human race would be freed from the captivity and dominion of the devil by Christ and would be led back to their homeland of paradise if they professed faith in the holy Trinity. (4) The fourth sign was that in one day there were 1030 slaves who did not want to return to their own masters after having been released from captivity; this foretells that those who do not want to return to Christ from their vices will perish eternally. (5) The fifth sign was a new star rising in the East, under the guidance of which the Magi reached Christ, whose marvelous brilliance, exceeding all stars, signifies the grace of God, through which not only those from among the Jews but also many more from among the heathens are brought to life, which is Christ. (6) The sixth sign is a great ring around the sun shining with golden radiance the whole day of Christ's nativity, signifying him whose ambit likewise embraces the most excellent universe. (7) The seventh sign was that all that same day in the city of Rome a stream of oil flowed abundantly across the Tiber, signifying the freely bestowed mercy of God, by which Christ came to seek out and save the human race, which had become lost. And these seven signs symbolize the seven gifts of the Holy Spirit.]

Four of these portents – the ring around the sun, the stream of oil, the restoration of slaves to their masters, and the payment of tribute to the emperor – occur in one or both of the Vercelli homilies. There is no mention of Augustus in the Pseudo-Hrabanus text, but the reference to a single prince who rules the world and the *pax admirabilis* both seem indebted to the Augustan scheme found in Orosius, the *De divinis officiis*, the *Catechesis Celtica*, and Vercelli V.

In his study of Hrabanus's homiliary, Étaix noted in passing that similar texts on the signs of the nativity can be found in other south German homiliaries of the ninth century, especially those descended from the Homiliary of Mondsee, compiled by Lantperhtus, the abbot of Saint-Michel de Mondsee in the diocese of Salzburg, between 811 and 819.[38] I have not yet examined any of these manuscripts myself to see if I can locate examples of what Étaix had in mind, but I can confirm that a text very close to the Pseudo-Hrabanus *De septem signis* appears in Munich, Bayerische

---

38 Étaix, 'L'homéliaire composé par Raban Maur,' 230–1. The Mondsee homiliary, preserved in Vienna, Österreichische Nationalbibliothek lat. 1014 (s. ix, Mondsee), is most fully discussed by H[enri] Barré, 'L'homiliaire carolingien de Mondsee,' *Revue Bénédictine* 71 (1961): 71–107, who at 85–6 identifies seven homiliaries that descend from the Mondsee homiliary. A briefer notice of the collection is given by Barré in *Les homéliaires carolingiens de l'école d'Auxerre: Authenticité – inventaire – tableaux comparatifs – initia*, Studi e testi 225 (Vatican City: Biblioteca Apostolica Vaticana, 1962), 25–7.

Staatsbibliothek, Clm 5257, an eleventh-century Bavarian manuscript whose contents offer numerous parallels to earlier Hiberno-Latin material.[39] On 29v, following a short question-and-answer dialogue in the *Joca monachorum* mode and a series of etymologies, appears the following text, which in some respects resembles an estranged sibling of the Pseudo-Hrabanus *De septem signis*, although the seven miracles are in a different order and they are not subjected to a numerological interpretation:

Multa signa ante natiuitatem suam Deus praemisit. (1) Primum signum erat quod princeps unus, id est Cesar Augustus, per omnem orbem regnabat quod ante non fuerat. (2) Secundum signum erat pax ammirabilis super omnem terram. (3) Tercium signum erat quod ipso Cesare concedente unusquisque homo ad propriam rediit patriam et censum singuli profitebantur reddere Cesari quod dragma appellabatur, trium habens denariorum pensionem, significans quod rex noster Dominus Iesus Christus a nobis fidem sancte Trinitatis requirit. (4) Quartum signum noua stella. (5) Quintum signum circulus magnus aureo splendens fulgore circa solem tota die natiuitatis Christi. (6) Sextum signum quod tota illa die natalis Domini riuulus olei in urbe Roma trans Tiberim largiter fluebat. (7) Septimum signum quod unusquisque sub Cesare Auguste rediit ad propria et qui hoc facere nolebant omnes uno die pariter perierunt, fere .xxx. milia hominum.[40]

[Before his birth, God sent many signs in advance. (1) The first sign was that a single prince, namely Caesar Augustus, was reigning throughout the whole world, which had not happened before. (2) The second sign was a wondrous peace over all the earth. (3) The third sign was that in deference to Caesar's own wishes, each man returned to his own native land, and they conducted a public census [whereby] each rendered unto Caesar what was called a drachma, having the value of three denarii, signifying that our king [and] Lord Jesus Christ demands from us faith in the holy Trinity. (4) The fourth sign was a new star. (5) The fifth sign was a great ring around the sun shining with golden radiance the whole day of Christ's birth. (6) The sixth sign was that all that day of Christ's nativity in the city of Rome a stream of oil flowed in abundance across the Tiber. (7) The seventh sign was that everyone under

---

39 The manuscript's contents are inventoried by C. Halm and G. Laubmann, *Catalogus codicum latinorum Bibliothecae Regiae Monacensis* 1.3 (Munich: Sumptibus Bibliothecae Regiae, 1873), 2. The question-and-answer dialogue entitled *Disputatio puerorum* at 24r–26r is discussed by Wright, *The Irish Tradition in Old English Literature*, 63, 64, 67, 77, 91, 92n189, and 93.

40 I rely here on a transcription of the passage that was generously provided to me by Charles D. Wright, to whom I am most grateful.

Caesar Augustus returned to their own homeland, and all those who did not want to do so perished one day all at once, about thirty thousand men.]

Yet another example comes from a Christmas sermon in the Cambridge, Pembroke College 25 homiliary, which is especially intriguing because as students of the Vercelli homilies are well aware, this manuscript is an eleventh-century version of an earlier Latin sermon collection that was known in England by the second half of the tenth century, when it was consulted by the authors of at least eight Old English homilies, including Vercelli homilies III, XIX, XX, and XXI, which all translate texts from the Pembroke collection.[41] The original ninth-century collection from which Pembroke 25 descends is a Carolingian collection known as the Homiliary of Saint-Père de Chartres, so called because the earliest extant manuscript witness was produced at the abbey of Saint-Père-en-Vallée at Chartres in the late tenth or early eleventh century.[42] Nine copies or redactions of this homiliary are known to survive today either whole or in part, and even though the original collection was probably first assembled somewhere in Frankish territory during the ninth century,[43] six of its nine surviving copies were produced in England, so we have abundant evidence that the texts in this homiliary were circulating in England and were being read and translated from the tenth century onward.[44] The Christmas sermon has not been printed or commented on before, although an outline of its contents was given by J.E. Cross in his 1987 monograph on the Pembroke 25

---

41 The connections with the Vercelli homilies are demonstrated in detail by James E. Cross, *Cambridge Pembroke College MS. 25: A Carolingian Sermonary Used by Anglo-Saxon Preachers*, King's College London Medieval Studies 1 (London: King's College London, 1987), 91–173.

42 The contents of this manuscript, Chartres, Bibliothèque municipale 25 (44), are described in the *Catalogue général des manuscrits des Bibliothèques publiques de France. Départements – Tome XI: Chartres* (Paris: E. Plon, Nourrit et cie, 1890), 11–12. The contents of the original collection from which the Chartres manuscript descends are reconstructed on the basis of five manuscripts by Barré, *Les homéliaires carolingiens de l'école d'Auxerre*, 17–25.

43 François Dolbeau, 'Du nouveau sur un sermonnaire de Cambridge,' *Scriptorium* 42 (1988): 255–7, suggests that the original collection was compiled somewhere in the vicinity of Tours.

44 The six surviving versions of this collection of English origin or provenance that have come to light are Cambridge, Pembroke College 25 (s. xi² or xiᵉˣ, Bury St Edmunds); Cambridge, St John's College 42, 13r–62v and 70v–71v (s. xii, Worcester?); Canterbury, Cathedral Library, Add. 127/12 (s. xiⁱⁿ); Lincoln, Cathedral Library 199 (C. 3. 3), 213r–345v (s. xiiᵐᵉᵈ); London, BL, Royal 5. E. XIX, 21r–36v (s. xiᵉˣ, Salisbury); and Oxford, Balliol College 240, 56r–136r (s. xiv).

collection.[45] This text is crucial for the present discussion since its list of portents overlaps not only with both Vercelli V and VI but with the *Old English Martyrology* as well. The Pembroke 25 sermon identifies seven portents that are said to have taken place during the reign of Augustus: a golden ring about the sun, a fountain of oil that flowed from morning till evening, the cancellation of debts, a solar eclipse, an earthquake, an end to war, and a talking ox in Rome and a talking lamb in Egypt:

In illius ergo Augusti tempore multa signa /11r/ et prodigia facta sunt ad Christi presignandam regis aeterni natiuitatem: (1) In illius enim tempore circulus aureus circa solem apparuit, quod significat quoniam ipse nasceretur cuius potestas et lux et pulchritudo et sapientia circumdaret omnem potestatem et omnem lucem et omnem pulchritudinem et omnem sapientiam in celo et in terra. (2) In illius iterum tempore fons olei manauit in Roma et fluxit a mane usque ad uesperum, quod significat unctionem Christi ad baptismum et doctrinam eius, qua omnes imbueret ad credendum per baptismum. (3) In eius tempore omnia debita regis laxata sunt ab eo, quia in eius tempore saluator nasceretur qui peccata omnibus debita per baptismum humano generi indulgeret. (4) In eius tempore sol obscuratus est, lumine per totum mundum separatus, et post obscurationem ortus est lucide, quod significat quoniam Christus nasceretur per totum mundum lucens ablata totius orbis gentilitate. (5) In eius tempore terrae motus factus est magnus, quia ad aduentum Christi cum sederit in sede maiestatis sue in die iudicii omnia trement. (6) In eius tempore bella ab orbe terrarum cessauerunt, quod significat quia in eius tempore natus esset qui pacem omnibus intulisset et pacem inter deum et hominem fecisset, inter corpus et animam, inter angelos et homines. (7) In eius tempore animalia fari humana locutione non dubitatur. Bos enim in Roma sub misterio natiuitatis eius locutus est, nihilominus et agnus in Egypto humana usus est loquela. Haec autem omnia facta sunt, fratres dilectissimi, ad significandam Christi natiuitatem ut elimenta intelligerent et animalia testificarentur aduentum eius.[46]

---

45 Cross, *Cambridge Pembroke College MS. 25*, 20–1 (art. 5).

46 This is the passage as it reads in Pembroke 25, 10v–11v. I have not collated it with the other copies of this sermon in Oxford, Balliol College 240, 60v–61v, and Cambridge, St John's College 42, 15r–v. Furthermore, two additional copies of this sermon have been identified by Jan Machielsen, *Clavis Patristica Pseudepigraphorum Medii Aevi*, IA–B: *Homiletica* (Turnhout: Brepols, 1990), nos. 2315 and 5323, in Paris, Bibliothèque Nationale, lat. 2025 (s. xii), 132v–33r, and Melk, Stiftsbibliothek, 218 (s. xii vel xv), 78r–v, and another is identified by Raymond Étaix, *Homéliaires patristiques latins: Recueil d'études de manuscrits médiévaux*, Collection des Études Augustiniennes,

[In the time of this Augustus, therefore, many signs and prodigies occurred foretokening the nativity of Christ the eternal king. (1) For in his time a golden ring appeared around the sun, which signifies that he would be born whose power and light and beauty and wisdom would encompass all power and all light and all beauty and all wisdom in heaven and on earth. (2) Again in his time a fountain of oil poured forth in Rome and flowed from morning till evening, which signifies Christ's anointing at baptism and his teaching, by which he initiated all into believing through baptism. (3) In his time all debts to the king were erased by him, for in his time the Saviour would be born who would forgive the sins and debts for all through baptism for the human race. (4) In his time the sun was darkened, cut off from its light throughout the entire world, but rose brightly after its eclipse, which signifies that Christ would be born shining through the entire world once the heathendom of the whole world was removed. (5) In his time there was a great earthquake, for all will tremble at Christ's coming, when he will sit in the seat of his majesty on the Day of Judgment. (6) In his time wars on earth ceased, which signifies that in his time the one was born who would introduce peace to all and would make peace between God and man, between body and soul, between angels and men. (7) There is no doubt that in his time animals spoke with human language, for an ox in Rome spoke at the observance of his birth, and a lamb in Egypt, no less, made use of human speech. All these things happened, most beloved brothers, to signify Christ's nativity so that the elements would understand and the animals would testify to his coming.]

These last two details, the talking ox and lamb, occur in both the *Old English Martyrology* and Patrick of Dublin's *De mirabilibus Hiberniae*, but nowhere else that Cross knew of, a fact that prompted him to suggest that these two talking animals became affixed to the Christmas portents in an Insular milieu. If Michael Lapidge is right in thinking that the Latin *Vorlage* of the *Old English Martyrology* was compiled in the 730s by Acca of Hexham, then our talking ox and lamb were already making their way across northern England by the second quarter of the eighth century.[47]

Another example appears in an unpublished Christmas sermon in Salisbury, Cathedral Library 9, 48v–49r, entitled *[De] tempore Natiuitatis Christi et eius miraculis*. Salisbury 9 is a florilegium of monastic texts copied

---

Série Moyen-Âge et Temps modernes 29 (Paris: Institut d'Études Augustiniennes, 1994), 210, in Paris, Bibliothèque Nationale, lat. 11702 (s. xii, Corbie), 3r.

47 Michael Lapidge, 'Acca of Hexham and the Origin of the *Old English Martyrology*,' *Analecta Bollandiana* 123 (2005): 29–78.

in two stages at Salisbury at the end of the eleventh and the beginning of the twelfth century. Its contents include, tellingly, excerpts from the Irish *Reference Bible*, the *Liber questionum in evangeliis*, the Vienna *Commentary on Luke*, and several other texts of at least suspected Irish origin or Irish influence that are known principally from copies transmitted in continental manuscripts of the eighth and ninth centuries.[48] Some of the texts in this manuscript were known in England at a much earlier date, and eleventh- or twelfth-century English copies can be identified for a few, but it would be difficult to find another English manuscript of any period that contains as concentrated a collection of exegetical texts with a Hiberno-Latin background as Salisbury 9. The outer edges of this manuscript are unfortunately eaten away by mould and damp, so that portions of the text are now lost, especially in the lower three-quarters of each page, where as many as two or three words are missing from the beginning or end of each line of this sermon. In the passage reproduced below, that missing text is indicated by ellipses in square brackets, or by square brackets enclosing a provisional guess at what some of that lost text may have been. Even with these gaps in the text, however, one can readily see that this sermon recounts ten portents that are said to have taken place in the year of Christ's birth, some of which echo the language of the *Catechesis Celtica*, while others match up more closely with the Pembroke 25 sermon:

---

48 On the date, scribes, and contents of Salisbury 9, see E. Maunde Thompson, 'Catalogue of the Manuscripts in the Cathedral Library of Salisbury,' in *A Catalogue of the Library of the Cathedral Church of Salisbury* (London: Spottiswoode, 1880), 4–5; Heinrich Schenkl, *Bibliotheca Patrum Latinorum Britannica*, 3 vols. in 1 (Vienna: Tempsky, 1891–1908; repr. Hildesheim: Georg Olms, 1969), no. 3608; Teresa Webber, *Scribes and Scholars at Salisbury Cathedral c. 1075–c. 1125* (Oxford: Clarendon, 1992), 148–9 and 160–2; the review of Webber's *Scribes and Scholars* by Thomas N. Hall in *Analytical and Enumerative Bibliography* n.s. 8 (1994): 136–7; Richard Gameson, *The Manuscripts of Early Norman England (c. 1066–1130)* (Oxford: OUP, 1999), 148; and Helmut Gneuss, *Handlist of Anglo-Saxon Manuscripts: A List of Manuscripts and Manuscript Fragments Written or Owned in England up to 1100*, MRTS 241 (Tempe, AZ: ACMRS, 2001), no. 699. One item in the manuscript (at 78r–79v) is a rare copy of the Hiberno-Latin *Homilia de die iudicii* (*BCLL*, no. 1252; *CPL*, no. 793) printed by Donatien de Bruyne, 'Fragments retrouvés d'apocryphes priscillianistes,' *Revue Bénédictine* 24 (1907): 326–7, from an eighth-century collection that has since been shown to exhibit abundant close parallels to Irish and Hiberno-Latin (and Anglo-Saxon) literature; for details and further references, see Charles D. Wright's entry on 'Apocrypha Priscillianistica' in *Sources of Anglo-Saxon Literary Culture: The Apocrypha*, ed. Frederick M. Biggs, Instrumenta Anglistica Mediaevalia 1 (Kalamazoo: Medieval Institute Publications, 2007), 73–4.

(1) [I]n hoc anno circulus aureus circa solem apparuit, [significat so]lem iustitie nascente<m>. Mundialis sol tremuit et letatur, [significa]t lucidam doctrinam Christi circumdare<t> humanam [...]am, et significat coronam uite eterne clariorem hac [luce f]uturum ubi *fulgebunt iusti sicut sol.* (2) In hoc anno [fons olei] in Roma fluxit et taberna meritoria per totum diem non [...] oleum terrenum unguenti celestis gradus tenuit et [...]st unctum spiritali oleo de quo dictum est: *unxit te [Deus Deus tuu]s oleo letitie,* et reliqua. Significat Christum de carne [...] ortum suum. Significat doctrinam eius ortam in [mundum, ole] um enim cunctis liquoribus carnis est, sicut doctri[na eius om]nibus doctrinis pulchrior. (3) In hoc anno bos [in Roma loc]utus est. Significat gentes loquuturas in [...]iutionem tempore Christi dicentes: *Pater noster* [...]. (4) In hoc anno omnia debita soluta sunt /49r/ a rege. Significat Christum nasciturum, in cuius tempore om[nia debita] peccatorum relaxata sunt. (5) In hoc anno sol caligine teneb[rosa] obscuratus est. Significat quia sol uerus post caliginem ueren[dum] nasceretur. (6) In hoc anno post famem in gentem abundan[tia panis] orta est. Significat panem uite post famem uerbi d[omini], ut est *ego sum panis uiuus qui de celo descendi.* (7) In hoc an[no terrae] motus factus est. Significat Christum terre`na´ omnia comi[nantem] et creaturas in iudicio conquassantem et *celum sicut li[ber inuolutus],* et reliqua. (8) In hoc anno serui ad dominos redacti su[nt. Signi]ficat regem regentem omnes creaturas in precipitium sib[...], de quo Psalma <a>it: *quoniam Dominus excelsus terribilis.* (9) In hoc [anno] nullus armis indigebat, quia pax erat de qua propheta [ait:] *conflabunt gladios suos in uomeres.* Significat [pa]cificum nasciturum de quo dicitur: *auferens bella* et c[etera]. (10) In hoc anno, facta pace cum Part`h´is, Iani porte clause [fuerunt], quod significat quia in eius tempore nasceretur ill[e qui omnem] gentilitatem concluderet cuius pax omnia exsupera[ret ...].

[(1) In that year a golden ring appeared around the sun, which signifies the sun of justice being born. The earthly sun trembled and rejoiced, which signifies the clear teaching of Christ that would encompass human [...] and signifies a crown of eternal life brighter than this light, [a crown] yet to come, when *the just will shine like the sun* (Matt. 13:43). (2) In that year a fountain of oil flowed in Rome and at an inn throughout the entire day not [...] earthly oil had the status of heavenly ointment and [...] anointed with spiritual oil, of which it is said: *God your God has anointed you with the oil of gladness,* and so forth (Psalm 44:8 [LXX]). This signifies Christ, who [...] his birth from the flesh. It signifies the teaching of him born into the world, for oil is more [precious?] than all fluids of the flesh, just as his teaching is more beautiful than all teachings. (3) In that year an ox in Rome spoke. This signifies the people who will speak in [...] the time of Christ saying: *Our Father* [...]. (4) In that year all debts were erased by the king. This signifies Christ, about to be born, in whose time all debts of sins were alleviated. (5) In that year the sun was obscured by a shadowy darkness. This signifies that the true sun would be born after a fearful darkness. (6) In that year, after a famine among the people, an abundance of bread arose. This signifies the bread of life after the famine of the word of the Lord, that is: *I am the living bread which came down from heaven* (John 6:51). (7) In that year there was an earthquake. This signifies Christ, threatening all earthly things, and creatures trembling in judgment, and *heaven rolled up like a book*, and so forth (Apoc. 6:14). (8) In that year slaves were led back to their masters. This signifies the king ruling all creatures in the fall [...], concerning which the Psalm says: *For the Lord is high, terrible* (Psalm 46:3 [LXX]). (9) In that year no one had need of weapons, for there was a peace concerning which the prophet spoke: *They melted down their swords into ploughshares* (Isaias 2:4). This signifies that the peaceful one was about to be born of whom it is said: *making wars to cease*, etc. (Psalm 45:10). (10) In that year, after peace was made with the Parthians, the gates of Janus were closed, which signifies that in his time the one would be born who would shut up every heathenism, whose peace would exceed all things [...].

The very last portent, the closing of the gates of Janus, appears elsewhere only so far as I know in Orosius, the *Catechesis Celtica*, and the *Reference Bible*, whereas portent number 3 gives us another rare example of the talking ox in Rome (if my reconstruction of the missing text at that point holds up), a detail that as we have seen occurs also in the *Old English Martyrology*, Patrick of Dublin, and the Pembroke 25 homiliary. The sixth portent, the vanquishing of famine by an abundance of bread, is parallelled only in the *Catechesis Celtica* and the *Liber questionum in evangeliis*, which argues strongly for its invention by an Irish or Breton author. It may also be significant that of the eight events reported in both the Salisbury 9 sermon and the *Catechesis Celtica*, seven appear in the same order in both texts.

One final example needs to be addressed before I hazard an explanation that will attempt to make sense of this chaotic tangle of data, and that is the Christmas sermon in the Old Icelandic Homily Book, which Tveitane first recognized as including several parallels for the portents in Vercelli V and VI, although he did not print the relevant passage in full, and he made no effort to probe these connections beyond his assertion that 'very nearly the exact source of this whole miracle story' in the Icelandic sermon can be found in the *Catechesis Celtica*.[49] The Old Icelandic Homily Book has not

---

49 Tveitane, 'Irish Apocrypha in Norse Tradition?' 123. Tveitane was less interested in the Icelandic sermon than he was in the Christmas sermon in the Old Norwegian Homily Book, ed. Gustav Indrebø, *Gamal norsk homiliebok. Cod. AM 619 4°*, Norsk historisk kjeldeskrift-institutt Skrifter 54 (Oslo: Jacob Dybwad, 1931), 31–5. As Tveitane noted,

had the attention from students of Old English homilies in recent years that it properly deserves, even though it has long been known that the contents of the Icelandic collection include Icelandic translations of Latin texts that go back to exemplars that were introduced into Scandinavia by English missionaries in the tenth and eleventh centuries.[50] One clear sign of the English ties to the contents of the Icelandic Homily Book is afforded by a penitential sermon in the Homily Book rubricated for Ash Wednesday. This sermon, as Joan Turville-Petre demonstrated over forty years ago, is an Icelandic translation of a Latin composite text that was independently translated into Old English as what we now refer to today as Belfour Homily VI and Vercelli Homily III, with a partial translation also embedded in Vercelli Homily XX.[51] These three Old English homilies translate the same Latin penitential sermon that underlies the Icelandic penitential sermon, and the Latin sermon that underlies them all circulated exclusively, so far as we know, in the Homiliary of Saint-Père de Chartres, the parent collection from which Pembroke 25 descends. The copy in Pembroke 25 is in fact the earliest copy that has been identified, and all other copies are in manuscripts of the Saint-Père Homiliary that were written in England. The circumspect Donald Scragg, in his edition of the Vercelli homilies, shrewdly points out that the Latin sermon behind Vercelli III 'may, of course, have circulated independently of the collection,'[52] and this is indeed a possibility. But the fact remains that all known copies of this sermon did circulate as part of the collection, so it is a reasonable guess that the Icelandic translation likewise depends upon a copy that came to the translator in a version of the Homiliary of Saint-Père de Chartres, and very likely one that originated in England.

This indirect link between homilies in the Vercelli Book and those in the Old Icelandic Homily Book, all dependant on a version of the Saint-Père

---

both the Norwegian homily and Vercelli VI seem to demonstrate familiarity with a confused and watered-down version of the Christmas portents tradition, since they both report that on the night of Christ's birth the emperor Augustus travelled to Bethlehem with a great army (Indrebø, 32, ll. 3–6; Scragg, 129, ll. 33–6) and that some time before Christ's birth (eight years in the Norwegian homily, seven nights in Vercelli VI) the sun shone brightly at midnight (Indrebø, 32, ll. 26–8; Scragg, 129, ll. 22–4). The connections between the Old Norwegian and Old English homilies have since been more fully examined by Christopher Abram, 'Anglo-Saxon Influence in the Old Norwegian Homily Book,' *Medieval Scandinavia* 14 (2004): 1–35.

50 See Hall, 'Old Norse-Icelandic Sermons,' 672–3 and 678–81.

51 Joan Turville-Petre, 'Translations of a Lost Penitential Homily,' *Traditio* 19 (1963): 51–78.

52 *VH*, 71n1.

Homiliary, provides an essential context for reading the passage quoted below from the Christmas sermon in the Icelandic Homily Book, which identifies seven portents at the Nativity. Like the analogous passages in Vercelli V and the Pembroke 25 sermon, this passage begins by situating these signs within the reign of Augustus. The seven signs are Augustus's arrival in Rome in a chariot, a ring about the sun, a fountain of oil, the forgiveness of debts, an unprecedented peace during which no one carried weapons, an earthquake, and the rising of the sun at midnight contrary to its normal behaviour. The full passage reads:

A tíþ Augustus urþo margar iarteíner þær er syNdo at Cristr var boreN i ríki hans: (1) Augustus kom i uphafe rikis síns meþ Tiberio syne sínom í Rómaborg i eiNi kerro. síþan er hann feck ríki fyr utan haf. Sva kom Cristr i kerom mis-cuNar siNar til heíms þessa at styra heime þessom sem fyR. oc nú oc a vallt meþ goþlegom faoþor í eiNom vilia oc í eiNe vesningo. (2) J ríki Avgustvs vas séN goþlegr hringr umb sól. sa er mercþe at sa mønde boreN verþa í hans hrike er hans móttr. fægrþ oc liós. specþ. oc pryþe. oc crafster meonde yver bera oc ráþa mønde sólo oc tungle. oc aollom hlutom. (3) J ríki Avgustus spratt upp viþsmiors bruþr fra morne til aptans. sa er mercþe at i hans ríki mønde boreN verþa sa er es bruþr miscuNar oc viþsmior allrar sælo. (4) Þa er Augustvs kom i Rúmsborg oc gaf alla sculld þa er folket átte at giallda honom a þui áre. Sva at víso gefr oss dominus noster synþer órar oc scvllder fyr helga skírn oc fyr saNa iátning oc algorva iþron gleópa váRa. þeira er ver gerþom i gegn vilia hans. (5) J hans ríki gerþesc sva mikill friþr of allan heim. svát enge maþr bar hervópn. þuiat horvetna var friþr oc samþycke oc éitt ríki fyr þat boþasc friþsamt ríki svnar guþs lifanda sa er friþ gerþe a meþal himins oc iarþar oc hann gerþe eítt rike. (6) J ríki Avgustvs gerþesc landskiálfte mikill sa er merkþe. at i hans riki mønde verþa boreN sa er hreóra mætte af sinom crafste allar hǫfoþskepnor a dóms dege sicut scriptvm est: 'Stiornor mono falla af himne oc himna craftar mono hreórasc fyrer auglite drótteNs. þa er hann keomr at deóma of alla meN.' (7) Þat barsc at i hans riki at sól raN upp a miþre nótt i gegn eþle síno. Þat merkþe at a hans tíþ meoNde berasc saoN sól Cristr siálfr, sá er lyser allan heím af villo eílífs blindleíx, sem Malakias spámaþr sagþe: 'Yþr vGvNdom nafn domini mon upreNa sól retlætes'.[53]

[In the days of Augustus there were many signs that revealed that Christ was born during his reign: (1) At the beginning of his reign Augustus came to Rome in a chariot with his son Tiberius. Later, when he extended the kingdom beyond

53 *Homiliu-bók: Isländska homilier efter en handskrift från tolfte århundradet*, ed. Theodor Wisén (Lund: C.W.K. Gleerup, 1872), 46–7.

the sea, Christ likewise came to this world in the chariot of his mercy to rule this world as it was from the beginning and now and forever shall be with the divine Father according to one will and one essence. (2) During the reign of Augustus a divine ring was seen around the sun, which signified that he would be born during his reign, when he would be surpassingly fair and bright, wise and mighty and powerful, and he would rule the sun and moon and all things. (3) In the reign of Augustus a fountain of oil sprang forth from morning till evening, which signified that during his reign he would be born who is a fountain of mercy and the oil of all happiness. (4) Then Augustus came to Rome and forgave the debts which the people were obliged to pay him that year. So in this way our Lord forgives us for our sins and debts through holy baptism and true confession and full repentance of the crimes which we have committed against his will. (5) During his reign there was such a great peace over all the world that no one bore weapons because everything was peaceful and in concord and under one rule, for this betokens the peaceful reign of the Son of the living God, who made peace between heaven and earth and established one kingdom. (6) In the reign of Augustus there was a great earthquake, which signified that during his reign he would be born who will shake all the primal elements on Judgment Day with all his power, as it is written: '*Stars shall fall from the sky, and the angels of heaven will tremble before the face of the Lord when he comes to judge all men*' (Matt. 24:29). (7) It happened that during his reign the sun rose at midnight contrary to its nature. This signified that in his time it would come to pass that the sun, Christ himself, would appear, who illumines the whole world and purges the error of eternal blindness, just as the prophet Malachi said: '*Unto you that fear the name of the Lord shall the sun of righteousness arise*' (Malachi 4:2).]

Six of these signs will by now be recognizable as details popularized by Orosius and the *Catechesis Celtica*, with a heavy concentration of parallels in Vercelli V and VI and the Pembroke 25 sermon. Together with the Pembroke 25 sermon, the Icelandic sermon provides a rare instance of the earthquake presaging Doomsday; and only the *Catechesis Celtica*, Vercelli VI, and the Icelandic homily record the miracle of the sun rising and shining at midnight. Portent number 1 in the Icelandic sermon – the emperor Augustus's arrival in Rome in a chariot at the beginning of his reign – is parallelled only in the seventh-century Pseudo-Jerome *Expositio quatuor evangeliorum* and the eighth-century *Reference Bible*, but every other sign in the Icelandic has close parallels in one or both of the Vercelli homilies or the Pembroke 25 sermon or all three.

Table 1 attempts to summarize all this information and plot out the relationships among the various texts. In each case, if the signs are presented in a discernible order within the text, even if they are not explicitly enumerated, I have indicated their number in the sequence. If the signs are scattered throughout a work over multiple chapters or sections, as in Julius Obsequens and Orosius, or if they occur incidentally in a text outside of any discernible sequence, then I have simply given them a check mark. Immediately one can see that these sets of portents fall generally into two more or less distinct groups, one dominated at the top of the table by the *Catechesis Celtica* and its analogues, and the other dominated at the bottom by the *Old English Martyrology* and its analogues. Orosius appears to have furnished raw material for texts in both groups, although the *Catechesis Celtica* or a text very close to it must have acted as an intermediary for some of these details; and it is especially noteworthy that apart from Orosius, only the Verona homily, the Pembroke 25 sermon, and the Salisbury 9 sermon straddle both groups. J.E. Cross believed that the miracles in the *Old English Martyrology* and Patrick of Dublin represent a distinctively Insular tradition of nativity miracles, and if this is indeed true, then we have reason for thinking the Pembroke 25 sermon and the Salisbury 9 sermon were both composed in the British Isles or were written with the help of texts composed in the British Isles.

If Étaix was correct in observing that comparable lists of portents circulated in ninth-century south German homiliaries that have yet to be catalogued or published, then there can be no doubt that this table is incomplete and there are other texts not yet identified that would help fill in the picture. But the pattern that begins to emerge when we consider these witnesses together is that the essential outlines of the tradition were already beginning to come together by the late seventh century, when the Pseudo-Jerome *Expositio quatuor evangeliorum* was written, and that several competing sub-traditions were in circulation during the eighth and ninth centuries, when the next several texts listed at the top of the table were written. The table helps us see that the portents in the Verona homily conform closely (up to a point) with those in the *De divinis officiis* and with those in the Pseudo-Bede *Commentary on Luke*, that the Pseudo-Hrabanus text is almost a mirror image of the sermon in Clm 5257, that the portents in Vercelli V match up best with the *Catechesis Celtica*, and that all the portents in Vercelli VI are shared only by the *Catechesis Celtica* and the Old Icelandic Christmas sermon. The precise relationship between the Vercelli homilies, the *Catechesis Celtica*, the Pembroke 25 sermon, and

Some medieval accounts of the portents at Christ's birth

Portent	Julius Obsequens, Prodigiorum liber	Orosius, Historiae	Ps.-Jerome, Expositio quatuor evangeliorum	Liber questionum in evangeliis	Vienna Commentary on Luke	Irish Reference Bible	Verona homily I	Pseudo-Alcuin, De divinis officiis	Catechesis Celtica	Ps.-Hrabanus Maurus, De septem signis	Clm 5257 sermon	Old English Martyrology	Vercelli homily V	Vercelli homily VI	Pembroke 25 sermon	Salisbury 9 sermon	Patrick of Dublin, De mirabilibus Hibemiae	Old Icelandic Christmas sermon
Augustus comes to Rome in a chariot		1	1			3	1					1	1	1	1			1
Golden arc / ring(s) around the sun	√	2	7			4	1	1	6	7	5	1	3	2	1	1		2
Fountain / stream / wells flow with oil	√	3	6			5		2	7		6			2	2	2		3
River Tiber floods					3													
Augustus closes the gates of Janus	√					6		3				10	2					
Augustus / king forgives all debts	√		1			7	3	4				2	3	4	3	4		4
Sun rises / shines at midnight								5					2					7
Solar eclipse													4	5	4	5		
Abundance of bread; famine ends			2					6								6		
Earthquake			3			8		7						6	5	7		6

Sign									
Slaves restored to masters or killed	√	4, 5			7	4	3		8
Peace: no weapons	√		5	9	2	2	1	9	5
Peace: no wars	√	5	6	√	10	2	2		6
Men obliged to pay tribute to emperor		1, 2		√	3b	3		5	
One prince rules the world					1	1			
Prisoners freed					3a				
Star in the East			5		5	4			
Caesar declines title of 'lord'	√							5	
3 suns / 3 moons	√	√	7			1, 2			
Fiery / golden ball from heaven	√	√				3, 4			
Wheat grows on trees	√					5			
Blood flows from a loaf of bread	√					6			
Milk rains from heaven	√					7			
Egyptian lamb speaks like a man	√				8		7b		
Roman ox speaks to its plowman	√				9		7a	3	

the Old Icelandic sermon is still difficult to pin down, but one explanation that would fit this accumulation of evidence is that a ninth-century precursor to the Pembroke 25 sermon based on the *Catechesis Celtica* and transmitted via a version of the Saint-Père collection lies directly in the background of both Vercelli homilies V and VI and the Old Icelandic Christmas sermon. This hypothetical proto-text of the Pembroke 25 sermon would be especially convincing if it had two or three extra signs including the portent of universal peace characterized by an absence of weapons, since this is an integral feature of both Vercelli V and the Icelandic sermon. But even without this detail, an early and slightly fuller incarnation of the Pembroke 25 sermon would explain the presence of the earthquake in the Icelandic text and would also explain the various details which the two Vercelli homilies and the Icelandic sermon have in common. The role of the *Catechesis Celtica*, the *Reference Bible*, and other Irish and Irish-influenced texts in transmitting these portents deserves more careful attention than I am able to give it here since doing so properly would entail discussion of an even greater number of obscure texts and manuscripts around which doubt and controversy swirl, but I believe we are on safe ground in deducing that the Christmas portents tradition reflected in Vercelli V and VI was essentially formulated and popularized by Irish exegetes and their students working in the seventh, eighth, and ninth centuries based ultimately on a reading of Orosius.[54] I find myself, in other words, in the peculiar position of being able to offer up hope of vindicating Tveitane, whose argument for an Irish origin of the portents tradition was poorly articulated and almost completely without evidential support, but whose basic instinct seems to have been right. By the time these portents found their way into the Vercelli homilies and the Icelandic homily, they were no longer Irish property, but they retain unmistakable echoes of the exegetical methods, stylistic mannerisms, and rhetorical tropes (such

---

54 The popularity of the Christmas portents among Irish authors is further indicated by several Middle Irish texts in prose and verse on the wonders of Christ's birth, on which see Kuno Meyer, 'Die siebzehn Wunder bei Christi Geburt,' *Zeitschrift für celtische Philologie* 5 (1905), 24–5; Henrik Cornell, 'The Miracles of Christmas Eve,' in *The Iconography of the Nativity of Christ* (Uppsala: A.-B. Lundequist, 1924), 47–56; Vernam Hull, 'The Middle Irish Apocryphal Account of "The Seventeen Miracles at Christ's Birth,"' *Modern Philology* 43 (1945–6): 25–39; Martin McNamara, *The Apocrypha in the Irish Church* (Dublin: Dublin Institute for Advanced Studies, 1984), 49–51; and the recent editions and translations by Brian Ó Cuív and Caoimhin Breatnach, with discussion by Martin McNamara, in *Apocrypha Hiberniae I*, 542–617.

as the 'thought, word, and deed' triad) that are most fully realized in Irish and Hiberno-Latin literature of the early Middle Ages.[55]

I am convinced that the situation must be more complicated than I have made it out to be here. Occam's razor is rarely a valid tool in source study, and we must presume at least a small number of lost and unrecoverable pieces of the puzzle. But even if the full story remains incomplete, at least two points are thrust into relief by the consideration of these ten analogues from the Pseudo-Jerome *Expositio quatuor evangeliorum*, the *Liber questionum in evangeliis*, the Vienna *Commentary on Luke*, the Irish *Reference Bible*, the Verona homily, the Pseudo-Hrabanus *De septem signis*, the sermon in Clm 5257, the Pembroke 25 sermon, the Salisbury 9 sermon, and the Old Icelandic sermon. The first point is that the set of portents in Vercelli V is in broad agreement with a tradition current in Hiberno-Latin exegetical literature by the late seventh or early eighth century that was best represented by the tenth-century *Catechesis Celtica* and with an important later reflex in the Icelandic Homily Book, which like Vercelli V is probably dependent on a text transmitted via a version of the Carolingian Homiliary of Saint-Père de Chartres. The second is that Vercelli VI is also indebted to the same tradition at some level, but it has abandoned the Augustan framework and the pattern of symbolic interpretation that characterize the core of the tradition, and has freely selected and reshaped a number of the constituent elements, all of which might reasonably be taken as signs that the tradition was undergoing decay by the time it reached the author of Vercelli VI.

---

55 The literary history of the 'thought, word, deed' triad and its cultivation by Irish authors is most fully discussed by Patrick Sims-Williams, 'Thought, Word and Deed: An Irish Triad,' *Ériu* 29 (1978): 78–111. The best study of the rhetorical features of early Hiberno-Latin prose remains Wright, *The Irish Tradition in Old English Literature*.

The Source of Vercelli VII:
An Address to Women

SAMANTHA ZACHER

Without a doubt, Vercelli VII has been one of the least studied homilies in the Vercelli manuscript. Perhaps the main reason for this critical neglect has been an inability by earlier scholars to locate a source for the text, and so to provide Vercelli VII with a suitable literary context. But even assessing the style of the homily on its own terms, it can be seen that the composition stands out among those in the Vercelli Book for its seemingly acephalous beginning, its heavy reliance upon figurative conceits, and, most notably, its address to women. Such a claim to 'difference' may seem a tall order in the context of a collection so often classified as being sui generis,[1] most importantly for its intermixture of prose and poetry (some-times within the same composition),[2] and for its eclectic compilation of

---

1 Milton McC. Gatch made this claim, on the gounds that the homilies in the Vercelli Book do not present a full program for the liturgical calendar, in his *Preaching and Theology in Anglo-Saxon England: Ælfric and Wulfstan* (Toronto: UTP, 1977), 57. See too Mary Clayton, whose extensive re-examination of Carolingian homiliaries turned up no analogues for the arrangement of the Vercelli Book even among collections designated for preaching to the laity, in her 'Homiliaries and Preaching in Anglo-Saxon England,' *Peritia* 4 (1985): 227; repr. in Paul E. Szarmach, ed., *Old English Prose: Basic Readings* (New York: Garland, 2000), 151–98.

2 For examples of this phenomenon in the Vercelli Book, see especially Charles D. Wright, 'More Old English Poetry in Vercelli Homily XXI,' in *Early Medieval English Texts and Interpretations: Studies Presented to Donald G. Scragg*, ed. E. Treharne and S. Rosser, MRTS (Tempe, AZ: ACMRS, 2002), 245–62, and Samantha Zacher, 'Sin, Syntax, and Synonyms: Rhetorical Style and Structure in Vercelli Homily X,' *JEGP* 103 (2004): 53–76. For a general discussion of the sometimes tenuous differences between poetry and prose, see further see D.R. Letson, 'The Poetic Content of the Revival Homily,' in *The Old English Homily and Its Backgrounds*, ed. Paul E. Szarmach and Bernard Huppé (Albany: State Univ. of NY Press, 1978), 139–56, and also Samantha Zacher, 'The Style and Rhetoric of the Vercelli Homilies' (unpub. PhD diss., Univ. of Toronto, 2003), 25–9.

items assembled from disparate sources.[3] And yet, this paper seeks to shed new light on some of the more atypical features of Vercelli VII in two ways: first, by identifying the thus far elusive source, and second by considering whether comparison with the source-text can illuminate questions about the target audience of Vercelli VII itself, and perhaps even of the Vercelli Book as a whole.

In the most recent published edition of the Vercelli homilies, Donald Scragg echoes the views of all previous editors in noting that Vercelli VII 'has many of the hallmarks of a literal translation from Latin but no source has yet been found.'[4] Scragg's inference was undoubtedly correct, as closer analysis of the homily's use of what might be labelled 'anti-feminist rhetoric' places it squarely within a wider patristic context. However, the textual history of the homily is more far-reaching than has previously been anticipated. In fact, Vercelli VII proves to be a close rendering of exactly half of a Latin translation of John Chrysostom's Homily XXIX on the Epistle to the Hebrews (focusing on Hebrews 12:4–7), the Latin version of which was produced by one Mutianus Scholasticus (also known as Mutianus of Vivarium) at the instigation of Cassiodorus within a century and a half of Chrysostom's death in 407 (so placing Mutianus's version somewhere in the sixth century, most likely some time after 537).[5]

Before a comparative analysis of Vercelli VII and its Latin source can be performed, some groundwork must first be laid with respect to the composition and transmission history of Greek and Latin versions of Chrysostom's Homily XXIX on the Hebrews. John Chrysostom was a highly influential and extraordinarily prolific exegete, who wrote no fewer than thirty-four homilies on the Epistle to the Hebrews in 403 or 404,

---

3 For a general discussion of sources, see Donald Scragg's apparatus for individual homilies in his *VH*. Also see his 'The Compilation of the Vercelli Book,' *ASE* 2 (1973): 189–207; repr. in *Anglo-Saxon Manuscripts: Basic Readings*, ed. Mary P. Richards (New York: Garland, 1994), 317–43.

4 Scragg, *VH*, 133.

5 Chrysostom's Homily XXIX is printed by Migne in PG 63, cols. 203–8; Mutianus's Latin translation is printed in PG 63, cols. 419–26. See further Rev. Frederic Gardiner's introduction to his translation of Chrysostom's Epistle to the Hebrews in *NPNF*, 343. For a superior edition of the Greek texts, see *Sancti Patris Nostri Ioannis Chrysostomi Archiepiscopi Constantinopolitani Interpretatio Omnium Epistolarum Paulinarum per Homilias Facta*, ed. Frederick Field, 7 vols. (Oxford: J.H. Parker, 1845–62), vol. 7. The attribution to Mutianus is sanctioned by Hermann Josef Frede in his authoritative *Kirchenschriftsteller. Verzeichnis und Sigel*, 4th ed., Vetus Latina 1/1 (Freiburg: Herder, 1995), 646, and Frede's opinion is accepted in all supplements to his work, down to the most recent, by Roger Gryson, in *Kirchenschriftsteller. Verzeichnis und Sigel. Aktualisierungsheft 2004*, Vetus Latina 1/1D (Freiburg: Herder, 2004).

which were among the last items he composed at Constantinople.[6] Though these homilies are generally accepted as genuine,[7] the circumstances under which they were purportedly composed have led some scholars to question their authenticity. As is stated in a superscript contained in one of the earliest manuscripts for these homilies, the whole of the collection was apparently edited posthumously by Chrysostom's short-hand writer, his 'dearly-loved friend the Priest Constantine or Constantius,' who compiled the materials from stenographic notes taken down while Chrysostom was preaching.[8] However, the degree of Constantine's involvement in the process of writing these homilies is not so much of relevance to this study as is the fact that Constantine's transcription resulted in two distinct versions of Chrysostom's homilies on the Hebrews, namely, 'that originally taken down by the short-hand writer, and another when this had been polished and made neat at a subsequent time.'[9] It is this 'older,' and therefore presumably more authoritative version of Chrysostom's Homily XXIX that apparently served as the source for Mutianus's Latin translation.[10]

Measured against the scant historical evidence surrounding the composition of Chrysostom's homilies on the Hebrews, the conditions under which Mutianus translated the same homilies into Latin are relatively well documented in the writings of his contemporaries.[11] Cassiodorus himself reports in his *De institutione diuinarum litterarum* (book 1, chapter 8) that

---

6   The question of date and authorship with respect to the homilies attributed to Chrysostom is complicated by the fact that Chrysostom himself did not publish all of his own homilies. For a summary of the debates concerning both the year and place of composition, see P. Allen and W. Mayer, 'The Thirty-Four Homilies on the Hebrews: The Last Series Delivered by Chrysostom in Constantinople?' *Byzanţion* 65 (1995): 310.

7   The PG itself counts these as part of Chrysostom's canon, though this view has not been accepted by Maurice Geerard, et al., *Clavis Patrum Graecorum*, 6 vols. with suppl. (Turnhout: Brepols, 1974–2003), 2: 528 (no. 4440).

8   *NPNF*, 343. Also see Allen and Mayer, 'The Thirty-Four Homilies on the Hebrews,' who point out (313) that Chrysostom's homilies on the Hebrews present the only collection for which a 'superscript stating the identity of the editor is attached in the manuscripts.'

9   *NPNF*, 343.

10 See further Ingrid Wilhelmsson, *Studien zu Mutianus dem Chrysostomosübersetzer* (published PhD diss., Lund: Håkan Ohlssons Boktryckeri, 1944), esp. at 1–4.

11 For a recent bio-bibliographical treatment of Mutianus of Vivarium, see Rodrigue LaRue et al., *Clavis Scriptorum Graecorum et Latinorum*, 2nd ed., 26 vols. in 10 (Trois-Rivières, Quebec: Université du Québec, Service de la bibliothèque, 1996), vol. 8, M–421. See further Jean-Paul Bouhout, 'Les traductions latines de Jean Chrysostome du Ve au XVIe siècle,' in *Traduction et traducteurs au Moyen Âge: Actes du colloque international du CNRS organisé à Paris, Institut de recherche et d'histoire des textes, les*

Mutianus was personally commissioned by him to provide a translation of Chrysostom's collection on Hebrews for the use of his monks at Vivarium, a project intended to remedy the absence of a suitable Latin commentary on the epistle.[12] Though the name Mutianus is not well known to modern Anglo-Saxon scholars, there is good evidence to suggest that Mutianus's Latin translation of Chrysostom's Hebrews circulated widely in the medieval period: several book catalogues from the ninth century onwards mention this translation,[13] with the earliest known copy surviving in a significantly corrupted seventh-century palimpsest.[14] In addition, as James O'Donnell has asserted, 'there are little traces up and down the middle ages of the survival of various Vivarian influences, as in the case of Cluny, where we know Mutianus' version of Chrysostom on Hebrews was included in the annual round of reading in the refectory.'[15] Significantly,

---

26–28 mai 1986, ed. Geneviève Contamine, Documents, études et répertoires (Paris: Éditions du CNRS, 1989), 31–50, esp. at 34.

12 Cassiodorus reports this commission in his *De institutione diuinarum litterarum*, book 1, chapter 8: 'Ad Hebraeos uero epistulam quam sanctus Iohannes Constantinopolitanus episcopus triginta quattuor omeliis Attico sermone tractauit, Mutianum uirum disertissimum transferre fecimus in Latinum, ne epistularum ordo continuus indecoro termino subito rumperetur' (*Cassiodori Senatoris Institutiones*, ed. R.A.B. Mynors, 2nd ed. [Oxford: Clarendon Press, 1961], 29; cf. PL 70, col. 1120]). For further discussion of Mutianus's commission by Cassiodorus, see James J. O'Donnell, 'Old Age and Afterlives,' in *Cassiodorus* (Berkeley: Univ. of California Press, 1979), 250, and Walter Berschin, *Greek Letters and the Latin Middle Ages: From Jerome to Nicholas of Cusa*, rev. and ed. Jerold C. Frakes (Washington: Catholic University of America Press, 1988), 77–8 and 302n19.

13 See Eduard Riggenbach, *Die ältesten lateinischen Kommentare zum Hebräerbrief: Ein Beitrag zur Geschichte der Exegese und zur Literaturgeschichte des Mittelalters*, Historische Studien zum Hebräerbrief 1 (Leipzig: A. Deichert, 1907), 6–11, and specifically for lists of manuscripts containing Mutianus's Latin translation, see 11n1. Eleven manuscripts containing the Latin translation are likewise treated (skeletally) by Albert Siegmund, *Die Überlieferung der griechischen christlichen Literatur in der lateinischen Kirche bis zum zwölften Jahrhundert*, Abhandlungen der Bayerischen Benediktiner-Akademie 5 (Munich: Filser, 1949), 98. The Latin translation is also briefly treated in Geerard, *Clavis Patrum Graecorum*, 2: 528 (no. 4440). For further discussion of the transmission history of Mutianus's work, see Pierre Courcelle, *Les lettres grecques en Occident: De Macrobe à Cassiodore*, 2nd ed. (Paris: E. de Boccard, 1948), 376–7, and more recently (with some updating) his *Late Latin Writers and Their Greek Sources*, trans. Harry E. Wedeck (Cambridge, MA: Harvard Univ. Press, 1969), 396–400.

14 See E.A. Lowe, 'An Uncial (Palimpsest) Manuscript of Mutianus in the Collection of A. Chester Beatty,' in *Palaeographical Papers, 1907–1965* (Oxford: Clarendon Press, 1972), 233.

15 O'Donnell, 'Old Age and Afterlives,' 250; cf. Joan Evans, *Monastic Life at Cluny, 910–1157* (Hamden, CT: Archon Books, 1968), 98.

Mutianus's translation was the only medieval Latin text of Chrysostom's Hebrews to circulate in this way. Though a second Latin translation was made by Mutianus's contemporary, the African bishop Facundus, the latter translation survives in only a smattering of quotations contained within the author's *Ad Iustinianum*, and the work can be ruled out as the source for the Old English text.[16]

By contrast with Mutianus, the influence of Chrysostom in Anglo-Saxon England is extraordinarily well documented from the earliest period:[17] Bischoff and Lapidge note with regard to the late seventh-century material deriving from Theodore's teaching that Chrysostom is 'quoted more frequently by name – seven times – than any other authority in the Canterbury biblical commentaries.'[18] Both Alcuin and Bede name Chrysostom as a source,[19] and Alcuin quotes from a Latin version of Chrysostom's Homilies on Hebrews in his *Aduersus Felicem*, and again in his *Contra haeresim Felicis*; significantly, both of these references derive explicitly from the translation by Mutianus.[20] However, Alcuin's debt to Mutianus is still richer than has been acknowledged. It is clear that Alcuin quotes heavily from Mutianus's Latin translation in his own commentary on Hebrews (which goes up to chapter 10 of the Epistle), and in so doing

---

16 A single paragraph of a rather literal Latin translation of Chrysostom's Homily on Hebrews was composed by Facundus (CCSL 90a, 347), but it will be clear from the analysis below that precisely what connects Mutianus's Latin rendering and the Old English version in Vercelli VII are the shared divergences from the original Greek; it stretches the imagination to suppose that were Facundus's version to have survived in its entirety it would contain precisely the same differences from Chrysostom's Greek. I thank Paul Remley for pointing out to me the limited survival of Facundus's version.

17 For a general survey, see J.D.A. Ogilvy, *Books Known to the English, 597–1066* (Cambridge, MA: Medieval Academy of America, 1967), 110–11.

18 B. Bischoff and M. Lapidge, *Biblical Commentaries from the Canterbury School of Theodore and Hadrian*, CSASE 10 (Cambridge: CUP, 1994), 214.

19 Cf. Peter Godman, ed., *Alcuin: The Bishops, Kings, and Saints of York* (Oxford: Clarendon Press, 1982), 122, l. 1546 and 123–4n1546; D. Hurst, ed., *In Lucae euangelium expositio*, CCSL 120, 28, l. 346.

20 Scholars have acknowldged references to Mutianus's translation in at least two works by Alcuin, though the debt appears to be far greater than has been previously recognized. See especially Alcuin's *Aduersus Felicem* (see PL 101, col. 170) and *Contra heresim Felicis* (see *Liber Alcuini Contra Haeresim Felicis: Edition with an Introduction*, ed. Gary B. Blumenshine, Studi e testi 285 [Vatican City: Biblioteca Apostolica Vaticana, 1980], 83; cf. PL 101, col. 108). For critical discussion of Alcuin's citations of Mutianus and their reception, see Wilhelmsson, *Studien zu Mutianus*, 3, and Ogilvy, *Books Known to the English*, 110.

appears to have set a trend for biblical commentators following him.[21] The most immediate influence can be seen in the work of his student Hrabanus Maurus, who completes Alcuin's work by providing commentary for the remaining chapters of the epistle, likewise citing and borrowing from Mutianus's translation throughout.[22] Despite the frequency of these citations, it is doubtful that even careful scrutiny of these Latin commentaries would have brought to light the source of Vercelli VII, since only scattered portions of Mutianus's translation of Chrysostom's Homily XXIX are quoted verbatim in them, and it is clear that the author of the Old English text had independent and direct access to a substantially complete version of Mutianus's translation. The evidence for widespread knowledge of Mutianus's work in Anglo-Saxon England thus provides an important addendum to the findings of Helmut Gneuss, whose *Handlist of Anglo-Saxon Manuscripts* records no known surviving copies of manuscripts containing Mutianus's translation before the eleventh-century. Since, as Helmut Gneuss and Michael Lapidge have both shown, Latin versions of several other of Chrysostom's works survive in manuscripts dating from the eighth century to the eleventh, we can now surmise the knowledge of Mutianus's work as well.[23] The fact that Vercelli VII represents in its entirety

---

21 For a list of additional commentators and authors who drew on the translations of Mutianus (including most notably Smaragdus of Saint-Mihiel and Haymo of Auxerre), see Riggenbach, *Kommentare zum Hebräerbrief*, esp. 24–51, and Wilhemsson, *Studien zu Mutianus*, 3.

22 In a recent conference paper ('The Commentary on Hebrews Attributed to Alcuin,' delivered 5 August 2006) Michael Fox addressed the role of Hrabanus's commentary in completing the work of his teacher Alcuin, and demonstrated his heavy reliance upon Mutianus's translation. Fox's important work provides additional proof of the knowledge of Mutianus's work in the early medieval period, though not necessarily in Anglo-Saxon England.

23 See Gneuss, *Handlist*, nos. 457, 581, and 819, and also now Michael Lapidge, *The Anglo-Saxon Library* (Oxford: OUP, 2006), esp. at 32, 145, 177, 218, 230, 316, and 317. In addition to the manuscripts cited by Gneuss, other Latin texts of Chrysostom include a copy of *De muliere Chananaea* (*CPG* 4529), which appears in Worcester, Cathedral Library, F. 92 (Gneuss, *Handlist* 763), fols. 206r–13r (now discussed by Lapidge); also, a Latin translation of his *Homilia 3, De laudibus s. Pauli* (*CPG* 4344) appears in Salisbury, Cathedral Library, 179 (Gneuss, *Handlist* 753), fols. 81r–82r. I am grateful to Tom Hall for pointing out these additional references. For the further discussion of other Latin translations of Chrysostom's homilies (not including that on Hebrews), see, for example, W. Wenk, *Zur Sammlung der 38 Homilien des Chrysostomus Latinus*, Wiener Studien, Beiheft 10 (Vienna, 1988); and A. Wilmart, 'La collection des 38 homélies latines de Saints Jean Chrysostome,' *Journal of Theological Studies* 19 (1917–18): 305–27; I thank Rosalind Love for these further references.

a close rendition of Mutianus's Latin version of Chrysostom's Homily XXIX on Hebrews provides the best evidence for Chrysostom's indirect influence on the Old English homiletic tradition.

The closeness of Vercelli VII to its source in Mutianus's Latin translation of Chrysostom's homily can best be seen through direct textual comparison. The appendix provided below presents for the first time a parallel edition and translation of Vercelli VII (based largely on Scragg's edition) and Mutianus's Latin translation of Chrysostom's text (based on the edition in the Patrologia Graeca).[24] In offering these parallel texts, two imponderables must be acknowledged from the outset. Though as the line-by-line analysis indicates, the Old English homily provides an almost complete and generally faithful rendering of the Latin source material cited, the possibility must nevertheless be reserved that the precise version of Mutianus's text consulted by the Old English translator may eventually come to light. Such a finding, however, would only sharpen the parallelisms recorded in the appendix and discussion below. Second, it is almost certain from the textual evidence provided in what follows that Vercelli VII is not an original translation, but rather is a copy of a copy. However, since Vercelli VII presents the only surviving vernacular witness to this text, except in those few cases where scribal errors can manifestly be shown to derive from transmission, all changes, additions, and omissions made with respect to the Old English adaptation of Mutianus's text are treated as the work of the Vercelli VII author.

In the remaining portions of this essay, the general dependence of Vercelli VII upon Mutianus's text will be tested by investigating three main areas of concentration: corruptions in the Old English text that may be elucidated or corrected by comparison with Mutianus's text; textual omissions, additions, and changes that especially highlight the Old English homilist's method of adaptation; and, finally, a consideration of the 'antifeminist' portions of the text, as a means of raising some probing questions about both the target audience of the homily, and ostensibly that of the Vercelli Book at large.

By far the clearest evidence that the original Old English translator consulted directly a version of Mutianus's text is the fact that numerous

---

24 The appendix is divided into sections primarily according the sentence structure of the Old English text. Though it will be evident from the layout of the Old English text in the appendix that Scragg's emendations have on the whole been maintained (in square brackets), on occasion I make changes to the Old English (enclosed in angle brackets) where the syntax seems particularly strained.

transmission errors in the Old English text can be explained and (where necessary) corrected with recourse to the Latin source. The following emendations are not intended to 'erase' differences between the two texts, but rather to introduce judicious modifications where the sense in the Old English is otherwise badly strained. A few illustrative examples will serve. For example, in section 12, the Old English author enumerates the following list of prophets who were said to be 'made famous' (following the Latin *claruisse*, which means both 'made bright' and 'made famous') by trial. Scragg's text is as follows (italics are supplied for emphasis):

> Geþenceað eac Iosep 7 Moyses [7] *Ieremiah* 7 Dauid 7 Eliam 7 Samuel 7 ealle ða halegan witegan, witodlice ealle hie wæron þurh geswinc gebyrhte.
> [Consider also Joseph and Moses and Jeremiah and David, and Elijah, and Samuel, and all the holy prophets, certainly they were all made famous through trial.]

This Old English inventory of biblical men may now be compared with the parallel Latin text presented by Mutianus:

> Num Ioseph uultis ut dicam? <Num> ipsum Mosen, num *Iesum Naue*, num Dauid, num Heliam, num Samuelem, num prophetas? Nonne uniuersos istos ex tribulationibus reperies claruisse?
> [Surely you don't want me to speak of Joseph? Or Moses himself? Or Joshua, or David, or Elijah, or Samuel, or the prophets? Won't you find that every single one of them was made famous by trials?]

Although the original manuscript reading for the list in Vercelli VII apparently included the name *Iesunaue* (as reported by Förster in his 1932 edition, who had access to the line before it was defaced by reagent), this reading was rejected by Scragg in favour of the more familiar *Ieremiah*. However, comparison with the Latin shows that the seemingly odd manuscript rendering *Iesunaue* is to be favoured, as it merely presents a bastardized form of the Latin *Iesum naue* (*Iesus naue* in the nominative case), a widely accepted alternative name for Joshua in patristic writings. Given that Joshua was historically Moses's successor, the manuscript reading makes better sense chronologically within this list of biblical leaders, and Scragg's emendation is to be rejected.

In other cases it is possible to use Mutianus's text in order to supply words that may have dropped out through eyeskip in the Old English translation. One such example can be found in section 7, which tells of the sufferings of Abraham (here again Scragg's text follows):

Geþencað nu hwylca þa wyrda wæron ær ðam flode, 7 hwylce Abrahames forlætu wæron, 7 hu he his wifes ðolode, 7 he hire bereafod wæs, 7 hu mis-licra frecennessa he oft aræfnode ægðer ge on gefeohtum ge on hungrum. [Think now what events came before the flood, and what Abraham's losses were, and how he suffered of his wife, and he was bereft of her, and how he often suffered various dangers both in battles and in (times of) hunger.]

The more detailed Latin explanation reads as follows:

Num uultis, ut dicam quae circa diluuium contigerunt? An uultis ut Abrahae demigrationes frequentes enarrem, aut direptionem eius uxoris, aut diuersa pericula, bella numerosa, fames tantas et tales?
[Surely you don't want me to speak of what happened around the time of the Flood? Or do you want me to describe Abraham's frequent wanderings, or the snatching away of his wife or the various dangers, the numerous wars, so many hungers of such a type?]

In comparing the two renderings, it seems distinctly odd that the Old English homilist would have chosen to denigrate Sarah by writing that Abraham 'suffered of his wife' ('his wifes ðolode'). Indeed, comparison with the Latin text proves to be instructive, as the parallel Latin attributes the source of Abraham's sorrow to the 'direptionem eius uxoris' ('snatching away of his wife'), a detail incorporated ultimately from Genesis 12.13–16 and 20.2–7, which narrates Sarah's double kidnapping by Pharaoh after Abraham pretends to be her brother. A possible remedy for the Old English text is to supply the word *reaflac* as an appropriate object of the verb, to complete the elusive phrase '7 hu he his wifes <reaflac> ðolode' ('and how he suffered <the snatching away> of his wife'). One can imagine that such a term may have fallen out of the text as a result of eye-skip, given the repetition in such close proximity of the visually similar roots –*ræf*- or -*reaf*- in *ræfnede* (in section 6), *bereafod* and *aræfnode* (in section 7), and again *ræfnode* (in section 8).

A more problematic example can be found in section 43, where the homilist discusses a series of injuries attributed to bodily overindulgence. Scragg's text is as follows:

Gif ðu þa ilcan olectunge þam lichoman [dest, þæs lichoman] hiw fægere bið þonne hit ær wæs.
[If you (do) the same indulgences to the body, the form (of the body) will be fairer than it was previously]

Si autem ab eis recedens, aliter temetipsum tractas, tunc et pulchritudo tibi corporis generatur.
[If, however, withdrawing from them, you treat yourself differently, then the beauty of your body is produced for you.]

Judging from the syntax of the Old English passage alone, Scragg's emendations are both economic and viable. However, comparison with the Latin demonstrates a different cause and effect than the one conveyed by Scragg, as we are told that the act of 'withdrawing from,' rather than 'engaging in,' delights is what makes the body beautiful. Since the general attitude towards overindulgence is negative in both the Latin and Old English, it may be sensible to alter Scragg's *dest* to *framadest*, meaning 'put away,' a form which is found in section 55, where we find the similar statement that 'eal þæt man ofer riht þygeð mid unyðnesse, hit him mon sceal framadon' ('Everything that is taken wrongfully without ease, it must be put away [from the body]').

Indeed, there are other cases in which negative clauses in the Latin are transmitted as faulty positive statements in the Old English. For example, in section 13, the Old English posits a rhetorical question concerning the consequences of idleness (using Scragg's text):

Hwæt, wene ge þæt ge mægen þurh idelnesse becuman to ðære biorhtnesse þe Godes þa gecorenan mid geswince geearnodon? Butan twion ge magon gif ge willað.
[Lo, do you expect that you may through idleness come to the brightness which God's chosen earned with trial? Without a doubt you can, if you want to.]

By contrast with this improbable statement, we find in the Latin the following scenario:

Dic enim mihi, tu ex otio et deliciis uis clarus existere? Sed hoc penitus non ualebis.
[Tell me, do you wish to be famous from laziness and pleasure? But you will absolutely not be able to do this.]

While the Latin answers prudently that it is impossible to achieve fame through laziness, the Old English offers a resounding 'butan twion ge magon gif ge willað' ('without a doubt you may if you wish'). Given the homily's altogether pessimistic view of indulgences, it seems necessary to supply a qualifying *ne*, as this element could easily have dropped out in transmission (see section 13).

Comparison with the Latin also permits occasional emendation of the Old English where words have been omitted. For example, in section 29 we find an explication of Matthew 11:8, which appears as a verse quotation in the preceding Section 28 (in the Latin and Old English). The Old English passage shows considerable corruption (quoted here from Scragg's text):

> On heofenum þæt ðonne is þa þe for Godes [lufan] swylce habban nellað (ll. 52–3).
> [In heaven, those then are the ones who for the (love) of God wish not to have such]

Scragg sensibly inserts the noun *lufan* in order to make sense of the genitive *Godes*. But the emended passage still leaves unresolved the object *swylce* ('such') at the end of the line. Comparison with the Latin text provides further clarification, as it states that:

> Qui uero non habent talia uestimenta, in caelis sunt.
> [Those who do not have such clothing are in heaven.]

The Old English is improved by the insertion of the noun <hrægl> so that the text reads 'swylce <hrægl> habban nellað' ('wish not to have such <clothing>'). Here again, we can assume that the object *hrægl* dropped out through eye-skip, since the same word appears in both the preceding and following sentences (see sections 27 and 29). The emended passage both clarifies and reinforces the important connection between soft clothes and sin.

Interestingly, there is at least one clear example in the Old English where the text does not match up with the PG version of Mutianus's translation as printed by Migne. This asymmetry provides a potential entry point for further research into the various versions of the source text that may have been available to the Old English author. In the portion of the Latin homily discussing women, in section 31, the following exploration of female weakness is offered:

> Quod enim sub umbraculis degunt quod oleo unguntur, quod frequentibus lauaeris utuntur, quod assidue unguentis abundantibus et aromatibus perfunduntur, et iacent in straminibus delicatis, hoc est quod eas tales efficit.

[Because they spend time under sunshades, because they smear themselves with oil, because they take frequent baths, because they cover themselves carefully with copious unguents and perfumes and lie on delicate beds, that is what makes them like that.]

The parallel section in Vercelli VII reads as follows:

Of hira liðan life hie bioð swa tyddre, for þan þe hie symle inne bioð 7 noht hefies ne wyrceaþ 7 hie oft baðiað 7 mid wyrtgemangum smyriað 7 symle on hnescum beddum hy r[e]stað.

[They are so weak on account of their soft lifestyle, because they are always inside, and they do not perform heavy work, and they bathe frequently, and smear themselves with unguents, and they always lie on soft beds.]

It seems noteworthy that the Old English author substitutes the phrase '7 noht hefies ne wyrceaþ' ('they do not perform heavy work') for the Latin *oleo unguntur* ('they smear themselves with oil'), since a similar expression of indolence can be found in the Greek of Chrysostom (as ἡ ἀργίᾳ). Either the phrase was not in the Latin version(s) consulted by Migne, or else it simply dropped out in his preparation of the text. The latter seems a possibility, since a parallel reference to 'heavy work' occurs elsewhere in Vercelli VII (in section 34) in the context of 'þe cyrliscu wiorc 7 hefegu on symbel wyrceaþ' ('who always perform churlish and heavy work'), in this case translating Mutianus's Latin 'quae in agris agunt uitam' ('who live their lives in the fields'). That section 31 of Vercelli VII is still following Mutianus, however, is clear, since the vernacular author mimics Mutianus's subsequent reference to the action of women lying (*iacent*) on soft beds (*straminibus delicatis*), in Old English 'symle on hnescum beddum hy r[e] stað,' a detail which is changed from the reference to the bed alone in Chrysostom.[25] Such a comparison of the surrounding details in the passage points to the likelihood that the exact version consulted by the Vercelli author was not at a distant remove from that edited in the PG.

Though the study of such minutiae is valuable for establishing the profound connection between the Old English and Latin texts, it is useful to discuss

---

25 For an analogous discussion of the abuse of luxury items, especially the misuse of aromas and luxuriating in beds (*reste*), see Vercelli X.220–30, and my discussion of this passage in 'Sin, Syntax, and Synonyms,' 70–2.

some of the more sizeable changes, omissions, and additions found in the Old English homilist's adaptation of Mutianus's text. The following presents a summary of the portions common to both translations (listed by section according to the appendix, and adapted from Scragg's edition):[26]

1–2   Opening address concerning the importance of learning and toil;
3–16   Catalogue of men in the Bible who attained distinction through toil;
17–26   Catalogue of men and nations in the Bible who led an indulgent and idle life;
27–9   Discussion of Mt. 11:8 in reference to the luxury of soft clothes;
30–45   Address to women, and a conceit comparing soft and indolent women to overly pampered trees;
46–9   Conceit likening the temperate body to a fair and cleaned house;
50–5   Conceit comparing the glutton to a dung-heap [and allusion to Rm. 13:14];
56–70   Discussion of the effects of gluttony and the attraction of temperance;
71–2   Conceit comparing the emergence of gluttony from sinful desires to the production of worms in a stagnant pool;
73   Final exhortation to avoid gluttony and embrace temperance.

As can be seen from the above synopsis, the homily presents a series of antitheses that continually reinforce the virtues of toil and affliction, and the vices of indolence and indulgence. But despite the homily's methodical symmetry, it is by no means flatly two-dimensional in its technique: in both the Latin and Old English we can detect a style that modulates skilfully and interestingly between forms of exegesis, exhortation, and lengthy and topically interconnected conceits. Though the Old English author generally follows the rhythms of the Latin text, one governing stylistic change can be found in the conversion of Chrysostom's signature question-and-answer format (maintained in the Latin) into a series of imperatives that encourage the audience to 'understand'; (*ongitað*; section 7), 'think' (*geþencað*; sections 7, 12, 19, and 21), 'remember' (*gemunað*; sections 8, 9, 18, 20 [preceded by *and*], 24, and 25), and 'hear' (*gehyrað*; section 27), as well as strings of intensifying adjectives that occur in the initial position,

---

26 Some 121 of the 207 lines of Mutianus's version printed in PG overlap with the vernacular version rendered in Vercelli VII.

such as 'certainly' *witodlice* (sections 2 [second sentence], 5, 22, 29, 67 [second sentence], and 70), and *soðlice* ('truly'; section 2). The frequency and regularity with which these reminders and intensifiers occur throughout the homily creates an insistent rhetorical effect that is highlighted in the Vercelli manuscript through regular punctuation and capitalization that marks off just those clauses.[27]

The truncation of the Latin source in Vercelli VII poses interesting questions about the completeness of the homily as it was bound into the Vercelli Book. The vernacular text begins abruptly with the phrase *Butan tweon* ('without a doubt'), an opening phrase which is unparalleled in Old English homilies, highlighted especially in the context of the Vercelli Book, where eight of the twenty-three homilies begin with the traditional 'men þa leofestan.'[28] Scragg's discussion of the relation of Vercelli VII to other neighbouring materials in the Vercelli manuscript also seems to indicate that Vercelli VII is acephalous: Scragg persuasively postulates that Vercelli VII is copied from an earlier exemplar, since the preceding homily in the manuscript is marked by the Roman numeral II 'at the right-hand end of the last line of text of Vercelli VI'; this homily in the manuscript marks the first of four homilies numbered with consecutive Roman numerals, thus apparently linking Vercelli VII–X. It is therefore generally assumed on the basis of this evidence that the Old English scribe was copying from a single, now lost, exemplar for these homilies, and that Vercelli VII itself presents an imperfect copy. However, while it has always been assumed that the missing Roman numeral I in the Vercelli manuscript represents a wholly different homily in the exemplar, comparison with the Greek and Latin versions of the homily may offer an enticing (albeit entirely speculative) proposition: the companion piece for this grouping in the exemplar may yet turn out to be a lost Old English translation of the first half of Mutianus's homily. An analogy for this type of arrangement may perhaps be drawn from within the Vercelli Book itself, where Vercelli XII, set for the second day in Rogationtide, refers back to the previous sermon in Vercelli XI by means of the opening phrase: 'girsandæg we wæron manode'

---

27 I was able to see the punctuation much more clearly in my direct consultation of the manuscript, and I am grateful to the Vassar College Turner Fund for providing me with the grant money to conduct this research. Many of the grammatical details are still visible in the facsimile prepared by Celia Sisam, ed. *The Vercelli Book*, EEMF 19 (Copenhagen: Rosenkilde and Bagger, 1976), fols. 56r–59r.

28 Also see Vercelli II, IV, XV, XVI, XIX, XX, and XXI. Vercelli III contains the variant *broðor þa leofestan*.

('yesterday we were reminded').[29]

Though it cannot finally be known whether the Old English translator intentionally pruned the homily down to nearly half its original length or whether he consulted an incomplete copy, it is nevertheless possible to gauge other seemingly deliberate authorial decisions made with regard to the treatment of the source text. As can be seen from the appendix, a pattern seems to emerge in the homilist's adaptation of materials from the Latin: while at the beginning of the homily whole passages are rendered line by line (and often word for word), as the homilist continues his translation, he increasingly condenses his argument so that some of the more long-winded conceits, exhortations, and explanations are expunged for the sake of economy. This pattern can be seen in the following examples, chosen for their differing degrees of verbal and rhetorical parallelism with the Latin text. Comparison of the opening address in Vercelli VII with the corresponding Latin passage reveals a strong lexical equivalence with the Latin source. These lines are particularly informative since they set up the main theme of Vercelli VII. The parallel passages (in sections 1–2) read as follows:

> Butan tweon, lar is haligdomes dæl, 7 ealles swiðost gif hio hyre gymeleste framadrifeð 7 ælce gitsunge afyrreð 7 þyssa woruldlicra þinga lufan gewanige 7 þæt mod to Godes lufan gehwyrfeð, 7 gedet þæt hit ealle ða lustfulnesse þysses andweardan lifes onscunað. Soðlice sio lar mid geswince hio sceal þa forenemnedan þing forðbringan. Witodlice ealle Cristes þa gecorenan þurh geswinc 7 þurh lare hie wurdon geweorðode þe we nu nemnan magon.
>
> [Without a doubt, teaching is a portion of holiness, and even more so if it drives away its negligence, and removes each type of avarice, and diminishes the love of things of this world, and turns the mind to the love of god, and makes it so that it shuns all the desire of this present life. Truly, teaching together with trial shall bring forth those aforementioned things. Certainly all the chosen of Christ became honoured through trial and through teaching, whom we may now name.]

The Old English author establishes a parallel hierarchy of sins that are vanquished by learning or discipline, roughly in the same order as that presented in the Latin:

---

29 See too the fragmentary opening of Vercelli XXIII on the Life of Saint Guthlac (which contains an elusive reference to a '[fore]sprecnan iglande,' 'aforementioned island'). The statement is often held to refer to a homily containing an earlier portion of the life of St Guthlac.

Disciplina ergo participatio sanctitatis est, et maxime, si ita negligentiam pellit, cupiditates excludit, saecularium rerum amores amolitur, animam conuertit, facit eam omnia huius uitae culpare: hoc quippe est quod tribulatio: cum haec fiunt, nonne sanctum perficitur? Nonne spiritualem ad se gratiam pertrahit? Consideremus iustos, unde cuncti claruerint: nonne per tribulationes? Enumeremus, si placet …

[Therefore discipline is the participation of holiness, and especially if in that way it drives away negligence, shuts off desires, removes the love of worldly things, changes the soul, makes it blame all things of this life. This indeed is what is a trial: when these things happen, is not a holy thing made perfect? Does it not bring spiritual grace to itself? Let us consider the just, how they all became famous: was it not through trials? Let us count them, if that suits …]

Despite the clear parallelism between the versions, it is evident even in this short passage that the translation is not merely mechanical. A substantial lexical change made by the Vercelli homilist is the expansion of the Latin phrase *animam conuertit* to include *to Godes lufan* as the goal for conversion. This addition seems stylistic, and may be paralleled by another reference to the love of God in section 28 (which has been omitted in the MS, but which Scragg correctly postulates is required to complete the sense of the passage); in both examples, the Old English homilist's aim seems to be to reinforce the religious or divine connotation of otherwise secular 'virtues' like 'love' or 'brightness.' Other syntactical changes include the substitution of an intensifying adverb *witodlice* for the subjunctive verb *consideremus* and the parallel loss of subjunctive *enumeremus* as the phrase is absorbed into a relative clause in the Old English. Though these minor grammatical changes do not radically alter the meaning of the text, as we shall see over the course of the homily as a whole, such accretive changes characterize the idiosyncratic style of the Old English homilist.

The ensuing body of the homily also follows closely the text by Mutianus in terms of its content and rhetoric. By far the most interesting points of correspondence can be seen in the homilist's handling of figurative conceits, which uniquely occupy the main rhetorical focus of Vercelli VII. A particularly full description in the Old English is evidenced in the conceit detailing the comparison of the body to a house (in sections 46–9), where there is notable verbal and rhetorical symmetry with the Latin:

Hwæt, ge witon ðæt ælc hus bið þe fægere þe hit man hwitað. Swa eac bið ælc lichoma ðe fægerra þe hine þære sawle scima gebyrhtet. Sona se lichoma sceal bion unfæger, þonne he mid unrotnesse 7 mid sare aseted bið, ða cumað of

ðam liðan olehtunge. For ðan ic lære þæt we flion þa liðnesse 7 flion [þa ole-
htunge] þysse worulde, ac hie synt swiðe swete.
[Lo, you know that each house is that much the fairer when one whitens it.
So also is the body that much fairer when the radiance of the soul brightens
it. Immediately the body shall be ugly when it is beset with unhappiness and
with sorrow, which come from soft indulgence. Therefore I teach that we
should flee those softnesses, and flee (those indulgences) of this world, though
they are very sweet.]

As in the Old English, the conceit in the Latin is offered as a means of
elucidating how toil (in this case upkeep of body and soul) results in
brightness of the soul:

Scitis autem quia sicut domum pulchram cum quis eraserit, efficit pul-
chriorem: sic etiam faciem pulchram splendor animae superueniens amplius
conuenustat; si uero in moestitia sit et doloribus constituta, deformis effici-
tur. Moestitia namque et moerores aegritudines faciunt et dolores; aegritu-
dine autem delicatudines corporis generantur, quae deliciis constant. Proinde
et ob hoc fugite delicias, si quid mihi obeditis et creditis. Sed uoluptatem,
inquis, habent deliciae. Sed non tantam uoluptatem, quantas difficultates atque molestias.
[However, you know that just as when someone scrapes down a beautiful
house, he makes it more beautiful: so too the brilliance of the soul coming
from above adorns more handsomely a beautiful face; if in truth (the soul) is
established in sadness and feelings of grief, it is made deformed. In fact, sadness and sorrows generate sicknesses and feelings of grief; however in sickness the delicate features of the body are generated, which are established in
delights. So for that reason flee from delights, if you listen to me and believe
me at all. But you say that delights give pleasure. But not so much pleasure as
difficulties and annoyances.]

The simile in both translations begins superficially by comparing the with-
ering body to an aging and decaying façade, and then builds a complex
layering effect, which hinges syntactically upon the three-fold repetition
of the element –fæger- ('fair') in the Old English and (though in a slightly
different order), of pulchr- ('beautiful') in the Latin. While the Old English
homilist does not translate the string of five Latin items beginning with
delic- ('luxury'), there is nevertheless a provocative parallelism formed by
the repetition of the elements lið- ('soft') and olehtung- ('indulgence') in
the parallel sections of the Old English. Other omissions seem designed to

cut down on the wordiness of the description: while the vernacular text translates the first doublet containing the pair *moestitia … doloribus* as *unrotnesse … sare*, the second reference to the same is economically omitted. And yet, there is one significant discrepancy between the two passages: while the Latin discusses the corruption of the soul, the Old English manifestly concentrates on the body. The difference, however, is potentially explainable through a close consideration of the Latin syntax. In Mutianus's text, it can be assumed that because *constituta* is feminine, it must refer to *anima*; the Old English translator, however, seems wrongly to assume that it refers to *corpus*, which is neuter. Despite this change in focus, the message of the simile is not radically disturbed, since both renderings agree that a remedy can be found for the sick soul or body only in their removal from all softness in the world that does not provide a true home. And while the Vercelli simile is so obviously indebted to its Latin source, the comparison nevertheless powerfully conveys sentiments that are recognizably Anglo-Saxon: the comparison of the body to a home beset by calamity is a virtual commonplace in Old English literature, as can be seen from various analogues contained in (for example) *The Phoenix* (ll. 199–207), *The Meters of Boethius* (VII.29–39), and Vercelli X.206–8. It is perhaps the enduring currency of such comparisons that explain its attractiveness here to the author of Vercelli VII.

A similar parallelism can be found in the scatological conceit contained in Vercelli (sections 51–6), which compares the glutton (who is 'soft' in body and mind) to dung:

Þonne ne don we swa, ac hlysten we þæs apostoles lare, Paulus; he cwæð: '*Ne do ge þæs flæsces giman on his willan.*' Wyrse is, þæt mon ðæs ofer riht bruce þonne hine mon on feltungrepe wiorpe. On þære grepe he wiorðeð to meoxe. Butan tweon, þæs lichoman sceaða on þære wambe he wiorðeð to þam ilcan, and eac ðam licho[ma]n to mettry[m]nesse. Eal þæt man ofer riht þygeð mid unyðnesse, hit him mon sceal framadon. Ac þysses nu feawa gymaþ. Forneah ealra manna mod sint on oferflowende willan onwended.

[Then let us not do so, but let us listen to the teaching of the apostle, Paul. He said: *make not provision for the flesh in its desires*. It is worse to enjoy it wrongfully than to cast it into a dung-pit. In the pit it will turn to dung. Without a doubt, that enemy of the body will turn to the same (dung) in the belly, and indeed to the weakening of the body. Everything that is taken wrongfully without ease, it must be put away (from the body). But few now think about this. The minds of nearly all men are turned towards overflowing desire.]

The homilist has visibly truncated the fulsome Latin prose, making it tighter and more succinct:

> Non itaque deliciemur deliciis corporis, sed audiamus Paulum dicentem: Carnis curam ne perficiatis in concupiscentiis. Tale namque est in uentrem cibos mittere, quale si quisquam eos in cloacam proiiciat; magis autem non tale est, sed multo peius. Hic enim fimum tantum operatur sine tua laesione; illic autem plurimos morbos, plurimasque procreat aegritudines. Nutrimentum enim nisi ex sufficientia non fit, quae ualeat sine labore digeri: cum uero plus exuberat, quam reficiendi corporis ratio postulat, non solum nutrimentum nullum, sed etiam corruptio generatur. Sed nullus attendit haec: preoccupatae sunt omnium mentes superflua uoluptate.
>
> [Let us not therefore be delighted by the delights of the body, but let us hear Paul saying: *make not provision for the flesh in its desires.* For to send food into the stomach, that is as if someone were to throw it into the privy. Rather it is not like that, but much worse; for in the latter case indeed such dung is produced without harming you, while in the former case it may cause very many weaknesses, and very many diseases. Indeed, nourishment does not happen unless from sufficiency, which is able to be digested without labour. When in truth [nourishment] is more abundant than the reason of feeding the body requires, not only is no nourishment generated, but indeed corruption. But no one heeds these things: the minds of all are preoccupied with superfluous desire.]

While the Latin translation uses both paronomasia (*deliciemur ... deliciis*) and alliteration (*carnis ... curam ... concupiscentiis*) to generate a sense of excess at the beginning of this passage, the Old English translator embellishes the same notion through a strategic use of tautology: in addition to the repetition created by the compound *feltungrip*, whose two constituent elements mean 'dung-hill' and 'privy,'[30] the homilist repeats these elements in *grepe* and *meox*, mimicking verbally the kind of foul 'overflowing' (*oferflow-*) described in the passage. Though the biblical reference localizes the simile to Rm. 13:14, the sentiments expressed in the passage are again found elsewhere in Anglo-Saxon texts: indeed, similar comparisons of the sinner to a dung-hill can be found in Ælfric's *CH* I.vii.240–6, where Ælfric compares beasts who rot in dung to 'fleshly men' (*flæsclice menn*) who 'end their days in the stench of their lust' ('on stence heora galnysse

---

30 See further the entries in the *Dictionary of Old English A–F*, CD-ROM (Toronto: PIMS, 2003), svv. *fel-tun* and *feltun-grep*.

geendiað heora dagas'), and in *CH* II.xxvii.187–91, where Ælfric compares the unrepentant sinner to a swine (*swyn*) that 'returns to the dung-heap after washing' ('cyrð to meoxe æfter his ðweale').[31]

If there are abundant points of contact between Vercelli VII and Mutianus's translation, discussion of the omissions found in the vernacular text helps further to characterize the idiosyncratic style of the Old English adaptor. Sizeable omissions include those found in sections 10, 36, 38, 44, 60, and 68. On the whole, these exclusions seem to avoid perceived repetitions or else to pare down difficult Latinate constructions. Such certainly seems to be the case for the excluded conceit (in section 38), which likens the soft body to the broken string of an instrument. Though from an aesthetic point of view the omission of this elegant conceit seems regrettable, the figure in the Latin nevertheless jarringly interrupts the address to women, severing it from the discussion of women's sins that follows (beginning in section 39). A similar omission is found in section 50, where the Vercelli VII homilist drops a lengthy discussion of the repercussions of gluttony that is padded out with gastronomic symptoms like 'distentionem et opressionem mentis ... somnum morti consimilem' ('swelling and oppression of mind ... and a sleep very like death') as well as *stomachi cruditatem* ('indigestion of the stomach'), 'praeclusionem spiritus interioris' ('obstruction of the inner spirit [or breath]'), and 'molestiam ructationis indigestae' ('the annoyance of undigested belching'). The case could easily be made here that the homilist omits the passage because it regurgitates the message already expressed in the above-cited scatological conceit.

By contrast with the frequent omissions, there are relatively few noteworthy additions to Mutianus that are found in Vercelli VII, and the majority of these seem to present hortatory expansions. One particularly interesting embellishment in the Old English version occurs in section 19, where Mutianus mentions 'Diues ille qui peruritur in camino ignis' ('that rich man who is burnt in the furnace of fire'), but the author of Vercelli VII

---

31 Also compare with the passage in chapter 28.197.23 of Alfred's translation of Gregory the Great's *Pastoral Care*, which likens Saul's hastening to the toilet as he is pursued by David (literally *to feltune*, 'to the dung-heap'), to 'evil lords' (*yflan hlafurdas*) who cannot dismiss evil thoughts in their hearts without 'bursting out in foul works' (*utaberstað on fullicum weorcum*); in Henry Sweet, ed., *King Alfred's West-Saxon Version of Gregory's Pastoral Care* (Oxford: EETS o.s. 45, 50, 1967–8), 196–7. See too the description of the unrighteous who lie forsaken just as a pile of dung in chapter XXXVI of the Old English version of Boethius's *Consolation of Philosophy* (ed. Walter John Sedgefield, *King Alfred's Old English Version of Boethius*), 104.4.

instead exhorts his audience to 'geþenceað þonne Ladzarus [7] þone wel-
egan þe her dæghwamlice symlede 7 is ðær nu singallice cwelmed' ('consider Lazarus [and] the wealthy man who here daily feasted and who is
there now continuously afflicted'). This apparently explanatory gloss
greatly enhances the homiletic effect of the Old English, as it forces the
link between sin on earth and eternal punishment as a consequence.
Overall, however, these additions seem geared to keep the vernacular
translation close to the source-text.

The extent to which figurative conceits (a signature feature of Chrysostom's
homilies) play an atypically important role in the structuring of the Old
English homily has already been demonstrated. An equally curious and
central feature is the homily's lengthy address to women, which in the Old
English translation appears mid-way through the homily. The homilist
first introduces the subject of women through several oblique references
contained in the two catalogues of biblical men (derived from both
Mutianus and his Greek source): the first reference appears in the aforementioned discussion of Abraham's grief at the loss of his wife (in section 7),
an affliction which is cited precisely in order to underscore his virtue. The
second, as a point of antithesis, contains a more lengthy description of
anonymous men in the Bible who committed sins of lust with respect to
beautiful women (section 24). The latter discussion feeds into an exegetical
explanation of Matthew 11:8, which focuses on the abuse of luxurious
dress and soft clothing (sections 27–9), a weakness associated particularly
with women in the homily.

    However, the dedicated treatment of women begins properly in sec-
tion 30, where the Old English homilist asks:

> For hwon wene ge þæt wif swa sioce syn of hyra gecynde? Ac hit is swa: of
> hira liðan life hie bioð swa tyddre, for þan þe hie symle inne bioð 7 noht
> hefies ne wyrceaþ 7 hie oft baðiað 7 mid wyrtgemangum smyriað 7 symle on
> hnescum beddum hy r[e]stað.
> [Why do you expect that women are so sick from their condition? But it is so:
> they are so weak on account of their soft lifestyle, because they are always
> inside, and they do not perform heavy work, and they bathe frequently, and
> smear themselves with unguents, and they always lie on soft beds.]

The use of the Old English term *gecynde* in this passage has in the past
seemed especially perplexing for editors and translators, since the surrounding context does not sufficiently elucidate the meaning of the term.

Scragg offers the helpful gloss 'childbirth [or perhaps menstruation].'[32] However, comparison with Mutianus's Latin offers an alternative:

Nam unde putatis, aut ex quali ratione mulieres sic esse debiles et infirmas? Num ex conditione sexus tantum? Nequaquam, sed etiam ex conuersatione et educatione. Quod enim sub umbraculis degunt quod oleo unguntur, quod frequentibus lauaeris utuntur, quod assidue unguentis abundantibus et aromatibus perfunduntur, et iacent in straminibus delicatis, hoc est quod eas tales efficit.

[From what cause or from what kind of reason do you think that women are so weak and feeble? Surely not from the condition of their sex alone? Not at all, but also from their lifestyle and upbringing. Because they spend time under sunshades, because they smear themselves with oil, because they take frequent baths, because they cover themselves carefully with copious unguents and perfumes and lie on delicate beds, that is what makes them like that.]

The word *gecynde* substitutes for Mutianus's phrase 'ex conditione sexus,' which in turn translates Chrysostom's φύσις, meaning 'sex.' The discussion of 'sex' in this manner has led Chrysostom's contemporary critics to read into this passage a misogynistic or anti-feminist subtext that is sometimes seen to be characteristic of Chrysostom's homilies.[33] Indeed, Chrysostom's association of women's sex (φύσις) with weakness serves elsewhere to establish the idea that women are the 'weaker vessel' (in Greek τo ἀσθενές σκεῦος), both with respect to their physicality and

---

32 *VH*, 42. Scragg's inference seems a good one, since verbal parallels can be made between the simile comparing women to withered plants and various medical explanations for menstruation. Isidore, *Etymologiae* XI.i.140–1 cites a particularly illuminating etymology for *menstrua* ('menstruation') that may convey a thematic connection: 'cuius cruoris contactu fruges non germinant, acescunt musta, moriuntur herbae, amittunt arbores fetus, ferrum rubigo corripit, nigrescunt aera' ('having touched whose blood, fruits will not grow, vintages turn sour, herbs die, trees lose their seeds, rust damages iron, bronze vessels grow blackened').

33 For arguments exploring Chrysostom's alleged misogyny and use of anti-feminist rhetoric, see especially Elizabeth A. Clark, *Jerome, Chrysostom, and Friends* (New York: Edwin Mellen, 1979 [1982]), 31n125 and 158–247, as well as her *Women in the Early Church* (Wilmington, DE: Michael Glazier, 1983); David C. Ford, *Women and Men in the Early Church: The Full Views of St John Chrysostom* (South Canaan, PA: St Tikhon's Seminary Press, 1996), 38–246; and Efthalia Makris Walsh, 'Overcoming Gender: Virgins, Widows, and Barren Women in the Writings of St. John Chrysostom, 386–97' (unpub. PhD diss., the Catholic Univ. of America, 1994). I thank Andy Orchard for assistance with Chrysostom's Greek.

their moral fortitude.[34] But while Chrysostom and Mutianus clearly blame women's 'education' and 'upbringing' as the culprit of their weakness, discounting their liability by nature, the Old English text as it appears in the manuscript argues just the opposite, stressing that the fault derives especially from their native temperament. Either the Old English homilist has again misconstrued a negative phrase in the Latin (as above in section 13), or else the change is more sinister and poignant in its criticism of women. Since Vercelli VII elsewhere chastises the luxuriant lifestyles of women, it seems prudent to emend the negative phrase in the Old English (as in section 30) to 'Ac hit <nis> swa' ('but it is [not] so').

The passage in isolation reveals little about the attitude of the Old English translator; however, the examination of several further passages in the Old English better illuminates this issue. The continuing sections 32–3 of the homily present another complex and carefully strung conceit, this time likening women to pampered trees:

> Eac ðu meaht þe bet ongytan þæt ic þe soð secge gif ðu genimst on hwylcum orcearde 7 on windigre stowe hwylc treow 7 hyt asettest on hleowfæste stowe 7 on wæterige stowe. ðonne meaht ðu gesion þæt hit sona forleoseð þa fægernesse þe hit hæfde on his agenre stowe.
>
> [Also, you might better understand that I am telling you the truth if you take a certain tree in a certain orchard and in a windy place, and set it in a sheltered place and in a wet place, then you might see that it immediately loses the fairness which it had in its own place.]

The terms of the comparison bear fruitful comparison with the Latin:

> Et ut melius hoc agnoscas, attende quod dico: ex horto aliquo in eremo constituto, qui uentis et tempestatibus uerberatur, sume arbustum aliquod, et pone in opaco et aquoso loco, et uidebis quod multum a fortitudine et dignitate sua mutabitur, quam habebat in hoc loco unde constat esse translatum.
>
> [And so that you may understand this better, pay heed to what I say: take a shrub from a garden established in the desert, buffeted by winds and tempests, and put it in a dark and wet place, and you will see that it will be much

---

34. For this argument made in the context of Chrysostom's homily, see further Ford, *Women and Men in the Early Church*, 96–7. For parallel uses of this phrase, see Ford's citation (96n30) of Chrysostom's Homily XXVI on 1 Corinthians (PG 61, col. 222D), his Letters to Olympias XII.1 (in Sources chrétiennes 13, 2nd ed., 324), and also Homily IX on Phillipians (PG 62, col. 252C).

changed with regard to the strength and worth that it had in the place from where it was taken.]

In both the Old English and Latin conceits, a correlation is set up between the cause of overindulgence and the effects of indolence on the body; just as women smear their bodies with perfumes and oils making themselves weak, so trees grow flaccid in their over-tended environment. But while Mutianus (following Chrysostom) highlights the potential loss of 'fortitudine et dignitate' ('strength and worth'), the author of Vercelli VII emphasizes instead the loss of *fægernesse* ('beauty'). Though the substitution in the Old English arguably serves a larger rhetorical purpose in that it echoes the opening sequence of the homily (in section 24), where men are said to have been 'captivated' by women's beauty and thus condemned to hell, the harsher criticism of women's behaviour in the Old English (even if derived from another version of the source-text) nevertheless is difficult to ignore.[35]

While Chrysostom's homilies (fairly or unfairly) have been stigmatized for their virulent anti-feminist rhetoric, it is perhaps surprising to find such sentiments amplified in the Old English (since, as we shall see below, such statements are not common in these homilies). Although what follows in the homily does not eradicate these strains of anti-feminism, nevertheless by the end of this segment (in sections 34–42) it is possible to detect a general softening of this rhetoric in both the Old English and Latin, so that in the former, the following qualification is found:

Þenc eac be ðam wifum þe cyrliscu wiorc 7 hefegu on symbel wyrceaþ. Þonne cnawest ðu þæt hie bioð halran 7 cafran þonne þa weras þe on idelnesse lifiað. Nu sio idelnes swa swiðe þam lichoman dereð, ne tweoge þe na þæt hio þære sawle ne sceððe, for þan þe sio sawl sceal nyde habban smittan þæs lichoman unþeawa 7 hio swiðe mænige 7 mislice sceaþe him onfehð. For ðon ic halsie

---

35   The issue is of course more complex than I have space here to discuss. Comparison with an excerpt from Chrysostom's sermon on 'How to Choose a Wife' further reveals this complexity: 'Along with virtue in their souls, the maidens of ancient times used to have great vigour in their bodies. Their mothers did not raise them as mothers do now, corrupting them with frequent baths, perfumed ointments, cosmetics, soft garments, and many other such influences, making them weaker than they should be' (as cited by Ford, *Women and Men in the Early Church*, 97n31). As in the passage for this homily on Hebrews quoted above, Chrysostom highlights an important paradox: while women are naturally made more susceptible to enticement by luxuries, they need not be weak if they are educated properly.

þæt we urne lichoman 7 sawle mid geswincum gestrangien, nalæs mid idel-
nessum tohælen. Ne sprece ic þas word to eow [we]rum anum ac to wifum.
Eawla, wif, to hwan wenest ðu þines lichoman hæle [geican] mid smyringe 7
oftþweale 7 oðrum liðnessum? Of ðam cymeð unhælo, nals mægen.
[Think also about the women who always perform churlish and heavy work.
Then you may know that they are healthier and stronger than those men who
live in idleness. Now idleness so greatly harms the body, do not doubt that
[idleness] does not harm the soul, because the soul must out of necessity have
the pollution of the body's sins and [the soul] receives very many and various
injuries from [the body] Therefore I ask that we strengthen our bodies and
souls with toil, and let us not make them weak with idlenesses. I do not speak
these words to you men alone, but to women. Alas, woman, why did you
expect to increase the health of your body with the smearing of (unguents),
and frequent bathing, and other softnesses? From those things comes sickness, not at all strength.]

The message in the Old English that women can be made even more resili-
ent than men if they toil and do not fall into the trap of luxury by and large
echoes that found in the Latin:

Quia uerum et certum est hoc, attende mulieres, quae in agris agunt uitam:
fortiores namque uiris sunt, qui sunt in ciuitatibus constituti; et si eas permit-
tas cum illis athletico more certare, multos huiusmodi uiros illae sine dubio
superabunt. Corpore namque molli reddito et delicato, necesse est et animam
participare ex corporis morbo. In multis namque compatiuntur et afficiuntur
operationes animae passionibus et affectionibus corporis ... Propterea obsecro, ut nostrum corpus forte reddamus, nec illud delicatum et aegrotabile faciamus. Non ad uiros tantum, sed etiam ad mulieres mihi est sermo. Quid
illud saepius lauas, quid deliciis corrumpis, et gracile facis, o mulier? Quid
fortitudinem eius debilitas? Deliciae quippe lassitudinem faciunt, non
fortitudinem.
[Because this is true and certain: pay attention to the women who live their
lives in the fields; for they are stronger than men who are brought up in cities;
and if you were to allow them to contend with them in an athletic contest,
they would doubtless surpass many men of that kind. For with the body having been rendered soft and delicate, it is necessary that the soul participates in
the disease of the body. For in many folk the workings of the soul suffer
alongside and are affected by the passions and feelings of the body ...
Therefore, I implore you that we render our body strong, and not make it
delicate and prone to sickness. My sermon is not only for men, but also for

women. Why do you wash [your body] too often, why corrupt [it] with delicacies, and make [it] frail, O woman? Why do you spoil its strength? Indeed, luxuries cause tiredness, not strength.]

Though the compliment to women in both texts is obviously back-handed (since once again it presumes an inherently gendered weakness), the treatment of women is here overall more empowering.[36] But while both texts issue a somewhat more equalizing message to women, the conditions under which such a reversal might be made differ significantly in the two texts: while the Old English stipulates that the women who toil in the countryside can be stronger than 'þa weras þe on idelnesse lifiað' ('men who live in idleness'), the Latin specifies that they can be stronger than men 'qui sunt in ciuitatibus constituti' ('who have been brought up in cities'). Though the vernacular translation at first seems to present a significant departure from the Latin, comparison with the remaining portion of the Latin quotation demonstrates that the Old English author in fact summarizes his source, since the original likewise closes by contemplating the inferior condition of the weakened male body when it is rendered soft (molli reddito). Given the homily's running commentary on the softness of women's bodies, this inverse portrayal of the softened male body appears

---

36 As Ford has argued, this issue is complicated elsewhere in Chrysostom's writings by the fact that in his view the greater potential for weakness in women is precisely what allows them to 'overcome greater obstacles in reaching the same level as even the most virtuous men' (Ford, Women and Men in the Early Church, 97). A parallel passage in Chrysostom's Homily XIII on Ephesians helps better to explain this logic: 'Maidens not yet twenty years old, who have spent their whole time in inner chambers, in a delicate and soft way of life... themselves soft in their nature [πᾳλᾳι κᾳι αυτᾳι την φυσιν], and rendered yet more tender by their overindulgence ... yea, these very ones, in a moment, seized with Christ's flame, have put off all that indolence and even their very nature, have forgotten their delicateness of youth, and like so many noble wrestlers, have stripped themselves of that soft clothing, and rushed into the midst of the contest ... So far does their zeal surpass their very nature [ουτω κᾳι φυσεως ανωτερον η προθυμιᾳ]' (As quoted from Ford, 97). Though once again the women are shown to exhibit a tendency towards weakness on account of their 'sex' [φὺσις], they are able to display a transcendent spiritual vigour. See further Ford, 98, who cites the following analogue from Chrysostom's Homily VII on St Matthew (PG 57.88D [NPNF 1, X, 54]): 'For the war against the devils and his powers is common to them [women] and the men, and in no respect does the delicacy of their nature [το της φυσεως πᾳλον] become an impediment in such contests, for not by bodily constitution [σωμᾳτων φυσει], but by mental choice [ψυχης προᾳιρεσει] are these struggles decided. Wherefore in many cases women have actually been more forward in the contest than men and have set up more brilliant trophies.'

particularly effeminizing. Here, in the context of the homily's persistent meditation on labour and indolence, the Old English passage seems (at least in this one instance) to be more praiseworthy.

But however we interpret the precise anti-feminist underpinnings of this address, the address to a specifically female audience only poses further questions concerning the use and transmission of this homily both within and beyond the Vercelli Book. Beginning with Chrysostom's source-text, there does not seem any reason to doubt that this author intended his homily to be used as an actual address to women. It is clear from both internal evidence gathered from Chrysostom's own writings, and also from evidence assembled by his ancient and modern biographers that Chrysostom's homilies were used in preaching to women on such themes as marriage, re-marriage, divorce, virginity, participation in the church, female preachers, barrenness, sex, and dress (to name just a few), and the evidence is compiled extensively on the basis of both internal evidence found in Chrysostom's own writings and also that assembled by his ancient and modern biographers.[37] By contrast, we know (from the evidence rehearsed above) that Mutianus's immediate target audience was the monks at Vivarium, who may perhaps have benefited from the homily's general appeal against idleness and its injunctions against all manner of 'soft' living.

The question remains, then, as to whether the author of Vercelli VII intended his homily for use in a preaching context analogous to that of either its ultimate or immediate source. Unfortunately, such evidence is not readily available from a consideration of its manuscript context. Though it might be tempting to reject the address to women in Vercelli VII as a coincidence of translation, parallels elsewhere in the Anglo-Saxon corpus caution against such an easy dismissal. In Old English homilies, for example, numerous non-gender-specific commentaries can be found on

---

37 For a discussion of audience in relation to Chrysostom's homilies on the Hebrews in particular, see Pauline Allen, 'The Homilist and the Congregation: A Case Study of Chrysostom's Homilies on the Hebrews,' *Augustinianum* 36.2 (1996): 397–442. For a discussion of female audiences in relation to Chrysostom's homilies, see especially Philip Rousseau, '"Learned Women" and the Development of a Christian Culture in Late Antiquity,' *Symbolae Osloenses* 70 (1995): 116–47; Ford, *Women and Men in the Early Church*, 200–37; and Agnes Cunningham, 'Women and Preaching in the Patristic Age,' in *Preaching in the Patristic Age: Studies in Honor of Walter J. Burghardt, S.J.*, ed. David Hunter (New York: 1989), 53–72, with comments about Chrysostom's addresses to women at 59, 60, 62–3, and 67.

the subject of the evils of luxury and sumptuous dress.[38] Saints' lives and homilies likewise sermonize indirectly about such topics as women's obedience, faithfulness, deceit, transvestism, modesty, infanticide, and vanity.[39] An even closer parallel may be found in Aldhelm's prose *De uirginitate*, which continually (if not obsessively) entertains the subject of women's abuse of pampering, overindulgence, and luxuries as a means of issuing practical advice to the *well-born nuns at Barking Abbey*.[40] As in Vercelli VII, this Latin text notably contains a comparable (though unrelated) conceit comparing women to trees,[41] as well as a parallel discussion of Matt. 11:8 as a means of elucidating the dangers presented to women who wear luxurious clothes.[42] In addition, several addresses to women can

---

38 See Robert DiNapoli, *An Index of Theme and Image to the Homilies of the Anglo-Saxon Church* (Hockwold cum Wilton: Anglo-Saxon Books, 1995), commentaries on 'clothing,' 27, and also on 'wealth,' 93.

39 This list is compiled from DiNapoli, *Index of Theme and Image*, 94–5.

40 See Michael Lapidge and Michael Herren, eds., *Aldhelm, the Prose Works* (Cambridge: D.S. Brewer, 1979), 51–8; the translations below are derived from this edition.

41 Aldhelm presents an almost inverse simile of that found in Vercelli VII, here likening virgins to budding flowers (*De uirginitate* XVIII): 'O praeclara uirginitatis gratia, quae uelut rosa senticosis exorta surculis purpureo flore rubescit, et nunquam defectu dirae mortalitatis marcescit, et licet moribundae carnis fessa fragilitas fatiscat, et propinquante fati termino cernua curuaque uetustate senescat, haec sola in modum iucundae pubertatis usquequaque uirescit et iugiter adolescit!' ('Oh radiant grace of virginity, which like a rose grown from thorny saplings blushes with a crimson flower, and never withers with the defect of dire mortality, and even though the tired fragility of the moribund flesh droops and, with the end of death approaching, grows old with bent and bowed senility, [virginity] alone in the manner of blissful youth continually flourishes and constantly matures!').

42 Aldhelm, *De uirginitate* LV: 'Vnde Gregorius peruigil pastor, et paedagogus noster, noster inquam, qui nostris parentibus errorem tetrae gentilitatis abstulit et regenerantis gratiae normam tradidit, cum euangelicum explanaret dictum: Ecce qui mollibus uestiuntur in domibus regum sunt, adiunxit: Nemo ergo existimet in studio uestium peccatum deesse, quia si hoc culpa non esset, nequaquam Petrus apostolus per epistolam suam feminas a pretiosarum uestium appetitu compesceret, dicens: Non in ueste pretiosa. Quod si hoc culpa non esset, nullo modo Ioannem Dominus de uestimenti asperitate laudasset. Pensate quae culpa sit hoc etiam uiros appetere a quo curauit pastor Ecclesiae et feminas prohibere' ('Whence Gregory, the watchful shepherd and our teacher – "our" I say, because (it was he) who took away from our forebears the error of abominable paganism and granted them rule of regenerative grace – when he was explaining the evangelical dictum "Behold, they that are clothed in soft garments are in the houses of the kings" [Matt. 11:8], added: "Let no one think, therefore, that sin is absent from the concern for fine clothing, since, if this were not a fault, Peter the apostle in his letter would not have constrained women from the longing for precious garments, saying 'not in precious garments' since, if this were not a fault, the Lord

be found in other Old English homilies, for example, in Ælfric's *Purification of the Virgin*, and in his paraphrase of Judith.[43] The presence of similar topoi in other Anglo-Saxon texts certainly highlights the provocative currency of the issues raised by Vercelli VII within an Anglo-Saxon context. If it is difficult to speculate about the target audience for individual homilies, it is perhaps even more challenging to do so with respect to the use and transmission of the Vercelli collection as a whole. While the current consensus holds that the Vercelli Book must have served as a reading book for private devotion, the extremely fraught question remains as to its intended readership. Kenneth Sisam's earlier claims for a primarily monastic audience have more recently been challenged by scholars such as Charles D. Wright and Éamonn Ó Carragáin, both of whom have put forward compelling cases for a secular clerical readership.[44] Given the evidence of Vercelli VII, it

---

would not have praised John for the roughness of his dress. Consider what a fault it would be for men to want what the shepherd of the Church took care to avert even women from!" [Hom. in euang. I.v.3].'

43 For a direct address to laywomen (*ge wif*), see especially Ælfric's homily on the Purification of the Virgin (*CH* I.9), which urges women to follow the example of the chaste widow Anna (Peter Clemoes, ed., *Ælfric's Catholic Homilies: The First Series Text*, EETS s.s. 17 [Oxford: OUP, 1997], 255, l. 188). Also see Ælfric's paraphrase of the biblical book of Judith, in Bruno Assmann, ed., *Angelsächsische Homilien und Heiligenleben*, BaP 3 (1889; repr. with a supplementary intro. by Peter Clemoes, Darmstadt: Wissenschaftliche Buchgesellschaft, 1964), 102–16; Mary Clayton has argued this work is aimed at a single virgin living within a community of *nunnan* (who were not cloistered but living under a rule in accordance with a vow of chastity) in 'Ælfric's *Judith*: Manipulative or Manipulated?' *ASE* 23 (1994): 215–27. Likewise, although it does not strictly present an address to women, the preface to Ælfric's *Admonitio ad filium spiritualem*, explains that he has translated this work of moral instruction for both monks and nuns ('to munecum and eac to mynecenum') who are living according to the Benedictine Rule. For treatment of this preface, see further Jonathan Wilcox, ed., *Ælfric's Prefaces*, Durham Medieval Texts 9 (Durham: Durham Medieval Texts, 1994), 52, 122. I thank Tom Hall for bringing these references to my attention; see now his 'Preaching at Winchester in the Early Twelfth Century' *JEGP* 104.2 (2005): 189–218. Also see his essay on 'Wulfstan's Latin Sermons,' in *Wulfstan, Archbishop of York: The Proceedings of the Second Alcuin Conference*, ed. Matthew Townend, Studies in the Early Middle Ages 10 (Turnhout: Brepols, 2004), 93–139, which discusses the potentially Wulfstanian *Sermo ad uiduas*, in Copenhagen, Kongelige Bibliotek, G.K.S. 1595 (HG 814), fols. 49v–50v.

44 See Kenneth Sisam, 'Marginalia in the Vercelli Book,' in his *Studies in the History of Old English Literature* (Oxford: Clarendon Press 1953; repr. 1962), 118. Charles D. Wright, 'Vercelli Homilies XI–XIII and the Anglo-Saxon Benedictine Reform: Tailored Sources and Implied Audiences,' in *Preacher, Sermon, and Audience in the Middle Ages*, ed. Carolyn Meussig (Leiden: Brill, 2002), 203–27; and Éamonn Ó Carragáin, 'Rome, Ruthwell, Vercelli: *The Dream of the Rood* and the Italian Connection,' in *Vercelli tra*

seems likely that such studies are moving in the correct direction by proposing an audience that does not obviate the presence of women. Moreover, the address in Vercelli VII calls much needed attention to what we might think of as the silent gaps in reader response where women and preaching texts are concerned. The Vercelli manuscript already offers two extraordinary heroic paradigms for strong women in the poem *Elene* and in the homily devoted to the purification of Mary in Vercelli XVII; we can now add Vercelli VII to this group, as the homily manifestly concerns itself with the behaviour and spirituality of women. But even if we cannot finally ascertain what the target audience of the homily might look like (if there was ever imagined to be one), we are now certainly in the position to make this claim about its textual history: in its long journey from early-fifth-century Constantinople to tenth-century Anglo-Saxon England, and in its transmission from Greek to Latin to Old English (as well as its passage from some unidentified exemplar to the Vercelli Book), Vercelli VII may indeed be said to have lost some of its original strength and dignity. But as an excellent example of the power of Old English prose, we might well suggest that in its many transplantings Vercelli VII has yet acquired a new beauty of its own.

oriente ed occidente tra tarda antichità e medioevo, ed. Vittoria Docetti Corazza, Bibliotecha Germanica: studi e testi, 6 (Alessandria: Edizioni dell'Orso, 1998), 59–100. I am eager to thank those who have read and commented on this paper in the four years since I first wrote it. I give special thanks to my co-editor, Andy Orchard, whose comments are always supremely helpful. I also wish to give hearty thanks to Paul Remley, as well as to Tom Hall and Donald Scragg for their extremely learned and generous references and suggestions.

Appendix:
Vercelli VII and Mutianus Scholasticus's Translation
of John Chrysostom, Homily XXIX on the Epistle to the Hebrews

The following table shows the correspondences between Vercelli VII and Mutianus's Latin translation. Line numbers for Vercelli VII refer to *VH* ([ ] represent Scragg's emendations, and <> represent my own).[45]

	Vercelli VII	Vercelli translation	Mutianus	Mutianus translation
1	Butan tweon, lar is haligdomes dæl, 7 ealles swiðost gif hio hyre gymeleste framadrifeð 7 ælce gitsunge afyrreð 7 þyssa woruldlicra þinga lufan gewanige 7 þæt mod to Godes lufan gehwyrfeð, 7 gedet þæt hit ealle ða lustfulnesse þysses andweardan lifes onscunað (ll. 1–4).	Without a doubt, teaching is a portion of holiness, and even more so if it drives away its negligence, and removes each type of avarice, and diminishes the love of things of this world, and turns the mind to the love of god, and makes it so that it shuns all the desire of this present life.	Disciplina ergo participatio sanctitatis est, et maxime, si ita negligentiam pellit, cupiditates excludit, saecularium rerum amores amolitur, animam conuertit, facit eam omnia huius uitae culpare:	Therefore discipline is the participation of holiness, and especially if in that way it drives away negligence, shuts off desires, removes the love of worldly things, changes the soul, makes it blame all things of this life.
2	Soðlice sio lar mid geswince hio sceal þa forenemnedan þing forðbringan (ll. 5–6). Witodlice ealle Cristes þa gecorenan þurh geswinc 7 þurh lare hie wurdon geweorðode þe we nu nemnan magon (ll. 5–7).	Truly, teaching together with trial shall bring forth those aforementioned things. Certainly all the chosen of Christ became honoured through trial and through teaching, whom we may now name.	hoc quippe est quod tribulatio: cum haec fiunt, nonne sanctum perficitur? Nonne spiritualem ad se gratiam pertrahit? Consideremus iustos, unde cuncti claruerint: nonne per tribulationes? Enumeremus, si placet:	This indeed is what is a trial: when these things happen, is not a holy thing made perfect? Does it not bring spiritual grace to itself? Let us consider the just, how they all became famous: was it not through trials? Let us count them, if that suits:

---

45 The Old English text of Vercelli VII is based upon *VH*, 133–8. The Latin text of Mutianus derives from PG 63, cols. 419–26.

	Old English	Translation	Latin	Translation
3	Þara wæs Abel on fyrmþe middangeardes 7 oðer Noe (ll. 7–8).	Of those, Abel was at the beginning of the earth, and the second Noah.	ab ipso initio Abel, ipsum Noe:	Abel from the very beginning, then Noah,
4	Ne mæg se rihtwisa man bion butan geswince gemang þam unrihtwisan (ll. 8–9).	Nor may the righteous man be without trial among the unrighteous.	non enim potest, cum solus sit in multitudine malignorum iustus, tribulationibus non affligi.	for a just man cannot be unafflicted by trials when he is alone in a crowd of wicked men.
5	Witodlice Noe ana wæs rihtwis betweox eall manna cyn, 7 he for his rihtwisnesse Gode licode (ll. 9–10).	Truly Noah alone was righteous among all of mankind, and he for his righteousness pleased God.	Noe quippe, inquit, solus perfectus erat in generatione sua, et Deo placuit. [Gn. 6:9]	It says that Noah alone was righteous among all of mankind, and he for his righteousness pleased God
6	Ongitað nu hwæt ic eow secge: gif ge nu bioð geswencte, þe swa manigra haligra manna mægenu to bysene habbað, hwæt wenst ðu <þæt>[46] he ana ræfnede betweoh arleasum butan ælcere bysene? (ll. 11–13).	Understand now what I say to you: if you are now afflicted, who have as an example the virtues of so many holy men, what do you expect <that> he suffered alone among the impious without any example?	Intellige namque mihi quod dico. Si nunc tam plurimos habentes, quorum debemus aemulari uirtutem, sic affligimur: quid putas patiebatur ille solus in tanto numero pessimorum?	Understand what I am saying. If now, considering so very many men, whose virtue we ought to emulate, we are thus afflicted: what do you think he suffered, that one man in such a great number of very wicked men?

---

46 MS *hwæt*. Scragg keeps the MS reading despite the strain it creates upon the syntax.

	Vercelli VII	Vercelli translation	Mutianus	Mutianus translation
7	Gepencað nu hwylca þa wyrda wæron ær ðam flode, 7 hwylce Abrahames forlætu wæron, 7 hu he his wifes <reaflac>[47] ðolode, 7 he hire bereafod wæs, 7 hu mislicra frecennessa he oft aræfnode ægðer ge on gefeohtum ge on hungrum (ll. 14–17).	Think now what events came before the flood, and what Abraham's losses were, and how he suffered <the snatching away> of his wife, and he was bereft of her, and how he often suffered various dangers both in battles and in [times of] hunger.	Num uultis, ut dicam quae circa diluuium contigerunt? An uultis ut Abrahae demigrationes frequentes enarrem, aut direptionem eius uxoris, aut diuersa pericula, bella numerosa, fames tantas et tales?	Surely you don't want me to speak of what happened around the time of the Flood? Or do you want me to describe Abraham's frequent wanderings, or the snatching away of his wife, or the various dangers, the numerous wars, so many hungers of such a type?
8	Gemunað eac hwylce ehtnesse Isac æghwanon ræfnode, 7 hu he hyra þeawe þeowode 7 oðre men to his geswinces leane fengon (ll. 17–19).	Remember also what persecutions Isaac suffered everywhere, and how he suffered their customs, and other men took reward for his toil.	Num uultis ut reuoluam quanta Isaac pertulerit? Exagitabatur undique, et persequutiones patiebatur, laborabat mercenaria seruitute, aliis fructum laboris eius sumentibus.	Surely you don't want me to recount what huge things Isaac endured? He was battered everywhere, he suffered persecutions, he laboured in hired service, while others took the fruit of his labour.
9	Gemunað eac Iacobes mænigfealdan geswinc (l. 19).	Remember also the manifold trials of Jacob.	Num uultis ut Iacob uobis producam in medium?	Surely you don't want me to bring up Jacob before you?
10			Et omnia quidem eius enarrare necessarium esse non puto, sed testimonium eius proferre opportunum prorsus existimo:	Indeed, I don't think it necessary to describe everything about him, but I reckon it wholly appropriate to put forward his testimony.

---

47 My addition is designed to render the Old English closer to the Latin. The noun *reaflac* seems most fitting since it seems possible that the term dropped out through eye-skip as a result of the surrounding terms *ræfnede* (in section 6), *bereafod* and *aræfnode* (in section 7), and again *ræfnode* (in section 8).

	Old English	Translation	Latin	Translation
11	Be ðam geswincum he wæs sprecende to Faraone 7 ðus cwæð: 'Lytle syndon mine dagas 7 awyrgede. Ne becomon hy na to minra fædera dagum' (ll. 20–2).	About those trials he was speaking to Pharaoh and said thus: *few are my days and evil. and they are not come up to the days of my fathers.*	ipse quippe loquens cum Pharaone: *Modici*, inquit, *et maligni facti sunt dies mei, et non peruenerunt ad dies patrum meorum.* [Gn. 47:9]	For he himself speaking with Pharaoh said *'few are my days and evil. and they are not come up to the days of my fathers.'*
12	Gebenceað eac Iosep 7 Moyses [7] <Iesunaue>[48] 7 Dauid 7 Eliam 7 Samuel 7 ealle ða halegan witegan, witodlice ealle hie wæron þurh geswinc gebyrhte (ll. 22–4).	Consider also Joseph, and Moses, and <Joshua>, and David, and Elijah, and Samuel, and all the holy prophets, truly they were all made famous through trial.	Num Ioseph uultis ut dicam? <Num> ipsum Mosen, num Iesum Naue, num Dauid, num Heliam, num Samuelem, num prophetas? Nonne uniuersos istos ex tribulationibus reperies claruisse?	Surely you don't want me to speak of Joseph? <Or> Moses himself? Or Joshua, or David, or Elijah, or Samuel, or the prophets? Won't you find that every single one of them was made famous by trials?
13	Hwæt, wene ge þæt ge mægen þurh idelnesse becuman to ðære biorhtnesse þe Godes þa gecorenan mid geswince geearnodon? Butan twion ge <ne> magon gif ge willað (ll. 25–7).[49]	Lo, do you expect that you may through idleness come to the brightness which God's chosen earned with trial? Without a doubt you <cannot>, if you want to.	Dic enim mihi, tu ex otio et deliciis uis clarus existere? Sed hoc penitus non ualebis.	Tell me, do you wish to be famous from laziness and pleasure? But you will absolutely not be able to do this.

48 Scragg (*VH*, 134) supplies *Ieremaie*, since the MS reading is obscured by reagent. The better reading seems to be *Iesunaue*, as originally suggested by Förster.

49 Since the sense in the Latin is emphatically negative, the Old English is here emended; however, in several other places the Old English author renders a negative Latin construction into a positive statement. cf. especially Table 30–1.

	Vercelli VII	Vercelli translation	Mutianus	Mutianus translation
14	Ic eow secge be ðam apostolum, ealle hie wæron geswencte maran geswincum þonne ænige oðre men (ll. 27–8).	I say to you about the apostles: they were all afflicted with greater trials than any other men.	Num apostolos uultis ut dicam? Sed etiam ipsi omnes, quantum ad tribulationem pertinet, caeteros superarunt.	Surely you don't want me to speak of the apostles? Each of them surpassed others with respect to trials.
15	Ða him eac Crist sylf foresæde: 'On þyssum middangearde ge habbað geswinc,' 7 eft he cwæð: 'Ge wepað 7 hiofað 7 þes middangeard gefyhð' (ll. 28–31).	Then Christ himself foretold to them: 'In this earth you will have trials.' And again he said: 'You will weep and you will grieve, but the world will be glad.'	Sed etiam Christus hoc dixit: In mundo, inquit, tribulationem habebitis [Io. 16:33]; et iterum, Uos plorabitis et lugebitis, mundus autem gaudebit. [Io. 16:20]	Even Christ said this thing: 'In this earth,' he said, 'you will have trials,' and again, 'You will weep and you will grieve, but the world will be glad.'
16	Neara 7 wiðerdene is se halega weg, swa swa dryhten sylf cwæð: 'Witodlice is se weg neara [þe to life gelædeð]' (ll. 31–2).[50]	Narrow and straight is the holy way, just as the Lord himself said, 'Truly is the way narrow [which leads to life].'	Et quia uia salutis arcta est et angusta, ipse Dominus uitae hoc dixit: Arcta est, inquit, et angusta uia, quae ducit ad uitam. [Mt. 7:14]	And because the way to salvation is straight and narrow, the Lord of life said this thing: 'Straight,' he said, 'and narrow is the way that leads to life.'
17	Þa ð[e] þa ruman wegas swiðe dysiglice h[ealda]ð, ne becumað hie na to life, ac he hie gelædeð to forwyrde (ll. 32–4).	Those [who hold] the spacious ways very foolishly, they will not come to life, but it will lead them to perdition.	Tu autem spatiosam quaeris: et quomodo non est istud absurdum? Propterea non adipisceris uitam, quia per aliam ingrederis uiam, sed ad perditiones uenies; illuc namque descendens iter elegisti.	But you seek the spacious way, and how is that not foolish? Moreover, you will not achieve life, because you are travelling a different path, but you will come to perdition, because you have chosen the way leading down there.

50 The portion in square brackets has been omitted in the MS.

	Old English	English	Latin	English
18	Gemunað eac þa ðe eall hira lif on þisse worulde on olehtungum lifedon (ll. 34–5).	Remember also those who all their lives lived in this world in delights.	Uultis etiam ut producamus in medium eos, qui in deliciis conuersati sunt, a nouissimis ad primos superius recurrentes?	Do you want me to bring up those who passed their lives in delights, describing them in reverse order from the most recent to the first?
19	Geþenceað þonne Ladzarus [7] þone welegan þe her dæghwamlice symlede 7 is ðær nu singallice cwelmed (ll. 35–6).	Consider Lazarus [and] the wealthy man who here feasted daily and who is there now continuously afflicted.	Diues ille qui peruritur in camino ignis;	That rich man who is burnt in the furnace of fire;
20	And gemunað Iudeas þe hira lif eall hyra wambe to forlore forgeafon. Be ðam wæs cweden þæt hyra wamb wære hyra god (ll. 37–8).	And remember the Jews who all their lives gave their bellies to destruction. About them it was said that their belly was their god.	Iudaei qui uitam suam uentri donauere perdendam, quorum deus uenter est; [Phil. 3.19]	the Jews who gave their stomachs to be lost, whose god is their stomachs.
21	Geþenceað eac þara þe in Sodome for hira unalyfedum gewilnungum forwurdon, 7 þara þe on Noes dagum wæron (ll. 38–40).	Think also of those who in Sodom on account of their unlawful desires perished, and of those who were in the days of Noah.	uel illi qui in eremo otium requirentes perierunt, sicut etiam in Sodomis, propter gastrimargiam consumpti sunt: et illi qui temporibus Noe fuerunt,	or those who perished wanting luxury in solitude, so too in Sodom they were consumed through their gluttony, or those who lived in the time of Noah,

	Vercelli VII	Vercelli translation	Mutianus	Mutianus translation
22	Witodlice be ðam þe ðam yðan life lyfedon on Sodome hit wæs gecweden ðætte *on hlafes fylnesse flowen*[51] (ll. 401).	Certainly about those who lived the easy life in Sodom it was said that they flowed away in the surfeit of bread.	nonne quia humidam et dissolutam persequuti sunt uitam? *In saturitatem, inquit, panis defluxerunt* [Ez. 16:49], de iis qui in Sodomis habitabant.	did they not lead a debauched and dissolute life? The Bible says of those that lived in Sodom that they flowed away in a surfeit of bread.
23	Þonne sio fylnes ðæs hlafes unriht wyrceð, hwæt is to cweðanne be ðam mænigfealdum smeamettum? (ll. 42–3).	When the surfeit of bread causes evil, what is to be said about those manifold delicacies?	Si autem panis saturitas tantum iniquitatis operatur, quid dicendum est de aliis condimentis?	If a surfeit of bread caused such evil, what is there to say of other foodstuffs?
24	Gemunað hu Esaw his dagas on ehtnesse lædde, 7 hu ða ðe ær in þam ryne Godes bearn wæron þurh ænlicra wifa sceawunga to fyrenlustum gehæfte on helle gehruron (ll. 43–5).	Remember how Esau spent his days in persecution, and how those ones, who before in that time were the sons of God, were captivated through the viewing of beautiful women, and fell into Hell?	Quid Esau? Nonne in uitio degebat? Quid illi, qui aspectu pulchrarum captiuati sunt mulierum, qui erant in numero filiorum Dei, et per <hoc> praeceps ad infernum libidinis deciderunt?	What about Esau? Didn't he spend his life in vice? What about those among the sons of God who were captivated by the appearance of beautiful women, and as a result fell headlong into a Hell of lust?

51 We can now identify the source for the Old English passage as Ez. 16:49.

25 Gemunaþ eac hu þa
forwurdon þe mid
wodheortnesse willan to
wæpnedmannum hæmed
sohton, 7 eallra Babilone 7
Egypta cyninga
ealle hie swiðe ungesæliglice
hira lif geendedon 7 nu
syndon on ecum witum
(ll. 46–9).

Remember also how
they perished, who with a
lusting of frenzy, sought
sex with men, and all
of Babylon, and all the
kings of Egypt who very
unhappily ended their lives
and now are in eternal
punishments.

Quid illi, qui in masculos
insano furore ferebantur?
Quid omnes reges gentium,
Babyloniorum, Aegyptiorum,
nonne uitam male atque
infeliciter terminauerunt?
Nonne in tormentis existunt?

What about those who
were brought to men by
a crazy madness? What
about all the kings of the
gentiles, the Babylonians,
the Egyptians: did they not
end their lives badly and
unhappily? Are they not
in torment?

26 Eac swylce þa ilcan witu
syndon gearuwe þam
mannum þe nu swylcum lifum
lifiað swylce hie lyfedon
(ll. 49–50).

Also the same torments
are prepared for men who
now live such lives as they
had lived.

Sed nunc, dic mihi, nonne
talia iterum fiunt?

But now tell me: do such
things not happen again?

27 Gehyrað eac hwæt Crist
cwæð, *þæt þa þe mid
hnescum hræglum gegyrede
wæron, [on cyninga husum
wæron]* (ll. 51–52).[52]

Hear also what Christ
said: *that those who were
clothed in soft clothes
[were in the palaces of
kings]*

Aduerte Christum dicentem:
*Qui mollibus uestibus
induuntur, in domibus regum
sunt* [Mt. 11:8]:

Pay heed to Christ when
he says: '*Those who are
clothed in soft clothing,
they are in the palaces
of kings.*

---

52 Quotation marks are supplied here; though Scragg's addition of the fuller Vulgate passage is maintained here, it need not be
presumed that the author included the entire quotation.

	Vercelli VII	Vercelli translation	Mutianus	Mutianus translation
28	On heofenum þæt ðonne is þa þe for Godes [lufan] swylce <hrægl>[53] habban nellað (ll. 52–3).	In heaven, those then are the ones who for the [love] of God wish not to have such <clothing>.	qui uero non habent talia uestimenta, in caelis sunt.	Those who do not have such clothing are in heaven.
29	Witodlice ægðer ge hnesce hrægl ge gehwylce hnescnesse þysse worulde no þæt an þa unfæstrædan ac eac þa fæstrædan 7 þæra soðfæstra sawla gewemmeð (ll. 53–6).	Certainly both soft clothing and each softness of this world harms not the inconstant alone, but also the constant and the souls of the righteous.	Molle namque uestimentum etiam ueram animam dissoluit, diffundit et frangit: ac si asperum habeat corpus et forte, citius per delicatam conuersationem molle perficitur.	For soft clothing destroys, dismays, and breaks the true soul: and if one has a brisk and strong body, it is quickly made soft through a delicate lifestyle.
30	For hwon wene ge þæt wif swa sioce syn of hyra gecynde? (ll. 56–7).	Why do you expect that women are so sick from their condition?	Nam unde putatis, aut ex quali ratione mulieres sic esse debiles et infirmas? Num ex conditione sexus tantum?	From what cause or from what kind of reason do you think that women are so weak and feeble? Surely not from the condition of their sex alone?

53 Scragg's addition of the noun *lufan* is certainly necessary to make sense of the genitive *Godes*. However, in viewing the Latin it seems possible that *hrægl* should also be supplied.

31 Ac hit <n>is swa: of hira liðan life hie bioð swa tyddre, for þan þe hie symle inne bioð 7 noht hefies ne wyrceaþ 7 hie oft baðiað 7 mid wyrtgemangum smyriað 7 symle on hnescum beddum hy r[e]staþ (ll. 57–9).

But it is <not> so: they are so weak on account of their soft lifestyle, because they are always inside, and they do not perform heavy work, and they bathe frequently, and smear themselves with unguents, and they always lie on soft beds.

Nequaquam, sed etiam ex conuersatione et educatione. Quod enim sub umbraculis degunt quod oleo unguntur, quod frequentibus lauaeris utuntur, quod assidue unguentis abundantibus et aromatibus perfunduntur, et iacent in straminibus delicatis, hoc est quod eas tales efficit.

Not at all, but also from their lifestyle and upbringing. Because they spend time under sunshades, because they smear themselves with oil, because they take frequent baths, because they cover themselves carefully with copious unguents and perfumes and lie on delicate beds, that is what makes them like that.

32 Eac ðu meaht þe bet ongytan þæt ic þe soð secge gif ðu genimst on hwylcum orcearde 7 on windigre stowe hwylc treow 7 hyt asettest on hleowfæste stowe 7 on wæterige stowe (ll. 60–2).

Also, you might better understand that I am telling you the truth if you take a certain tree in a certain orchard and in a windy place, and set it in a sheltered place and in a wet place,

Et ut melius hoc agnoscas, attende quod dico: ex horto aliquo in eremo constituto, qui uentis et tempestatibus uerberatur, sume arbustum aliquod, et pone in opaco et aquoso loco,

And so that you may understand this better, pay heed to what I say: take a shrub from a garden established in the desert, buffeted by winds and tempests, and put it in a dark and wet place,

33 ðonne meaht ðu gesion þæt hit sona forleoseð þa fægernesse þe hit hæfde on his agenre stowe (ll. 62–3).

then you might see that it immediately loses the fairness which it had in its own place.

et uidebis quod multum a fortitudine et dignitate sua mutabitur, quam habebat in hoc loco unde constat esse translatum.

and you will see that it will be much changed with regard to the strength and worth that it had in the place from where it was taken.

	Vercelli VII	Vercelli translation	Mutianus	Mutianus translation
34	Þenc eac be ðam wifum þe cyrliscu wiorc 7 hefegu on symbel wyrceaþ (ll. 64–5).	Think also about the women who always perform churlish and heavy work.	Quia uerum et certum est hoc, attende mulieres, quae in agris agunt uitam:	Because this is true and certain: pay attention to the women who live their lives in the fields;
35	Þonne cnawest ðu þæt hie bioð halran 7 cafran þonne þa weras þe on idelnesse lifiað (ll. 65–6).	Then you may know that they are healthier and stronger than those men who live in idleness.	fortiores namque uiris sunt, qui sunt in ciuitatibus constituti;	for they are stronger than men who are brought up in cities;
36			et si eas permittas cum illis athletico more certare, multos huiusmodi uiros illae sine dubio superabunt.	and if you were to allow them to contend with them in an athletic contest, they would doubtless surpass many men of that kind.
37	Nu sio idelnes swa swiðe þam lichoman dereð, ne tweoge þe na þæt hio þære sawle ne sceððe, for þan þe sio sawl sceal nyde habban smittan þæs lichoman unþeawa 7 hio swiðe mænige 7 mislice sceaþe him onfehð (ll. 66–9).	Now idleness so greatly harms the body, do not doubt that [idleness] does not harm the soul, because the soul must out of necessity have the pollution of the body's sins and [the soul] receives very many and various injuries from [the body]	Corpore namque molli reddito et delicato, necesse est et animam participare ex corporis morbo. In multis namque compatiuntur et afficiuntur operationes animae passionibus et affectionibus corporis.	For with the body having been rendered soft and delicate, it is necessary that the soul participates in the disease of the body. For in many folk the workings of the soul suffer alongside and are affected by the passions and feelings of the body.

№	Old English	Latin	Translation
38		Etenim in aegritudinibus aliter nos habemus, propter quod morbo mollescimus; et iterum cum ualemus, aliter nos habemus. Sicut enim in chordis contingit: cum enim sunt ipsi sonitus molles et delicati et non conuenienter extenti, etiam etiam ars deprauatur, et cogitur uitio seruire chordarum: sic etiam fit in corpore: multas ab eo anima suscipit laesiones multasque necessitates. Quando enim multa opus habuerit ad sui curationem, amaram anima sustinet seruitutem.	For we conduct ourselves differently in illnesses, because we become soft through sickness, and when we are well again, we conduct ourselves differently. Just as happens with musical strings: for when the sounds are soft and delicate, and not properly stretched, the artistry is diminished, and compelled to serve the imperfection of the strings. It happens thus in the body: the soul picks up many wounds and many obligations from it. For when [the body] paid close attention to its own care, the soul has bitter servitude.
39	For ðon ic halsie þæt we urne lichoman 7 sawle mid geswincum gestrangien, nalæs mid idelnessum tohælen (ll. 69–71).	Propterea obsecro, ut nostrum corpus forte reddamus, nec illud delicatum et aegrotabile faciamus.	Therefore I ask that we strengthen our bodies and souls with toil, and let us not make them weak with idlenesses. / Therefore I implore you that we render our body strong, and do not make it delicate and prone to sickness.
40	Ne sprece ic þas word to eow [we]rum anum ac to wifum (ll. 72–3).	Non ad uiros tantum, sed etiam ad mulieres mihi est sermo.	I do not speak these words to you men alone, but to women. / My sermon is not only for men, but also for women.

	Vercelli VII	Vercelli translation	Mutianus	Mutianus translation
41	Eawla, wif, to hwan wenest ðu þines lichoman hæle [geican] mid smyringe 7 oftþweale 7 oðrum liðnessum? (ll. 73–4).	Alas, woman, why did you expect to increase the health of your body with the smearing [of unguents], and frequent bathing, and other softnesses?	Quid illud saepius lauas, quid deliciis corrumpis, et gracile facis, o mulier! Quid fortitudinem eius debilitas?	Why do you wash [your body] too often, why corrupt it with delicacies, and make it frail, O woman! Why do you spoil its strength?
42	Of ðam cymeð unhælo, nals mægen (l. 74).	From those things comes sickness, not at all strength.	Deliciae quippe lassitudinem faciunt, non fortitudinem.	Indeed, luxuries cause tiredness, not strength.
43	Gif þa ilcan olectunge þam lichoman [<frama>dest, þæs lichoman][54] hiw fægere bið þonne hit ær wæs (ll. 75–6).	If you [<put away>] the same indulgences from the body, the form [of the body] will be fairer then it was previously.	Si autem ab eis recedens, aliter temetipsum tractas; tunc et pulchritudo tibi corporis generatur,	If, however, withdrawing from them, you treat yourself differently, then the beauty of your body is produced for you,
44			quando secundum rationem et ualet et habitum obtinet salutarem.	when it grows strong according to reason and obtains a healthy condition.
45	Gif ðu þonne his lustum symle fulgæst, þonne ne mæg he nawðer ne his mægen ne his fægernysse [gehealdan], ac symle bið sioc 7 unrot (ll. 76–8).	If you then follow [the body's] lust, then it may not keep either its strength nor its fairness, but it will always be sick and unhappy.	Si uero plurimis illud circumsepias morbis, neque flos uel uigor aderit corporis, neque habitus salutaris, sed semper moestum erit et languidum.	If in truth you hedge it in with very many sicknesses, there will not be the flower and vigour of the body, but it will always be sad and weak.

54 The sense of *framadest* is closer to the Latin and preserves Scragg's emendation. This term is borrowed from section 55, where it states that 'Eal þæt man ofer riht þygeð mid unyðnesse, hit him mon sceal framadon.'

46	Hwæt, ge witon ðæt ælc hus bið þe fægere þe hit man hwitað (ll. 78–9).	Lo, you know that each house is that much the fairer when one whitens it.	Scitis autem quia sicut domum pulchram cum quis eraserit, efficit pulchriorem:	However, you know that just as when someone scrapes down a beautiful house, he makes it more beautiful:
47	Swa eac bið ælc lichoma ðe fægerra þe hine þære sawle scima gebyrhtet (ll. 79–80).	So also is the body that much fairer when the radiance of the soul brightens it.	sic etiam faciem pulchram splendor animae superueniens amplius conuenustat.	so too the brilliance of the soul coming from above adorns more handsomely a beautiful face.
48	Sona se lichoma sceal bion unfæger, þonne he mid unrotnesse 7 mid sare aseted bið, ða cumað of ðam liðan olehtunge (ll. 80–2).	Immediately the body shall be ugly, when it is beset with unhappiness and with sorrow, which come from that soft indulgence.	Si uero in moestitia sit et doloribus constituta, deformis efficitur. Moestitia namque et moerores aegritudines faciunt et dolores; aegritudine autem delicatudines corporis generantur, quae deliciis constant.	If in truth [the soul[55]] is established in sadness and feelings of grief, it is made deformed. In fact, sadness and sorrows generate sicknesses and feelings of grief; however, in sickness the delicate features of the body are generated, which are established in delights.
49	For ðan ic lære þæt we flion þa liðnesse 7 flion [þa olehtunge] þysse worulde, ac hie synt swiðe swete (ll. 82–83).	Therefore I teach that we should flee those softnesses, and flee [those indulgences] of this world, though they are very sweet.	Proinde et ob hoc fugite delicias, si quid mihi obeditis et creditis. Sed uoluptatem, inquis, habent deliciae. Sed non tantam uoluptatem, quantas difficultates atque molestias.	So for that reason flee from delights, if you listen to me and believe me at all. But you say that delights give pleasure. But not so much pleasure as difficulties and annoyances.

55 Assuming that because *constituta* is feminine, it must refer to *anima*. The Old English translator seems wrongly to assume that it refers to *corpus*, which is neuter.

Vercelli VII	Vercelli translation	Mutianus	Mutianus translation
50 Sume men synt ðe him þyncð þæt nawðer ne æt ne drync ne genihtsumige, ær he oð ða hracan ful sie, 7 þonne þa oferfylle hyra gemynd forleosað (ll. 84–6).	There are some men to whom it seems that neither food nor drink might suffice, before they are full up to the throat, and then gluttony destroys their minds.	Huc accedit quia uoluptas illa, usquequo linguam uel gulam tangit, apparet; cum autem mensa remota fuerit, uel postquam erit cibus assumptus, similis eris ei-qui nihil illius attigerit: magis autem, multoque amplius peiorem grauedinem ex illis cibis et distentionem et opressionem mentis habiturus atque somnum morti consimilem; forenses etiam iuges habebis uigilias propter stomachi cruditatem et praeclusionem spiritus interioris, et per molestiam ructationis indigestae, et plurimum maledicturus es tuum uentrem, cum deberes magis intemperantiae uitium atque immoderationis arguere.	It has come to this point because that pleasure is apparent, in so far as it touches the tongue and the throat; but when the table is taken away, or after the food has been consumed, you will be like a man who has touched none of it: yet more, as one about to have far worse heaviness from that food, and swelling and oppression of mind and a sleep very like death; you will have public and indeed continual restlessness on account of the indigestion of the stomach and obstruction of the inner spirit and through the annoyance of undigested belching, and you will curse most of all your belly, when you ought rather to blame the vice of intemperance and immoderation.

51	Þonne ne don we swa, ac hlysten we þæs apostoles lare, Paulus; he cwæð: 'Ne do ge þæs flæsces giman on his willan' (ll. 86–7).	Then let us not do so, but let us listen to the teaching of the apostle, Paul. He said: make not provision for the flesh in its desires.	Non itaque deliciemur deliciis corporis, sed audiamus Paulum dicentem: Carnis curam ne perficiatis in concupiscentiis. [Rm. 13:14]	Let us not therefore be delighted by the delights of the body, but let us hear Paul saying: make not provision for the flesh in its desires.
52	Wyrse is þæt mon ðæs ofer riht bruce þonne hine mon on feltungrepe wiorpe (ll. 88–9).	It is worse to enjoy it wrongfully than to cast it into a dung-pit.	Tale namque est in uentrem cibos mittere, quale si quisquam eos in cloacam proiiciat; magis autem non tale est, sed multo peius;	For to send food into the stomach, is as if someone were to throw it into the privy. Rather it is not like that, but much worse;
53	On þære grepe he wiorðeð to meoxe (l. 89).	In the pit it will turn to dung.	hic enim fimum tantum operatur sine tua laesione;	for in the latter case indeed such dung is produced without harming you,
54	Butan tweon, þæs lichoman sceaða on þære wambe he wiorðeð to þam ilcan, and eac ðam licho[ma]n to mettry[m]nesse (ll. 89–91).	Without a doubt, that enemy of the body will turn to the same [dung] in the belly, and indeed to the weakening of the body.	illic autem plurimos morbos, plurimasque procreat aegritudines.	while in the former case it may cause very many weaknesses, and very many diseases.
55	Eal þæt man ofer riht þygeð mid unyðnesse, hit him mon sceal framadon (ll. 91–2).	Everything that is taken wrongfully without ease, it must be put away [from the body].	Nutrimentum enim nisi ex sufficientia non fit, quae ualeat sine labore digeri: cum uero plus exuberat, quam reficiendi corporis ratio postulat, non solum nutrimentum nullum, sed etiam corruptio generatur.	Indeed, nourishment does not happen unless from sufficiency, which is able to be digested without labour. When in truth [nourishment] is more abundant than the reason of feeding the body requires, not only is no nourishment generated, but indeed corruption.

	Vercelli VII	Vercelli translation	Mutianus	Mutianus translation
56	Ac þysses nu feawa gymaþ. Forneah ealra manna mod sint on oferflowende willan onwended (ll. 92–3).	But few now think about this. The minds of nearly all men are turned towards overflowing desire.	Sed nullus attendit haec: preoccupatae sunt omnium mentes superflua uoluptate.	But no one heeds these things: the minds of all are preoccupied with superfluous desire.
57	Fedað iowre lichoman on riht 7 forlætað þa oferfylle. Ne sceal man swiðor etan þonne se maga gemyltan mæge (ll. 94–5).	Feed your body in moderation, and abandon gluttony. Nor must one eat more than the stomach can digest.	Vis nutrire corpus? Reseca quod est superuacaneum, et quod sufficiat subministra, quantum poterit stomachi decoctio maturare:	Do you wish to nourish the body? cut back what is unnecessary, and supply what suffices, as much as the absorption of the stomach is able to digest:
58			ne magis ex cibis abundantibus opprimatur, ne demergas et obruas quod posset sufficere.	lest it be more oppressed by abundant provisions, lest you overwhelm and bury what ought to suffice.
59	Se goda mete ægðer deð, ge þone lichoman fedeð ge þæt mod gladað to ælcere hælo, 7 ælce untrymnesse he flymeð ægðer ge ðam innoðe ge ðam mode. Helpeð þæt se mete hreðe 7 wel mylteð þe se [maga] ðygeð (ll. 95–8).	Good food does both things: it feeds the body and gladdens the mind to each wellness, and puts to flight each weakness, both in the stomach and in the mind. It helps that the food is quickly and well digested which the stomach tastes.	Sufficientia quippe et nutrimentum et uoluptas est: nihil enim sic iucundum est, sicut cibus bene digestus et decoctus:	Sufficiency is of course both nourishment and pleasure: for nothing is so pleasant as food well digested and absorbed:

	Old English	Translation	Latin	Translation
60			nihil enim sic salutem, nihil sic sensuum acumen operatur: nihil sic aegritudinem fugat, sicut moderata refectio. Sufficientia quippe cum nutrimento et sospitatem simul etiam procreat et uoluptatem:	for nothing so produces health, nothing so produces a sharpening of the senses, nothing so puts to flight disease as eating in moderation. Of course sufficiency with nourishment also generates both health and pleasure at the same time.
61	7 of ðære oferfylle cumaþ manige mettrymnessa (ll. 98–9).	And from that gluttony comes many weaknesses.	abundantia uero morbum facit, et molestias ingerit, et aegritudines generat. Quod enim facit fames, hoc etiam plenitudo facit ciborum, magis autem multo peiora.	Indeed abundance causes sickness, and introduces annoyances, and produces diseases. For what hunger causes, that also abundance of food causes, but rather much worse things.
62	**Nis sio oferfyll þon betere þe se hunger. We flioð þone hunger 7 lufiað þæt no betere nis, ða oferfylle (ll. 99–100).**	**Gluttony is not the better than hunger. We flee hunger, and love that which is no better, [namely] gluttony**	[compare 65 below]	[compare 65 below]
63	Se hunger þone lichoman sona acwelleð 7 alyseð of ðam witelica[n] life (ll. 100–1).	Hunger immediately kills the body and frees it from the life of punishment.	Fames quippe in paucis diebus aufert hominem, et liberat ex hac uita poenali;	Hunger of course in a few days carries a man off and frees him from this life of punishment;

	Vercelli VII	Vercelli translation	Mutianus	Mutianus translation
64	Sio oferfyll þone lichoman untrumnessa fylleð 7 gedeð þæt he afulað 7 hine þonne æt nyxstan mid swiðe hreowlice deaðe fornimeð (ll. 102–3).	Gluttony fills the body with weaknesses and makes it so that it becomes foul, and in the next moment seizes it with a very cruel death.	excessus uero ciborum consumit, et putrefacit corpus humanum, et macerat aegritudine diuturna, et tunc eum morte crudeli consumit.	in truth the excess of food consumes, and putrefies the human body, and wears it down with lasting disease, and then consumes it with cruel death.
65	[compare 62 above]	[compare 62 above]	**Nos autem famem quidem inoptabile quoddam fugiendumque putamus, et ad indigestiones confugimus, quas multo uidemus esse peiores. Unde igitur iste morbus ad homines, unde hic furor?**	**We however indeed think hunger an undesirable thing and something to be escaped from, and we flee to indigestions, which we consider to be much worse. Whence therefore is that disease for men, whence this madness?**
66	Ne lære [ic] þæt men hy hungre acwellan, ac ðæt hy swa mycles brucen swa him ægðer ge to hæle ge to fostre helpan mæge (ll. 104–5)	I do not teach that men torture themselves with hunger, but rather that they enjoy as much as may help them both for health and for sustenance.	Non dico ut se homines crucient, sed ut tantum nutriantur, quantum illis et uoluptatem pariat et salutem, et corpori nutrimentum competens subministret,	I do not say that men should torture themselves, but that they nourish [themselves] as much as brings them both pleasure and health, and furnishes proper nourishment to the body,
67	þæt þone lichoman lyste þære sawle worcum fulgan. Witodlice ne mæg sio oferfyl næniþþinga to þære sawle þwerian, ac hio þære sawle 7 þæs lichoman geferscipe gewemmeð (ll. 105–8).	so that it pleases the body to fulfil the works of the soul. Certainly gluttony may not serve the soul in any wise, but it harms the fellowship of soul and body.	ut opus sit corpus nostrum operationibus animae obsequium sui muneris exhibere, dum suam tenet bene compagem, et concinnum sibi constat ex suis operibus uniuersis.	so that it may be necessary that our body give the service of its gift to the actions of the soul, while it holds its framework well, and stands well-ordered from all its own operations.

68

Cum uero exudans deliciis fuerit factum, compagem suam et concinnantiam non ualet ex diffluentia retinere; subintrans quippe humorum redundantia totum dissoluet penitus et effundit. *Carnis*, inquit Apostolus, *curam ne perfeceritis in concupiscentiis* [Rm. 13:14]. Bene dixit: materies namque est cibus cupiditatibus inhonestis.

When indeed it has become sweaty through delights, it is not able to keep its framework and structure from flowing away; the overflow of waters entering in by all means will destroy it all utterly and it pours away. The Apostle says, *let you not provide care of the flesh in desires*. He spoke well: for food is the material for wicked desires.

69

Ac þeah ðe hwa eallra manna wisost sie, gif he his luste fulgæð, he hine genyðerað, oððe ðurh unrihthæmed oððe ðurh oðer yfel (ll. 108–10).

But though anyone be the wisest of all men, if he fulfils his desire, he debases himself, either through adultery or through another evil.

Ac si in philosophia quisquam cunctis emineat, tamen si deliciatur, necesse est ut aliquid uel ex cibis uel ex uino patiatur, ut flammam excitet ampliorem. Hinc fornicationes, hinc adulteria.

As if someone surpasses all in philosophy, if nevertheless he is enticed, it is necessary that he suffers something either from food or wine, so that he kindles a greater flame. From this come fornications, from this come adulteries.

	Vercelli VII	Vercelli translation	Mutianus	Mutianus translation
70	Witodlice, ne mæg sio hungriende wamb ænne unrihtlust acennan ne sio gemetegode fyl þon ma (ll. 110–11).	Indeed, the hungering belly may not give rise to one evil desire, any more than may moderated sufficiency.	Etenim uenter esuriens amorem non ualet procreare; magis autem neque sufficientia, si fuerit moderata.	Because the hungering stomach is not able to generate love; but rather neither [does] sufficiency, if it is moderated.
71	Ac of þære oferfylle cumað þa unrihtan lustas gelice 7 on meresteallum wyrmas tyddriað, 7 of ðære gemetegunge god wiorc gelice 7 of clænre eorðan gode wæstmas (ll. 111–14).	But from gluttony come those illicit desires just as also in stagnant water worms propagate, and from moderation [come those] good deeds just as also from that pure earth [come those] good fruits.	Quae uero generat absurdas cupiditates, illa est abundantia, quae se deliciis tradit. Sicut enim terra, quae ualde humecta est, generat uermes, et fimus cum compluitur, uel cum plurimum sibi humorem retinet; terra uero quae libera est ab humoribus, fructuum foecunditate decoratur, si ex abundantia non corrumpatur aquarum; ac si etiam non colatur, ultro tamen gramina subministrat; si uero colatur, fructuum foecunditate pollebit.	That which generates foolish lusts, is abundance, which surrenders itself to delights. For just as the earth, which is very wet, generates worms, and dung when it rains, or when it retains a lot of fluid in itself; in truth, the earth which is free from fluids is decorated with the richness of fruits, if it is not corrupted by an abundance of water; but even if it is not cultivated, nevertheless it further supplies grass; if in truth it is cultivated, it will be fertile with the richness of fruits.

72 For þan ic lære þæt we urne lichoman mid oferfylle ne gewemmen, ac mid gemetegunge gefrætewigen (ll. 114–15),

Therefore I teach that we not harm our bodies with gluttony, but that we adorn it with moderation,

Obsecro igitur ne nostrum corpus uitiosum et inutile faciamus, neque ei uitia inseramus, sed praeparemus ei fructus utiles et arbusta fructuosa, nec ea dissoluamus per immoderationem ciborum: immoderatio quippe pro fructibus uermes facit. Sic etiam insita nobis cupiditas, si eam deliciarum inundationibus ebries, cupiditates generat turpes et uoluptates admodum turpiores.

I therefore ask that we not make our body full of vice and useless, and not plant sins in it, but let us prepare for it useful fruits and fruit-bearing plants, and let us not dissolve it through the immoderation of food: immoderation certainly generates worms in place of fruits. So also our innate desire, if you moisten it with the floods of delights, it generates disgraceful lusts and still more disgraceful desires.

73 ⁊ us fram awiorp[en] þa wol, ⁊ geearnien ⁊ onfon þa god þe us gehatene synt on þam[56] hælendan Criste ⁊ mid þam halegan gaste in ealra worulda woruld (ll. 115–18).

and that we cast away from ourselves that pestilence, and that we earn and receive those good things which are promised to us in the Saviour Christ and with the Holy Spirit forever.

Abiiciamus itaque hanc luem, ut possimus adipisci bona quae promissa sunt, in Christo Iesu Domino nostro, cum quo Patri gloria, una cum sancto Spiritu, nunc et semper, et in saecula saeculorum. Amen.

Let us cast away this plague, so that we are able to obtain those good things which are promised, in Jesus Christ our Lord, with whom to the Father, together with the holy spirit, be glory now and always, forever. Amen.

56 Scragg's interpolated 'toweardan rice mid þam' has been removed here, since the phrase proves not to be in the Latin.

Vercelli Homily XV
and *The Apocalypse of Thomas*

CHARLES D. WRIGHT

The Apocalypse of Thomas, an apocryphal revelation of Christ concerning the travails that will usher in the last times and the cosmological signs that will occur on each of the seven days preceding the Day of Judgment, survives in three distinct Latin versions and four independent Old English translations, as well as a Middle Irish poetic version;[1] information about the Old English versions is set out in table 1. In a recent essay I printed in parallel-column format six previously unknown or neglected Latin texts of *Thomas*, discussed their relationship to the previously published versions, and drew attention to certain readings that help to reconstruct the lost Latin sources of the Old English translations.[2] Space did not permit a

---

1 For the Middle Irish version appended to the *Saltair na Rann*, see W.W. Heist, *The Fifteen Signs before Doomsday* (East Lansing: Michigan State College Press, 1952), 1–21.

2 Charles D. Wright, 'The Apocalypse of Thomas: Some New Latin Texts and Their Significance for the Old English Versions,' in *Apocryphal Texts and Traditions in Anglo-Saxon England*, ed. Kathryn Powell and Donald Scragg (Cambridge: Boydell and Brewer, 2003), 27–64. Quotations from *Thomas* below are from a critical edition I am currently preparing, but I have cited whichever manuscript is closest to Vercelli XV for a given passage, with select variants in brackets. Since it is easy to locate the corresponding passages in the older editions of individual manuscripts (cited in the following notes) I have not supplied the page and line references to these editions. For translations of the interpolated and non-interpolated versions, see M.R. James, *The Apocryphal New Testament* (1924; repr. with revisions Oxford: Clarendon Press, 1953), 555–62. The translation in J.K. Elliott's new edition of James's collection (Oxford: Clarendon Press, 1993), 645–51, is modernized but essentially the same. An independent translation of the non-interpolated version by A. de Santos Ontero is also valuable, but like James he provides only brief footnotes drawing attention to some of the most significant variant readings; see Edgar Hennecke and Wilhelm Schneemelcher, *New Testament Apocrypha*, 5th ed., trans. R.McL. Wilson, 2 vols. (Louisville: Westminster/John Knox, 1991–2), 2:

Table 1
The Old English Versions of *The Apocalypse of Thomas*

Abbreviated name	*DOE* short title	Cameron no.	Manuscript(s)
Vercelli XV	HomU 6	B.3.4.6	Vercelli, Biblioteca Capitolare CXVII [Ker no. 394 art. 17; Scragg MS A]
Corpus 41	HomU 12	B3.4.12	Cambridge, Corpus Christi College 41 [Ker no. 32 art. 12; Scragg MS D]
Bazire–Cross 3	HomS 44; HomS 33	B3.2.44; B3.2.33	Cambridge, Corpus Christi College 162 [Ker no. 38 art. 37; Scragg MS G]; Oxford, Bodleian Library, Hatton 116 [Ker no. 333 art. 26; Scragg MS T]
Blickling VII	HomS 26	B3.2.26	Princeton Univ., Scheide Library 71 [Ker no. 382 art. 7; Scragg MS B]

Note: Short titles and numbers are those assigned by the Dictionary of Old English *List of Texts and Editions*. References for the manuscripts are to Ker, *Catalogue*, by item and article number, and D.G. Scragg's *sigla* of the manuscripts of anonymous homilies, 'The Corpus of Vernacular Homilies and Prose Saints' Lives before Ælfric,' *ASE* 8 (1979): 223–77.

detailed comparison of the surviving Latin versions with each Old English translation. In the present essay, therefore, I will examine the Old English version of *Thomas* in Vercelli Homily XV, focusing on what appear to be the homilist's alterations and additions to his source.[3] The most significant of these changes, I will suggest, reflect the homilist's efforts to pre-empt sceptical reactions to the revelation and to link apocalyptic expectation to the spread of clerical corruption. I will also suggest that an end-time prophecy which the homilist seems to have added to his source – attributing widespread corruption to 'young kings, young popes, young bishops and young ealdormen' – may constitute a disaffected secular cleric's response to the Benedictine Reform movement.

The homilist's changes become apparent only when his translation is compared with his source. The actual manuscript of *Thomas* used by the

---

748–52. For translations into German and Italian, see M. Geerard, *Clavis Apocryphorum Novi Testamenti* (Turnhout: Brepols, 1992), 210.

3 In lieu of a line-by-line comparison (which I defer for a critical edition of *Thomas* in preparation) I have grouped the most substantive alterations into seven general categories (below, 162). For new Latin parallels for particular readings in Vercelli XV, see Wright, 'Some New Latin Texts,' 44–6.

Vercelli homilist has not survived, but we can approximate it by comparing variant readings in the surviving manuscripts. It will therefore be necessary first to survey the manuscript transmission of the Latin versions of
Thomas and to assess Vercelli XV's relation to the divergent recensions of
the work.

I. The Latin Manuscript Transmission of *The Apocalypse of Thomas*

The surviving Latin manuscripts of *Thomas* transmit three different versions: non-interpolated, interpolated, and abbreviated. What appears to be
the primitive form of the apocalypse, the so-called non-interpolated version, survives in one very early fragment and one much later complete
copy:

> *Non-interpolated Version*:
> B: Naples, Biblioteca Nazionale Vittorio Emanuele III, lat. 2 (Vindobon.
> 16), fol. 60, lower script (s. v^2; *CLA* III.396) [fragment].[4]
> N: Munich, Bayerische Staatsbibliothek Clm 4563 (s. xi$^{med.}$), fol. 40.[5]

This so-called non-interpolated version lacks a historical-prophetic introduction (corresponding to Vercelli XV, ll. 3–70) found in four other
manuscripts:

> *Interpolated Version*:
> M: Munich, Clm 4585 (s. ix^1), fols. 65v–67v.[6]
> P: Vatican City, Biblioteca Apostolica, Pal. lat. 220 (s. ix^1), fols.
> 48v–53r.[7]

---

4 Ed. Edmund Hauler, 'Zu den neuen lateinischen Bruchstücken der Thomasapokalypse
und eines apostolischen Sendschreibens im Codex Vind. Nr. 16,' *Wiener Studien* 30
(1908): 308–40; earlier ed. J. Bick, 'Wiener Palimpseste, I,' *Sitzungsberichte der Wiener
Akademie der Wissenschaften*, phil.-hist. Kl. 159, Abh. 7 (1908): 97–8.

5 Ed. P.L. Bihlmeyer, 'Un texte non interpolé de l'Apocalypse de Thomas,' *Revue
Bénédictine* 28 (1911): 270–82. For further details on the manuscripts, see Wright, 'Some
New Latin Texts.'

6 Ed. F. Wilhelm, *Deutsche Legenden und Legendare* (Leipzig: J.C. Hinrichs,1907),
40*–42*.

7 This version was discovered by Dobschütz, but the text has never been printed in its
entirety, only as selected variants (supplied by Dobschütz) by Hauler, Bihlmeyer, and
Max Förster (see n. 11 below). The manuscript also contains Redaction XI of the *Visio
Pauli*, and a collection of Hiberno-Latin sermons; see Charles D. Wright, *The Irish
Tradition in Old English Literature*, CSASE 6 (Cambridge: CUP, 1993), 111, and the
references cited there.

V: Verona, Biblioteca Capitolare I (1) (s. vi–vii), fols. 403v, 404v (addition of s. vii; *CLA* IV.472) [fragment].[8]
W: Würzburg, Universitätsbibliothek M.p.th.f. 28 (s. viii[4/4]; *CLA* IX.1408), fols. 57r–58v.

MP alone transmit the interpolation in full; the fragmentary V has only the opening, while W deletes most of the prophecies and substitutes material derived from Lactantius's *Epitome diuinarum institutionum*.[9] Immediately following the interpolation in MP is an *Ego sum* proclamation by Christ (= Vercelli XV, ll. 72–4; on the homilist's treatment of this speech see below, 165–6); the corresponding speech in the non-interpolated BN follows immediately after the opening admonition *Audi Thomas* ... From this point the two versions run roughly parallel for the remainder of the apocalypse.

A broad *terminus post quem* for the interpolated version is provided by its thinly disguised references to events of the first half of the fifth century.[10] It is uncertain how much earlier the non-interpolated version might be; guesses range from the third to the fourth century.[11] There is no evidence that it was translated from a Greek original, although the possibility cannot be ruled out. The interpolated introduction, however, was almost certainly composed in Latin, for it alludes cryptically (albeit transparently) to the emperors Honorius and Arcadius by saying that their names begin with the eighth and first letters of the alphabet – which is true of 'Honorius' only in the Latin alphabet.[12]

---

8 Ed. M.R. James, 'Notes on Apocrypha. I: *Revelatio Thomae*,' *Journal of Theological Studies* 11 (1910): 288–90; idem, 'The *Revelatio Thomae* Again,' *Journal of Theological Studies* 11 (1910): 569. A more accurate transcript of fol. 403v was given by E. Carusi and W.M. Lindsay in *Monumenti paleografici Veronesi*, fasc. II (Rome: Biblioteca Apostolica Vaticana, 1934), 11 (with a facsimile of the entire page as plate 24; part of fol. 403v is also reproduced in *CLA*). The text continues on fol. 404v, but unfortunately only parts of a few words are legible.

9 See Wright, 'Some New Latin Texts,' 33.

10 These are most fully (though often very speculatively) explicated by Hauler, 'Zu den neuen Bruchstücken.' The *terminus post quem* could be as early as 423, the year of Honorius's death – again assuming that the allusion has been correctly interpreted – and possibly as late as the 450s, if we take seriously the suggestions of Hauler for the other prophecies. A *terminus ante quem* is afforded by the reference to the work (as 'Reuelatio quae appellatur Thomae') in the *Decretum Gelasianum* (495/96), ed. E. von Dobschütz, *Das Decretum Gelasianum*, Texte und Untersuchungen 38/4 (Leipzig: J.C. Hinrichs, 1912), 12 and 53.

11 See Förster, 'A New Version of the Apocalypse of Thomas in Old English,' *Anglia* 73 (1955): 12.

12 See James, *New Testament Apocrypha*, 556, n.1.

In addition to the interpolated and non-interpolated versions, there are also six 'abbreviated' texts that have only the list of signs. Abbreviated texts are found in the following manuscripts:

Abbreviated Versions:

A: Munich, Bayerische Staatsbibliothek Clm 8439 (s. xv), fol. 191.[13]

T: Toronto, Fisher Rare Book Library, Collection of 190 Pieces of Vellum (current shelfmark 'MS 45'), fragment 24–25 (s. ix²).[14]

R: Vatican City, Biblioteca Apostolica, Reg. lat. 49 (s. x^ex.), fol. 52v.

H: Oxford, Bodleian Library, Hatton 26, part II (s. xiii^in.), fol. 88r.

E: Einsiedeln, Stiftsbibliothek 319 (s. x²), pp. 155–6.

O: Vienna, Österreichische Nationalbibliothek 1878 [part B] (s. xii), fols. 161v–62r.

With relatively few exceptions (primarily in A) the readings of the abbreviated texts agree with manuscripts of the interpolated version, which suggests that they were created by deletion of the introduction from interpolated texts; in effect, the abbreviated versions are 'de-interpolated.' They have all diverged significantly, however, from the interpolated text or texts upon which they were based, and as a result there is a broad variational division separating not only the interpolated and non-interpolated versions, but also the abbreviated and non-abbreviated versions. Among the abbreviated texts, three sub-groups can be distinguished, consisting of **AT**, **EO**, and **RH**, but all three share enough distinctive readings to suggest that they may derive from a common abbreviated archetype. I am not prepared, however, to rule out the possibility that one or more of these groups developed independently by a parallel process of removing the introduction.[15]

To summarize the relationship between the three recensions, the non-interpolated version appears to be the primary one; the 'interpolated' version was created by the addition of a series of *ex eventu* prophecies to the originally brief introduction; and the abbreviated versions were created by

---

13 Ed. Walther Suchier, *L'Enfant Sage (Das Gespräch des Kaisers Hadrian mit dem klugen Kinde Epitus)*, Gesellschaft für romanische Literatur 24 (Dresden: Max Niemeyer, 1910), 272.

14 **TRHEO** are ed. Wright, 'Some New Latin Texts,' 54–64 (on the manuscripts see 35–40).

15 The group **AT** in particular stands somewhat apart from **RHEO**, while **T** is unique among the abbreviated versions in retaining the dramatic context of a revelation of Christ to Thomas, and is the only one to retain the sentence beginning *Audi Thomas*.

the removal of virtually the entire expanded introduction from an inter-polated text or texts.[16]

II. The Relation of Vercelli XV to the Latin Versions of *The Apocalypse of Thomas*

The basic affiliations of the Old English versions of *Thomas* were identi-fied by Max Förster, who edited Vercelli XV in 1913 and the Corpus 41 homily in 1955.[17] Förster had access to proof sheets from an unpublished edition of *Thomas* by Ernst von Dobschütz, consisting of diplomatic tran-scripts of **BVM** as well as of **P**, whose text still has never been printed in its entirety.[18] Moreover, Förster was the first to draw attention to the abbrevi-ated text **A**, which had escaped Dobschütz's notice. In his 1913 edition of Vercelli XV, Förster attempted to approximate the homilist's source with a composite Latin text of *Thomas* based on **M** (his **M¹**), with selected vari-ants in brackets from **BP** and **N** [his **M²**] where they afforded closer paral-lels; conjectural emendations made to accommodate the Old English translation were highlighted typographically. In his 1955 edition of Corpus 41, Förster printed a more elaborate composite Latin text, now including readings from **V** and **A**, but keyed to the Corpus 41 translation. Förster did print selected variants relevant for the other Old English ver-sions, including Vercelli XV, but he did not include those portions of the interpolated introduction that were not translated by the Corpus 41

---

16 The hypothesis that the historical-prophetic introduction is an interpolation seems well founded, but is not beyond doubt, and some scholars have preferred the more neutral designations 'longer' and 'shorter.' The main arguments in favour of interpolation were concisely summarized by James, *New Testament Apocrypha*, 562. Marcel Dando has argued that the longer recension is the original: 'L'Apocalypse de Thomas,' *Cahiers d'Études Cathares* 28 (1977): 5 and 42.

17 Förster, 'Der Vercelli-Codex CXVII nebst Abdruck einiger altenglischer Homilien der Handschrift,' in *Festschrift für Lorenz Morsbach*, ed. F. Holthausen and H. Spies, Studien zur englischen Philologie 50 (Halle: Max Niemeyer, 1913), 116–28; idem, 'A New Version.' Förster had drawn attention to three of the Old English adaptations of *Thomas* in 'Der Vercelli-Codex,' and Rudolf Willard noted the fourth in his *Two Apocrypha in Old English Homilies*, Beiträge zur englischen Philologie 30 (Leipzig: Bernhard Tauchnitz, 1935), 2.

18 On Dobschütz's edition see Wright, 'Some New Latin Texts,' 29 and n. 9. In addition to the proof sheets consulted by Förster, Dobschütz's *Nachlass* includes an unfinished handwritten draft edition, which I have transcribed and will make use of in an edition I am currently preparing.

homilist. Thus, the composite text in the 1913 edition is not a complete record of the variants (since Förster was not then aware of **V** or **A**), while the composite text in the 1955 article skips over a substantial portion of the interpolated introduction that was translated by the Vercelli homilist.

It was left to D.G. Scragg in his 1992 edition of the Vercelli homilies to combine the material from the two composite texts printed by Förster into a complete source apparatus for Vercelli XV.[19] In doing so, however, Scragg omitted Förster's brackets and *sigla* indicating which readings were from which manuscripts, as well as the italics marking Förster's own conjectural emendations. This is a defensible economy in a large-scale critical edition of twenty-three homilies, but the resulting text does not afford an adequate basis for detailed comparative source analysis. Scragg's plain-text version of Förster's composite apocalypse was in turn the basis of Mark Atherton's line-by-line source analysis of Vercelli XV for *Fontes Anglo-Saxonici*,[20] which inevitably has the same limitations. Naturally Scragg and Atherton did not discuss passages left untranslated by the homilist, but what a vernacular author may have omitted from a Latin source can be crucial to understanding his methods, purposes, and biases.[21] Even if editors cannot afford to print such passages in their apparatus, source scholars and critics cannot afford to ignore the content obscured by editorial ellipses.

Förster noted that both Vercelli XV and Corpus 41 have material corresponding to the interpolation.[22] Vercelli XV translates most of the interpolation, while Corpus 41 translates just a few brief passages. Förster also stated that Blickling VII had 'a few general statements' from the interpolation, but he did not specify these and I find nothing in the homily that derives from it. Nor are there any traces of the interpolation in Bazire–Cross 3. But the absence of the interpolation is not the same thing as

---

19 *VH*, 253–8.

20 Mark Atherton, 'The Sources of Vercelli Homily XV (C.B.3.4.6),' 1996, *Fontes Anglo-Saxonici: World Wide Web Register*, at http://fontes.english.ox.ac.uk/; also available in CD-ROM: David Miles, Rohini Jayatilaka, and Malcolm Godden, *Fontes Anglo-Saxonici: A Register of Written Sources Used by Anglo-Saxon Authors. CD-ROM Version 1.1* (Oxford: Fontes Anglo-Saxonici Project, 2002). I am grateful to Dr Jayatilaka for sending me a print-out of the complete entry.

21 For an example, see Charles D. Wright, 'Vercelli Homilies XI–XIII and the Anglo-Saxon Benedictine Reform: Tailored Sources and Implied Audiences,' in *Preacher, Sermon and Audience in the Middle Ages*, ed. Carolyn Muessig (Leiden: Brill, 2002), 203–28.

22 Förster, 'A New Version,' 11–12 (the quotation following is from 12).

affiliation with the 'non-interpolated' version represented by **BN**. I have argued elsewhere that the Latin sources of Blickling VII and Bazire–Cross 3 were abbreviated texts that had already removed the characteristic interpolation from the interpolated version.[23] This conclusion is supported by the character of the readings of the Old English versions for the list of signs, which agree almost exclusively with manuscripts of the interpolated and/or abbreviated versions whenever these differ substantively from the non-interpolated version. Readings that appear to reflect something in **BN** are usually found in the interpolated text **P**, or in at least one of the other interpolated or abbreviated texts, a fact that undermines Förster's contention that in individual readings within the list of signs Vercelli XV often agrees more closely with the non-interpolated version.[24] Indeed, in my previous essay I concluded that 'there seem to be no readings in any of the Old English homilies that correspond exclusively with the non-interpolated version.'[25]

One apparent exception I noted is the phrase *mycel þreatnes* ('great affliction,' ll. 4–5), which corresponds (save for the difference in number) to **N**'s reading *necessitates magnae*, where the interpolated texts read *siccitas magna* (**VMW**, *om.* **P**). The immediate context of this phrase, however, is otherwise much closer to the interpolated version (including several additional items in the list of travails), while the 'interpolated' reading *siccitas magna* could easily have been altered from **necessitas magna* (which would correspond more precisely to the singular *mycel þreatnes*) in the Vercelli homilist's lost source manuscript.[26]

---

23 Wright, 'Some New Latin Texts,' 43.
24 Förster, 'Der Vercelli-Codex,' 77. In almost every case where his composite text incorporates a reading from **N** (his **M²**), however, the reading is shared with the interpolated text **P** or **M** (his **M¹**). Förster's reading *'sequuntur'* (paralleling *folgað*, l. 85; ms. *folgiað*) is an emendation of **N**'s *adsecuntur*, which he contrasts with **M**'s *sequebantur*; but present-tense forms (*sequuntur /secuntur* or *sequentur*) are also found in **PW** and all the abbreviated versions. In the description of the sixth day Förster switches to **N** for his base text, but only because **M** breaks off at that point and he could not reproduce Dobschütz's unpublished text of **P** *in extenso*, but only in the form of select variants.
25 Wright, 'Some New Latin Texts,' 43.
26 See Wright, 'Some New Latin Texts,' 43, n.82; the phrase *necessitates multae* does appear in **MP** at a later point. The Corpus 41 reading *micel wæta* may distantly reflect the variant *siccitas magna*, though as Förster noted ('A New Latin Version,' 19n22), the meaning is precisely the opposite. Willard therefore suggested emending to *micel unwæta*.

There is, however, another apparent 'non-interpolated' reading that I failed to account for. As Förster recognized, the Vercelli homilist's reference to 'dissension' between two kings and two brothers ('þurh þæt þonne ariseð unsehtnesse betweoh twam cyningum 7 twam gebroðum,' ll. 8–9) reflects a passage in the introduction of N: 'Tunc erunt participationes in saeculo inter regem et regem' ('then there will be divisions in the world between king and king'; the corresponding passage in the fragmentary B is defective here). Although much of the material from the 'non-interpolated' introduction is retained in the interpolated version, none of the surviving interpolated texts includes this prophecy. This does not, I think, indicate that the Vercelli homilist had access to a non-interpolated version of *Thomas*, from which he translated just two distinctive readings (this sentence and possibly the phrase *necessitates magnae*). Against these two 'non-interpolated' parallels are many readings that agree with one or more interpolated texts *against* BN. Again, since the Vercelli homilist does translate the interpolation, it is obvious that his main source-text was an interpolated one. It is far more likely, then, that the Vercelli homilist's interpolated text belonged to a distinct line of transmission that happened to have retained one or two isolated readings that now appear (due to the exiguous and random survival of Latin manuscripts) to be exclusive to the 'non-interpolated' version.

The lost source of Vercelli XV, then, was an interpolated version of *Thomas* similar to MP, which alone transmit all the 'historical' prophecies, as well as the series of imprecations beginning *Vae illis* ... (for this passage see below, 167). Yet it agreed with BN against MPVW in a few readings that are closer to the archetypal interpolated text (and therefore to the lost non-interpolated text used by the interpolator). If Förster greatly overstated the degree to which Vercelli XV agreed in details with the non-interpolated version, he nonetheless rightly concluded 'daß dem Angelsachsen eine bessere und ursprünglichere Textform der längeren Rezension [i.e., the interpolated version] vorgelegen hat.'[27]

It is, of course, possible that the Vercelli homilist consulted (or remembered) other Latin versions of *Thomas*, or other OE translations that have not survived;[28] but in default of concrete evidence for use of multiple

---

27 Förster, 'A New Latin Version,' 77.
28 Moreover, one cannot in this case attribute the heterogeneity to separate developments and cross-pollination within the vernacular tradition, for the four surviving Old English versions show no trace of interdependence or of mutual reliance on lost vernacular translations.

versions it is simpler to assume that he had access to only a single copy of a now lost interpolated Latin version. But was the homilist translating directly from a copy of *Thomas*, or from a Latin sermon that had already conflated *Thomas* with material from other sources (including an apocryphal narrative of the delivery of the damned through the intercession of Mary, Michael, and Peter)?[29] The distinction makes a difference, for if there was an intermediate Latin source, many of the apparent alterations to *Thomas* might be due to its compiler rather than to the Vercelli homilist himself. We know that Old English homilists sometimes used such intermediate sources,[30] but it is rarely possible to detect them on the basis of internal evidence alone. Förster did in fact postulate an intermediate Latin source for Vercelli XV, on the grounds that the Anglo-Saxon homilist himself would not have conflated the two apocryphal narratives, thereby representing the 'Delivery of the Damned' as a continuation of the revelation to Thomas.[31] But a lacuna in the Vercelli Book text deprives us of the transition between these two sources,[32] so it is impossible to say whether or not it was signalled overtly. In any case, unsignalled transitions from one source to another are not uncommon in OE vernacular homilies, and we need not assume that the most recently named authority is being credited with everything that follows until a different authority is named. An intermediate source cannot be ruled out, but neither can it be presumed. In what follows, therefore, I tentatively attribute such changes as appear to have been made to *Thomas* to the intervention of the Vercelli homilist.

---

29 On this section of the homily and its analogues in Old English see Mary Clayton, 'Delivering the Damned: A Motif in Old English Homiletic Prose,' *MÆ* 55 (1986): 92–102; eadem, *The Cult of the Virgin Mary in Anglo-Saxon England*, CSASE 2 (Cambridge: CUP, 1990), 253–8. Clayton argues persuasively that the motif is based ultimately on a version of the apocryphal *Transitus Mariae*. See also Thomas D. Hill, 'Delivering the Damned in Old English Anonymous Homilies and Jón Arason's *Ljómur*,' *MÆ* 61 (1992): 75–82; and David F. Johnson, 'A Scene of Post-Mortem Judgement in the New Minster *Liber Vitae*,' *OEN* 34/1 (Fall 2000): 26–30.

30 Latin sermons in the Homiliary of St. Père de Chartres or 'Pembroke Homiliary,' for example, which for the most part are patchworks of patristic and early medieval sources, were the immediate source for a number of Old English homilies. See J.E. Cross, *Cambridge Pembroke College MS. 25: A Carolingian Sermonary Used by Anglo-Saxon Preachers*, King's College London Medieval Studies 1 (London: King's College, 1987).

31 Förster, 'Der Vercelli-Codex,' 76.

32 *VH*, 251, comparing Vercelli XV with other OE homilies that include the 'Delivering the Damned' narrative, suggests that the lacuna may have included the *Ego te homo* speech of Christ based on Caesarius of Arles.

III. The Vercelli Homilist's Alterations and Additions

According to D.G. Scragg, 'the homilist translated slavishly. He added very little, and what does appear to be his own is repetitive in vocabulary and idea.'[33] I agree that independent addition was generally not the homilist's modus operandi, and that he often does translate quite closely; yet I would qualify Scragg's characterization of the translation as 'slavish,' with reference to a variety of alterations and additions detailed below. The homilist also makes one extended addition (a passage Scragg calls 'the speech of men alive at Doomsday,' discussed below, 169–70) that affords a rare glimpse into an Anglo-Saxon preacher's effort to pre-empt any sceptics among his audience, and he appears to have added a prophecy (discussed below, 172–80) that alludes obliquely to the ecclesiastical politics of the Benedictine Reform movement.

Many of the homilist's substantive alterations can be grouped into the following broad categories:[34] (1) deletion of anachronisms; (2) explanatory and summarizing statements; (3) rhetorical embellishments; (4) biblical additions and doctrinal emendations; (5) moralizing asides; (6) authenticating devices; and (7) politically motivated and possibly topical revisions.

(1) *Deletion of anachronisms.* Once the fifth-century events alluded to in the interpolated introduction had become distant history, the 'prophecies' were liable to be deleted, as they were in W and in all the abbreviated versions. It is all the more remarkable, then, that the Vercelli homilist gamely attempted to translate them. That he did so suggests he took them seriously as prophecy, and either failed to recognize their late-antique historical context, or was untroubled by the lapse of time between these putative end-time events and his own day. The homilist does, however, remove certain obvious anachronisms. Most notably he omits the one prophecy that could readily be identified as an allusion to specific historical emperors, that identifying Arcadius and Honorius by means of a transparent alphabet cipher (see above, 153). He does translate a reference to Roman soldiers (*Romanis militibus*) as *Romanisce þeode* (l. 44), but he omits or alters two more concretely anachronistic references to a 'Caesar.' In one case he translates the phrase 'and they will be subjected to Caesar

---

33 *VH*, 252. Förster ('Der Vercelli-Codex,' 77) stated that 'Die altenglische Übersetzung ist übrigens meist so wörtlich, daß sie stellenweise zur Textrekonstruktion verwandt werden kann.' ('Incidentally, the Old English translation is so literal that it can be used as a witness in places for reconstructing the source-text.')

34 There are other kinds of alteration, of course, but these categories capture many of them.

[*subjecti Cesari* **V**; *subiecta Ces(s)aris* **MP**] as they had been before' as 'and they will be subjugated in their cities as they had been before' ('7 hie beoð on hiora ceastrum underðeodde swa hie ær wæron,' ll. 13–14). It is possible that his manuscript read *castris for cesari(s)*, or (as Scragg suggests) that *ceastrum* is a scribal substitution induced by the appearance of the same word later in the sentence. But in another passage the homilist translates a reference to a 'golden image of Caesar' ('imaginem aureum Cesaris' **P**; **M**'s *i. a. cesserit* is an obvious error) simply as a 'golden image' (*gyldene anlicnesse*, l. 33), so it is more likely that he purposely deleted both references. Elsewhere he leaves untranslated (or translates only in very generic terms) references to specifically Roman civil offices for which there was no Anglo-Saxon equivalent. Thus, he renders *priores urbium* ['leaders of cities' = *curiales*?] simply as *manige men* (l. 16),[35] and he reduces the sequence 'Reges terrae et principes et tribuni et omnes locuples commouebuntur' (**M**; *om.* **PW**: 'The kings of the earth and princes and tribunes and all the wealthy will be troubled') to *eorðcyninge* (l. 50 'earthly king'), passing over *principes* as well as the more specifically Roman *tribuni*.[36]

(2) *Explanatory and summarizing statements.* Occasionally the homilist makes explicit the implicit causal relation between two statements in the Latin source. After the reference to the 'golden image of Caesar' being placed in the churches, for example, the Latin has an independent clause 'Tunc abundabunt martyria' (**P**: 'then martyrdoms will abound'); the homilist translates this as 'Bið þonne on þa tid martyra genihtsumnesse' and then explains why there will be an abundance of martyrs: 'for ðam þingum þæt man cwelmeð þa mæran þe nellað gebiddan to ðam hæðenan onlicnesse' (ll. 34–6: 'because they kill the glorious persons who are not willing to pray to the heathen image').[37] Again, on the fifth day the Latin states that angels will be looking down upon the earth and that all men will flee into the

---

35 For the tentative equation with *curiales* see R.W. Burgess, 'Hydatius and the Final Frontier: The Fall of the Roman Empire and the End of the World,' in *Shifting Frontiers in Late Antiquity*, ed. R.W. Mathisen and H.S. Sivan (Aldershot: Variorum, 1996), 332. Otto B. Schlutter, 'Some Remarks on Max Förster's Print of Some Old English Homilies Contained in *Vercelli Codex XCVII*,' *Neophilologus* 15 (1929): 268, suggests that the homilist's text may have read 'plures [scil. homines] urbium.'

36 The Latin list of rulers is, however, drawn from Apoc. 6:15. While the homilist has an equivalent for *reges terrae*, he makes *eorðcyninge* dative singular and attaches it to the previous sentence, as if his Latin source read *regi terrae*, as Förster indeed reconstructed it.

37 **M**'s corrupt 'una audauit martyria' suggests an original * 'unde habundabunt martyria'; if so, the homilist's 'for þam þingu' may have been prompted by *unde*.

mountains to hide themselves; the homilist translates this closely but also spells out the obvious affective cause of their flight: '7 þonne ealle men æfter þan sona mid mycle egesan swiðe geþreade beoð ...' (ll. 121–2: 'and then all men immediately thereafter will be very oppressed with great fear ...').

In two cases the homilist specifies which signs will occur on the day before Judgment Day. The first of these, following the signs of Saturday, is unproblematic, since this is the last day (Monday being the first) preceding the Sunday of Judgment.[38] Directly addressing *Broðor mine*, he concludes the sequence by explaining that 'þis sindon þæs Sæternesdæges tacno, 7 þa mihtlican þa þe geweorðað ær ðam myclan dryhtnes domes dæge' (ll. 135–7: 'these are the signs of Saturday, and the powerful ones that will take place before the great day of the Judgment of the Lord').[39] Curiously, however, the homilist had earlier stipulated that the dissension between the two kings and brothers would happen on the day before Judgment Day: '7 þæt gewyrðeð on þam dæge ær se mycla dæg bio' (ll. 9–10: 'and that will happen on the day before the great day [of Judgment]'). This is one of the signs from the non-interpolated version, but in the interpolated version and in Vercelli XV it is followed by the rise and fall of several other kings, all of whose reigns must precede the week leading up to Judgment, the homilist's relative chronology is impossible, and inscrutable.

(3) *Rhetorical embellishments*.[40] These tend to be opportunistic rather than independent; that is, the homilist usually works off something that directly translates the Latin, but simultaneously evokes an established vernacular rhetorical device, which he then develops. The simplest form of embellishment takes the form of synonymous doublets, a recurrent feature of 'rhythmical prose' in Old English homilies, as Otto Funke has shown, though many of the homilist's doublets do not alliterate.[41] Funke

---

38 On the sequence of days in Vercelli XV and the other OE versions of *Thomas*, see Wright, 'Some New Latin Texts,' 42.

39 The homilist also marks the end of the first day by saying 'These are the signs of Monday,' and he concludes the description of each succeeding day (except for Friday) with a similar summarizing statement. The non-abbreviated Latin texts (except for **W**) have corresponding comments 'Ista sunt signa primae (secundae, etc.) diei' at the end of each day, but among the abbreviated texts only **E** does so consistently, though **H** also does for the first three days and **O** does for the second, fourth, and seventh.

40 By 'rhetorical embellishments' I refer only to added material that is couched in a heightened rhetorical form; naturally there are various rhetorical effects (such as alliteration) in the homilist's rendering of the Latin, but these would have to be the subject of another study.

41 Funke, 'Studien zur alliterierenden und rhythmisierenden Prosa in der älteren altenglischen Homiletik,' *Anglia* 80 (1962): 33.

cites three examples from Vercelli XV (l. 25, 'gewitene 7 oftogene'; l. 64, 'winnað 7 swincað'; l. 95, 'gefealden 7 tolesen'), and there are others (l. 24, 'gewiteð 7 forwyrðeð'; l. 63, 'tiliað 7 strynað').[42] There are also paired items that involve more loosely related terms (l. 101, 'geseon 7 witan'; l. 102, 'ure lareowas 7 ure boceras'; l. 106, 'sægde 7 lærde'; l. 124, 'oferfeallen 7 bewrigen'; ll. 126–7, 'gesceapen wæs 7 geworden'). In the section following the part dependent upon *Thomas*, the homilist pairs *sarig* and *dreorig* no fewer than three times (ll. 143, 150–1, 162).

Occasionally the homilist constructs more elaborate lists of synonyms employing homoeoteleuton. The sign *mycel geomrung* (l. 81, 'great lamentation' = *murmur magnum*), for example, is extended with a series of synonyms rhyming on *–ung*: '7 þær bið mycel wanung 7 granung 7 murnung 7 sworetung' (ll. 81–2: 'and there will be great lamentation and groaning and complaint and moaning'). The Corpus 41 homilist in translating the same sign employs a doublet ('gnornung 7 geomrung'), and similar doublets and occasionally longer runs similar to the Vercelli homilist's are common in vernacular descriptions of hell, often in contexts where *geomrung* translates *fletus* in the biblical phrase 'fletus et stridor dentium' ('weeping and gnashing of teeth,' Mt. 8:12, 13.42; Lk. 13:28).[43] The rhyming doublet 'wanung 7 granung' (or in reverse order) is particularly common. The Vercelli homilist himself employs a similar run (again including

---

42　A search of the *DOE Corpus* indicates that these are not common pairings, but 'winnað and swincað' occurs in Assmann XIV (pairings of the nouns *gewinn* and *geswinc* are more common); 'sægde 7 lærde' occurs in Bede 4, 'secgan and læran' in HomM 14.2.

43　A *DOE Corpus* proximity search (Fragmentary) of *wanung* near *granung* yields 10 matches, excluding Vercelli XV, e.g., HomS 42 (Baz–Cr) 28 and 47, 'mycele wanunge and granunga and geomerunga;' 'wanung and granung and toða gristbitung'; HomM 8 (Murfin) 70, 'Ne þær naht elles nis gehyred butan wanung 7 granung 7 grisbitung of toþe'; HomU 15 (Robinson) 19, 'geomrung and þoterung ... granung and gnornung'); HomU 35.1 (Nap 42) 290, 'þær is sorgung and sargung and a singal heof; ... þær is wanung and granung'); WHom 13.86, 'ðær is sorgung 7 sargung, 7 a singal heof; þær is wanung 7 granung.' Particularly interesting is a line in a Doomsday sequence in HomU32, edited as poetry by E.G. Stanley, '*The Judgement of the Damned* (from Cambridge, Corpus Christi College 201 and Other Manuscripts), and the Definition of Old English Verse,' in *Learning and Literature in Anglo-Saxon England*, ed. Michael Lapidge and Helmut Gneuss (Cambridge: CUP, 1985), 384, l. 25: 'hæþenra granung 7 reafera wanung,' where *reafera wanung* seems to have been substituted for *heriga fyll* in the corresponding passage in Vercelli II and XXI, probably owing to the influence of this stock collocation, as Stanley (388) suggests. Some additional examples with other words ending in *–ung* can be found by means of a proximity search (fragmentary) of *ung & + ung*. For examples in Wulfstan, see Andy Orchard, 'Crying Wolf: Oral Style and the *Sermones Lupi*,' *ASE* 21 (1992): 248.

'wanunge 7 granunge') in a later part of the homily (ll. 187–9) not depend-ent upon *Thomas*: 'Eala, broðor mine, hwæt, ðær mæg gehyran micel sorh 7 mycel wanung 7 mycel sworetung 7 mycel wop 7 toða gristbitung 7 þone hludestan sarigcerm 7 þone sarigestan stefn 7 þone sarigestan wanunge 7 granunge' ('Alas, my brothers, lo, there one may hear great sorrow and great lamentation and great moaning and great weeping and gnashing of teeth and the loudest cry of pain and the most sorrowful lamentation and groaning').[44]

In addition to lists employing homoeoteleuton, the homilist also con-structs anaphoric lists. He concretizes the abstract Latin phrase *talia qua-lia* ('such things,' referring to the terrors of the Friday before Judgment), for example, with a sequence based on *þyllic* that employs an alliterating doublet, *weorc*[45] and *wite* (though the terms are separated by a third, non-alliterating element): 'þyllic weorc 7 þyllic egesa 7 þyllic wite' (ll. 126–7: 'such pain and such terror and such torment').[46] In his list of 'young' of-ficials whose vices contribute to the evils of the last days (discussed more fully below, 172) he repeats the adjective *iung* four times: '7 on iunge cyn-ingas 7 on iungan papan 7 on iungum bisceopum 7 on iungum ealdor-mannum' (ll. 7–8: 'and in young kings and young popes and young bishops and young ealdormen').

Another kind of rhetorical embellishment involves *Wa bið* and *Wa þam þe* exclamations, but I will discuss the relevant passages under the headings 'moralizing asides' and 'authenticating devices.'

---

44 Funke ('Studien,' 30) draws attention to these two passages. In his note on the latter
    passage (*VH*, 265) Scragg draws attention to grammatical difficulties and also the
    repetition of *wanung*, and suggests that the words *micel sorh* to *gristbitung* 7 are a
    scribal addition; yet the similarity with the previous list suggests that the sequence is
    authorial, if perhaps corrupted in transmission. It is, however, possible that both lists
    were added at some point in the transmission of the homily.

45 Scragg apparently takes *weorc* as the neuter noun meaning 'deed, action,' which is
    certainly possible in view of the Latin 'Fiunt talia qualia nunquam facta sunt'; but the
    parallelism with *egesa* and *wite* suggests it is the Anglian masculine noun *wærc* ('pain').
    Cf. R.D. Fulk, 'Old English *weorc*: Where Does It Hurt? South of the Thames,' *ANQ*
    17.2 (Spring 2004): 6–12. Somewhat surprisingly, the pair *weorc/wærc* and *wite* is not
    very common, but there are a few examples in both poetry and prose (*Genesis A* ll. 1040
    and 2746; *Genesis B* l. 292; LawWi B14.3.2).

46 Parallel phrases built on *þyllic* occur in HomU 40 (Nap 50) 182; PPs (prose) 10.7;
    LawIICn 7.1. The word *þyllic* seems to have been a favourite of the homilist's, as he
    uses it three more times in another passage of his own composition, the 'speech of men
    alive at Doomsday' (see 169 below).

(4) *Biblical additions and doctrinal emendations.* In at least two instances the homilist adds biblical material. When translating a reference to the darkening of the sun and moon, for example, he is reminded of Job 3:4 ('dies ille vertatur in tenebras,' 'that day will be turned to darkness') and adds the phrase '7 eall hit bið on þeostra gecyrred' (l. 58: 'and it will all be turned to darkness'). In response to the signs of Friday, men flee into the mountains to hide themselves from the angels (or from the 'powers of heaven'), and implore the earth to open up and swallow them ('Utinam terra aperiret se et deglutiret nos' **N**; the readings of the other manuscripts vary somewhat, but only **NPRHEO** have a form of *deglutire* or *conglutire*). The homilist translates this exclamation fairly closely (ll. 122–5; with –*glutiret* cf. *forswelge*),[47] but recognizes the parallel with Apoc. 6:15–16 and brings it more closely into line with the biblical text by omitting the reference to the angels or powers of heaven (in the Apocalypse men are said to flee instead 'from the face of the one sitting on the throne and from the wrath of the lamb') and by having the men also beg the mountains and hills to fall upon and cover them so they might no longer live ('We halsiað eow, muntas 7 dena, þæt ge us oferfeallen 7 bewrigen, þæt we næfre eft cwice sien,' ll. 123–4; cf. Apoc. 6:16 'et dicunt montibus et petris cadite super nos'; Lk. 23:30 [= Hos. 10:8] 'tunc incipient dicere montibus cadite super nos et collibus operite nos').[48]

Given his apparent credence in his source as the revealed words of Christ, the homilist's willingness to alter subtly the divine name that Christ bestows upon himself in the first-person proclamation 'ego sum pater omnium spirituum' is remarkable. Instead of translating *pater* (in all surviving Latin versions that include the speech) directly with *fæder*, he substitutes *nerigend*: 'ic eom ... eallra gasta nerigend' ('I am ... the saviour of all spirits,' ll. 72–3). Evidently conscious of the dubious trinitarian implications of Christ's terming himself the 'father of all spirits,'[49] he substitutes a standard

---

47 As noted above (162), however, he makes explicit the fear that motivates their flight; he also adds to their exclamation the clause 'þæt we næfre eft cwice arisan,' repeated almost verbatim from the previous line, 'þæt we næfre eft cwice sien' (there is no corresponding phrase in *Thomas* or in the biblical sources for these exclamations).

48 Blickling VII, ed. Richard Morris, *The Blickling Homilies of the Tenth Century*, EETS o.s. 58, 63, 73 (1874–80; repr. one vol., London: OUP, 1967), 93, l. 33, similarly adds, 'and þonne hie cweþaþ to þæm dunum and to þæm hyllum: "Feallaþ ofor us, and us bewreoþ and gehydað ..."'

49 De Santos Otero, in Hennecke-Schneemelcher, *New Testament Apocrypha*, 2: 751n5, compares the phrase *tu animarum pater* in a Priscillianist tract. Heb. 12:9 uses the term *pater spirituum* for God the Father.

(though primarily poetic) Christological epithet, perhaps borrowed from the popular homily Vercelli X, which uses the same expression.[50] Yet he has just insisted that the *ic eom* speech is 'the utterance of the mouth of the almighty Lord himself' (l. 71). How did the homilist reconcile such an intervention in what he evidently regarded as the *ipsissima uerba* of Christ, to the extent of a divine name change? Presumably he felt that translating *pater* as *nerigend* was not a falsification, but a legitimate equivalent (one perhaps authorized by the dogma of *communicatio idiomatum* as well as Christ's statement 'Ego et Pater unum sumus,' Jn 10:30: 'I and the Father are one') that would neither require explanation nor risk scandalizing the more doctrinally competent members of his audience.

(5) *Moralizing asides.* These are mostly of a very general kind, such as 'for þan hie þonne bioð forlætene þonne sio tid cymeð' (ll. 68–9, 'for that reason they will be forsaken when that time comes'), and 'For ðan manegum men bið swiðe mycel nydþearf ær þære tide þæt hie to Gode gehwyrfen' (ll. 75–6, 'for many men therefore there is very great need that they turn to God before that time'). In both of these cases the homilist uses a *for ðan*-clause to subordinate his own comment to a passage from his source. Syntactically independent additions are usually brief, such as the clauses '7 Godes æwe beoð gefylde' (l. 18, 'and God's law will be overthrown') and '7 he sylf mid forwyrðeð!' (l. 66, 'and he will perish himself at the same time'), the latter added to a 'Wa þam mannum' ('Woe to the men') exclamation, apparently to clarify that the fire will not only burn up houses and lands but their inhabitants as well.

The homilist's more substantial moralizing asides take the rhetorical form of 'Wa ðam þe' or 'Wa us' exclamations. This was a well-established feature of vernacular homiletic rhetoric,[51] and there are also some poetic examples (*Beowulf* 183b, *The Wife's Lament* 52b, and *Solomon and Saturn* 327).[52]

---

50 Vercelli X, l. 20: 'ealra gasta nerigend' (part of a list of divine epithets). The word *ner(i)-gend* has a poetic flavour, occurring only rarely in OE prose.

51 Andy Orchard, *A Critical Companion to 'Beowulf'* (Cambridge: D.S. Brewer, 2003), 153n112, cites Blickling Homily V, l. 104; Napier XXX, ll. 99 and 203; and Napier XLIV, l. 345. Further examples can be accessed in the *DOE Corpus* by a simple search for the Latin word *vae* (*uae/ ve*) and of *wa* [the spelling *wae* is rare outside the Lindisfarne and Rushworth Gospels] + *bið/ biþ*, *eow*, *þe/ ðe*, and *us*. Many of the Old English prose examples are modelled directly on Latin *Vae tibi/uobis/illi(s)/qui* phrases in the Bible and the Fathers.

52 See Haruko Momma, 'The "Gnomic Formula" and Some Additions to Bliss's Old English Metrical System,' *NQ* n.s. 36 (1989): 423–6 (I owe this reference to Andy

But even here the homilist has followed a cue in his source, for his 'Wa þam þe' exclamations echo an initial series of 'Wa þam mannum' exclamations (ll. 60–8) based on Latin *Vae illis* imprecations (found in **MP** alone). The homilist builds on this rhetorical precedent later, first at the conclusion of the signs of Wednesday, and then at the conclusion of the signs of Friday. Both cases involve speeches by men who witness the signs of the days in question. In the speech concluding the signs of Friday, the homilist translates the content of the speech fairly closely except for adding the anaphoric list noted above that expands the Latin phrase *talia qualia*. He then caps the speech off with his own third-person exclamation 'Wa ðam þe ðis eal sceal gebidan' (l. 111: 'Woe to him who must experience all this'), intended to suggest that, since the end is near, anyone (including those in his audience) might experience these terrors and find themselves saying similar things.

The homilist's most elaborate addition, also built upon a sequence of first-person *Wa us* exclamations, comes in the 'speech of men alive at Doomsday,' but since the speech as a whole serves as a dramatic authenticating device, it will be discussed under the next heading.

(6) *Authenticating devices.* Several of the homilist's substantive interventions reveal his concern to authenticate the content of the revelation. When translating Christ's *ego sum* speech,[53] the homilist may be responsible for the redundant introductory clause, which has no parallel in the Latin: 'Þis is þonne þæs ælmihtigan dryhtnes sylfes muðes cwide, ⁊ he ðus wæs cweðende' (ll. 71–2, 'This then is the utterance of the mouth of the almighty Lord himself, and he was saying as follows ...'). Nor is there any Latin parallel for the direct-speech introduction ('Þæt is soð þæt ic secge ...,' l. 73: 'That is true what I say ...') to Christ's statement 'ealle þas tacenu bioð æt þysse worulde

---

Orchard). The formula Momma discusses includes a variety of substitutions both positive and negative (*Wel bið/ Eadig bið; Dol bið/ Earm bið*; etc.). For the positive form Momma suggests the Beatitudes as a possible source, but does not rule out vernacular origins.

53 In Scragg's punctuation the conclusion of the *ego sum* speech, '⁊ eac bið swiðe mycel hungor ⁊ swiðe micle adle ofer ealle eorðan' (ll. 74–5) marks the end of Christ's discourse, but in the Latin the entire apocalypse, including the list of the signs of the seven days preceding Judgment, is part of Christ's discourse (or letter). It is true that in Vercelli XV there are shifts in 'focalization,' notably when the homilist slips into his own voice and addresses the audience with the phrase 'Broðor mine ...' (l. 135, as he does also in the second half of the homily, ll. 187 and 198); but I think we are still to understand that the revelation as a whole is in Christ's own words (as the punctuation of Förster and Szarmach implies).

ende geætywde' ('all these signs will be revealed at the end of this world' =
PMW *Haec [Septem haec* **M**] *sunt signa in fine [finitionem* **MW**] *seculi huius*).
Given the homilist's manifest respect for his source – authorized as it was by
the apostle Thomas and preserving in direct speech Christ's prophecies regarding the Last Judgment – it may seem bold of him to have put words in
His mouth; yet the homilist is merely invoking a phrase that Christ often
uses in the Gospels to introduce a prophetic utterance, *Amen dico uobis* ...,
which is generally translated in Old English as 'soð ic eow secge ...' The purpose of these added clauses is clearly to reinforce the authenticity of Christ's
speech against potential doubters.

The fact that Thomas was a famous doubter convinced only by a physical sign granted him by Christ makes him an ideal vehicle for a revelation
of the Signs of Judgment, and particularly for a homily that challenges
those who would doubt the revelation itself. Vercelli XV is the only one of
the four OE versions that identifies its source as a revelation of Christ to
Thomas,[54] and the only surviving version of *Thomas* that specifies that
Christ's revelation was prompted by a question from Thomas concerning
when the Antichrist would appear ('se halga Thomas, Godes apostol, ac-
sode urne dryhten hwænne Antecristes cyme wære,' ll. 1–2). Corpus 41
introduces the apocalypse with the generic *Sægeð*, whose subject is either
impersonal or is to be understood as 'the book,' while the authors of
Blickling VII and Bazire–Cross 3 assume the text's authority in their own
voice.[55] Apocalyptic revelations do sometimes take the form of a reply by
Christ to questions by one or more apostles,[56] and the version of *Thomas*
known to the Vercelli homilist may have attempted to clarify the context
of Christ's speech by assimilating it to this established tradition (or the
homilist may have done so himself).

The 'speech of men alive at Doomsday,' which concludes the signs of
Wednesday, is the homilist's only extended addition (longer than a single
clause or short sentence) to his source. As Scragg notes,[57] this speech expands considerably on a brief sentence in the Latin, the formulation of

---

54 In **NBVMPT** the revelation begins *Audi Thomas* ..., but with no indication that Thomas
    has asked anything. **P** alone introduces Christ's statement with *Iesus dixit Thomas [de]*
    dii iudicii, which corresponds generally to 'Ða wæs dryhten sprecende to him 7 ðus
    cwæð ...' (l. 3).
55 Blickling Homily VII, ed. Morris, 95–7; Bazire–Cross 3, in *Eleven Old English*
    Rogationtide Homilies, ed. Joyce Bazire and J.E. Cross (Toronto: UTP, 1982), 49–50.
56 E.g., the Questions of Bartholomew and the Apocalypse of Peter (trans. James, *New*
    Testament Apocrypha, 167 and 511–12).
57 *VH*, 252n2.

which varies considerably in the manuscripts. In the non-abbreviated versions men exclaim that the end is at hand and they will perish; **N** couches this statement in the first-person plural, 'Putamus finis adpropinquabit ut pereamus' ('We think that the end is near, that we shall die') while **PMW** combine the first-person singular *Puto* with the first-person plural *pereamus*. In Vercelli XV we have instead a series of three first-person *Wa us* exclamations, the second of which corresponds generally in content to the Latin, though this time the Latin does *not* involve an analogous *Vae nobis* formula: '7 nu we magon geseon 7 witan witodlice ðæt nu nealæceð ure endedæge ...' (ll. 100–10: 'and now indeed we can see and understand that now our day of death approaches'). The homilist then concludes the speech with a third-person exclamation almost identical to the one that concludes the speech of men on Friday: 'Wa ðam þe ðæt eall sceal gebidan' (l. 128: 'Woe to him who has to experience all that').

The unanimous testimony of the surviving Latin texts suggests that this expanded speech was never part of the Latin tradition of *Thomas*; it is a late homiletic insertion made either by the Vercelli homilist's immediate source or more likely by the homilist himself. The men who witness the signs of Judgment are made to regret (explicitly and repetitively) their previous mockery when *lareowas* and *boceras* ('teachers' and 'scholars') had tried to forewarn them:

7 þonne cweðað ealle men: 'Wa us nu earmingas 7 swa synfullan þæt we æfre þis sceoldon gebidan. Wa us þæs þæt we æfre gestrynde wæron oððe geborene. 7 nu we magon geseon 7 witan witodlice ðæt nu nealæceð ure endedæge, swa us oft sægdon ða ðe ure lareowas 7 ure boceras wæron, þæt ðas tacno sceoldon cuman þe we nu geseoð 7 gyt sceolon, 7 we him dydon to bysmere ða hie us þillic sægdon. Wa us nu earmingas þæt we nu lifiað to lange on swylcum ege þæs we næfre ne wendon, þonne man us oft þyllic toweard sægde 7 lærde hu we sceoldon to Gode gecyrran 7 ure earman sawle alysan of helle wite. Ac we his ne rohton, ac we lufedon micle swiðor ura wamba fylnesse 7 on ure gold 7 on ure glengnesse 7 on ure myclan gestreone 7 on reaflacum 7 on gitsunge. Swiðor we þæt lufedon þonne we dydon Godes beboda, 7 þyllic þe we nu geseoð.' (ll. 98–111)

[And then all men will say: 'Woe to us wretches and men so sinful that we ever had to experience this. Woe to us that we were ever conceived or born. And now we are able to perceive and truly know that our last day approaches, as those who were our teachers and scholars often told us that these signs would come which we see now and are yet to see, but we mocked them when they said such things to us. Woe to us wretches that we now live too long in such terror as we never expected, when we were often forewarned and taught how we should turn to God and redeem our poor souls from hell torment. But we didn't care about it, but much rather loved the fullness of our bellies and our gold and our adornment and our great treasure and plundering and avarice. We loved [to do] that rather than fulfil God's commandments, and such things as we now see.']

Himself one of the *lareowas* who warns his congregation of the signs of Judgment, the homilist pre-empts anyone who would mock his own authority by placing sceptical statements in the mouths of men who discover too late the truth of the prophecies they had scorned. Warnings of the terrors of the last days are his primary strategy for motivating penance and reform, but that strategy is staked upon the audience's literal acceptance of the revelation and its imminent (yet not precisely dated) fulfilment. There is obvious irony in the fact that he defends the literal veracity of his source by falsifying it; yet it is only in this speech that he makes an extended substantive addition. Moreover, as Scragg points out, even here the homilist repeats words and phrases from earlier translated passages (including the *Wa* formula he had already used in translating the Latin *Vae illis* sequence). That he himself considered the apocalypse to be literally true is suggested by his close translation even of obscure (and textually corrupt) prophecies that he could not possibly have understood. The signs of Judgment demand literal acceptance, and the homilist adds no new signs of his own (though he seems to have allowed himself one very significant embellishment in his list of corrupt 'young' officials).[58] The speech of men alive at Doomsday, however, like the later speech concluding the signs of Friday, is not itself a sign, but is merely representative of what men will say in response to the appearance of the signs. This leaves the homilist free to imagine what else might be said, and he exploits the opening to forestall scepticism concerning the text he is translating.

(7) *Politically motivated and possibly topical revisions.* The homilist's most tendentious alterations to his source occur within a sequence castigating 'masspriests' (= *sacerdotes*), where he not only adds condemnations of their wealth (*wela*) and perverted teaching (*lar*) not found in the surviving Latin manuscripts, but also twice shifts the burden of guilt assigned in the Latin to the people (*populus*) to the masspriests instead. The first part of the homilist's prophecy of the masspriests' corruption corresponds to a

---

58   He may also have suppressed the signs of the fifth day in order to fit the entire sequence into one week; see Wright, 'Some New Latin Texts,' 41.

series of statements in the interpolated texts, the first of which does not refer specifically to the *sacerdotes*: 'each one will say whatever pleases him' ('unusquisque quod illi placet loquatur' **VP**; also **MW** with minor variants). The next two statements in the Latin *do* refer to the *sacerdotes*: 'My priests/bishops will not have peace among themselves' (*inter se* **VM**; *in terre* **PW**); and 'they will sacrifice to me with a deceitful mind.' The Vercelli homilist makes the subject of all three statements *minra mæssepreosta*, who 'please each another [*ælc oðrum*] in their speech, do not maintain peace among themselves [*him betweonum*, agreeing with **VM**] and sacrifice[59] to me with very deceitful mind' (ll. 9–13). The following statement, 'þonne gesyhð þæt folc þæt þa mæssepreostas bioð mid unriht gefyllede ymbe heora welan' ('then the people will see that the masspriests will be filled with injustice regarding their wealth,' ll. 13–14), differs radically from **MPVW**, which say that the *sacerdotes* 'will see the people' (*populum*, **MVW**) 'withdrawing from the house of God.' Förster accordingly emended P's corrupt 'uidebunt hominis sacerdotes' to 'uidebunt homines sacerdotes,' making *homines* the subject and *sacerdotes* the object; yet the change of subject may be due to the homilist, once again shifting the burden of guilt from the people to the masspriests. In any case, he seems to have introduced an entirely new complaint regarding the masspriests' wealth. Again, in lines 26–8, his statement '7 leasunga 7 gymeleasnessa Godes beboda bi[o]ð þonne gemeted on ðam mæssepreostum' ('and deception and heedlessness of God's commands will be encountered in the masspriests') recasts in more emphatically negative terms what the Latin phrases as a lack of a positive quality: 'priestly integrity will not be [or: will scarcely be] found' ('sacerdocium integrum non inuenietur' (**P**; *s. i. minime inuenitur* **M**, *s. i. minime inue*[*ni*]*tur* **W**). Finally, in the sequence '7 heora blis 7 heora lar bið eall to tælnesse geþeoded, 7 heora gefea gewiteð 7 forwyrðeð' (ll. 23–4: 'and their bliss and their teaching will be wholly applied to calumny, and their joy will pass away and perish') there is nothing corresponding to 'heora lar bið eall to tælnesse geþeoded' in the Latin ('laetitia periit et gaudium recedit' **M**, om. *et* **W**, om. *recedit* **P**: 'happiness will pass away and joy will disappear'). In the homilist's manuscript it is

---

59 Reading *ons*[*æcg*]*að* with Förster and Scragg (ms. *onsacað*). Since all Latin manuscripts have a form of *sacrificare*, the emendation is well founded; but *onsacan* is often used to translate Latin (*ab*)*negare* in contexts referring to denial of God (cf. Bosworth–Toller, s.v.), so the unemended form may have been understood this way by the Vercelli Book scribe and any subsequent readers. Alternatively, *onsacan* may be a variant form of *onsecgan*. Cf. the gloss *litaturus* for *onsacende*, ClGl 1 (cited from the *DOE Corpus*).

possible that the words *letitia periit* in the order **periit letitia* had generated a scribal error **peritia* (whence *lar*); but the extension appears to be another example of the homilist's intensification of his source's condemnation of *sacerdotes*.

To judge from these interventions it appears that the homilist wished to link apocalyptic expectation more closely to clerical corruption. The homilist's condemnation of the *wela* of masspriests[60] might reflect a Benedictine bias against secular clergy, but a non-monastic priest or bishop could also have been motivated to warn his own clergy of the spiritual danger of excess wealth, particularly at a time of crisis. (The example of Gildas's *De exidio Britanniae* suffices to show that a diatribe against a particular group's moral failings need not have been penned by their enemies.) The term *mæssepreostas*, in any case, directly translates *sacerdotes*.

Yet masspriests are not the homilist's only target. His statement that the vices of iniquity, malice, and envy will appear 'ofer eall middanngeard, 7 on iunge cyningas 7 on iungan papan 7 on iungum bisceopum 7 on iungum ealdormannum' (ll. 6–8) has no parallel in any surviving Latin version and is probably the homilist's addition, especially since there are no references to a 'pope' in any Latin version of *Thomas*, only to *sacerdotes* (which originally designated bishops as well as priests).[61] The fourfold repetition of the adjective *iung* is obtrusive, and appears calculated to draw attention to the homilist's specification of the more general warning in *Thomas*. Apparently the homilist viewed with alarm the prospect of the most senior lay and ecclesiastical offices being occupied by youthful (or perhaps 'new' and inexperienced?) tenants.[62] Assuming for the moment (with Scragg) that *iung* refers to age,[63] young kings would not be remarkable at any time, but the reference to 'young popes' seems rather pointed (not to

---

60 This seems the most likely interpretation of ll. 13–14 in context, but for an alternative possibility see n. 86 below.

61 The homilist consistently translates the term *sacerdotes* as *mæssepreostas*, and the surviving versions of *Thomas* never use the term *episcopus*, which would almost certainly have been the Latin equivalent for *bisceop* if the homilist were translating a Latin source at this point.

62 In the Latin the list of vices is followed by the statement that each person will say what is pleasing to him, but in Vercelli XV the vices are linked instead to these 'young' malefactors and represented as the cause of dissension between the two kings and two brothers: '7 þurh þæt þonne ariseð unsehtnesse betweoh twam cyningum 7 twam gebroðrum ...' (ll. 8–9, corresponding to the 'non-interpolated' reading 'Tunc erunt participationes in saeculo inter regem et regem'; see above, 158).

63 Scragg's glossary, s.v. *geong*, gives only the sense 'young.'

mention implausible) for a generic complaint, and the list smacks of the kind of 'vaticinia ex euentu' that this apocalyptic genre encourages. As the homilist's most substantive and concrete addition to the prophecies it may, therefore, be circumstantial rather than merely conventional.

At the time the Vercelli Book was written (about the middle of the second half of the tenth century), the unlikely circumstances prophesied had, indeed, quite recently obtained. Pope John XII was only eighteen when elevated to the papacy in 955 by Roman noblemen in fulfilment of a promise made to his father Alberic upon his death a year earlier. John's sexual depravity 'gave great scandal to Christendom.'[64] He died in 964 (reportedly of a stroke while in bed with a married woman) after having betrayed his former ally Otto I, who temporarily deposed him in 963. At the time, Otto was married to Edith, daughter of King Æthelstan, so these events would have been of considerable interest in Anglo-Saxon England. John's direct intervention in Anglo-Saxon ecclesiastical affairs was, moreover, dramatic and decisive, for he was the young pope who, at the behest of the then twenty-year-old King Edgar,[65] authorized the expulsion of the secular clerics from the Old Minster at Winchester. (I follow the consensus view that the papal letter to Edgar is probably genuine, but since it has been declared a forgery by Julia Barrow, I address the problem of its authenticity

---

64 Quotation from *The Oxford Dictionary of the Christian Church*, ed. F.L. Cross and E.A. Livingston, 3rd ed. (Oxford: OUP, 1997), 884. For John XII see also J.N.D. Kelly, *The Oxford Dictionary of Popes* (Oxford: OUP, 1986), 126–7. John's vices may have been exaggerated by his enemies, but I am concerned only with his contemporary reputation, not his actual character.

65 Edgar had become king in 959 at the age of sixteen. The Old English text 'King Edgar's Establishment of Monasteries,' ed. and trans. in D. Whitelock, M. Brett, and C.N.L. Brooke, *Councils & Synods with Other Documents Relating to the English Church, I: A.D. 871–1204* (Oxford: Clarendon Press, 1981), 146, is rather defensive regarding the king's youth, attributing the following expression of wonderment to the elders who remembered his predecessors: 'Hit is la formicel Godes wunder þæt þysum cildg-eongum cynincge þus gesundfullice eallu þing underþeodde synt on his cynelicum anwealde; his foregengan, þe geþungen wæron on ylde 7 on gleawscype swiþe bescawede 7 forewittige, [7] on ænegum gewinne earfoþwylde, næfre þisne andweald on swa micelre sibbe smyltnesse gehealdan ne mihton, naþor ne mid gefeohte, ne med scette' ('It is indeed a very great miracle of God that all things in his royal domain are thus prosperously subjected to this youthful king; his predecessors, who were mature in age and very prudent and farseeing in wisdom (and) hard to overcome in any strife, never could maintain this dominion in so great peace and tranquility, neither by battle, nor by tribute'). A king's youthfulness could cut both ways, of course; the *Anglo-Saxon Chronicle* (D, E) for 975 blames the 'anti-monastic reaction' during Edward's reign on the king's youth (*Councils & Synods*, 160).

in an appendix, below, 182–4). In moving against the clerks the young king Edgar also had the approval of his *witan*, which had assembled along with prominent ecclesiastics to consider the fate of the secular clergy in 964.[66] Edgar's *witan* included several young ealdormen appointed by Eadwig or Edgar between 956 and 962, among them Byrhtnoth (956–91) and Æthelwine *Dei amicus* (962–92), both prominent champions of the monks[67] (although another, Ælfhere of Mercia [956–83], was to lead the 'anti-monastic reaction' after Edgar's death in 975).

And what of 'young' bishops? Unfortunately, we do not know the dates of birth of any of the three major reforming bishops who acted in concert with Edgar and his *witan* against the clerks. Æthelwold was likely in his mid-fifties when consecrated as bishop of Winchester in 963,[68] but Oswald, who had been an 'adolescent' during the episcopacy of his uncle Oda (941–58),[69] must have been considerably younger, probably still in his thirties, when consecrated bishop of Worcester in 961. The case of Dunstan is vexed, but it is possible, perhaps even likely, that when first elevated to the episcopacy of London he had barely reached his thirties. The argument

---

66 See Eric John, 'The Beginning of the Benedictine Reform in England'; the main source for this meeting is Byrhtferth of Ramsey's *Vita S. Oswaldi* (997–1002), ed. J. Raine, *Historians of the Church of York*, 3 vols., Rolls Series 71 (London, 1879–94), 1: 427.

67 We naturally think of Byrhtnoth as the *eald geneat* who died heroically at Maldon in 991, but in the period 957–63 he was still a young man. D.G. Scragg, *The Battle of Maldon* (Manchester: Manchester University Press, 1981), 15, guesses that Byrhtnoth was born about 930, in which case he would have been in his mid-to-late twenties when appointed as ealdorman.

68 Æthelwold was born during the reign of Edmund (899–924), and was an *adolescens* during Æthelstan's reign (924–39). See *Wulfstan of Winchester: The Life of St Æthelwold*, ed. Michael Lapidge and Michael Winterbottom (Oxford: Clarendon Press, 1991), xlii–xliii. Even if we do not assume that Æthelwold was at least thirty when ordained priest (between 934/5 and 939), an *adolescentia* (normally reckoned as lasting from fourteen to twenty-eight, as Lapidge and Winterbottom note) would put him in his twenties during the 930s.

69 According to Byrhtferth of Ramsey, Oswald was raised in the household of his uncle Oda of Canterbury (archbishop from 941–58) as an *adolescens* and tutored there by the Frankish scholar Frithegod (active c. 950, apparently left England after Oda's death), *Vita S. Oswaldi*, ed. Raine, 410. On Frithegod's tutelage of Oswald see Michael Lapidge, 'A Frankish Scholar in Tenth-Century England: Frithegod of Canterbury / Fredegaud of Brioude,' *ASE* 17 (1988): 46–65; repr. in Lapidge, *Anglo-Latin Literature 900–1066* (London: Hambledon Press, 1993), 159 and n. 15. Byrhtferth reckons *adolescentia* as between fourteen and twenty-eight in the 'Ramsey Computus' diagram: *Byrhtferth's Enchiridion*, ed. Peter S. Baker and Michael Lapidge, EETS s.s. 15 (Oxford: OUP, 1995), 374.

compels me, in the words of John of Wallingford, to 'tug the rope of controversy' in a matter that John himself deemed *inutile*.[70]

Dunstan's birth is usually given as c. 909/10, mainly on the grounds that he should have been at least thirty when ordained as a priest, sometime prior to his election as abbot of Glastonbury (c. 940–6).[71] As Nicholas Brooks has noted, however, 'We certainly do not need to suppose that in appointing to the major churches of the kingdom, West Saxon kings were much concerned with canonical niceties in the early tenth century.'[72] Moreover, Dunstan's biographer B., writing in the decade 995–1005, states that Dunstan 'was born' (*oritur*) as a *puer strenuus* during the reign of Æthelstan (924–39).[73] Brooks has shown that 'there can be little doubt that B. meant that Dunstan was *born* whilst Athelstan was on the throne.'[74] As Brooks points out, 'it would then follow that Dunstan had been a youth of at most fourteen or fifteen when rejecting the attractions of the secular life and choosing to be professed as a monk; he would have been a young man of at most twenty-two when made abbot of Glastonbury.'[75] It would

---

70 'sed super hoc [the matter of Dunstan's birth], quia inutile est, non multum trahimus ex alterutraque parte funem' (quoted by J. Armitage Robinson, *The Times of Saint Dunstan* [Oxford: Clarendon Press, 1923], 93).

71 Wulfstan of Winchester informs us (c. 8) that Dunstan was ordained on the same day as Æthelwold: *Life of St Æthelwold*, ed. Lapidge and Winterbottom, xlii and 14n4, and above, n. 68.

72 N. Brooks, 'The Career of St Dunstan,' in *St Dunstan: His Life, Times and Cult*, ed. Nigel Ramsey, Margaret Sparks, and Tim Tatton-Brown (Woodbridge: Boydell Press, 1992), 5.

73 *Memorials of St. Dunstan*, ed. William Stubbs, Rolls Series 63 (London, 1874), 6. On B. see Michael Lapidge, 'B. and the *Vita S. Dunstani*,' in Lapidge, *Anglo-Latin Literature 900–1066*, 279–91. Lapidge (282) states that B. was 'almost certainly' wrong in placing Dunstan's birth in Æthelstan's reign, and speculates that this may have been due to his inability to locate any books regarding English kings prior to Æthelstan. A spirited defence of a birthdate c. 909 was made by Robinson, *The Times of Dunstan*, 92–5.

74 Brooks, 'The Career,' 3 (emphasis in the original). Leslie A. St. L. Toke, 'Some Notes on the Accepted Date of Saint Dunstan's Birth,' in *The Bosworth Psalter*, ed. F.A. Gasquet and Edmund Bishop (London: George Bell and Sons, 1908), 131–43, had argued that *oritur* refers only to Dunstan's coming into prominence during Æthelstan's reign; but Brooks points out that B. goes on to describe Dunstan's christening, naming, and childhood.

75 'The Career,' 5. The upper limit of twenty-two assumes his appointment to the abbacy came at the end of Edmund's reign (946). According to Wulfstan of Winchester (*Life of St Æthelwold*, ed. Lapidge and Winterbottom, 15), Æthelwold went to Glastonbury to study with 'abbot' Dunstan; this was presumably some time after Æthelstan's death on 27 October 939 (cf. Lapidge and Winterbottom, 14n4), but it is unclear how much later. Brooks concludes cautiously: 'In the absence of direct evidence we are unable to

also follow that Dunstan was no more than thirty-five when consecrated as archbishop of Canterbury in 959, having already been bishop of London and of Worcester.

B. knew Dunstan personally and had worked with him closely prior to 960, so his testimony cannot lightly be dismissed. It is, admittedly, difficult to square with the testimony of others that Dunstan was an old man by the 980s. In a poem written about 986, Abbo of Fleury describes him as a *senex* (in contrast to *iuuenes*, referring to his students); and again in his *Passio S. Eadmundi Regis et Martyris*, written at Dunstan's request while Abbo was at Ramsey (985–7), he refers to Dunstan's venerableness (*antiquitas*) and 'snow-white' hair.[76] Similarly, in the *Epistola specialis* to his *Narratio metrica de S. Swithuno* (992–4, revised after 996) Wulfstan of Winchester describes Dunstan as 'angelic with snowy-white hair' (*canicie niueus ... angelicus*) when the *witan* assembled in 980 to consecrate the foundations of Æthelwold's reconstructed Old Minster.[77] Had Dunstan been born in the first year of Æthelstan's reign (as asserted by eleventh-century additions to the *Anglo-Saxon Chronicle*),[78] he would have been sixty-two in 986, and may well have been white-haired by his late fifties; but *senectus* was usually reckoned to begin at seventy.[79]

Let us assume for the moment, however, that B. was right in placing Dunstan's birth during the reign of Æthelstan. In that case Dunstan must have been ordained uncanonically, for even if he was born in 924, he would have been made a priest some time between the ages of eleven and fifteen, depending on the exact date of his ordination (934/5–9). Now, in the late 930s, as Brooks suggests, the early dedication to a clerical career of a highly recommended youth belonging to an influential family may not have

---

determine whether B. failed to indicate Dunstan's youthfulness when he entered the monastic life and when he was made abbot, or whether he was misinformed about the time of his birth' (5).

76 See Abbo's poem 'Summe sacer,' l. 26, ed. Scott Gwara, 'Three Acrostic Poems by Abbo of Fleury,' *JMLat* 2 (1992): 216 (for the date of the poem, see 205n15); and for the *Passio Eadmundi*, *Three Lives of English Saints*, ed. Michael Winterbottom (Toronto: PIMS, 1972). In the *Passio*, Abbo refers to an incident when Dunstan was a *iunior* during Æthelstan's reign, but unfortunately does not specify in what part of his reign it occurred.

77 Wulfstan's *Narratio* is edited by Michael Lapidge, *The Cult of St Swithun*, Winchester Studies 4.ii (Oxford: Clarendon Press, 2003), 376 (l. 72); I owe this reference to Professor Lapidge.

78 See Toke, 'Some Notes,' who shows that the references to the date of Dunstan's birth as 924/5 in manuscripts of the Anglo-Saxon *Chronicle* are later insertions.

79 Isidore, *Etymologiae* XI.ii.3, ed. W.M. Lindsay (Oxford: Clarendon Press, 1911).

been extraordinary or scandalous. But by 959, when Dunstan (still under thirty-five, and a vocal opponent of clerical irregularity) was consecrated archbishop of Canterbury, his non-canonical ordination would be a potentially embarrassing skeleton in his closet. Of course, the reigning pope was in no position to deny him the pallium on that account (and was willing to countenance his pluralities); but canonical irregularities in Dunstan's own career would hardly have been viewed charitably by his clerical adversaries.[80] If we accept this scenario – which seems inescapable if B. was right about Dunstan's birth – then later references by Benedictine partisans to Dunstan's advanced age in the early 980s could well have been defensive rear-guard efforts to quash any lingering gossip. If by that time Dunstan was in his late fifties or early sixties and grey-haired, this might even have seemed plausible.[81]

The reference to 'young' bishops in Vercelli XV could thus be a polemical salvo aimed at Dunstan and Oswald, both perhaps still in their late thirties, or just barely forty, in 964. OE *iung/geong* can, of course, also mean 'new,' 'fresh,' or 'inexperienced,' 'raw,'[82] and in that sense the political and ecclesiastical regime in Anglo-Saxon England in 964 was decidedly *iung*: Edgar became king of Mercia and Northumbria in 957, but king of the English only in 959; Dunstan was installed as archbishop in the same year (having been appointed to the sees of London and Worcester just two years earlier), while Oswald and Æthelwold became bishops still later, in 961 and 963 respectively. The *witan* with whom the king and his bishops met in 964 included several ealdormen appointed by Edgar or Eadwig. The secular clergy observing (and protesting) the events of 963/4 must surely have felt that the old establishment had been swept away by 'new men' who had the support of a young pope – one who had looked the other way

---

80 Dunstan was in fact criticized by a secular canon for his pluralities, requiring his biographers to concoct some very resourceful justifications for a circumstance it was impossible to deny.

81 B. was himself a secular canon who had resided in Liège during the period of the expulsions. His *Vita*'s innocent candour regarding Dunstan's date of birth may have been one of the reasons that B. failed to gain the patronage he sought. Adelard's drastically revised version (before 1012; ed. Stubbs, *Memorials*, xxx–xxxi, xli–xlii) omits the reference to Dunstan's birth. For the suggestion that B. had returned to England before Dunstan's death, see Michael Winterbottom, 'The Earliest Life of St Dunstan,' *Scripta Classica Israelica* 19 (2000): 163–79; Lapidge believes that he spent the remainder of his career at Liège.

82 On the semantic range see Heiner Bouwer, *Studien Zum Wortfeld um* eald *und* niwe *im Altenglischen* (Heidelberg: Carl Winter, 2004), 347–70. Bower focuses primarily on poetry and interlinear glosses, and does not refer specifically to this passage in Vercelli XV.

with respect to Dunstan's pluralities and then signed off on his agreement with Edgar and his ealdormen to deprive them of their livings.

A topical allusion to the Benedictine Reform, and specifically to the expulsions of the clerks by King Edgar, Pope John XII, Archbishop Dunstan, and Edgar's ealdormen, would require dating the homily after 964 (unless the allusion were interpolated), leaving at most a decade or two between its composition and its copying in the Vercelli Book. There is no internal evidence for an earlier date, though there are some textual corruptions in the Vercelli Book copy that suggest it is more than one remove from the original, and if Scragg's conclusions about the origins of the homily and of the Vercelli Book itself are sound, we have to allow time for a copy of an Anglian text to make its way to a library in the south-east.[83] This need not have required more than one or two decades, however, and the reference to 'young popes' is explicable historically only after the election of John in 955. Since Mercia was at the centre of the 'anti-monastic reaction' in 975,[84] it would not be surprising to encounter a negative perspective on the expulsions and confiscations in an Anglian homily written after 964. The suggestion should not be pressed; but even if Vercelli XV was composed before the Reform and the reigns of Edgar and John XII, its references to the iniquity, malice, and envy of young/new kings, popes, bishops, and ealdormen might readily be *interpreted* topically by readers after 964, particularly if, as Eamonn Ó Carragáin has argued, the Vercelli Book was a compilation for secular canons.[85] For such readers, as members of the clerical estates victimized (from their point of view) by the Benedictine Reform expulsions and confiscations, there would no doubt be satisfaction in defining their opponents apocalyptically.[86]

---

83 See *VH*, lxxiv–lxxix, 252 and n. 4; and Scragg's earlier essay 'The Compilation of the Vercelli Book,' *ASE* 2 (1973): 189–207, repr. in *Anglo-Saxon Manuscripts: Basic Readings*, ed. Mary Richards (New York: Garland, 1994), 317–43 (here 335–6).

84 See D.J.V. Fisher, 'The Anti-Monastic Reaction in the Reign of Edward the Martyr,' *Cambridge Historical Journal* 10 (1950–2): 254–70.

85 Ó Carragáin, 'Rome, Ruthwell, Vercelli: "The Dream of the Rood" and the Italian Connection,' in *Vercelli tra oriente ed occidente tra tarda antichità e medioevo*, ed. Vittoria Dolceti Corazza (Alessandria: Edizioni dell'Orso, 1999), 93–7.

86 The sentence 'þonne gesyhð þæt folc þæt þa mæssepreostas bioð mid unriht gefyllede ymbe heora welan' (ll. 13–14), which I have translated above (171) as 'then the people will see that the masspriests will be filled with injustice regarding their wealth' is susceptible to another interpretation: 'and then the people will see that the masspriests will be unjustly cast down on account of their wealth.' The homilist uses *gefyllan* in the sense 'cast down' just four lines later: '7 Godes æwe beoð gefylde' (l. 18).

With prophecies of this sort topical interpretation can easily become a parlour game;[87] yet just eight folios earlier in the Vercelli Book, in Homily XI, occurs a remarkable condemnation of corrupt kings, bishops, and ealdormen for plundering churches and 'holy orders,' and in this case it is clear that the homilist is speaking not of an apocalyptic future but of recent history and local conditions:

Nu syndon þa Godes cyrican bereafode 7 þa wiofeda toworpene þurh hæðenra manna gehresp 7 gestrodu, 7 þa weallas syndon tobrocene 7 toslitene 7 þa godcundan hadas syndon gewanode for hyra sylfra gewyrhtum 7 geearnungum. 7 nalas þæt an Godes þeowas ane syndon, ac eac swylce cyningas 7 bisceopas 7 ealdormen, þa þe ðysse þeode rædboran syndon, hie habbað þa godcundan hadas 7 þæt Godes folc gestroden 7 bereafod for leasum tyhtum 7 lyðrum metsceattum. 7 we þonne nu for ure ealra gewyrhtum þas egeslican þing 7 þas ondrysenlican her on worulde þrowigað. (ll. 90–9)

[God's churches are now despoiled and the altars cast down by the plundering and robbery of heathen men, and the walls are broken and breached and the spiritual orders diminished on account of their own deeds and deserts. And not only God's servants alone, but also kings and bishops and ealdormen, who are counselors of the people, have robbed and plundered the spiritual orders and the people of God because of false charges and corrupt bribes. And we are now suffering these terrible and dreadful things here in the world because of our own deeds.]

I have suggested elsewhere that the author of Vercelli XI was a secular priest or canon whose complaints about the depredations of churches and 'holy orders' were prompted by the reforming bishops' cooperation with King Edgar and powerful ealdormen in the expulsions of the clerks and confiscations of their property.[88] I am not aware that these passages in

---

87 It would be tempting to refer the dissension between two kings 'and two brothers' (it is not clear whether this means a pair of kings and a pair of brothers, or a pair of kings who are also brothers) to the division of the kingdom between the young kings and brothers Eadwig and Edgar in 957. As I have noted above, the phrase '7 twam gebroðrum' is not paralleled in *Thomas* and might be the homilist's elaboration of the prophecy. On the other hand, if we take literally the homilist's statement that this *unsehtnes* will occur 'on the day before the great day [of Judgment],' he could not have been alluding to a recent event.

88 'Vercelli Homilies XI–XIII and the Benedictine Reform,' 222–6.

Vercelli XI and XV have ever been directly compared, but two such consecutive diatribes implicating kings, bishops, and ealdormen in precipitating an ecclesiastical calamity could hardly have been penned or read in the decades following 964 without evoking the Reform movement and its aftermath. It is most unlikely that homilists associated with or sympathetic to the Reform movement would have characterized a coalition of secular and spiritual power in such negative terms,[89] but the hostile perspective (as well as the guarded, non-specific plural form in which both passages are couched, without reference to any particular king, bishop, or ealdorman) would be entirely consistent with clerical (non-monastic) authorship following the monastic ascendancy.

To conclude with the implications of Vercelli Homily XV's use of *The Apocalypse of Thomas*, the homilist's credulous acceptance of his apocryphal source (did he even know it was uncanonical?) is just the kind of attitude that Ælfric was later to condemn as *micel gedwyld* ('great error') when opposing the dissemination of apocryphal texts and heterodox beliefs in English books.[90] Indeed, the homilist himself was aligned with those whom Ælfric castigated as *gedwolmen* ('heretics') for teaching that the Virgin Mary 'and certain other saints' would each rescue a portion of the damned from hell after the Last Judgment – the very doctrine set forth in the second half of Vercelli XV.[91] Ælfric attributes this unorthodox doctrine to men 'who wished to remain always in their fleshly desires and did not want to earn eternal life through hardships' ('on heora flæsclicum lustum symle licgan woldon. and noldon mid earfoðnyssum þæt ece lif

---

89 Two conceivable monastic contexts would be the immediate aftermath of Dunstan's expulsion by Eadwig in 956 and the 'anti-monastic' reaction following the death of Edgar in 975. In their attacks on the clerics, however, the monks were never coy about identifying themselves in explicit and triumphant terms, and the lack of any reference to monks or monasteries in both Vercelli XI and XV all but rules out a monastic diatribe against the pre-Reform era or the 'anti-monastic' reaction. I have not undertaken a close examination of the sermon's vocabulary, but some of the homilist's preferences diverge from distinctive 'Winchester' usage, e.g., *wuldorhelm* (l. 38) instead of *wuldorbeag*; *onsæcgað* (l. 12; ms. *onsacað*) instead of *offriað* or *bringað*. For these 'Winchester words' see the 'Index of Old English Words' in Mechthild Gretsch, *The Intellectual Foundations of the English Benedictine Reform*, CSASE 25 (Cambridge: CUP, 1999).

90 *Ælfric's Catholic Homilies: The First Series*, ed. Peter Clemoes, EETS s.s. 17 (London: OUP, 1997), 174. See Malcolm Godden, 'Ælfric and the Vernacular Prose Tradition,' in *The Old English Homily and Its Background*, ed. Paul Szarmach and B.F. Huppé (Albany: State University of New York Press, 1978), 99–117.

91 *Ælfric's Catholic Homilies: The Second Series*, ed. Malcolm Godden, EETS s.s. 5 (Oxford: OUP, 1979), 333, ll. 184–95. See Clayton, 'Delivering the Damned.'

geearnian'), a characterization reminiscent of the reformers' attacks against the clerks for licentiousness and refusal to live according to regular discipline.[92] Whether or not he was a member of the secular clergy, the Vercelli homilist would certainly have disputed this characterization. His intention was not to encourage a life of idle pleasure, or to promulgate heresy, or indeed even to promote 'apocrypha.'[93] In his own way he was as rigorous a moralist as Ælfric, if not as rigorous a theologian; if he accepted uncritically apocryphal narratives such as the Signs of Doomsday and the Delivering of the Damned, his intention was rather to inspire fear of Judgment on the one hand and reverence for Mary, Michael, and Peter on the other, thereby giving his audience a powerful inducement to repent but also reason to hope. The Vercelli homilist took these writings on faith and for gospel, and sought to combat the very scepticism that Ælfric was to encourage. In the short term the Vercelli homilist's attitude prevailed, for vernacular versions of *Thomas* continued to be copied into the eleventh and early twelfth centuries – even migrating from such anonymous and often apocryphal collections as Vercelli, Blickling, and Corpus 41 to the predominantly Ælfrician collections in CCCC 162 and Hatton 116 (Bazire–Cross 3). Yet by that time *Thomas* had begun to lose its purchase on the medieval imagination and library shelf, retaining barely a toe-hold even in Latin, with only three abbreviated copies surviving from the twelfth century through the fifteenth; it then passed out of knowledge for some five centuries, until its scholarly recovery in the twentieth.[94]

---

92 The reformers as a group, however, did not avoid 'pre-Reform' apocryphal traditions as consistently as Ælfric, whose attitude in this regard seems to have been atypical, as Mary Clayton and Joyce Hill have stressed. See Clayton, 'Ælfric and the Nativity of the Blessed Virgin Mary,' *Anglia* 104 (1986): 288–92; and Hill, 'Reform and Resistance: Preaching Styles in Late Anglo-Saxon England,' in *De l'Homélie au sermon: Histoire de la prédication médiévale*, ed. Jacqueline Hamesse and Xavier Hermand (Louvain-la-Neuve: Université catholique de Louvain, 1993), 15–46.

93 On the definition of and attitudes towards apocrypha in Anglo-Saxon England, see Frederick M. Biggs, 'An Introduction and Overview of Recent Work,' in *Apocryphal Texts*, ed. Powell and Scragg, 1–25.

94 This was not, I think, due to any distaste for its lurid signs of Doom, but rather to competition with the much more widely disseminated 'Fifteen Signs before Doomsday,' which had the advantage of attribution to a church Father (Jerome). I would like to thank Frederick M. Biggs, Thomas N. Hall, Thomas D. Hill, and Michael Lapidge for their comments and suggestions on this paper.

Appendix
The Authenticity of the Letter of John XII to King Edgar

The papal letter cited above (p. 173, n. 65) was recently edited and translated by Alexander R. Rumble, in *Property and Piety in Early Medieval Winchester: Documents Relating to the Topography of the Anglo-Saxon and Norman City and Its Minsters*, Winchester Studies 4.iii (Oxford: Clarendon Press, 2002), 233–7 (no. XXXIII). The text is also edited and translated by Whitelock, *Councils & Synods*, 109–13 (no. 29). For the date (before early November 963) and attribution to John XII (rather than John XIII), see Thomas Symons, 'Notes on the Life and Work of St Dunstan, II,' *Downside Review* n.s. 80 (1962): 357–8, whose view (asserted but not really argued) is accepted by Whitelock and Rumble, though Whitelock leaves open the possibility that the letter may not be genuine. See also Eric John, 'The Beginning of the Benedictine Reform in England,' in his *Orbis Britanniae and Other Studies* (Leicester: Leicester University Press, 1966), 249–64; Lapidge and Winterbottom, eds., *Wulfstan of Winchester: Life of St Æthelwold,* xlvi ('apparently genuine'), and Mechthild Gretsch, *The Intellectual Foundations of the English Benedictine Reform*, CSASE 25 (Cambridge: CUP, 1999), 236. The letter has also been accepted as a genuine papal privilege, but with attribution to John XIII rather than John XII, by H. Zimmermann, *Papsturkunden 896–1046*, 3 vols., Denkschriften der Österreichischen Akademie der Wissenschaften, Phil.-Hist. Klasse 174, 177, 198 (Vienna, 1984–5), 1: 416–18 (no. 212) (suggesting a date of 971), and by Wilhelm Levison, *England and the Continent in the Eighth Century* (Oxford: Clarendon Press, 1946), 196–8. Whitelock noted, however, that John XIII (who became pope on 1 October 965) 'would hardly send a letter permitting the ejection of the canons so long after this had taken place on 20 February 964' (p. 110).

Julia Barrow has recently argued that the letter is a Canterbury forgery dating between the 1070s and 1120s: see Barrow, 'English Cathedral Communities and Reform in the Late Tenth and the Eleventh Centuries,' in *Anglo-Norman Durham 1093–1193*, ed. David Rollason, Margaret Harvey, and Michael Prestwich (Woodbridge, Suffolk: Boydell, 1994), 37–8 (I am grateful to Dr Barrow for drawing my attention to her essay and discussing the matter with me). As Barrow points out, Æthelwold, whom the letter terms a *coepiscopus*, was not consecrated until 29 November 963, and John was deposed just few days later (4 December). John returned to Rome the following February, but Barrow argues that there would not have been enough time for Æthelwold to have conveyed such a request to Rome. John remained pope until his death on 14 May 964, however, and the letter may have been a post-facto confirmation (represented as prior approval) of actions taken when John had been unable to respond to Edgar's request. Whitelock preferred to date the letter before John's flight from Rome, on the grounds that Edgar would be unlikely to act without papal approval; but he might well have done so in the circumstances of a contested papacy of uncertain resolution and duration. Dating the letter between February and May 964 would also account for the reference to Æthelwold as *coepiscopus*, which Whitelock had to explain as anticipatory: 'if it was known at Rome that he was bishop-elect, it may have been thought unnecessary to wait until news of his consecration had been received before using this title' (*Councils & Synods*, 111). In any case, it is Dunstan, not Æthelwold, whom the letter authorizes to expel the clerks.

An additional problem is the relation between the letter and the *Regularis Concordia*, which was not written until 965. Barrow, citing F. Liebermann, 'Aethelwolds Anhang zur Benediktinerregel,' *Archiv für das Studium der neueren Sprachen und Literaturen* 108 (1902): 375–7, states that the letter makes use of the *Regularis Concordia*. Yet Liebermann merely refers to Stubbs, who says that the language of the letter is reminiscent of the *Regularis Concordia*, but does not cite any specific parallel. The most striking is the provision in both for the election of a bishop by the monks serving a cathedral church, but as Whitelock suggests, Æthelwold would have known the papal letter. Whitelock further suggests that 'the abuse of the secular canons reminds one of various passages in Winchester writings, but may have been influenced by the letter to which the pope is replying.' An alternative explanation (that the papal letter was not issued until 967), as Barrow notes, was offered by Hanna Vollrath, *Die Synoden Englands bis 1066* (Paderborn: F. Schöningh, 1985), 449–53.

Barrow raises a new objection, however, that she considers decisive. The writer refers to Edgar's *imperii dignitas*, whereas the papal formulary, the *Liber Diurnus*, distinguishes between kings and emperors, and does not ascribe *imperium* to the former. According to Barrow, genuine papal letters of this period addressed to kings observe this distinction. Yet Edgar clearly considered his rule an *imperium*, as is shown by the phrase *imperii mei* in charters generally regarded as authentic (S674, S679, S712, S755, S782; cf. S717; I have used the *New Regesta Anglorum* database, at http://www.trin.cam.ac.uk/sdk13/chartwww/NewRegReg.html, to search forms of the word *imperium* in the charters of Edgar, excluding those regarded as doubtful or spurious). Surely protocol would allow reference to the *imperii dignitas* of a correspondent who regarded himself as ruling an *imperium*, unless the claim were disputed. (Edgar's *imperium* was hardly in competition with Otto's.) Moreover, since the alleged forger clearly *was* familiar with the *Liber Diurnus*, why would he have committed such a blunder?*

Barrow has, to be sure, raised legitimate questions as to the letter's authenticity, but they are not, in my view, sufficient to overturn the consensus in its favour. Even if the surviving text of the letter is a forgery, it may still have been based upon a genuine original (as forgeries often were). Stubbs (who printed the letter with attribution to John XIII) stated that he could not vouch for its authenticity, but added that if it were a forgery it must be an early (pre-Conquest) one, since after the Conquest the Winchester monks claimed that the church had always been monastic (*Memorials*, 364n1). Stubbs's claim that there is no evidence that cathedral clerks were termed *canonici* (as in the papal letter) 'until the eve of the Conquest' is simply wrong: cf. Rumble, *Property and Piety*, 236n8, and the references cited there.

---

* On Edgar's imperial pretensions, see now Julia Crick, 'Edgar, Albion, and Insular Dominion,' in *Edgar, King of the English 959–975: New Interpretations*, ed. Donald Scragg (Woodbridge: Boydell Press, 2008), 158–70.

The 'Homiletics' of the Vercelli Book Poems: The Case of *Homiletic Fragment I*

JONATHAN T. RANDLE

Of the six poetic texts in the Vercelli Book, none has been so neglected by modern scholars as *Homiletic Fragment I*. Perhaps because of its fragmentary nature or its pious tone, only three extended analyses of the poem have been produced in the past fifty years.[1] As the modern title implies, however, the poem sits squarely within the homiletic context of the Vercelli Book as a whole.[2] Its theme, namely, the deceitfulness of men in the present age, is a relatively commonplace homiletic motif; and the quotation in the poem of a biblical text subsequently explicated has parallels in the exegesis of a biblical pericope found widely in Old English homiletic prose.[3]

Of the poem itself, only the final forty-seven lines now remain of the original text, with the loss of a single leaf containing the end of *Soul and Body I* and the beginning of *Homiletic Fragment I*.[4] The truncation of the text poses difficulties, especially with regard to its rhetorical structure.

---

1 For the three extended analyses of the poem, see T.D. Hill, 'The Hypocritical Bee in the Old English "Homiletic Fragment I," Lines 18–30,' *NQ* 213 (1968): 123; N.D. Isaacs, *Structural Principles in Old English Poetry* (Knoxville: Univ. of Tennessee Press, 1968), 99–106; and P. Pulsiano, 'Bees and Backbiters in the Old English *Homiletic Fragment I*,' *ELN* 25.2 (December 1987): 1–6.

2 The present title of the poem, *Homiletic Fragment I*, was given by Krapp in his 1932 edition of the Vercelli Book poems (ASPR 2). Twenty-five years earlier, F. Holthausen, 'Zur Textkritik Altenglischer Dichtungen,' *Englische Studien* 38 (1907): 201, referred to the poem as a 'sermon,' calling it by the title *Predigt über ps. 28,3*.

3 Lines 9–15a are apparently a loose translation of Psalm 27:3; see below. The use of a scriptural text (the 'pericope') is an important homiletic stylistic and structural device, as will be discussed.

4 See C. Sisam, ed., *The Vercelli Book: A Late Tenth-Century Manuscript Containing Prose and Verse, Vercelli Biblioteca Capitolare CXVII*, EEMF, 19 (Copenhagen: Rosenkilde and Bagger, 1976), 17.

Such problems are compounded by the fact that no source – direct or otherwise – has been identified. Here, it will be suggested that *Homiletic Fragment I* was based on a lost homiletic text, given the number and frequency of what may be called 'homiletic elements' within the poem. Through an examination of several features in *Homiletic Fragment I* (including theme, structure, metre, and diction), a series of criteria are isolated which can aid in the definition and identification of other 'homiletic verse' in Old English.

Generally speaking, the theme of *Homiletic Fragment I* is the deceitfulness of slandering and backbiting men; Grein went so far as to title the poem *Bi manna lease* ('On the falseness of men').[5] The focus is on those who speak fair words, though they harbour guile in their hearts (lines 3–6):

> Eorl oðerne   mid æfþancum
> ond mid teonwordum   tæleð behindan,
> spreceð fægere beforan,   ond þæt facen swa þeah   5
> hafað in his heortan,   hord unclæne.
>
> ['One man blames another from behind with insults and vicious words, speaks well to his face, but has malice in his heart, a dirty store.']

Deceivers such as these are called *þam synfullum* ('the sinful,' line 9b) and *þam ligewyrhtum* ('the liars,' line 11b), but it is not merely such smooth-speaking backbiters whom the poet complains against. The composer of *Homiletic Fragment I* widens his focus to include those deceptive men who make vows and pledge oaths with no intention of fulfilling them (lines 12–15a and 24–7):

> þam þe ful smeðe   spræce habbað,
> ond in gastcofan   grimme geþohtas,
> gehata ð holdlice,   swa hyra hyht ne gæð,
> wære mid welerum.   15
>
> ...
>
> Swa bioð gelice   þa leasan men,
> þa ðe mid tungan   treowa gehataþ   25

---

5 C.W.M. Grein, ed., *Bibliothek der angelsächsischen poesie*, 3 vols. (Goettingen 1858–64), 2: 142. The poem is similarly titled in C.L. Wrenn, *A Study of Old English Literature* (London: Harrap, 1967), 244; see also G.K. Anderson, *The Literature of the Anglo-Saxons* (Princeton: Princeton Univ. Press, 1957), 174, where the poem is called *The Failings of Man*.

fægerum wordum,   facenlice þencaþ,
þonne hie æt nehstan   nearwe beswicaþ.

['Those who have speech full smooth, and bitter thoughts in their hearts, who promise loyally a pact with their lips, though their intention does not follow it … So they are like those false men, who with their tongue promise pledges with fair words, think maliciously, when they finally play their petty tricks.']

This theme – the negative portrayal of deceitful men who betray their pledges of fidelity – is commonplace in Old English verse: examples dealing with the loyalty owed to one's lord are found in both *Beowulf* (ll. 2884–91) and *The Battle of Maldon* (ll. 185–201);[6] examples dealing with deceit and the breaking of pledges are found in *Precepts* (ll. 29–31) and *Vainglory* (ll. 31b–6a). Similar themes of deceit, slandering, and treachery also appear widely in Old English prose. Prohibitions against such treachery and backbiting appear in the law codes of (for instance) Ine,[7] Alfred,[8] Æthelred,[9] and Cnut.[10] In these last two instances, since it is probable that

---

6 For discussions of this heroic 'ideal' in *Beowulf* and *The Battle of Maldon* (among other texts), see R. Woolf, 'The Ideal of Men Dying with Their Lord in *Germania* and in *The Battle of Maldon*,' *ASE* 5 (1976): 72–4; see also R. Frank, 'The Battle of Maldon and Heroic Literature,' in *The Battle of Maldon AD 991*, ed. D. Scragg (Oxford: Blackwell, 1991): 196–207, esp. 204–6.

7 Heavy fines of compensation are levied against those who practise deceit in Ine [13]; see F. Liebermann, ed., *Die Gesetze der Angelsachsen*, 3 vols. (Halle: Niemeyer, 1903–16), 1: 94–5.

8 Alfred quotes a verse from Exodus 23 which advises vigilance against 'false men'; see Alfred [El.40] in Liebermann, ed., *Gesetze*, 1: 0–1: 'Leases monnes word ne rec ðu no þæs to gehieranne, ne his domas ne geðafa ðu, ne nane gewitnesse æfter him ne saga ðu.' An exhortation to fulfil oaths is represented by Alfred's first law: 'Æt ærestan we lærað, þæt mæst ðearf is, þæt æghwelc mon his að ond his wed wærlice healde' (Alfred [Af 1]; see Liebermann, ed., *Gesetze*, 1: 46).

9 For instance, in the twenty-seventh canon of Æthelred's laws from 1014 (VIII Æthelred, ed. Liebermann, *Gesetze*, 1: 266), an admonition against false priests occurs: 'Gif mæssepreost ahwar stande on leasre gewitnesse oððe on mænan aðe oððe þeofa gewita and geweorhta beo, þonne sy he aworpen of gehadodra gemanan and þolige ægðer ge geferscipes ge freondscipes ge æghwilces wurðscipes, buton he wið God and wið men þe deoplicor gebete' ('If a mass-priest stands in any way in false witness or in a wicked oath or is an adviser or abettor of thieves, then he should be expelled fom the ranks of consecrated men, and forfeit companionship and friendship and every honour, unless he the more seriously make amends to God and men').

10 See, for instance, Cnut, 1020 [14]: 'for ðam þe ealle biscopas secgað, þæt hit swyþe deop wið God to betanne, þæt man aðas oððe wedd tobrece' ('For all bishops say, that it is a very serious matter to atone before God, when oaths or pledges are broken'); see Liebermann, ed., *Gesetze*, 1: 274. See further II Cnut [6] and [7], in which murderers

archibishop Wulfstan was responsible for drafting the law codes of both Æthelred and Cnut,[11] it comes as no surprise that similar exhortations occur in Wulfstan's homilies, particularly in his *Sermo Lupi*.

In his sermon, Wulfstan observes that there has been little loyalty among men, even though they speak fair words ('þæt lytle getreowþa wæran mid mannum, þeah hy wel spæcan').[12] The betrayal and deceit which is symptomatic of Wulfstan's England receives due attention,[13] and specific mention is made of those who shamefully attack and 'stab others in the back' ('ælc oþerne æftan heaweþ sceandlican onscytan,' ll. 69–70), echoing *Homiletic Fragment I*, ll. 3–4 cited above. Ælfric, Wulfstan's contemporary, also encourages his audience to avoid treachery and guile in his SERMO DOMINICA X POST PENTECOSTEM,[14] and the same exhortation is found throughout the homilies of Ælfric, whether through direct address to the audience or through the *exempla* of the saints.[15] The anonymous homilists, too, included similar denunciations. In most instances, treachery and guile are associated with the devil and his 'smooth speech' which brought about the Fall of Man.[16] The homilist of Blickling Homily V, for

---

and perjurers are both condemned and linked together through the alliteration of *manslagan* and *manswaran*, on the one hand, and *licceteras* and *leogeras*, on the other; see Liebermann, ed., *Gesetze*, 1: 312. On Wulfstan's alliterative style, see (for instance) D. Bethurum, ed., *The Homilies of Wulfstan* (Oxford: Clarendon Press, 1957), 87–98, and A. Orchard, 'Crying Wolf: Oral Style and the *Sermones Lupi*,' *ASE* 21 (1992): 244–9.

11 On Wulfstan's drafting of these codes, see (for instance) D. Whitelock, 'Archbishop Wulfstan, Homilist and Statesman,' *TRHS*, 4th ser. 24 (1942): 25–45.

12 See *WH* XX (EI).12–13.

13 Ibid., ll. 59–76, 95–9, and 138–41. Note that, as with Cnut's secular law code mentioned above, perjury and the breaking of oaths is equated with murder in Wulfstan: 'her syndan mansworan and morþorwyrhtan' (ll. 162–3) ('Here are oath-breakers and murderers').

14 *Supp.* XVI: 'Ne sceole we na mid facne us freond gewyrcan' (l. 155) ('We must not make friends through wickedness'); 'Þus we sceolon geearnian þa upplican wununge mid þyllicum dædum, urum Drihtne to lofe, mid nanum andsætum facne, ne mid ænigum swicdome' (ll. 199–201) ('Thus we must earn a dwelling above with such deeds, to our Lord's praise, with no hateful wickedness, nor with any treachery').

15 See, for instance, 'ac we sceolon … awendan … ure heortan fram facne' (*CH* I.VI.103–6) ('but we must … turn … our hearts from wickedness'); 'God … forbead facn and reaflac' (*CH* II.VII.57–8) ('God … forbade wickedness and plundering'); ('Blessed was the man in whom no wickedness dwelt'); and 'Eadig wæs se wer on þam ne wunode nan facn' (*LS* XXXI.302) ('This is truly a blessed man, who never had wickedness or evil in his heart'). This last quotation, from the *Life* of St Martin, is also found in a slightly altered form in *VH* XVIII.215–16: 'Þis is soðlice eadig wer, ne wæs næfre facen ne inwit in his heortan.'

16 See esp. *BH* I, pp. 3–5, and *VH* XIV.7–9, 17–20.

example, explicitly encourages his audience to strive for heaven by abandoning deceit and treachery; the homilist draws a distinction between the man who speaks truthfully and the deceiver, whom the homilist implicitly compares with the devil.[17]

The poet of *Homiletic Fragment I* has added to this thematic tradition in Old English literature by presenting deceitfulness as concomitant with the sinful degeneration of the world (ll. 31–2a). The poem begins in midthought, with those who slander and hold deceit in their hearts being presented as the cause of sorrow, which taints the joys of men (ll. 1–6). They are like bees which, though they carry honey in their mouths, have a poisonous sting in their tails (ll. 18–23). Just so, the combination of fair speech and treacherous thoughts in the deceiver can secretly wound (ll. 24–30). This single example of deceit is representative of the state of the world under the influence of the devil, for no one keeps true love and peace with his neighbour as God commands (ll. 31–9). The text concludes with an exhortatory passage calling the audience to strive to do better, so that they can enjoy heaven when God brings about an end to earthly life (ll. 43–7). In order to emphasize the centrality of this theme of deceitfulness, the composer of *Homiletic Fragment I* employs three prevalent techniques – biblical quotation, aural repetition, and the central metaphor of the bee.

---

17 *BH* V.55: 'Dauid se sealmsceop ... þus cwæþ: "Se mon se þa soþfæstnesse mid his muþe sprecþ, ond hie on his heortan georne geþencþ, ond he hi fullice gelæsteþ, ond he afylleþ þa inwitfullan word of his tungan, þæt beoþ þa men þa þe Godes rices geleafan habbað ond healdaþ; forþon hi noldan heora nehstan beswican þurh þa facenfullan word." Maniges mannes wise bið þæt he wile symle to his nehstan sprecan þa word þe he wenþ þæt him leofoste syn to gehyrenne, ond þonne hwæþere þencþ hu he hine eþelicost beswican mæge þurh þa swetnesse þara worda; deofles wise bið þæt he wile symle þone unwaran man beswican þurh þa swetnesse þara synna' ('David the Psalmist ... spoke as follows: "The man who speaks the truth with his tongue, eagerly thinks it in his heart, truly performs it, and puts aside deceitful words from his tongue, he is one of those men who have and hold belief in God's kingdom, because they would not decieve their neighbours with wicked words." It is the practice of many a man always to tell his neighbour the words which he thinks will be most pleasant to hear, and then nonetheless plots how he might betray him most easily through the sweetness of those words; it is the practice of the devil that he will always betray the unwary man through the sweetness of sins'). Such a technique of verbal parallelism is also evident, as we shall see, in *Homiletic Fragment I*; moreover, the focus on deceit and guile in the closing lines of this passage parallels a similar focus in *Homiletic Fragment I* ('tæleð behindan, / spreceð fægere beforan,' ll. 4b–5a), while the quotation from Psalm 15:3–4 provides a further point of comparison. Note also the verbal parallel between the final clause of the scriptural quotation in the homily ('forþon hi noldan heora nehstan beswican') and line 27 of *Homiletic Fragment I*: 'þonne hie æt nehstan nearwe beswicaþ.'

Perhaps the most immediate means of focusing the attention of his audience on this theme is the paraphrase and expansion in lines 8–15a of a verse from the Psalter:

> Forðan se witiga cwæð:
> 'Ne syle ðu me ætsomne   mid þam synfullum
> in wita forwyrd,   weoruda dryhten,   10
> ne me on life forleos   mid þam ligewyrhtum,
> þam þe ful smeðe   spræce habbað,
> ond in gastcofan   grimme geþohtas,
> gehatað holdlice,   swa hyra hyht ne gæð,
> wære mid welerum.'   15

['Just as the prophet said: "Do not put me into the destruction of punishments alongside the sinful, Lord of Hosts, nor destroy me in life with those liars who have speech full smooth, and bitter thoughts in their hearts, who promise loyally a pact with their lips, though their intention does not follow it.']

This excerpt is a versified amplification of Psalm 27:3: 'Ne simul trahas me cum peccatoribus et cum operantibus iniquitatem ne perdas me; qui loquuntur pacem cum proximo suo, mala autem in cordibus eorum' ['Draw me not away together with the wicked; and with the workers of iniquity destroy me not: Who speak peace with their neighbour, but evils are in their hearts'].[18] The *peccatoribus* ['wicked'] and *operantibus iniquitatem* ['the workers of iniquity'] of the biblical text correspond to the *synfullum* ('sinful,' l. 9b) and *ligewyrhtum* ('liars,' l. 11b) of *Homiletic Fragment I*. This appeal to a scriptural authority as a sort of *apologia* or justification for the message of the poem is a common feature in many Old English texts, and indeed other homilies seem to be composed of nothing more than citations and applications of scriptural and patristic authorities. Vercelli Homily III, a Lenten penitential homily in the same manuscript, is one example of such a text. Following his Latin source, the homilist cites several biblical texts throughout the work.[19] Moreover, the homilist makes

---

18 See the discussion of the relationship between the Psalm and the verse paraphrase in, for instance, ASPR 2, xxxix; Anderson, *Literature*, 174–5; Stanley B. Greenfield and Daniel G. Calder, *A New Critical History of Old English Literature* (New York: New York University Press, 1986), 267–8; and Isaacs, *Structural Principles*, 99–100. The theme of deceit and the prayer against liars and oath-breakers is a common one in the Psalms; see Psalms 12:3–4, 30:18–19, 33:12–15, and 35:1–4, among others.

19 See, for example, *VH* III.11–13: 'Ðy we sceolon symle wunian on þære godcundan lufan ond ures nehstan, þæt he symle on us þurhwunige, for þam, swa swa Iohannes cwæð:

extensive use of patristic sources, occasionally drawing on the Fathers in lengthy chains of quotations.[20] As even the most cursory glance at other Old English homilies will suggest, the appeal to textual authority – whether scriptural or patristic – was often of primary importance to the Anglo-Saxons.[21] In quoting a biblical text, the poet of *Homiletic Fragment I* not only provides a prominent means of stating and substantiating his theme – that of deceit – but he also places his poem within the Old English homiletic tradition.

The theme of deceit is likewise emphasized through the use of aural repetition. The contrast between the fair words and the treacherous inner thoughts of the deceiver is developed in the alliterative coupling of forms of *fæger* ('fair, attractive') and *facen* ('treachery, guile') three times in the fragment (here in bold; ll. 3–6, 15b–18a, and 24–6):[22]

Eorl oðerne   mid æfþancum
ond mid teonwordum   tæleð behindan,
spreceð **fægere** beforan,   ond þæt **facen** swa þeah   5
hafað in his heortan,   hord unclæne.
     ...
Wea bið in mode,   15
siofa synnum fah,   sare geblonden,

"God is seo soþe lufu, ond se þe wunaþ on ðære soðan lufan, he wunaþ on Gode ond God wunað on him"' ('For that reason, we must always dwell in the love of God and of our neighbour, so that he always dwells in us, for, just as John said: "God is that true love, and he who dwells in that true love, he dwells in God and God dwells in him"'); *VH* III.40–2: 'Be þæra synna andettnesse Salomon cwæð: 'Se ðe his scylda gehydeð, ne bið he na geriht. Se ðe soðlice hie geandet ond hie þonne forlæt, se bið mildheortnesse begytend' ('Concerning the confession of those sins, Solomon said, 'He who hides his sins shall not at all be set right. He who truly confesses them and forsakes them, he shall be one who obtains mercy'). See further *VH* III.44–6, 48–50, 66–80, 107–10, and 130–1.

20 Ibid., ll. 89–100. In this case, a passage which is printed as a single paragraph in Scragg's edition is composed almost entirely of quotations from patristic sources, namely Isidore, Jerome, and Augustine.

21 Such an appeal to authority is often found in the first lines of a homily, such as is seen in *VH* V.1 ('Her segð þis halige godspel') or *VH* VI.1 ('Her sagað ymb ðas mæran gewyrd'). As in *VH* III quoted above, patristic sources are often named; see *VH* VIII.1–2 ('Men ða leofestan, manað us ond myndgað on þyssum bocum sanctus Gregorius, se halega writere'). See also *CH* I.XXXVI.167 ('Se wisa augustinus trahtnode þis godspel').

22 See now Antonette diPaolo Healey, 'Questions of Fairness: Fair, Not Fair, and Foul,' in *Unlocking the Wordhord: Anglo-Saxon Studies in Memory of Edward B. Irving, Jr*, ed. Mark C. Amodio and Katherine O'Brien O'Keeffe (Toronto: UTP, 2003), 252–73.

gefylled mid **facne**,   þeah he **fæger** word
utan ætywe.

...

Swa bioð gelice   þa leasan men,
þa ðe mid tungan   treowa gehataþ   25
fægerum wordum,   **facenlice** þencaþ.
['One man blames another from behind with insults and vicious words,
speaks well to his face, but has malice in his heart, a dirty store ... There shall
be woe in his mind, a heart stained with sins, filled with malice, though he
shows fair words on the outside ... So they are like those false men, who with
their tongue promise pledges with fair words, think maliciously.']

With similar diction, the contrast between *fæger* and *facen* is also emphasized elsewhere in Old English literature; moreover, particularly in homiletic literature, the two words seem frequently to refer to the contrast
between speech and thought, just as in *Homiletic Fragment I*. In his
Admonitio ad filium spiritualem, Ælfric encourages his 'spiritual children'
to be forthright with each other, harbouring no guile or deceit. In doing so,
he echoes the distinction made in the Vercelli poem: 'Ne lufa ðu ðinne
broðor mid gehiwodre heortan ðæt ðu hine kysse and kepe him hearmes
forðam ðe se fakenfulla fægere word sprecð oft and on his modes digolnysse
macað syrwunga' ['Do not love your brother with a feigned heart, so that
you kiss him and keep him from harm, since the treacherous man often
speaks fair words, and the hidden places of his mind plots tricks'].[23] In describing the Fall of Man, an anonymous homily found in Oxford, Bodleian
Library, Bodley 340 makes an analogous comparison between the beauty
of Paradise (*neorxnawonges fægernysse*) and the deceit (*facne*) of that old
enemy the devil (*se ealda feond*), through which man was deprived of
Eden.[24] King Alfred's prose translation of Psalm 13:5 uses corresponding vocabulary:[25]

---

23 H.W. Norman, ed., *The Anglo-Saxon Version of the Hexameron of St. Basil ... and the
    Anglo-Saxon Remains of St. Basil's Admonitio ad filium spiritualem* (London 1848), 44–6.
24 The homily, entitled IN SABBATO SANCTO (Cameron B3.2.25) has been transcribed
    by the *DOE*; the relevant quotation is found in ll. 346–52: 'Uton gemunan hu sarlice
    and hu geomorlice se ealda feond manncynnes, ure þa ærestan ealdras, Adam and Efan,
    neorxnawonges fægernysse bereafode, and heo mid his facne and inwite beswac and
    forlærde, þæt heo on ðære byrignysse þæra beweredra blæda heora scyppendes bebod
    ælmihtiges Godes awegan and oferferdon.'
25 Patrick P. O'Neill, ed., *King Alfred's Old English Prose Translation of the First Fifty
    Psalms*, Medieval Academy Books 104 (Cambridge, MA: Medieval Academy of
    America, 2001), 112.

Hi synt byrgenum gelice: seo byð utan fæger, and innan ful. Heora tungan wyrcaþ mycel facn, þeah hi fægere sprecon; heora geþeaht and heora willa and heora weorc byð swylce þære wyrrestan nædran attor, þa mon "aspis" hæt. ['They are like burials, which are fair on the outside and foul within; their tongues produce great wickedness: though they speak fairly, their thoughts, and their wishes, and their deeds are like the poison of the worst snake, which is called an asp.']

In addition to the focus on deceptive speech in this last quotation, it is of interest to note Alfred's use of a comparison with the asp, 'the worst snake,' in his description of these deceivers. Just so, in *Homiletic Fragment I*, the primary theme of deceit is highlighted through the use of a similar comparison with the natural world.

This most engaging comparison is found in lines 18b–30 of *Homiletic Fragment I*, where the poet comments on his biblical text quoted in lines 9–15a by comparing the *synfullum* and *ligewyrhtum* of the psalm to bees (*HF1*, lines 18b–23):

> Ænlice beoð,
> swa ða beon berað   buta ætsomne
> arlicne anleofan,   ond ætterne tægel   20
> hafað on hindan,   hunig on muðe,
> wynsume wist. Hwilum wundiaþ
> sare mid stinge,   þonne se sæl cymeð.

['They are incomparable, just as the bees bear both together, exquisite food, honey in the mouth, joyful sustenance, and they have a poisoned tail behind. Sometimes he wounds sorely with his sting, when the opportunity arises.']

It is this vivid metaphor, along with a related *hapax legomenon* (*hunig-smæccas*, l. 28b), which has occasioned nearly all the scholarly commentary on the poem.[26] Although the precise function of the bee metaphor in the structure of the original poem cannot be known with certainty, it was certainly important enough in the eyes of the poet for him to devote at least thirty lines of his text (1b–30) to the development and interpretation of this image. In fact, the entire poetic fragment can be seen as an explication of the bee metaphor: lines 1b–18a describe the relationship between individuals – the deceitful slanderers and their neighbours – and include the quotation from Psalm 27; lines 18b–30 present the bee metaphor and

---

26 See n. 1 above.

its interpretation with reference to the deceivers of the first section; and lines 30–47 explain the metaphor as it relates to the wider context of the world in this present age.

Given the emphasis on deceit through the conspicuous means of the biblical quotation, the aural repetition, and the development of and commentary on the extended metaphor, it is certain that the poet of *Homiletic Fragment I* saw his portrayal of slanderers and oath-breakers as the primary topic of his composition. The fact that this theme is also prevalent throughout the homiletic literature of the Anglo-Saxons suggests a further defining and unifying context for the poem. Yet a secondary theme is also evident in the poem which suggests both a further correlation with such a homiletic context and, more importantly, a unity within the poem's most immediate context, the Vercelli Book manuscript.

The theme of repentance seems to have been a conspicuous concern of the Vercelli Book compiler.[27] *Homiletic Fragment I* conforms to this thematic preoccupation in the Vercelli Book by including a five-line concluding exhortation which stresses the need of both the poet and the audience to consider the state of the world and, by implication, the state of our own souls (ll. 43–7):

Uton to þam beteran,   nu we bot cunnon,
hycgan ond hyhtan,   þæt we heofones leoht
uppe mid englum   agan moton   45
gastum to geoce,   þonne god wile
eorðan lifes   ende gewyrcan!
['Let us think and hope on the better part, now we know a remedy, so that we
may have the light of heaven above with the angels, as a consolation for souls,
when God wishes to cause an end to life on earth.']

We note a distinctive change of syntax beginning in line 43, with the first-person plural verb form *uton*. This change to a collective 'we' is repeated by the use of the first-person plural nominative form, *we*, twice more in the five-line passage (ll. 43b and 44b). The descriptive tone of the first forty-two lines of the text is abandoned in favour of a more personal and prescriptive conclusion, in which the poet emphasizes our own accountability in a

---

27 See, for instance, Éamonn Ó Carragáin, 'How Did the Vercelli Collector Interpret *The Dream of the Rood?*' in *Studies in English Language and Early Literature in Honour of Paul Christophersen*, ed. P.M. Tilling, Occasional Papers in Ling. and Lang. Learning 8 (Coleraine: New Univ. of Ulster, 1981), 63–104.

corrupt world. This type of syntactical change is also used elsewhere in Old English homiletic texts to provide a similar means of emphasis and focus. For instance, in Vercelli Homily I, a narrative version of the Passion of Christ which 'is related almost verbatim from one or more of the Gospels,'[28] the homilist acts as narrator by concentrating on the depiction of the trial, death, and burial of Christ. Having completed his narration, the homilist concludes by encouraging the audience to meditate on the preceding account; his inclusion of first-person plural forms (here in bold) suggests the 'corporate' nature of his conclusion (*VH* I.297–301):

> Ac **utan we** nu for þan a singalice **ussum** dryhtne hælendan Criste þanc secgan eallre þære eaðmodnesse þe se heofonlica cyning ælmihtig drihten in þas halgan tid eallum mancynne gecyðde. **Utan we** hine nu lufigan ofer eall oðre þing, swa **we** nu **gehyraþ** þæt he **us** lufode ond **us** hyldo to worhte.
>
> ['But let us now therefore always continuously say thanks to our Lord Saviour Christ for all the humility which the heavenly king almighty God revealed to all mankind in this holy time. Let us now love him above all other things, just as we now hear that he loved us and brought favour to us.']

Here the homilist has departed from the narrative tone of the homily by utilizing first-person plural pronouns and verb forms (particularly *we* and *utan*), distinguishing the conclusion of the text from the preceding lines in which nouns and verbs occur almost exclusively in third-person forms.[29] Moreover, there are additional passages in both the Vercelli homilies and further Old English homiletic texts which suggest that such a concluding section, in which an exhortation to repentance displays an alteration of syntax from predominantly third-person forms to first-person plural forms, was a homiletic commonplace.[30]

In addition to such changes of syntax, the poet also focuses on the theme of repentance in *Homiletic Fragment I* through an implicit reference to the

---

28 Scragg, *VH*, 1, suggests that the homily 'follows very closely the account of the Passion in John 18 and 19, with frequent references to other Gospels, particularly Matthew 26 and 27, to provide additional explanation of motive and intent.'

29 Although forms such as *we*, *us*, and *ure* occur earlier in the homily, they are either used descriptively (as in *ure dryhten*, *VH* I.3) or in the speeches of characters (as in one of the speeches of Caiaphas, *VH* I.10–12, which includes phrases such as *þonne we æfre ær gesawon, gif we hine forlætaþ*, and *ure land ond ure þeode*).

30 See, for instance, *VH* II.107–13, *VH* VI.86–91, and *VH* X.263–5. The same call to repentance is evident in the homilies of Ælfric and Wulfstan: see *CH* I.VII.253–8; *CH* II.XIX.298–300; and *WH* XX(EI).186–201.

Day of Judgment. It has previously been demonstrated that, in addition to (and often in conjunction with) the theme of repentance, the Judgment Day theme is a unifying motif in the Vercelli Book, occurring in both the prose and verse texts.[31] In the final lines of the penitential conclusion to *Homiletic Fragment I*, the poet reminds the audience that God will bring this earthly life to an end (ll. 46b–7). This particular motif, the reminder of God ending the world at the apocalyptic Day of Judgment, is found elsewhere in Old English homiletic literature, often placed in the context of a call to repentance.[32]

That such a penitential conclusion occurs in the poem is a crucial factor in any attempt to reconstruct the precise structure of the original, complete text of *Homiletic Fragment I*. Although this hypothetical structure cannot be known with certainty, it seems that most scholars have disregarded the fragmentary nature of the extant poem when analysing the structure of the text. Isaacs, for instance, states that *hunigsmæccas* (l. 28b) is the 'central metaphor of the poem' which 'sustains the structure of this forty-seven-line ... fragment ... If the poem as it exists appears to be as nearly complete a structure as its statement warrants, we may give the poet due benefit of the doubt and suppose that not much is missing.'[33] What is most striking about Isaacs's analysis is that, while examining the 'statement' of *Homiletic Fragment I*, he completely ignores the homiletic context of the poem, which can suggest an alternate organizing principle.

One of the most characteristic and widespread forms of homiletic structure may be called a 'tripartite' structure, beginning with a pericope, which is then followed by the homilist's commentary on the scripture and concluded by a general admonition to the audience. Such a structure is exactly what is found in the extant text of *Homiletic Fragment I*: there is a pericope in the form of the scriptural paraphrase from Psalm 27 (ll. 8–15a), a general

---

31 Ó Carragáin, 'Vercelli Collector,' 66: 'The key to the use for which the collection was intended is to be found in the clearly-defined preoccupations of the collector. He ... ensured throughout his collection a regular recurrence of texts describing the Last Judgement.'

32 See, for instance, *Soul and Body I*, ll. 12b–14; see also *CH* I.I.289–93, *CH* I.XXII.132–44, *CH* II.XXIV.142–4, *LS* XXIX.44–5, and *Supp.* XVIII.45–6. For a discussion of the Judgment Day theme in Anglo-Saxon verse, see G.D. Caie, *The Judgment Day Theme in Old English Poetry* (Copenhagen: Nova, 1976). Milton McC. Gatch provides a convenient discussion of the occurrence of the theme in homiletic texts; see his *Preaching and Theology in Anglo-Saxon England: Ælfric and Wulfstan* (Toronto: UTP, 1977), esp. 61–116, and 'Eschatology in the Anonymous Old English Homilies,' *Traditio* 21 (1965): 117–65.

33 *Structural Principles*, 100. Pulsiano follows Isaacs by suggesting that the poem 'gains its structural unity' from the bee metaphor. See 'Bees and Backbiters,' 1.

commentary on the passage and the establishment of the didactic metaphor (ll. 15b–42), and, finally, a concluding exhortation (ll. 43–7). Although this straightforward interpretation ignores the first seven lines of the poem, as well as any text which might have been lost on the preceding folio, it offers further evidence in support of homiletic influence on the poem. The extant text of *Homiletic Fragment I* seems therefore a 'mini-homily' in this regard. Of these three sections, the concluding lines share the most stylistic parallels with homiletic texts and merit closer analysis. Such concluding exhortations, generally expressed in first-person pronouns and verb forms, occur not only throughout the corpus of Anglo-Saxon homilies, as we have seen, but also in a number of poetic texts.[34]

So, for instance, the Old English poem *The Judgment Day I* concludes with the following exhortation (ll. 114–19):

Oncweþ nu þisne cwide: cuþ sceal geweorþan
þæt ic gewægan ne mæg   wyrd under heofonum,   115
ac hit þus gelimpan sceal   leoda gehwylcum,
ofer eall beorht gesetu   byrnende lig.
Siþþan æfter þam lige   lif bið gestaþelad;
welan ah in wuldre   se nu wel þenceð.

['Now utter this speech: it shall become known that I cannot avoid fate under the heavens, but it must happen thus for every one, burning flame over all the bright dwellings. Then after that flame, life will be strengthened; he has wealth in glory, who now thinks well.']

As in *Homiletic Fragment I*, this passage contains an exhortation addressed to the audience, encouraging them to think on their future in heaven (ll. 118–19). Moreover, what is remarkable about this closing exhortation from *The Judgment Day I*, and what may offer an indication of the intended overall structure of *Homiletic Fragment I*, is that this conclusion to the poem is linked with its opening passage through a series of verbal echoes and thematic parallels (*JD1*, ll. 1–4):

Ðæt gelimpan sceal,   þætte lagu floweð,
flod ofer foldan;   feores bið æt ende
anra gehwylcum.   Oft mæg se þe wile
in his sylfes sefan   soð geþencan.

---

34 For poetic parallels, in addition to those mentioned in the previous discussion, see *The Fates of the Apostles*, ll. 115–22; *The Phoenix*, ll. 667–77; and *The Partridge*, ll. 12–16.

['It shall happen that the liquid shall flow, a flood over the earth; that will be at the end of life for everyone. Often one who is willing to can consider the truth in his own mind.']

The phrase 'Ðæt gelimpan sceal' in the first line is echoed by verse 116a, 'ac hit þus gelimpan sceal,' emphasizing the inevitability of the events which the poet describes in the body of his text. Lines 1b and 2a, the flooding of the earth by water, complement the burning flame of line 117. However, while the 'flod ofer foldan' brings in its wake the destruction of life for all, the Apocalyptic flames have the opposite effect.[35] The poet then progresses to the central message of *Judgment Day I*, the need of the individual to contemplate truth, which effectively closes both passages. The repetition of the verb (ge-)*þencan* serves as an aural link between the two passages, while a similar modal consistency is established by the repetition of *mæg* (ll. 3b, 115a). This type of verbal parallelism can also be seen in other Old English verse texts, such as *The Wanderer*, where the opening and concluding sections of the poem are strongly linked through repetition.[36] In both of these cases the first lines of the poem, in addition to providing verbal echoes with the exhortation at the conclusion, also serve to establish the homiletic intent of the poet. It is possible, therefore, that the missing portion of *Homiletic Fragment I* included just such a 'preface' which would have introduced the theme of deceit. The progression, in the initial lines of the fragment, from the general *sorh cymeð* (l. 1b) to the specific *Eorl oðerne ... tæleð behindan* (ll. 3–4) seems to indicate that these lines could feasibly belong to such an introductory passage.

If one takes such parallelism into account, some intriguing hypotheses regarding the extant structure of *Homiletic Fragment I* emerge when the text is compared with the observed structure of some of the Old English prose homiletic texts. Speaking of the Vercelli homilies, Paul Szarmach states the following:[37]

---

35 The parallels between *anra gehwylcum* (l. 3a) and *leoda gehwylcum* (l. 116b), on the one hand, and 'feores bið æt ende' (l. 2b) and 'lif bið gestaþelad' (l. 118b), on the other, support this relationship.

36 This aural link in *The Wanderer* is formed through repetition of *are gebideð* (l. 1a) / *are seceð* (l. 114b), and *Swa cwæð eardstapa* (l. 6a) / *Swa cwæð snottor on mode* (l. 111a).

37 P.E. Szarmach, 'The Vercelli Homilies: Style & Structure,' in *The Old English Homily & Its Backgrounds*, ed. P.E. Szarmach and B.F. Huppé (Albany: SUNY Press, 1978), 252.

[A] sufficiently full central episode or exposition can in effect be a homily within a homily and can also appear elsewhere with its own rubric. OE writers in different periods were aware of the structural feature called here the 'center' … [T]here is therefore a form one might label the 'concentric homily,' which consists of a number of motifs or themes that prepare for a narrative or dramatic center by anticipating the style and content of the center.

At least five of the homilies in the Vercelli Book reflect this type of concentric structure,[38] and it is also evident in the homilies of Ælfric.[39] Moreover, the same sort of rhetorical patterning is evident, on a smaller scale, in additional Old English verse texts.[40]

Homiletic Fragment I seems to be built around this same type of structure. As Isaacs mentions, several elements in the text prepare the audience for what he sees as the central focus, the metaphor encapsulated in *hunigsmæccas* (l. 28b).[41] A more coherent structure results, however, if one extends the central metaphor of the poem to include lines 18b–30. The arrangement of the preceding and following lines can then be demonstrated to be verbally and thematically dependent on this central passage. To begin with, just as the composer uses verbal echoes to emphasize the theme of deceit (as we have seen), he also uses this type of repetition to structure his concentric text. Such repetitions occur, in the first instance, between the first two sections of the poem. The duplication of *fæger* and *facen*, mentioned above in conjunction with the thematic analysis of the text, is one such example of the structural use of verbal parallelism. The two words are paired chiastically twice in the first section of the text, at lines 5 ('spreceð fægere beforan, ond þæt facen swa þeah') and 17 ('gefylled mid

---

38 Ibid., 244; Szarmach lists Homilies IX, X, XIX, XX, and XXI.

39 See, for instance, A.E. Nichols, 'Methodical Abbreviation: A Study in Ælfric's Friday Homilies for Lent,' in *The Old English Homily & Its Backgrounds*, ed. Szarmach and Huppé, 169, where Ælfric's homily for the First Friday of Lent (*Supp.* II) is described as having a 'central metaphor: man lies ill, and the Healer comes to make him physically hale and spiritually whole.' The lines preceding this central metaphor, dealing with Christ's healing of a paralytic at the Pool of Bethsaida (John 5:1–15), thematically prepare the audience for the metaphoric exegesis at the homily's centre.

40 See a discussion of the concentric 'envelope pattern' in A.C. Bartlett, *The Larger Rhetorical Patterns in Anglo-Saxon Poetry* (New York: Columbia Univ. Press, 1935), 9–29.

41 *Structural Principles*, 100–1. Isaacs suggests that lines 18b–22, 'the simile which precedes' the *hunigsmæccas* metaphor, are instrumental in preparing the audience for the metaphor. He also sees lines 1–2 as 'the broadly generalized statement of the situation which is imaged forth in the metaphor: the obverse of sweetness is inevitably a sting.'

facne, þeah he fæger word'). This repetition amply prepares the audience for the recurrence of the dichotomy in the second, central section of the poem (ll. 18b–30): 'fægerum wordum, facenlice þencaþ' (l. 26). There is a further, though tenuous, verbal repetition evident between *behindan* (l. 4b) and *on hindan* (l. 21a), yet this slight aural echo is enriched by what appears to be a play on words by the composer. In line 4b, the backbiter is described as one who 'slanders' or 'derides' behind another (*tæleð behindan*). In the second section of the poem, the metaphorical bee is described as having a poisonous tail behind: 'ætterne tægel / hafað on hindan' (ll. 20b–1a). The fact that, in the larger thematic intent of the poem, the slandering (*tæleð*) of the deceiver is equated with the stinging tail (*tægel*) of the bee in the metaphor only serves to reinforce the self-conscious paronomasia in the two passages.

Two additional examples of verbal parallelism found in the first two sections of the poem merit note. In the first section, the 'smooth speech' of the lie-workers is emphasized: 'ful smeðe spræce habbað' (l. 12). In the interpretation of the bee metaphor which makes up the second section of the text, the deceivers are described similarly: 'smeðne sybcwide, ond in siofan innan' (l. 29). As Isaacs states, '[T]he *smeðe spræce* (12) anticipates the *smeðne sybcwide* (29a) … thus directly associating the *witiga*'s quotation with the central metaphor.'[42] A second verbal parallel is likewise used to prepare the audience for the central metaphor, while also anticipating the concluding section of the text. The coming of sorrow in line 1b of the text (*sorh cymeð*) anticipates both the diction and the illustrative essence of the bee metaphor (ll. 22b–3):

> Hwilum wundiaþ
> sare mid stinge,   þonne se sæl cymeð.
> ['Sometimes he wounds sorely with his sting, when the opportunity arises.']

The repetition of *sorh/sare* ('grief'/'grievously') and *cymeð* ('comes') establishes a sense of the ominous inevitability of sorrow in the world, a

---

42 *Structural Principles*, 102. This parallel is all the more striking in that the adjective *smeðe*, 'smooth,' is not used anywhere else in such an apparently deliberate manner as it is here; in fact, *Homiletic Fragment I* contains the only two poetic attestations of the word. With reference to speech, *smeðe* is used in two prose texts: Ælfric's Letter to Sigeweard ('Her we magon gehiran, þæt se Hælend lufað swiðor þa dæde þonne þa smeðan word'; see S.J. Crawford, ed., *Exameron Anglice or The Old English Hexameron*, BaP 10 (Hamburg: Wissenschaftliche Buchgesellschaft, 1921), ll. 955–6) and the 'Seven Sleepers' homily ('ne miht þu us na swa bepæcean mid þinan smeðan wordan'; *LS* XXIII.602–3).

point which the composer is at pains to make in the concluding section of the poem (ll. 31–47).

The central position of the bee metaphor is further established when one considers this final section of *Homiletic Fragment I*. Having made his point about the individual deceiver and his resemblance to the stinging bee, the composer then extends the application of his metaphor to include the world (*þes middangeard*, l. 31a). The two outer sections of the poem (ll. 1–18a and 31–47), each closely related to the bee metaphor, are also linked through verbal repetition, and thereby a comparison is established between the single backbiter and the entire race of man (ll. 15b–16):

> Wea bið in mode,
> siofa synnum fah,   sare geblonden
> ['Woe is in the heart, a mind guilty with sins, sorely mingled.']

In the final section of the poem a similar diagnosis is made concerning the world, which is 'mingled with evil': 'Swa is nu þes middangeard mane geblonden' (l. 31b).[43] Further, in the central section of the text, just as the slanderers wound *þurh deofles cræft* (l. 30a), the current state of the world is caused by *se ealda* (l. 32b), or the devil. The extension and application of the bee metaphor is also indicated by a further verbal parallel between the final two sections of the poem (ll. 18b–22a and 40–2):

> Ænlice beoð,
> swa ða beon berað   buta ætsomne
> arlicne anleofan,   ond ætterne tægel   20
> hafað on hindan,   hunig on muðe,
> wynsume wist.
>
> ...
>
> Forðon eallunga   hyht geceoseð,   40
> woruld wynsume,   se ðe wis ne bið,
> snottor, searocræftig   sawle rædes.

---

43 As with *smeðe* in lines 12 and 29, the repetition here of *geblonden* seems to have both an aural and a structural significance. The word is used nine other times in poetic texts (and not at all in prose) most often to denote either the clash of natural forces (*Andreas*, l. 424b; *Metres* 5, l. 19a; *Metres* 20, l. 81) or, more interestingly for the present purposes, the blending or spreading about of a poison (*Christ and Satan*, l. 128b; *Guthlac*, l. 668b, and *Riddles* 23, l. 8b).

['They are incomparable, just as the bees bear both together, exquisite food, honey in the mouth, joyful sustenance, and they have a poisoned tail behind ... Wherefore he entirely chooses hope, the joyful world, who is not wise, clever, and cunning in the counsel of the soul.']

Here the poet compares the honey of the bee, which only a fool would seek without considering the stinging tail, to the 'joyful world,' which is chosen by the one 'who is not wise, clever, and cunning in the counsel for the soul.'[44] The repetition of *wynsum* in this context links the concluding section of the poem back to the central passage, thus strengthening the aural relationship between the two sections, as well as confirming the suggestion of a concentric structure in the text. It is of interest to note that the word *wynsum* occurs frequently throughout the corpus of Old English prose and verse, often in alliterative conjunction with *wlitig*.[45] Moreover, there seems to be a precedent for the use of *wynsum* as a structural element in verse texts. In *The Phoenix*, for instance, the formula *wyrta wynsum* occurs four times (ll. 194a, 196a, 529a, and 653), and this repetition serves to link the initial portion of the poem (ll. 1–380, loosely based on the *De aue Phoenice* attributed to Lactantius) with the two subsequent interpretive and allegorical portions dealing with the Resurrection (ll. 381–588) and with Christ (ll. 589–677).[46] This use of structural and lexical parallelism, comparable to the use of *wynsum* in *Homiletic Fragment I*, seems to suggest that the poet intentionally included certain aural echoes in order to emphasize the concentric relationship between the sections of his poem.

Given the preceding evidence, it seems likely that the composer of *Homiletic Fragment I* deliberately utilized a structure in his poem which reflects the structure observed in some Old English homilies. The pericope–exegesis–exhortation sequence is found in many homilies of the medieval

---

44 The use of the phrase *sawle rædes* in this context is significant, for the phrase occurs additionally in some Old English homilies: 'we a sculon bion ymbhydige ure sawle rædes' (*VH* X.55); 'eac to ure sawle ræde' (*VH* XVII.103); 'we scylon beon ymbhydige and gemyndige sawle rædes' (Napier XLIX, p. 253, ll. 16–17). The phrase is also used in a similar context in the *Metres of Boethius* (*Metres* 21, l. 5).

45 See, for instance, *Christ and Satan* 213a, *Christ* 910a, and *Phoenix* 203a and 318a. The conjunction of the two words may be based, in part, on a similar juxtaposition in Psalm 146:1, where the phrase *wynsum and wlitig* is found glossing the Latin *iucunda decoraque*; see, for instance, the gloss for this verse in A.C. Kimmens, ed., *The Stowe Psalter*, TOES 3 (Toronto: UTP, 1979).

46 Further examples of repetition with *wynsum* are found in *The Panther* (ll. 45 and 65) and *Riddles* 84 (ll. 20 and 26).

period, and a related progression from the individual to the universal is also evident in homiletic texts, whether in prose or verse. Moreover, the use of a concentric structure in the poem, with various elements of the central metaphor being anticipated and commented upon in the outer two sections, is also indicative of homiletic literature. The exhortative and so-called homiletic conclusion of the text is appropriate to its overall tenor, but it is by no means the only structural element which suggests an affinity with homiletic prose.

Of all such structural elements in *Homiletic Fragment I*, the central metaphor, which likens deceivers to the bee which has honey in its mouth but a stinging tail behind, has received more attention from scholars than any other aspect of the text. T.D. Hill was the first to suggest that the comparison between the bee and the hypocritical deceivers derived from 'patristic biblical exegesis,' specifically that of Gregory the Great, who included the image in his *Homiliae in Ezechielem*.[47] Hill suggests that the image was 'fairly widely current during the early Middle Ages' by referencing further uses of the image in a letter, again from Gregory, and in the writings of Eucherius of Lyons.[48] Following Hill, Phillip Pulsiano indicated a further series of patristic texts – including commentaries on Psalms 27 and 117 from Augustine and Cassiodorus – which he considered to be useful as either source material or contextual analogues for *Homiletic Fragment I*.[49] These sources highlight the use of the bee as a 'type' of hypocrite in patristic literature, but ignore one of the most salient uses of the bee in

---

47 Hill, 'Hypocritical Bee,' 123. Gregory begins his discussion of the bee with a quotation from Psalm 117:12 ('circumdederunt me sicut apes, et exarserunt sicut ignis in spinis') ('they surrounded me like bees, and they burned like fire among thorns'); he then proceeds to comment on the hypocritical nature of the bee: 'Apes enim in ore mel habent, in aculeo caudae vulnus. Et omnes qui lingua blandiuntur, sed latenter ex malitia feriunt, apes sunt, quia loquendo dulcedinem mellia proponunt, sed occulte feriendo vulnus inferunt' ('For bees have honey in their mouths, but a wound in the point of their tail. And all those who speak kindly with their tongues, but strike secretly out of malice, are bees, because they put forward honey by speaking sweetness, but they cause a wound by striking furtively'). Note the paronomasia in Gregory's use of *feriunt ... feriendo ... inferunt*. See Gregory, *Homiliae in Ezechielem* I.9 (PL 76.879–80).
48 For the relevant quotations, see Gregory, *Epistolae* VII.27 (PL 77.882) and Eucherius of Lyons, *Liber formularum spiritualis intelligentiae* I.5 (PL 50.751).
49 According to Pulsiano, the texts in question lead to the suggestion that the poet of *Homiletic Fragment I* was identifying his 'deceivers' with the Jews who persecuted Christ. This interpretation of the relationship between the poem and its potential sources offers a further unifying theme in the Vercelli Book, that of the Passion of Christ; see 'Bees and Backbiters,' 5–6.

medieval didactic literature, in the prose *De uirginitate* by the Anglo-Saxon Aldhelm:[50]

> Apis, inquam, propter peculiaris castimoniae privilegium pudicissimae virginitatis tipum et ecclesiae portendere speciem indubitata scripturarum auctoritate asstipulatur, quae florentes saltuum cespites ineffabili praeda depopulans dulcia natorum pignora, nesciens coniugiiillecebrosa consortia, fetosa quadam suavissimi suci concretione producit:[51]
> ['The bee, I say, by virtue of the special attribute of its peculiar chastity, is by the undoubted authority of the scriptures agreed to signify a type of virginity and the likeness of the Church: robbing the flowering fields of pastureland of an ineffable booty she produces her sweet family and children, innocent of the lascivious coupling of marriage, by means of a certain generative condensation of a very sweet juice.']

Aldhelm, writing in the late seventh century to the nuns at Barking, gives to them as a model the bee which, 'by virtue of the special attribute of its peculiar chastity,' procreates asexually. The identification of bees with virginity is common in medieval exegesis, occurring (for instance) in texts which comment on the doctrine of the Virgin Birth of Christ. Thus Ælfric, writing three centuries after Aldhelm, makes the following comparison with the Virgin Mary in a sermon for Christmas (*CH* II.I.83–90):

> Nis nan wifhades mann hire gelica. for ði naðer ne ær ne siððan næs nan mæden þæt bearn gebære. and syððan mæden þurhwunode buton hire anre; Sindon þeahhwæðere sume gesceafta þe tymað buton hæmede. and bið ægðer ge seo moder mæden. ge seo dohtor þæt sind beon; Hi tymað heora team mid clænnysse; Of ðam hunige hi bredað heora brod. and beoð acennede þa geongan mid mægðhade. and ða yldran wuniað on mægðhade;
> ['No human being in the form of a woman is her like, for neither before nor since was there a virgin who bore a child and afterwards remained a virgin except her alone. Yet there are some creatures who reproduce asexually, and can be not only mother and virgin but daughter: they are bees. They produce their progeny in purity. They breed their brood from honey, and the young are born from virginity, and the parents dwell in virginity.']

---

50 *Aldhelmi Opera*, 233. See further Augustine Casiday, 'St Aldhelm's Bees (*De uirginitate prosa* cc. IV–VI): Some Observations on a Literary Tradition,' *ASE* 33 (2004): 1–22.
51 See M. Lapidge and M. Herren, trans., *Aldhelm: the Prose Works* (Cambridge: D.S. Brewer, 1979), 62. The point, that bees create asexually and therefore are models for virgins, is also made by Eucherius of Lyons ('Apis forma virginitatis, sive sapientiae').

Bees here are given a place of prominence in the order of Nature: they are categorized as the only other example, apart from Mary, of creatures which *tymað buton hæmede.* The bee image in Anglo-Saxon England, therefore, is in the first instance identified with the chaste life of virgins.

A further metaphorical use of bees as a positive 'type' occurs again in the work of Aldhelm. Immediately following the previous quotation from the prose *De uirginitate*, he is quick to suggest that the nuns may benefit from another lesson to be learned from the bees. Emphasizing the 'harmonious fellowship' (*concordi sodalitate*) which exists among the members of a hive, Aldhelm focuses on the obedient relationship between the bees and their rulers:[52]

> Illud etiam commemorandum de apum concordi sodalitate et theatrali quodam spectaculo stupendum autumo, ultroneum videlicet voluntariae servitutis affectum, quem erga suorum obsequia principum exercere noscuntur. Nonne sub huiuscemodi contemplationis intuitu omnis monasticae conversationis disciplina et regularia coenubiorum instituta simillima collatione declarentur? ['This also is to be remembered, I suggest, concerning the harmonious fellowship of the bees, and to be admired as some theatrical spectacle – I mean the spontaneous inclination to voluntary servitude which they are known to exercise in obedience to their rulers. In respect of this sort of consideration, are not all the disciplines of the monastic way of life and the regular practices of monasteries indicated by an extremely close comparison?']

Again, later in the same passage, Aldhelm suggests that the bee, because of both its virginal nature and its obedient service, gives an example to all mortals living in 'the vale of tears.' To this theme of devout obedience might be added a final and related image of bees used by Aldhelm; namely, the industry of the bee. Once again, in the prose *De uirginitate*, Aldhelm encourages his readers to consider the bee:[53]

> solertissimae apis industriam praedictis exemplorum formulis coaptari posse uberrima rerum experimenta liquido declarant ... Nam quemadmodum examen arta fenestrarum foramina et angusta alvearii vestibula certatim per turmas

---

52 See R. Ehwald, ed., *Aldhelmi Opera*, MGH AA15 (Berlin: Weidmann, 1919), 234, and Lapidge and Herren, *Prose Works*, 62–3. A similar image is used by Aldhelm in his *Epistula ad Wilfridi abbates* (*Aldhelmi Opera*, 501–2), in which he encourages the abbots of Wilfrid to remain faithful to their leader while in exile. He urges the abbots to consider the bees, who devotedly follow their leader and king whether he departs from or returns to his beloved home.

53 See *Aldhelmi Opera*, 231–2; Lapidge and Herren, *Prose Works*, 61.

egressum amoena arvorum prata populatur, eodem modo vestrum, ni fallor, memoriale mentis ingenium per florulenta scripturarum arva late vagans bibula curiositate decurrit.

['the richest experience of life clearly declares that the industry of the highly ingenious bee might be adapted to the aforementioned schemes of examples … For just as the swarm, having left in companies and throngs the restricted openings of the windows and the narrow entrance-halls of the beehive, pillages the beautiful meadows of the countryside, in the same way your remarkable mental disposition – unless I'm mistaken – roaming widely through the flowering fields of scripture, traverses (them) with thirsty curiosity.']

The metaphor set forth here, namely, that the contemplation and study of the scriptures (and, later in the same passage, that of metrics and history) is to be compared with the swarm of bees which 'pillages the beautiful meadows of the countryside,' is repeated by Aldhelm in his *Epistula ad Ehfridum*. In a passage of this highly rhetorical letter, he states that the traffic between Ireland and England of biblical scholars mimics the swarm of bees which ferries its burden through the flowers to the honeycomb: so, too, do scholars store their arts *in alueariis sofiae*.[54] However, none of these examples are immediately relevant to the use of the 'hypocritical' bee in *Homiletic Fragment I*; rather, they are all positive images, accentuating the beneficial lessons to be learned from the bee. Like the bee in the Vercelli poem, though, the use of bees as observed in the literature of Anglo-Saxon England has a 'sting' as well.

Ælfric, for instance, states in a sermon on the Nativity of Christ that bees, creatures which he earlier compared with the Virgin Mary in a similar context, are born of rotting flesh: 'ac us secgað lareowas þæt of fearres flæsce, fule stincendum, beoð beon acende, þæt hi cuce swa fleoð.'[55] This tradition probably originates from the circumstances surrounding the riddle of Samson in the book of Judges: 'et post aliquot dies revertens ut acciperet eam declinavit ut videret cadaver leonis et ecce examen apium in ore leonis erat ac favus mellis … dixitque eis de comedente exivit cibus et de forte est egressa dulcedo nec potuerunt per tres dies propositionem solvere' (Judges 14:8 and 14). Despite its biblical basis and its didactic context, however, this reference is not immediately comparable to the bee in

---

54 See *Aldhelmi Opera*, 490–1.
55 *Supp.* I.268–70. This passage in Ælfric is based on Isidore, *Etymologiae*, XII.viii.2. It is of interest here that Ælfric contradicts his assertion, quoted earlier, that bees are born from honey; see n. 51 above.

Homiletic Fragment I. A more fruitful comparison can be made between the poem and the following passage from the *Metres of Boethius* (*Metres* 18, ll. 5–11):

> Hwæt, sio wilde beo,   þeah wis sie,   5
> anunga sceal   eall forweorðan
> gif hio yrringa   awuht stingeð.
> Swa sceal sawla gehwilc   siððan losian,
> gif se lichoma   forlegen weorðeð
> unrihthæmede,   bute him ær cume   10
> hreow to heortan,   ær he hionan wende.
> ['Behold: the wild bee, even though she may be wise, shall completely lose all, if she stings anything in anger. So shall each soul be lost, if the body become embroiled in adultery and fornication, unless repentance should previously come to the heart, before one have passed from here.']

This passage, according to Isaacs, seems to repeat the sentiment expressed in lines 22b–3 of *Homiletic Fragment I*: 'Hwilum wundiað / sare mid stinge þonne se sæl cymeð.'[56] The suggested parallels between the two passages are superficial, however. There is no mention of deceit or hypocrisy on the part of the bee in the Boethian passage, as there is in *Homiletic Fragment I*; on the contrary, the sting of the bee is a straightforward result of its anger. Again, although in both poems the bee is used as a metaphorical type, the focus is markedly different in each case. While in *Homiletic Fragment I* the bee is used to emphasize the wickedness of deceivers, the bee in the above *Metre* highlights the guilt and coming destruction of those who sin through fornication (*unrihthæmede*, l. 10a) – a didactic inversion of the association of the bee with virgins, seen earlier. Finally, there is no specific mention in *Homiletic Fragment I* of the death of the bee – or the sinner, for that matter – as there is in the above passage. Nevertheless, the portrayal of the bee in a negative context, as well as the emphasis on the bee's sting, is comparable to the Vercelli poem.

A more convincing parallel for the use of the bee in *Homiletic Fragment I* is found, once again, in the works of Aldhelm, who has a five-line enigma on the bee (*Ænigma* XX):[57]

---

56 See *Structural Principles*, 101.
57 See *Aldhelmi Opera*, p. 106; M. Lapidge, and J.L. Rosier, trans., *Aldhelm: the Poetic Works* (Cambridge: D.S. Brewer, 1985), 74.

Mirificis formata modis, sine semine creta
Dulcia florigeris onero praecordia praedis;
Arte mea crocea flavescunt fercula regum.
Semper acuta gero crudelis spicula belli
Atque carens manibus fabrorum vinco metalla.   5
['Formed in wondrous ways and engendered without seed, I load my sweet
inwards with booty from flowers. Through my craft the food of kings grows
golden with honey. I always brandish the sharpened arrow-points of fierce
warfare and (yet), lacking hands, I surpass the metal-work of smiths.']

As with the quotations from *De uirginitate*, Aldhelm here begins by emphasizing the 'miraculous' asexual procreation of bees (l. 1), a point which
is missing from the extant text of *Homiletic Fragment I*. Yet, upon further
analysis, this short text provides a series of close parallels with the Vercelli
fragment.

In *Homiletic Fragment I*, the bee metaphor focuses on the dual nature
of the bee, existing as it does with 'honey in the mouth' (l. 21b) and 'a
poisonous tail' (l. 20b). These same two qualities are mentioned in the
above quotation from Aldhelm. The bee is said to stow away (*onero*) in its
sweet breast (*dulcia ... praecordia*) the pollen of the flower (l. 2). The stinging tail of the bee is likewise depicted through martial imagery in line 4, in
which the bee's sting is metaphorically referred to as the 'sharpened spears
of war' (*acuta ... spicula belli*) which are carried continually by the bee –
even while kings enjoy the taste of honey in their food (l. 3), a reference
which resembles the *hunigsmæccas* of *Homiletic Fragment I*.

Similarly, although the diction of this riddle is fairly straightforward
and yields a simple (though metaphorical) meaning in most cases, Aldhelm
has employed some word forms which could be interpreted in multiple
senses. In two instances, this ambiguity of diction bears striking resemblances to the use of the bee metaphor in *Homiletic Fragment I*. In describing the weaponry of the bee, Aldhelm makes use of the neuter plural
form of the adjective *acutus* (*acuta*, l. 4), meaning 'sharp.' However, just as
in *Homiletic Fragment I*, where *þa leasan men* wound *þurh deofles cræft*,
acuta in Aldhelm's riddle can also refer to the intellect, in which case the
meaning would be 'crafty' or 'subtle.' There is also an ambiguity in the use
of the word *creta* in line 1 of the riddle. Context demands the interpretation of this form of *cretus* as a past participle of the verb *cresco*, meaning
'to come into being.' *Cretus* can also be interpreted as a participle of the
verb *cerno*, however, with the resulting meaning 'to discern, perceive, or
comprehend.' In this sense, *creta* would parallel the *-smæccas* element of

the compound *hunigsmæccas* in *Homiletic Fragment I*, for *-smæccas*, too, has an extended meaning of 'to understand' or 'perceive.'[58]

While a direct connection between Aldhelm's riddle and *Homiletic Fragment I* cannot be established on such tenuous grounds, there are nevertheless reasons for viewing the texts as belonging to the same tradition in Anglo-Saxon England. The amibiguous diction in Aldhelm's poem firmly identifies that text within the Anglo-Latin riddle tradition, which is full of such wordplay. The use of similar ambiguous diction, as well as the 'central' metaphor, in *Homiletic Fragment I* can also be seen as a development from this same riddle tradition, for metaphor and ambiguity is at the heart of the riddle.[59] Thus the aforementioned texts, especially the riddle of Aldhelm, share a degree of similarity with *Homiletic Fragment I* in their depiction of bees and exist as analogues to the bee metaphor. A final parallel for the metaphor in the poem originates from a theme in the Psalter which, on the surface, has nothing whatsoever to do with bees. Previous commentary on the relationship between *Homiletic Fragment I* and the Psalms has resulted in the suggestion that two verses from the Psalms influenced the composer of the poem.[60] To these verses might be added a third, as we shall see.

As mentioned earlier, Alfred's translation of Psalm 11:2 (his Psalm 13:5) exhibits some similarities of diction with *Homiletic Fragment I*.[61] This translation, which differs significantly from its Latin source in its mention of graves and of the poison of the asp,[62] seems to be typical of Alfredian

---

58 In Ælfric's *Grammar*, for instance, the verb *sapio* is glossed by both *ic wat* and *ic gesmæcce*. See J. Zupitza, ed., *Ælfrics Grammatik und Glossar*, Sammlung englischer Denkmäler 1 (Berlin: Weidmann, 1880), 221, l. 9. It seems that in Old English, as in Latin, there was a similarity between verbs which denoted tasting and verbs which denoted understanding or wisdom.

59 See, for instance, Greenfield and Calder, *New Critical History*, 269: 'The riddles elaborate metaphorically upon their subjects with the deliberate ambiguities that are their generic essence.' Further, it will be remembered that one of the interpretations of the bee in Anglo-Saxon England actually sprang from the riddle of Samson in the scriptures.

60 The relationship between *Homiletic Fragment I* and Psalm 27:3 has already been commented upon, while both Hill ('Hypocritical Bee') and Pulsiano ('Bees and Backbiters,' 3–5) suggest that a further defining context for the poem is gained when one considers Psalm 117:12.

61 See above, n. 25.

62 The Latin text reads as follows: 'frustra loquuntur unusquisque proximo suo labium subdolum in corde et corde locuti sunt' ('Every one utters lies to his neighbour; with flattering lips and a double heart they speak').

translations, which have long been recognized as a combination of 'dependence and originality' when it comes to his sources.[63] However, his interpolations into the above verse of the Psalter, far from being Alfredian 'creations,' can be explained simply by further references within the Psalms.

The first difference noted between Alfred's translation and his Latin source, namely, the likening of the sinful to the asp, is not an artistic invention of Alfred's; rather, the same image is found elsewhere in the Psalter (Psalm 139).[64] Here David implores God to save him from the 'man of violence' who plots evil in his heart, and who has the poison of asps under his lips. Yet there is no specific mention in this Psalm of deceivers, which raises questions about why Alfred would associate this later verse with his translation of Psalm 13. Likewise, the source for the second interpolation in Alfred's translation is found elsewhere in the Psalter.[65] Like Alfred's Psalm 13, these verses compare the throats of sinners to open graves ('sepulchrum patens est guttur eorum'). Moreover, such a sinner is called *virum dolosum*, which emphasizes the theme of deceit as is found in the Alfredian translation from Psalm 13.

Although these two potential source passages are located at opposite ends of the Psalter, it is of interest to note that the verses in question do occur in close proximity in a single passage, but in the New Testament rather than the Old. In the Epistle to the Romans, the Apostle Paul comments on the sinfulness of man under the law by quoting a number of specific verses from the Psalter (Romans 3:12–18):

---

63 See, for instance, J. Bately, 'The Nature of Old English Prose,' in *The Cambridge Companion to Old English Literature*, ed. M. Godden and M. Lapidge (Cambridge: CUP, 1991): 75.

64 Psalm 139:2–4: 'Eripe me Domine ab homine malo a viro iniquo eripe me qui cogitaverunt iniquitates in corde tota die constituebant proelia acuerunt linguam suam sicut serpentis venenum aspidum sub labiis eorum' ('Deliver me, O Lord, from the evil man: rescue me from the unjust man. Who have devised iniquities in their hearts: all the day long they designed battles. They have sharpened their tongues like a serpent: the venom of asps is under their lips').

65 Psalm 5:7 and 10–11: 'odisti omnes qui operantur iniquitatem perdes omnes qui loquuntur mendacium virum sanguinum et dolosum abominabitur Dominus ... quoniam non est in ore eorum veritas cor eorum vanum est sepulchrum patens est guttur eorum linguis suis dolose agebant iudica illos Deus decidant a cogitationibus suis secundum multitudinem impietatum eorum expelle eos quoniam inritaverunt te Domine' ('Thou hatest all the workers of iniquity: thou wilt destroy all that speak a lie. The bloody and the deceitful man the Lord will abhor ... For there is no truth in their mouth: their heart is vain. Their throat is an open sepulchre: they dealt deceitfully with their tongues: judge them, O God. Let them fall from their devices: according to the multitude of their wickednesses cast them out: for they have provoked thee, O Lord').

omnes declinaverunt simul inutiles facti sunt non est qui faciat bonum non est usque ad unum sepulchrum patens est guttur eorum linguis suis dolose agebant venenum aspidum sub labiis eorum quorum os maledictione et amaritudine plenum est veloces pedes eorum ad effundendum sanguinem contritio et infelicitas in viis eorum et viam pacis non cognoverunt non est timor Dei ante oculos eorum.

['All have turned out of the way: they are become unprofitable together: there is none that doth good, there is not so much as one. Their throat is an open sepulchre: with their tongues they have dealt deceitfully. The venom of asps is under their lips. Whose mouth is full of cursing and bitterness, their feet swift to shed blood, destruction and misery in their ways, and the way of peace they have not known. There is no fear of God before their eyes.']

Of interest to the present argument is the fact that Paul has chosen the two references previously seen (from Psalms 5 and 139), thereby linking deceitful men with the poison of the snake. It seems likely, then, that Alfred has relied upon this particular Pauline passage in order to establish his comparison between graves, deceivers, and the asp; yet it should also be evident that deceit in the Psalms is, in the first instance, identified with the *aspis* rather than with the *apis*.[66]

It is such a learned tradition, found in the Psalms, the writings of (for instance) Augustine and Gregory from the patristic era, and the literature of Aldhelm and other writers from Anglo-Saxon England, which provides the most convincing source material for the bee metaphor in *Homiletic Fragment I*. Even if none of these parallels can be identified as a proper source for the poem, they nonetheless provide a useful context for analysing the bee image in Anglo-Saxon England. In using the striking image of the hypocritical bee, the poet of *Homiletic Fragment I* appears to have drawn upon a wide range of material, most of which is patristic, and a good portion of which is homiletic. Such a reliance on prose sources is indicative (though not exclusively so) of homiletic verse in Old English; yet it is in more conspicuous elements, such as metre and diction, that the evidence for prosaic and homiletic influence on this verse text is most convincing.

---

66 The similarity in orthography between *aspis* and *apis* should not be overlooked here. There may be, in *Homiletic Fragment I*, an element of paronomasia in the choice of the bee to indicate deceitful men; similar puns occur throughout the corpus of Old English literature, and wordplay seems to have been a hallmark of some Old English composers. See, for instance, R. Frank, 'Some Uses of Paronomasia in Old English Scriptural Verse,' *Speculum* 47 (1972): 207–26.

There are certain lines and verses in *Homiletic Fragment I* which, according to the traditional 'rules' governing Old English metre, contain abnormal, or at least unusual, metrical forms. These departures would seem to suggest either that the composer of *Homiletic Fragment I* was unfamiliar with such guidelines (which is doubtful), or else that he deliberately adopted a relaxed approach to metrical composition and, by doing so, distanced himself from the more orthodox metre observed elsewhere in Old English poetry. The first example of such unusual metrical forms occurs in line 8 ('Forðan se witiga cwæð'), which exists as a single (or stray) half-line. The context does not suggest that any material has been lost from the passage, either before or after line 8, which could possibly emend the verse. Similar phrases, such as 'forðan þe se hælend cwæð' or 'forðam se witega cwæð' are attested in prose,[67] while other analogues ('swa swa se witega cwæð,' for instance) are more numerous, occurring both in prose and verse.[68] In most attestations, these analogues are used as direct introductions to quotations (as might be expected), so it is doubtful, given the fact that the paraphrase from Psalm 27 begins immediately after line 8, that another verse was omitted after the 'stray' half-line. Moreover, as *witiga* is the only fully stressed word in the half-line (and would therefore alliterate in a line of normal metre),[69] it is of interest to note that line 8 continues the alliterative scheme of line 7 (on *w*-). The use of continued alliteration is observed in other cases of single half-lines in Old English verse, and the frequency of such stray verses, especially in the texts of the Junius Manuscript, prompted Bliss to suggest that such single half-lines could be viewed as intentional on the part of the poet, 'particularly if a short line has either double or continued alliteration.'[70]

---

67 See, for instance, *LS* XVI.337–40: 'forðan þe se hælend cwæð þus on his godspelle, [In patientia uestra possidebitis animas uestras]; þæt is on Engliscre spræce, On eowrum geðylde ge habbað eowre sawla soðlice gehealdene.'

68 The only other poetic occurrences of such analogues are *swa se witega cwæð*, from one of the *Metrical Charms* ('For Unfruitful Land,' l. 37a); and *swa se waldend cwæð*, found in *The Judgment Day I* (l. 94a), a poem which – as noted previously – owes much to the Old English homiletic tradition. Similar forms occur more than forty times in homiletic texts, mostly in the homilies of Ælfric, with the most attested forms being *swa swa se witega cwæð* (twenty-four times); *swa swa se apostol cwæð* (ten times); and *swa swa se hælend cwæð* (five times).

69 See T. Cable, *The English Alliterative Tradition* (Philadelphia: Univ. of Pennsylvania Press, 1991), 22.

70 A.J. Bliss, 'Single Half-Lines in Old English Poetry,' *NQ* 216 (1971): 449. Within the Vercelli Book there are further examples of single half-lines in *Soul and Body I* (l. 110) and in the metrical portions of *VH* II and *VH* XXI; see E.G. Stanley, 'The Judgement of

Although the presence of such a metrically 'incomplete' form does not argue exclusively for the influence of prose texts on *Homiletic Fragment I*, the frequency of further unorthodox alliterative patterns in the poem suggests a standard of composition which is rather more liberal (in metrical terms, at least) than the 'strict rules' which govern alliteration in Old English verse.[71] The most obvious instance of atypical alliteration in *Homiletic Fragment I* is found in line 40: 'Forþan eallunga hyht geceoseð.'[72] As the line stands, there is no alliterative pattern; neither have previous editors suggested any emendation to the text at this point which would correct the lack of alliteration. One possible emendation which immediately suggests itself would be to include OE *a*, 'ever,' in the b-verse, producing a line which reads 'Forþan eallunga [a] hyht geceoseð.' Since *eallunga* tends to alliterate elsewhere in Old English verse,[73] the suggestion appears to be justified. Yet this emendation fails to resolve the initial unorthodox metre, for it results in three stresses in the b-verse in a combination which is unattested elsewhere in verse. This lack of alliteration in line 40, then, also seems to indicate a relaxed approach to the rigid guidelines of alliteration mentioned above.

---

the *Damned* (from Cambridge, Corpus Christi College 201 and Other Manuscripts) and the Definition of Old English Verse,' in his *A Collection of Papers with Emphasis on Old English Literature*, Publications of the Dictionary of Old English 3 (Toronto: PIMS, 1987), 352–83. Additional examples occur in *Andreas* (ll. 1036, 1040, and 1434) and *Elene* (ll. 22, 451, 518 and 1276). There is also such a stray half-line in *The Dream of the Rood* (l. 76).

71 See, for instance, A.J. Bliss, *An Introduction to Old English Metre* (Oxford: Blackwell, 1962), §14: 'The rules governing alliteration in OE poetry are very strict.' As we have seen, however, such rigidity is uncharacteristic of the examples of homiletic verse in the Vercelli Book.

72 The only examples comparable to line 40a of *Homiletic Fragment I* occur in a single prose text: 'and for þy eallunga flæsclice we ne beoþ ymbsnidene for þon þe on ymbsnidenesse hiwe behatenum fulwihtes geryne we syn geclænsude. Þæs restedæges ænethwile idle we tellaþ for þon þe eallunga þone onwrigenan hyht reste þære ecean we habbaþ ... Þa bigengu þæs niwan monan we na ne healdaþ for þon þe eallunga on criste niwre gesceafte þa ealdan forþ gewitun and efne hi wærun gewordene niwe.' The text in question is a gloss of Isidore's *De miraculis Christi*; see A.S. Napier, ed., *Old English Glosses, Chiefly Unpublished* (Oxford: Clarendon Press, 1900), 206, ll. 15–20 and 207, ll. 34–6.

73 For the attestations in verse, see the following: 'þæt se him eallunga owiht ne ondrædeð' (*Christ*, l. 922); 'hæfdan hi eallunga ut aworpen' (*Paris Psalter* 77.45, l. 3); 'æfre gestillan ne eft eallunga' (*Metres* 11, l. 26); 'þæt hit ænige eallunga fordo' (*Metres* 20, l. 130); 'ac hio bið eallunga an hire selfre' (*Metres* 20, l. 220); 'ond þa unþeawas eallunga ne magon' (*Metres* 22, l. 26); 'ælc eorðlic ðing, eallunga forsion' (*Metres* 24, l. 7); 'Ðis is eallunga min agen cyð' (*Metres* 24, l. 49); 'þe he hine eallunga ær underþiodde' (*Metres* 25, l. 66); 'eallunga to him æfre onwendan' (*Metres* 26, l. 116); 'þridde is tohope þam þe eallunga' (*Instructions*, l. 261).

Such an approach is again evident in line 12 of the poem ('þam þe ful smeðe spræce habbað'), which contains another example of unusual alliterative patterning. Here, *smeðe* and *spræce* appear to be the two alliterating stresses in the line; yet, according to a traditional view of Old English verse composition, 'The consonant groups <u>sc</u>, <u>sp</u> and <u>st</u> are treated as single consonants; that is, each alliterates only with itself, not with either of the others or with <u>s</u> followed by a vowel or by any other consonant.'[74] On the other hand, such a relaxed attitude to the alliteration of *s*-groups is often found in prose texts, as in some Old English homilies. Ælfric, for instance, writes of the passion of St Stephen using the same type of alliterative pattern (here in bold) as that found in *Homiletic Fragment I*: 'Se wisa agustinus **spræc** ymbe ðas rædinge and **smeade** hwi se halga cyðere stephanus cwæde þæt he gesawe mannes bearn standan æt godes swiðran.'[75] A similar tendency is found in the anonymous Old English homilies, such as in line 94 of Vercelli Homily VIII, where the alliteration on sm- and st- (here in bold) is emphasized by the use of a more artistic pattern of alternating alliteration on l- (here underlined): 'ond þær is <u>l</u>ufu ond **smyltnes** ond syngal <u>l</u>ioht ond swete **stenc**' (l. 94).[76]

In addition to such unorthodox patterns observed above, the composer of *Homiletic Fragment I* has added several more 'artistic' alliterative touches to the poem, perhaps in an attempt to compensate for what might be viewed as metrical or alliterative 'deficiencies' elsewhere in his composition. These more poetic ornaments can be categorized according to the use of interlinear alliteration.[77] In the first instance, there are alliterative patterns which establish links between successive lines of the poem, as we have seen before in the case of lines 7–8 (here, and in the quotations which

---

74 Bliss, *Introduction*, §14.

75 *CH* I.III.60–2. See also *LS* XXXIV.100: 'Hi smeadon þa mid glædnysse, and embe Godes willan spræcon.' Alliteration on sc- and st- also appears to have been 'legitimate' in Ælfric's rhythmical prose; see *Supp.*, p. 111.

76 Further *s*-group alliterating pairs are found in P. Gonser, ed., *Das angelsächsische Prosa-Leben des heiligen Guthlac*, Anglistische Forschungen 27 (Heidelberg: Winter, 1909), 156, ll. 37–8 ('And he þa semninga se biscop on midre þære spræce, þe hi heom betwux smeadon'); Napier XLVI, p. 233, ll. 13–14 ('þonne lærð us godes engel stilnesse and gemetlice spræce and smeaunge ymbe godes beboda'); and Napier LIX, p. 307, l. 19 ('and godes lara and laga smeagean and spirian').

77 A useful study of such interlinear alliteration is found in A. Orchard, 'Artful Alliteration in Anglo-Saxon Song and Story,' *Anglia* 113 (1995): 429–63. In the discussion which follows, the terms used to refer to the different alliterative schemes ('back-linked,' 'strong-linked,' and so on) are borrowed from Orchard.

follow, alliterating elements within a given line are printed in bold, while those which participate in interlinear alliteration are underlined):

Byð þonne þæs **w**ommes ge**w**ita **w**erouda dryhten.
Forðan se **w**itiga cwæð:
['He is then a witness to the stain, the Lord of Hosts. For which reason the prophet said ...']

As mentioned above, the continued alliteration on w- in these three verses suggests a connection between the two lines. Such is also the case in lines 10–11 of the poem, in which a back-linked alliterative pattern, again on w-, is evident:

in **w**ita for**w**yrd, **w**eoruda dryhten,
ne me on life forleos mid þam lige**w**yrhtum
['... into the ruin of punishments, Lord of Hosts, and do not abandon me in life, among the workers of lies.']

In addition to the use of back-linked alliteration in these lines, the poet has intensified the connection between the two lines by using similar alliterative patterns in the two a-verses. Both verses 10a and 11a exhibit double alliteration, and both include *for-* compounds in which the second element (-*wyrd* in line 10a and -*leos* in line 11a) participates in the double alliteration of the verse. A third example of alliteration which links consecutive lines is found in lines 28–9 of the poem, which exhibit weak-linked alliteration:

hafað on gehatum hunig**sm**æccas,
smeðne sybcwide, ond in siofan innan
['he has among his enemies the taste of honey, a smooth speech of peace, and inside his heart ...']

In this case, the non-alliterating element in the b-verse of line 28 (-*smæc-cas*) is linked, through alliteration on *sm-*, to the non-alliterating word in the a-verse of line 29 (*smeðne*). The technique of variation, so distinctive a feature of Old English poetry, is here supplemented through interlinear alliteration. The resulting connection between the two lines serves to clarify any confusion which might result from the use of the 'taste of honey' metaphor: the *hunigsmæccas* in line 28 is linked to, and therefore equated with, the *smeðne sybcwide* of line 29. All these examples suggest an effort on the part of the composer to 'dress up' his poetry, or to highlight relationships between verses, through the use of certain ornamental effects.[78]

In addition to alliterative patterns which suggest relationships between successive lines of *Homiletic Fragment I*, there are also patterns which form links among several lines in the poem. For example, following the biblical paraphrase in lines 9–15a, there occurs a series of lines which exhibit a flourish of such artistic alliterative patterns (*HF1*, ll. 15b–23):

> Wea bið in mode,   15
> siofa synnum fah,   sare geblonden,
> gefylled mid facne,   þeah he fæger word
> utan ætywe. Ænlice beoð,
> swa ða beon berað   buta ætsomne
> arlicne anleofan,   ond ætterne tægel   20
> hafað on hindan   hunig on muðe,
> wynsume wist. Hwilum wundiaþ
> sare mid stinge,   þonne se sæl cymeð.
>
> ['There shall be woe in his mind, a heart stained with sins, mixed with pain, filled with malice, though he shows fair words on the outside. They are incomparable, just as the bees bear both together, exquisite food, honey in the mouth, joyful sustenance, and they have a poisoned tail behind. Sometimes he wounds sorely with his sting, when the opportunity arises.']

In this case, as can be seen, almost every line exhibits some sort of alliterative relationship to either the preceding or following lines: end-linked alliteration on *b*- occurs in lines 15b–16; back-linked alliteration is found in lines 18–19 (vocalic) and again in lines 21–2 (on *h*-); and strong-linked alliteration occurs in lines 18–19 (on *b*-) and again in lines 19–20 (vocalic). In addition to these more common types of interlinear alliteration, a less well-attested type occurs in lines 16–17, in which the non-alliterating element in the a-verse of the first line (*fah*, line 16) participates in the alliterative scheme (on *f*-) of the second line (line 17). This succession of lines, interrelated through alliteration, occurs at the central point of the poem, where the composer establishes his comparison between the deceitful men and the hypocritical bee.

---

78 The fact that such techniques are also used in Old English homiletic prose is indicated by Orchard, who cites a short homily (Napier XXXI) as evidence of such intentional and ornamental alliteration; see 'Artful Alliteration,' 459–62.

The structural importance of the passage has already been noted, and the thematic significance of the passage to the poem as a whole is further emphasized by this ornamental and rhetorical flourish.

In short, neither the metrical 'defects' of *Homiletic Fragment I* nor the particular alliterative embellishments of the poem can be used, on their own, to suggest a prosaic or homiletic context or origin for the poem. Nevertheless, many of the unusual alliterative and metrical forms have parallels in prose texts; so, too, do the instances of 'extra' or 'ornamental' alliteration. The recurrence of these unusual forms seems to suggest a synthesis of techniques of composition which might find its origin in the indistinct 'borderland' between prose and verse texts in Old English. Rather than being (on metrical grounds) simply 'debased poetry,' *Homiletic· Fragment I* exhibits a range of metrical qualities which suggest influence from both prose and poetry. There are elements which are reminiscent of the most rhetorically complex Old English poems; these exist alongside metrical anomalies which suggest the most pedestrian of prose texts. The poem exhibits a blend of prosaic and poetic metrical qualities which suggests an effort on the part of the composer to combine the two traditions, and it is this type of blending which should be noted as a hallmark of Old English homiletic verse.

Like the metrical and alliterative anomalies cited above, many of the lexical and syntactical forms in *Homiletic Fragment I* suggest that the composer was aware of and, indeed, familiar with Old English prose. However, the identification of 'poetic' or 'prosaic' diction in Old English literature must be approached with caution. There are numerous difficulties in trying to establish whether or not a given word in the corpus of Old English literature is 'prosaic' or 'poetic' – not the least of which is the fact that the extant corpus by no means represents all of the Old English literature which was composed.[79] Such a caveat must be borne in mind throughout the following analysis; nevertheless, in certain instances, it is possible to suggest that the poet of *Homiletic Fragment I* avoided word forms which are attested elsewhere in Old English verse.

Some words and phrases found in the poem, for instance, are found elsewhere only in prose texts. In the case of *teonwordum* (l. 4a), there are only three other attestations of forms of *teonword* in Old English literature, all of which occur in prose texts. First, *teonwordum* is found in the

---

79 On the difficulties of labelling Old English words as 'prosaic' or 'poetic,' see E.G. Stanley, 'Studies in the Prosaic Vocabulary of Old English Verse,' *NM* 72 (1971): 385–418.

Alfredian translation of the Gregory the Great's *Dialogi*.[80] In this passage, the spiteful talk is identified with *þa hæðenan weras* who use their words to persecute the holy Sanctulus. The context here does not provide any close parallels with the use of *teonwordum* in *Homiletic Fragment I*, but the identification with heathens is worthy of note. Although it is the *eorl* (l. 3a) who speaks with *teonwordum* in the Vercelli poem, this *eorl* is later compared, as we have seen, with *þam synfullum* (l. 9b), *þam ligewyhtum* (l. 11b) and *þa leasan men* (l. 24b) – all of which, to the Christian mind, could be descriptions of the heathen. Second, in an anonymous homiletic *Life* of St Mildred, the homilist makes a telling comparison between the noblemen of his day and the saint.[81] Here *teonwordum* is equated with *ofermettum*, *woruldprydum*, *nyðum*, and *æfeste*: again, qualities which are frequently associated with the sinful. Moreover, the homilist's complaint about the negative traits of noblemen in the world 'now' is reminiscent of *Homiletic Fragment I*. In the poem, once again, it is the *eorl* who speaks with *teonwordum*, just as in the homily. Likewise, it is the present world which is filled with crimes: 'Swa is <u>nu</u> þes middangeard mane geblonden' (l. 31). Finally, an occurrence of *teonwordum* is found in the Old English Heptateuch, in a passage which translates Numbers 13:33–4 and which has further lexical parallels with *Homiletic Fragment I*.[82] In this passage, the band of Israelite warriors which Moses sent out to reconnoitre the promised land of Canaan delivers an unfavourable report about the land (and its inhabitants), fostering doubt and dissension among the Israelites and eventually inciting the wrath of God.[83] Likewise, in *Homiletic Fragment I*, the poet, quoting the psalmist, recognizes God's intent to give the sinful over to the tormenting destruction which their sins have brought upon them (ll. 9–11). In the biblical translation, *teonwordum* is placed in juxaposition

---

80 H. Hecht, ed., *Bischof Wærferths von Worcester Uebersetzung der Dialoge Gregors des Grossen*, BaP 5 (Leipzig and Hamburg: Wissenschaftliche Buchgesellschaft, 1900–7), 250, ll. 19–22.

81 M. Förster, 'Die altenglischen Beigaben des Lambeth-Psalters,' *Archiv* 132 (1914): 334, ll. 19–21.

82 S.J. Crawford, ed., *The Old English Version of the Heptateuch*, EETS o.s. 160 (London: OUP, 1922), 317. The verses are transposed here; compare the original order of Numbers 13:33–4 in the Vulgate: 'dextraeruntque terrae quam inspexerant apud filios Israhel dicentes terram quam lustravimus devorat habitatores suos populum quem aspeximus procerae staturae est ibi vidimus monstra quaedam filiorum Enach de genere giganteo quibus conparati quasi lucustae videbamur.'

83 Following this episode, the Israelites were condemned to forty years of wandering in the desert; see Numbers 14:32–4.

with *tældon*, a form of the verb *tælan*. This is exactly the same relationship as that found in line 4 of the Vercelli poem: 'ond mid teonwordum tæleð behindan.'

The attestation of *teonword* largely in prose texts suggests a limited frame of lexical reference for the composer of *Homiletic Fragment I*; but, as was mentioned earlier, judgments about the 'prosaic' nature of such vocabulary should be approached with caution. Analogous to *teonword*, however, there exist two words (*teoncwide* and *teonhete*), either of which could have been used by the composer of *Homiletic Fragment I* without any metrical or alliterative difficulties, and both of which are attested else-where in verse.[84] Moreover, in some of these verse attestations, the two other *teon-* compounds are linked by alliteration with forms of (*ge-*)*teal-don* or analogous nominal forms, just as in *Homiletic Fragment I*. In *Andreas*, for instance, the helmsman-Christ assures Andrew that 'Ne frine ic ðe for tæle ne ðurh teoncwide' (l. 633).[85] Such attestations highlight the lexical choice of the composer of *Homiletic Fragment I* by suggesting that *teoncwide* and *teonhete*, attested elsewhere primarily in poetry, could be used in a more or less identical context as *teonword*, and with no loss of meaning. While the identfication of *teonword* as a prosaic word form can-not be definite, such a suggestion does seem convincing, especially given the two synonymous terms found elsewhere in poetry. This suggestion is strengthened by additional evidence which highlights further examples of diction in the Vercelli poem which might be called 'prosaic.'

For instance, there are additional examples of phrases or half-lines in *Homiletic Fragment I* which are found elsewhere only in prose texts. Perhaps the most convincing of these is found in the exhortative conclud-ing section of the poem. *Uton to þam beteran* in line 43a is a phrase which is found, albeit in a slightly different form, only in prose (and primarily in homiletic) texts. The progression *uton ... to þam beteran* occurs four times in Old English homilies,[86] while a similar construction occurs in a Rogationtide homily from Oxford, Bodleian Library, Hatton 114.[87] These

---

84 Forms of *teoncwide* and *teonhete* occur six times in verse texts: *Andreas*, ll. 633b and 771a (both *teoncwide*); *Guthlac*, l. 448a (*teoncwidum*); *Juliana*, l. 205a (*teoncwide*); *Exodus*, l. 224b (*teonhete*), and *Paris Psalter* 147.2, l. 1a (*teonhete*).

85 See, further, *Exodus* (l. 224) and *Juliana* (l. 205).

86 See, for example, an unpublished homily transcribed by the *DOE* (Cameron B3.2.7, l. 188); Napier XLIX, p. 265, l. 4; *VH* X.263; and B. Thorpe, ed. and trans., *Ancient Laws and Institutes of England*, 2 vols. (London, 1840), 394–400, l. 140.

87 See *RH* 11.38–43, where *to þam beteran* occurs in a conditional clause which is dependent on the *uton*-clause: 'Uton we þonne forðon, men þa leofestan, geornlice

homiletic texts are useful not only in an effort to contextualize the verse in *Homiletic Fragment I*, but they are also significant in that they help to clarify the meaning of the half-line. As line 43a appears in the poem, there is an ellipsed verbal infinitive, one of the hallmarks of Old English poetic syntax and an example of the typical Old English economy of diction which is evident in so many verse texts.[88] Based on the homiletic attestations of 'uton … to þam beteran' mentioned above, the 'missing' infinitive is undoubtedly a verb such as *wendan* or *cyrran*, both meaning 'to turn'; the resulting meaning in line 43 would thus be 'let us turn to the better.'[89]

A second prosaic phrase in the poem (though it might be called 'biblical' in this case) is found in line 39b, *swa him god bebead*. This phrase is found, verbatim, in only three other texts: it occurs in two homilies of Ælfric and in the Old English Heptateuch. Interestingly, though, the two homiletic passages in which the phrase occurs are themselves translations or retellings of scriptural passages. In Ælfric's homily entitled DE INITIO CREATURAE, the phrase occurs in a passage of the text which recounts the story of Noah; the reference itself, 'he dyde þa swa him god bebead,' derives from one of two verses in the biblical account.[90] Similarly, in his homily for the first Sunday in September, Ælfric recounts the story of Job; the passage in question comes near the end of the homily (*CH* II.XXX.190–3):[91]

Elifaz ða and baldað and sofar. ferdon ongean to heora mæge iobe. and didon swa swa him god bebead. and drihten underfeng IOBES ansyne. and heora synne ðurh his ðingrædene forgeaf.

---

tiligean þæt we for his lufe and for his willan us sylfe and ures lichaman lustas and willan on us sylfum cwylmen, and þæt we eac for his lufon and for his willan ealle þa lustfulnessa þissere andweardan tide and ðissere gewitendan forseon and forhycgan, þæt we of ðam wacran and of þam wyrsan to þam beteran and to þam selran becuman moton.'

88 See B. Mitchell, *Old English Syntax*, 2 vols. (Oxford: Clarendon Press, 1985), §§3966–8.

89 Although the infinitives *hycgan* and *hyhtan* ('to think' and 'to rejoice,' respectively) occur in line 44a, it is likely that they are to be seen as belonging with the auxiliary *cunnon* (l. 43b) rather than the imperative *uton* (l. 43a). Such an interpretation of lines 43–4a would result in a translation as follows: 'Let us (turn) to the better, now (that) we are able to consider and rejoice in a remedy.'

90 See *CH* I.I.189–90. The two verses in question are Genesis 6:22 ('facit ergo Noe omnia quae praeceperat illi Deus') and Genesis 7:5 ('facit ergo Noe omnia quae mandaverat ei Dominus').

91 These lines are a loose paraphrase of Job 42:9: 'abierunt ergo Eliphaz Themanites et Baldad Suhites et Sophar Naamathites et fecerunt sicut locutus fuerat ad eos Dominus et suscepit Dominus faciem Iob.'

['Eliphaz and Baldad and Sophar went to their kinsman Job, and they did just as God ordered them, and the Lord assumed the appearance of Job, and forgave them their sins.']

In a passage which we have seen before in conjunction with the use of *teonword* and *tældon* in *Homiletic Fragment I*, the phrase *swa him god bebead* occurs at the beginning of the translation of Numbers 13 from the Old English Heptateuch: 'Æfter ðam ðe Moyses, se mæra heretoga, mid Israhela folce, swa swa him God bebead, ofer ða Readan Sæ ferde.'[92] Although these three prose references are the only other attestations of *swa him god bebead* in Old English literature, it is interesting to note that similar formulaic systems are also found, both in prose and in verse.[93] Attested variations in verse texts include *swa him metod bebead* (*Gen* 965b), *swa him se eca bebead* (*Gen* 2370b, 2897b), and *swa him dryhten bebead* (*And* 1695), while prose texts contain such variations as *swa him Crist bebead* and *swa him se hælend bebead*, in addition to inversion of the nominative and accusative forms to produce *swa God him bebead* (among others).[94] Presumably, one of the attested poetic variations for God (*metod, se eca,* or *dryhten*) would have been acceptable both stylistically and metrically in a poetic context.[95] Again, as in the case of *teonwordum* above, caution must be exercised in drawing conclusions, but it seems curious that the composer of *Homiletic Fragment I* should choose to include in his verse text a syntactical construction which is rather pedestrian, and one which lacks the

---

92   See Crawford, ed., *Heptateuch*, 315.
93   A formulaic system is defined as 'a group of verses usually sharing the same meter and syntax in which one word, usually stressed, is constant and the other stressed word or words may be varied to suit the alliterative and/or narrative context.' See A. Riedinger, 'The Old English Formula in Context,' *Speculum* 60 (1985): 294–317, at 305, for an analysis of such formulaic systems.
94   See, for instance, *VH* V.49–50 ('ond hira lar wæs gesæd geond ealne middangeard to eorðan gemærum, swa him Crist bebead'); an unpublished homily for Palm Sunday transcribed by the *DOE* (Cameron B3.2.18.3, l. 32: 'þa dydon þa þegnas swa him se hælend bebead, and gegearwodon him þær þa Eastron') and Crawford, ed., *Heptateuch*, 127 (Genesis 17:23: 'Abraham soðlice ymbsnað hys sunu Ismahel on þone ylcan dæg, swa swa God him bebead').
95   It might be argued that the use of *god* in line 39b is determined by the presence of *gastlice* in the previous verse; however, a similar meaning could be obtained by the use of *inneweard* and *eca*, which would yield 'inneweard lufe swa him eca bebead.' The alliteration of *inneweard* is attested elsewhere in Old English verse; see, for instance, *Beowulf* 998 and *Christ and Satan* 136.

more evocative or 'traditional' poetic vocabulary. Consideration of one final lexical choice on the part of the composer will help to resolve this enigma.

At the point in *Homiletic Fragment I* where the poet departs from the bee metaphor and turns his attention to a complaint against the present state of the world, there occurs a series of two a-lines which contain alliterating couplets of finite verbs (*HF1*, ll. 31–3):

> Swa is nu þes middangeard   mane geblonden,
> wanað ond weaxeð. Wacað se ealda,
> dweleð ond drefeð   dæges ond nihtes
> ['So now is this middle-earth mingled with crime, it waxes and wanes; the Old One watches day and night, lurks and disturbs.']

Individually, these words seem to hold no great significance; they (and their related forms) are distributed over a wide variety of texts.[96] Even when the verbs are taken together in pairs there seems to be nothing conclusive about the attestations; *dweleð* and *drefeð* occur together only here, while *wanað* and *weaxeð* – though found together in a number of texts – most often occur, as one might expect, in discussions about the moon.[97] What is intriguing about these two verses in *Homiletic Fragment I* is best explained by reference to another example of 'homiletic verse' in Old English; namely, the so-called sermon of Hrothgar from *Beowulf* (ll. 1700–84). Speaking of this 85-line portion of the heroic poem, Peter Clemoes suggests that the poet might have drawn on 'vernacular preaching' for certain images in the text, such as the devil's arrows (*Beowulf*, ll. 1743b–4), while also drawing on such preaching for rhetorical techniques, particularly (for our purposes) in the coupling of alliterative finite verbs.[98] It seems likely that the poet of *Homiletic Fragment I*, like the *Beowulf*

---

96 See, for example: 'Weaxað and wridað, wilna brucað' (*Genesis* 1532); 'he ne wanað swaþæh nan þing his' (*LS* I.46); 'Forðæm sua sua unwærlicu ond giemeleaslicu spræc menn dweleð' (H. Sweet, ed., *King Alfred's West-Saxon Version of Gregory's Pastoral Care*, EETS o.s. 45 and 50 (London: OUP, 1871; repr. in 1 vol., 1958), 89, l. 7); and 'þone deofol þe ealle men bregeð and ealle woruld drefeð' (*WH* V.95–6).

97 See *CH* I.X.52 ('Se mona deð ægðer ge wyxð ge wanað'); *CH* II.XII.429–30 ('and se mona … is hwiltidum weaxende. hwiltidum wanigende'); and H. Henel, ed., *Ælfric's De Temporibus Anni*, EETS o.s. 213 (London: OUP, 1942), ch. 1, l. 35 ('Se mona ðe weaxð and wanað'; see also ch. 3, l. 9: 'Dæghwomlice þæs monan leoht bið weaxende oððe wanigende').

98 P. Clemoes, *Interactions of Thought and Language in Old English Poetry*, CSASE 12 (Cambridge: CUP, 1995), 43–4.

poet, is drawing upon the same tradition of alliterating finite verbs evident in the vernacular homilies. Occurring in close succession in the second half of the poem (a section which, as has already been shown, is filled with examples of lexical and structural elements also found in homilies), these two alliterating couplets offer further convincing evidence which suggests a relationship between *Homiletic Fragment I* and the tradition of vernacular homiletic composition in Anglo-Saxon England. The lexical issues presented above indicate, when considered cumulatively, that this relationship was viewed by the composer of *Homiletic Fragment I* as neither inappropriate nor inadequate for the treatment of his theme.

The intention in this discussion has not been to demonstrate that *Homiletic Fragment I* is, or can be called, homiletic; such a label is taken for granted. Rather, if *Homiletic Fragment I*, despite its fragmentary state, can offer some evidence in support of a descriptive definition of 'homiletic verse,' then we are presented with a series of broad criteria which can indicate a homiletic origin for, or homiletic influence on, a given verse text. In the first instance, the theme of a poem may generally indicate a close relationship to Anglo-Saxon homiletic material. Second, a poem's structure can often indicate homiletic influence. In many instances, one can see a direct correlation between the structure of a poetic text and that of a homily. Such is the case, for example, in *Homiletic Fragment I*, where the tripartite structure of the poem can be shown to reflect the classical homiletic structure of pericope–exegesis–exhortation. Although the structure of the poem is more difficult to assess owing to the fragmentary nature of the text, the composer's use of rhetorical technique offers some indications of the poem's conjectured structure. Finally, the more 'immediate' aspects of a poem, including word choice, syntax, and metre, can often provide a commentary on the sources of influence upon the poem (or upon the poet). Because of the apparently systematized regularity of recognizable metrical patterns in the corpus of Old English verse, substantial departures from the metrical 'norms' are conspicuous. Such departures include unmetrical lines, or lines with debased poetic metre, as well as stray half-lines, all of which are attested in *Homiletic Fragment I*. Within the confines of this metrical system, word choice must have been a pre-eminent concern of the composer – so much so that scholars have attempted, with varying degrees of success, to define an Old English poetic 'word-hoard.'[99] For this reason, words in a poem which are unattested elsewhere in poetic

---

99 See, for instance, M.S. Griffith, 'Poetic Language and the Paris Psalter,' *ASE* 20 (1991): 167–86.

texts, but found in prose texts, suggest an affinity (deliberate or not) with these prose texts. All these poetic 'abnormalities' could be used by a composer to evoke a range of responses from his audience. As primarily aural effects, one imagines that any irregularities in the metre and diction of a poem would be subject to an almost immediate reaction from the listener familiar with Old English poetic conventions. The 'homiletic tone' so often mentioned in commentaries on Old English didactic poems may consequently be due more to the skill of the poet in manipulating these aural effects than to any negligence or indiscretion on his part. To put it in terms with which the poet of *Homiletic Fragment I* would surely have sympathized, homiletic poems in Old English can be said to possess the outward form of traditional vernacular verse, but their inner qualities suggest a completely different type of influence, namely, that of the prose homiletic tradition.

The Dream of the Rood: Cross-References

ANDY ORCHARD

Even now, when arguments continue about its age and integrity, *The Dream of the Rood* is for most modern readers one of the most central and celebrated examples of Old English verse extant, and there is growing evidence that its considerable poetic power was also appreciated in Anglo-Saxon England itself. The 156-line poem that survives entire (though not quite intact) in a single copy in the Vercelli Book (from line 6 of folio 104v through to the bottom of folio 106r) appears to have at least two epigraphical reflexes in stone and silver, in that it has been argued that echoes of parts of the text are also found in poetic inscriptions on both the eighth-century Ruthwell Cross (albeit that the date of the inscription and the form of the monument have both been disputed)[1] and the eleventh-century Brussels Reliquary Cross.[2] Likewise, as we shall see, it has long been

---

1 For the most recent argument in favour of a late date for the inscription, see Patrick W. Conner, 'The Ruthwell Monument Runic Inscription in an Eleventh-Century Context,' *RES*, n.s. 59 (2007): 25–51; cf. Eric Gerald Stanley, 'The Ruthwell Cross Inscription: Some Linguistic and Literary Implications of Paul Meyvaert's Paper "An Apocalypse Panel on the Ruthwell Cross,"' in his *A Collection of Papers with Emphasis on Old English Literature* (Toronto: PIMS, 1987), 384–99. For the notion that what was originally erected at Ruthwell was not a cross at all, but simply a monument, see Fred Orton, 'Northumbrian Identity in the Eighth Century: The Ruthwell and Bewcastle Monuments; Style, Classification, Class, and the Form of Ideology,' *Journal of Medieval and Early Modern Studies* 34 (2004): 95–145; Fred Orton, 'Rethinking the Ruthwell and Bewcastle Monuments: Some Deprecation of Style; Some Consideration of Form and Ideology,' in *Anglo-Saxon Styles*, ed. Catherine Karkov and George Hardin Brown (Albany: SUNY Press, 2003), 31–67.

2 For an important overview, which directly opposes the views of Orton, Stanley, and Conner noted above, see the many publications of Éamonn Ó Carragáin, especially his *Ritual and the Rood: Liturgical Images and the Old English Poems of the 'Dream of the*

noticed that words, phrases, and themes from *The Dream of the Rood* can be matched at apposite moments in a range of surviving Anglo-Saxon texts in both Latin and Old English and in prose and in verse, again suggesting that the poem may have had a wider currency in Anglo-Saxon England than is sometimes supposed.

Such fleeting indications that other Anglo-Saxon authors, perhaps over several centuries, may have sought to transmit and transmute echoes of *The Dream of the Rood* also chimes with the impressive range of internal parallels, ambiguities, and apparently deliberate *double entendres* that have often been detected in the poem itself.[3] Together, both the internal and external parallels suggest that *The Dream of the Rood* is best regarded as the well-crafted and fully integrated work of a highly skilled and apparently widely regarded poet rather than the augmented and composite text that modern readers have occasionally claimed.[4] This chapter will consider a number of parallels and echoes both within and beyond the Vercelli text, and attempt not only to suggest how *The Dream of the Rood* was read and reread and copied and consciously recalled by a variety of

---

Rood' Tradition (London and Toronto: The British Library and UTP, 2005). See too Annemarie E. Mahler, '*Lignum Domini* and the Opening Vision of *The Dream of the Rood*: A Viable Hypothesis?' *Speculum* 53 (1978): 441–59, for the notion that the opening vision of *The Dream of the Rood* recalls a reliquary cross.

3 See, for example, Neil D. Isaacs, 'Progressive Identifications: The Structural Principle of *The Dream of the Rood*,' in his *Structural Principles in Old English Poetry* (Knoxville: Univ. of Tennessee Press, 1968), 3–18; Eugene R. Kintgen, 'Echoic Repetition in Old English Poetry, Especially The Dream of the Rood,' *NM* 75 (1974): 202–23; Carol B. Pasternack, 'Stylistic Disjunctions in the *Dream of the Rood*,' *ASE* 13 (1984): 167–8; and Susan Irvine, 'Adam or Christ? A Pronominal Pun in *The Dream of the Rood*,' *RES*, n.s. 48 (1997): 433–47.

4 On the carefully integrated structure of the poem as a whole, see in particular the ingenious (and sometimes over-ingenious) comments of David R. Howlett, 'The Structure of *The Dream of the Rood*,' *Studia Neophilologica* 48 (1976): 301–6. See too Faith H. Patten, 'Structure and Meaning in *The Dream of the Rood*,' *English Studies: A Journal of English Language and Literature* 49 (1968): 385–401; and N.A. Lee, 'The Unity of *The Dream of the Rood*,' *Neophilologus* 56 (1972): 469–86. For the notion of *The Dream of the Rood* as a composite text, see, for example, Peter Orton, *The Transmission of Old English Poetry*, Westfield Publications in Medieval and Renaissance Studies 12 (Turnhout: Brepols, 2000), 159–60.

artists and artisans during the Anglo-Saxon period, but also to consider the changing range of ways in which we are challenged to view the Vercelli text today.

Perhaps fittingly in view of its apparently multiple incarnations in the medieval period, the poem has appeared in many forms in recent years, and has been edited and anthologized in whole or in part many times;[5] likewise, it has generated a bewildering amount of scholarly debate.[6] Aside from the usual discussions, standard in Anglo-Saxon studies, of the poem's

---

5 Important editions include John Mitchell Kemble, ed., *The Poetry of the Codex Vercelliensis* (London, 1856); Albert. S. Cook, ed., *The Dream of the Rood* (Oxford: Clarendon Press, 1905); George P. Krapp, ed., *The Vercelli Book*, ASPR 2 (New York: Columbia Univ. Press, 1935); Bruce Dickins and Alan S.C. Ross, ed., *The Dream of the Rood* (London: Methuen, 1934); and Michael Swanton, ed., *The Dream of the Rood* (Manchester: Manchester Univ. Press, 1970).

6 Some highpoints of the mass of secondary scholarship would doubtless include Rosemary Woolf, 'Doctrinal Influence on *The Dream of the Rood*,' *Medium Ævum* 27 (1958): 137–53; J. Burrow, 'An Approach to *The Dream of the Rood*,' *Neophilologus* 43 (1959): 123–33; Dame Helen Gardener, '*The Dream of the Rood*,' in *Essays and Poems Presented to Lord David Cecil*, ed. W.W. Robson (London: Constable, 1970), 18–36; C.J. Wolf, 'Christ as Hero in *The Dream of the Rood*,' *NM* 71 (1970): 202–10; Paul B. Taylor, 'Text and Texture of *The Dream of the Rood*,' *NM* 75 (1974): 615–22; A.D. Horgan, '*The Dream of the Rood* and Christian Tradition,' *NM* 79 (1978): 1–20; Edward B. Irving, Jr, 'Crucifixion Witnessed, or Dramatic Interaction in *The Dream of the Rood*,' in *Modes of Interpretation in Old English Literature: Essays in Honour of Stanley B. Greenfield*, ed. Phyllis Rugg Brown, Georgia Ronan Crampton, and Fred C. Robinson (Toronto: UTP, 1986), 101–13; Peter Clemoes, 'King and Creation at the Crucifixion: The Contribution of Native Tradition to *The Dream of the Rood* 50–6a,' in *Heroes and Heroines in Medieval English Literature: A Festschrift Presented to André Crépin on the Occasion of His Sixty-Fifth Birthday*, ed. Leo Carruthers (Cambridge: D.S. Brewer, 1994), 31–43; Harksoon Yim, 'Dual Perspectives in *The Dream of the Rood*,' *Publications of the Mississippi Philological Association* 1999, 1–6; Jane Roberts, 'Some Relationships between *The Dream of the Rood* and the Cross at Ruthwell,' *Studies in Medieval English Language and Literature* (Tokyo) 15 (2000): 1–25; Elaine M. Treharne, "Hiht wæs geniwad': Rebirth in *The Dream of the Rood*,' in *The Place of the Cross*, ed. Catherine E. Karkov, Sarah Larratt Keefer, and Karen Louise Jolly (Woodbridge: Boydell Press, 2006), 145–57; and Frederick M. Biggs, '*The Dream of the Rood* and *Guthlac* B as a Literary Context for the Monsters in *Beowulf*,' in *Text, Image, Interpretation: Studies in Anglo-Saxon Literature in Honour of Éamonn Ó Carragáin*, ed. Jane Roberts and Alastair Minnis (Turnhout: Brepols, 2007), 289–301.

supposed unity and structure,[7] its metre,[8] its place in the manuscript,[9] its relationship to the liturgy or other Latin sources,[10] such as The Gospel of Nichodemus or the Passio Andreae,[11] basic questions still remain about such a fundamental aspect as the very genre of The Dream of the Rood: is it dream-vision, riddle, homily, or some combination of the three?

Before considering such generic issues, however, the sheer artistry and brilliance of the surviving poem in the Vercelli Book should be highlighted, since the poet seems deliberately to toy with expectations, a trait that may

---

7 Anthony R. Grasso, 'Theology and Structure in The Dream of the Rood,' Religion and Literature 23 (1991): 23–38; Bernard F. Huppé, The Web of Words: Structural Analyses of the Old English Poems 'Vainglory,' 'The Wonder of Creation,' 'The Dream of the Rood,' and 'Judith' (Albany: SUNY Press, 1970), 64–112; Faith H. Patten, 'Structure and Meaning in The Dream of the Rood,' English Studies: A Journal of English Language and Literature 49 (1969): 385–401; N.A. Lee, 'The Unity of The Dream of the Rood,' Neophilologus 56 (1972): 469–86; Howlett, 'The Structure of The Dream of the Rood.' See too Swanton, ed., The Dream of the Rood, 76: 'In the past, scholars have found different parts of these concluding lines unsatisfactory for various reasons, supposing what they considered to be stylistic or thematic breaks to indicate a later redactor's hand ... The final words here are ... no more out of place than Cynewulf's signatures, or the homiletic endings to the Wanderer or Seafarer, which also at one time were considered to have been later additions.' Note the use of the term 'homiletic' here.

8 Robert D. Stevick, 'The Meter of the Dream of the Rood,' NM 68 (1967): 149–68; Constance B. Hieatt, 'A New Theory of Triple Rhythm in the Hypermetric Lines of Old English Verse,' MP 67 (1969): 1–8.

9 See now Samantha Zacher, Preaching the Converted: The Style and Rhetoric of the Vercelli Book Homilies, TASS (Toronto: UTP, 2009).

10 Howard Rollin Patch, 'Liturgical Influence in The Dream of the Rood,' Publications of the Modern Language Association of America 34.2 (1919): 233–57; Éamonn Ó Carragáin, 'Crucifixion as Annunciation: The Relation of The Dream of the Rood to the Liturgy Reconsidered,' English Studies: A Journal of English Language and Literature 63.6 (1982): 487–505; Julia Bolton Holloway, 'The Dream of the Rood and Liturgical Drama,' Comparative Drama 18.1 (1984): 19–37; Earl R. Anderson, 'Liturgical Influence in the Dream of the Rood,' Neophilologus 73.2 (1989): 293–304; Thomas D. Hill, 'The Cross as Symbolic Body: An Anglo-Latin Liturgical Analogue to The Dream of the Rood,' Neophilologus 77.2 (1993): 297–301; Murray McGillivray, 'Dream of the Rood 9–12 and the Christmas Liturgy,' NQ 52.1 (2005): 1–2.

11 Cf. Robert Emmet Finnegan, 'The Gospel of Nicodemus and The Dream of the Rood, 148b–156,' NM 84 (1983): 338–43. The notion that some version of the Latin Passio Andreae underlies certain aspects of The Dream of the Rood is highlighted by the inclusion of a translation of the relevant part of the Passio in D.G. Calder and M.J.B. Allen, Sources and Analogues of Old English Poetry: The Major Latin Sources in Translation (Cambidge: D.S. Brewer, 1976), 56–7; cf. Malcolm Godden, Ælfric's Catholic Homilies: Introduction, Commentary, and Glossary, EETS s.s. 18 (Oxford: OUP, 2000), 319.

have made the text all the more appreciated in its day. It is surely fitting that a poem that exploits so successfully notions of comparison and contrast should have been so long and widely perceived to be playfully ambiguous in its diction; there are throughout the poem a number of very different perspectives at play.[12] In this context, it may be significant that the poem uses the conjunction *hwæð(e)re* ('yet,' 'however,' 'nevertheless') no fewer than nine times, eight of them in the first half of the poem, and seven of those in the speech of the Cross, so adding to the enigmatic flavour of that portion of the poem.[13] Indeed, such frequent usage strongly sets apart *The Dream of the Rood* from other Old English poems extant.[14]

It is as if the poet is offering us a series of alternative perspectives, a kaleidoscopic and necessarily fractured vision of a wonder that cannot be completely encompassed. A few examples of what seem to be deliberately ambiguous terminology will highlight the artistry of the whole. So, for example, the form *beswyled* (l. 23a) seems to derive from the verb *beswyllan* ('to soak, drench'), but may perhaps also suggest the verb *besyllan* ('to sully, defile; stain, soil'), in somewhat the same way that the term *fah* (l. 13b) appears to play on the twin meanings 'stained' and 'guilty,' a pun widespread in Old English literature.[15] Likewise, the homographs *stefn* ('trunk, root'; l. 30a) and *stefn* ('voice'; l. 71b)[16] are both exploited in a way which seems particularly apposite in a poem which is, after all, about a speaking tree. In a similar vein, the repeated use of the term *beam* ('beam') at lines 6a, 97b, 114b, and 122a, signifying both a wooden object and a ray of light, is singularly appropriate in discussing a wooden cross wrapped round with light, just as the parallel fourfold repetition of the word *beacen* ('sign, beacon') at lines 6b, 21b, 83a, and 118b evidently plays on the notion of a sign or symbol that in the vision is suffused with light.[17] The connection between the two terms is emphasized through the parallel observations of

---

12 See, for example, Michael J. Swanton, 'Ambiguity and Anticipation in *The Dream of the Rood*,' *NM* 70 (1969): 407–25.

13 At ll. 18a, 24a, 38b, 42b, 57a, 59b, 70a, 75b, and 101b. See further W.F. Bolton, 'Connectives in *The Seafarer* and *The Dream of the Rood*,' *Modern Philology* 57 (1960): 260–2.

14 Cf. the distribution in the four signed poems of Cynewulf (whose links with *The Dream of the Rood* are discussed below): there is a single use of the adverb *hwæðre* in *Elene* 719b, two in *Christ B* 453b and 709b, and one in *Juliana* 517b.

15 Cf. *DOE*, s.v. *fāh¹*, *fāg¹* and *fāh²*, *fāg²*.

16 The latter form does not appear in the Vercelli Book, but all subsequent editors have accepted Kluge's emendation in order to supply the necessary alliteration.

17 Cf. *DOE*, s.v. *bēam*; *beacen*.

the Cross on the one hand that 'menn ofer moldan, ond eall þeos mære gesceaft, / gebiddaþ him to þyssum beacne' ('men over the earth, and all this famed creation pray to this beacon'; ll. 82–3a), and the similar assertion of the Dreamer on seeing the vision of the Cross that 'Gebæd ic me þa to þan beame' ('then I prayed to that beam'; l. 122a). The apparently loaded use of the compound *reordberend* ('speech-bearers') at lines 3a and 89b is a further case in point; what has often been seen as a lazy use of a tired and clichéd kenning for 'mankind' (distinguished from other creatures by possessing a voice) gains added force in a poem where the only thing to talk is a speaking tree. Again, the verb in line 101a, 'Deað he þær byrigde' is ambiguous, and could be interpreted as 'he tasted death there' (as in ll. 113b–14a 'deaðes wolde / biteres onbyrigan')[18] or 'he buried death there.'[19] In short, there seem so many possibilities for felicitous ambiguity built into the fabric of *The Dream of the Rood* that it seems likely that the poet is consciously exploiting such *doubles entendres* for artistic effect, blurring boundaries, and inviting his audience to make connections and identifications that deepen an already rich text.

Such a policy of creative ambiguity and identification seems also to have extended to the poet's depiction of his main characters. There are three protagonists in *The Dream of the Rood*, namely Christ, the Cross, and the dreamer, and patterns of repetition strongly suggest that it was the poet's firm intention to identify each with the others, both separately and collectively.[20] The identification of Christ and the Cross is, of course, easily achieved through their shared suffering and experience, underlined by the at first glance otiose assertion by the Cross that at the Crucifixion 'Bysmerodon hie unc butu ætgædere' ('they reviled the two of us both together' [l. 48a]), where the unique dual form in the poem (*unc*) is 'unpacked' by repetition of the immediately following forms *butu* ('both') and *ætgædere* ('together'); essentially the same half-line 'Bismærædu uŋket men ba ætgad[..]' appears on the Ruthwell monument (l. II.3).[21] Further

---

18 In the manuscript, *wolde* has been corrected from *þrowode*.

19 *DOE* distinguishes the homographs as *byrgan*¹ and *byrgan*².

20 See further Neil D. Isaacs, 'Progressive Identifications: The Structural Principle of *The Dream of the Rood*,' in *Structural Principles in Old English Poetry*, ed. Neil D. Isaacs (Knoxville: Univ. of Tennessee Press, 1968), 3–18. See too Constance B. Hieatt, 'Dream Frame and Verbal Echo in *The Dream of the Rood*,' *NM* 72 (1971): 251–63. For a further identification implicit in the text, namely, between Christ and Adam, see Irvine, 'Adam or Christ?'

21 The text of the Ruthwell poem here and below is taken from ASPR 2, 115, using the following transliteration: 'Runes which are no longer visible, or which cannot be

thematic identification of Christ and the Cross is achieved through the dreamer's observation of the Cross 'þæt hit ærest ongan / swætan on þa swiðran healfe' ('that it first began to bleed on the right side' [ll. 19b–20a]), an evident echo of Christ's own wound.

The identification of the dreamer and the Cross is highlighted through a series of verbal parallels, beginning with the dreamer's comment immediately after his observation of the bleeding Cross that 'Eall ic wæs mid sorgum[22] gedrefed' ('I was entirely afflicted with sorrows' [l. 20b]), a half-line that is directly echoed by the assertion of the Cross itself after seeing first hand the Crucifixion ('Ic þæt eall beheold' ['I saw it all' (l. 58b)]) that 'Sare ic wæs mid sorgum[23] gedrefed' ('I was sorely afflicted with sorrows' [l. 59a]). Shortly before the Cross speaks, the dreamer asserts that during his vision he was a passive observer, using a carefully formulated phrase adorned with cross-alliteration ('Hwæðre ic þær licgende lange hwile' ['Yet I [was] lying there for a long time' (l. 24)]).[24] Shortly before the Cross turns to make a direct address to the dreamer, it too notes that after the Crucifixion, buried (again in echo of Christ himself) in a pit alongside the two crosses that had carried the thieves, it too was reduced to a passive observer, using what seems clearly a parallel and equally carefully formulated phrase, also adorned with cross-alliteration ('Hwæðre we þær greotende[25] gode hwile' ['Yet we [were] weeping there for a good time' (l. 70)]).

A similar technique is apparent in the poet's most audacious identification, that of the dreamer and Christ. After Christ has been taken down

---

identified, are here represented by points within square brackets; runes which are incomplete, but which can be identified with some confidence, are represented by italic letters' (ASPR, cxxii–cxiii). I have also consulted the very useful (if in places conflicting) editions of the Ruthwell text as given by Howlett, 'Inscriptions and Design,' 85–91, and Ó Carragáin, *Ritual and the Rood*, xxi–xxix. The identification of the Cross and Christ found here in the Ruthwell text is unusual: as we shall see, the inscription prefers to focus on the role of the Cross alone in the Crucifixion.

22 The manuscript reads *surgum*, but the emendation is universally accepted.

23 The word *sorgum* is missing in the manuscript, but is easily supplied both from the earlier parallel and (through a less circular argument) from the Ruthwell Cross, where it appears as 'S[...] ic w[.]s mi[.] so[.]gum gidrœ[..]d'.

24 See further Andy Orchard, 'Artful Alliteration in Anglo-Saxon Song and Story,' *Anglia* 113 (1995): 437–8.

25 The manuscript reads *reotende* ('weeping'): a reading which although it violates the normal rules of alliteration, is nonetheless retained by several editors, including Grein, Bütow, and Bolton. Other editors (Cook and Kemble) have opted for *geotende* ('dripping'): with still others split between *hreotende* ('weeping'; favoured by Swanton) or its synonym *greotende* (Krapp).

from the Cross, and has been abandoned by his followers, the Cross notes that 'Reste he ðær mæte weorode' ('He rested there with a small company' [l. 69b]). The phrase 'mæte weorode' has long puzzled commentators, who have rightly wondered what possible company the solitary Christ might have at this point. As has often been noted, however, the phrase is also found in the dreamer's own description of himself towards the end of the poem, where he tells of his yearning to pray to the Cross 'þær ic ana wæs / mæte werede' ('Where I was alone, with a small company' [123b–4a]); these are the only two examples of the phrase to have survived in Old English,[26] leading most commentators to interpret the former occurrence in the light of the latter, as an example of litotes.[27] Yet while the uniqueness of the phrase underlines the identification, one might fairly note that in the second occurrence of the phrase the fact that it occurs in parallel variation with the simple term *ana* ('alone') would seem to violate the principle of 'specifying variation,' wherein the more specific variant generally follows rather than precedes.[28] A better question might be to ask what constitutes Christ's 'company' (*we[o]rod*) in the first example, one surely answered by alliteration in the very next line, itself already identified as important in the progressive identifications of the text: ('Hwæðre *we* þær greotende gode hwile' ['Yet *we* [were] weeping there for a good time' (l. 70)]). Christ seems alone at this point, but in fact has a retinue of three crosses for company, just as the dreamer may seem alone, but is accompanied throughout by both Christ and the Cross.

There is, finally, one unifying half-line that appears three times in the poem, namely, *elne mycle* ('with great zeal'), which is used once each of the activities of Christ (l. 34a), the Cross (l. 60a), and the dreamer (l. 123a). The fact that in the latter two cases that phrase appears alongside another that serves to identify pairs among this triad of protagonists (namely, 'Sare ic wæs mid sorgum gedrefed' [59a; cf. 20b] and 'mæte werede' [124a; cf. 69b]) only seems to confirm the fact that the poet expects his audience to make specific connections between his characters.

If, then, the poet of *The Dream of the Rood* seems consciously to blur the boundaries between the main characters depicted, as well as to exploit

---

26 A phrase apparently signally the opposite, namely, *we(o)rod unmæte* ('no small troop'), is found in *Andreas* 1219b and 1682b.

27 Typical is the comment of Swanton, ed., *Dream of the Rood*, 128, that 'it is probably interpreted as a simple case of OE litotes.'

28 Fred C. Robinson, *'Beowulf' and the Appositive Style* (Knoxville: Univ. of Tennessee Press, 1985), 61–3.

the artistic possibilities offered by ambiguous diction, so too it might be argued that he seems deliberately to mix and merge generic distinctions. The poet of *The Dream of the Rood* seems to have produced a text that is an intentional conflation of the dream-vision, the homiletic, and the enigmatic, and just as the poet identified his three main characters, so too did he blend generic distinctions elsewhere kept separate. Perhaps the most generally accepted classification of the text, encapsulated in the modern title, is that the poem represents an early manifestation of the genre of poetic dream-vision that was to prove so popular in later medieval English texts; but there seem as many differences as similarities in the comparisons offered.[29] Certainly, the language of the first part of the poem in particular (up to line 78) privileges the notion that a vision, or rather a series of visions, is involved, as the following sequence of lines attests, with the obvious parallelism picked out in bold italics, as throughout this paper:

'***Geseah ic*** wuldres treow ... wynnum scinan' (ll. 14b and 15b)
['***I saw*** the tree of glory ... joyfully shine']
'***Geseah ic*** þæt fuse beacen / wendan wædum ond bleom' (ll. 21b–2a)
['***I saw*** that eager beacon change its coverings and colours']
'***Geseah ic*** þa frean mancynnes / efstan elne mycle' (ll. 33b–4a)
['***I saw*** the lord of mankind hasten with great zeal']
'***Geseah ic*** weruda god / þearle þenian' (ll. 51b–2a)
['***I saw*** the god of hosts cruelly stretched out'][30]

In each case, the phrase *Geseah ic* ('I saw') begins the b-line, although it will be noted that the first two examples are spoken by the dreamer, and refer to the Cross, the second two by the Cross, and refer to Christ; such a change of perspectives, is, as we have already seen, a recurring feature of

---

29 See, for example, Constance B. Hieatt, 'Dream Frame and Verbal Echo in the *Dream of the Rood*,' *NM* 72 (1971): 251–63; A. C. Spearing, *Medieval Dream-Poetry* (Cambridge: CUP, 1976); Andrew Galloway, 'Dream-Theory in *The Dream of the Rood* and *The Wanderer*,' *RES* n.s. 45 (1994): 475–85; Antonina Harbus, 'Dream and Symbol in *The Dream of the Rood*,' *Nottingham Medieval Studies* 40 (1996): 1–15; and Bret A. Wightman, 'A Vision of Sanctity: The Spectacle of *The Dream of the Rood*' (unpub. PhD diss., Lehigh Univ., 1999).

30 Anne L. Klinck, 'Christ as Soldier and Servant in *The Dream of the Rood*,' *Florilegium* 4 (1982): 109–16, argues that while the phrase *þearle þenian* (l. 52a), used of Christ, is usually interpreted as 'cruelly stretched out' (though this is to take the verb form as a variant of the more normal *þennan*, and to take the infinitive in its passive sense), the verb form might also be understood as a variant of *þegnian* ('to serve'), so depicting Christ in the role of suffering servant.

the poem. Likewise, it is notable that the word *gesyhð(e)* ('vision'; always in an oblique case) should also appear four times in the poem, each time as the final word in an a-line (ll. 21a, 41a, 66a, and 96a). Though these lines are far from being the only ones which include references to sight or vision,[31] the sheer formal parallelism, heavily predominant in the first half of the poem, surely invites notice.

But if the first part of the poem, with its focus on the visual and the in-dividual demonstrates tight control over its repeated patterning, so too do the closing lines, which are equally remakable in this respect (*The Dream of the Rood*, ll. 131b–56):[32]

```
                    Nah ic ricra feala
freonda on foldan,   ac hie forð heonon
gewiton of worulde dreamum,   sohton him wuldres cyning,
lifiaþ nu on heofenum   mid heahfædere,
wuniaþ on wuldre,   ond ic wene me                        135
daga gehwylce   hwænne me dryhtnes rod,
þe ic her on eorðan   ær sceawode,
on þysson lænan   life gefetige
ond me þonne gebringe   þær is blis mycel,
dream on heofonum,   þær is dryhtnes folc               140
geseted to symle,   þær is singal blis,
ond me þonne asette   þær ic syþþan mot
wunian on wuldre,   well mid þam halgum
dreames brucan.   Si me dryhten freond,
se ðe her on eorþan   ær þrowode                         145
on þam gealgtreowe   for guman synnum.
He us onlysde   ond us lif forgeaf,
heofonlicne ham.   Hiht wæs geniwad
mid bledum ond mid blisse   þam þe þær bryne þolodan.
Se sunu wæs sigorfæst   on þam siðfate,                  150
mihtig ond spedig,   þa he mid manigeo com,
gasta weorode,   on godes rice,
```

---

31 See too ll. 4a, 9b, 11a, 18b, 25a, 36b, 46b, 58b, 64a, and 137b; obviously, all but the last of these references appear in the first half of the poem.

32 For a similar analysis of this passage, which I repeat in its essentials below, see Andy Orchard, 'Re-Reading *The Wanderer*: The Value of Cross References,' in *Via Crucis: The Way of the Cross. A Festschrift for James E. Cross*, ed. Thomas N. Hall (Morgan-town: West Virginia Univ. Press, 2002), 13–16.

anwealda ælmihtig,   englum to blisse
ond eallum ðam halgum   þam þe on heofonum ær
wunedon on wuldre,   þa heora wealdend cwom,   155
ælmihtig god,   þær his eðel wæs.
[I do not have many powerful friends on earth, but they have gone forth
hence from the joys of the world, sought the King of Glory; they live now in
heaven with the High Father, dwell in glory. And I look forward each day to
when the Lord's cross, which I have previously seen here on earth, will fetch
me from this transitory life and bring me then where there is great bliss, joy
in heaven, where there is the Lord's folk seated at the feast, where there is
continual bliss, and he will then place me where I afterwards might dwell in
glory, delight in joy fully among those sainted ones. May the Lord be my
friend, he who previously suffered here on earth on that gallows-tree for the
sins of man. He redeemed us and gave us life, a heavenly home. Hope was
renewed, with glory and with bliss, for those who endured the burning there.
The Son was secure in victory on that expedition, mighty and successful,
when he came with a multitude, a troop of spirits into God's kingdom, the
almighty sole ruler, to bliss among the angels and all the saints who previously dwelt in glory, when their ruler came, almighty God, where his homeland was.]

These closing lines clearly smack of homiletic concerns widely attested in
Anglo-Saxon sermons, and as many commentators have noted, tie *The
Dream of the Rood* closely into the broader themes of the Vercelli Book as
a whole.[33] The (again) fourfold patterned references to heaven in consecutive b-lines (*þær is … þær is … þær is … þær ic*, ll. 139–42) offer perhaps the
most obvious examples of repeated diction that contrasts the earthly life
with the life to come, and the same point is made by the dreamer's insistence that while he has no powerful friends on earth ('Nah ic ricra feala
freonda on foldan,' ll. 131b–2a), he hopes to find a friend in the Lord ('Si
me dryhten freond,' l. 144b). Likewise, in the mention here of 'this transitory life' ('þysson lænan life,' l. 138); the effect of separating adjective and

---

33 See in particular Éamonn Ó Carragáin, 'How Did the Vercelli Collector Interpret *The
Dream of the Rood?*,' in *Studies in English Language and Early English Literature in
Honour of Paul Christophersen*, ed. P. M. Tilling, Occasional Papers in Lang. and Lang.
Learning 8 (Coleraine: New Univ. of Ulster, 1981), 63–104. See too Jennifer Elise
Merriman, 'The Rhetoric of the End Times in Old English Preaching' (unpub. PhD
thesis, Pennsylvania State Univ., 2004), esp. chapters 1 ('The Vercelli Book: Towards a
Rhetoric of Old English Eschatology,' 20–58) and 4 ('*The Dream of the Rood* and the
Rhetoric of Inner Conversion,' 148–81).

noun across the caesura not only serves to underline the instability of life on earth, but it is also clearly deliberate, since it is likewise found the only other time the phrase is used (l. 109).

Other patterns of repetition in this passage again underline the notion that the poet has carefully moulded his material to offer a contrast between this life and the next: the alternation in (again) four a-lines of heaven and earth (*on heofenum ... on eorðan ... on heofonum ... on eorþan*, ll. 134a, 137a, 140a, and 145a) seems all the more pleasing since in the corresponding b-lines the word for God remains the same (*dryhtnes ... dryhtnes ... dryhten*, ll. 136b, 140b, and 144b); central to this sequence is a pair of lines linked by verbal repetition and rhyme in which the dreamer contrasts his own vision of the cross ('þe ic her on eorðan ær sceawode,' l. 137) with Christ's suffering on the same cross ('se ðe her on eorþan ær þrowode,' l. 145), a conceit which neatly summarizes the theme of the whole piece, and returns us to the notion of a vision reported for homiletic purpose. Similarly, the intense raptures of heaven are emphasized through the interwoven repetition of words for 'bliss' (*blis*, ll. 139, 141, 149, and 153) and 'joy' (*dream*, ll. 133, 140, and 144); neither word appears elsewhere in the poem at all. Careful patterning is again evident in the echoing references in three self-contained a-lines to those dwelling in heaven's glory in the present ('wuniaþ on wuldre,' l. 135), in the future ('[syþþan mot] wunian on wuldre,' l. 143), and in the past ('wunedon on wuldre,' l. 155). With its firm focus on the contrast between this world and the next, then, it might well be argued from these closing lines that *The Dream of the Rood*, like its companion pieces in the Vercelli manuscript, is a homiletic text.

In combining aspects of a dream-vision with the device of a talking object (so-called prosopopoeia),[34] the author of *The Dream of the Rood* appears also to be gesturing towards the genre of the Old English riddles, many of which are either of the two commonest forms beginning 'I saw' (*Ic [...] (ge) seah*) or 'I am' (*Ic eom*);[35] in combining the experience of the cross and the vision of the dreamer, the author of *The Dream of the Rood* manages to fit both perspectives into the text. The same kinds of progressive identification through repetition that are apparent both in the dream-vision proper and in the homiletic conclusion to the poem have also been recognized in the initial

---

34 The classic discussion remains Margaret Schlauch, '*The Dream of the Rood* as Prosopopoeia,' in *Essays and Studies in Honour of Carleton Brown*, ed. P.W. Long (New York: New York Univ. Press, 1940), 23–34.

35 See, for example, Andy Orchard, 'Enigma Variations: The Anglo-Saxon Riddle-Tradition,' in *Latin Learning and English Lore: Studies in Anglo-Saxon Literature for Michael Lapidge*, ed. Katherine O'Brien O'Keeffe and Andy Orchard, 2 vols. (Toronto: UTP, 2005), 1: 284–304.

section that with further fourfold identification describes the cross itself and moves the audience from the *syllicre treow* ('quite wondrous tree'; l. 4b),[36] to the *wuldres treow* ('tree of glory'; l. 14b), to the *wealdendes treow* ('ruler's tree', l. 17b),[37] to the *hælendes treow* ('saviour's tree'; l. 25b). All of these are perspectives offered by the dreamer; not until line 44 does the Cross, after initially describing the brutal process that uprooted it and made it into what it became,[38] finally announce itself as a rood-tree (*rod*), the significance of which is signalled by alliteration, displacement of natural syntax, and chiastic structure (as well as punctuation and capitalization in the Vercelli Book): 'Rod wæs ic aræred · ahof ic ricne cyning' ('as a rood was I raised up: I carried up the powerful king').[39]

With regard to the use of prosopopoeia that is shared by the author of *The Dream of the Rood* and the Old English *Riddles*, it is important to recall that the same device is also found in Anglo-Latin *enigmata* ('riddles,' or perhaps better 'mysteries'), and that the scheme itself is discussed in detail by Aldhelm (who died in 709 or 710) in the introduction to his own set of 100 *Enigmata*, the earliest datable such texts to have survived from Anglo-Saxon England. Aldhelm, writing at the end of the seventh century, offers several biblical precedents for the practice, as follows (*De metris* 7):[40]

> Porro quod eadem muta insensibilium rerum natura, de qua enigma clancu-lum et latens propositio componitur, quasi loqui et sermocinari fingitur, hoc et in sacris litterarum apicibus insertum legitur, quia nonnunquam rationabi-lis creatura irrationabilium gestu et personis utitur, et e diverso irrationabilis

---

36 The use of the comparative neuter adjectival form *syllicre* here often excites critical attention (see, for example, Swanton, ed., *Dream of the Rood*, 104), but may be another example of authorial indirection, since the same form equates to the feminine genitive or dative singular of the positive adjective. Clearly, given the neuter gender of *treow* ('tree'), it is the comparative form that is required; but given the existence of a feminine homophone *treow* ('faith'), an audience might be forgiven for supposing briefly that a 'wondrous faith' was being discussed, until the lack of an oblique ending (the feminine genitive or dative form would be *treowe*) made plain that it was a tree. Such playful and artistic use of appropriate homophones (in a poem which after all is about both a tree and a faith) is, as we have seen above, found elsewhere in the poem.

37 The manuscript reads *wealdes*, a reading that has been defended as meaning both 'tree of the forest' and 'tree of power.' Assuming an antecedent form such as *wealdēdes*, with scribal haplography, would account for the form.

38 The same often painful self-description by an object of how it was created is a common feature of the Exeter Book *Riddles*; see, for example, *Riddle* 24 ('Holy Bible'; ASPR 3, 193–4).

39 See further George S. Tate, 'Chiasmus as Metaphor: The *Figura Crucis* Tradition and *The Dream of the Rood*,' *NM* 79 (1978): 114–25.

40 R. Ehwald, ed., *Aldhelmi Opera*, MGH AA 15 (Berlin: Weidmann, 1919), 76–7.

sensus vivacitate carens intellectualium gestu et voce fungitur: quemadmo-
dum in libro Iudicum diversa lignorum genera articulata hominis voce lo-
quentia monarchum quaesisse referuntur (*Ierunt*, inquit, *ligna ungere super
se regem*) ubi et singillatim, sicut supra iam diximus, ficus et vitis simulque
oliva, et ad extremum ramnus igne proprio flammisque voracibus Libani ce-
dros consumpturus iuxta ritum humanae locutionis profari perhibentur.
Huius etiam tropi figuram in quarto Regum volumine Ioas Israeliticae plebis
gubernaculo potitus ad Amasiam regalibus imperii sceptris fulgentem, cum
furibundo cavillationis ludibrio et probroso gannaturae subsannantis elogio
crudeliter componens *Carduus*, inquit, *Libani misit ad cedrum quae est in
Libano, dicens: Da filiam tuam filio meo uxorem* et reliqua; et psalmista *omnia ligna silvarum exsultasse.*
[Moreover, as far as the same silent nature of inanimate objects, concerning
which a secret enigma and masking arrangement are found, as if it is por-
trayed as talking or speaking, this too is found written in the letters of sacred
scripture, where occasionally a rational creature adopts the attitude and pos-
ture of irrational ones, and by contrast an irrational creature lacking the
power of sense adopts the manner and voice of sentient beings: such as when
in the Book of Judges various kinds of trees are said to have sought a ruler
speaking with the articulated voice of man: 'The trees went to anoint a king
over them' [Judg. 9:8]. Then one by one, as I have said before, the fig-tree and
the vine and the olive-tree, and finally the bramble, which was about to con-
sume the cedars of Lebanon with its own fire and greedy flames, are said to
have spoken after the pattern of human speech [Judg. 9:15]. Likewise, in the
fourth Book of Kings, Joas, endowed with the governance of the people of
the Israelites, cruelly composed a figure of this trope with furious mockery of
derision and shameful speech of snarling scorn against Amasius, resplendent
with the royal sceptre of authority, when he said 'A thistle of Libanus sent to
a cedar tree, which is in Libanus, saying: Give thy daughter to my son to wife
[4 Kings 14:9], and so on; and the psalmist brought the animate to the inanimate metaphorically, saying 'All the trees of the woods rejoice' [Ps. 95:12].]

This rather lengthy passage, from a text which was apparently read especially during the earlier part of the Anglo-Saxon period,[41] is of considerable

---

41 For evidence that Bede knew Aldhelm's *De metris*, see Michael Lapidge, *The Anglo-
Saxon Library* (Oxford: OUP, 2006), 193; a letter from Leofgyth in the Bonifatian
correspondence also shows familiarity with the work: see Michael Tangl, ed., *Die Briefe
des heiligen Bonifatius und Lullus*, MGH ES (Berlin: Weidmann, 1916), 52–3. See too
Michael Lapidge and Andy Orchard, 'Aldhelm,' in *Sources of Anglo-Saxon Literary*

interest with regard to the possible impetus for *The Dream of the Rood*, since, as Bruce Braswell has pointed out,[42] it illustrates the rhetorical device of prosopopoiea (without, however, using the term) by considering both its relationship to the genre of the enigma or riddle and to its biblical precedents. The latter are particularly intriguing in that the three examples given here from the Old Testament Books of Judges, Kings, and Psalms all depict speaking trees, just like the talking cross in *The Dream of the Rood*; still more impressive is the focus in the first biblical passage on the claims for dominion of four different kinds of tree, since it was to become a commonplace of patristic tradition that Christ's Cross was itself composed of four different kinds of wood.[43]

It is indeed tempting to suggest that this passage from Aldhelm might have offered literary inspiration to the author of *The Dream of the Rood*, especially when it is remembered that the Ruthwell Cross, which apparently echoes part of the poem, lies at the very edge of the ancient kingdom of Aldfrith of Northumbria, to whom Aldhelm's *Enigmata* were sent, apparently along with the dedicatory letter that contains this very passage.[44] The relationship of *The Dream of the Rood* with the verses inscribed on the Ruthwell Cross is an intriguing one, notwithstanding the continuing

---

Culture, ed. Frederick M. Biggs, Thomas D. Hill, and Paul E. Szarmach (forthcoming). An eighth-century fragment from Anglo-Saxon England of the so-called *Epistola ad Acircium* (a longer text which contains the *De metris*) now survives in Miskolc, Lévay József Library, and an excerpt from the *Epistola* is also found in Paris, Bibliothèque Sainte-Geneviève, MS 2410, a manuscript dated s. x^{ex}–xi^{in}: See Helmut Gneuss, *Handlist of Anglo-Saxon Manuscripts: A List of Manuscripts and Manuscript Fragments Written or Owned in England up to 1100*, MRTS 241 (Tempe: Arizona Center for Medieval and Renaissance Studies, 2001), nos. 850 and 903.

42 Bruce Karl Braswell, '*The Dream of the Rood* and Aldhelm on Sacred Prosopopeia,' *Mediaeval Studies* 40 (1978): 461–7.

43 *Collectanea Pseudo-Bedae*, ed. Michael Lapidge and Martha Bayless, Scriptores Latini Hiberniae 14 (Dublin: DIAS, 1998), 178–9 and 271 (no. 372: 'DE QUATVOR LIGNIS CRUCIS').

44 Cf. Braswell, '*The Dream of the Rood* and Aldhelm on Sacred Prosopopeia,' 466–7, who suggests that *The Dream of the Rood* was composed at or for the court of King Aldfrith; David Howlett, 'Inscriptions and Design of the Ruthwell Cross,' in *The Ruthwell Cross: Papers from the Colloquium Sponsored by the Index of Christian Art, Princeton University, 8 December 1989*, ed. Brendan Cassidy, Index of Christian Art, Occasional Papers 1 (Princeton, NJ: Department of Art and Archaeology, Princeton Univ., 1992), 92–3, goes further, and proposes Aldhelm himself as the author of *The Dream of the Rood*.

debate over the date of that inscription,[45] the authorship of which has been variously ascribed to the court of King Aldfrith of Northumbria and to his baptismal sponsor and, apparently, cousin Aldhelm himself.[46] It is perhaps sufficient here to note that not only is the Ruthwell Inscription regularly used to emend what seems obviously defective in the Vercelli Book text,[47] but that, as we shall see, it also contains other readings that suggest that it is an extract from a longer text that is close to, but not identical with, that found in the later manuscript.[48] The notion that what is inscribed on the Ruthwell Cross (whenever that inscription may have occurred) is an extract from an earlier and familiar text may also help explain the undoubted difficulty of reading the runes as currently arranged in groups of two to three runes aligned vertically, with a single word customarily filling several lines.[49] The implication is that if the text itself was familiar, it might nonetheless survive unfamiliar transmission.

The Ruthwell poem, in so far as it can be reconstructed with any certainty, is unusual in a number of respects, not least of which is that not all of its lines are made up of paired and alliterating half-lines, as are all but one of the lines in *The Dream of the Rood*.[50] Indeed, in the opening line of the

---

45 Cf. Swanton, p. 39: 'The essential literary identity of the two texts cannot be questioned; the verbal parallel is too close to be accounted for simply by the use of common material.' See too Jane Roberts, 'Some Relationships between *The Dream of the Rood* and the Cross at Ruthwell,' *Studies in Medieval English Language and Literature* 15 (2000): 1–25.

46 On the close relationship between Aldhelm and Aldfrith, as well as the liklihood that both were trained at Iona by Admonán, see now Michael Lapidge, 'The Career of Aldhelm,' *Anglo-Saxon England* 36 (2007): 15–69.

47 So the word *sorgum* is supplied in line 59.

48 Cf. Howlett, 'Inscriptions and Design, ' 85: 'The text established by collation of the cross and drawings suggests that the source of the Ruthwell poem was similar to, but distinct from, lines 39–65 of *The Dream of the Rood* in the Vercelli Book.' See too Daniel Paul O'Donnell, 'Manuscript Variation in Multiple-Recension Old English Poetic Texts: The Technical Problem and Poetical Art' (unpub. PhD diss., Yale Univ., 1996), 245–9 and 292–305. For the alternative view, namely, that the Vercelli text represents an expansion of the Ruthwell version, see Orton, *Transmission of Old English Poetry*, 144–9.

49 See, for example, R.I. Page, *An Introduction to English Runes* (London: Methuen, 1973), 150: 'So odd does [the Ruthwell inscription] appear that I incline to think it may be not be part of the original design for the cross, and to wonder if these runes were added by a later carver who had less command over the space he had to fill.'

50 The exception is the self-alliterating line 76, *freondas gefrunon* ('friends discovered'). Some editors have been tempted to supply another half-line, but the sense is complete as it stands.

reconstructed Ruthwell poem, we find a self-alliterating half-line that is reflected in a pair of alliterating half-lines in the Vercelli text. The Ruthwell
version, with parallel phrasing again highlighted in bold italics, reads as follows: '[+ ond]*geredæ hinæ god alme3ttig* '(I.1: 'god almighty stripped himself'); the cognate line in *The Dream of the Rood* reads: 'On*gyrede hine* þa
geong hæleð þæt wæs *god ælmihtig*' (l. 39: 'Then the young hero, who was
god almighty, stripped himself'). The difference is striking, masking as it
does a concern within *The Dream of the Rood* as a whole to identify fully
the divine and human aspects of Christ, as described above. Instead, the
Ruthwell poem, which tends to focus firmly on the the drama of the
Crucifixion itself, matches its self-alliterating half-line with an alliterative
pair that again offers an abbreviated version of what is found in the Vercelli
text. The Ruthwell version reads '*þa he walde on galgu gistiga*' (I.2: 'when
he wished to climb onto the gallows'), while that in the Vercelli Book includes a number of other details (lines 40b–1): '*Gestah he on gealgan* heanne,
/ modig on manigra gesyhðe, *þa he wolde* mancyn lysan' ('he climbed onto
the lowly gallows, bold in the sight of many, when he wished to redeem
mankind'). The medial half-line in the Vercelli text ('*modig* on manigra gesyhðe') may indeed be reflected in the self-alliterating half-line that constitutes the next rather damaged verse in the Ruthwell text, generally
reconstructed as *modig f[ore] [allæ] men* ('bold before all people'), although
given that the phrase *god ælmihtig* appears in the preceding line of the
Ruthwell poem there may also be a further parallel in line 93 of *The Dream
of the Rood*, which reads '*ælmihtig god for* ealle *menn*' ('almighty god, before all people'). The collocation of phrases seems intriguing, given the clear
aural echoes involved (in *The Dream of the Rood*, which would include
modig + *manigra* … *man-* … *menn*; a similar line with the same aural resonance is found in *Resignation* 175a ['*modig fore* þære mengo']), and may
suggest oral or memorial transmission.

The same sense that some of the parallels between the Ruthwell and
Vercelli poems result from a shared archetype transmitted orally is heightened when two further passages are compared. The third section of the
Ruthwell poem describes the moment of Crucifixion in words which map
closely onto what is recorded in the Vercelli Book (III.1–3):

> + *kri[s]t wæs on rodi*
> *hweþræ þer fus[æ]   fêarran kw[o]mu*
> *[æ]þþilæ* til anum   *ic þæt al bi[êald]*
> [Christ was on the cross; but nobles hastening came together there from afar;
> I beheld it all.]

Given that again the Ruthwell text begins with a stray half-line, it seems very close to what is found in *The Dream of the Rood* (ll. 56b–8):

> Crist *wæs on rode.*
> *Hwæðere þær fuse   feorran cwoman*
> *to* þam *æðelinge.   Ic þæt eall be*heold.
> [Christ was on the cross; yet they came from afar to the prince: I beheld it all.]

The difference lies in the echoing terms [*æ*]*þþilæ* (III.3), which in the Ruthwell version refers to Christ's followers, and *æðelinge* (l. 58a), which in the Vercelli version refers to Christ himself. It may be that the Vercelli poem reflects an earlier stage in the transmission, given that the nobility of Christ is reflected elsewhere in *The Dream of the Rood* through cognate terms, notably in the closing words of the text, which speak of Christ returning 'þær his eðel wæs' (l. 156b: 'where his homeland was'), presumably the most suitable destination for an *æðeling*. Again, however, what seems at issue is an oral and memorial transmission of a shared and well-known text.

Yet the Ruthwell poet appears to have selected his words with care, focusing attention on the Crucifixion, rather than on Christ; there is no reference to the dreamer at all. The Ruthwell text is clearly composed of four sections, the first of which describes Christ mounting the Cross, the second and third of which describe the Crucifixion itself, and the fourth of which describes the deposition from the Cross. In apparently paring down some reflex of the Vercelli text for his inscription, the Ruthwell poet seems to have made a point of retaining those parts of the narrative that accord most closely with the Passion narratives in the Gospels of Matthew and John.[51] In this context, it is also interesting to note that an anonymous homily for Palm Sunday (HomS 18, Cameron no. B3.2.18) found in three separate eleventh-century manuscripts and offering a vernacular rendering of Matthew 26–7, appears to have several significant verbal and thematic parallels with *The Dream of the Rood*.[52] In speaking of the Deposition of

---

51 Cf. Howlett, 'Inscriptions and Design,' 90: 'The designer [of the Ruthwell text] quoted words and phrases which recall the Passion narratives of Matthew and John, as well as the Benedictine Office. Later Old English translations of these Latin texts afford remarkable echoes of words and phrases in the Ruthwell poem.' Howlett's observations also of course accord well with the notion that it was *The Dream of the Rood* rather than the Ruthwell text that was the better known.

52 See further Dorothy M. Horgan, '*The Dream of the Rood* and a Homily for Palm Sunday,' *NQ* 29.5 (1982): 388–91 and (independently) Aidan Conti, 'An Anonymous

Christ from the Cross, for example, the homily adds to the Gospel account the fact that when Joseph and Nichodemus go to take down Christ, '7 hi sona to ðære rode becomon 7 heo him sona to aleat' ('and they immediately approached the Cross, and it bowed down to them'); compare 'hnag ic hwæðre þam secgum to handa' (*Dream* 59; 'yet I bent down to the men's hands'). More striking still is the (again, extra-evangelical) detail that Joseph and Nichodemus place Christ in a tomb 'þe wæs *gecorfen* on ðam *beorhtan stane*' ('which was carved in that bright stone'); one might compare '*curfon* hie þæt of *beorhtan stane*' (*Rood* 66: 'they carved it from bright stone'), and further note that in extant Old English this collocation is uniquely shared by these texts. The fact that one of the manuscripts containing this homily, Oxford, Bodleian Library, Bodley 340, not only comes from the same putative milieu as the Vercelli Book (namely, the south-east of England, specifically Rochester or Canterbury), but in fact contains five common items, only strengthens the connection;[53] neither of these shared details, one might note, is found in the Ruthwell text, again suggesting that it is the longer Vercelli version that comes closest to the putative archetype.

A similar conclusion is suggested by the inscription on the Brussels Reliquary Cross, which is much briefer than that found at Ruthwell, and includes only two lines of verse, as follows:[54]

> *Rod* is min nama. *Geo ic ricne cyning*
> bær *byfigynde*, *blode bestemed*.
> [Rood is my name. Once, trembling, drenched in blood, I bore the powerful king.]

The phrase *ricne cyning* is uniquely shared between the Brussels inscription and *The Dream of the Rood* 44 (which has further echoes: '*Rod* wæs ic aræred. Ahof *ic ricne cyning*'; the *Geo* of the Brussels text may derive from *Dream* 28a: 'Þæt wæs geara *iu*'); the parallel passage from the Ruthwell poem reads '*ic riicnæ ᚳyniᚾc*' (II.1). Apart from the Brussels inscription, the phrase *blode bestemed* appears four times in extant Old English, in *Exodus* 449b (*blode bestemed*); *The Dream of the Rood* 48b

Homily for Palm Sunday, *The Dream of the Rood*, and the Progress of Ælfric's Reform,' *NQ* 48.4 (2001): 377–80.
53 The items in question are *VH* I, III, V, VIII, and IX, variant-versions of which from Bodley 340 are printed by Scragg in his edition.
54 Text from ASPR 6, 115, ll. 1–2.

(*blode bestemed*); *Christ* C 1085b (*blode bistemed*); *Beowulf* 486b (*blode bestymed*); again, it also appears in the parallel passage from the Ruthwell poem (*ic* [...] *miþ blodæ* [.]*istemi*[.]). The Brussels Cross proclaims that it 'bore [Christ] trembling' (*'bær byfigynde'*), an apparent echo of *The Dream of the Rood* 42, where the Cross proclaims, 'I trembled when the warrior embraced me' (*'Bifode* ic þa me se beorn ymbclypte'); the added similarity of the sounds *bær* and *beorn* is intriguing, especially when it is recalled that the only time the word *beran* ('to bear') is used in *The Dream of the Rood* it likewise appears collocated with the noun *beorn* (line 32: *'Bæron* me ðær beornas on eaxlum' ['Warriors bore me there on their shoulders']). It seems possible that the author of the two verses of the Brussels inscription is basing his text on an extract from *The Dream of the Rood* (ll. 42–4), but has also conflated other words and associations (*iu* and *bær-/beorn-*) from elsewhere in the poem, perhaps through mis-remembering the text. The fact that both the inscriptions from Ruthwell and Brussels appear largely to be based on rather localized and evidently adapted passages of *The Dream of the Rood* (ll. 42–4 for Brussels; ll. 39–65 for Ruthwell) may again support the notion that both inscriptions repre-sent extracts from a longer text that was widely known.

In the same context, it is notable that Tatwine (who died in 735, and who drew heavily on Aldhelm's *Enigmata* in composing his own),[55] should describe the Cross of Christ in terms that seem also to echo certain aspects of *The Dream of the Rood* in his enigma 9 (*de cruce Christi* ['On the Cross of Christ']):[56]

Versicolor cernor nunc; nunc mihi forma nitescit.
Lege fui quondam cunctis iam *larbula* servis;
Sed modo *me* gaudens *orbis veneratur et ornat.*
Quique meum gustat fructum iam sanus habetur,
Nam mihi concessum est insanis ferre salutem.   5
Propterea sapiens optat me *in fronte* tenere.
[Now I seem changeable in colour; now my shape shines. Once by law I was already a terrifying spectre for all servants, but now the world rejoicing hon-ours and adorns me. Whoever tastes my fruit is already considered healed, for

---

55 See, for example, Andy Orchard, *The Poetic Art of Aldhelm*, CSASE 8 (Cambridge: CUP, 1994), 252–4 and 286–7.

56 W.F. Bolton, 'Tatwine's *De Cruce Christi* and *The Dream of the Rood*,' *Archiv für das Studium der neueren Sprachen und Literaturen* 200 (1963): 344–6; F. Glorie, ed., *Collectio-nes Aenigmatum Merovingicae Aetatis*, CCSL 133 (Turnhout: Brepols, 1968): 176.

I have been granted to bring health to the unhealed; moreover the wise man chooses to keep me in front.]

The notion that the Cross is seen to be 'changeable in colour' is matched in *The Dream of the Rood*, where the Cross is likewise seen to 'change its coverings and colours' (*'wendan wædum ond bleom;'* l. 22a),[57] and the self-description of Tatwine's Cross as on the one hand a 'terrible spectacle' (*larbula*) established 'by law' (*lege*), presumably a reference to a gallows-tree, and on the other something widely honoured and adorned around the world ('me ... orbis veneratur et ornat'; l. 4) again finds a resonance in two connected passages in *The Dream of the Rood*. In the first of these, the Cross says that 'strong enemies took me there, made me there a spectacle, commanded me to raise up their criminals' ('Genaman me ðær strange feondas, / geworhton him þær *to wæfersyne, heton* me heora *wergas hebban*'; ll. 30b–1); the second reads as follows (ll. 80b–3a):

> Is nu sæl cumen
> þæt *me weorðiað* wide ond side
> *menn ofer moldan,* ond eall þeos mære gesceaft,
> gebiddaþ him to þyssum beacne.
> [The time has now come that people far and wide across the world, and all this glorious creation, pray to this sign.]

It may also be relevant that line 82 (*'menn ofer moldan* ond eall þeos mære gesceaft') is the only one in the whole poem that is repeated verbatim: it also occurs at line 12, just after a discussion of the Cross as more than just a 'criminal's gallows' ('fracodes gealga', l. 10b), and just before a detailed description of the ornamentation of the Cross, appropriately set off in a perfect envelope-pattern (*wuldres treow ... geweorðode ... weorðlice wealdendes treow*), which reads as follows (ll. 14b–17):

> Geseah ic wuldres treow,
> wædum *geweorðode,* wynnum scinan,
> *gegyred* mid golde; gimmas hæfdon
> *bewrigene weorðlice* wealdendes treow.
> [I saw the tree of glory, adorned with coverings, shining joyfully, decked with gold; gems had ornately covered the ruler's tree.]

---

57 James Smith, 'The Garments that Honour the Cross in *The Dream of the Rood*,' *Anglo-Saxon England* 4 (1975): 29–35.

It is as if Tatwine, recalling certain connected passages from *The Dream of the Rood*, has constructed his *enigma* with an audience familiar with the vernacular text in mind; certainly, such a view would also help to explain the reference in Tatwine's *enigma* to keeping the cross 'in front' (*in fronte*): *The Dream of the Rood* says that 'no one need be fearful, who carries the best of signs on their chest' (ll. 117–18: 'Ne þearf ðær þonne ænig anforht[58] wesan / þe him ær *in breostum* bereð beacna selest'). But the combined connections, though suggestive, are hardly conclusive.

However, Tatwine is not the only Anglo-Latin poet to have produced celebratory verses on an enigmatic and decorated cross: at some point in the early ninth century, Aediluulf, presumably writing in the North of England, and perhaps at no great remove from Ruthwell itself,[59] describes a monk having a dream-vision of a cross, beginning with the following lines (*De abbatibus* 22.32–4 [723–5]):[60]

> *Crux ueneranda nitens* praecelso stipite surgit
> Vertice de mensae, nimium candente smaragdo.
> *Aurea cum gemmis* flauescit lamina fuluis.
> [A venerable shining cross rises up on a lofty stem from the edge of the altar, with very brilliant emerald; a golden layer grows yellow with tawny gems.]

Aediluulf here focuses on just one aspect of the decorated Cross, whereas *The Dream of the Rood* describes an object bedecked with both gold and gore; the latter perpsective also features in a poem composed a generation earlier by Alcuin, trained at York but writing on the Continent, who crisply captures the same contradiction between a brilliant cross and one spattered with blood in an extended poetic reverie on the cross (*carmen* 112) that includes the line 'Crux sacrata dei *fulgescit sanguine* summi' (l. 7: 'The holy cross grows brilliant with the blood of God on high'). Such images seem to have had considerable currency in Anglo-Saxon verse.

Yet if several Anglo-Latin texts offer intriguing evidence of parallels with *The Dream of the Rood* to go alongside the reflexes of the text that have been detected in the Ruthwell and Brussels inscriptions, as well as in

---

58 The manuscript reads *unforht*, but the emendation is generally accepted.
59 See in particular Michael Lapidge, 'Aediluulf and the School of York,' in *Lateinische Kultur im VIII. Jahrhundert: Traube-Gedenkschrift*, ed. A Lehner and W. Berschin (St Ottilien: Eos Verlag), 161–78.
60 Cf. Alistair Campbell, ed., *Æthelwulf: De abbatibus* (Oxford: Clarendon Press, 1967), 56–7, esp. n. 2.

some later homiletic and liturgical texts, it is also notable the extent to which words and phrases from *The Dream of the Rood* can be matched at appropriate moments in a strictly limited range of surviving Old English verse. So, for example, the opening lines of *The Dream of the Rood* have a close parallel, both verbally and conceptually, in the description of a similar dream-vision in *Daniel. The Dream of the Rood* begins as follows, with parallels again indicated by bold italics (*Dream* 1–3):

> Hwæt! Ic swefna cyst   secgan wylle,
> ***hwæt***[61] me ***gemætte***   to midre nihte,
> syðþan ***reordberend   reste wunedon***!
> ['Listen: I will tell of the best of dreams, which I dreamed in the middle of the night, after the speech-bearers remained in their beds.']

One might well compare the description of the first dream-vision of Nebuchadnezzar, and recall that a later dream–vision of Nebuchadnezzar actually concerns a tree (*Daniel* 120–3):

> Het þa tosomne sinra leoda
> þa wiccungdom widost bæron,
> frægn þa ða mænigeo   ***hwæt*** hine ***gemætte***,
> þenden ***reordberend   reste wunode***.
> [He ordered those of his people who practised magic most widely to come, and asked them what he dreamt, once the speech-bearer remained in his bed.][62]

This is the only occurrence of the term *reordberend* in *Daniel*, which appears twice in *The Dream of the Rood*, where, as we have seen, it seems to have a particular purpose in highlighting the paradox of a speaking tree. It is useful to consider the biblical source for this passage (Daniel 2:1–3):

> in anno secundo regni Nabuchodonosor vidit Nabuchodonosor somnium et conterritus est spiritus eius et somnium eius fugit ab eo. praecepit ergo rex ut convocarentur arioli et magi et malefici et Chaldei et indicarent regi somnia sua qui cum venissent steterunt coram rege.

---

61 The manuscript reads *hæt*, though all editors have accepted the emendation.
62 The alternative is to suppose that (as elsewhere in the extant poetry) *reordberend* is a plural form, and that *wunode* is a plural with loss of -*n*, as in (for example) *Beowulf*, ll. 905a, 1408a, and 2164b. See further, Robert T. Farrell, ed., *Daniel and Azarias* (London: Methuen, 1974), 54.

[In the second year of the reign of Nabuchodonosor, Nabuchodonosor had a dream, and his spirit was terrified, and his dream went out of his mind. Then the king commanded to call together the diviners and the wise men, and the magicians, and the Chaldeans: to declare to the king his dreams: so they came and stood before the king.]

Certainly, there is no warrant in the source for describing the king as a 'speech-bearer,' and while the vernacular parallel is striking, it seems ultimately inconclusive: there is no way to decide on the relative chronology of the texts, even supposing that the congruence signals a direct relationship, as opposed to simple happenstance or independent reliance on a text, texts, or tradition now lost.

A rather better case for a direct literary connection with the *The Dream of the Rood* can be made with Cynewulf's *Elene*, which is not only also preserved in the Vercelli Book, but contains another poetic dream-vision of the Cross, namely, Constantine's famous vision before the Battle of the Milvian Bridge, as follows (*Elene* 88b–92a):[63]

> *Geseah* he frætwum **beorht**
> wliti *wuldres treo*   ofer wolcna hrof,
> *golde* geglenged   (*gimmas* lixtan);   90
> wæs se blaca **beam**   bocstafum awriten,
> **beorhte** ond **leohte**.
> [He saw, bright with adornments, the beautiful tree of glory over the vault of the skies, decorated with gold (gems shone); the gleaming beam was inscribed with letters brightly and lightly.]

This self-contained passage, marked off by envelope-patterning through the repeated term 'bright' (*beorht* [88b] ... *beorhte* [92a]), finds a close parallel in a rather longer passage describing the dreamer's first vision of the Cross in (*Dream of the Rood* 4–17):[64]

> Þuhte me þæt ic *gesawe*   syllicre *treow*
> on lyft lædan,   *leohte* bewunden,   5
> *beama beorhtost*.   Eall þæt beacen wæs

---

63 The manuscript reads *gelenged* at line 90a, and two letters (*on*?) have been erased before *awriten* in line 91b.

64 The manuscript reads *wealdes* at line 17b, a reading as the genitive of the homographs *weald* ('forest') and *weald* ('power').

begoten mid *golde. Gimmas* stodon
fægere æt foldan sceatum,   swylce þær fife wæron
uppe on þam eaxlegespanne.   Beheoldon þær engel dryhtnes ealle,
fægere þurh forðgesceaft.   Ne wæs ðær huru fracodes gealga,   10
ac hine þær beheoldon   halige gastas,
men ofer moldan,   ond eall þeos mære gesceaft.
Syllic wæs se sige*beam*,   ond ic synnum fah,
forwunded mid wommum.   *Geseah* ic *wuldres treow*,
wædum geweorðode,   wynnum scinan,   15
gegyred mid *golde*;   *gimmas* hæfdon
bewrigene weorðlice   wealdendes *treow*.
[It seemed to me that I saw a quite marvellous tree, lifted into the sky, wound
round with light, the brightest of beams. All that beacon was dripping with
gold. Gems stood fair at the corners of the earth, and likewise there were five,
up on the shoulder-bar. All beheld there the messenger of the lord, fair
throughout future creation. That was no criminal's gallows, but holy spirits,
men across the world, and all this famed creation, beheld it there. Marvellous
was the victory-beam, and I stained [or 'guilty'] with sins, wounded with
flaws. I saw the tree of glory, honoured with cloths, shining with joys,
adorned with gold; gems had honourably covered the ruler's tree.]

One might note that this passage too is based around a rather complex
envelope-pattern (*gesawe ... treow ... golde ... gimmas*; *gesawe ... [wuldres]*
treow ... golde ... gimmas) that in fact lies at the heart of the parallel passage from *Elene*. The Latin source for that section of *Elene* reads as follows: 'Et intendens in caelum uidit signum crucis Christi ex lumine claro
constitutum, et desuper litteris aureis scriptum titulum' ('And looking
into the sky he saw the Cross of Christ set up in bright light, and an inscription written on the top in golden letters'). Although one might argue
that all the elements of brilliance and gold are already present in the source,
it is important to note that the Latin specifies that it is the inscribed letters
themselves that are gold, rather than the whole cross, as in *Elene* and *The*
Dream of the Rood, both of which texts also emphasize that the cross is
'the tree of glory' (*wuldres treo* [*Elene* 89a]; *wuldres treow* [*Dream* 14b]),
and that the cross is decorated not just with gold, but with gems (*golde ...*
gimmas [*Elene* 90]; *golde gimmas ... golde ... gimmas* [*Dream* 7 and 16]).
Both of these details are missing from the Latin. Moreover, the phrase
wuldres treo(w) ('tree of glory', l. 14b) is uniquely shared in the extant
corpus by *The Dream of the Rood* in the passage just cited, and in *Elene*,
where it occurs four times in all (at ll. 89a, 827b, 866b, and 1251b); again,
in each case there seems little warrant for the phrase in the Latin source.

This passage from *The Dream of the Rood* also introduces the first occurrence of the compound *sigebeam* ('victory-beam,' l. 13a; the same form appears later at 127a). In extant Old English poetry, the term likewise occurs only here in *The Dream of the Rood* and in *Elene*, where it appears no fewer than seven times (at ll. 420b, 444a, 665b, 846b, 860b, 964b, and 1027a), alongside what are evidently related compounds, likewise unique in poetry to *Elene*, namely, *sigebeacen* ('victory-beacon'; at ll. 168b, 887a, 974a, and 1256a) and *sigorbeacen* ('victory-beacon'; at 984b).[65] Indeed, at two points in *Elene*, the cross is described as *selest sigebeacna* ('best of victory-beacons,' l. 974a)[66] and *selest sigebeama* ('best of victory-beams' l. 1027a),[67] both formulations that have parallels in the designations *beacna selest* ('best of beacons') and *wudu selesta* ('best of trees'), found in *The Dream of the Rood* at lines 118b and 27b. It is important to stress that none of these *sige-/sigor-* compounds in *Elene* have anything corresponding to notions of victory in the Latin source, which strongly suggests that this heavily repeated feature is a device of Cynewulf's own choosing, inspired from outside his immediate Latin source.

Further signs that it is Cynewulf who in *Elene* is borrowing from *The Dream of the Rood*, rather than the other way around, stem from the observation that a key passage in the latter, occurring precisely at the midpoint of the poem, and in the context of the Cross concluding its description of the Crucifixion, seems evidently echoed in some lines in *Elene* that again have no warrant in the Latin source. The passage in question from *The Dream of the Rood* reads as follows (*Dream* 78–80a):

> *Nu ðu miht gehyran, hæleð min se leofa,*
> *þæt ic bealuwara weorc gebiden hæbbe,*
> *sarra sorga.*
> [Now you can hear, my dear young man, what deeds of evil-doers I have endured, painful sorrows.]

---

65 The term *sigebe(a)cn* is also found in a number of prose texts, glossaries, and, intriguingly, on the Bewcastle Cross, the relationship of which to the Ruthwell Cross remains a matter of hot debate.

66 The manuscript reads *sigebecna*, with another *a* inserted above the line before the *c*.

67 It may be worth noting that the phrase *selest sigebeama* is preceded by a description of Elene decorating the cross with gold and gems ('Heo þa rode heht / golde beweorcan ond gimcynnum,' ll. 1022b–3) that is certainly sanctioned in the source ('collocans praetiosam crucem auro ac lapidibus pretiosis'), but which represents only the second time that the collocation of gold and gems occurs in the poem (the first is during Constantine's vision, at line 90, where, as discussed above, there is no such collocation in the source). Cynewulf may have aniticpated Elene's decoration of the Cross in his description of the original vision.

The phrase 'hæleð min se leofa' ('my dear young man') is repeated a few lines later (*Dream* 95b), when the Cross instructs the dreamer to explain his vision to the rest of mankind, and to explicate it; in other words, these lines come precisely at the transition from dream-vision to homily discussed above. The parallel passage from *Elene* comes in the context of a lengthy speech that describes the mercy of Christ despite all the agonies he suffered at the Crucifixion, and reads as follows (*Elene* 511–16):

> *Nu ðu meaht gehyran,   hæleð min se leofa,*
> *hu* arfæst is   ealles wealdend,
> þeah we æbylgð wið hine   oft ge*wyrc*en,
> synna wunde,   gif we sona eft
> þara *bealu*dæda   bote gefremmaþ   515
> ond þæs unrihtes   eft geswicaþ.
>
> [Now you can hear, my dear young man, how merciful is the ruler of everything, although we may often commit wickedness against him, with the wound of sins, if we immediately afterwards make amends for those evil deeds, and afterwards cease from wrong.]

The striking identity of the opening lines of these passages is underscored by the general context, which emphasizes the agony of the Crucifixion; it may also be significant that both these passages contain the only *bealu-* ('evil') compounds to be found in either poem. There is nothing whatsoever in the Latin source of *Elene* to suggest this passage, and so it is tempting to suggest that Cynewulf is here echoing *The Dream of the Rood* directly. By contrast, when we consider other reflexes of the same striking opening phrase elsewhere in Old English verse, a still more complex picture emerges.

Alongside both *The Dream of the Rood* and *Elene* in the Vercelli Book we find precisely the same striking opening phrase echoed (uniquely in extant Old English verse) in two passages from *Andreas* which themselves have a self-evident connection in terms of subject-matter and language. The first of these passages comes at the end of a speech by Andreas describing the wonders of Christ to Christ himself, who at this stage is disguised as a helmsman (*Andreas* 595–600):

> *Nu ðu miht gehyran,   hyse leofesta,*   595
> *hu* us *wuldres weard   wordum* ond dædum
> lufode in life,   ond þurh *lare* speon
> to *þam fægeran gefean,*   þær freo moton,
> eadige mid englum,   *eard weardigan,*

þa ðe æfter deaðe   dryhten secað.   600
['Now you can hear, dearest youth, how the guardian of glory loved us in life
with words and deeds, and through his teaching has drawn us to that fair
delight where they may be allowed free and blessed among the angels, to
dwell in their homeland, those who after death seek the lord.]

The whole passage is a tissue of Cynewulfian borrowings unique in the extant corpus of Old English: apart from the lines already indicated, *Andreas*
595b (*hyse leofesta*) matches *Elene* 523b (*hyse leofesta*); *Andreas* 596a (*wuldres weard*) matches both *Elene* 84a (*wuldres weard*) and *Chrsit B* 527a
(*wuldres weard*); *Andreas* 598a (*to þam fægeran gefean*) matches *Elene* 948a
(*þone fægran gefean*); and *Andreas* 599b (*eard weardigan*) matches both
Christ B 772b (*eard weardien*)[68] and *Juliana* 20a (*eard weardade*).

The second passage, by contrast, contains no new Cynewulfian borrowings, and seems to have been modelled solely on the earlier passage in
the same poem (*Andreas* 811–14):

Nu ðu miht gehyran,   hyse leofesta,
hu he wundra worn   *wordum* cyðde,
swa þeah ne gelyfdon   *larum* sinum
modblinde menn.
[Now you can hear, dearest youth, how he revealed a multitude of miracles
through his words, even though the men blind at heart did not pay heed to his
teachings.]

The links between these two passages from *Andreas* extend beyond their
opening lines and the general context of a discussion of Christ's life, no
necessary aspect of which is enshrined in the overlapping words. Both
passages also preserve an interest in the contrast between words and deeds,
as well as an emphasis on Christ's teaching, with the result that the first
three lines of each passage seem very close in both structure and sound –
the later passage evidently an aural echo of the former and the phrase
lufode in life (*Andreas* 597a) apparently paralleled by *gelyfdon* (*Andreas*
813a).[69] If Cynewulf is echoing *The Dream of the Rood* in *Elene*, the

---

68 Interestingly, the Exeter Book scribe originally wrote *weardigen*, and then sub-puncted
the *g* for deletion.
69 For this common wordplay, which is especially frequent in Cynewulf's works, see
Eugene R. Kintgen, '*Lif, lof, leof, lufu*, and *geleafa* in Old English Poetry,' *NM* 78
(1977): 309–16; Kintgen also includes a number of examples from *Andreas*.

Andreas poet seems initially to be echoing *Elene* (as he seems to do abundantly elsewhere),[70] and then to be pursuing parallels of his own. Such progressive identifications (with *Elene* drawing on *The Dream of the Rood*, then *Andreas* drawing on *Elene*, then *Andreas* drawing on itself) are matched both by the identifications so evident within *The Dream of the Rood*, and by those that have been signalled here in other texts and contexts. Together, such evident echoes surely suggest a lengthy and complex transmission-history for the poem that survives in the Vercelli Book.

There seems, then, little doubt that generations of Anglo-Saxon authors, in both Latin and Old English, both at the beginning of the period and at the end, converted artistically the matter of the Cross into pious, precious, and precocious verse and prose, and I would argue that *The Dream of the Rood* is crucial (as it were) to our understanding of that process. I would suggest that *The Dream of the Rood* and its reflexes, whether on stone, on silver, or on skin, together provide an index of the ways in which some of the finest Old English verse that has survived could adapt and change, in the course of a lengthy journey that may have lasted up to three centuries and which both transmitted and transmuted an already kaleidoscopic text through the minds and mouths of a number of poets to the hands and hearts of a number of sculptors and scribes.

Three aspirations suggest themselves, inspired by the poem itself: I hope first that the above analysis will have helped to demonstrate the superior skill of whoever wrote *The Dream of the Rood*, as well as the poet's extraordinary sensitivity to similarities of diction and character and generic form; I hope second to have fostered a similar level of sensitivity for modern readers of a poem that is in my view one of the greatest monuments of Anglo-Saxon England; and I hope third that I have shown enough to suggest that at least some Anglo-Saxons found it so, and sought to echo its scintillating words in ways that make sense only if the poem was widely known. But then I may be dreaming.[71]

---

70 For a detailed analysis, see Alison M. Powell, 'Verbal Parallels in *Andreas* and Its Relationship to *Beowulf* and Cynewulf' (unpub. PhD diss., Univ. of Cambridge, 2002), 283–99 ('Appendix C'), which lists 149 parallels uniquely shared between *Andreas* and the four signed poems of Cynewulf; nearly eighty of the parallels Powell detects connect *Andreas* and *Elene* directly.

71 My deepest thanks to Samantha Zacher, who helped me dream, and without whom this rude piece would never have been written.

Vercelli Homilies XIX–XXI, the Ascension Day Homily in Cambridge, Corpus Christi College 162, and the Catechetical Tradition from Augustine to Wulfstan

MICHAEL FOX

The anonymous homilies known as Vercelli XIX–XXI and the Ascension Day homily in CCCC 162 (Tristram III) are the work of a single author.[1] That author, in providing homilies for Rogationtide and Ascension Day, attempts to interweave themes and hortatory messages appropriate to the season with basic Christian instruction. In other words, the author's aim is at once to convince listeners and readers[2] of the spiritual importance of the

---

1 For Vercelli XIX–XXI, all citations are taken from D. Scragg, ed., *The Vercelli Homilies*, EETS o.s. 300 (Oxford: OUP, 1992), and translations are adapted from L.E. Nicholson, ed., *The Vercelli Book Homilies: Translations from the Anglo-Saxon* (Lanham, MD, and London: Univ. Press of America, 1991); for the Ascension Day homily in CCCC 162, pp. 431–41, from the dissertation of H. Tristram, *Vier altenglische Predigten aus der heterdoxen Tradition, mit Kommentar, Übersetzung und Glossar sowie drei weiteren Texten im Anhang* (Freiburg im Breslau: n.p., 1970) (item III) [in citations, in both Latin and Old English, abbreviations have been silently expanded and orthography, punctuation, and capitalization have been regularized]. On problems with Tristram's text, see J. Cross, *Cambridge Pembroke College MS 25: A Carolingian Sermonary Used by Anglo-Saxon Preachers*, KCLMS I (London: King's College, 1987), 174–5. On the manuscript CCCC 162 and its contents, see D. Scragg, 'Cambridge, Corpus Christi College 162,' in *Anglo-Saxon Manuscripts and Their Heritage*, ed. P. Pulsiano and E. Treharne (Aldershot and Brookfield, VT: Ashgate, 1998), 71–83.

2 On the possible audiences of these homilies, see Charles Wright's observations about Vercelli XI–XIII (also Rogationtide homilies) in 'Vercelli Homilies XI–XIII and the Benedictine Reform: Tailored Sources and Implied Audiences,' in *Preacher, Sermon and Audience in the Middle Ages*, ed. C. Muessig (Leiden: Brill, 2002), 203–27. In discussing what might be appropriate for a clerical community or lay audiences, Wright observes that 'one version of the *Canons of Edgar* specifies the Rogation Days as one of the three occasions when priests should remind the people to pay tithes' (210; D. Whitelock, ed. and trans., *Councils and Synods with Other Documents Relating to the English Church, I: A.D. 871–1204, Part I: 871–1066* [Oxford: Clarendon Press, 1981], 331). Though not

season and to rehearse as many of the most significant events of Christian history and foundations of the faith as possible. In the latter aim, the author was influenced by a long tradition of catechetical writing, the most significant example of which is Augustine's *De catechizandis rudibus* (*DCR*), but perhaps also by a developing sense of what sort of sermon was appropriate for Rogationtide. As Milton Gatch has suggested, the three Rogation Days became a common occasion for the preaching of 'general catechetical and parenetic or hortatory sermons,'[3] and the fact that twenty-four Old English Rogationtide sermons are extant demonstrates just how significant the event was in the Anglo-Saxon preaching cycle.[4]

Vercelli XIX–XXI have long been recognized to be related. As homilies for the three days of prayer and fasting leading up to Ascension Day, they have an obvious and immediate relationship (as, it would seem, Vercelli

---

mentioned in Vercelli XI–XIII – and Wright takes this as evidence against an exclusively lay audience – Vercelli XX.28–30 does mention tithing, which may indicate that this set of sermons was intended originally for at least a partially lay audience.

3   M. McC. Gatch, *Preaching and Theology in Anglo-Saxon England* (Toronto: UTP, 1977), 51 (also cited, with reference to Vercelli XI–XIII, by Wright, 'Vercelli Homilies XI–XIII,' 209). Gatch's suggestion is that this was a development of the 'late-Saxon church,' but the evidence of Vercelli XIX–XXI and Tristram III suggests that it may have begun at least before Ælfric and Wulfstan. Gatch also comments that Rogation Days 'seem to receive peculiar emphasis in England as preaching days' (*Preaching*, 201n37). For a detailed explanation of Roman and Gallican tradition and the confusion of the Major Litany (25 April) and the Minor Litany (the Monday, Tuesday, and Wednesday preceding Ascension Day), see J. Hill, 'The *Litaniae maiores* and *minores* in Rome, Francia and Anglo-Saxon England: Terminology, Texts and Traditions,' *Early Medieval Europe* 9 (2000): 211–46. Hill's survey of the common topics of Rogationtide homilies demonstrates just how strikingly unusual the contents of the latter set in the Vercelli Book are. Bedingfield explains the rather large corpus of Rogationtide material in Anglo-Saxon England: 'The festival, consisting of three days of processions, attracted such a large body of preaching material partly because its prescribed topics were quite broad, and the sorts of sermons that might be written "for any time of the year" tended to migrate toward this dramatic penitential period' (M. Bradford Bedingfield, *The Dramatic Liturgy of Anglo-Saxon England* [Woodbridge: Boydell, 2002], 191). The association of teaching with Rogationtide may be explained by the 'metaphor of the spiritual lamps,' which appears in three Old English Rogationtide homilies, and comes ultimately from Caesarius's *Sermo* CCXV. This connection is traced by Gordon Sellers ('The Old English Rogationtide Corpus: A Literary History,' unpub. PhD diss., Loyola Univ., 1996, pp. 126–51). For the relationship of Rogationtide homilies to the liturgy, see S.J. Harris, 'The Liturgical Context of Ælfric's Homilies for Rogation,' in *The Old English Homily: Precedent, Practice and Appropriation*, ed. A. Kleist (Turnout: Brepols, 2007), 143–69.

4   For a detailed discussion of the Old English tradition, see Sellers, 'Rogationtide Corpus.'

XI–XIII and Ælfric's *CH* I.18–I.20 and *CH* II.19–22). Donald Scragg first argued, on the basis of similar introductions and 'intimate' linguistic features, that the three formed a separate unit in the Vercelli collection. He suggested that all three homilies, which he termed 'composite homilies,' might have been 'compiled by the same person,' perhaps from an exemplar in a late West Saxon collection.[5] Paul Szarmach, describing the homilies as *Kompilationspredigten* and as 'concentric homilies,' suggested that each had been composed according to the same formula – 'introduction, an appropriate number of preparatory motifs, a central narrative episode or exposition, and a closing' – most likely by the same person.[6] James Cross and Joyce Bazire, in their edition of the Old English Rogationtide homilies, cast some doubt on the question of common authorship, suggesting that Vercelli XIX and Vercelli XX evince different attitudes towards their sources and different methods of compilation: their pairing in the manuscript, they noted, could be only for reasons of liturgical season.[7] However, this was before the discovery, by James Cross, of the relationship between Cambridge, Pembroke College 25 and Vercelli XIX–XXI and Tristram III.[8] The matter seems currently to rest with Donald Scragg's most recent work on the subject, which restates with new evidence the claim for common authorship. Considering phraseology, lexical items, and the common use of the Carolingian homiliary of St Père de Chartres, he argues that Vercelli XIX–XXI and Tristram III are the work of the same author, an author who perhaps worked in a Canterbury library during Dunstan's pontificate, 959–88.[9]

Assuming Szarmach and Scragg are correct about the authorship of these homilies, the suggestion which needs now to be examined in detail

---

5   D. Scragg, 'The Compilation of the Vercelli Book,' *ASE* 2 (1973): 194–5 and 203–4.

6   P. Szarmach, 'The Vercelli Homilies: Style and Structure,' in *The Old English Homily and Its Backgrounds*, ed. P. Szarmach and B.F. Huppé (Albany: State Univ. of New York Press, 1978), 244 and 248.

7   J. Bazire and J. Cross, eds, *Eleven Old English Rogationtide Homilies* (Toronto: UTP, 1982), 25. See also Cross, *Pembroke College MS 25*, 92–3.

8   Cross examines the relationship of Cambridge, Pembroke College MS 25 to several Old English homilies (*Pembroke College MS 25*). See also P. Szarmach, 'Pembroke College 25, Arts. 93–95,' in *Via Crucis: Essays on Early Medieval Sources and Ideas in Memory of J.E. Cross*, ed. T.N. Hall with assistance from T.D. Hill and C.D. Wright (Morgantown: West Virginia Univ. Press, 2002), 295–325.

9   D. Scragg, 'An Old English Homilist of Archbishop Dunstan's Day,' in *Words, Texts and Manuscripts: Studies in Anglo-Saxon Culture Presented to Helmut Gneuss on the Occasion of His Sixty-Fifth Birthday*, ed. M. Korhammer, with K. Reichl and H. Sauer (Cambridge and Rochester, NY: D.S. Brewer, 1992), 181–92.

was first made in a general article by Virginia Day.[10] Day looked at the model *narrationes* suggested by Augustine in his *De catechizandis rudibus* and found, in Latin and Old English examples, echoes of Augustine's guidelines for educating catechumenates. Of Vercelli XIX, she states: 'This homily does not include an outline of the complete cycle [of Christian history], from creation to Doomsday, but, as an introduction to Rogationtide penitential themes, the homilist describes the Trinity and its powers of creation, the creation of heaven, earth and the angels, the fall of the angels, the creation and fall of man and his ultimate redemption.'[11] Though Day refers only to Vercelli XIX.1–48, I believe the influence of Augustine's instructions for presenting Christian history may be found in all four homilies, which, considered in sequence, show an ordered progression of historical events and themes, and which continually make reference to the fundamental importance of the creation and fall of angels and men. A detailed examination of Augustine's model *narrationes* and the tradition of catechetical instruction, including the related works of Ælfric and Wulfstan, confirms the conclusions of Szarmach and Scragg and establishes that the author of the four homilies was the first to attempt to follow the traditional guidelines of Augustine in a series of vernacular sermons, and thus to anticipate what Ælfric and Wulfstan would later do in single occasional sermons.[12]

---

10 Virginia Day, 'The Influence of the Catechetical *narratio* on Old English and Some Other Medieval Literature,' *ASE* 3 (1974): 51–61.

11 Ibid., 56.

12 This catechetical model has also been used to attempt to identify the principle of unity behind the works of Oxford, Bodleian Library, Junius 11. Day mentions the similarity of Bede's account of Cædmon's compositions to Augustine's directions, and isolates the opening of *Genesis A* (1–102) and perhaps *Christ and Satan* (1–18) as influenced by the *narratio* ('Influence,' 54–5). J.R. Hall, however, extends the influence to all the works of Junius 11, and includes a synoptic table for Augustine's *DCR*, Wulfstan's homily (Bethurum VI) and all five poems of Junius 11 (see 'The Old English Epic of Redemption: The Theological Unity of MS Junius 11,' *Traditio* 32 [1976]; 185–208; repr. in R. Liuzza, ed., *The Poems of MS Junius 11* [London and New York: Routledge, 2002], 20–52). Other scholars, such as Marjorie Sue Allen and Phyllis Portnoy, have suggested that the liturgy is a more likely source, and Hall later responds to criticisms of his argument (see '"The Old English Epic of Redemption": Twenty-Five-Year Retrospective,' in *The Poems of MS Junius 11*, ed. Liuzza, 53–68). However, that the story of the creation and fall might be a suitable introduction for many kinds of instruction is proved, for example, by the opening of *Guthlac B*, in which lines 1–53a (819–71a) are devoted to the creation and fall of Adam and Eve as a prelude to the story of Guthlac and his death.

The Latin Background: Augustine, Martin, and Pirmin[13]

De catechizandi rudibus,[14] a work from the middle of Augustine's career, was probably written after the *Confessiones*, and concurrently with the early portions of *De Genesi ad litteram*, around 405. The work was composed specifically for Deogratias, deacon of Carthage, who had asked Augustine for some advice on how to instruct candidates for the catechumenate. Deogratias was having difficulty determining how to present Christian belief (the *modus narrationis*), including where to begin and end the narration and what supplemental material to add to the end of the narrative.[15] Augustine sent Deogratias a lengthy set of instructions and two

---

13 The Latin background is in fact far more complex than this heading suggests. In addition to these authors, one ought also to consider many other unedited or unstudied Latin sermons, including the so-called *Homilia sacra* (ed. G. Elmenhorst, in *Gennadii Massiliensis presbyteri liber de ecclesiasticis dogmatibus* [Hamburg, 1614], 47–55, and also recently edited by G. Constable, 'The Anonymous Early Medieval Homily in MS Copenhagen GKS 143,' in *Ritual, Text and Law: Studies in Medieval Canon Law and Liturgy Presented to Roger E. Reynolds*, ed. K.G. Cushing and R.F. Gyug [Aldershot and Burlington, VT: Ashgate, 2004], 161–70); the sermons attributed to Boniface in PL 89.843–72 (see Bouhout, 'Alcuin,' 184–91); the sermon 'Venus, a Man,' partially edited by Levison (W. Levison, *England and the Continent in the Eighth Century* [Oxford: OUP, 1946], 302–14); the works of Eligius of Noyon (n. 47, below); and the sermon 'Necessarium est enim' (first edited by W. Scherer, 'Eine lateinische Musterpredigt aus der Zeit Karls des Grossen,' *Zeitschrift für deutsches Alterthum* [sic] 12 [1865]: 436–46, but see now Bouhot, 'Alcuin,' 183–4). Constable notes the closely associated nature of many of these works in his study of the *Homilia sacra*: 'It would take too much space to demonstrate here the many textual resemblances and relationships between the homily, the works of Caesarius and Martin [of Braga], and the *Scarapsus*' (163).

14 All citations from *DCR* are from I.B. Bauer, ed., *De catechizandis rudibus*, CCSL 46 (Turnhout: Brepols, 1969), 115–78; all translations, from J.P. Christopher, trans., *St Augustine: The First Catechetical Instruction* (Westminster, MD, and London: Newman Press and Longmans, Green and Co., 1962).

15 'Petisti me, frater Deogratias, ut aliquid ad te de cathechizandis rudibus, quod tibi usui esset, scriberem. Dixisti enim, quod saepe apud Carthaginem, ubi diaconus es, ad te adducuntur qui fide christiana primitus imbuendi sunt, eo quod existimeris habere catechizandi uberem facultatem, et doctrina fidei et suauitate sermonis: te autem pene semper angustias pati, idipsum quod credendo Christiani sumus, quo pacto commode intimandum sit; unde exordienda, quo usque sit perducenda narratio; utrum exhortationem aliquam terminata narratione adhibere debeamus, an praecepta sola, quibus obseruandis cui loquimur nouerit christianam uitam professionemque retineri' ('You have asked me, Brother Deogratias, to write something to you on the instruction of candidates for the catechumenate that may be of use to you. For you tell me that at Carthage, where you are a Deacon, those who are to be grounded in the rudiments of the Christian faith are often brought to you, because you are supposed to possess great

model *narrationes*, one long and one short. First of all, Augustine answers Deogratias's queries:

Narratio plena est, cum quisque primo catechizatur ab eo quod scriptum est: 'In principio fecit Deus caelum et terram,' usque ad praesentia tempora ecclesiae. Non tamen propterea debemus totum pentateuchum, totosque iudicum et regnorum et Esdrae libros, totumque euangelium et actus apostolorum, uel, si ad uerbum edidicimus, memoriter reddere, uel nostris uerbis omnia quae his uoluminibus continentur narrando euoluere et explicare; quod nec tempus capit, nec ulla necessitas postulat: sed cuncta summatim generatimque complecti, ita ut eligantur quaedam mirabiliora, quae suauius audiuntur atque in ipsis articulis constituta sunt, et ea tamquam in inuolucris ostendere statimque a conspectu abripere non oportet, sed aliquantum immorando quasi resoluere atque expandere, et inspicienda atque miranda offerre animis auditorum: cetera uero celeri percursione inserendo contexere. Ita et illa quae maxime commendari uolumus aliorum submissione magis eminent; nec ad ea fatigatus peruenit quem narrando uolumus excitare, nec illius memoria confunditur quem docendo debemus instruere.[16]
[The narration is complete when the beginner is first instructed from the text 'In the beginning God created heaven and earth,' [Gen. 1:1] down to the present period of church history. That does not mean, however, that we ought to repeat verbatim the whole of the Pentateuch, and all the books of Judges and Kingdoms and Esdras, and the entire Gospel and the Acts of the Apostles (if we have learned them by heart), or relate in our own words all that is contained in these books, and thus develop and explain them; for which neither time serves nor any need calls. But we ought to present all the matter in a general and comprehensive summary, choosing certain of the more remarkable facts that are heard with greater pleasure and constitute the cardinal points in history; these we ought not to present as a parchment rolled up and at once snatch them out of sight, but we ought by dwelling somewhat upon them to untie, so to speak, and spread them out to view, and offer them to the minds of our hearers to examine and admire. But the remaining details we

---

ability in catechizing, by reason both of your thorough training in the faith and the charm of your style; but that you are almost always perplexed to discover how suitably to present that truth, the belief in which makes us Christians; where to begin the narration, to what point it should be brought down, and whether at the close of the narration an exhortation should be added, or precepts only, in the observance of which he to whom we are speaking may know that the Christian life and passion are maintained') (*DCR* I.1).
16 *DCR* III.5.

should weave into our narrative in a rapid survey. In this way not only are the points which we desire most to emphasize brought into greater prominence by keeping others in the background, but also he whose interest we are anxious to stimulate by the narration does not reach them with a mind already exhausted, and we avoid confusing the memory of him whom we ought to instruct by our teaching.]

As the *narratio* progresses, however, one must also keep in mind the *finis praecepti* – 'caritas de corde puro et conscientia bona et fide non ficta' (1 Tim. 1:5) – and remember that the scriptures written before the coming of Christ were written for no other reason than to announce his coming and to prefigure the Church to be; the scriptures written after, to tell of Christ and to counsel love.[17]

Augustine's first model *narratio* is lengthy, and begins not with Gen. 1:1, but rather with observations on what the Christian life means and what reasons some men have for wishing to become Christian. The creation of the world and man and his fall (interspersed with comments which look ahead to the birth of Christ) are recounted in detail, and, though the fall of the angels is not mentioned separately, it is cited as a parallel to the fall of man.[18] Augustine discusses the cities of the righteous and the just; Noah; Nineveh (and here the focus is repentance); idol worship after the Flood; devout citizens of the holy city, specifically Abraham; the people in Egypt; the parting of the Red Sea; forty years in the desert; the law; the Promised Land and Jerusalem; King David (from whose seed came Christ); Babylon versus Jerusalem; the restoration of the temple; the five ages of the world to the coming of Christ; the life, death, and ascension of Christ; Paul's work to convert; and the Last Judgment. Augustine concludes with an exhortation which is again quite protracted.[19]

In the shorter version of the *narratio*, equal in length roughly to the concluding exhortation of the longer, Augustine opens with remarks on the transience of earthly life and observes the reciprocal roles of Adam and Christ: one, having consented to his wife, brings death into the world; the other brings eternal life. Augustine comments on the Flood, stressing how

---

17 *DCR* III.6–IV.8. Augustine succinctly describes the relationship between the two testaments: 'In ueteri testamento est occultatio noui, in nouo testamento est manifestatio ueteris' ('In the Old Testament the New is concealed, and in the New the Old is revealed') (*DCR* IV.8).

18 *DCR* XVIII.30.

19 *DCR* XVI.24–XXV.49.

the Church is foreshadowed in the ark; the role of Abraham in Christ's coming; the birth, resurrection, and ascension of Christ; and Judgment Day. The shorter *narratio* also ends with an exhortation steadfastly to endure and not to yield to the devil, for God does not permit his servants to be tempted beyond what they are able to withstand.[20]

The popularity of *De catechizandis rudibus* is difficult to ascertain,[21] in part because the types of work in which its influence might appear are quite varied, including both handbooks for the treatment of catechumenates (which might include descriptions of what the *narrationes* ought to contain – Augustine's 'narratio plena est' passage – as well as related material on baptism, virtues, and vices, etc.) and *narrationes* based on the Augustinian model.[22] Though Eugippius includes five chapters of material from *DCR* in his *Excerpta ex operibus sancti Augustini* (ch. CLXXXVI–CXC), including *DCR* III.6–IV.7 and the complete shorter *narratio* (though none of the longer),[23] verbatim quotation from *DCR* is not widespread, and the only nearly complete reproduction of the work by a named author (so far as I know) is found in the first book of Hrabanus Maurus's *De ecclesiastica disciplina*.[24] J.P. Christopher notes that Bede and Alcuin used the work (along with *De doctrina christiana*) as a textbook,[25] but there is, I believe, no extant manuscript evidence of the work from Anglo-Saxon England.[26] Even citations are relatively rare: for example, J.D.A.

---

20 *DCR* XXVI.52–XXVII.55.
21 Bauer lists nineteen manuscripts, but only four from the ninth century (and nothing earlier) (*De catechizandis rudibus*, 117–20).
22 In the composition of *narrationes*, of course, the nature of the genre would tend to allow writers to produce works which followed Augustine in structure, but not necessarily in specific content. Day further suggests that many catechetical *narrationes* 'presumably ... would have been in the vernacular and mostly would not have been written down at all' ('Influence,' 52).
23 Eugippius includes, in order, DCR III.6–IV.7 (ch. CLXXXVI), IX.13 (ch. CLXXXVII), X.15 (ch. CLXXXVIII), XIV.20, XIV.22 (ch. CLXXXVIIII), and XVI.24, XXVI.52–XXVII.55 (ch. CXC). See P. Knöll, ed., *Eugippii excerpta ex operibus s. Augustini*, CSEL 9, Pars I (Vienna, 1885).
24 Hrabanus Maurus, *De ecclesiastica disciplina*, PL 112.1191–1262. The first book, *De sacris ordinibus*, consists mainly of passages from *DCR*, including *DCR* III.5–IV.7 (the 'narratio plena est' passage) and *DCR* XVI.24–XXVII.55 (both model *narrationes*). See also below, n. 27.
25 Christopher, *First Catechetical Instruction*, 9.
26 Helmut Gneuss finds no manuscripts or fragments of the work which were in England before 1100; see his *Handlist of Anglo-Saxon Manuscripts: A List of Manuscripts and Manuscript Fragments Written or Owned in England up to 1100* (Tempe, AZ: ACMRS, 2001).

Ogilvy lists one citation in a letter of Alcuin to Charlemagne (796), and Michael Lapidge's *The Anglo-Saxon Library* and the database of the *Fontes Anglo-Saxonici* contain two and three references, respectively, all to one of Ælfric's homilies.[27] However, Alcuin's mention of *DCR* supports the idea that Augustine's ideas had more influence than the words he used, and Alcuin's summary of how to educate an adult is informative:

Igitur ille ordo in docendo uirum aetate perfectum, diligenter, ut arbitror, seruandus est, quem beatus Augustinus ordinauit in libro, cui de catecizandis rudibus titulum praenotauit. Primo instruendus est homo de animae inmortalitate et de uita futura et de retributione bonorum malorumque et de aeternitate utriusque sortis. Postea: pro quibus peccatis et sceleribus poenas cum diabolo patiatur aeternas, et pro quibus bonis vel benefactis gloria cum Christo fruatur sempiterna. Deinde fides sanctae Trinitatis diligentissime docenda est, et aduentus pro salute humani generis filii dei domini nostri Iesu Christi in hunc mundum exponendus; et de mysterio passionis illius, et ueritate resurrectionis et gloria ascensionis in caelos et futuro eius aduentu ad iudicandas omnes gentes et de resurrectione corporum nostrorum et de aeternitate poenarum in malos et praemiorum in bonos, mox – ut praediximus – mens nouella firmanda est. Et hac fide roboratus homo et praeparatus baptizandus est. Et sic tempore oportuno saepius euangelica praecepta danda sunt per sedulae praedicationis officium, donec adcrescat in uirum perfectum et digna efficiatur Spiritui sancto habitatio et sit perfectus filius Dei in operibus misericordiae, sicut pater noster caelestis perfectus est; qui uiuit et regnat in trinitate perfecta et unitate benedicta, Deus et Dominus per omnia saecula saeculorum.[28]

[So I believe we should be careful to keep the order in teaching adults which St Augustine laid down in his book *De catechizandis rudibus*. A man must first be taught about the immortality of the soul and the future life and rewards for

---

27 J.D.A. Ogilvy, *Books Known to the English, 597–1066* (Cambridge, MA: Medieval Academy of America, 1967), 82; the references in Michael Lapidge (*The Anglo-Saxon Library* [Oxford: OUP, 2006], 252) and in the *Fontes Anglo-Saxonici* database (CD-ROM Version 1.1; http://fontes.english.ox.ac.uk) are all to Ælfric's *CH* II.4 (see below, 268).

28 *Epistolae karolini aeui* II, ed. E. Dümmler, MGH Epist. 4 (Berlin, 1895), *Ep.* 110, 158–9; trans. in S. Allott, *Alcuin of York: His Life and Letters* (York: William Sessions, 1974), 73–4. It has been suggested that Alcuin's summary here comes not directly from *DCR*, but rather from Eugippius's *Excerpta* (A. Etchegaray Cruz, 'Le rôle du *De catechizandis rudibus* de Saint Augustin dans la catéchèse missionnaire dès 710 jusqu'à 847,' *Studia Patristica* 11 [1972]: 319–20).

good and evil and both kinds of eternity, later the particular sins for which he must suffer eternal punishment with the devil and the good deeds for which he may enjoy everlasting glory with Christ. Then belief in the Holy Trinity must be carefully taught and the coming of the Son of God, our Lord Jesus Christ, into the world for the saving of mankind must be expounded, with the mystery of his passion, the truth of his resurrection and ascension into heaven and his coming to judge all nations; also the resurrection of our bodies and the eternity of punishment for the wicked and reward for the good must later be instilled into the novice's mind. After this preparation and strengthening in the faith, he should be baptized. The teaching of the gospel must be given in preaching frequently at suitable times, till he grows into the perfect man and is made a worthy dwelling for the Holy Spirit and a perfect son of God in works of mercy, as our heavenly Father is perfect, who lives and reigns in the perfect trinity and blessed unity, God and Lord, world without end.]

Clearly, during Charlemagne's attempts to convert the Saxons and Avars, at least, Alcuin felt that the general outline of what the catechumenate needed to be taught had been best described by Augustine.[29] In the absence of further direct links to Anglo-Saxon England, we do, however, have two intermediate authors, almost certainly influenced by *DCR*, who were known and quoted by the Anglo-Saxons: Martin of Braga and Pirmin.[30] Martin's *De correctione rusticorum* (*De corr. rust.*) – a title which immediately aligns the work with the didactic tradition as set out by Augustine[31] – was written around 573 or 574, and Claude Barlow notes

---

29 For the historical background to this letter – Alcuin's advice that Charlemagne take a more lenient approach with the Avars than he had with the Saxons – see M. Garrison, 'Praesagum nomen tibi: The Significance of Name-wordplay in Alcuin's Letters to Arn,' in *Erzbischof Arn von Salzburg*, ed. M. Niederkorn-Bruck and A. Scharer (Munich: R. Oldenbourg, 2004), 114. The general progress from pagan to catechumen to baptism is further described in Alcuin's *Ep.* 134. In the context of early ninth-century catechizing, see also the so-called *Ordo de catechizandis rudibus*, which may have been inspired by Alcuin's letter. See J.-P. Bouhot, 'Alcuin et le *De catechizandis rudibus* de Saint Augustin,' *Recherches Augustiniennes* 15 (1980): 176–240 (which includes an edition of one version of the text and notes to previous editions); and the entry in the Alcuin *Clauis*, item ALC 74 (CCCM, *Clauis scriptorum Latinorum medii aeui*, *Auctores Galliae 735–987, Tomus II, Alcuinus*, ed. M.-H. Jullien and F. Perelman [Turnhout: Brepols, 1999]).

30 Evidence that Ælfric and Wulfstan knew these two writers is discussed below.

31 This title, however, was given to the work for the *editio princeps*: Martin's own phrase is 'pro castigatione rusticorum' (*De corr. rust.* I). On the title of the work, see Barlow

that 'the general pattern of the *De correctione rusticorum* is modelled on the instructions given by Augustine in his *De catechizandis rudibus*.' In addition to Augustine's *DCR*, Barlow posits that Martin used *De ciuitate Dei* (material on the angels) and the sermons of Caesarius of Arles as sources, though he was able to find few direct parallels.[32]

Like Augustine's text, Martin's was written to answer a specific request, in this case, that of Bishop Polemius, who was concerned with the origin of idols and their sins, and with how to chastise those rustics who cling to pagan superstition and prefer to worship demons over God.[33] The sermon proper begins with a very clear statement of purpose:

Desideramus, filii karissimi, adnuntiare uobis in nomine domini quae aut minime audistis aut audita fortasse obliuioni dedistis. Petimus ergo caritatem uestram ut, quae pro salute uestra dicuntur, adtentius audiatus. Longus quidem per diuinas scripturas ordo dirigitur, sed ut uel aliquantulum in memoriam teneatis, pauca uobis de pluribus commendamus.[34]

[We desire, my dearest children, to report to you in the name of the Lord things which you have never heard or perhaps have heard and forgotten. We ask your favour, that you listen with greater attention to matters which are spoken for your salvation. It would take a long time to go completely through

---

(C. Barlow, ed., *Martini episcopi Bracarensis opera omnia* [New Haven: Yale Univ. Press, 1950]), 159–60. All citations from the work are taken from Barlow's edition. For an introduction to Martin and the religious context of the work (especially Martin's remarks on pagan practices), see S. McKenna, *Paganism and Pagan Survivals in Spain up to the Fall of the Visigothic Kingdom* (Washington: Catholic Univ. of America, 1938), 75–107. An excellent overview of Martin's text and its reception by late Merovingian authors, especially, is given by Yitzak Hen, 'Martin of Braga's *De correctione rusticorum* and Its Uses in Frankish Gaul,' in *Medieval Transformations: Texts, Power, and Gifts in Context*, ed. Esther Cohen and Mayke B. de Jong (Leiden: Brill, 2001), 35–49.

32 Barlow, *Martini*, 163–4.

33 Martin advises Polemius that he must start at the beginning of worldly history, and compose the address in the appropriate language: 'Sed quia oportet ab initio mundi uel modicam illis rationis notitiam quasi pro gustu porrigere, necesse me fuit ingentem praeteritorum temporum gestorumque siluam breuiato tenuis compendii sermone contingere et cibum rusticis rustico sermone condire' ('Since it is necessary to offer them some small explanation for those idols' existence from the beginning of the world to whet the appetite, as it were, I have had to touch upon a vast forest of past times and events in a treatise of very brief compass and to offer the rustics food seasoned with rustic speech') (*De corr. rust.* I).

34 *De corr. rust.* II; translation from C. Barlow, *Iberian Fathers, Volume I: Martin of Braga, Paschasius of Dumium, Leander of Seville* (Washington: Catholic Univ. of America Press, 1969), 71–2.

the divine scriptures, but let us touch upon a few of many points, in order that you may keep at least a little in your memories.]

The sermon then moves immediately into the creation, the fall of the angels, and the creation of man in order to fill the empty seats in heaven. Martin describes the flood and the restoration of the human race, but notes, as Augustine does, that the worship of creatures, and particularly idols, arises again almost immediately. Where Martin's text differs most from Augustine's plan is in the central chapters. Martin discusses idolatry and the worship of nature at length (in terms which will be familiar to readers of Ælfric and Wulfstan), including the classical gods and the unfortunate practice of naming the days of the week after those same gods. After quickly relating the life of Christ,[35] Martin discusses the judgment of Last Days and the choice that every man has for that moment. However, the text does not end there. Martin gives an example of a catechism for baptism – a reminder of the compact made with God to renounce the devil and all idols – and refers to the Apostle's Creed and *Pater Noster* before offering a general exhortation to keep the precepts of God and be ready on the day of judgment. Even more so than Augustine's model narration, therefore, Martin's covers fundamental aspects of Christianity, though the clear focus throughout is on recalling those new Christians who, since baptism, have reverted to pagan practices.

Pirmin's *Scarapsus* (or the *Dicta Pirminii*),[36] written probably between 710 and 724, adopts its overall form and some detail directly from Martin, but frequently diverges from Augustine and Martin in its desire to offer more information about life as a Christian. Gall Jecker's edition of the text suggests that Pirmin incorporated a wide range of sources: unlike Martin, who appears to have composed an original sermon more or less from

---

35 Martin's transition to the life of Christ, in fact, is presented in such a way that the Incarnation seems to be God's answer to demonic deception and worship (see *De corr. rust.* XIII).

36 For the text, see G. Jecker, *Die Hiemat des hl. Pirmin, des Apostels der Alamannen,* Beiträge zur Geschichte des alten Mönchtums und des Benediktinerordens, Heft 13 (Münster: Verlag der Aschendorffschen Verlagsbuchhandlung, 1927). For the latest work on the manuscript tradition of the text, see E. Hauswald, 'Die handschriftliche Überlieferung des *Scarapsus* (*Dicta Priminii*),' in *Ireland and Europe in the Early Middle Ages: Texts and Transmission / Irland und Europa im früheren Mittelalter: Texte und Überlieferung,* ed. Próinséas Ní Chatháin and M. Richter (Dublin: Four Courts, 2002), 103–22. J.-P. Bouhot regards the attribution to Pirmin with scepticism, and suggests that the work may have been composed in the seventh century ('Alcuin,' 180-1).

memory, Pirmin has put together an elaborate and literary manual of instructions for the new Christian. Pirmin's address does not take the form of an epistolary treatise, but rather begins with a series of scriptural citations on the need for, and the efficacy of, preaching and the rest that can be found in the Lord. Quoting Martin, Pirmin also promises to offer parts of scripture which may be held in the memory as an aid to salvation.[37]

The early part of the history comes almost directly from Martin:[38] for example, material on the fall of the angels and the birth of demons is reproduced almost verbatim, as is the section on the placement of man in paradise and the account of the flood and the preservation of the human race through the three sons of Noah. At this point, however, the accounts diverge. Where Martin continues into his lengthy account of idol worship after the flood, Pirmin, quoting scripture frequently,[39] turns instead to the

---

37 'Fratres karissimi, spiritus sanctus per prophetas, sacerdotes et leuitas et omnes doctores aeclesiae catholice admonet, dicens: "Clama, ne cesses, quasi tuba exalta uocem tuam et adnuntia populo meo peccata eorum" [Isa. 58:1]. Et iterum: "Si non adnunciaueris iniquo iniquitatem suam, ipse in peccatis suis morietur, sanguinem autem eius de manu tua requiram" [Ezek. 3:18, 33:8]. Et dominus in euangelio ait: "Euntes in mundo uniuerso, predicate euangelium" [Mk. XVI.15]. Et uos, fratres, qui ad ecclesiam conuenitis, dominus per prophetam dicit: "Venite, fili, audite me, timorem domini docebo uos" [Ps. 33:12]. Et iterum: "Hodie, si uocem eius audieritis, nolite obdurare corda uestra" [Ps. 94:8]. Et dominus in euangelio: "Venite ad me omnes, qui laboratis et honerati estis, et ego uos reficiam" [Matt. XI.28] dicit dominus. Petimus ergo, karissimi, caritatem uestram, ut, que pro salute uestra dicuntur, attentius audiatis. Longus quidem per diuinis scripturis ordo degeritur, sed uel ut aliquantulum in memoria teneatis, pauca uobis de pluribus commendamus' ('Dearest brothers, the Holy Spirit, through the prophets, priests, and deacons, and all the Doctors of the Catholic Church gives us advice, saying "Cry, cease not, lift up thy voice like a trumpet, and shew my people their wicked doings". And again: "If thou declare not his wickedness to the wicked: the same wicked man shall die in his iniquity, but I will require his blood at thy hand." And the Lord says in the gospel: "Go ye into the whole world, and preach the gospel." And as you, brothers, who come together to the church, the Lord speaks through the prophet: "Come, children, hearken to me: I will teach you the fear of the Lord." And again: "Today if you shall hear his voice, harden not your hearts." And the Lord says again in the gospel: "Come to me, all you that labour, and are burdened, and I will refresh you." So, dearest, we seek your love, so that you may hear more attentively those things that are said for your salvation. A lengthy sequence is set out in holy scripture, but so that you can keep a part of that in your memory, let us recommend a few things out of many') (*Scarapsus* I).

38 For a list of Pirmin's borrowings from Martin, by chapter, see Barlow, *Martini*, 166–7.

39 Even in the early scriptural history, Pirmin adds quotations from Genesis to Martin's account of the fall of man. Overall, Pirmin is much more interested in giving a sense of the words of scripture than is Martin.

law as given to Moses and God's attempts to steer humanity back to the faith through the prophets and, finally, Christ. In the course of relating the life of Christ and the activities of the apostles, Pirmin lists the names of the apostles, gives the complete *Pater Noster*, compares the temptation of Christ and the temptation of Adam, and relates the composition of the Apostle's Creed. Only in the second part of the work does Pirmin return to Martin, incorporating much of his material on baptism, before launching into a very detailed and interesting discussion of the *principalia uitia*[40] – supported mainly by citations from the Old and New Testaments – the commandments, and how a Christian ought to live. The work is much longer than Martin's *De correctione rusticorum*, and the focus much more upon those precepts which every Christian must follow.[41]

Ælfric and Wulfstan

Turning to the Old English tradition, we have, in Ælfric's *De initio creaturae* (*CH* I.1), the clearest example of a single sermon, designed for any occasion (*quando uolueris*), which attempts to relate the highlights of Christian history.[42] The sermon begins with an explanation of the Trinity before launching into a narrative account of the creation and fall of the angels[43] and the significant events of the Old and New Testaments. Interspersed with a faithful rendering of events in Genesis 1–3, Ælfric discusses the origin and abilities of the devil, the reason for the creation of Adam and Eve, the devil's motivation for the temptation and the origin of the soul. The increase in population and the flood are followed by a discussion of the building of the tower of Babel and the worship of images. However, Ælfric explains, one family never bent to idols, and a description of the line of Sem leads into the

---

40 Pirmin's discussion of the vices is especially interesting given the treatment of the vices in Vercelli XX; the Old English homilist may well have been influenced by Pirmin, or a work like it, in his decision to include such material. Where Pirmin offers several cautions from scripture for each vice, however, Vercelli XX reproduces the descriptions from Pembroke 25, item 93, which are derived ultimately from Alcuin.

41 In evaluating the content of three sermons obviously derived from Martin of Braga's *De correctione*, one of which is Pirmin's, Hen observes that each 'explain[s] the Creed in clear, concrete terms, and simplif[ies] [its] message by using a series of contrasts, such as demons versus God, pagan versus Christian, old versus new, and damnation versus redemption' ('Martin,' 42).

42 P. Clemoes, ed., *Ælfric's Catholic Homilies. The First Series. Text*, EETS s.s. 17 (Oxford: OUP, 1997).

43 For an analysis of Ælfric's various presentations of angelic history, see M. Fox, 'Ælfric on the Creation and Fall of the Angels,' *ASE* 31 (2002): 175–200.

annunciation, life of Christ, the seduction of the Jews through the devil's teaching, the harrowing of Hell, and the ascension. To conclude, Ælfric briefly mentions the Last Judgment and then exhorts his listeners to merit eternal life through good works.

While the range of Ælfric's material generally resembles that of Augustine, Martin, and Pirmin, there are some obvious and immediate differences. Unlike Martin and Pirmin, Ælfric does not combine scriptural history with pastoral advice: Ælfric is content to move in a logical and systematic way through historical events. In this focus, Ælfric's sermon seems to follow Augustine's model *narrationes*. As Malcolm Godden has noted, however, 'there are no obvious sources for this sermon.'[44] Evidence elsewhere suggests that Ælfric knew Augustine's *DCR* – the context in which it appears to have been a source (*CH* II.4) is particularly interesting, as Ælfric relates Old Testament highlights[45] – and he uses Martin's *De correctione rusticorum* in *De falsis diis* (Pope XXI),[46] *De auguris* (LS XVII, appropriately, a 'sermo in laetania maiore'), and perhaps also for details in *CH* I.6 on the placement of the start of the new year,[47] but there is nothing to suggest that Ælfric knew Pirmin.[48]

---

44 M. Godden, *Ælfric's Catholic Homilies: Introduction, Commentary and Glossary*, EETS s.s. 18 (Oxford: OUP, 2000), 8.

45 'The homily expounds the Gospel for the day, John II.1–11, on the marriage at Cana and Christ's first miracle. Interpreting the six water-vessels as the six ages of the world and the wine as the spiritual truth hidden in the events of those ages, Ælfric is able to use the occasion to convey the major events of the Old Testament ... and their significance for the Christian faith' (Godden, *Ælfric's Catholic Homilies*, 371).

46 Pope notes the influence of Martin on lines 72–180, but also states: 'What is not so clear [as the influence upon the aforementioned lines] is that Martin's sermon sets the pattern for the entire homily by putting the attack on false gods in the perspective of man's relation to the true God from Adam to the present.' Pope also sees this 'historical perspective' in *De initio creaturae* (J.C. Pope, ed., *Homiles of Ælfric: A Supplementary Collection*, EETS o.s. 259–60 [Oxford: OUP, 1967–8], 671). On Martin and Ælfric (including an appendix of parallel passages), see also David F. Johnson, 'Euhemerisation versus Demonisation: The Pagan Gods and Ælfric's *De falsis diis*,' in *Pagans and Christians: The Interplay between Christian Latin and Traditional Germanic Cultures in Early Medieval Europe*, ed. T. Hofstra, L.A.J.R. Houwen, and A.A. MacDonald (Groningen: E. Forsten, 1995), 35–69.

47 Lapidge, *Anglo-Saxon Library*, 263.

48 Godden, *Ælfric's Catholic Homilies*, 8. However, Ælfric's preface to the first series of Catholic homilies has, near its conclusion, a sequence of scriptural citations which resembles the opening of Pirmin's *Scarapsus* (quoted above, n. 37). The ultimate source for the combination of Ezekiel 3:18–19 and Isaiah 58:1 in exhortations about preaching seems to be Caesarius of Arles, who frequently employs this formula (see G. Morin, ed., *Sancti Caesarii Arelatensis sermones*, CCSL 103–4 [Turnhout: Brepols, 1953], *Sermones* I [p. 2], IV [22], V [26], LVII [251], CLXXXIII [744], and CCXXX [912]), but Eligius of Noyons (who also knew and used Martin's *De corr. rust.*, on which see

In other words, rather than borrow from prior authors, Ælfric has here taken a model for the presentation of Christian history and adapted it for his own purposes, as an introduction, it would seem, to his collection of homilies. The homily by Wulfstan known as Bethurum VI is likely an adaptation of Ælfric's *De initio creaturae*, and seems also to have been intended to be the opening item of a series of sermons.[49] Wulfstan, however, rather than beginning without preamble, shows the influence of his sources, as, using verses from Ezekiel 3:18–19 and Isaiah 58:1, he focuses on the importance of preaching: the sermon is clearly intended to serve as a model for preachers.[50] After establishing the need for preaching and its effect on the souls of the common folk, bishops, and priests, Wulfstan, adapting the words of Martin (perhaps via Pirmin), encourages his listeners to pay attention to a selective account of scriptural history:

Leofan men, ic bidde eow þæt ge geþyldelice hlystan þæs ðe ic eow nu secgan wille. Hit is lang to areccene þæt we on bocum ymbe Godes wundra rædað. Nu wille ic þeah be suman dæle scortlice hit eow sum asecgan.[51]

Barlow, *Martini*, 165–6) also uses it in his sermon *De supremo iudicio*, preserved by Audoenus of Rouen (B. Krusch, ed., *Praedicatio Eligii de supremo iudicio, Passiones uitaeque sanctorum aeui Merouingici*, MGH *Scriptores rerum Merouingicarum*, tomus IV [Hannover: Weidmann, 1902], 749–61); the sermon also appears twice in the PL, as book II, cap. xv of the *Vita Eligii* by Audoenus of Rouen (PL 87.477–594) and as the treatise *De rectitudine catholicae conuersationis* (PL 40.1169–90) – though the PL versions preserve passages Krusch feels are not part of the sermon – and it is under the final title that Bethurum notes the influence of Eligius on Wulfstan (Bethurum Xb and Xc). Wulfstan uses the formula to open Bethurum VI.

49 The rubric of the sermon, of course, is 'incipiunt sermones Lupi episcopi,' but, in CCCC 201 and Hatton 113, two closely related manuscripts, the sermon is also found near the beginning, after short items on creation and Adam, and the ages of the world. CCCC 201, after a fragment of a translation of the *Regularis concordia* (pp. 1–7), begins with Napier I (*Adam se æresta man*, pp. 8, 9) and Napier LXII (*De aetatibus mundi*, pp. 9, 10) before Bethurum VI; Hatton 113 opens with a work Ker calls *De initio creaturae*, ff. 1–3 (related to CCCC 201), and Napier LXII again, Old English and Latin (*Be frumsceafta*), ff. 3–4. See N.R. Ker, *A Catalogue of Manuscripts Containing Anglo-Saxon* (Oxford: Clarendon Press, 1957).

50 The source here is either Ælfric's Old English preface to the first series of *Catholic Homilies*, or, more likely, the opening of Pirmin's *Scarapsus*. Jost, for his part, does not believe that Wulfstan used the preface (K. Jost, *Wulfstanstudien* [Bern: A. Francke, 1950], 55n8). See above, n. 37. However, Ezekiel and Isaiah were significant influences on Wulfstan (see Bethurum XVIa and XVIb; and the discussion in J. Wilcox, 'The Wolf on Shepherds: Wulfstan, Bishops, and the Context of the *Sermo Lupi ad Anglos*,' in *Old English Prose: Basic Readings*, ed. P.E. Szarmach [New York and London: Garland, 2000], 395–418).

51 Bethurum VI.21–4.

[Beloved men, I ask that you patiently attend to what I wish now say to you. It takes a long time to relate what we read about the wonders of God in the Bible. Nevertheless, I wish now briefly to explain some part of it to you.]

Wulfstan then narrates the story of creation, the angelic fall, the creation and fall of Adam and Eve, Cain and Abel, Noah and the flood, the resurgence of evil after the flood (and here Wulfstan discusses the nature and role of the devil, and refers to idol worship), and the various connections of the line of Sem to the coming of Christ (including Abraham, Moses, David, and Mary),[52] before shifting from Old Testament concerns to New by noting the years which have passed between the creation of Adam and the birth of Christ. For the benefit of unlearned men, Wulfstan explains how it might be that one born so late could have created all things: this discussion of the Trinity leads into a section about Christ, and the remainder of the sermon gives a summary of Wulfstan's broader eschatological homilies.[53]

Thus, though the inspiration for his homily was likely Ælfric, Wulfstan's primary source for the content of the homily seems to have been Pirmin.[54] Choosing to follow the general structure of Martin and Pirmin, Wulfstan introduces his homily with a short account of the importance of preaching and the need to know scripture, gives an account of Christian history (with much more emphasis on New Testament events than Ælfric), and concludes with other material related to the Christian life. Wulfstan, then, clearly shares the concerns of Martin and Pirmin; his so-called catechetical homilies (Bethurum VII–X), which cover baptism, the *Pater Noster* and Creed, the gifts of the Holy Spirit at confirmation, and the duties of Christian living, confirm this.[55] In addition, Wulfstan constantly reminds his audience of the

---

52 Wulfstan includes details about Zedekiah and Cyrus, king of Persia, which may, as Bethurum suggests, reflect his use of Ælfric's *On the Old and New Testament* (D. Bethurum, ed., *The Homilies of Wulfstan* [Oxford: Clarendon Press, 1957]), 298–9).

53 Bethurum, *Homilies*, 298.

54 Wulfstan's debt to Pirmin has been thoroughly documented by Karl Jost, who notes that Wulfstan uses the *Scarapsus* as a source twice. Wulfstan uses the first part of Pirmin for the beginning of Bethurum VI and the second part as the main source for the related sermons Bethurum Xb (Latin) and Xc (Old English) (Jost, *Wulfstanstudien*, 47). Only one manuscript of the *Scarapsus* which may have been in Anglo-Saxon England before 1100 survives, but the collection of texts in Oxford, Bodleian Library, Bodley 572 (2026), saec. ix[1] [Gneuss 583.3] – which Gneuss calls a 'penitential collection' – suggests how Pirmin's work might have been received.

55 Bethurum, *Homilies*, 299. One might compare the emphasis on the *Pater Noster* and Creed in Martin and Pirmin (perhaps again influenced, at least in the latter case, by Augustine's *De symbolo ad catechumenos*) with the Old English treatments in Ælfric

devil's presence and adds a discussion of the Antichrist which we do not find in Ælfric.[56] This distinction has been noted by Malcolm Godden, who suggests that, overall, 'where Ælfric tended to relate human sinfulness back to free will and personal responsibility, Wulfstan tended to attribute it to the work of the devil.'[57] In the single sermons here under discussion, however, Ælfric and Wulfstan are mainly interested in presenting scriptural history, and do not, unlike Martin and Pirmin, introduce such topics as baptism, the Pater Noster, and the Creed.

Vercelli XIX–XXI and Tristram III

Vercelli XIX begins with a brief discussion of the Trinity (1–11)[58] and contains an account of the creation, the fall of the angels, the creation of Adam and Eve, and their fall (12–48). The passage on the fall of the angels, which Scragg suggests may come from a lost vernacular source,[59] is of especial interest:

Ærest on frymþe he geworhte heofonas and eorðan and sæ and ealle þa þinc þe on him syndon, and ealle þa englas þe on heofonum syndon. And ealle þa ðe of englum to deoflum forsceapene wurdon, ealle he hie of him sylfum mid his oroðe utableow[60] – and þone þe he foremærostne hæfde ofer ealle þa oðre

---

(CH I.XIX and I. XX) and Wulfstan. Though learning these two prayers is commonly the first task of the new Christian, even Bede comments on their importance, and notes that he himself has translated them into English for the benefit of unlearned priests (*Epistola ad Ecgbertum* V, ed. C. Plummer, in *Venerabilis Baedae Opera Historica*, 2 vols. [Oxford: OUP, 1896], 1: 405–23).

56 Wulfstan refers constantly to the 'deofles lare' (53, 72–3, 82, 86, 115, 181), which is behind every evil act from the fall of Adam and Eve to the death of Christ: 'Ælc yfel cymð of deofle and ælc brot and nan bot' ('Every evil comes from the devil, and every harm, and no remedy') (82–3).

57 M. Godden, 'The Relations of Wulfstan and Ælfric: A Reassessment,' in *Wulfstan: Archbishop of York: The Proceedings of the Second Alcuin Conference*, ed. M. Townend (Turnhout: Brepols, 2004), 373–4.

58 The source for the opening of Vercelli XIX has been identified as the first lines of the opening item of Pembroke 25 (Scragg, *Vercelli Homilies*, 315), which also includes a few lines on Adam's expulsion from paradise. For an outline of Pembroke 25, item 1, see Cross, *Pembroke College MS 25*, 19.

59 Scragg, *Vercelli Homilies*, 311. Day ('Influence,' 56) also notes that there are two passages in Vercelli XIX which closely resemble passages in Martin and Pirmin (Vercelli XIX.30–1 and *De corr. rust.* V [*Scarapsus* IV]; Vercelli XIX.19–20 and *De corr. rust.* III [*Scarapsus* II]).

60 For the significance of the word 'utableow,' see T.D. Hill, 'When God Blew Satan Out of Heaven: The Motif of Exsufflation in Vercelli Homily XIX and Later English Literature,' *Leeds Studies in English* n.s. 16 (1985): 132–41.

englas þe Lucifer wæs haten, þæt ys on ure geþeode 'leohtberend' gereht, ac he eft, þa he hine sylfne his scyppende gelicne don wolde and him þrymsetle on norðdæle heofona rices getimbrian wolde, of ðam he ricene afeoll. And ealle þa ðe æt ðam ræde mid him wæron and him æfter besawon, ealle hie wurdon·of englum to deoflum forsceapene and on helle bescofene, þær hie on ecnesse witu þoliað, for ðam þe hie forhogedon hira scyppend, ælmihtigne God.[61]

[First, in the beginning, he created the heavens and the earth and the sea and all the things which are in them, and all those angels which are in the heavens and all those which were transformed from angels to devils – he blew all of them from himself with his breath – and that one whom he considered foremost over all other angels, he who was called Lucifer, which is interpreted 'Lightbearing' in our language. But he then, afterwards, wished to make himself like his creator and wished to build himself a throne in the northern portion of the kingdom of heaven: he fell from there quickly, and all those who were with him in that plan and followed him, all of them were transformed from angels to devils and shoved into hell, where they suffer punishments eternally because they neglected their creator, almighty God.]

To judge from the repetition (in line 49) of the opening – 'men þa leofestan' – it would seem that the author regarded these first forty-eight lines as the introductory unit of his homily (and, by extension, of his four homilies). What Szarmach has called the 'central episode' of the homily is an account of the story of Jonah and the Ninevites (105–48), the relevance of which lies in the three-day fast of the Ninevites (also mentioned in the discussion of fasting in Vercelli III) and the homilist's emphasis on God's mercy, which has already been stressed with reference to Rogationtide.[62] An account of the origin of the 'gangdagas' is given: the bishop Mamertus of Vienne, seeing his people decimated by disease, ordered a three-day period of fasting and prayer which resulted in an end to that 'sudden death' (149–64). The homily concludes with an exhortation to each man to do what seems best and a description of the joy of eternal life.

Vercelli XX picks up the discussion of Rogation Days and makes some general observations on church attendance (1–15) before a brief illustration of the efficacy of prayer in the story of Elijah from James 5:17–18

---

61 Vercelli XIX.12–23.
62 See also Paul E. Szarmach, 'Three Versions of the Jonah Story: An Investigation of Narrative Technique in Old English Homilies,' *ASE* 1 (1972): 183–92.

(16–22).[63] The homily contains a conventional list of sins to be avoided and then addresses the benefits of fasting and, in particular, almsgiving, which is linked with the opening of Vercelli XIX by a reference to devils and angels: 'And heo geþeoded þone mann þe hy begæd Godes englum, and hine ascyred fram deoflum, and heo ys unoferwinnendlic weall ymb þa sawle, and heo framadrifð deoflu and englas togeladað on fultum'[64] ['And it [almsgiving] joins the man who practises it to God's angels, and separates him from devils, and it is an insurmountable wall around the soul, and it drives away devils and summons angels for help']. The three kinds of almsgiving are discussed before the homilist continues with an exhortation to avoid the eight capital sins (57–179), a list which derives ultimately from Alcuin's *De uirtutibus et uitiis*.[65] Pride is 'cwen ealra yfela,' the beginning of all sin (Sir. X.15), and the cause of the angelic fall; gluttony, the second capital sin, is the cause of the expulsion of Adam and Eve from Eden. The homily concludes with a brief warning against love of worldly goods (180–8) and a contrast of the pain of hell with the desirability of heaven (189–203).

Vercelli XXI opens with an exhortation to love God and our neighbours just as ourselves (Luke 10:27; Mark 12:30–1) – precisely what Augustine feels is the central message of all scripture[66] – and stresses the need for humility and the avoidance of evil (1–28). In many ways, the opening of Vercelli XXI recapitulates the hortatory themes of Vercelli XIX and XX: fasting, almsgiving, request for the mercy of God, and the qualities after which man should strive. On Judgment Day, we are told, the souls of the

---

63 The two common pericopes for Rogationtide are Luke 11:6–13 and James 5:16–20. Elijah is also mentioned in this context in Vercelli III.133–5, and thus may also have been included via Pembroke 25, item 22, which seems to be the source for the quotation from Augustine which follows soon after (see below).

64 Vercelli XX.46–9. This reference is also found in Vercelli III.145–51, where it is attributed to Augustine, and probably is inspired by the Latin homily in Pembroke 25, item 22.

65 On Alcuin's *De uirtutibus et uitiis*, Cambridge, Pembroke College 25 and Vercelli XX, see Szarmach, 'Pembroke College 25,' as well as his 'The Latin Tradition of Alcuin's *Liber de uirtutibus et uitiis*, cap. xxvii–xxxv, with Special Reference to Vercelli Homily XX,' *Mediaevalia* 12 (1989 for 1986): 13–41.

66 'Diligamus Dominum Deum nostrum ex toto corde, ex tota anima, ex tota mente nostra et proximum nostrum sicut nosmet ipsos. Propter quae duo praecepta caritatis sensisse Moysen, quidquid in illis libris sensit' ('Let us love the Lord God with our whole heart, with our whole soul, with our whole mind, and our neighbour too. [I reckon] Moses felt the same two impulses, whatever he felt in those books of his') (Augustine, *Confessiones* XII.xxv.35, ed. L. Verheijen, CCSL 27 [Turnhout: Brepols, 1981]).

righteous will be clothed with the twelve strengths of the soul (57–84). There is a reminder of Christ's sacrifice and the harrowing of Hell, and the listener is encouraged to make suitable gifts in return (87–115), which agains leads us to a comment on Doomsday and the eternal reward available to us (116–25). Because of our foundation in Adam, we are subject to death and to final judgment: again we are told what sins to avoid and how to act – a passage for which Scragg has commented on the alliteration and suggested dependence on a poetic source (128–41) – and the most compelling words are reserved for the sin of pride:

Þurh oferhygednesse englas wurdon iu forsceapene to deoflum and bescofene eac on helle grund, þær hie sceolon on worulda woruld witu þolian, for ðam þe hie forhogedon heofona wealdend and sigora syllend, and him sylfum þær rice mynton. Ac him se ræd ne geþah, ac se stiðmoda cyning, dryhten ælmihtig, awearp of ðam setle þone modigan feond and of ðam wuldre eac þæs heofonlican rices ealle þa þe mid him æt ðam ræde wæron. Hie wiston þe geornor, witum besette on þære byrnendan helle, wið hwæne hie winnan ongunnon.[67]

[On account of pride were the angels formerly transformed into devils and shoved also to the bottom of hell, where they shall suffer pain eternally because they neglected the ruler of the heavens and the giver of victories and intended to have a kingdom [or power] for themselves there. But that plan did not benefit them; rather, the resolute king, the almighty lord, threw that proud fiend from the throne and from the glory of the heavenly kingdom also all those who were with him in that plan. They knew then, most clearly, beset by punishments in that burning hell, against whom they had begun to fight.]

67 Vercelli XXI.141–9. This passage closely resembles that in Vercelli XIX (quoted above) in word and detail: both share the relatively unusual use of the verb *bescufan* here with Ælfric's *CH* I.24, in which he is expounding the parable of the lost drachma in Luke 15:8–10: 'Þæt teoðe [host of angels] wearþ mid modignysse forscyldgod and hi ealle to awyrigedum deoflum wurdon awende and of þære heofonlican blisse to hellesuslum bescofene' (*CH* I.24, 78–81). Ælfric's homily closely follows Gregory's *Homilia in euangelia* XXXIV, the *locus classicus* for medieval angelology, but this passage is an addition to his source (Godden, *Ælfric's Catholic Homilies*, 195). Charles D. Wright isolates this passage for analysis as verse ('More Old English Poetry in Vercelli Homily XXI,' in *Early Medieval English Texts and Interpretations: Studies Presented to Donald Scragg*, ed. E. Treharne and S. Rosser [Tempe, AZ: MRTS, 2002], 245–62), a possibility which has interesting implications for our understanding of the transmission of material on the fall of the angels in Anglo-Saxon England (see Fox, 'Ælfric,' 197–9). This passage was also incorporated into the composite homily 'Be rihtan cristendome' (A. Napier, ed., *Wulfstan: Sammlung der ihm zugeschriebenen Homilien* [Berlin: Weidmann, 1883], item XXX).

The homily concludes with a version of Vercelli II, the pseudo-poetic description of the possible horrors of Judgment Day, a reiteration of the opening exhortation from Luke 10:27 and a list of the joys of the heavenly kingdom, a list which echoes the closing lines of both Vercelli XIX and XX.

Tristram III begins with an explanation of Ascension Day and related New Testament events. Quoting scripture frequently, the author moves from the fear of Herod and the Jews of Christ to events after his resurrection – including Christ's commandments to baptize and to preach – and to the ascension itself. From a reasonably close but selective paraphrase of Acts 1:4–11, the author moves to an invocation of the Lord:

'Eala, þu geworhtest heofones and eorðan, and sæ and ealle gesceafta, and þu ðe gesceope þone forman mann Adam, þone þe deofol beswac mid facenfullum swicdome, and hyne man syððan ut of neorxnawange anydde and hine sona gehæftne mid him to suslum geteah. Þone þu drihten god and us ealle mid þinum agenum blode alysdest and he eft to neorxnawanges gefean wearð gelædd þe he ær of wearð adrifen. We biddað þe nu ða ælmihtig drihten þæt þu for þinum mæran upstige us ece ræste forgife þonne þu cymst to ðam þæt þu wylt deman ealre worulde and heofonware and hellware on þinra haligra eðle þær ðe bið niwe lofsang gesungen þæt is on heofona rices wuldre.'[68]

['Lo, you created heaven and earth, the sea and all creation, and you yourself shaped the first man, Adam, that one whom the devil deceived with crafty fraud, and forced out of paradise, and, confined, immediately led into torment with him. You, Lord God, with your own blood redeemed Adam and us all, and he was led again to the joy of paradise, from which he had previously been driven. We ask you now, almighty Lord, that you for your great ascension grant us eternal rest, when you come that you shall judge all the world, the citizens of heaven and the citizens of hell, in your holy land, where there will be a new song of praise sung, that is, in the glory of the heavenly kingdom.']

---

68 Tristram III.51–65. Cross suggests that the prayer may have a liturgical source (*Pembroke College MS 25*, 176); Tristram recognizes thematic similarities between this passage and the opening of Vercelli XIX and notes in each the creation-fall-redemption-judgment pattern first mentioned by Peter Clemoes with respect to Ælfric's writings (Tristram, *Vier altenglische Predigten*, 289–90; P. Clemoes, 'The Chronology of Ælfric's Works,' in *The Anglo-Saxons: Studies in Some Aspects of Their History and Culture Presented to Bruce Dickens*, ed. P. Clemoes [London: Bowes and Bowes, 1959], 225; repr. in Szarmach, *Old English Prose*, 40–1).

Though the prayer has possible models in scripture,[69] the content, in its mention of Adam and the devil, especially, seems to have been chosen by the author to echo the preceding Rogationtide sermons. Immediately, we are again told to give glory and rejoice because of the Lord's ascension: the author mentions the defeat of the devils, the final judgment, the fact that all men were in hell as a result of the sin of Adam, and the eternal condition of the righteous and the damned. The author, paraphrasing 1 Peter 2:21–3, cautions us not to be afraid of Judgment Day and reiterates the events of the ascension, this time including the vision of Christ in heaven and a vision of souls in torment as things seen by the disciples in order that we may be instructed. We must desire heaven and guard against hell, the torments of which are illustrated by passages from the Visio Pauli.[70] After more advice to live justly and forgo earthly things, the author starts into the 'grandis honor' ('micel wurðmynt') portion of the homily, defining great honour with many different scriptural examples which culminate in a repetition of the ascension scene and a prayer of the apostles. The homily concludes with a reminder to look after ourselves spiritually and to do good works, as Judgment Day may soon be upon us.

   The sources of these homilies and their relationship to the homiliary of St Père de Chartres have been amply discussed by Donald Scragg and James Cross. In each of the four homilies, the majority of the text seems to depend on translated and reorganized material from earlier Latin or vernacular homilies. If we ignore the process of selection and adaptation,[71] it remains to be pointed out which passages in the four homilies do not originate in the author's main source. Though there are several short passages and transitional paragraphs with no obvious source, three passages are particularly significant: Vercelli XIX.12–45, Vercelli XXI.125–48, and

---

69   For example, the opening resembles that of the prayers in 2 Esd. 9:5–38 and Acts 4:24–30.

70   Tristram, Vier altenglische Predigten, 295–6; Cross, Pembroke College MS 25, 177. The fact that Ælfric denounces the Visio at the opening of one of his Rogationtide homilies may suggest that he is reacting against a tendency to include such apocryphal material in homilies of the season (see CH II.20, 1–18, in Ælfric's Catholic Homilies. The Second Series. Text, ed. M. Godden, EETS s.s. 5 [Oxford: OUP, 1979]), and, as Godden points out, Bazire-Cross V also 'shows parallels with the Visio' (Godden, Ælfric's Catholic Homilies, 529).

71   Comprehensive source information is available in the apparatus to Scragg's edition and in Cross's work (for Tristram III). The use of the St Père homiliary, however, does vary between homilies. While Vercelli XIX and XXI show a considerable range of items used and reorganization of text, Vercelli XX and Tristram III rely mainly on one (Vercelli XX; item 93) or two (Tristram III; items 41 and 42) items in the collection.

Tristram III.49–65.[72] Each of these passages contains a condensed version of Christian history, moving, with some variation, from creation, to the fall of man, to the devil as tempter, if not to the angelic fall (only in the passages from Vercelli XIX and XXI), to the effect of the sin of Adam, redemption, and Judgment Day (only in the passages from Vercelli XXI and Tristram III).

In addition, in the selection and ordering of material, the author seems to have intended, as much as possible within the framework of his occasion, to move from the beginning of scriptural history through to Judgment Day,[73] and to incorporate basic Christian instruction. Paul Szarmach has observed that the central episodes of Vercelli XIX–XXI are the story of Jonah, the explanation of the eight capital sins, and the 'semipoetic presentation of the Day of Judgement.'[74] To these central episodes, we might add important references (at least) to the creation sequence in Genesis 1–3 and the New Testament commandments of Luke 10:27. The Ascension Day homily, in turn, focuses on Christ's role as redeemer and judge, and how we ought to live: though shot through with admonitory images, the final homily in the set is a celebration of Christ and the great honour which is available to us, if we simply follow his example.

Conclusions

When Augustine describes how the fundamentals of the faith ought to be presented to catechumenates, he focuses on the communication of Christian history, though precepts and admonitions also have a place in the narration. In order to instruct most effectively, the sermon should present interesting highlights in a manner which does not simply march details past the audience, but rather spreads out the whole of Christian history that the symmetry of God's plan might also be seen. While the concerns of later authors were not the same as those of Augustine, this general principle – that the relevance of particular details in the scriptural account to one another, and to Christian life overall, should be demonstrated – seems to have been heeded.

---

72 All three are cited, at least in part, above. In Vercelli XXI, we might also add the extensive material on the Last Judgment which follows, and which also appears in Vercelli II.

73 Scragg has commented on Vercelli XIX–XXI: 'They form an organized set, beginning in homily XIX with the Trinity and the Creation, and concluding in homily XXI with a long description of the terror of the Last Judgement' (*Vercelli Homilies*, 310).

74 Szarmach, 'The Vercelli Homilies,' 244.

However, authors also clearly felt free to adapt the basic guidelines of Augustine's model *narratio* to their own immediate needs. Martin uses the framework of scriptural history to attempt to steer apostates away from pagan gods and practices and back to the Christian faith; Pirmin, by contrast, uses the same outline of scriptural history as an introduction to the fundamental tenets of the faith. Martin's *De correctione rusticorum*, especially, seems to me to have been an excellent model for the use of a general history in the context of a specific aim or occasion. Ælfric and Wulfstan are closer to Augustine, in that both are primarily interested in outlining only scriptural history, though, even here, we have evidence of the idiosyncratic interests of each, and the concerns of Martin and Pirmin (to present material on basic prayers such as the Creed and *Pater Noster*) are dealt with in other sermons.

In the case of Vercelli XIX–XXI and Tristram III, we see an author who, given the opportunity to compile a series of sermons for Rogationtide and Ascension Day, decides to combine material appropriate to the occasion with the sort of general outline of scriptural history which Augustine recommends. There is evidence of an organized progression from creation to Last Judgment in Vercelli XIX–XXI, and the concluding Ascension Day homily shows the relevance of the material in the three preceding homilies to the life and salvation of the individual Christian. The most important historical events for these occasions are clearly the creation and fall of angels and men, and the birth and career of Christ: the homilist carefully and skilfully demonstrates their significance, and provides his audience with four extremely rich homilies for one of the most important preaching occasions of the year.

That the occasion should merit such fundamental instruction may be illustrated by the example of Ælfric in his first series of homilies: where the author of Vercelli XIX–XXI and the Ascension Day homily in CCCC 162 chooses to include Christian history, both past and still to come, as a topic appropriate to the season, Ælfric instead offers homilies on the gospel pericope of Luke 11:5–13 (*CH* I.18), followed by the Lord's Prayer (*CH* I.19), a general homily on the Catholic faith (*CH* I.20) – 'Ælc cristen man sceal æfter rihte cunnan ægþer ge his pater noster ge his credan'[75] ['Every Christian man should, according to what is right, know both his *Pater Noster* and his Creed'] – and a reasonably close exposition of the Ascension (*CH* I.21). Though the material is almost completely different, the fundamental importance of what each homilist has to say is evident:

---

75 *CH* I.20, 1–2.

Rogationtide is an occasion not only for explaining the origins and purpose of the season, but also for reintroducing the fundamental articles of the Christian faith. After all, as our author himself warns, those who do not wish to hear the teachings of scripture (and the apostles) shall find that woe descends unrelentingly upon them.[76]

76 Tristram III.145–9. I would like to thank Andy Orchard and Samantha Zacher for their hospitality at the University of Toronto in September 2002 and for their skilful editing, and Stephen Harris for his particularly close reading of a draft version of this paper.

The Reburial of the Cross in the Old English *Elene*

MANISH SHARMA

The central theme of *Elene* is conversion – through the cross and, by extension, through Christ. By means of a series of encounters with the ultimate icon of Christianity, first Constantine and Elene, then Judas, then all the Jews accede to the spiritual truth that the cross signifies. The attainment of this spiritual truth is represented throughout the text by the metaphorics of movement. Robert Stepsis and Richard Rand, for instance, have argued that the theme of the poem is 'a simple yet fundamental one concerning the power of the cross, and through the cross, of Christ, to effect the reconciliation of the two realms of darkness and light and the *movement*, through the revelation of the cross, from one condition to the other' (my emphasis).[1] Similarly, Jackson J. Campbell states of the arrangement of *Elene* that it incorporates 'the movement from dark to light, from death to life, from earthly troubles to heavenly glory.'[2] The figurative shift from ignorance to knowledge and darkness to light parallel the literal movement from confinement to release by means of which Judas is liberated from his incarceration and the cross is discovered. Both of these episodes belong to what Earl Anderson has called 'a pattern of movement from

---

1 R. Stepsis and R. Rand, 'Contrast and Conversion in Cynewulf's *Elene*,' *NM* 70 (1969): 274. Stepsis and Rand oppose the kinetic quality of *Elene* to the earlier view of the poem 'being constructed around a series of contrasts – darkness versus light, concealment versus revelation, blindness versus sight.' See also S.B. Greenfield and D.G. Calder, *A New Critical History of Old English Literature* (New York: New York Univ. Press, 1986), 113–18, who discuss this kinetic dimension of *Elene*.

2 J.J. Campbell, 'Cynewulf's Multiple Revelations,' in *Cynewulf: Basic Readings*, ed. R.E. Bjork (New York and London: Garland, 1996), 229–50.

restriction to expansiveness.'[3] The typological reflex of this movement is of course the progression from confinement within the bondage of Judaic law (or the letter) towards the freedom of the Spirit. While Stepsis and Rand, Campbell, and Anderson express what has become a typical view of *Elene*'s fundamental structure, it may be that critics have been premature in ascribing a single, unidirectional movement to the poem's narrative line. It may be argued, in fact, that the metaphorical vectors of *Elene* are bidirectional; the movement of liberation and revelations is accompanied by a movement back within confinement, darkness, and secrecy that culminates in the problematic image of the reburial of the cross – an image that cannot be accounted for wholly by recourse to typology.

The bidirectionality of movement in the poem is first apparent in the case of Constantine's conversion. He is the first to experience conversion in *Elene*, though, indeed, the question might legitimately be posed as to whether his conversion is truly an 'experience' at all. Gordon Whatley, for one, comments on Constantine's 'spontaneous acceptance of the cross' and his 'rapid understanding of its significance.'[4] The immediacy and totality of his compliance with the heavenly messenger's commands and the subsequent enthusiasm with which he investigates his new-found faith contrast sharply with the prolonged distress suffered by Judas when confronted by another (earthly) messenger: the formidable Elene. It is evident, therefore, that Constantine wastes no time in acquiescing to the angel's demands:

---

3 E.R. Anderson, 'Wisdom and Compunction,' in his *Cynewulf: Structure, Style, and Theme in His Poetry* (Rutherford, NJ: Fairleigh Dickinson Univ. Press; London: Associated Univ. Presses, 1983), 161; Anderson observes 'the pattern of movement from restriction to expansiveness' present in the depiction of Constantine's warfare against the barbarians and 'repeated with the confinement of Judas in the pit, followed by his conversion and release' and 'the resurrection of the Cross from its narrow grave at Calvary.' For Anderson, 'these incidents project, through setting, the objective correlatives of the changing mental states in Constantine, Judas, and Elene as their spirits, under the intellectual and emotional force of the Cross, move, liberated, from spiritual darkness to sapiential light.'

4 G. Whatley, 'The Figure of Constantine the Great in Cynewulf's *Elene*,' *Traditio* 37 (1981): 168. See further Anderson, 'Constantine and the Christian *Ordo*,' in his *Cynewulf: Structure*, 126–33. For a discussion of Constantine's dream-vision in *Elene*, see A. Harbus, 'Text as Revelation: Constantine's Dream in *Elene*,' *Neophilologus* 78 (1994): 645–53. On the historical conversion of Constantine, see A.H.M. Jones, *Constantine and the Conversion of Europe* (London: Hodder and Stoughton, 1948); and A. Alföldi, *The Conversion of Constantine and Pagan Rome* (Oxford: Clarendon Press, 1948).

> He wæs sona gearu
> þurh þæs halgan hæs   – hreðerlocan onspeon –
> up locade   swa him se ar abead
> fæle friðowebba. (85–8)
> [He was immediately ready by means of the holy one's command – he opened
> his breast-lock – he looked up as the messenger, the true peace-weaver, bade
> him.]

The immediacy of Constantine's preparedness is reinforced by the alliteration in line 86: the command of the angel (*halgan hæs*) permeates him without resistance as he at once opens his heart and mind to the revealed wisdom of God (*hreðerlocan onspeon*), while sound-play links the opening of the 'breast-lock' to Constantine's upward look (*up locade*). The metaphor of 'opening,' by contrast, does not occur in the Latin account of Constantine's turn to the heavens:[5] 'intendens in coelum uidit signum Crucis Christi' ('straining towards the heavens, he saw the sign of the Cross of Christ').[6] The account of Constantine's conversion in *Elene* parallels that of Nebuchadnezzar in *Daniel*, where the formerly proud king is said to have *up locode* (l. 622) in a gesture of newfound humility upon accepting God's mastery. Gradon compares *hreðerlocan onspeon* in *Elene* to line 79 of *Juliana* (*ferðlocan onspeon*), where the context indicates that speech is the action described; such a rendering is unlikely in *Elene* unless it is the angel speaking, though Constantine seems quite clearly to be the

---

5 On the source of the Old English *Elene*, see P.O.E. Gradon, ed., *Cynewulf's 'Elene'*, rev. ed. (Exeter: University of Exeter Press, 1977), 15–22; and M.C. Bodden, ed., *The Old English Finding of the True Cross* (Cambridge: D.S. Brewer, 1987), 36–47. For the purposes of comparison in this chapter, I will use, along with Bodden's edition, the *Acta Cyriaci*, from the *Acta Sanctorum*, May, vol. 1, ed. G. Henschen and D. Papebroche (Antwerp, 1680), which accompanies her edition of the Old English homily on the Invention of the Cross found in Oxford, Bodleian Library, Auct. F.4.32. For the reasons against using A. Holder's edition of the *Inuentio* (Leipzig, 1889), which admittedly uses a manuscript preserving an earlier version of the legend (Paris, Lat. 2769 [MS A]), see Bodden, ed, *True Cross*, 58 (Bodden does, however, supplement her readings of the *Acta Cyriaci* from this edition). See too now Stephan Borgehammar, *How the Holy Cross Was Found: From Event to Medieval Legend*, Bibliotheca Theologiae Practicae 47 (Stockholm: Almqvist & Wiksell, 1991). Nevertheless, as stated by Daniel G. Calder, *Cynewulf* (Boston: Twayne, 1981), 105, 'in matters of detail no absolute statements concerning the relation of source and poem are possible.'
6 Bodden, ed., *True Cross*, 62.

subject of *onspeon*.[7] Campbell offers a more satisfactory explanation, noting that 'the phrase is consummately appropriate as part of an asyndetic series of clauses. "He opened his heart" to the vision, as he so patently does in the context of the entire passage; miraculous manifestations, after all, require spiritual receptiveness.'[8] Moreover, the introduction of the theme of containment and the container with the conversion of Constantine resonates elsewhere when we take into consideration Judas's incarceration, which precipitates his conversion, within the *hearmloca* ('grief-stronghold') at line 695. It may be instructive, therefore, to investigate the other occurrences of the element -*loca* in the poem.

The wise men of Constantine's kingdom tell the king after he has inquired about the nature of the sign that permitted his victory over the heathen forces that Christ 'alysde leoda bearn of locan deofla' ('freed the children of men from the devils' stronghold [181]). The next occurrence of *loca* is also intimately connected with this episode in salvation history, as Judas's father recounts the details of Christ's interment: 'þreo niht siððan in byrgenne bidende wæs under þeosterlocan' ('for three nights afterwards he was waiting in the tomb down within a dark stronghold' [483–4]). Finally, within the poet's prayer, which begins once the story of Judas ends and thanks God for knowledge that has been granted, the speaker states that God has 'unbound the bone-container, unwound the breast-lock, unlocked the skill of poetry' ('bancofan onband, breostlocan onwand, leoðucræft onleac' [1249–50]). The threefold repetition of the *on*-prefix coupled with a compound or verb containing *loc-* (*leac-*) reminds us of *hreðerloca onspeon* at line 86 and links God's gift to the poet to the 'gift' of Christian faith given to Constantine.

In three of the above examples the theme of containment occurs in a negative context: the 'grief-stronghold' of Judas, the 'dark stronghold' of Christ's tomb, and hell as the 'stronghold' of the devil. In every case, on the other hand, 'release' or 'opening' is assigned a positive function in anticipation of the climactic Invention of the Cross. The antinomy of containment and release established by the element -*loca* is founded securely on the oppositions that the text strives to create: darkness and light; evil and good; ignorance and knowledge; death and rebirth.

---

7 Gradon, ed., *Elene*, 29. See also E. Ekwall's review of Cook's *Elene*, *Anglia* 33 (1922): 61–7, at 65.
8 Campbell, 'Multiple Revelations,' 233.

The metaphorical space of the 'breast-lock' in the depiction of Constantine's conversion, furthermore, appears to correspond to the literal space of the *hearmloca* in the depiction of Judas's conversion. In both conversion experiences, we are presented with a bounded space (the *-loca*) that is breached in the course of acquiring the new faith. Similarly, the *breostloca* of the speaker in the epilogue of *Elene* is opened so that the gift of poetry can emerge. There is, however, an important distinction in the case of Constantine: he is the passive recipient of new knowledge and opens his heart so that the angel's message may enter his *breostloca*. Judas, by contrast (like Christ out of his tomb and like the souls Christ frees from hell) physically exits the pit of his incarceration. The ascription of a single movement to the text (for example, from darkness to light, bondage to freedom, restriction to expansiveness) is perhaps deliberately weakened by Cynewulf's description of the initial stage of Constantine's conversion: instead of movement out of the metaphorical space of the *loca*, a dynamic always positively valorized (as revelation, light, and freedom), we have the opposite, as the *breostloca* is breached by an external agency.

Perhaps a more striking illustration of this movement 'against the grain' of the text occurs in the account of Judas' baptism:

> Swylce Iudas onfeng
> æfter fyrstmearce   fulwihtes bæð
> ond geclænsod wearð   Criste getrywe
> lifwearde leof;   his geleafa wearð
> fæst on ferhðe   siððan frofre gast
> wic gewunode   in þæs weres breostum,
> bylde to bote. (1032–8)
> [Thus Judas, after an appointed interval, received the immersion of baptism and, faithful to Christ and beloved by the Guardian of life, was cleansed; his faith became fixed in his heart when the Holy Ghost occupied a dwelling in the breast of that man and impelled him towards repentance.]

We can easily discern Cynewulf's artistry in this passage: interlinear alliteration on *f* between lines 1032 and 1033 is matched by interlinear alliteration on *b* between lines 1037 and 1038; *geclænsod wearð* at line 1034 anticipates *geleafa wearð* at line 1035; at line 1035, in addition, sound-play establishes a link between 'life' (*lif*), 'love' (*leof*), and 'faith' (*geleafa*) – characterizing the baptism as a metaphorical 'return to life' enabled both by Judas's new-found belief and God's love channelled through the Holy

Ghost.[9] The Latin version of Judas's baptism in the *Act Cyriaci* is spare by comparison and makes no mention of the Holy Ghost: 'Judas autem accipiens incorruptionis baptismum in Christo Jesu, de praecedentibus signis ostensus est fidelis, et commendauit eum Episcopo qui illo tempore erat adhuc Jerosolymis, et baptizauit eum in Christo' ('Moreover, Judas, receiving the baptism of purity in Jesus Christ, was shown to be faithful concerning the preceding signs, and she [Elene] entrusted him to the Bishop who at that time was still in Jerusalem, and he baptized him in Christ').[10] The Holy Ghost does enter Judas, however, prior to his riposte to the devil in the Old English Homily on the Invention: 'Iudas wearð þa gefylled mid þam Halgan Gaste' ('Judas became then filled with the Holy Ghost'). The contrast with Cynewulf's elaborate description, nevertheless, is striking. Here we see the *breost* as a site of enclosure which resists the surface movement of the text out of entombment. For, as with the initial stage of Constantine's conversion, the metaphorical space of Judas's breast, the *wic*, is subject to invasion by an external agency who takes up residence therein.

The only other instance of the term *wic* in the poem, in fact, occurs in a similar context to describe a parallel movement by the Holy Ghost into Elene – nowhere present in the Latin but closely resembling the Old English homily's description of the Holy Ghost filling Judas. The passage from *Elene* reads:

> Heo gefylled wæs
> wisdomes gife,   ond þa wic beheold
> halig heofonlic gast,   hreðer weardode,
> æðelne innoð,   swa hie ælmihtig
> sigebearn godes   sioððan freoðode. (1142–6)
>
> [She was filled with the gift of wisdom and the heavenly Holy Ghost occupied that dwelling, took up residence in that noble heart and mind; thus, the almighty victory-son of God afterwards protected her.]

As with Constantine and Judas, therefore, an external agency takes up residence within the figurative boundaries of Elene's 'heart and mind.' The

---

9 For the wider use of such paronomastic puns in *Elene*, see, for example, Samantha Zacher, 'Cynewulf at the Interface of Literacy and Orality: The Evidence of the Puns in *Elene*,' *Oral Tradition* 17.2 (2002): 346–87.

10 Bodden, ed., *True Cross*, 94.

text manifests a further movement into containment (implicating the three major figures in the poem in this dynamic) even as the narrative moves towards release. The evidence suggests that the assignation of a unidirectional movement to *Elene* may be premature. Movement into containment in the above passages describes a vector which runs directly counter to the governing tropes of revelation, disclosure, and exodus upon which Cynewulf's version of the Invention of the Cross is founded, complicating any characterization of *Elene* as manifesting a straightforward progression towards liberation, revelation, and light.

But the most telling instance of this regressive movement towards enclosure is the fate of the cross itself, subsequent to its invention. The discovery of the cross in *Elene* marks the climax of the text's depicted movement from confinement to freedom, from ignorance to knowledge, from light to darkness, and from the Mosaic law of the Jews to the Spirit of Christian understanding. In both Latin and Old English versions, once it has been exhumed the cross is decorated with precious metals and jewels and a shrine is raised upon the site of its discovery. Again, it is instructive to view the manner with which Cynewulf elaborates upon his putative source. The relevant Latin passage describing the adornment of the cross reads: 'cum magno autem studio collocans pretiosam Crucem, auro et lapidibus pretiosis, faciens loculum argentem, in ipso collocauit Crucem Christi' ('and with great zeal setting the precious Cross with gold and precious stones, making a silver container in which she placed the Cross of Christ').[11] The focus of Cynewulf's elaboration appears to be the image of the silver container (*loculum argentem*) provided by the Latin:

> heo þa rode heht
> golde beweorcean   ond gimcynnum,
> mid þam æðelstum   eorcnanstanum,
> besettan searocræftum   ond þa in seolfren fæt
> locum belucan   þær þæt lifes treo,
> selest sigebeama   siððan wunode
> æðele, unbrece. (1022–8)

[She commanded the Cross to be encased in gold and cunningly set around with precious gems and the noblest stones and locked around with fastenings in a silver vessel where that tree of life, the best of victory-trees, remained afterwards, noble, inviolable.]

---

11 Ibid., 92.

While the Latin account of the adornment of the cross does little to suggest the 'enclosed' status of the now-decorated relic, in the Old English we are presented with three consecutive verbs with a *be-* prefix: *beweorcean*, *besettan*, and *belucan*.[12] The *be-* prefix has two attested functions in Old English: it operates either as a deprivative or in the same way as the preposition 'about.' The function of the prefix in the three verbs cited from the above passage is clearly the latter, and the cross is represented here, as opposed to the Latin, as completely surrounded and encased by gold, gems, and silver fetters. The stress on containment and enclosure is augmented further by an instance of paronomasia, as the cross is described not only as 'locked around' but literally as 'locked around with locks' (*locum belucan*). The phrase recalls the negative associations of the enclosed space of the *loca*, which must be opened in order for Christian truth to advance: here of course is the opposite dynamic, and the very symbol of Christian truth is enclosed.[13]

The term *belucan*, in particular, carries some profoundly negative associations in the remainder of the extant poetic corpus, particularly in the biblical poetry.[14] In *Daniel*, line 695, Baltassar and his court are described ominously as *belocene*, trapped by their fast impending doom and locked in spiritual stasis with no opportunity for redemption. The occurrences of *belucan* in *Exodus* are especially relevant: the verb is applied to the Egyptians at lines 43 and 457, stressing their spiritual bondage and contrasting the liberation of the Israelites. It seems deliberate in *Exodus* that *belucan* is countered by its precise antonym, the verb *onlucan* at line 523, which describes the liberation of spiritual knowledge from the bondage of the letter – precisely what is meant to be symbolized by the Invention of the Cross in *Elene*. In *Elene*, moreover, we see the verb *onlucan* used to describe the opening of the poet's heart by God in the epilogue (l. 1250) in

---

12 Nor does the Homily on the Invention stress at all the confinement of the cross or mention that it is 'locked': 'And hio þa halgan Cristes rode bewyrcan het mid golde and mid seolfre and mid diowurþum gimmum' ('And she commanded that the holy cross of Christ be wrought with gold and silver and with precious jewels' [Bodden, ed., *True Cross*, 92–3]). On the jewels associated with the cross in *The Dream of the Rood* and other Anglo-Saxon crosses, see now Éamonn Ó Carragáin, *Ritual and the Rood: Liturgical Images and the Old English Poems of 'The Dream of the Rood' Tradition* (London and Toronto: British Library and UTP, 2005), 339–54.

13 The possibility remains, of course, that *belucan locum* is merely a mistranslation of the Latin *loculum* ('small container').

14 We should note also that in its only other occurrence in extant verse in the Paris Psalter 88.42, *loc* describes the fetters of hell.

order to permit true knowledge in the form of poetry to emerge. The previously locked container of Cynewulf's heart in this context had confined knowledge within, rendering it inaccessible and useless both to Cynewulf and to those who might learn from it.

The motif of useless and inaccessible treasure recalls *Beowulf* 2277, where it is said of the dragon resting atop his hoard that 'ne byð him wihte ðy sel' ('he was none the better for it').[15] In an interesting parallel with *Elene*, after the dragon's gold has been won by the hero before his death, it is reburied within Beowulf's barrow and becomes again 'swa unnyt swa hit æror wæs' ('as useless as it previously was' [3168]).[16] We should note, then, that the cross is compared to buried treasure prior to its exhumation when it is called a *goldhord* at line 790.[17] Thus, the locking of the cross by Elene suggests the disturbing possibility that the relic has reacquired the ambiguous status of hidden treasure – especially when we consider that *un*locking the heart of the speaker in the epilogue permits the precious treasure of poetry to attain for Cynewulf its potential in the economy of divine truth.

---

15 On the dragon's treasure in *Beowulf*, see E.R. Anderson, 'Treasure Trove in *Beowulf*: A Legal View of the Dragon's Hoard,' *Mediaevalia* 3 (1978 for 1977): 141–64; T.M. Andersson, 'The Thief in *Beowulf*,' *Speculum* 59 (1984): 493–508; H.R.E. Davidson, 'The Hill of the Dragon: Anglo-Saxon Burial Mounds in Literature and Archaeology,' *Folk-Lore* 61 (1950): 169–85; L.V. Grinsell, 'Barrow Treasure in Fact, Tradition and Legislation,' *Folk-Lore* 78 (1967): 1–38; and C. Knipp, '*Beowulf* 2210b–2323: Repetition in the Description of the Dragon's Hoard,' *NM* 73 (1972): 775–85.

16 See E.I. Condren, '*Unnyt* Gold in *Beowulf* 3168,' *PQ* 52 (1973): 296–9.

17 Arthur Gilchrist Brodeur, *The Art of 'Beowulf'* (Berkeley: University of California Press, 1960), 261, states that the term *goldhord* is used with 'striking inappropriateness' to describe the cross; Catharine A. Regan, 'Evangelicalism as the Informing Principle of Cynewulf's *Elene*,' *Traditio* 29 (1973): 27–52, at 280, however, argues that 'the compound is a striking metaphor which not only signifies Cynewulf's attitude towards the Cross – which is sustained throughout the poem – but, without modifying that tone, connotes the redemptive merits gained by Christ's death on the Cross.' John P. Hermann, *Allegories of War: Language and Violence in Old English Poetry* (Ann Arbor: University of Michigan Press, 1989), 109, argues contrary to Regan that 'the *goldhord* of tradition also associates the cross with the worldly power this symbol of the crucifixion produced for Constantine, and for the English Church as well. The Anglo-Saxon *goldhord* was not desired as capital in the modern sense, but as a representation of past victories, as well as of the future victories its distribution to warriors would make possible. A conventional sublatory reading like Regan's necessarily spiritualizes the *goldhord*, removing gold to a symbolic plane where only religious associations are presumed relevant.' On the cross as treasure, see further Anderson, 'Civitas Dei Peregrinans,' in *Cynewulf*, 152–3.

At the most literal level, then, the adornment of the cross in the Old English appears to bear an almost sinister resonance – suggesting a return to bondage and confinement after a brief space of liberation following the Invention, and matching the regressive movement implicit in Constantine's conversion, the confirmation of Judas's faith, and the movement of the Holy Ghost into Elene. For Catherine Regan, this troubling passage is smoothed over by recourse to a typological interpretation. She observes that in Judas's prayer to God to reveal the true cross, he begs that God might reveal the cross to him as he revealed to Moses the bones of Joseph (ll. 784–7). Regan thus argues that 'just as Joseph's bones were disinterred only to be reburied as he had wished in the Promised Land, so too will the Cross be resurrected only to be reburied in jewels by Elene.'[18] Rather than effacing the seemingly problematic imagery of the reburial of the cross with a typological solution, it might be illuminating to explore its ramifications and find some motivation for this paradoxical urge in the text to conceal the relic, returning it to the dark secrecy from which it was just exhumed.

The locking of the cross has some important implications for the presentation of the Jews in *Elene* as 'trapped' by their adherence to the Old Law. Tom Hill sees the confrontation between Elene and the Jews in the text as 'patterned typologically,' so that it 'is not simply a conflict between individuals but rather the confrontation of two kinds of wisdom – the wisdom of the word and the law of the Jews, and the Christian wisdom of Elene.'[19] The adherence of the Jews to the *littera* of Mosaic law is traditionally represented by means of the imagery of confinement, bondage, darkness, and seclusion. According to Anderson, 'The movement from "narrow" to "roomier" understanding has a paradigm in the doctrine of the supersession of the Old Law by the New, and in the corresponding progression from legalistic preoccupation with the "letter" to a sapiential concern for the "spirit" of the Law.'[20] So Paul writes in Romans 7:6: 'nunc autem soluti a lege morientes in quo detinebamur ita ut serviamus in novitate spiritus et non in vetustate litterae' ('But now we are discharged from the law, dead to that which held us captive, so that we are slaves not under the old written code but in the new life of the spirit'). As Varda Fish has observed, patristic commentary also allegorizes the bondage of Judaic law; for Fish, then, Judas's experience in the pit 'metaphorically reflects his spiritual condition under the Old Law' and 'is a figure for the Jews' situation under the Old Law.'[21]

---

18 Regan, 'Evangelicism,' 47–8.
19 Hill, 'Sapiential Structure,' 212.
20 Anderson, *Cynewulf*, 161.
21 Fish, 'Theme and Pattern,' 12.

The dynamic of containment and release which informs the major themes of *Elene* is implicit in one important form within this opposition of the Old Law and New. According to the Pauline metaphor, the container of the letter must be breached in order for Christian understanding to proceed forth; the release of Judas from confinement, then, represents on the allegorical plane in *Elene* his movement out of the bondage of both law and letter. Traditionally, it is contemplation of the cross which permits spiritual understanding to emerge from the enclosure of the literal. Accordingly for Augustine, 'Crux Domini nostri clauis fuit qua clausa aperirentur' ('the Cross of our Lord was the key by which the enclosure [of the Law] was opened').[22] Augustine's words resemble the opening of the Advent Antiphon, where Christ himself is understood as a key: 'O clavis David, et sceptrum domus Israel; qui aperis, et nemo claudit, claudis, et nemo aperit' ('O key of David, and sceptre of the land of Israel; you who open and none closes, you who close and none opens').[23] Of course in the Old English *Exodus* we are supplied with the metaphor of the 'keys of the spirit' (*gastes cægon* [525]) that permit wisdom to emerge from the container of the literal. The image of unlocking the spirit from the bondage of the letter by means of the cross (and, by extension, Christ) is the likely inspiration for Cynewulf's declaration that God has *leoðucræft onleac* ('unlocked the craft of poetry') at line 1250 in the epilogue of *Elene*. How are we to assess, then, the image of the locked cross? The symbol by which spiritual meaning is unlocked (*onlucan*) from the metaphorical container of the letter is itself locked (*belucan*) by Elene in the literal container of its adornment; we are presented, therefore, with the curious figure of a key within a gilded and locked box.

The hermeneutic powers of the cross demand that its regressive movement back into confinement in *Elene* be examined in those terms. Thus, while the surface vectors of the text insist on a revelatory movement towards spiritual meaning away from the bondage of the letter, the locking of the cross seems to insist on the inaccessibility of the spiritual interior and the inescapability of the fetters of the literal level of meaning. The cross, instead of being the key which opens a metaphorical container, becomes itself contained in a literal enclosure as Elene's adornment inverts the dynamic of Christian interpretation. The regressive movement back towards the bondage of the letter is emphasized by a subtle alteration to the *Acta Cyriaci*. When Constantine first spies the cross, before grasping

---

22 CCSL 38.518.
23 Cf. A.S. Cook, ed., *The Christ of Cynewulf* (Boston: Ginn and Co., 1900), 76.

its Christian meaning, the scene is described in the Latin text as follows: 'et intendens in coelum uidit signum Crucis Christi, ex lumine claro constitutum' ('and turning [upwards] he saw the sign of the Cross of Christ in the sky having been outlined by a bright light').[24] Cynewulf's elaboration is noteworthy:[25]

> geseah he frætwum beorht
> wliti wuldres treo   ofer wolcna hrof
> golde geglenged;   gimmas lixtan. (88–90)
> [He saw, bright with ornate treasures, the shining tree of glory over the roof of clouds, adorned with gold; gems gleamed.]

While in the *Acta* the cross is described only as illuminated, for Constantine in *Elene* the cross appears gilded and bejewelled, anticipating its adornment after its exhumation. As observed above, Constantine's proleptic vision is only of the literal object and does not encompass its spiritual meaning. Nevertheless, Calder states of Constantine's vision that 'Cynewulf's "poetic elaborations" constitute a vision of the ultimate reality the Cross embodies; here the Cross is not just a holy relic with special powers to protect the emperor against the invading Huns. Cynewulf's first presentation of the Rood does not simply serve a military function, but symbolizes the whole Christian order.'[26]

But the fact that the adorned cross in this early episode can only be perceived by Constantine on the literal level reflects the metaphorical circumstances of its later adornment, which suggest a movement back into the confinement of the letter. Constantine's inability at this point to penetrate to the inner truth of the cross 'adorned with gold, gleaming with gems' looks forward to the ramifications of its later confinement, whereby the cross is 'encased in gold and cunningly set around with precious gems and the noblest stones and locked around with fastenings in a silver vessel' (in ll. 1023–6).

Any reckoning of this regressive movement back towards the literal must take into consideration Cynewulf's attempted transformation of his source material. There is in the *Acta Cyriaci*, as in *Elene*, an opposition created between the spiritual knowledge of Christianity and Judaic law,

---

24 Bodden, ed., *The True Cross*, 62.
25 Gradon, ed., *Elene*, 30, supplies *geglenged* for the unlikely manuscript reading *gelenged*, meaning 'extended' or 'lengthened.'
26 Calder, *Cynewulf*, 107–8.

though in the Latin version, by contrast to the Old English, it is not a major theme. Speaking to the Jews, Helena simply states in the Latin: 'sed quia repellentes omnem sapientiam, eum qui uolebat de maledicto vos redimere maledixistis' ('but because you repudiated all wisdom, you cursed him who desired to redeem you from evil'). We clearly can understand *sapientia* in this context to refer to 'spiritual wisdom.' The 'evil' of which the Jews are guilty, moreover, is seen by Helena to be within their 'law': 'et lucem tenebras existimastis et ueritatem mendacium, peruenit in uos maledictum quod est in lege uestra scriptum' ('and you judged darkness to be light and truth to be falsehood, the evil which is written in your law came into you').[27] So, while the opposition between the letter and the spirit is not presented in explicit terms in the *Acta*, nevertheless we can find in the Latin account the probable source for Cynewulf's stark thematic contrast.

But notwithstanding this implicit opposition in the Latin version between *lex* and *sapientia*, previous scholars have argued that the *Acta* represents, in direct contrast to *Elene*, a quest only for the literal object of the cross and not a movement towards its spiritual meaning. For inherent in the figure of the cross itself is the dichotomy of the letter and the spirit; the cross is simultaneously a literal instrument of torture and the spiritual means to salvation, as most famously depicted in *The Dream of the Rood*. Hence, Regan states:

It seems reasonable to assume that the monk must have approached saints' lives meditatively, as he approached Scripture, because of the firm habit of meditation he had formed through extensive daily practice (from 1200 to 1500 hours of reading per year). He must have reflected on the spiritual significance of the saints' life – in other words his attention must have been directed not only to the *letter* but also to the *spirit* of the work. A close reading of *Elene* suggests that Cynewulf, very likely a monk himself, had approached the *Acta Cyriaci* in the same way that any monk must have approached a saint's life in the *lectio divina*. Thus *Elene* can best, and most logically, be comprehended as the product of the poet's meditation on the *Acta Cyriaci*, not merely as a versification of his Latin source.[28]

For Regan, therefore, the relationship between the Latin and Old English versions of the Invention is analogous to the relation between letter and

---

27 Bodden, ed., *The True Cross*, 72.
28 Regan, 'Evangelicism as the Informing Principle,' 252–3.

spirit – itself a thematic concern of both works. Varda Fish argues similarly for Cynewulf's interest in the spiritual meaning of the Invention legend as opposed to the literal account provided by the *Acta*, stating: 'The quest for the cross in the Old English poem, then, does not seek a merely physical object, *as in the Latin legend*, but a symbol of true wisdom in which letter and spirit, sign and significance are simultaneously present' (my emphasis).[29] It can be argued that the awareness the Latin version of the Invention legend displays regarding the Jews' repudiation of spiritual wisdom and their adherence to the letter of the law creates a kind of contradiction in the text: if the Christian quest for the cross in the Latin text is a quest only on the literal plane, as Fish and Regan have suggested, then the opposition between Christian wisdom and Judaic law is compromised. In other words, Helena in the Latin version excoriates the Jews for their adherence to the letter, while simultaneously pressing them for the means to pursue the literal.

Cynewulf's *Elene* can be read, therefore, as an attempt to avoid the contradiction of the Latin text by spiritualizing the quest for the cross. If the quest is no longer merely for the physical relic but for Christian *sapientia*, then the terms of the contradistinction between the Jews and the Christians (bearing far more thematic significance in the Old English text) would, on the surface, appear stable. For Regan it is clear that Elene 'conceives of the Cross as a symbol, a sign of salvation, and not as a relic.'[30] Fish concurs, stating: 'Cynewulf transformed the search for a physical object into a quest for spiritual perception.'[31] Fish observes further that descriptions of the object of Elene's quest, such as *wisdom onwreon* ('to reveal wisdom' [674]), *soð gecyðan* ('to speak the truth' [588]), and *onwreon wyrda geryno* ('to reveal the mystery of the events' [589]), imply that 'Elene's quest goes beyond the revelation of the physical *beacen* of the cross and that it leads us to a new spiritual perception of the *beacen*.'[32] By adding this figural dimension to the quest for the cross, Cynewulf seems to dodge a contradiction which resides in his probable Latin source – where the letter is repudiated even as the literal is pursued.

But the regressive movement we have observed in *Elene* creates a problem in Cynewulf's Old English allegoresis that is precisely parallel to that which we see in the Latin source-text. By means of the series of movements

---

29 Fish, 'Theme and Pattern,' 19.
30 Regan, 'Evangelicism as the Informing Principle,' 42.
31 Fish, 'Theme and Pattern,' 4.
32 Ibid., 8.

back into containment, particularly the locking of the cross, the text institutes a movement back within the bondage of the literal. The dynamic by which Christian wisdom is meant to transcend Judaic knowledge (emergence from confinement) is reversed and the oppositional structure ('littera et spiritus') which characterizes the opposition between the Old and the New in *Elene* is destabilized. Avoidance of the apparent contradiction in the source-text by spiritualizing its quest is thus thwarted and the straightforward movement of the narrative towards the unlocked truth of the spirit in *Elene* is rendered problematic by an undercurrent of movement which insists on the persistence of confinement and the letter. In the same manner, the Latin version of the Invention simultaneously rejects and pursues the literal. The movement from the letter to the spirit in *Elene*, therefore, thematizes Cynewulf's own movement from meditation upon the literal Latin account to his spiritualized version: neither movement can escape entirely the terms of the letter but, instead, is directed inevitably back within its confines. It is ironic, then, that Cynewulf should add to his source the eschatological conversion of the Jews to Christianity (ll. 1115–24) – attempting to eliminate the distinction between the two peoples under the banner of Christian liberation while this distinction has already been attenuated by the imagery of confinement which infiltrates the text's depiction of conversion and Invention.[33]

We could say, then, that the Old English text resists the poet's own attempt to choose the bread instead of the stone. Indeed, Judas's rhetorical question upon facing the threats of Elene, which posit a choice between just these two alternatives, is relevant to this textual dilemma and requires some examination. When the queen is pressing Judas for the location of the cross and threatens him with death unless he responds truthfully, Judas replies:

Hu mæg þæm geweorðan   þe on westenne
meðe ond meteleas   morland trydeð,
hungre gehæfted   ond him hlaf ond stan
on gesihðe bu geweorðað
stearc ond hnesce,   þæt he þone stan nime
wið hungres hleo,   hlafes ne gime,

---

33 On the motif of the eventual conversion of the Jews at the Day of Judgment, see A.V. Talentino, 'Causing City Walls to Resound: *Elene* 151b,' *PLL* 9 (1973): 189–93; and E.R. Anderson, 'Cynewulf's *Elene* 1115b–24, The Conversion of the Jews: Figurative or Literal?' *ELN* 25 (1988): 1–3.

gewende to wædle   ond þa wiste wiðsæce,
beteran wiðhycge   þonne he bega beneah. (611–8)
[How can it be when someone is treading the march-land wastes, exhausted
and without food, oppressed by hunger, and a loaf and a stone, one hard, one
soft, both come into view together, that he would choose the stone for relief
of his hunger and not heed the loaf, return to want and forgo the food, reject
the better when he had both things available?]

Judas's question to Elene in the Old English is a significant elaboration of
the Latin version: 'Et quis in solitudine constitutus, panibus sibi appositis,
lapides manducat?' ('When someone in solitary confinement has loaves set
before him, will he eat stones?').[34] Critical focus on these lines and the corresponding passage in the Latin has called attention to a number of potential biblical allusions. T.D. Hill sees a parallel with Christ's first temptation
in the desert (Matt. 4:3 and Lk. 4:3), where Satan tempts Christ, who is
famished after forty days of fasting, to change a stone into a loaf of bread.[35]
E.G. Whatley rejects Hill's suggestion and offers what is the more plausible citation of the parable of the fish and the serpent and the bread and the
stone ('Is there any among you who, if your child asks for bread, will give
a stone? Or if the child asks for a fish, will give a snake?' [Matt. 7:9]).[36] For
Whatley, moreover, the exegetical associations of bread and stone reflect
also Judas's impending choice between the old dispensation and the new.
Augustine's interpretation of the parable is thus relevant: 'Panis intelligi-
tur caritas propter majorem appetitum, et tam neccessarium ut sine illa
caetera nihil sint, sicut sine pane mensa inops. Cui contraria est cordis
duritia, quam lapidi comparauit' ('Bread is understood as love by means of
the greater appetite, and is necessary to such an extent that without it the
other things shall be nothing, just as without bread the table is destitute.
To which is opposed the hardness of the heart, which he compared to

---

34 Bodden, ed., *True Cross*, 82.
35 Hill, 'Sapiential Structure,' 218–20; See also, by the same author, 'Bread and Stone,
    Again: *Elene* 611–18,' *NM* 81 (1980): 252–7. Matt. 4:3 reads (Lk. 4:3 is almost identical):
    'si filius Dei es, dic ut lapides isti panes fiunt' ('if you are the son of God, command
    these stones to become loaves of bread'). Hill also directs attention to the short account
    of the temptation in Mk. 1:12–13.
36 E.G. Whatley, 'Bread and Stone: Cynewulf's *Elene* 611–18,' *NM* 76 (1975): 550–60.
    Matt.7:9 in the Vulgate reads: 'Aut quis est ex vobis homo, quem si petierit filius suus
    panem, numquid lapidem porriget ei? Aut si piscem petierit, numquid serpentem
    porriget ei?' Whatley also directs attention to Lk. 11:11, which contains the fish/serpent
    contrast but does not mention the bread/stone contrast, replacing it with egg/scorpion.

stone').[37] Nourishing bread is equivalent to the spiritually nourishing *caritas* of the new dispensation, while the Jews in their rejection of Christ and adherence to the Law were traditionally described as 'hard-hearted' (*duri cordis*); furthermore, while bread represented the spiritual kingdom of Christ, stones signified the earthly and carnal kingdom of the Jews.[38] According to patristic authors, bread was equivalent to the spiritually nourishing *caritas* of the new dispensation and represented the kingdom of Christ, while stones signified the earthly and carnal kingdom of the Jews and their incarceration in the Law. Of course, at this point in the narrative, Judas is unaware of the irony intrinsic to his implied choice of the bread.

An important manipulation evident in Judas' response to Elene is how Cynewulf, contrary to his possible sources, provides a kinetic element to its imagery. The *Acta Cyriaci* presents a static depiction of a choice between two options: 'When someone in solitary confinement has loaves set before him, will he eat stones?' Cynewulf, however, incorporates a sense of physical movement and quasi-exilic imagery within the situation represented in Judas's response – giving us a figure treading the march-land somewhat like Grendel. As Whatley rightly observes, moreover, Judas is using 'a kind of proverb or parable to express his willingness to cooperate. In his reply Judas means to give the impression that he has no alternative but to choose. Who would choose a stone if he could avoid starvation with a loaf of bread.' Thus, 'Judas's rhetorical parable is mere rhetoric, designed to convince Elene that since she has him in her power, and since he wants to live, he intends to cooperate with her.'[39] Judas's misleading rhetorical question in *Elene*, therefore, appears to assert one thing (i.e., that he will cooperate), but preserves the possibility, by suspending resolution for the time being, that the opposite will become reality.

The imagery set forth in his question appears to reveal more about the poem itself than seems intentional, just as Judas himself is unaware of the ironic implications of his implied choice of the bread and rejection of the stone. On the one hand the kinetic imagery presented in the question suggests a *movement* towards the bread of the new dispensation; however, by the very suspension of closure intrinsic to its rhetorical mode, Judas's question simultaneously preserves the possibility of movement in the opposite direction towards the stone of Mosaic law and the letter. At this point in the

---

37 PL 35.1342.
38 Whatley, 'Bread and Stone,' 555–6.
39 Ibid., 552.

narrative, in fact, Judas has no intention of choosing 'the bread' and cooperating with Elene. Judas's misleading rhetoric implicitly acknowledges the bidirectional movement of the text, and the parable intended to represent, at Judas's expense, the transcendence of Judaic ignorance provides us, ironically, with an allegory for the inescapability of the letter.

The Journey Motif in the Poems of the Vercelli Book

PATRICK MCBRINE

Crist sylf foresæde: 'On þyssum middangearde ge habbað geswinc,' ond eft he cwæð: 'Ge wepað ond hiofað ond þes middangearde gefyhð.' Neara ond wiðerdene is se halega weg, swa swa dryhten sylf cwæð.
[Christ himself proclaimed: 'You will have toil in this world,' and then he said: 'You will weep and lament, and this world will rejoice.' Narrow and steep is the holy way, just as the Lord himself said.]   *VH* VII.29–32

All of the poetry in the Vercelli Book is concerned with the quest for Heaven, as Christ's disciples make literal and figurative journeys (the terms used include *sið* ['journey'] and *lifes weg* ['the path of life']) that test the limits of their faith. The language associated with journeying in the manuscript is a recurring series of words that highlights progressive stages of the road to salvation. In particular, terms such as *sið* ('journey'), *geomor* ('sad' or 'troubled'), *frofor* ('solace'), *hyht* ('hope'), and *dream* ('joy') define moments of joyful expectation or miserable uncertainty as individuals struggle to find their way. Each of the six Vercelli poems, namely, *Andreas, The Fates of the Apostles, Soul and Body I, Homiletic Fragment I, The Dream of the Rood*, and *Elene*, uses several or all of these words as part of a larger thematic message: the course of this life is harsh and sorrowful, yet faith and hope will lead to eternal bliss. This message appears throughout the poetry of the manuscript and, characterized by a particular language, allows us to view the poems as a collection with a number of shared interests.

The Fates of the Apostles, Cynewulf's shortest signed poem, is certainly the most succinct treatment of the journey motif in the Vercelli Book. Here Cynewulf recounts all twelve 'fates' (i.e., deaths) of the apostles in just 122 lines. Despite its title, however, the poem also concerns the narrator, whose own sadness figures prominently in both the opening and closing lines of the poem. Each of the lives of the apostles is a triumphant victory over the afflictions of mortal existence, yet the narrator himself finds no consolation for his own heartache in the process of recounting the fates of the apostles. Constance B. Hieatt first noted the importance of the term *sið* ('journey') as a unifying element in the poem, and D.G. Calder has recognized the journey as a dominant image in *Fates*, yet more remains to be said about the narrator's description of himself as 'sad' (*geomor*) in relation to this motif.[1]

In the opening lines of the poem the narrator says (1–2): 'Ic þysne sang siðgeomor fand / on seocum sefan' ('Travel-weary, I have composed [literally 'found'] this poem with a sick heart').[2] This is the only occurrence of the word *siðgeomor* in the surviving corpus of Old English, and though 'travel-weary' may be too colloquial a translation, it does suit the emphasis Cynewulf places on journeying in the poem.[3] The *sið* element is undoubtedly a metaphor for the narrator's journey through life, while the word *geomor* binds this particular moment of it to sadness. The closest parallel to this opening appears in the *Wife's Lament*, a poem in the Exeter Book, where passionate love is the catalyst for sorrow and song (1–2): 'Ic þis giedd wrece bi me ful geomorre, / minre sylfre sið' ('This song, my own journey, I have composed about myself, very sad'). The journey in *The Wife's Lament* is confined to the woman's personal experience, while the narrator of *The Fates of the Apostles* tries to place his own journey in the context of those who have gone before him. In fact, the prominence of the

---

1 See further Constance B. Hieatt, 'The *Fates of the Apostles*: Imagery, Structure, and Meaning,' repr. in *The Cynewulf Reader*, ed. Robert Bjork (New York: Routledge, 2001), 67–77; and Daniel G. Calder, *Cynewulf* (Boston: Twayne, 1981), 27–41 (esp. 33, 40); for general discussions of the poem's structure see also James L. Boren, 'Form and Meaning in Cynewulf's *Fates of the Apostles*,' in *The Cynewulf Reader*, ed. Bjork, 57–65; Alvin A. Lee, *The Guest-Hall of Eden* (New Haven: Yale Univ. Press, 1972), esp. 73–75; and E.R. Anderson, *Cynewulf: Structure, Style, and Theme in His Poetry* (New Jersey: Fairleigh Dickinson Univ. Press, 1983), 68–83.

2 All poems in Old English are cited by line number according to ASPR; all translations are my own.

3 Bosworth-Toller translates *siðgeomor* as 'sad and weary with travel' (879); Grein gives 'tristis de peregrinationibus' (609); and Sweet, 'sad from traveling' (155); J.R. Clark offers 'travel-weary' (308); cf. *siðfæt werig* in John C. Pope, ed., *Homilies of Ælfric: A Supplementary Collection*, 2 vols., EETS 259 (London: OUP, 1967–8), Feria VI in tertia ebdomada Quadragesimae (pp. 288–300), l. 260. The closest parallel to the word *siðgeomor* in Old English verse appears in *Genesis A* (67–9): 'Waldend sende / laðwendne here on langne sið, / geomre gastas' ('The Lord sent the hateful host [of angels] on a long journey, wretched spirits').

word *siðgeomor* in the opening lines of the poem, and the subsequent focus on voyage metaphors in *The Fates of the Apostles*, announces an unmistakable relationship between the narrator's troubled *sið* and those of the apostles.

We may safely assume, then, that the poem represents at some level the narrator's desire to come to terms with his own sorrow by comparing it with that of the apostles. Consider, for example, the lives of John and James, whose mortal suffering is rewarded with heavenly joy in the afterlife (30–7):

> He in Effessia   ealle þrage   30
> leode lærde,   þanon lifes weg
> siðe gesohte,   swegle dreamas,
> beorhtne boldwelan.   Næs his broðor læt,
> siðes sæne,   ac ðurh sweordes bite
> mid Iudeum   Iacob sceolde   35
> fore Herode   ealdre gedælan,
> feorh wið flæsce.
> [All his time in Ephesus, he (John) taught the people; from there he sought the way of life, the journey, and the joys of Heaven – that bright splendid dwelling! Nor was his brother careless or slow in the journey, but among the Jews by the bite of the sword James had to part with his life, spirit from flesh, and died because of Herod.]

Here the *lifes weg* (31) and *sið* (32; also 24) are metaphors for death, figurative roads to the kingdom of God; and the joys of Heaven (*swegle dreamas* [32]) and the bright halls of the Lord (*beorhtne boldwelan* [33]) represent the rewards of a faithful life. Each of the fates of the apostles is a reiteration of this formula – life, suffering, death, joy – and each of their glorious ascensions stands in contrast to the narrator's wretched misery. The last two journeys in the poem, the voyages of Simon and Thadeus into Persia (*land Persea / sohton siðfrome Simon ond Thaddeus* [76]), follow the same path from mortal suffering to celestial deliverance;[4] the conclusion to their lives is also the end of the main narrative, and may stand as the conclusion to all the lives in the poem (79–84):

---

4 Cf. *Andreas*, where the helmsman (Christ) describes the Heaven-bound journeys of the faithful (640–2): 'Gastas hweorfon, / sohton siðfrome swegles dreamas, / engla eðel þurh þa æðelan miht' ('Souls eager for the journey have turned, sought out Heaven's joys and the homeland of angels through that noble might'). See also Joseph D. Wine, *Figurative Language in Cynewulf* (New York: Peter Lang, 1993), 45.

Æðele sceoldon
ðurh wæpenhete   weorc þrowigan,   80
sigelean secan,   ond þone soðan gefean,
dream æfter deaðe,   þa gedæled wearð
lif wið lice,   ond þas lænan gestreon,
idle æhtwelan,   ealle forhogodan.   84
[These noble men had to suffer torment from weapon-hatred, to seek their
reward for victory and that true happiness, joy after death, when life was
parted from limb; and they turned away from all fleeting treasures and empty
prosperity.]

The victorious reward (*sigelean* [81]) granted to Simon and Thadeus is joy
(*dreame* [82]), that same joy that John and James receive in Heaven (*swegle
dreamas* [32]); and their true happiness (*soðan gefean* [81]) surpasses all
the transient wealth and prosperity (*gestreon* [83] ... *æhtwelan* [84]) of
this world.

In contrast to what are ultimately happy endings, the narrator at the end
of the poem is still troubled by the same gloom he shows in the opening
lines;[5] his last resort is to beg his audience for its prayers (90–114):

Nu ic þonne bidde   beorn se ðe lufige   90
þisses giddes begang   þæt he geomrum me
þone halgan   heap helpe bidde
friðes ond fultomes.   Hu ic freonda beþearf
liðra on lade,   þonne ic sceal langne ham
eardwic uncuð,   ana secan   95
                         ...
Sie þæs gemyndig   mann se ðe lufie
þisses galdres begang,   þæt he geoce me
ond frofre fricle.   Ic sceall feor heonan,
an elles forð,   eardes neosan,   110
sið asettan,   nat ic sylfa hwær,
of þisse worulde.   Wic sindon uncuð,
eard ond eðel,   swa bið ælcum menn
nemþe he godcundes   gastes bruce.

5 See further Robert C. Rice, 'The Penitential Motif in Cynewulf's *Fates of the Apostles*
and Its Epilogues,' *ASE* 6 (1977): 105–19.

[Now I beseech the one who may delight in the course of this poem, that he beseech that holy troop for peace and protection for woeful me. O how I shall need kind friends on that journey, when I must seek out a lasting home, an unknown dwelling on my own ... may he be mindful of this, who delights in the course of this poem, and seek help and the aid of comfort for me. I must go far from here, forward elsewhere on my own, to seek out a land, to set out on a journey; I know not where myself, but from this world. The dwellings are unknown to me, the country and the native land; so it is for each man, unless he possesses a divine soul.]

Note the reappearance of the adjective *geomor* in line 91, which creates a large envelope pattern, returning the audience to *siðgeomor* at the opening of the poem; this repetition frames the narrative and gives unity to the poem as a whole. To the narrator's initial feeling of sadness, Cynewulf now adds a sense of emotional isolation or exile. The narrator says that he is alone (*ana, an* [95, 99]), and bound to seek out (*secan, neosan* [95, 99]) an unknown dwelling place (*eardwic uncuð, wic uncuð* [95, 101]) without the assurance of reaching Heaven's bright halls. Seeking peace and protection (*friðes ond ful-tomes* [93]), help and comfort (*geoce ... ond frofre* [109–9]), the narrator is like the solitary journeyman of the *Wanderer*, an elegiac figure.[6] The kind of exile in that poem is similar to the narrator's spiritual journey in *Fates*, and Andy Orchard has recently made a strong case for the convergence of secular and Christian paths in the *Wanderer*.[7] The closing lines of *The Fates of the Apostles* therefore exhort the audience to pray more eagerly (*georno to Gode cleopigan* [115]), so that they may joyfully reach that greatest of all hopes (*hyhta mæst* [118]), which is Heaven. The prominence of *hyht* here at the end of the poem is significant, because, as we shall see, it is one of the most enduring consolations for earthly cares throughout the poetry of the Vercelli Book.

If we look beyond the manuscript, we find Cynewulf's narrator expressing the same introspective despondence in the Exeter Book. In the epilogue to Cynewulf's *Juliana*, the narrator shows the same anxiety about the afterlife as he does in *The Fates of the Apostles*, and the language is very similar (699–712):

---

6 See further 'The Wanderer, in *The Exeter Book* (ASPR 3), 134–7.
7 See further Andy Orchard, 'Re-Reading *The Wanderer*: The Value of Cross-References,' in *Via Crucis: The Way of the Cross. A Festschrift for James E. Cross*, ed. Thomas N. Hall (Morgantown: West Virginia University Press, 2002), 1–26. For a general introduction to elegy see further Ann Klinck, *The Old English Elegies* (Montreal: McGill–Queen's Univ. Press, 1992).

       Min sceal of lice
sawul on siðfæt,   nat ic sylfa hwider,   700
eardes uncyðu;   of sceal ic þissum,
secan operne   ærgewyrhtum,
gongan iudædum.   Geomor hweorfeð
·ᚳ·ᚾ·ᚷ·ᚠ·   Cyning biþ reþe,
sigora syllend,   þonne synnum fah   705
·ᛖ·ᚹ·ᚢ·   acle bidað
hwæt him æfter dædum   deman wille
lifes to leane. ·ᛚ·ᚹ· beofað,
seomað sorgcearig.   Sar eal gemon,
synna wunde,   þe ic siþ oþþe ær   710
geworhte in worulde.   þæt ic wopig sceal
tearum mænan.

[My soul must [venture] from its body on a journey – I know not where myself, but to an unknown land. From this [world], I must go seek another according to my former deeds and works of old. Sorrowful, *cyn* (? = 'humanity') will pass away, and the king, the giver of victories, will be harsh when, marked by sin, *ewu* (? = 'sheep') will await in terror what He will decree for them as a reward for life according to their deeds. *LF* (? *lagu-feoh*= 'earth's flood-bound wealth') will quake and lie at rest, sorrowful. I remember all the pain, the wounds of sins, which now or then I did in the world. Woeful, I shall lament that with tears.][8]

As in *Fates*, Cynewulf emphasizes the journey (*siðfæt* [700]), which again is a metaphor for death; we also find the same doubt expressed in the same terms about the destination of that journey: '*sið asettan, nat ic sylfa hwider*' (700), which the narrator in *Fates* says verbatim (100). In addition, the 'unknown land' (*eardes uncyðu* [701]) of *Juliana* echoes the *eardwic uncuð* (93) and the *wic ... uncuð, eard ond eðel* (112) of *Fates*. The word *geomor* is also used here (703), perhaps with reference to humanity (*cyn*), though undoubtedly intertwined with the runic symbols spelling Cynewulf's own name, inviting the audience to decipher some inextricable relationship between the author and the words of the epilogue.[9] Absent in

---

8 For a discussion of the problems associated with translating Cynewulf's runes see further Ralph Elliot, 'Cynewulf's Runes in *Juliana* and *The Fates of the Apostles*,' in *The Cynewulf Reader*, ed. Bjork, 293–307.

9 See further Dolores Warwick Frese, 'The Art of Cynewulf's Runic Signatures,' in *The Cynewulf Reader*, ed. Bjork, 323–45.

Fates is the emphasis on mortal deeds found in *Juliana* (*ærgewyrhtum* ...
dædum ... *ær geworhte in worulde* [702, 707, and 711]), which also appears
in *Elene*, another of Cynewulf's poems in the Vercelli Book. Considering
the repeated language and themes in these two epilogues, then, it is clear that
Cynewulf is deeply interested in the earthly struggle against physical and
spiritual adversity, a subject to which he persistently returns and often in
relation to this journey motif.

Following *The Fates of the Apostles* in the Vercelli Book are thirteen homilies (VI–XVIII) and then a group of three short poems, *Soul and Body I*,
Homiletic Fragment I, and *The Dream of the Rood*. *Soul and Body I* is a
dramatic poem in which a condemned soul rebukes its body for a life of sin.
Personification is the main rhetorical device here, though metaphor also
plays a role. The opening lines of the poem exhort all individuals (*hæleða
æghwylc* [1]) to consider their soul's journey or suffer the consequences in
the afterlife. In contrast to *The Fates of the Apostles*, which emphasizes joy
after a life of hardship, *Soul and Body I* focuses on the eternal sorrows resulting from a life of sinful indulgence. Here is how the poem opens (1–9):

> Huru, ðæs behofað   hæleða æghwylc
> þæt he his sawle sið   sylfa geþence,
> hu þæt bið deoplic   þonne se dead cymeð,
> asyndreð þa sybbe   þe ær samod wæron,
> lic ond sawle!   Lang bið syððan   5
> þæt se gast nimeð   æt Gode sylfum
> swa wite swa wuldor,   swa him on worulde ær
> efne þæt eorðfæt   ær geworhte.
> Sceal se gast cuman   geohðum hremig.
> [Truly, it befits each one of us to consider the soul's journey, how grave it will
> be when death comes, and tears asunder those kin who were once together,
> the soul and body! It will be long afterwards that the soul will receive from
> God himself torment or triumph, depending on what his body has done for
> him in the world before. So the soul will come seething in anguish.]

This is not the glorious ascension of apostles, but the ruinous fall of the
sinful into Hell. In *Soul and Body I*, the consequence of wasting a life in
the service of the body's sensual pleasures is everlasting sorrow and regret.
There is a close parallel to this opening at the end of *Christ II*, the only
other signed poem of Cynewulf appearing in the Exeter Book; the journey
metaphor there is likewise applied to the shared existence of the soul and
body (815–20):

Forþon ic leofra ghwone   læran wille,   815
þæt he ne agæle   gæstes þearfe,
ne on gylp geote,   þenden God wille
þæt he her in worulde   wunian mote,
somed siþian   sawel in lice,
in þam gæsthofe.   820
[So I want to teach each of the dear people, so that he not neglect the soul's
need, nor blurt out in boasting, as long as God wishes that he may be permitted to remain here in the world, and for the soul to travel together in the
body, the spirit's dwelling.]

This partnership of body and soul is extremely common in Old English
literature, especially in homiletic prose, and the poet is surely picking up
on that tradition here.[10] The personified *gast* in the case of *Soul and Body I*
is also alone on a journey ('ic ana ... siðode' [55]), like the narrator of *Fates*,
although its final dwelling place is by no means uncertain, as it is in *Fates*
(103–7):

Fyrnað þus þæt flæschord,   sceall þonne feran onweg,
secan Hellegrund,   nallæs heofondreamas,
dædum gedrefed.   Ligeð dust þær hit wæs,   5
ne mæg him ondsware   ænige gehatan,
geomrum gaste,   geoce oððe frofre.
[So (the soul) will revile that flesh-hoard, when it must journey onward, seek
the depths of Hell, not at all heavenly joys, and be tormented by its previous
deeds. The dust will lie where it was, nor may it (the body) command any
answer from it (the soul), no help or comfort, from that wretched spirit.]

As surely as Simon and Thadeus are bound for heavenly joys in *The Fates of
the Apostles* (*swegle dreamas* [32]), so in contrast is the sinful soul doomed
to the fires of Hell, where heavenly bliss is nowhere to be found ('hellegrund,
nallæs heofondreamas' [4]). There is no hope for the troubled soul (*geomrum gaste* [107]), as with the troubled narrator of *The Fates of Apostles* (*geomrum me* [91]), that any help or comfort ('geoce oððe frofre' [107]) may be
had for the soul's grief. Hope is reserved for the faithful spirit in *Soul and
Body I* (127), which merits comfort and assurance: 'it will be more hopeful
when the holy soul goes to the flesh, surrounding it with comfort' ('Þonne

---

10 For some of the more dramatic scenes between God and the soul and body in the
Vercelli homilies see further especially Vercelli IV (124–287), but also X (101–10).

bið hyhtlicre þæt sio halige sawl / færeð to ðam flesce, frofre gewunden'). At the end of the poem good souls (gastas gode [132]) return to their bodies, offering words of encouragement (156–7): 'Wolde ic þe ðonne secgan þæt ðu ne sorgode, / forðan wyt bioð gegæderode æt Godes dome' ('I want to tell you that you do not have to be sad, for we two will be together at God's judgment'). So, the poem closes with a message of hope, the same message we find at the end of The Fates of the Apostles, despite the emphasis both poems place on sorrow in this life or the next.

In Homiletic Fragment I, many of the same themes are reiterated, although the narrator relies more on direct homiletic exhortation than personification or metaphor.[11] It is true that some verses have been lost between folios 103 and 104 of the manuscript, which contained the final lines of Soul and Body I and the beginning of this piece, but not much has been lost, and the surviving verses coincide with the preceding themes.[12] The opening lines of the poem evoke The Fates of the Apostles by placing emphasis on earthly sorrow: 'sorh cymeð / manig ond mislic in manna dream' ('sorrow comes much and variously upon the joys of men' [1]). Here joy itself (dream) takes the place of the journey metaphor found in the preceding poems (the sið), and the focus turns to the importance of the average individual's earthly deeds (as we find at the end of Juliana). Through a series of admonitions, a prophet-figure (witega [8]) warns the reader of sinful men, the kind of men who speak with 'hunige on muðe' (21) but who are 'marked by their own sins and sorely afflicted' (siofa synnum fah sare geblonden [16]). The faithful man, says the prophet, should embrace spiritual love (gastlice lufe [39]), and wisely attend to the needs of the soul, lest he choose the sins of the world (40–2): 'Forþan eallunga hyht geceoseð, / world wynsume, se ðe wis ne bið, / snottor, searocræftig sawle rædes' ('for he will choose hope altogether, a pleasure-filled world, if he is not wise, prudent, and skilful for the teaching of the soul'). The sense of the word hyht in this instance is surely negative: this is not the hope of the faithful, who struggle and strive to please God, but the blind hope of the idle, who put their trust in this world and ignore their souls. The narrator encourages them to turn to the better way, 'to think and hope that we may possess Heaven's light' ('hycgan ond hyhtan, þæt we heofones leoht ... agan moton' [44]). Again, the concluding emphasis falls upon that same spirit of hopefulness seen at the end of Soul and Body I and The Fates of the Apostles.

---

11 See the essay by Jonathan Randle above, 185–224.
12 See further ASPR 1, xxxviii–xxxix, for a discussion on the loss of leaves between folios 103 and 104.

In *The Dream of the Rood*, there is a much closer relationship between the narrator and the subject matter of the poem than we have seen thus far.[13] In *Soul and Body I* and *Homiletic Fragment I*, a prophet-figure (*witega*) dispenses wisdom from a distance, while Cynewulf's narrator in *The Fates of the Apostles* never relates his own sorrow to that of the poem's chief protagonists. This is not the case in *The Dream of the Rood*. At first, the dreamer is struck only by his own sinfulness in relation to the glorious rood (13–20): ('Syllic wæs se sigebeam, ond ic synnum fah, / forwunded mid wommum … eall ic wæs mid sorgum gedrefed' ('wondrous was that triumphant cross, and I marked by sins, wounded by misdeeds … I was entirely afflicted with sorrow'). This is the same grief-stricken egotism that dominates Cynewulf's narrator in *Fates* and *Elene*, but through his interaction with the personified cross, the narrator of *The Dream of the Rood* discovers a life of sorrow to which he can relate. Using the very same language as the dreamer, the cross tells how it, too, was once overcome with grief (59): 'Sare ic wæs mid sorgum gedrefed.' By repeating the phrase, *sorgum gedrefed*, the poet makes a deliberate connection between the dreamer and the rood that does not exist, for example, between the narrator and Christ's disciples in *The Fates of the Apostles*. Once the poet has made this connection, it is apparent that the dreamer is on the same path as the rood towards the revelation of Christ's love and the fulfilment of heavenly joy. In fact, the dreamer is so inspired by the story of Christ and the redemptive power of the cross, 'through which every spirit shall seek the kingdom of Heaven from this earthly path' ('ac ðurh ða rode sceal rice gesecan / of eorðwege æghwylc sawl' [119–20]), that he awakens, literally, from his grief and becomes eager for the journey to Heaven (122–6):

> Gebæd ic me þa to þan beame   bliðe mode,
> elne mycle,   þær ic ana wæs
> mæte werede.   Wæs modsefa
> afysed on forðwege,   feala ealra gebad   125
> langunghwila.
> [I entrusted myself to that cross with a joyful heart, with great zeal, where I was alone with little company. My heart was eager for the onward way, and I suffered many moments of longing.]

So, now with a joyful heart (*bliðe mode* [122]), the dreamer longs to join Christ in Heaven; and though he is alone, *ana* (123), like Cynewulf's

---

13 See the essay by Andy Orchard above, 225–53.

narrator (93) and the wretched spirit of *Soul and Body I* (55), the dreamer is possessed of a feeling of hopefulness which they both lack (127–9):

> Is me nu lifes hyht
> þæt ic þone sigebeam   secan mote
> ana oftor   þonne ealle men,
> well weorþian.
> [There is now hope for me in life that I might seek out that triumphant cross alone more often than all men, and honour it well.]

The dreamer is like one of Cynewulf's apostles, looking forward to joy (*dream*) and the fellowship of the saintly hosts – that same heavenly flock that Cynewulf honours in *The Fates of Apostles* ('þone halgan heap' [90]). The dreamer says, 'þær ic syþþan mot wunian on wuldre, well mid þam halgum dreames brucan' ('there I may dwell in glory afterward and fully experience joy among those saints' [42–4]). Possessed by new inspiration and joyfulness, the narrator of the *Dream of the Rood* ends the poem with a proliferation of words for 'bliss,' culminating in Christ's own victorious journey (*siðfate*) into Heaven (139–53): 'þær is blis micel ... þær is singal blis ... hiht was geniwad / mid bledum ond blisse ... Se sunu wæs sigorfæst on þam siðfate ... englum to blis' ('there is great bliss ... there is eternal bliss ... hope was renewed with inspiration and bliss ... the son was firm in glory on that journey ... as bliss for angels'). Note that the final lines again place strong emphasis on the journey to Heaven and hope ('hiht was geniwad'). The *Dream of the Rood*, therefore, presents a model road for Christians, in which the grief of mortal existence is reversed by Christ's sacrifice and victorious journey into Heaven.

Struggle and redemption are also central themes in *Andreas*, Vercelli's first and longest poem, where the apostles Andrew and Matthew strive to save themselves and their persecutors, the cannibal Mermedonians. Matthew's journey (*æðelinges sið* [44]) is undertaken to convert the flesh-eating Mermedonians, but this trip goes terribly wrong, and the saint quickly finds himself blinded, drugged, and imprisoned. Here Matthew is resolute (*onmod* [54]) and praises God defiantly in his heart ('herede in heortan heofonrices weard' [52]), but he also cries out in despair (54–67):

> Eadig ond onmod,   he mid elne forð
> wyrðode wordum   wuldres aldor,   55
> heofonrices weard,   halgan stefne,

of carcerne.   Him wæs Cristes lof
on fyrhðlocan   fæste bewunden.
He þa wepende   weregum tearum
his sigedryhten   sargan reorde   60
grette, gumena brego,   geomran stefne,
weoruda wilgeofan,   ond þus wordum cwæð:
'Hu me elþeodige   inwitwrasne
searonet seowað!   A ic symles wæs
on wega gehwam   willan þines   65
georn on mode;   nu ðurh geohða sceal
dæde fremman   swa þa dumban neat.

[Blessed and resolute, with courage he praised the prince of glory continually in words, the guardian of Heaven's kingdom with a holy voice from his cell. The praise of Christ was firmly bound within his breast. Then, weeping with weary tears, he addressed his Lord of victory, leader of men, with sorrowful speech, and [called out to] the generous God of hosts with a sad voice, saying: 'Help me! A foreign people sows hateful bonds and cunning snares for me! I have always been eager in my heart to do your will in every way; now, in anguish, I am forced to act like speechless beasts do.']

Note the juxtaposition of *halgan stefne* (56) and *geomran stefne* (61); Matthew's voice is a holy one, devoted to God, but also one that is weakened by doubt and hopelessness. Only God's brilliant voice (in contrast to the sad voice of Matthew) brings healing and comfort to the sorrowful laments of the saint: 'he his maguþegne under hearmlocan / hælo and frofre beadurofum abead beorhtan stefne ... ne beo ðu on sefan to forht' ('he offered healing and comfort to his servant with a brilliant [or clear] voice ... do not be too fearful of heart' [94–8]). Note here the same comforting message that is given to the good souls in *Soul and Body I* (156–7). Here, too, is the same comfort (*frofre*) that Cynewulf's narrator prays for in *The Fates of the Apostles* (*frofre* [109]). With God's intervention, then, Matthew is emboldened for a time ('ða wæs Matheus miclum onbryrded / niwan stefne' [122–3]), but he slips back into despair before Andreas arrives to rescue him. Matthew still offers praise to God in prison (*secgan dryhtne lof* [1006]), but left alone in the gloom of his cell, he is once more helpless to contain his sorrow (1007–8): 'He ðær ana sæt / geohðum geomor in þam gnornhofe' ('There he sat, alone in anguish, miserable in that wretched cell'). The recurrence of the word *geomor* reminds the reader of Matthew's earlier grief (*geomran stefne* [61]); the weight of sorrow is also strongly emphasized by the three alliterating words for sadness, 'geohðum ... geomor ... gnornhof' (8).[14] Only with his deliverance from prison is hope finally renewed for the sorrowful Matthew ('hiht was geniwad' [1010]).

The hero Andreas is subject to this same human vulnerability. From the beginning, Andreas tries to avoid making the perilous journey at all, saying that he does not have the time to go or really know the way (190–3). God immediately rebukes the saint for this hesitation, telling Andreas that he has no choice but to make the journey (203–14): 'Eala, Andreas, þæt ðu a woldest / þæs siðfætes sæne weorþan ... (211) Ne meaht ðu þæs siðfætes sæne weorðan ... gif ðu wel þencest / wið þinne waldend wære gehealdan.' ('Alas, Andreas, that you would be cowardly in that journey ... you cannot be cowardly in the journey ... if you intend to keep your pact with the Lord'). In the parallel account of the life of Andreas in *The Fates of the Apostles*, the saint does not 'waver before the might of any king on earth' ('Ne þreodode he fore þrymme ðeodcyninges, / æniges on eorðan' [18]), but here he is afraid of the journey (*siðfætes sæne* [211]), unlike the apostle James in *Fates* ('næs ... siðes sæne' [33–4]). Andreas's fear is justified, however, since he ends up in the same prison from which he rescues Matthew and subject to the same torments. In terms that invite the reader to recall Matthew's earlier plight, Andreas calls out to the Lord, unable to endure further torture from the Mermedonians (1398–1400):

> Ongan þa geomormod   to Gode cleopian,
> heard of hæfte,   halgan stefne
> weop werigferð.
> [Then, sorrowful, he began to call out to God, bravely from his fetters and with a holy voice he wept, weary-hearted.]

Here is that same holy voice reduced to grief (*halgan stefne* [1399]) and the weary-hearted weeping (*weop weriferð* [1400] that are expressed by Matthew earlier in the poem ('halgan stefne ... wepende weregum tearum' [56–9]). The word *geomormod* (1398) is also present, which connects the sorrowful lament of Andreas to the woeful voice of Matthew (*geomran stefne* [61]). So great is the sorrow of Andreas, however, that he compares his own suffering to that of Christ. Calling out to the Lord, Andreas begs Christ to remember his own death upon the cross and the plea He made to

---

14 Prison and Hell are often described in the same terms in poetry as a *hof* or *ham* of some kind, especially one that restricts; see, for example, *Juliana, engan ham* (323, Hell), *grornhofe* (324, Hell), *reongan ham* (530, Hell), *engan hofe* (532, Juliana's cell).

His Father (1406–13): 'Hwæt, þu sigora weard ... mid Iudeum geomor wurde ... ond cwæde ... fæder engla ... hwæt forlætest ðu me?' ('Lo you, Lord of victories, became sad among the Jews and said, 'father of angels, why have you forsaken me?'). Using a rhetorical strategy similar to that in *The Dream of the Rood*, where the repetition of *sorgum gedrefed* connects the dreamer to the cross, the *Andreas* poet uses the word *geomor* to relate Andreas's suffering to that of Christ.[15] Of course, Andreas is not asked to make the ultimate sacrifice, and God has already told him that the Mermedonians will not be allowed to 'deal death to his body' ('ne magon hie ... þinne lichoman ... deaðe gedælan' [1215–17]). As promised, God brings healing and comfort to the afflictions of the faithful saint (1462–7): 'þa com dryhten God ... ond frofre gecwæð ... heht his lichoman / hales brucan' ('Then the Lord God came ... and spoke words of comfort to the saint and commanded his body to be healed'). Again, here is the same *frofor* (1465) that God brings to Matthew and which is sought and cherished by the individuals in the poems already mentioned.

Now, unlike Matthew and Andreas, the Mermedonians do not place their hope in God at all; nor do they have any interest in the soul's journey or the path to salvation (154–6):

> Feorh ne bemurndan,
> grædige guðrincas,   hu þæs gastes sið
> æfter swyltcwale   geseted wurde
> [They did not care about the spirit, greedy battle-warriors, how the soul's journey might be set after death.]

The Mermedonians are doing exactly the opposite of what the poet of *Homiletic Fragment I* exhorts, which is to give thought to the soul's journey (1–2). Until the flood at the end of the poem, a metaphorical baptism, the Mermedonians are ravenously sinful (1072–3): 'wendan ond woldon wiðer-hycgende / þæt hie on elþeodigum æt geworhton' ('they expected and wished, being perverted, to make food out of those foreigners'). The focus of the Mermedonians is firmly set upon this world, because they desire only human flesh (113–15): 'þeod wæs oflysted, / metes modgeomre' ('the people were filled with longing, desperate in their hearts for food'). The term *modgeomre* is conspicuous here, the inverse form, *geomormod*, being applied to Andreas (1398); and although the source of grief is different from anything

---

15 See too Frederick M. Biggs, 'The Passion of Andreas: *Andreas* 1398–1491,' *Studies in Philology* 85 (1988): 413–27.

we have seen thus far, the anguish of the Mermedonians is profound and genuine. What is more, the word *modgeomor* is used like the word *geomor* in *The Fates of the Apostles* to create a thematic envelope pattern. This pattern occurs after the conversion of the Mermedonians and after Andreas has instructed them in Christianity, 'the true path of life' ('lærde þa þa leode on geleafan weg' [1680]). Following their conversion, the Mermedonians set aside their hunger for human flesh, and desire only the fellowship and teaching of the saint. When Andreas prepares to leave, the Mermedonians suffer anguish (*geomriende geohðu* [1695]), and are full of grief at the prospect of being separated from him (1708): 'mæcgas modgeomore. Þær manegum wæs hat æt heortan hyge weallende' ('the people [were] sorrowful. Many a heart was welling hot in its breast').[16] This is the second and only other occurrence of the word *modgeomor* in the Vercelli Book, and its repetition reminds the reader of the Mermedonians' former hunger for flesh (*metes modgeomre* [115]). That hunger has now changed, and the people's craving, once only for the sinful consumption of human flesh – a perversion of the feast of the Holy Communion – has become spiritual in nature. Their former gluttony has been replaced by a genuine and wholesome desire for the Christian way of life (*geleafan weg* [1680]) and spiritual food.[17] A similar communion metaphor appears in *Soul and Body I*, where the soul chastises the body for glutting itself on earthly meat and drink, while the soul thirsts for the spiritual blood and body of Christ (39–41): 'Wære þu þe wiste wlonc ond wines sæd; / þrymful þunedest ond ic ofþyrsted wæs godes lichoman gæstes drinces' ('You were proud of eating and full of wine; you boasted gloriously and I was thirsting for the body of God and blood of the spirit'). The *Andreas* poet therefore places cannibalism in the context of worldly gluttony, suggesting that all forms of selfish consumption are sinful. In *Andreas* we find the same aversion to earthly indulgence, the same message

---

16 See further the lament of the sailors in *Andreas* (405–6): 'Hwider hweorfað we hlafordleas, / geomormode, gode orfeorme / synnum wunde, gif we swicað þe?' ('Where shall we turn, sad at heart, deprived of your goodness, wounded by sins, if we abandon you?'). For other poems in which *geomormod* in particular signals the fear or reality of exile, see, for example, *Beowulf* (2894 and 3018–20); *Genesis A* (858–9 and 927–31) *The Wife's Lament* (1, 17, 19, and 42); *Judith* (147); *The Phoenix* (139, 353, 412, and 517, 556); *Christ I* (90, 124, 154, and 173), *Christ II* (499 and 535); *Descent into Hell* (52); and *Resignation* (95).

17 See further Robert Boenig, *Saint and Hero: Andreas and Medieval Doctrine* (London: Bucknell Univ. Press, 1991), esp. chapter 3, 'Andreas, the Eucharist and Vercelli,' 55–77; and David Hamilton, 'The Diet and Digestion of Allegory in *Andreas*,' *ASE* 1 (1972): 147–58.

of caution that we see throughout the Vercelli Book; that is, do not put your hope in this world. The journeys of Andreas and Matthew are therefore part of their own spiritual progress towards Heaven, although their suffering is secondary to their mission of converting the Mermedonians.

This theme of conversion is of central importance in Vercelli's final poem, *Elene*, where visions of the cross inspire the poem's chief characters to set out on the Christian journey.[18] On the eve before his battle with the Huns and Hrethgoths, emperor Constantine is troubled by thoughts of defeat, and his heart is weighed down with care (*modsorge wæg* [61]). When at last he falls asleep, a messenger from Heaven appears and reveals a symbol (*sigores tacen* [85]) with which he may overcome his enemies. The revelation of the cross here has the same redemptive effect on Constantine as it does upon the narrator of the *Dream of the Rood*, and the emperor awakens at once from his previous sorrow (96–8): 'Cyning wæs þy bliðra / ond þe sorgleasra, secga aldor, / on fyrhðsefan, þurh þa fægeran gesyhð' ('the king, the prince of men, was the happier and the less sorrowful at heart because of that fair vision'). Soon afterward, Constantine learns about the life and passion of Christ and turns to Christianity (191). Notice how Cynewulf focuses on comfort and hopefulness in describing Constantine's new state of mind (195–7):

> Wæs him niwe gefea
> befolen in fyrhðe,   wæs him frofra mæst
> and hyhta nihst   heofonrices weard.
> [A new joy entered his heart, and the guardian of Heaven's kingdom became the greatest of comforts and nearest of hopes for him.]

This is the very same language of hopefulness that Cynewulf uses at the end of *The Fates of the Apostles* (115–22) and which continues to highlight shared interests of the poems of this manuscript.

In fact, Elene herself is described in terms similar to Cynewulf's apostles. In the scene where Constantine commands her to go in search of the cross, for example, the emperor is like God and Elene a faithful apostle (219–24):

> Elene ne wolde
> þæs siðfates   sæne weorðan,   220
> ne ðæs wilgifan   word gehyrwan,

---

18 See further the essay by Manish Sharma above, 280–97.

hiere sylfre suna,   ac wæs sona gearu,
wif on willsið,   swa hire weoruda helm,
byrnwiggendra,   beboden hæfde.
[Elene did not wish to be slow in the journey, nor to despise the words of her
gracious giver, her own son; rather she was ready at once, the woman on that
wished-for journey, as the lord of the hosts, of armed men, had commanded.]

Were it not for the specific references to Elene and her son ('hiere sylfre
suna' [222]), this passage might refer to any of the pilgrims in *The Fates of
the Apostles*; like the apostle James, who is undaunted by his mission ('næs
... siðes sæne' [34]), Elene herself does not hesitate ('ne ... siðfates sæne'
[219–20]). Furthermore, the epithet applied to Constantine, *weoruda helm*
(223), is evocative of many such formulaic epithets for God elsewhere. In
Andreas, for example, the Lord is the *weoruda drihten* (173) when he
sends Andreas across the sea to rescue Matthew ('þu scealt feran ... siðe
gesecan' [174–5]); unlike Elene, Andreas is afraid to make the journey ('ne
meaht ðu þæs siðfætes sæne' [204, 211]). Note the repeated use of the
phrase *siðfætes sæne*, related to all the individuals here. The more important issue, however, is that Cynewulf empowers Elene with a strength of
character that rivals that of the apostles themselves. In Old English, *ellen*
means 'strength' or 'courage,' and Anglo-Saxon audiences of *Elene* could
not have missed the play on words associated with the poem's heroine.[19]

Elene is a bold and resolute ambassador of the Christian faith, and she
is determined to carry out her mission; in fact, she is the voice of Christianity
itself in the second half of the poem.[20] Her efforts are frustrated, however,
by the poem's chief antagonists. From the beginning, Cynewulf harshly
condemns the Jewish people for the crucifixion of Christ (210–11): 'þæs
hie in hynðum sculon/ to widan feore wergðu dreogan!' ('for that they
must suffer torment forever in humiliation'). The tension between Elene
and the Jewish elders is developed in a series of meetings, the council sequence of the poem, in which Elene continually condemns the elders as
she demands that they find someone who can reveal the location of the

---

19 For definitions of the word *ellen* see further *DOE*.
20 See further Catherine A. Regan, 'Evangelicism as the Informing Principle in Cynewulf's
    Elene,' *Traditio* 54 (1973): 27–52, repr. in *The Cynewulf Reader*, ed. Bjork, 251–80. See
    also Thomas D. Hill, 'Sapiential Structure and Figural Narrative in the Old English
    Elene,' ibid., 207–28 (originally in *Traditio* 27 [1971]: 159–77), and Joseph Wittig,
    'Figural Narrative in Cynewulf's *Juliana*,' ibid., 147–69, who views Juliana as a possible
    figural character for the Church (esp. 158–62).

cross.[21] Threatened with death, the elders hand over Judas, whose name accords with *Iudea cyn* (290), making him an ideal typological figure.[22] From this point forward the conflict between Christianity and Judaism is reduced to the interaction between Elene and Judas. Ultimately, Judas is left with the choice of cooperating or dying ('swa life swa deað' [606]), and he is troubled not just by the loss of his life but the loss of his faith as well (627–31):

Iudas maðelode,   (him wæs geomor sefa)
hat æt heortan   ond gehwæðres wa,
ge he heofonrices   hyht swa mode
ond þis ondwearde   anforlete,   630
rice under roderum,   ge he ða rode ne tæhte.
[Judas spoke up, his heart was troubled and burned within his breast – and the grief of either choice! – that he must give up his inner hope of the heavenly kingdom, and forfeit this present kingdom beneath the heavens, if he did not reveal the cross to her.]

The language here, especially the use of the word *geomor* in relation to spiritual dispondence, is very Cynewulfian; note the familiar emphasis on hope and the heavenly kingdom (629). For Judas and the whole Jewish people, sorrow is ended only at conversion, and just as with emperor Constantine and the narrator in *The Dream of the Rood*, it is the vision of the cross that renews joy for Judas (839–42):

Þa wæs modgemynd   myclum geblissod
hige onhyrded,   þurh þæt halige treo,
inbryrded breostsefa,   syððan beacen geseh,
halig under hrusan.
[Then his spirit was greatly overjoyed, his breast emboldened, by that holy tree, and his heart was inspired when he saw that holy symbol beneath the earth.]

Just moments later, the Jewish people likewise rejoice when they behold the power of the cross to resurrect a lifeless body (889–92):

---

21 Note the recurrent use of the verb *nægan* ('to harass') throughout this sequence (287, 385, 559).
22 For the figural significance behind the character of Judas see further Thomas Hill, 'Sapiential Structure and Figural Narrative,' 211; Regan, 'Evangelicism as the Informing Principle in Cynewulf's *Elene*,' 257–62; and Calder, *Cynewulf*, 110.

þær wæs lof hafen
fæger mid þy folc.   Fæder weorðodon,
ond þone soðan   sunu wealdendes
wordum heredon.
[There praise was raised fairly among that people. They worshipped the father and glorified the true son of the Lord with words.]

As in *Andreas*, one of the central concerns of *Elene* is conversion; and although the journey motif is less prominently expressed in terms of the word *sið*, there is still a strong emphasis on the act of conversion as a means to end earthly grief and renew hope and joy.

Cynewulf does return to the *sið* metaphor at the end of *Elene*, however. In the epilogue to the poem he once again returns to his narrator-persona for reflection and conclusion. Now, old and wise with the knowledge of years, the narrator of *Elene* looks back upon his life with a contented spirit (1236–51):

> ...
> Ic wæs weorcum fah,
> synnum asæled,   sorgum gewæled,
> bitrum gebunden,   bisgum beþrungen,   1245
> ær me lare onlag   þurh leohtne had
> gamelum to geoce,   gife unscynde
> mægencyning amæt   ond on gemynd begeat,
> torht ontynde,   tidum gerymde,
> bancofan onband,   breostlocan onwand,   1250
> leoðucræft onleac.   Þæs ic lustum breac,
> willum in worlde.
> [I was marked by my deeds, bound by sins, overwhelmed by sorrow, constrained and oppressed by bitter troubles, before the almighty king granted me wisdom (*lar*) through that bright symbol as a comfort to an old man; He granted uncorrupted grace, and poured it into my consciousness, revealed its brightness, increased it at times, unbound my body, opened up my heart, and unlocked my skill for poetry. This I have used with passion and joy in the world.]

Like the narrator of the *Dream of the Rood* (and *Juliana*), the poet-persona of *Elene* has suffered through many earthly cares ('Ic wæs weorcum fah, / synnum asæled, sorgum gewæled' [1242–3]), and ultimately finds solace in the cross, a comfort for his old age ('þurh leohtne had / gamelum to geoce' [1245]). The narrator of *Elene* sees that his own journey is near its end, and if we believe him to be the same narrator as the one in *The Fates of the Apostles*, it is here at last that he finally finds peace of mind.

All the Vercelli poems strive to leave this impression of hopefulness, despite their persistent emphasis on earthly sorrows. There is just enough grief in the poetry, just enough fear for the future, to stress the importance of living well in this world. The journey motif is the ideal way to focus on the inevitability of suffering without making it the final destination of existence. Many of the Vercelli homilies, such as Vercelli VII (quoted at the opening of this discussion), contain similar passages, where life is described as a voyage; the rhetorical function of the motif in these cases is also not to discourage but persuade the audience to prepare their souls for Heaven. The judgment-day homilies in Vercelli (notably II, IV, VIII, and IX) also juxtapose the passing joys and cares of this world against the eternity of salvation or damnation.[23] Much remains to be said about the relationships between the verse and prose texts of the manuscript, but for the moment, this discussion has shown at least one point of convergence among the poems of the Vercelli Book.

---

23 See, for example, the *her-þær* topos, one of the most common rhetorical devices in the homilies, which is used to contrast the transience of this world with the eternity of Heaven (for example, *VH* IV.1–56 and IX.1–15).

The Vercelli Book and Its Texts:
A Guide to Scholarship

PAUL G. REMLEY

The following bibliography, extracted from a lengthy work in progress and revised for the present collection, contains eight sections: Vercelli Book (pp. 319–28); *Andreas* (pp. 328–46); *The Fates of the Apostles* (pp. 346–51); *Soul and Body I* (pp. 351–6); *Homiletic Fragment I* (pp. 356–7); *The Dream of the Rood* (pp. 357–78); *Elene* (pp. 378–92); and *Vercelli Homilies* (pp. 392–415). The new work just mentioned is a revised edition of *A Bibliography of Publications on Old English Literature to the End of 1972*, by Stanley B. Greenfield and Fred C. Robinson (Toronto: UTP, 1980), an edition which has been updated to take in scholarship appearing since 1972. The revised edition is currently in preparation under the direction of Professor Andy Orchard and myself. All new entries have been based directly on the original works or have been checked against multiple independent reports. The identification of neglected items has been aided considerably by reference to the following sources: the annual bibliographies in *Anglo-Saxon England* and the *Old English Newsletter*; the *MLA International Bibliography*; the *International Medieval Bibliography*; *OCLC WorldCat*; and *Iter: Gateway to the Middle Ages and Renaissance*. Above all, the painstaking work of Professor Carl T. Berkhout, in his annual contributions to the first two of these publications from 1976 through 2000, has bolstered the integrity of the final production. The assistance of Professor Thomas N. Hall is gratefully acknowledged for the later entries.

It became clear at an early stage of preparation that the length of this guide would increase exponentially if an attempt were made to follow up promising references in works cited in the existing compilation of entries, and then to follow up references uncovered in those sources, and so on. Moreover, it seemed impractical and quite possibly inappropriate to offer a full analysis of the literature treating the Cynewulfian canon, the Ruthwell Cross, *Soul and Body II*, and other related topics, or to catalogue the editions of individual poems appearing in pedagogical works. Finally, the possibility of summarizing the wide range of materials now available online – and in other electronically encoded formats – had to be rejected out of hand. Such an undertaking will be the proper brief of another sort of compilation altogether. Nevertheless, I have sought to cover certain types of print materials exhaustively, most notably those that refer to the Vercelli Book, its verse, or its prose at the level of the wording of their titles. Moreover, I have tried to seek out and to record significant scholarly treatments of the manuscript and its texts, regardless of length or larger context, whenever they have entered my purview. Specifically, with regard to the *Vercelli Homilies*, an effort has been made in entry **834** to bring together references to existing editions of texts offering later witness to individual homilies, editions of the most important analogues, and other relevant texts. I should be grateful to users of this guide for any advice regarding presentation or omissions that might be taken into account in the preparation of the compendious bibliography noted above.

Vercelli Book

FACSIMILE EDITIONS

- [Cooper, Charles Purton, et al., eds.] ca. 1834–7. See item **18**. [Fols. 43r, 49r (initial), 75v (before damage).]
1 Wülker, Richard P., ed. *Codex Vercellensis. Die angelsächsische Handschrift zu Vercelli in getreuer Nachbildung.* Leipzig: von Veit, 1894. Pp. viii + 87. [Partial, reduced facs., including reproductions of eighty-three pp. containing verse; photography by Ludwig Lange; credited to 'R. Wülker.'] Reviews: [Anon.], *Nation* 60 (1895): 73; B. Assmann, *Beiblatt zur 'Anglia'* 6 (1896): 103; K.D. Bülbring, *Museum. Tijdschrift voor filologie en geschiedenis* 3 (1895): 93–4.
2 Förster, Max, intro. *Il Codice Vercellese con omelie e poesie in lingua anglosassone. Per concessione del ven. Capitolo metropolitano di Vercelli la prima volta interamente riprodotto in fototipia.* Rome: Danesi, 1913. Pp. 70 + [6] + [272]. [Fols. 1–136 in reduced facs., augmented by facs. of 29v, 133v, at full size, on two folded leaves; photographed in the course of restoration in the Biblioteca Apostolica Vaticana, ca. 1911–12; intro. credited to 'Prof. dott. Massimiliano Foerster.'] Reviews: R. Brotanek, *Beiblatt zur 'Anglia'* 26 (1915): 225–38; B. Fehr, *Deutsche Literaturzeitung* 36 (1915): cols. 2589–90; W. Keller, *ASNSL* 139 (1919): 233–5; F. Klaeber, *JEGP* 18 (1919): 476–80.

3 Sisam, Celia, ed. *The Vercelli Book: A Late Tenth-Century Manu-script Containing Prose and Verse, Vercelli Biblioteca capitolare CXVII.* EEMF 19. Copenhagen: Rosenkilde and Bagger, 1976. Pp. 60 + [10] + [2] + [272]. [Includes quiring diagram on folded leaf.] Reviews: M.-C. Garand, *Scriptorium* 32 (1978): 166–7; H. Gneuss, *Anglia* 103 (1985): 455–61; M. Lehnert, *Deutsche Literaturzeitung für Kritik der internationalen Wissenschaft* 105 (1984): cols. 515–17.

STUDIES

4 [Anon.] Inventory of cathedral library at Vercelli. Manuscript. 1426. [Possible reference to Vercelli Book as *liber omeliarum antiquis-simum* [sic] *non habens principium nec finem.* See item 3, p. 45.]
5 Leone, Giovanni Francesco. Inventory of cathedral library at Vercelli. Manuscript. 1602. [Pub. in item 10, 4: 567–70; probable reference to Vercelli Book as *liber Gothicus, sive Langobardus,* with comment 'eum legere non valeo.' See item 10, 4: 568, and, further, 41, p. 1547.]
6 [Anon.] Record of pastoral visitation to cathedral at Vercelli. Manu-script. 1664. [Possible reference to Vercelli Book as a volume [*in*] *lingua Hebraica uel ignota conscriptum.* See item 3, p. 45.]
7 Bianchini, Giuseppe Maria. Letter to Carlo Vittorio delle Lancie. Manuscript. 1748. [Pub. in item 10, 4: 554–60. Contains earliest known remarks treating Vercelli Book at some length, citing Latin phraseology from *Vercelli Homilies* VI, XV–XVIII, and offering an inaccurate transcript of some forty-seven words of OE from *Vercelli Homily* XVI. See further item 2, pp. 40–2.]
8 — Inventory of cathedral library at Vercelli. Manuscript. 1750. [Pub. in item 10, 4: 562–6. Contains entry for Vercelli Book, 4: 565: '(CXVII) Codex saeculi X. Liber ignotae linguae. Videtur *liber Homiliarius per anni circulum,* ut constat ex nonnullis rubricis latine conscriptis; linguae Theotiscae.' See further item 41, p. 1547.]
9 [Anon.] Inventory of cathedral library at Vercelli. 1768 × 1778. Two copies extant in manuscript. [Includes entry describing Vercelli Book: 'CXVII 42 / Codex membran. in fol. saec. IX vel X. nitide et distincte exscriptus Saxonico charactere. De eo specimen damus, ut de idio-mate etiam judicent eruditi. Theotisco idiomate conscriptum esse conjicimus: Verum otium nobis non fuit rem penitius considerare.' For full text, see item 41, pp. 1547–8.]
10 De Gregori, Gaspare. *Istoria della vercellese letteratura ed arti.* 4 vols. in 3. Turin: Chirio e Mina, 1819–24. Pp. 560, [311], 308, 584. [In vol. 4,

pub. in 1824, De Gregori prints a series of texts providing evidence for consultation of the Vercelli Book from the seventeeth century to the eighteenth. See items **5, 7–8**. All vols. are attributed to 'G. De-Gregory.']

11 Blume, Friedrich. *Iter Italicum.* 4 vols. Berlin: Nicolai, 1824–36. Vol. 1, pp. xxx + 272. 1824. Vol. 2, pp. vii + 247. 1827. Vol. 3, pp. iv + 230. 1830. Vol. 4, pp. x + 364. 1836. [In vol. 1, subtitled *Archive, Bibliotheken und Inschriften in den sardinischen und österreichischen Provinzen*, Blume, then professor of law at Halle an der Saale, initiates modern study of the Vercelli Book with the first printed notice of his consultation of the manuscript, undertaken in the course of a visit to Vercelli over 27 Oct.–19 Nov. 1822: 'Vercelli,' 1: 87–101, citing, p. 99, 'Legenden oder Homilien in angelsäxischer Sprache'; see further items **12–13, 17, 19**.]

12 — 'Vermischte Nachrichten von italiänischen Bibliotheken und Archiven im Sommer 1822.' *Archiv der Gesellschaft für ältere deutsche Geschichtskunde* 5 (1824–5): 575–92. ['Vercelli,' pp. 585–9, with brief notice of 'Sammlung von Homilien in angelsächsischer Sprache,' p. 585. The present sect. of vol. 5 of the *Archiv* was pub. in 1825. The article is credited to 'Prof. Bluhme in Halle.' This notice was erroneously attributed to G.H. Pertz, author of the preceding article in the vol., in a range of later sources. See, e.g., the bibliographical ghosts in items **22**, pp. 189–90; **36**, p. 17; **53**, p. 22, no. 239.]

13 — 'Juristische Handschriften in Italien. Zugaben zum *Iter Italicum*.' *Rheinisches Museum für Jurisprudenz* (Göttingen) 4·(1832–3): 233–309, 327–80. [In fasc. 2 of vol. 4 of the periodical, pub. in 1832, Blume affirms, p. 234, that cited *homiliarum liber incognito sermone scriptus* is 'ein angelsächsisches Homiliarium.' He includes an inaccurate transcript of some thirty words from the incipit of *Vercelli Homily* XVII, embodying changes ascribed to Jacob Grimm and Wilhelm Grimm, who have also supplied a trans.; see item **2**, pp. 42–3; the two sects. of the article are credited to 'Blume.']

14 Maier, C. 'Beschreibung der Handschrift des Domcapitels zu Vercelli no. CXVII.' Adjunct to transcript of texts in Vercelli Book. Manuscript. 1833 or 1834. [Two-page description of Vercelli Book, now detached from transcript in item **16**; the present London, Lincoln's Inn, Misc. 225, 43r–v; first pub. in item **43**; reissued in **3**, pp. 48–9, with complete facs. as plates I–II.]

15 — 'Beilage zur Beschreibung des Cod. capit. Vercell. n. CXVII.' Adjunct to transcript of texts in Vercelli Book. Manuscript. 1833 or 1834. [Notes on quiring of Vercelli Book. The present London,

Lincoln's Inn, Misc. 312, 1r; now bound with transcript in item 16;
ed. in 43, pp. 3–4; facs. in item 3, plate III.]
16 — 'Cod. Vercell. capit. CXVII.' Transcript of texts in Vercelli Book.
Manuscript. 1833–4. [Product of an undertaking initiated in a letter
dated 18 Sept. 1832, sent by Johann Martin Lappenberg, archivist at
Hamburg and widely published historian, to Charles Purton Cooper,
Secretary to the Commissioners of the Public Records, in London.
The transcript produced by Maier had been commissioned by Sept.
1833 and was completed at Vercelli over Oct. 1833–Mar. 1834. Now
preserved as London, Lincoln's Inn, Misc. 312, fols. 2–136. See further
items 14–15; 18; 36; 43; 318; and esp. 3, pp. 48–9, with representative
facs. in plates IV–X.]
17 Blume, Friedrich. *Bibliotheca librorum manuscriptorum Italica.*
*Indices bibliothecarum Italiae ex schedis Maieri Eslingensis, Haenelii
Lipsiensis, Gottlingii Ienensis, Car. Wittii, suisque propriis, in suple-
mentum* [sic] *'Itineris Italici.'* Göttingen: Dieterich, 1834. Pp. iv +
272. ['Vercellae. Bibliothecae Capituli,' pp. 5–7; Blume, p. 6, offering
a comment on the script of the Vercelli Book, here treats *homiliarum
liber lingua Anglosaxonica elegantissime scriptus*, therein reproducing,
in all essentials, his notice in item 13. The work as a whole is credited
to 'Fridericus Blume i. C. Hamburgensis.']
18 [Thorpe, Benjamin, ed.] Untitled *editio princeps* of Vercelli poems. In
*Appendices to a Report on Rymer's 'Foedera' Intended to Have Been
Made to the Late Commissioners on Public Records,* [ed. Charles
Purton Cooper et al.], appendix B, pp. 47–138. 5 vols. in 3. Printed,
London: [Commissioners of the Public Records], ca. 1834–7. Pub.,
London: [Public Record Office], 1869. Comprising appendices A,
pp. [260] + 116, 93 plates (37 folded); B, pp. 165, 11 plates (8 folded);
C, pp. xiv + [158], 2 plates; D, pp. 542; E, pp. [366] + 160 (ends
incomplete). [Thorpe's ed., printed in 1834, is based on the transcript
made by C. Maier. See items 14–16 and, for the date of printing, item
3, p. 49 with n. 2. The plates, many using colour, include facsimiles of
fols. 43r, 49r (initial), 75v, the first and last of these offering images
unaffected by damage linked to the application of a reagent. The
work of the Commissioners of the Public Records was suspended in
1837. Sects. printed to that date were not distributed formally until
1869, but Thorpe's ed. did circulate before their release, forming the
basis of several editions of texts in the Vercelli Book; see items 69–70,
72, 341, 405, 408; cf. 480, 839, 841. The printed sects. were issued in
1869 as appendices '(A.),' '(B.),' '(C.),' '(D.),' accompanied by pt. 1

of the untitled appendix E and a fragment of pt. 2. The title given here has been taken verbatim from a sheet containing an explanation of the delayed release, signed by M.R. Romilly and dated 19 May 1869, which was inserted into the distributed vols. See further: (1) Thomas Rymer and Robert Sanderson, eds. *Foedera, conventiones, literae et cujuscunque generis acta publica, inter reges Angliae*. 3rd ed. Rev. George Holmes. 10 vols. The Hague: Neulme, 1739–45. Repr. Farnborough: Gregg, 1967. (2) Thomas Duffus Hardy. *Syllabus (in English) of the Documents Relating to England and Other Kingdoms Contained in the Collection Known as 'Rymer's "Foedera."'* 3 vols. London: Longmans, 1869–85. Repr. New York: AMS Press, 1974.]

19 Blume, Friedrich. *Iter Italicum*. Vol. 4. 1836. See item **11**. [In an addendum (printed on p. 133 of the present vol., referring back to vol. 1, p. 99), a note whose substance is credited to Jacob Grimm, Blume issues the earliest pub. reference to the Vercelli poems and the transcript produced by C. Maier (see items **14–16**): 'Das angelsäxische Homiliarium ist vor Kurzem, auf Veranstaltung englischer Geschichtsforscher, von (dem nun schon verstorbenen) Dr. Maier volständig abgeschrieben worden; es haben sich wichtige angelsäxische Lieder darin gefunden. (Jac. Grimm.).' The present vol. bears the subtitle *Vierter und lezter Band. Königreich Neapel, nebst Nachträgen und Registern zu allen vier Bänden und zur 'Bibliotheca librorum mss. Italica.'* (For the last work, see item **17**.)]

– Thorpe, Benjamin, ed. and trans. 1842. See item **341**. [Early notice of Vercelli Book in ed. of *Soul and Body I* and *II*.]

20 Gazzera, Costanzo. *Delle iscrizioni cristiane antiche del Piemonte e della inedita epigrafe di Rustico vescovo di Torino del settimo secolo discorso*. Turin: Stamperia reale, 1849. Pp. 149, 8 plates. [Includes comments on script and provenance in Vercelli, pp. 127–8; see further item **21**.]

21 – 'Delle iscrizioni cristiane antiche del Piemonte discorso.' *Memorie della Reale accademia delle scienze di Torino*, Classe di scienze morali, storiche e filologiche, ser. 2, 11 (1851): 131–277. [See pp. 255–6; printed version of lecture series delivered in Feb.–Apr. 1847; see further item **20**.]

22 Neigebaur, Ferdinand. 'Die Bibliothek des Erzbischöflichen Dom-Capitels zu Vercelli.' *Serapeum* 18 (1857): 177–90. [See esp. pp. 189–90.] Also pub. in Italian trans., 'La biblioteca del capitolo metropolitano di Vercelli.' *Rivista contemporanea* (Turin) 19 (1859): 119–33.

23 Wülker, Richard P. 'Über das Vercellibuch.' *Anglia* 5 (1882): 451–65.

24 — *Grundriss zur Geschichte der angelsächsischen Litteratur, mit einer Übersicht der angelsächsischen Sprachwissenschaft.* Leipzig: von Veit, 1885. Pp. xii + 532. [Sect. III.5, 'Das Vercellibuch,' pp. 237–43.]

25 Cook, Albert S. *Cardinal Guala and the Vercelli Book.* Univ. of California Lib. Bull. 10. Sacramento, CA: State Office, Superintendent of State Printing, 1888. Pp. 8. [See further item **26**.]

26 — 'Supplementary Note to *Cardinal Guala and the Vercelli Book.*' *MLN* 4 (1889): 212–13. [See item **25**.]

27 Krapp, George Philip. 'The First Transcript of the Vercelli Book.' *MLN* 17 (1902): 171–2.

 – Napier, A.S. 1906. See item **850**. [First pub. work drawing on a privately prepared transcript of *Vercelli Homilies*.]

28 Förster, Max. 'Der Vercelli-Codex CXVII nebst Abdruck einiger altenglischer Homilien der Handschrift.' In *Festschrift für Lorenz Morsbach*, ed. F. Holthausen and H. Spies, 21–179. Studien zur englischen Philologie 50. Halle an der Saale: Niemeyer, 1913. Also pub. separately: Halle an der Saale: Niemeyer, 1913. Pp. 163. [Study of the manuscript and its texts, sects. I–VI, VIII, with an ed., in sect. VII, of *Vercelli Homilies* II, VI, IX, XV, XXII; see further item **857**.] Review: R. Brotanek, *Beiblatt zur 'Anglia'* 26 (1915): 225–38.

 – — in 1913. See item **2**. [Facs. ed.; 'Introduzione,' pp. 7–70. Italian-language study of the manuscript and its texts in six sects. These generally follow item **28**, in sects. I–VI, but offer occasional amplifications in the commentary.]

29 Sisam, Kenneth. 'Epenthesis in the Consonant Groups *sl, sn*.' *ASNSL* 131 (1913): 305–10. [Orthography of scribal stints in Vercelli Book.]

30 Ricci, Aldo. 'Il codice anglosassone di Vercelli nel primo centenario della sua scoperta.' *Rivista delle biblioteche e degli archivi* 33 (1923): 13–19.

31 Pastè, Romualdo. 'Vercelli.' In Giuseppe Mazzatinti et al., *Inventari dei manoscritti delle biblioteche d'Italia*, 21: 73–129. Forlì *et alibi*: Bordandini et al., 1890–. ['Cod. CXVII. (Arab. 41),' p. 106 (no. 117). Vol. 21 was pub. in 1925].

32 Pasteris, Emiliano. *Attone di Vercelli. Ossia il più grande vescovo e scrittore italiano del secolo. Vita e opere, con un studio sulle sue prose ritmiche recentemente scoperte dall'autore.* Milan: Stamperia e tipografia industriale, 1925. Pp. vi + 218. [Discussion of provenance, p. 161.]

 – Krapp, George Philip, ed. 1932. See item **77**. [Treatment of Vercelli Book in intro. to ASPR ed.]

33 Herben, Stephen J., Jr. 'The Vercelli Book: A New Hypothesis.' *Speculum* 10 (1935): 91–4.

34 Ericson, Eston Everett. 'The Vercelli Book.' *N&Q* 171 (1936): 138. [Comments on theories addressing Italian provenance.]

35 Dilkey, Marvin C., and Heinrich Schneider. 'John Mitchell Kemble and the Brothers Grimm.' *JEGP* 40 (1941): 461–73. [Esp. at pp. 465–8.]

36 Ker, Neil R. 'C. Maier's Transcript of the Vercelli Book.' *MÆ* 19 (1950): 17–25.

37 Sisam, Kenneth. 'Marginalia in the Vercelli Book.' In his *Studies in the History of Old English Literature*, 109–18. Oxford: Clarendon Press, 1953. Corr. repr. 1962.

38 Ker, Neil R. *Catalogue of Manuscripts Containing Anglo-Saxon.* Oxford: Clarendon Press, 1957. Pp. lxiv + 567. [Vercelli Book, pp. 460–4 (no. 394).] Augmented repr. 1990.

39 Muinzer, Louis A. 1957. See item 318. [Transcript of Vercelli Book by C. Maier.]

40 Halsall, Maureen. 'Benjamin Thorpe and the Vercelli Book.' *ELN* 6 (1968–9): 164–9.

41 — 'Vercelli and the Vercelli Book.' *PMLA* 84 (1969): 1545–50.

42 Scragg, D.G. 'Initial *h* in Old English.' *Anglia* 88 (1970): 165–96. [Distribution of linguistically anomalous cases in Vercelli Book, pp. 172–5, 179; esp. on *Andreas*, *Soul and Body I*, and *Elene*, and on *Vercelli Homilies*.]

43 Halsall, Maureen. 'More about C. Maier's Transcript of the Vercelli Book.' *ELN* 8 (1970–1): 3–6.

44 Scragg, D.G. 'Accent Marks in the Old English Vercelli Book.' *NM* 72 (1971): 699–710. [Lists accent marks in texts of *Vercelli Homilies*, augmenting report on verse in ASPR.]

45 Erickson, Jon L. 'The Readings of Folios 77 and 86 of the Vercelli Codex.' *Manuscripta* 16 (1972): 14–23. [Damaged leaves containing text in *Vercelli Homilies* XIV, XVI.]

46 Avonto, Luigi. *L'Ospedale di S. Brigida degli Scoti e il 'Vercelli Book.'* [Vercelli]: [n.p.], 1973. Pp. 29.

47 Cameron, Angus. 'A List of Old English Texts.' In *A Plan for the Dictionary of Old English*, ed. Roberta Frank and Cameron, 25–306. Toronto OE Ser. 2. Toronto: Univ. of Toronto Press, 1973. Pp. vii + 347. [See pp. 30 (items A.2.1–6: *Andreas*, *Fates of the Apostles*, *Soul and Body I*, *Homiletic Fragment I*, *Dream of the Rood*, *Elene*), 94–5 (items B.3.2.1–4, B.3.2.11: *Vercelli Homilies* V, XVI, VIII, IX, III

respectively), 97–100 (items B.3.2.24, B.3.2.34, B.3.2.36, B.3.2.38–40, B.3.2.43: I, XIX, XI, XX, XII, X, XIII), 102–3 (items B.3.3.10, B.3.3.17, B.3.3.19: XXIII, XVIII, XVII), 106–7 (items B.3.4.6–11: XV, XXII, II, IV, VI–VII), 114 (items B.3.5.11, B.3.5.13: XIV, XXI). Entries for the *Vercelli Homilies* include detailed citations of manuscripts and editions.]

48 Scragg, D.G. 'The Compilation of the Vercelli Book.' *ASE* 2 (1973): 189–207. Augmented reissue in *Anglo-Saxon Manuscripts: Basic Readings*, ed. Mary P. Richards, 317–43. Basic Readings in AS England 2. New York: Garland, 1994. ['Postscript,' p. 343.] Repr. New York: Routledge, 2001.

– Sisam, Celia, ed. 1976. See item **3**. [Facs. ed.; 'Introduction,' pp. 13–60.]

49 Temple, Elżbieta. *Anglo-Saxon Manuscripts, 900–1066.* Survey of Manuscripts Illuminated in the British Isles 2. London: Harvey Miller, 1976. Pp. 243. ['Vercelli, Cathedral, Codex CVII,' p. 55 (no. 28).]

50 Martin, Margaret. 'A Note on Marginalia in the Vercelli Book.' *N&Q* n.s. 25 (1978): 485–6. [Probable incipit of antiphon on 136v.]

51 Robinson, P.R. 'Self-Contained Units in Composite Manuscripts of the Anglo-Saxon Period.' *ASE* 7 (1978): 231–8. [Identification of three 'booklets' in Vercelli Book, p. 237.] Reissued in *Anglo-Saxon Manuscripts*, ed. Mary P. Richards, 25–35. See item **48**.

– Scragg, D.G. 1979. See item **928**. ['Vercelli, Biblioteca capitolare CXVII, the Vercelli Book,' in sect. 2.]

52 Szarmach, Paul E. 'The Scribe of the Vercelli Book.' *SN* 51 (1979): 179–88. [Also esp. for *Vercelli Homilies*.]

– Boenig, Robert E. 1980. See item **213**. [Includes discussion of Italian provenance.]

53 Greenfield, Stanley B., and Fred C. Robinson, using the collections of E.E. Ericson. *A Bibliography of Publications on Old English Literature to the End of 1972.* Toronto: Univ. of Toronto Press, 1980. Pp. [xxiii] + 437. [Vercelli Book, p. 22, nos. 237–58.]

54 Healey, Antonette di Paolo, and Richard L. Venezky. *A Microfiche Concordance to Old English: The List of Texts and Index of Editions.* Toronto: Dictionary of Old English Project, 1980. Pp. xviii + 201. [The contents of the Vercelli Book are treated under twenty-nine sigla. Verse: And, Fates, Soul I, HomFr I, Dream, El. *Vercelli Homilies*: (I) HomS 24; (II) HomU 8; (III) HomS 11; (IV) HomU 9; (V) HomS 1; (VI) HomU 10; (VII) HomU 11; (VIII) HomS 3; (IX)

HomS 4; (X) HomS 40; (XI) HomS 36; (XII) HomS 39; (XIII) HomS 43; (XIV) HomM 11; (XV) HomU 6; (XVI) HomS 2; (XVII) LS 19; (XVIII) LS 17; (XIX) HomS 34; (XX) HomS 38; (XXI) HomM 13; (XXII) HomU 7; (XXIII) LS 10.]

55 Gneuss, Helmut. 'A Preliminary List of Manuscripts Written or Owned in England up to 1100.' *ASE* 9 (1981): 1–60. [See p. 59 (no. 941); see further item **64**.]

– Ó Carragáin, Éamonn. 1981. See item **560**. [Role of collector.]

56 Fell, Christine E. 'Richard Cleasby's Notes on the Vercelli Codex.' *Leeds Stud. in Eng.* n.s. 12 (1981): 13–42; n.s. 15 (1984): 1–19. [Notes produced ca. 1837 in the light of texts printed in item **18**.]

57 Ohlgren, Thomas H. *Insular and Anglo-Saxon Illuminated Manuscripts: An Iconographic Catalogue c. A.D. 625 to 1100*. With contributions by Carl T. Berkhout et al., and with the assistance of William I. Bormann. New York: Garland, 1986. Pp. xx + 400. ['Vercelli, Biblioteca capitolare, Codex CXVII,' pp. 92–3 (no. 116).]

– Scragg, D.G. 1992. See item **834**. [Description of Vercelli Book in intro. to EETS ed. of *Vercelli Homilies*, pp. xxiii–xxv, under siglum 'A.']

– — 1994. See item **48**. [Augmented treatment of compilation of Vercelli Book.]

58 Zimmermann, Gunhild. *The Four Old English Poetic Manuscripts: Texts, Contexts, and Historical Background*. Anglistische Forschungen 230. Heidelberg: Winter, 1995. Pp. ix + 327. ['The Vercelli Book: The Impact of Christianity,' ch. 4.] Reviews: A. Hindorf, *ZAA* 44 (1996): 365–6; G. Knappe, *Anglia* 116 (1998): 523–5.

– Whatley, E.G. 1996. See item **1007**. [Ecclesiastical context.]

59 Heckman, Christina M. 'The Sweet Song of Satan: Music and Resistance in the Vercelli Book.' *Essays in Med. Stud.* (Chicago *et alibi*) 15 (1998): 57–70. [Discussion of passages alluding to music in the verse and prose of the Vercelli Book.]

60 Scragg, Donald G. 'The Significance of the Vercelli Book among Anglo-Saxon Vernacular Writings.' In *Vercelli tra Oriente ed Occidente. Atti delle Giornate di studio, Vercelli, 10–11 aprile 1997, 24 novembre 1997*, ed. Vittoria Dolcetti Corazza, 35–43. Bibliotheca Germanica, Studi e testi 6. Alessandria: Edizioni dell'Orso, 1998.

61 — 'Towards a New Anglo-Saxon Poetic Records.' In *New Approaches to Editing Old English Verse*, ed. Sarah Larratt Keefer and Katherine O'Brien O'Keeffe, 67–77. Cambridge: D.S. Brewer, 1998. [Discussion of problems affecting titles of poetic texts in Vercelli Book, pp. 70–1.]

62 — 'Vercelli Book.' In *Medieval England: An Encyclopedia*, ed. Paul E. Szarmach, M. Teresa Tavormina, and Joel T. Rosenthal, 755. New York: Garland, 1998.

63 — 'Vercelli Book.' In *The Blackwell Encyclopaedia of Anglo-Saxon England*, ed. Michael Lapidge et al., 459. Oxford: Blackwell, 1999.

64 Gneuss, Helmut. *Handlist of Anglo-Saxon Manuscripts: A List of Manuscripts and Manuscript Fragments Written or Owned in England up to 1100*. Med. and Renaissance Texts and Stud. 241. Tempe, AZ: Arizona Center for Medieval and Renaissance Studies, 2001. Pp. [viii] + 188. [See p. 145 (no. 941): 's. x²; SE England (Canterbury, St A[ugustine's]? Rochester?).']

— Ó Carragáin, Éamonn. 2001. See item **801**.

— Roberts, Jane. 2001. See item **1023**. [Context of *Elene* in Vercelli Book.]

65 Dolcetti Corazza, Vittoria. 'Codici della Biblioteca capitolare di Vercelli.' In *Antichità germaniche*, ed. Dolcetti Corazza and Renato Gendre, 1: 193–203. 2 vols. Bibliotheca Germanica, Studi e testi 10, 12. Alessandria: Edizioni dell'Orso, 2001–2.

66 Treharne, Elaine, and Susan Rosser, eds. *Early Medieval English Texts and Interpretations: Studies Presented to Donald G. Scragg*. Med. and Renaissance Texts and Stud. 252. Tempe, AZ: Arizona Center for Medieval and Renaissance Studies, 2002. Pp. xix + 391. ['Donald G. Scragg: Major Publications,' pp. xv–xvii.]

— Dockray-Miller, Mary. 2005. See item **278**. [On the 'eadgiþ erasure.']

67 — 'Female Devotion and the Vercelli Book.' *PQ* 83 (2006 for 2004): 337–54. [Hypothesis of female audience.]

Andreas

EDITIONS

68 [Thorpe, Benjamin, ed.] 'The Legend of St. Andrew.' 1834. In *Appendices to a Report on Rymer's 'Foedera,'* appendix B, pp. 47–89. See item **18**.

69 Grimm, Jacob, ed. *'Andreas' und 'Elene.'* Kassel: Fischer, 1840. Pp. lviii + 182. [Follows text in item **68**, introducing title *Andreas*.]

70 Kemble, John M., ed. and trans. *The Poetry of the Codex Vercellensis, with an English Translation*. 2 vols. Ælfric Soc. 5 and [14]. London: Ælfric Soc., 1843–56. Vol. 1, pp. xvi + 100. 1843. Vol. 2, pp. x + 110. 1856. [The ed. of *Andreas*, pub. in 1843, occupies the whole of vol. 1, with 'The Legend of St Andrew,' subtitle for the vol., first occurring

internally at p. xi; '*Elene* and Minor Poems,' the subtitle for vol. 2, occurs internally at p. iii.]

71 Ettmüller, Ludwig, ed. *Engla and Seaxna scôpas and bôceras. Anglosaxonum poëtae atque scriptores prosaici.* Bibliothek der gesammten deutschen National-Literatur von der ältesten bis auf der neuere Zeit I.28. Quedlinburg: Bassius, 1850. Pp. xxiv + 304. ['*Andrêas*,' pp. 148–56, following text in item **69**; also for *Elene*. The ed. is credited to 'Ludovicus Ettmüllerus.'] Reviews: [Anon.], *Literarisches Zentralblatt* 2 (1851): 693–4; [Anon.], *Zeitschrift für die österreichischen Gymnasien* 4 (1853): 922. Repr. Amsterdam: Rodopi, 1966.

72 Grein, Christian W.M., ed. *Bibliothek der angelsächsischen Poesie in kritisch bearbeiteten Texten und mit vollständigem Glossar.* 4 vols. in 2 pts. Göttingen: Wigand, 1857–64. Pt. 1. Texts: Vol. 1, pp. vi + [370]. 1857. Vol. 2, pp. iv + [416]. 1858. Pt. 2. Glossary: Vol. 3, pp. iv + 538. 1861. Vol. 4, pp. v + 804. 1864. [*Andreas*, 2: 9–52, with corrections at 2: 415–16. Apart from the ed. of *Soul and Body I* (and *II*) in vol. 1, the work treats all of the Vercelli poems in vol. 2. Vols. 1–2, containing the verse, were superseded by vols. cited in item **74**; vols. 3–4 (1861–4), containing the 'Glossar,' were reissued separately, from 1898, under their more familiar subtitle, *Sprachschatz der angelsächsischen Dichter.*]

73 Baskervill, W.M., ed. '*Andreas*': *The Legend of St. Andrew.* Boston: Ginn, 1885. Pp. x + 78. Reviews: [Anon.], *Academy* (London) 29 (1886): 12; J.W. Bright, *MLN* 1 (1886): 11–12; F. Kluge, *Englische Studien* 10 (1887): 117–18; J. Zupitza, *Deutsche Literaturzeitung* 6 (1885): 1587–9. 2nd ed. 1891 [under title: '*Andreas*': *A Legend of St. Andrew*]. Repr. 1900.

74 Wülker, Richard P., ed. *Die Verceller Handschrift, die Handschrift des Cambridger Corpus Christi Collegs CCI, die Gedichte der sogen. Cædmonhandschrift, Judith, der Hymnus Cædmons, Heiligenkalender und kleineren geistlichen Dichtungen.* Bibliothek der angelsächsischen Poesie 2. 1 vol. in 2 pts. Leipzig: Wigand, 1888–94. Pt. 1, pp. vi + vi + 1–[210]. 1888. Pt. 2, pp. [iv] + [211]–570. 1894. [*Andreas* in pt. 1, pp. 1–86, with the other Vercelli poems. This vol., with the two vols. that accompany it in the ser. Bibliothek der angelsächsischen Poesie (Kassel *et alibi*: Wigand, 1883–98), supersedes item **72**.] Reviews: W.M. Baskervill, *Amer. Jnl of Philol.* 8 (1887): 95–7 [consulting advance sheets of pt. 1]; O. Glöde, *Englische Studien* 21 (1895): 106–15; A. Schröer, *Literaturblatt für germanische und romanische Philologie* 10 (1889): cols. 52–3. Repr. Hamburg: Grand, 1922.

75 Krapp, George Philip, ed. *'Andreas' and 'The Fates of the Apostles':* *Two Anglo-Saxon Narrative Poems, Edited with Introduction, Notes, and Glossary.* Albion Ser. of AS and Middle Eng. Poetry. Boston: Ginn, 1906. Pp. lxxxi + 238. Reviews: [Anon.], *Academy* (London) 70 (1906): 362; [Anon.], *Athenaeum* 1906, pt. 2 (July–Dec.): 155; J.H.G. Grattan, *MLR* 2 (1907): 175–6; W.P. Ker, *Scottish Hist. Rev.* 5 (1907–8): 225; L. Pound, *Englische Studien* 37 (1907): 220–3.

76 Craigie, W.A., ed. *Early Christian Lore and Legend.* Specimens of AS Poetry 2. Edinburgh: Hutchen, 1926. Pp. iii + 78. [Excerpts, pp. 2–6, 15–31.]

77 Krapp, George Philip, ed. *The Vercelli Book.* ASPR 2. New York: Columbia Univ. Press, 1932. Pp. xciv + 152. [*Andreas* and the other Vercelli poems are treated serially in the intro. (pp. xi–lxxx), the ed. proper (pp. 3–102), and notes (pp. 105–52).] Reviews: B. Colgrave, *MLR* 28 (1933): 93–5; W.C. Greet, *Sewanee Rev.* 40 (1932): 511–12; H.S.V. J[ones], *JEGP* 32 (1933): 397; H. L[arsen], *PQ* 12 (1933): 318–19; K. M[alone], *MLN* 49 (1934): 352; [Anon.], *TLS* 2 June 1932: 410.

78 Magoun, Francis P., ed. *The Vercelli Book Poems Done in a Normalized Orthography and Edited.* Harvard OE Ser. 4. Cambridge, MA: Dept. of English, Harvard Univ., 1960. Pp. [vii] + 118. ['*Andreas*, or The Acts of St Matthew and St Andrew,' pp. 1–50. The edited text regularly indicates the length of vowels and dipthongs.] Review: N.E. Eliason, *MLR* 64 (1969): 382–3.

79 Brooks, Kenneth R., ed. *'Andreas' and 'The Fates of the Apostles,' Edited, with Introduction, Commentary, and Glossary.* Oxford: Clarendon Press, 1961. Pp. [lvi] + 184. Reviews: P. Bacquet, *EA* 18 (1965): 174–5; J.J. Campbell, *JEGP* 62 (1963): 678–80; R.P. Creed, *Speculum* 39 (1964): 499–501; K. Grinda, *ASNSL* 200 (1964): 297–9; C.A. Ladd, *N&Q* 208 n.s. 10 (1963): 432–3; K. Malone, *Revue belge de philologie et d'histoire* 42 (1964): 154–60; S. Potter, *MLR* 57 (1962): 404–5; M.L. Samuels, *RES* n.s. 14 (1963): 175–7; C. Schaar, *SN* 34 (1962): 331–4; [Anon.], *TLS* 4 May 1962: 322; R. Willard, *MP* 62 (1964–5): 45–51; R. Woolf, *MÆ* 37 (1963): 134–6. Repr. Oxford: Clarendon Press, 1998.

80 Campbell, Jackson J., and James L. Rosier, eds. *Poems in Old English.* New York: Harper and Row, 1962. Pp. ix + 147. [Excerpts, pp. 29–31.] Review: A. Renoir, *College Eng.* 25 (1963–4): 235.

81 Ravizza, Cristina, ed. and trans. *Andreas. Introduzione, traduzione, glossario e note.* Turin: Giappichelli, 1988. Pp. 351.

TRANSLATIONS

82 Kemble, John M., ed. and trans. 1843. See item 70.
83 Root, Robert Kilburn, trans. *'Andreas': The Legend of St. Andrew, Translated from the Old English*. Yale Stud. in Eng. 7. New York: Holt, 1899. Pp. xiii + 58. Reviews: G. Binz, *Englische Studien* 29 (1901): 114–15; J.M. Garnett, *Amer. Jnl of Philol.* 20 (1899): 443–4; *idem, PMLA* 18 (1903): 445–58, at p. 454; F. Klaeber, *Beiblatt zur 'Anglia'* 11 (1900): 69–74. Repr. Hamden, CT: Archon Books, 1970.
84 Cook, Albert S., and Chauncey B. Tinker, trans. *Select Translations from Old English Poetry*. Boston: Ginn, 1902. Pp. xi + 195. [Excerpts, pp. 133–8.] Repr. Westport, CT: Greenwood Press, 1970.
85 Hall, J[ohn] Lesslie, trans. *'Judith,' 'Phoenix,' and Other Anglo-Saxon Poems, Translated from the Grein-Wülker Text*. New York: Silver, Burdett, and Company, 1902. Pp. [ix] + 119. [Includes trans. of *Andreas*, pp. 60–119.] Review: J.M. Garnett, *PMLA* 18 (1903): 445–58, at p. 454.
86 Kennedy, Charles W., trans. 1910. See item 296. [*Andreas*, pp. 211–63; as 'Cynewulfian' verse.]
87 Gordon, R.K., trans. *Anglo-Saxon Poetry*. Everyman's Lib. London: Dent, 1926. Pp. xvi + 367. [*Andreas*, pp. 200–33.]
88 Olivero, Federico, trans. *'Andreas' e 'I fati degli apostoli.' Traduzione dall'anglosassone, con introduzione e note*. Turin: Libreria Fratelli Treves dell'Anonima libraria italiana, 1927. Pp. xlviii + 123. Reviews: [Anon.], *ASNSL* 153 (1928): 304–5; [Anon.], *RES* 4 (1928): 373. 2nd ed. as *'Andreas' e 'I fati degli apostoli.' Poemetti del IX secolo*. Turin: Società editrice internazionale, 1942. Pp. lxxi + 167.
89 Kennedy, Charles W., trans. *Early English Christian Poetry*. Oxford: Oxford Univ. Press, 1952. Pp. xii + 292. ['St. Andrew's Mission to Mermedonia,' in ch. 3.] Repr. London: Hollis, 1968.
90 — *An Anthology of Old English Poetry*. Oxford: Oxford Univ. Press, 1960. Pp. xvi + 174. [Excerpts, pp. 28–34.]
91 Bradley, S.A.J., trans. *Anglo-Saxon Poetry: An Anthology of Old English Poems in Prose Translation with Introduction and Headnotes*. Everyman's Lib. London: Dent, 1982. Pp. xxvi + 559. [*Andreas*, pp. 110–53.]
92 Ravizza, Cristina, ed. and trans. 1988. See item 81.
93 Boenig, Robert, trans. *The Acts of Andrew in the Country of the Cannibals: Translations from the Greek, Latin, and Old English*. Garland Lib. of Med. Lit., Ser. B, 70. New York: Garland, 1991. Pp. [xlvi] + 121. ['*Andreas*,' pp. 71–121.]

STUDIES

- Sweet, Henry. 1871. See item **429**. [Sees *Fates of the Apostles* as conclusion for *Andreas*, p. 16.]

94 Clement, Knut Jungbohn. 'Jacob Grimm's Erläuterungen zu *Andreas*.' In his *Forschungen über das Recht der salischen Franken vor und in der Königszeit. 'Lex Salica' und malbergische Glossen. Erläuterungen, nebst erstem Versuch einer vollständigen hochdeutschen Übersetzung*, ed. Heinrich Zoepfl, 41–56. Bibliothek für Wissenschaft und Literatur 3. Berlin: Grieben, 1876. [Criticism of item **69**, pp. 41–86]

95 Kern, H. 'Angelsaksische Kleinigheden.' *Taalkundige bijdragen* 1 (1877): 193–209. [*Andreas* 770 (*ælfæle*), p. 206; also for *Elene* and other verse.]

96 Fritzsche, Arthur. 'Das angelsächsische Gedicht *Andreas* und Cynewulf.' *Anglia* 2 (1879): 441–96. Also issued as Leipzig diss. Pub. Halle an der Saale: Karras, 1879. Pp. 58. [Also esp. for *Elene*.]

97 Zupitza, Julius. 'Kleine Bemerkungen.' *Anglia* 3 (1880): 369–72. [Textual notes on *Andreas* 145, 483.]

98 Kluge, Friedrich. 'Anglosaxonica.' *Anglia* 4 (1881): 105–6. [Commentary on *Andreas* 1661, and on other verse.]

99 Napier, Arthur S. 'Zu *Andreas* 1182.' *Anglia* 4 (1881): 411.

100 Lipsius, Richard Adelbert. *Die apokryphen Apostelgeschichten und Apostellegenden*. 2 vols. in 3 + suppl. vol. Braunschweig: Schwetschke, 1883–90. Pp. 1373, 431, vii + 262. [Discusses *Andreas* in vol. 1, pub. in 1883, at pp. 547–8.]

- Holtbuer, Fritz. 1884. See with item **101**.

101 — 'Der syntaktische Gebrauch des Genitives in "Andreas," "Gūð-lac," "Phönix," "Dem heiligen Kreuze" und "Höllenfahrt."' *Anglia* 8 (1885): 1–40. Also issued as Leipzig diss. Pub. Halle an der Saale: Karras, 1884. Pp. 42.

102 Ramhorst, Friedrich. *Das altenglische Gedicht vom heiligen Andreas und der Dichter Cynewulf*. Berlin diss. Berlin: Schade, 1885. Pp. 74. Reviews: [Anon.], *Academy* (London) 30 (1886): 210; A.S. Napier, *Deutsche Literaturzeitung* 7 (1886): 670–1; A. Schröer, *Englische Studien* 10 (1887): 118–22.

- Wülker, Richard P. 1885. See item **24**. ['*Andreas*,' pp. 187–9.]

103 Zupitza, Julius. 'Zur Frage nach der Quelle von Cynewulfs *Andreas*.' *ZDA* 30 (1886): 175–85.

104 Baskervill, W.M. 'Other Notes on the *Andreas*.' *MLN* 2 (1887): 151–2. [Esp. on *Andreas* 64, 145, 819, 1585.]

105 — 1887. See item **74**. [Review discussing advance sheets of Wülker's ed. of *Andreas*.]

106 Bright, James W. 'Notes on the *Andreas*.' *MLN* 2 (1887): 80–2. [Esp. on ll. 1, 4, 24, 51, 145, 301–3, 305, 483, 489, 496, 516, 523–4, 630, 770, 820, 857, 892, 1015, 1091, 1183, 1232, 1254, 1379, 1445, 1509, 1587, 1702.]

107 — 'Prof. Baskervill's Notes.' *MLN* 2 (1887): 152–3. [See item **74**, with reviews, and item **105**.]

108 Kent, Charles W. *Teutonic Antiquities in 'Andreas' and 'Elene.'* Leipzig diss. Halle an der Saale: Karras, 1887. Pp. [vi] + 65. Review: [Anon.], *Nation* 47 (1888): 11–12.

109 Cremer, Matthias. *Metrische und sprachliche Untersuchung der altenglische Gedichte 'Andreas,' 'Gūðlāc,' 'Phoenix' ('Elene,' 'Juliana,' 'Crist'). Ein Beitrag zur Cynewulffrage.* Bonn diss. Bonn: [n.p.], 1888. Pp. [iii] + 51.

110 Wülker, Richard P. 'Die Bedeutung einer neuen Entdeckung für die angelsächsische Literatur-Geschichte.' *Berichte über die Verhandlungen der königlich sächsischen Gesellschaft des Wissenschaften zu Leipzig, philologisch-historische Klasse* 40 (1888): 209–18. [On *Andreas* and *Fates of the Apostles*; believes former not written by Cynewulf.]

111 Napier, A[rthur S.] 'Collation der altenglischen Gedichte im Vercellibuch.' *ZDA* 33 (1889): 66–73. [*Andreas*, pp. 68–9.]

112 — 'Odds and Ends.' *MLN* 4 (1889): 137–40. [*Andreas* 254–5, p. 139.]

113 Reussner, Heinrich Adolf. *Untersuchungen über die Syntax in dem angelsächsischen Gedichte vom heiligen Andreas. Ein Beitrag zur angelsächsischen Grammatik,* I: *Das Verbum.* Leipzig diss. Halle an der Saale: Karras, 1889. Pp. [ii] + 63. [Only pt. issued.] Review: J.E. Wülfing, *Englische Studien* 19 (1894): 117–18.

114 Bauer, Hermann. *Über die Sprache und Mundart der altenglischen Dichtungen 'Andreas,' 'Guðlac,' 'Phönix,' 'Hl. Kreuz' und 'Höllenfahrt Christi.'* Marburg diss. Marburg: Universitäts-Buchdruckerei, 1890. Pp. 99.

– Deering, [Robert] Waller. 1890. See item **358**. [Judgment Day as theme; esp. at pp. 8, 50, 61, 75.]

115 Hinze, Wilhelm. *Zum altenglischen Gedicht 'Andreas.' 1. Teil.* Berlin: Gaertner, 1890. Pp. 40. [Only pt. issued.] Review: O. Brenner, *Englische Studien* 16 (1892): 87.

116 Holthausen, Ferdinand. 'Zu alt- und mittelenglischen Dichtungen.' *Anglia* 13 (1891): 357–62. [*Andreas* 489, 1092, p. 357; also on *Elene* and other verse.]

117 Cook, Albert S. 'Old English *scūrheard*.' *MLN* 7 (1892): 253. [Reply to item 119.]

118 Holthausen, Ferdinand. 'Zur Textkritik altenglischer Dichtungen.' *BGDSL* 16 (1892): 549–52. [*Andreas* 495–6, 717–19, 726–8, 943–7, 1080–2, 1179–80, 1404, at pp. 550–1; also for *Homiletic Fragment I* and other verse.]

119 Pearce, J.W. 'Anglo-Saxon *scūr-heard*.' *MLN* 7 (1892): 193–4. [*Andreas* 1133 and other verse; see further items 117, 120, 122–3, 135.]

120 — 'Old English *scūrheard*.' *MLN* 7 (1892): 253–4. [Reply to item 117.]

121 Cook, Albert S. 'A Note on the *Beowulf*.' *MLN* 8 (1893): 59. [Also treats *Andreas* 458–60.]

122 Hart, J.M. '*Scūr-heard*.' *MLN* 8 (1893): 61. [Comment on item 119.]

123 Palmer, Arthur H. '*Scūr-heard*.' *MLN* 8 (1893): 61. [Comment on item 119 and responses.]

124 Wack, Gustav. 'Artikel und Demonstrativpronomen in *Andreas* und *Elene*.' *Anglia* 15 (1893): 209–20.

125 Taubert, Eugen Max. *Der syntactische Gebrauch der Präpositionen in dem angelsächsischen Gedichte vom heiligen Andreas. Ein Beitrag zur angelsächsischen Grammatik.* Leipzig diss. Leipzig: Hoffmann, 1894. Pp. 52.

126 Sarrazin, Gregor. 'Noch einmal Kynewulfs *Andreas*.' *Beiblatt zur 'Anglia'* 6 (1895–6): 205–9.

127 Trautmann, Moritz. 'Der *Andreas* doch von Cynewulf.' *Beiblatt zur 'Anglia'* 6 (1895–6): 17–22.

128 — 'Zu Cynewulf's *Andreas*.' *Beiblatt zur 'Anglia'* 6 (1895–6): 22–3.

129 Cosijn, Peter J. 'Anglosaxonica. III.' *BGDSL* 21 (1896): 8–26. ['*Andreas*,' on many lines, pp. 8–21, and other verse.]

130 — 'Zu *Andreas* 575.' *BGDSL* 21 (1896): 252.

131 Sarrazin, Gregor. 'Neue *Beowulf*-Studien: I. König Hrodhgeirr und seine Familie. II. Das Skjöldungen-epos. III. Das Drachenlied. IV. Das Beowulflied und Kynewulfs *Andreas*.' *Englische Studien* 23 (1897): 221–67.

– Trautmann, Moritz. 1897. See item 307. [Contextual relationship of *Andreas* and *Fates of the Apsotles* in Vercelli Book.]

132 Buttenwieser, Ellen Clune. *Studien über die Verfasserschaft des 'Andreas.'* Heidelberg diss. Heidelberg: Geisendörfer, 1898. Pp. 87. Review: G. Binz, *Englische Studien* 29 (1901): 108–14.

133 Bourauel, Johannes B. 'Zur Quellen- und Verfasserfrage von "Andreas," "Crist" und "*Fata*."' *Bonner Beiträge zur Anglistik* 11

(1901): 65–132. Pt. 1 only ('Zur Quellenfrage') also issued as Bonn diss. Pub. Darmstadt: Otto, 1901. Pp. 46. Reviews: [Anon.], *Neue philologische Rundschau* (1902): 598–9 [signed by '-tz-']; [Anon.], *Neuphilologisches Centralblatt* 17 (1904): 268 [signed by 'Kasten']; G. Binz, *Zeitschrift für deutsche Philologie* 36 (1904): 505–8; A. Schröer, *Beiblatt zur 'Anglia'* 17 (1906): 40–2.

134 Skeat, Walter W. '*Andreas* and *Fata apostolorum*.' In *An English Miscellany: Presented to Dr. Furnivall in Honour of His Seventy-Fifth Birthday*, ed. [Anon.], 408–20. Oxford: Clarendon Press, 1901.

135 Krapp, George Philip. 'Miscellaneous Notes.' *MLN* 19 (1904): 232–4. ['*Scūrheard, Beowulf* 1033, *Andreas* 1133,' p. 234; see item **119**.]

136 — 'Notes on the *Andreas*.' *MP* 2 (1904–5): 403–10. [Esp. for ll. 15, 28, 36, 88, 109, 194, 198, 236, 356, 507, 865, 953, 1317–19, 1474, 1522, 1548–9.]

137 Förster, Max. 'Ae. *fregen* "die Frage."' *Englische Studien* 36 (1906): 325–8. [Includes comments on *Andreas* 254–6; see further item **144**.]

138 Sarrazin, Gregor. 'Zur Chronologie und Verfasserfrage angelsächsischer Dichtungen.' *Englische Studien* 38 (1907): 145–95. [Pt. 2, '*Andreas*,' pp. 158–70; also for Cynewulfian poems and other verse.]

139 Trautmann, Moritz. 'Berichtigungen, Erklärungen und Vermutungen zu Cynewulfs werken.' *Bonner Beiträge zur Anglistik* 23 (1907): 85–146. [Esp. for '*Andreas*,' pp. 107–37, with appendix 2, 'Zum *Andreas*,' pp. 142–3; also esp. for *Elene*, and for *Fates of the Apostles* and other verse.]

140 Grau, Gustav. *Quellen und Verwandtschaften der älteren germanischen Darstellungen des jüngsten Gerichtes.* Studien zur englischen Philologie 31. Halle an der Saale: Niemeyer, 1908. Pp. xiii + 288. ['*Andreas*,' pp. 131–45; also for *Soul and Body I* and *II, Dream of the Rood, Elene*.] Reviews: G. Ehrismann, *Anzeiger für deutsches Altertum* 35 (1911): 184–96; K. Guntermann, *Zeitschrift für deutsche Philologie* 41 (1909): 401–15; H. Hecht, *ASNSL* 130 (1913): 424–30; K. Helm, *Literaturblatt für germanische und romanische Philologie* 34 (1913): cols. 57–9; [Anon.], *Literarisches Zentralblatt* 61 (1910): 164–50 [signed by '-tz-'].

141 Klaeber, Frederick. 'Jottings on the *Andreas*.' *ASNSL* 120 (1908): 153–6.

142 Smithson, George A. *The Old English Christian Epic: A Study in the Plot Technique of the 'Juliana,' the 'Elene,' the 'Andreas,' and the 'Christ,' in Comparison with the 'Beowulf' and with the Latin Literature of the Middle Ages.* Univ. of California Pub. in Mod.

Philol. 1.4. Berkeley, CA: Univ. Press, 1910. Pp. 98. Reviews: H.L.S.
Creek, *JEGP* 10 (1911): 640–2; G. Sarrazin, *Deutsche Literaturzeitung*
32 (1911): 1255–6; A.R. Skemp, *MLR* 7 (1912): 379–81. Repr. New
York: Phaeton Press, 1971.

143 Trautmann, Moritz. 'Beiträge zu einem künftigen *Sprachschatz der
altenglischen Dichter.*' *Anglia* 33 (1910): 276–82. [On *gedræg* and
gedreag, brimcald, and *wopes hring*; esp. for *Andreas* 41–3, 1278,
1555, and for *Elene.*]

144 Förster, Max. 'Nochmals ae. *fregen* "Frage."' *ASNSL* 135 (1916):
399–401. [See item **137.**]

145 Monroe, B.S. 'Notes on the Anglo-Saxon *Andreas.*' *MLN* 31 (1916):
374–7. [On ll. 125–8, 301–3, 807–9, 846, 1124–5, 1358–9, 1460, 1605–6.]

146 Kock, Ernst A. *Jubilee Jaunts and Jottings: 250 Contributions to the
Interpretation and Prosody of Old West Teutonic Alliterative Poetry.*
Lunds universitets årsskrift n.s. 1, 14, no. 26. Lund: Gleerup, 1918.
Pp. iv + 82. [Contains notes on some thirty-five OE poems; on
Andreas, see pp. 1–7; for reviews, see item **53,** p. 93, no. 1104.]

147 Cook, Albert S. 'The Authorship of the O.E. *Andreas.*' *MLN* 34
(1919): 418–19.

148 Kock, Ernst A. 'Interpretations and Emendations of Early English
Texts: V.' *Anglia* 43 (1919): 298–312. [Contains twenty-one notes
on *Andreas,* pp. 298–303, and twenty-three others on *Fates of the
Apostles, Elene,* and other verse.]

–   Hamilton, George L. 1920. See item **314.** [Study of sources.]

149 Holthausen, Ferdinand. 'Zur altenglischen Dichtungen.' *Anglia* 44
(1920): 346–56. [Esp. at pp. 352–3, for *Andreas* 258, 320, 489, 829,
892, 942, 1111.]

150 — 'Zur altenglischen Dichtungen.' *Beiblatt zur 'Anglia'* 31 (1920): 25–32.
[*Andreas,* in numerous lines, pp. 27–8; also contains notes on *Fates of the
Apostles, Soul and Body I, Homiletic Fragment I,* and other verse.]

151 Kock, Ernst A. 'Interpretations and Emendations of Early English
Texts: VI.' *Anglia* 44 (1920): 97–114. [*Andreas* 1230, p. 97; also
contains notes on *Elene* and other verse.]

152 — 'Interpretations and Emendations of Early English Texts: VII.'
Anglia 44 (1920): 245–60. [See pp. 244–6, for *Andreas* 375, 914,
1102–3, and pp. 251–2 for ll. 218, 1355. Also includes notes on
Elene, Homiletic Fragment I, and other verse.]

153 Holthausen, Ferdinand. 'Zur altenglischen Gedichten.' *Beiblatt zur
'Anglia'* 32 (1921): 136–8. [*Andreas* 375, 914, at p. 137; also includes
notes on *Elene* and other verse.]

154 Kock, Ernst A. 'Interpretations and Emendations of Early English Texts: VIII.' *Anglia* 45 (1921): 105–31. [See pp. 105–7 for *Andreas* 81–3, 1035, 1526–7; also includes notes on *Elene* and other verse.]

155 — *Fornjermansk forskning.* Lunds universitets årsskrift n.s. 1, 18, no. 1. Lund: Gleerup, 1922. Pp. [iv] + 43. [On parallels in poetic style and diction between OE and other Germanic literatures; *Andreas*, p. 18.]

156 — 'Interpretations and Emendations of Early English Texts: IX.' *Anglia* 46 (1922): 63–96. [Treats some twenty-three lines or passages in *Andreas*; see also for *Fates of the Apostles* and other verse.]

157 Cook, Albert S. 'The Old English *Andreas* and Bishop Acca of Hexham.' *Trans. of the Connecticut Acad. of Arts and Sciences* 26 (1922–4): 245–332. [Esp. in sects. 6–9, 16–18.] Reviews: C. Bastide, *Revue critique* n.s. 92 (1925): 302; E. Ekwall, *Beiblatt zur 'Anglia'* 36 (1925): 321–2; H.M. Flasdieck, *Englische Studien* 61 (1927): 288–90; G.P. Krapp, *MLN* 40 (1925): 190–1; F. Liebermann, *ASNSL* 149 (1925): 105–7.

158 — 'Bitter Beer-Drinking.' *MLN* 40 (1925): 285–8. [*Andreas* 1533.]

159 Hoops, Johannes. 'Altenglisch *ealuscerwen, meoduscerwen.*' *Englische Studien* 65 (1930–1): 177–80. [Esp. for *Andreas* 1526.]

160 —, and Friedrich Klaeber. 'Altenglisch *ealuscerwen* und kein Ende.' *Englische Studien* 66 (1931–2): 1–5. [Also for *meoduscerwen.*]

161 Imelmann, Rudolf. '*Beowulf* 489f., 600, 769.' *Englische Studien* 66 (1931–2): 321–45. [Also on *Andreas*, in discussion of *scerwen*.]

162 Klaeber, Friedrich. 'Three Textual Notes.' *Englische Studien* 67 (1932–3): 340–3. [On *Andreas* 1532 and other verse.]

163 Krogmann, Willy. '*Ealuscerwen* und *meoduscerwen.*' *Englische Studien* 67 (1932–3): 15–23. [*Contra* Imelmann, item **161**.]

164 Holthausen, Ferdinand. 'Die Quelle der altenglischen Andreas-Legenden.' *Beiblatt zur 'Anglia'* 44 (1933): 90–1.

165 — 'Eine neue lateinische Fassung der Andreaslegende.' *Anglia* 62 (1938): 190–2.

166 Klaeber, Friedrich. '*Beowulf* 769 and *Andreas* 1526ff.' *Englische Studien* 73 (1938–9): 185–9. [On *ealuscerwen* and *meoduscerwen*.]

167 Kuriyagawa, Fumio. ['*Andreas* and *Beowulf*.'] *Stud. in Eng. Lit.* (Tokyo) 21 (1941): 155–68. [In Japanese.]

168 Klaeber, Friedrich. 'Zur Texterklärung altenglischer Dichtungen.' *Beiblatt zur 'Anglia'* 54–5 (1943–4): 170–6. [*Andreas* 1547–9, pp. 170–1.]

169 Schaar, Claes. 'Notes on *Andreas* and *Elene*.' *SN* 19 (1946–7): 310–13.

170 Brooks, K[enneth] R. 'Old English *wopes hring.*' *Eng. and Germanic Stud.* (Birmingham) 2 (1948–9): 68–74. [Treatment of *Andreas* 1280.]

171 Lumiansky, R[obert] M. 'The Contexts of O.E. *ealuscerwen* and *meoduscerwen.' JEGP* 48 (1949): 116–26. [Esp. for *Andreas* 1522–53, sect. II.]
   – Schaar, Claes. 1949. See item **316**. ['Cynewulfian' context; 'The *Andreas* Problem,' in sect. IV.1.]
172 Brooks, K[enneth] R. 'Two Textual Emendations in the Old English *Andreas.' Eng. and Germanic Stud.* (Birmingham) 3 (1949–50): 61–4. [On ll. 996–1000, 1529–35.]
173 Peters, Leonard J. 'The Relationship of the Old English *Andreas* to *Beowulf.' PMLA* 66 (1951): 844–63.
174 Smithers, G[eorge] V. 'Five Notes on Old English Texts.' *Eng. and Germanic Stud.* (Birmingham) 4 (1951–2): 65–85. [Esp. on *meoduscerwen* and other readings in *Andreas* 1526–7, 1532–5, in sect. 3.]
175 Holthausen, Ferdinand. 'Zu den ae. Gedichten der Hs. von Vercelli.' *Anglia* 73 (1956): 276–8. [Notes on *Andreas* 396, 669, 1080–2, and other verse.]
176 Crowne, David K. 'The Hero on the Beach: An Example of Composition by Theme in Anglo-Saxon Poetry.' *NM* 61 (1960): 362–72. [Esp. on *Andreas* 235–47.]
177 Sisam, Kenneth. 'OE. *stefn, stefna* "stem."' *RES* n.s. 13 (1962): 282–3. [Esp. on ll. 493–5.]
178 Page, R.I. 'Anglo-Saxon Runes and Magic.' *JBAA*, 3rd ser. 27 (1964): 14–31. [Discussion of *rūn* and related terms; also for *Elene* and other verse.] Augmented reissue in his *Runes and Runic Inscriptions: Collected Essays on Anglo-Saxon and Viking Runes*, ed. David Parsons, 105–25. Woodbridge: Boydell Press, 1995.
179 Schaar, Claes. 'The Old English *Andreas* and Scholarship Past and Present: A Review of a Review.' In *English Studies Presented to R.W. Zandvoort on the Occasion of His Seventieth Birthday*, ed. [Anon.], 111–15. Amsterdam: Swets and Zeitlinger, 1964. [Pub. as suppl. vol. to *ES* 45 (1964).]
180 Wolpers, Theodor. *Die englische Heiligenlegende des Mittelalters. Eine Formgeschichte des Legendenerzählens von der spätantiken lateinischen Tradition bis zur Mitte des 16. Jahrhunderts.* Tübingen: Niemeyer, 1964. Pp. xv + 470. ['*Andreas*,' sect. I.ii.6; also for *Elene* and other OE texts, in verse and in prose.]
181 Schabram, Hans. '*Andreas* und *Beowulf*. Parallelstellen als Zeugnis für literarische Abhängigkeit.' *Nachrichten der Giessener Hochschulgesellschaft* 34 (1965): 201–18.
182 Hill, Thomas D. 'Two Notes on Patristic Allusion in *Andreas.' Anglia* 84 (1966): 156–62.

183 Stanley, Eric G. '*Beowulf.*' In *Continuations and Beginnings: Studies in Old English Literature*, ed. Stanley, 104–41. London: Nelson, 1966. [Discussion of *Andreas*, pp. 110–14.]

184 Woolf, Rosemary. 'Saints' Lives.' 1966. In *Continuations and Beginnings*, ed. Eric G. Stanley, 37–66. See item **183**. [Discussion of *Andreas*, pp. 50–3; also for *Elene*.]

185 Brodeur, Arthur G. 'A Study of Diction and Style in Three Anglo-Saxon Narrative Poems.' In *Nordica et Anglica: Studies in Honor of Stefán Einarsson*, ed. Allan H. Orrick, 97–114. The Hague: Mouton, 1968. [Esp. for comparison of *Andreas* and *Beowulf.*]

186 Robinson, Fred C. 'Some Uses of Name-Meanings in Old English Poetry.' *NM* 69 (1968): 161–71. [*Andreas* 1605–6, pp. 162–5, and other verse.]

187 Hill, Thomas D. 'Figural Narrative in *Andreas*: The Conversion of the Mermedonians.' *NM* 70 (1969): 261–73.

188 Kühlwein, Wolfgang. '*Andreas*-Crux 1241 und *Beowulf*-Crux 849.' *BGDSL* 91 (1969): 77–81.

189 Mitchell, Bruce. 'Five Notes on Old English Syntax.' *NM* 70 (1969): 70–84. [Esp. for *Andreas* 271–5, 324–9, 474–80, 1114–16, 1284–90.]

190 Trahern, Joseph B., Jr. '*A defectione potus sui*: A Sapiential Basis for *ealuscerwen* and *meoduscerwen*.' *NM* 70 (1969): 62–9. [Esp. on *Andreas* 1526–35; also for ll. 21–5.]

191 Grosz, Oliver J.H. 'The Island of Exiles: A Note on *Andreas* 15.' *ELN* 7 (1969–70): 241–2.

–   Scragg, D.G. 1970. See item **42**. [Anomalous use of initial *h* in copy of *Andreas*, pp. 174, 179.]

192 Trahern, Joseph B., Jr. 'Joshua and Tobias in the Old English *Andreas*.' *SN* 42 (1970): 330–2. [Esp. for *Andreas* 1513–19; also for *Dream of the Rood*.]

193 Ingersoll, Sheila M. '*Scūr-heard*: A New Dimension of Interpretation.' *MLN* 86 (1971): 378–80. [See also item **119** and responses.]

194 Levine, Robert. 'Ingeld and Christ: A Medieval Problem.' *Viator* 2 (1971): 105–28. [See pp. 112–13 on *Andreas*, ll. 1401–28.]

195 Gober, Wallace G. '*Andreas*, lines 360–362.' *NM* 73 (1972): 672–4.

196 Hamilton, David. 'The Diet and Digestion of Allegory in *Andreas*.' *ASE* 1 (1972): 147–58.

197 Robinson, Fred C. 'Anglo-Saxon Onomastics in the Old English *Andreas*.' *Names* 21 (1973): 133–6.

198 Szittya, Penn R. 'The Living Stone and the Patriarchs: Typological Imagery in *Andreas*, lines 706–810.' *JEGP* 72 (1973): 167–74.

199 Casteen, John. '*Andreas*: Mermedonian Cannibalism and Figural Narrative.' *NM* 75 (1974): 74–8.

200 Unrue, John C. '*Andreas*: An Internal Perspective.' *In Geardagum* 1 (1974): 25–30.

201 Hamilton, David. '*Andreas* and *Beowulf*: Placing the Hero.' In *Anglo-Saxon Poetry: Essays in Appreciation, for John C. McGalliard*, ed. Lewis E. Nicholson and Dolores Warwick Frese, 81–98. Notre Dame, IN: Univ. of Notre Dame Press, 1975.

202 Stevick, Robert D. 'Arithmetical Design of the Old English *Andreas*.' 1975. In *Anglo-Saxon Poetry*, ed. Lewis E. Nicholson and Dolores Warwick Frese, 99–115. See item 201.

203 Allen, Michael J.B., and Daniel G. Calder, trans. *Sources and Analogues of Old English Poetry: The Major Latin Texts in Translation*. Cambridge: D.S. Brewer, 1976. Pp. xviii+ 235. ['*Andreas*,' sect. II.]

204 Hieatt, Constance B. 'The Harrowing of Mermedonia: Typological Patterns in the Old English *Andreas*.' *NM* 77 (1976): 49–62.

205 Hill, Thomas D. 'Hebrews, Israelites, and Wicked Jews: An Onomastic Crux in *Andreas* 161–67.' *Traditio* 32 (1976): 358–61.

206 Fujiwara, Yasuaki. 'Stress in *Andreas*.' *Stud. in Eng. Ling.* (Tokyo) 4 (1977): 304–7.

207 Sowa, Hosei. ['*Andreas* and Exegetical Criticism.'] *Stud. in Eng. Lit.* (Tokyo) 54 (1977): 3–17. [In Japanese; summary, *Stud. in Eng. Lit.* (Tokyo) Eng. no. 1978: 169.]

208 Walsh, Marie Michelle. 'The Baptismal Flood in the Old English *Andreas*: Liturgical and Typological Depths.' *Traditio* 33 (1977): 137–58.

209 Stevick, Robert D. 'Geometrical Design of the Old English *Andreas*.' *Poetica* (Tokyo) 9 (1978): 73–106.

210 Bridges, Margaret. 'Exordial Tradition and Poetic Individuality in Five OE Hagiographical Poems.' *ES* 60 (1979): 361–79. ['*Andreas* 1–13,' pp. 364–7; also for *Elene* and other verse.]

211 De Roo, Harvey. 'Two Old English Fatal Feast Metaphors: *ealuscerwen* and *meoduscerwen*.' *Eng. Stud. in Canada* 5 (1979): 249–61. [*Andreas* 1526, 1532–5, and other lines.]

212 Whitbread, L.G. '*Andreas*, lines 1513–16.' *N&Q* n.s. 26 (1979): 297–8.

213 Boenig, Robert E. '*Andreas*, the Eucharist, and Vercelli.' *JEGP* 79 (1980): 313–31. [Includes discussion of Italian provenance of Vercelli Book.]

214 Earl, James W. 'The Typological Structure of *Andreas*.' In *Old English Literature in Context: Ten Essays*, ed. John D. Niles, 66–89, 167–70. Cambridge: D.S. Brewer, 1980.

215 Lucas, Peter J. '*Andreas* 733b.' *N&Q* n.s. 28 (1981): 5–6.

216 Schabram, Hans. '*Andreas* 303A und 360B–362A: Bemerkungen zur Zählebigkeit philologischer Fehlurteile.' In *Geschichtlichkeit und Neuanfang im sprachlichen Kunstwerk. Studien zur englischen Philologie zu Ehren von Fritz W. Schulze*, ed. Peter Erlebach, Wolfgang G. Müller, and Klaus Reuter, 39–47. Tübingen: Narr, 1981.

217 Stevens, K. 'Some Aspects of the Metre of the Old English Poem *Andreas*.' *Proc. of the R. Irish Acad.* 81C (1981): 1–27.

218 Walsh, Marie M. 'St Andrew in Anglo-Saxon England: The Evolution of an Apocryphal Hero.' *Annuale Mediaevale* 20 (1981): 97–122.

219 Shimose, Michio. ['On *Andreas*.'] *Jnl of Kumamoto Women's Univ.* 34 (1982): 158–78. [In Japanese.]

220 Heinemann, Fredrik J. '*Ealuscerwen – meoduscerwen*, the Cup of Death, and *Baldrs draumar*.' *SN* 55 (1983): 3–10. [*Andreas* 1526 and contexts; also esp. for *Beowulf*.]

221 Hill, Thomas D. 'The *sphragis* as Apotropaic Sign: *Andreas* 133–44.' *Anglia* 101 (1983): 147–51.

222 Irving, Edward B., Jr. 'A Reading of *Andreas*: The Poem as Poem.' *ASE* 12 (1983): 215–37.

223 Wright, Charles D. 'Matthew's Hebrew Gospel in *Andreas* and in Old English Prose.' *N&Q* n.s. 30 (1983): 101–4.

224 Kiser, Lisa J. '*Andreas* and the *lifes weg*: Convention and Innovation in Old English Metaphor.' *NM* 85 (1984): 65–75.

225 Reddick, R.J. 'Old English *unlæd*: A Note on *Andreas*.' *ELN* 22.4 (1985): 1–10.

226 Calder, Daniel G. 'Figurative Language and Its Contexts in *Andreas*: A Study in Medieval Expressionism.' In *Modes of Interpretation in Old English Literature: Essays in Honour of Stanley B. Greenfield*, ed. Phyllis Rugg Brown, Georgia Ronan Crampton, and Fred C. Robinson, 115–36. Toronto: Univ. of Toronto Press, 1986.

227 Thrane, Torben. 'On Delimiting the Senses of Near-Synonyms in Historical Semantics: A Case-Study of Adjectives of "Moral Sufficiency" in the Old English *Andreas*.' In *Linguistics across Historical and Geographical Boundaries: In Honour of Jacek Fisiak on the Occasion of His Fiftieth Birthday*, ed. Dieter Kastovsky and Aleksander Szwedek, 671–92. 1 vol. in 2. Trends in Ling., Stud. and Monographs 32. Berlin: Mouton, 1986.

228 Donoghue, Daniel. *Style in Old English Poetry: The Test of the Auxiliary*. Yale Stud. in Eng. 196. New Haven, CT: Yale Univ. Press, 1987. Pp. xii + 234. [Extensive syntactic analysis of *Andreas*; see further item **244**.]

229 – 'On the Classification of B-Verses with Anacrusis in *Beowulf* and *Andreas.' N&Q* n.s. 34 (1987): 1–5.

230 Hall, J.R. 'Two Dark Old English Compounds: *ælmyrcan* (*Andreas* 432a) and *gūðmyrce* (*Exodus* 59a).' *Jnl of Eng. Ling.* 20 (1987): 38–47.

231 Nelson, Marie. 'The Old English *Andreas* as an Account of Benign Aggression.' *Med. Perspectives* (Richmond, KY, *et alibi*) 2.1 (1987): 81–9.

232 Biggs, Frederick M. 'The Passion of Andreas: *Andreas* 1398–1491.' *SP* 85 (1988): 413–27.

233 Porter, Nancy A. 'Wrestling with Loan-Words: Poetic Use of *engel, seraphim,* and *cherubim* in *Andreas* and *Elene.' NM* 89 (1988): 155–70.

234 Renoir, Alain. 'Oral-Formulaic Tradition and the Affective Interpretation of Early Germanic Verse.' In *Germania: Comparative Studies in the Old Germanic Languages and Literatures,* ed. Daniel G. Calder and T. Craig Christy, 113–26. Woodbridge: D.S. Brewer, 1988. [Comparison of *Andreas* and *Beowulf*; also for *Elene* and other Cynewulfian verse.]

235 Stevick, Robert D. 'The Manuscript Divisions of *Andreas.'* In *Philologia Anglica: Essays Presented to Professor Yoshio Terasawa on the Occasion of His Sixtieth Birthday,* ed. Kinshiro Oshitari et al., 225–40. Tokyo: Kenkyusha, 1988.

236 Waterhouse, Ruth. 'Self-Reflexivity and *wrætlic word* in *Bleak House* and *Andreas.' Jnl of Narrative Technique* 18 (1988): 211–25.

237 Hall, J.R. 'Old English *sæbeorg: Exodus* 442a, *Andreas* 308a.' *Papers on Lang. and Lit.* 25 (1989): 127–34.

238 Henrotte, Gayle A. 'The *Heliand* and *Andreas:* Jesus Stills the Waves.' In *Medieval German Literature: Proceedings from the Twenty-Third International Congress on Medieval Studies, Kalamazoo, Michigan, May 5–8, 1988,* ed. Albrecht Classen, 39–50. Göppinger Arbeiten zur Germanistik 507. Göppingen: Kümmerle, 1989.

239 Kolb, Eduard. 'Schiff und Seefahrt im *Beowulf* und im *Andreas.'* In *Meaning and Beyond: Ernst Leisi zum 70. Geburtstag,* ed. Udo Fries and Martin Heusser, 237–52. Tübingen: Narr, 1989.

240 Riedinger, Anita. '*Andreas* and the Formula in Transition.' In *Hermeneutics and Medieval Culture,* ed. Patrick J. Gallacher and Helen Damico, 183–91. Albany: State Univ. of New York Press, 1989.

241 Cronan, Dennis. 'Old English Water-Lands.' *ELN* 27.3 (1990): 6–9. [Aquatic terminology in *Andreas*; also on other verse and glosses.]

242 Rowland, Jenny. 'OE *ealuscerwen/meodoscerwen* and the Concept of "Paying for Mead."' *Leeds Stud. in Eng.* n.s. 21 (1990): 1–12.

[*Andreas*, esp. at pp. 9–12; comparison with Celtic traditions, as in *Gododdin*.]

243 Boenig, Robert. *Saint and Hero: 'Andreas' and Medieval Doctrine.* Lewisburg, PA: Bucknell Univ. Press, 1991. Pp. 133. Reviews: N.P. Howe, *Medievalia et Humanistica* n.s. 21 (1994): 133–8; M. Nelson, *JEGP* 92 (1993): 416–19; E.G. Whatley, *N&Q* n.s. 40 (1993): 516–18.

244 Donoghue, Daniel. 'Postscript on *Style in Old English Poetry*.' *NM* 92 (1991): 405–20. [Auxiliaries and other aspects of syntax in *Andreas* and other verse, pp. 405–8; see further item **228**.]

245 Henrotte, Gayle A. 'Jesus Asleep in the Boat: A Thrice-Told Tale.' In *De Gustibus: Essays for Alain Renoir*, ed. John Miles Foley, 250–65. New York: Garland, 1992. [Comparison with *Heliand*.]

246 Olsen, Alexandra Hennessey. 'The Aesthetics of *Andreas*: The Contexts of Oral Tradition and Patristic Latin Poetry.' 1992. In *De Gustibus*, ed. John Miles Foley, 388–410. See item **245**.

247 Cavill, Paul. '*Beowulf* and *Andreas*: Two Maxims.' *Neophilologus* 77 (1993): 479–87.

248 Ida, Hideho. 'Case Assignment in the Relative Clauses in *Andreas*.' *Doshisha Stud. in Eng.* (Kyoto) 60–1 (1993): 88–104.

249 — 'The Relative Pronouns in *Andreas*.' *Doshisha Stud. in Eng.* (Kyoto) 59 (1993): 67–86.

250 Riedinger, Anita R. 'The Formulaic Relationship between *Beowulf* and *Andreas*.' In *Heroic Poetry in the Anglo-Saxon Period: Studies in Honor of Jess B. Bessinger, Jr*, ed. Helen Damico and John Leyerle, 283–312. Stud. in Med. Culture 32. Kalamazoo, MI: Medieval Institute Publications, 1993.

251 Tkacz, Catherine Brown. 'Christian Formulas in Old English Literature: "næs hyre wlite gewemmed" and Its Implications.' *Traditio* 48 (1993): 31–61. [*Andreas* 1469–77 and related texts, in verse and in prose.]

252 Eto, Yasuharu. '*Andreas* 1229–52.' *Explicator* 52 (1993–4): 195–7.

253 Fee, Christopher. 'Productive Destruction: Torture, Text, and the Body in the Old English *Andreas*.' *Essays in Med. Stud.* (Chicago et alibi) 11 (1994): 51–62.

254 Clemoes, Peter. *Thought and Language in Old English Poetry.* CSASE 12. Cambridge: Cambridge Univ. Press, 1995. Pp. xvii + 523. [Esp. at pp. 250–72, in ch. 7, 'Vernacular Poetic Narrative in a Christian World.']

255 Foley, John Miles. 'The Poet's Self-Interruption in *Andreas*.' In *Prosody and Poetics in the Early Middle Ages: Essays in Honour of*

C.B. Hieatt, ed. M.J. Toswell, 42–59. Toronto: Univ. of Toronto Press, 1995.

256 Hermann, John P. 'Boniface and Dokkum: Terror, Repetition, Allegory.' *Medievalia et Humanistica* n.s. 22 (1995): 1–29. [*Andreas*, pp. 20–3.]

257 Macrae-Gibson, O.D., and J.R. Lishman. 'Computer Assistance in the Analysis of Old English Metre: Methods and Results: A Provisional Report.' 1995. In *Prosody and Poetics*, ed. M.J. Toswell, 102–16. See item **255**. [Also on *Elene* and other verse.]

–   Page, R.I. 1964. See item **178**. [Use of term *rūn*.]

258 Shaw, Brian. 'Translation and Transformation in *Andreas*.' 1995. In *Prosody and Poetics*, ed. M.J. Toswell, 164–79. See item **255**.

259 Watkins, Calvert. *How to Kill a Dragon: Aspects of Indo-European Poetics*. Oxford: Oxford Univ. Press, 1995. Pp. xiii + 613. ['The Germanic World,' sect. 43.2, for *Andreas* 1221–2.] Repr. 2001.

260 Kendall, Calvin B. 'Literacy and Orality in Anglo-Saxon Poetry: Horizontal Displacement in *Andreas*.' *JEGP* 95 (1996): 1–18.

261 Stévanovitch, Colette. 'Le menu des banquets dans la poésie vieil-anglaise.' In *Banquets et manières de table au Moyen Âge*, ed. [Anon.], 375–89. Sénéfiance 38. Aix-en-Provence: CUER MA, 1996. [Includes discussion of *Andreas*.]

262 Olsen, Karin. 'Animated Ships in Old English and Old Norse Poetry.' In *Animals and the Symbolic in Mediaeval Art and Literature*, ed. L.A.J.R. Houwen, 53–66. Mediaevalia Groningana 20. Groningen: Egbert Forsten, 1997. [*Andreas*, *Christ II* and *Guthlac B*.]

263 — 'The Dichotomy of Land and Sea in the Old English *Andreas*.' *ES* 79 (1998): 385–94.

264 Shippey, T.A., and Andreas Haarder, eds. *'Beowulf': The Critical Heritage* London: Routledge, 1998. Pp. xvii + 594. [Esp. in ch. 41, 'Jacob Grimm,' including a trans. of a letter discussing *Andreas*, *Elene*, *Beowulf*, and other verse in connection with his ed. in **69**; also for J.M. Kemble et al.]

265 Mora, María José. 'Un invierno entre los hielos: Los paisajes de la poesía anglosajona.' *Cuadernos del CEMyR* (La Laguna, Centro de estudios medievales y Renacentistas) 7 (1999): 225–42. [Also for *Beowulf* and other verse.]

266 Bammesberger, Alfred. 'Old English *unnan* in *Andreas*, line 298b.' *N&Q* n.s. 47 (2000): 409–11.

267 Herbison, Ivan. 'Generic Adaptation in *Andreas*.' In *Essays on Anglo-Saxon and Related Themes in Memory of Lynne Grundy*, ed. Jane Roberts and Janet Nelson, 181–211. King's College London

Med. Stud. 17. London: King's College, London, Centre for Late Antique and Medieval Studies, 2000.

268 Harbus, Antonina. 'A Mind for Hagiography: The Psychology of Resolution in *Andreas*.' In *Germanic Texts and Latin Models: Medieval Reconstructions*, ed. K.E. Olsen, A. Harbus, and T. Hofstra, 127–40. Mediaevalia Groningana n.s. 2. Louvain: Peeters, 2001.

269 Kelemen, Erick. '*Clyppan* and *cyssan*: The Formulaic Expression of Return from Exile in Old English Literature.' *ELN* 38.3 (2001): 1–19. [*Andreas* 1016 and twelve other occurrences, in verse and in prose.]

270 Abdou, Angela. 'Speech and Power in Old English Conversion Narratives.' *Florilegium* 17 (2002 for 2000): 195–212. [Esp. on *Andreas*, and on *Guthlac A* and *B*.]

271 Frank, Roberta. 'North-Sea Soundings in *Andreas*.' 2002. In item **66**, pp. 1–11.

272 Swisher, Michael. 'Beyond the Hoar Stone.' *Neophilologus* 86 (2002): 133–6. [Liminality in *Andreas*; also for *Beowulf* and OE prose.]

273 Cooke, William. 'Two Notes on *Beowulf* (with Glances at *Vafþrúðnismál*, *Blickling Homily 16*, and *Andreas*, lines 839–46).' *MÆ* 72 (2003): 297–301.

274 Dendle, Peter. 'Pain and Saint-Making in *Andreas*, Bede, and the Old English Lives of St Margaret.' In *Varieties of Devotion in the Middle Ages and Renaissance*, ed. Susan C. Karant-Nunn, 39–52. Arizona Stud. in the Middle Ages and the Renaissance 7. Turnhout: Brepols, 2003.

275 Wilcox, Jonathan. 'Eating People Is Wrong: Funny Style in *Andreas* and Its Analogues.' In *Anglo-Saxon Styles*, ed. Catherine E. Karkov and George Hardin Brown, 201–22. SUNY Ser. in Med. Stud. Albany: State Univ. of New York Press, 2003.

276 Bammesberger, Alfred. 'Old English *willan brucan* in *Andreas*, line 106b.' *N&Q* n.s. 51 (2004): 3–5.

277 Kabir, Ananya Jahanara. 'Towards a Contra-Modern Aesthetics: Reading the Old English *Andreas* against an Image of the Virgin of Guadalupe.' In *Signs of Change: Transformations of Christian Traditions and Their Representation in the Arts, 1000–2000*, ed. Nils Holger Petersen, Claus Clüver, and Nicolas Bell, 31–50. Textxet: Stud. in Comparative Lit. 43. Amsterdam: Rodopi, 2004.

– Scheil, Andrew P. 2004. See item **811**. ['Poetic Variations: *Andreas*,' pp. 228–38; treatment of Jews, esp. in the light of treatment of cannibals.]

278 Dockray-Miller, Mary. 'The *eadgiþ* Erasure: A Gloss on the Old English *Andreas*.' *ANQ* n.s. 18.1 (2005): 3–7.

279 Faerber, Robert. 'Les *Acta apocrypha apostolorum* dans le corpus littéraire vieil-anglais: *Acta Andreae.*' *Apocrypha* 16 (2005): 199–227. [Also esp. for *Fates of the Apostles.*]

280 Teresi, Loredana. '"Mangiatori d'uomini" e "mangiatori d'erba" nell'*Andreas*: Due modalità "mostruose" dell'alto Medioevo anglosassone.' In *'Fabelwesen,' mostri e portenti nell'immaginario occidentale. Medioevo germanico e altro*, ed. Carmela Rizzo, 303–25. Bibliotheca Germanica, Studi e testi 15. Alessandria: Edizioni dell'Orso, 2005.

281 Wightman, Bret A. '"I will never forsake you": The Divine Protection Theme in *Andreas.*' *In Geardagum* 25 (2005): 47–60.

282 Ida, Hideho. ['Is Jesus God or Man? A Comparative Study of Old English *Andreas* and Its Analogues.'] *Doshisha Stud. in Lang. and Culture* (Kyoto) 8.4 (2006): 679–90. [In Japanese.]

283 Johnson, David F. 'The *Crux usualis* as Apotropaic Weapon in Anglo-Saxon England.' 2006. In item **664**, pp. 80–95. [*Andreas*, pp. 87–9; also for *Elene.*]

284 Suzuki, Hironori. 'Effect of Alliteration on Constructions with Complex Predicates in Old English Poetry.' In *Textual and Contextual Studies in Medieval English: Towards the Reunion of Linguistics and Philology*, ed. Michiko Ogura, 179–92. Stud. in Eng. Med. Lang. and Lit. 13. Frankfurt: Peter Lang, 2006. [Analysis of *Andreas.*]

285 Fulk, R.D. 'Old English Meter and Oral Tradition: Three Issues Bearing on Poetic Chronology.' *JEGP* 106 (2007): 304–24. [Comparison of *Andreas* with *Beowulf* and other verse; also esp. on Cynewulfian verse.]

The Fates of the Apostles

EDITIONS

286 [Thorpe, Benjamin, ed.] 'The Fates of the Twelve Apostles, a Fragment.' 1834. In *Appendices to a Report on Rymer's 'Foedera,'* appendix B, pp. 90–2. See item **18**.

287 Kemble, John M., ed. and trans. 1856. See item **70**. [*Fates of the Apostles*, 2: 94–9, following title in item **286**.]

288 Grein, Christian W.M., ed. 1858. See item **72**. [*'Fata apostolorum,'* 2: 7–9.]

289 Wülker, Richard P., ed. 1888. See item **74**. ['Die Schicksale der Apostel,' pp. 87–91.]

290 Krapp, George Phillip, ed. 1906. See item **75**.
291 Craigie, W.A., ed. 1926. See item **76**. [*Fates of the Apostles*, pp. 31–3.]
292 Krapp, George Phillip, ed. 1932. See item **77**.
293 Magoun, Francis P., ed. 1960. See item **78**. [*Fates of the Apostles*, pp. 51–5.]
294 Brooks, Kenneth R. ed. 1961. See item **79**.

TRANSLATIONS

295 Kemble, John M., ed. and trans. 1856. See item **287**.
296 Kennedy, Charles W., trans. *The Poems of Cynewulf Translated into English*. London: Routledge, 1910. Pp. xii + 347. [*Fates of the Apostles*, pp. 197–9; also esp. for *Elene*, and for *Andreas* and *Dream of the Rood*.] Repr. New York: Peter Smith, 1949.
297 Gordon, R.K., trans. 1926. See item **87**. [*Fates of the Apostles*, pp. 197–9.]
298 Olivero, Federico, trans. 1927. See item **88**.
299 Kennedy, Charles W., trans. 1960. See item **90**. [Excerpt, p. 140.]
300 Bradley, S.A.J., trans. 1982. See item **91**. [*Fates of the Apostles*, Pp. 154–7.]
301 Boenig, Robert, trans. *Anglo-Saxon Spirituality: Selected Writings*. Classics of Western Spirituality 100. New York: Paulist Press, 2000. Pp. xviii + 330. ['Cynewulf: *The Fates of the Apostles*,' pp. 190–3. Also for *Dream of the Rood* and *Vercelli Homilies*.]

STUDIES

– Sweet, Henry. 1871. See item **429**. [Sees *Fates of the Apostles* as ending for *Andreas*, p. 16.]
– Wülker, Richard P. 1885. See item **24**. ['Schicksale der Apostel,' pp. 242–3.]
– — 1888. See item **74**. [*Andreas* and *Fates of the Apostles*.]
302 Napier, Arthur S. 'The Old English Poem *The Fates of the Apostles*.' *Academy* (London) 34 (1888): 153.
303 Cook, Albert S. 'The Affinities of the *Fata apostolorum*.' *MLN* 4 (1889): 4–8.
304 Kail, J. 'Über die Parallelstellen in der angelsächsischen Poesie.' *Anglia* 12 (1889): 21–40. [On studies by G. Sarrazin treating parallels in *Beowulf* and Cynewulfian verse; see further item **306**.]
– Napier, A[rthur S.]. 1889. See item **111**. [*Fates of the Apostles*, pp. 69–71.]

305 Sarrazin, Gregor. 'Die *Fata apostolorum* und der Dichter Kynewulf.'
     Anglia 12 (1889): 375–87.
306 — 'Parallelstellen in angelsächsischer Dichtung.' *Anglia* 14 (1892):
     186–92. [Reply to J. Kail, in item **304**.]
307 Trautmann, Moritz. 'Wer hat die "Schicksale der Apostel" zuerst für
     den Schluss des "Andreas" erklärt?' *Beiblatt zur 'Anglia'* 7 (1897):
     372–3. [For the hypothesis, see further item **429**.]
308 Brandl, Alois. 'Zu Cynewulfs *Fata apostolorum.*' *ASNSL* 100 (1898):
     330–4.
  – Bourauel, Johannes B. 1901. See item **133**. [Authorship and sources.]
309 Holthausen, Ferdinand. 'Zur Quelle der altenglischen *Fata apos-*
     tolorum.' *ASNSL* 106 (1901): 343–5.
  – Skeat, Walter W. 1901. See item **134**. [Relationship to *Andreas*.]
310 Barnouw, A.J. 'Die "Schicksale der Apostel" doch ein unabhängiges
     Gedicht.' *ASNSL* 108 (1902): 371–5.
311 Klaeber, Friedrich. 'Emendations in Old English Poems.' *MP* 2
     (1904–5): 141–6. [*Fates of the Apostles* 47–8, p. 146.]
  – Sarrazin, Gregor. 1907. See item **138**. [Pt. 1, 'Kynewulf,' pp. 145–58.]
  – Trautmann, Moritz. 1907. See item **139**. [Cynewulfian verse.]
312 Holthausen, Ferdinand. 'Zur altenglischen Literatur. XI.' *Beiblatt*
     zur 'Anglia' 21 (1910): 174–6. [See p. 175 for *Fates of the Apostles*,
     line 1; also on *Elene* and other verse.]
313 Perkins, R. 'On the Sources of the *Fata apostolorum.*' *MLN* 32
     (1917): 159–61.
  – Kock, Ernst A. 1918. See item **146**. [*Fates of the Apostles* 43–4, p. 7.]
  – — 1919. See item **148**. [On ll. 35–7, p. 303.]
314 Hamilton, George L. 'The Sources of *The Fates of the Apostles* and
     Andreas.' *MLN* 35 (1920): 385–95.
  – Holthausen, Ferdinand. 1920. See item **150**. [*Fates of the Apostles* 32,
     p. 28.]
  – Kock, Ernst A. 1922. See item **156**. [On ll. 84–5, p. 74.]
315 — *Plain Points and Puzzles: Sixty Notes on Old English Poetry.*
     Lunds universitets årsskrift n.s. 1, 17, no. 7. Lund: Gleerup, 1922.
     Pp. iv + 26. [*Fates of the Apostles* 103–5, p. 25; also for *Elene* and
     other verse.] Reviews: H.M. Flasdieck, *Beiblatt zur 'Anglia'* 33
     (1923): 223; F. Klaeber, *JEGP* 22 (1923): 313–15.
316 Schaar, Claes. *Critical Studies in the Cynewulf Group.* Lund Stud.
     in Eng. 17. Lund: Gleerup, 1949. Pp. 337. ['*Christ II* and the *Fata*
     apostolorum,' in ch. II; also esp. for *Elene*, and for *Andreas* and
     Dream of the Rood.]

317 Elliott, Ralph W.V. 'Cynewulf's Runes in *Juliana* and *Fates of the Apostles.*' *ES* 34 (1953): 193–204. Reissued in item **334**, pp. 293–307.

– Matsunami, Tamotsu. 1953. See item **330**. [Runic signatures.]

318 Muinzer, Louis A. 'Maier's Transcript and the Conclusion of Cynewulf's *Fates of the Apostles.*' *JEGP* 56 (1957): 570–87.

319 Diamond, Robert E. 'The Diction of the Signed Poems of Cynewulf.' *PQ* 38 (1959): 228–41. Reissued in item **334**, pp. 309–22.

320 Lehmann, Winfred P., and Virginia F. Dailey. *The Alliterations of the 'Christ,' 'Guthlac,' 'Elene,' 'Juliana,' 'Fates of the Apostles,' 'Dream of the Rood.'* Austin: Univ. of Texas, Dept. of Germanic Languages, 1960. Pp. vi + 401.

– Woolf, Rosemary. 1966. See item **184**, pp. 48–9. [Hagiographical context.]

– Whitbread, Leslie. 1967. See item **372**. [*Fates of the Apostles* 100–2, p. 472.]

321 Boren, James L. 'Form and Meaning in Cynewulf's *Fates of the Apostles.*' *Papers on Lang. and Lit.* 5 (1969): 115–22. Reissued in item **334**, pp. 57–65.

322 Hieatt, Constance B. 'The *Fates of the Apostles*: Imagery, Structure, and Meaning.' *Papers on Lang. and Lit.* 10 (1974): 115–25. Reissued in item **334**, pp. 67–77.

323 Calder, Daniel G. 'The *Fates of the Apostles*, the Latin Martyrologies, and the Litany of the Saints.' *MÆ* 44 (1975): 219–24.

324 Frese, Warwick Frese. 'The Art of Cynewulf's Runic Signatures.' 1975. In *Anglo-Saxon Poetry*, ed. Lewis E. Nicholson and Frese, 312–34. See item **201**. Reissued in item **334**, pp. 323–45.

325 Howlett, D.R. '*Se giddes begang* of *The Fates of the Apostles.*' *ES* 56 (1975): 385–9.

– Allen, Michael J.B., and Daniel G. Calder, trans. 1976. See item **203**. ['*The Fates of the Apostles*,' sect. III; Latin sources in trans.]

326 Ginsberg, Warren. 'Cynewulf and His Sources: *The Fates of the Apostles.*' *NM* 78 (1977): 108–14.

327 Rice, Robert C. 'The Penitential Motif in Cynewulf's *Fates of the Apostles* and in His Epilogues.' *ASE* 6 (1977): 105–19.

328 Russom, Geoffrey R. 'Artful Avoidance of the Useful Phrase in *Beowulf, The Battle of Maldon*, and *Fates of the Apostles.*' *SP* 75 (1978): 371–90.

329 Cross, J.E. 'Cynewulf's Traditions about the Apostles in *Fates of the Apostles.*' *ASE* 8 (1979): 13–75. Reissued in item **334**, pp. 79–94.

330 Matsunami, Tamotsu. 'Runic Passages in Cynewulf.' In *Old English Studies from Japan 1941–81*, ed. Tadao Kubouchi, William Schipper, and Hiroshi Ogawa, 65–74. *OEN* Subsidia 14. Binghamton, NY: Center for Medieval and Early Renaissance Studies, 1988. [Trans. of an article first pub. in Japanese in 1953.]

331 Wells, David A. 'Die Apostelverzeichnisse und die *Fata apostolorum* in der frühmittelhochdeutschen Literatur.' *ZDA* 120 (1991): 369–92. [Esp. at pp. 372–3.]

332 Gleason, Raymond E. 'The Riddle of the Runes: The Runic Passage in Cynewulf's *Fates of the Apostles*.' *Essays in Med. Stud.* (Chicago et alibi) 9 (1992): 19–32.

333 Rodrigues, Louis J. '"Cyn(e)wulf": More in Our Thoughts than in Our Prayers.' In *Papers from the VII International Conference of the Spanish Society for Medieval English Language and Literature*, ed. Bernardo Santano Moreno, Adrian R. Birtwistle, and Luis G. Girón Echevarría, 12–37. Cáceres: Servicio de Publicaciones, Universidad de Extremadura, 1995. ['The *Fates of the Apostles*,' sect. I.i.] Reissued in his '*The Dream of the Rood and Cyn(e)wulf*' and Other Critical Essays, 29–46. See item 641.

–   Cross, J.E. 1996. See item 1005. [*Fates of the Apostles* and other Cynewulfian verse, pp. 414–17.]

334 Bjork, Robert E., ed. *Cynewulf: Basic Readings*. Basic Readings in AS England 4. New York: Garland, 1996. Pp. xxv + 364. Repr. as *The Cynewulf Reader*. New York: Routledge, 2001.

335 García García, Fernando. '*The Fates of the Apostles* as a Rhetorical Exercise.' In *Medieval Studies: Proceedings of the Third International Conference of the Spanish Society for Medieval English Language and Literature*, ed. Luis Alberto Lázaro, José Simón, and Ricardo J. Sola, 129–39. Madrid: Universidad de Alcalá de Henares, 1996.

336 Bjork, Robert E. 'Cynewulf.' 1998. In *Medieval England: An Encyclopedia*, ed. Paul E. Szarmach et al., 227–9. See item 62.

337 Roberts, Jane. 'Cynewulf.' 1999. In *The Blackwell Encyclopaedia of Anglo-Saxon England*, ed. Michael Lapidge et al., 133–5. See item 63.

338 Anderson, James E., and Leslie D. Schilling. 'The *begang* of Cynewulf's *Fates of the Apostles*.' In *Essays on Old, Middle, Modern English, and Old Icelandic: In Honor of Raymond P. Tripp, Jr.*, ed. Loren C. Gruber, with Meredith Crellin Gruber and Gregory K. Jember, 23–47. Lampeter: Edwin Mellen Press, 2000.

339 McCulloh, John M. 'Did Cynewulf Use a Martyrology? Reconsidering the Sources of *The Fates of the Apostles*.' *ASE* 29 (2000): 67–83.
  – Faerber, Robert. 2005. See item **280**. [Treatment of Andrew.]
  – Fulk, R.D. 2007. See item **285**. [Metre and oral tradition.]

Soul and Body I

EDITIONS

340 [Thorpe, Benjamin, ed.] 'The Departed Soul's Address to the Body.' 1834. In *Appendices to a Report on Rymer's 'Foedera,'* appendix B, pp. 93–7, with erratum on p. 138. See item **18**. ['The Condemned Soul,' pt. 1, ll. 1–126; 'The Blessed Soul,' pt. 2, ll. 127–66.]
341 –, ed. and trans. *Codex Exoniensis: A Collection of Anglo-Saxon Poetry, from a Manuscript in the Library of the Dean and Chapter of Exeter, with an English Translation, Notes, and Indexes.* London: Pickering, 1842. Pp. xvi + 546. [Pub. for the Society of Antiquaries of London. Thorpe's work includes an ed. of 'A Departed Soul's Address to the Body,' pp. 367–77, with a trans. in parallel columns. This is presented in two parts: 'A Condemned Soul,' pp. 367–74, ed. from the Exeter Book, with variants cited from *Soul and Body I*, ll. 1–126; and 'A Blessed Soul (from the Vercelli MS.),' pp. 374–7, comprising *Soul and Body I*, ll. 127–66. In his notes, pp. 525–6, Thorpe observes that the 'second portion of this poem is not in the Exeter MS., and in the Vercelli MS., where alone it occurs, it is a fragment wanting an end.']
342 Kemble, John M., ed. and trans. 1856. See item **70**. [*Soul and Body I*, 2: 100–10, reproducing the title, division and subtitles introduced by Thorpe in item **340**.]
343 Grein, Christian W.M., ed. 1857. See item **72**. ['Reden der Seele an den Leichnam,' 1: 198–204, with 'nachträgliche Verbesserungen' at 2: 414; ed. of *Soul and Body I* and *II* comprising (1) an integral ed. of ll. 1–126, founded on the readings of the Vercelli Book, with variants in Grein's apparatus and emendations supplied from the Exeter Book, and (2) an ed. ('II. Nur im Cod. Vercell.') of ll. 127–66 of *Soul and Body I*.]
344 Wülker, Richard P., ed. 1888. See item **74**. ['Rede der Seele an den Leichnam,' pp. 92–107; ed. of *Soul and Body I* and *II* with parallel passages printed on facing pages.]

345 Krapp, George Phillip, ed. 1932. See item **77**.
346 Magoun, Francis P., ed. 1960. See item **78**. [*Soul and Body I*,
     pp. 56–61.]
347 Shippey, T.A., ed. and trans. *Poems of Wisdom and Learning in Old
     English*. Cambridge: D.S. Brewer, 1976. Pp. 152. ['*Soul and Body I*,'
     pp. 104–11.]
348 Moffat, Douglas, ed. and trans. *The Old English 'Soul and Body.'*
     Woodbridge: D.S. Brewer, 1990. Pp. [viii] + 103. [Parallel passages of
     Soul and Body I and *II* are ed. on facing pages, under the title 'The
     Damned Soul,' pp. 48–61; separate ed. of *Soul and Body I* 127–67,
     under the title 'The Blessed Soul,' pp. 62–4.] Reviews: J. Čermák,
     MÆ 60 (1991): 298; A.J. Frantzen, *Envoi* 3 (1992): 173–7; K. O'B.
     O'Keeffe, *Speculum* 67 (1992): 1012–13; E.A. Rowe, *Anglia* 110
     (1992): 177–81; E.G. Stanley, *RES* n.s. 43 (1992): 401–2; A. Wawn,
     MLR 87 (1992): 922–3.

TRANSLATIONS

349 Thorpe, Benjamin, ed. and trans. 1842. See item **341**. [Trans. of ll.
     125–64 of *Soul and Body I*.]
350 Kemble, John M., ed. and trans. 1856. See item **342**.
351 Gordon, R.K., trans. 1926. See item **87**. ['The Soul's Address to the
     Body,' pp. 310–13.]
352 Shippey, T.A., ed. and trans. 1976. See item **347**.
353 Moffat, Douglas, ed. and trans. 1990. See item **348**.

STUDIES

354 Rieger, Max. 'Zwei Gespräche zwischen Seele und Leib.' *Germania*
     (Stuttgart *et alibi*) 3 (1858): 396–407. [See esp. pp. 398–10 for *Soul
     and Body I*.]
355 Kleinert, Gustav. *Über den Streit zwischen Leib und Seele. Ein
     Beitrag zur Entwicklungsgeschichte der 'Visio Fulberti.'* Halle diss.
     Iserlohn: Bädeker, 1880. Pp. 80. Reviews: G. P[aris], *Romania* 9
     (1880): 311–14; H. Varnhagen, *Anglia*. 3 (1880): 569–81, at 577.
  – Napier, A[rthur S.] 1889. See item **111**. [*Soul and Body I*, p. 69.]
356 Bruce, J.D. 'A Contribution to the Study of "The Body and the
     Soul": Poems in English.' *MLN* 5 (1890): 193–201. [Cites ed. of *Soul
     and Body I* and *II* in item **343**.]

357 Buchholz, Richard. *Die Fragmente der 'Reden der Seele an den Leich-nam' in zwei Handschriften zu Worcester und Oxford, neu heraus-gegeben nebst einer Untersuchung über Sprache und Metrik, sowie einer deutschen Übersetzung.* Erlanger Beiträge zur englischen Philologie 6. Erlangen: Deichert, 1890. Pp. lxxvi + 28. [Brief consideration of *Soul and Body I* and *II* in sect. III, 'Quellenfrage.'] Reviews: M. Kaluza, *Literaturblatt für germanische und romanische Philologie* 12 (1891): cols. 12–16; J. Zupitza, *ASNSL* 85 (1890): 78–83.

358 Deering, [Robert] Waller. *The Anglo-Saxon Poets on the Judgement Day.* Leipzig diss. Halle an der Saale: Niemeyer, 1890. Pp. [vi] + 85. [Esp. at pp. 3–9, 17, 31, 36–9, 42, 45, 61, 80; also for *Andreas, Elene, Dream of the Rood.*] Reviews: O. Glöde, *Literaturblatt für german-ische und romanische Philologie* 13 (1892): cols. 118–21; R. W[ülker], *Literarisches Zentralblatt* 43 (1892): 723–4.

359 Batiouchkof, Thedor Dimitrievich. 'Le débat de l'âme et du corps.' *Romania* 20 (1891): 1–55, 513–78. [Discussion of *Soul and Body I* and *II*, esp. at pp. 2–9; the French article is an abridgment of an original ser. of articles in Russian, which also appeared as a book, *Spor dushi s tyélom: V pamyatnikach sredne-vikovoi literature. Opet istoricosrav-niteliavago izslyedavaniya.* St. Petersburg: Tip. V.S. Balasheva, 1891. Pp. 314.]

360 Zupitza, Julius. 'Zu "Seele und Leib."' *ASNSL* 91 (1893): 369–404. [Examines homiletic prose related to *Vercelli Homily IV* in connec-tion with Thorpe's hypothesis that a work in prose stands behind *Soul and Body I* and *II*.]

361 Klaeber, Fr[iedrich]. 'Zu altenglischen Dichtungen.' *ASNSL* 113 (1904): 146–9. [*Soul and Body I* 5–7, pp. 148–9; see also for *Elene*.]

362 Holthausen, F. 'Zur Textkritik altenglischer Dichtungen.' *Englische Studien* 37 (1907): 198–211. [See p. 198 for *Soul and Body I* 44–5, 47–8; see also on *Homiletic Fragment I, Dream of the Rood,* and other verse.]

  – Grau, Gustav. 1908. See item **140**. ['Reden der Seelen,' pp. 174–5, on *Soul and Body I* and *II*.]

363 Dudley, Louise. 'An Early Homily on the "Body and Soul" Theme.' *JEGP* 8 (1909): 225–53. [See esp. at pp. 239–53; also esp. for parallel texts cited in connection with *Vercelli Homily IV* in item **834**.]

364 — *The Egyptian Elements in the Legend of the Body and Soul.* Bryn Mawr College Monographs 8. Baltimore, MD: Furst, 1911. Pp. 179. [Includes discussion of *Soul and Body I* and *II*.]

– Holthausen, Ferdinand. 1920. See item **150**. [*Soul and Body I* 47–8, p. 28.]

365 Kurtz, Benjamin P. '*Gifer* the Worm: An Essay toward the History of an Idea.' *Univ. of California Pub. in Eng.* 2.2 (1929): 235–61. [*Soul and Body I* and *II*: on the former esp. at pp. 235–7.]

366 Oakden, J.P., with the assistance (in vol. 2 only) of Elizabeth R. Innes. *Alliterative Poetry in Middle English.* 2 vols. Manchester: Manchester Univ. Press, 1930–5. Pp. xii + 273, x + 403. [Subtitles: Vol. 1, *The Dialectal and Metrical Survey*; vol. 2, *A Survey of the Traditions*. Includes hypothesis of dependence of Worcester *Soul's Address to the Body* on archetype of *Soul and Body I* and *II*. See vol. 2, pp. 3–4.] Repr. Hamden, CT: Archon, 1968.

367 Willard, Rudolph. 'The Address of the Soul to the Body.' *PMLA* 50 (1935): 957–83. [*Soul and Body I* and *II*; also for *Vercelli Homilies IV, XI.*]

368 Heningham, Eleanor K. *An Early Latin Debate of the Body and Soul Preserved in MS Royal 7.A.III. in the British Museum* 6–8, New York Univ. diss., Menasha, WI: Banta, 1939. Pp. 83, 4 plates. [See esp. pp. 6–8, 13–14, 52–3; also for *Vercelli Homilies.*]

369 – 'Old English Precursors of the Worcester Fragments.' *PMLA* 55 (1940): 291–307. [*Soul and Body I* and *II*; also for *Vercelli Homilies.*]

370 Bolton, W.F., ed. *An Old English Anthology.* London: Arnold, 1963. Pp. [xi] + 178. ['*Soul and Body,*' pp. 121–4, from Exeter Book; includes comments on *Soul and Body I*.] Repr. Evanston, IL: Northwestern Univ. Press, 1996.

371 Smetana, Cyril. 'Second Thoughts on *Soul and Body I*.' *MS* 29 (1967): 193–205.

372 Whitbread, L. 'The Doomsday Theme in Old English Poetry.' *BGDSL* 89 (1967): 452–81. ['*Soul and Body,*' pp. 465–7; also for *Fates of the Apostles, Elene.*]

373 Hill, Thomas D. 'Punishment According to the Joints of the Body in the Old English *Soul and Body II*.' *N&Q* n.s. 15 (1968): 409–10. [Also for *Soul and Body I*; see further item **376**.]

374 Gatch, Milton McC. *Death: Meaning and Mortality in Christian Thought and Contemporary Culture.* New York: Seabury Press, 1969. Pp. viii + 216. [Pt. 2, ch. 5, 'The Early Medieval Tradition,' discusses *Soul and Body I* and *II*, and other verse.]

375 Gyger, Alison. 'The Old English *Soul and Body* as an Example of Oral Transmission.' *MÆ* 38 (1969): 239–44.

376 Hill, Thomas D. 'Punishment According to the Joints of the Body, Again' *N&Q* n.s. 16 (1969): 246. [See item **373**.]
377 Ferguson, Mary Heyward. 'The Structure of the *Soul's Address to the Body* in Old English.' *JEGP* 69 (1970): 72–80. [Includes brief comparison of *Soul and Body I* and *II*.]
 – Scragg, D.G. 1970. See item **42**. [Anomalous use of initial *h* in copy of *Soul and Body I*, pp. 172–3, 179.]
 – Allen, Michael J.B., and Daniel G. Calder, trans. 1976. See item **203**. ['*Soul and Body I* and *II*,' sect. IV; Latin sources in trans.]
 – Healey, Antonette diPaolo. 1978. See item **917**, pp. 45–8. [Context in corpus of OE.]
378 Orton, P.R. 'Disunity in the Vercelli Book *Soul and Body*.' *Neophilologus* 63 (1979): 450–60.
379 – 'The OE *Soul and Body*: A Further Examination.' *MÆ* 48 (1979): 173–97. [*Soul and Body I* and *II*.]
380 Marino, Cinzia. 'Il poema anglosassone *The Grave*.' Istituto universitario orientale, *Annali*, Filologia germanica (Naples) 24 (1981): 201–10. [*Soul and Body I* and *II*, pp. 204–5.]
 – Ó Carragáin, É. 1981. See item **560**. [Context in Vercelli Book.]
381 Frantzen, Allen J. 'The Body in *Soul and Body I*.' *Chaucer Rev.* 17 (1982): 76–88.
382 Moffat, Douglas. 'The MS Transmission of the OE *Soul and Body*.' *MÆ* 52 (1983): 300–2. [*Soul and Body I* and *II*.]
383 – 'The Worcester *Soul's Address to the Body*: An Examination of Fragment Order.' *Papers on Lang. and Lit.* 20 (1984): 123–40. [*Soul and Body I* and *II*, p. 130 with n. 18.]
384 – 'A Case of Scribal Revision in the Old English *Soul and Body*.' *JEGP* 86 (1987): 1–8. [*Soul and Body I* and *II*.]
385 – , ed. '*The Soul's Address to the Body*': *The Worcester Fragments*. Med. Texts and Stud. 1. East Lansing, MI: Colleagues Press, 1987. Pp. vii + 133. [Discussion of *Soul and Body I* and *II*, esp. at pp. 41–3; also esp. on *Vercelli Homily IV*.] Reviews: J. Johansen, *Eng. Stud. in Canada* 14 (1988): 343–7; E.G. Stanley, *Yearbook of Langland Stud.* 1 (1987): 150–2.
386 Gatch, Milton McC. 'Perceptions of Eternity.' In *The Cambridge Companion to Old English Literature*, ed. Malcolm Godden and Michael Lapidge, 190–205. Cambridge: Cambridge Univ. Press, 1991. [*Soul and Body I* and *II*.] Repr. in his *Eschatology and Christian Nurture: Themes in Anglo-Saxon and Medieval Religious*

Life, item V. Variorum Collected Stud. Ser. 681. Aldershot: Variorum, 2000.

387 Moffat, Douglas. 'Anglo-Saxon Scribes and Old English Verse.' *Speculum* 67 (1992): 805–27. ['Scribal Performance in the Versions of *Soul and Body*,' sect. 4; also esp. in sect. 5.]

388 Liuzza, Roy Michael. 'On the Dating of *Beowulf*.' In *'Beowulf'*: *Basic Readings*, ed. Peter S. Baker, 281–302. Basic Readings in AS England 1. New York: Garland, 1995. [Statistical analysis of textual variation in *Soul and Body I* and *II*.] Repr. as The *'Beowulf'* *Reader*. 2000.

389 Matto, Michael. 'The Old English *Soul and Body I* and *Soul and Body II*: Ending the Rivalry.' *In Geardagum* 18 (1997): 39–58.

390 Boudreau, Michael R. '*Soul and Body I* and *II*.' 1998. In *Medieval England: An Encyclopedia*, ed. Paul E. Szarmach et al., 706. See item **62**.

391 Hoek, Michelle. 'Violence and Ideological Inversion in the Old English *Soul's Address to the Body*.' *Exemplaria* 10 (1998): 271–85. [Treats passages common to *Soul and Body I* and *II*.]

392 Orton, Peter. *The Transmission of Old English Poetry*. Westfield Pub. in Medieval Stud. 12. Turnhout: Brepols, 2000. Pp. xvii + 223. ['*Soul and Body I* (SB1),' *ad indicem*, pp. 222–3.]

393 Fulk, R.D. 'On Argumentation in Old English Philology, with Particular Reference to the Editing and Dating of *Beowulf*.' *ASE* 32 (2003): 1–26. [Esp. at pp. 17–21.]

Homiletic Fragment I

EDITIONS

394 [Thorpe, Benjamin, ed.] 'A Fragment, Moral and Religious.' 1834. In *Appendices to a Report on Rymer's 'Foedera*,' appendix B, pp. 98–9. See item **18**.

395 Kemble, John M., ed. and trans. 1856. See item **70**. [*Homiletic Fragment I*, 2: 79–82, following title in item **394**.]

396 Grein, Christian W.M., ed. 1858. See item **72**. ['*Bi manna lease*,' 2: 142–3.]

397 Wülker, Richard P., ed. 1888. See item **74**. ['Predigtbruchstück über Psalm 28,' pp. 108–10.]

398 Krapp, George Phillip, ed. 1932. See item **77**.

399 Magoun, Francis P., ed. 1960. See item **78**. [*Homiletic Fragment I*, pp. 62–3.]

TRANSLATION

400 Kemble, John M., ed. and trans. 1856. See item **395**.

STUDIES

- Napier, A[rthur S.] 1889. See item **111**. [*Homiletic Fragment I*, p. 69; cited as 'Predigtbruchstück.']
- Holthausen, Ferdinand. 1892. See item **118**. [*Homiletic Fragment I* ll. 12, 40–1, p. 551; cited as 'Predigt über ps. 28 (*Be manna léase*).']
- —. 1907. See item **362**. *Homiletic Fragment I*, ll. 43–4, cited as 'Predigt über ps. 28.']
- —. 1920. See item **150**. [Line 40, p. 28; cited as 'Predigt über Psalm 28.']
- Kock, Ernst A. 1920. See item **152**. [Line 27, p. 253.]
401 Hill, Thomas D. 'The Hypocritical Bee in the Old English *Homiletic Fragment I*, lines 18–30.' *N&Q* n.s. 15 (1968): 123.
402 Isaacs, Neil D. 'The Old English "Taste of Honey."' In his *Structural Principles in Old English Poetry*, 99–106. Knoxville: Univ. of Tennessee Press, 1968.
403 Pulsiano, Phillip. 'Bees and Backbiters in the Old English *Homiletic Fragment I*.' *ELN* 25.2 (1987): 1–6.
- Wilcox, Jonathan. 1990. See item **602**.

The Dream of the Rood

EDITIONS

404 [Thorpe, Benjamin, ed.] 'The Holy Rood, a Dream.' 1834. In *Appendices to a Report on Rymer's 'Foedera,'* appendix B, pp. 100–4, with erratum on p. 138. See item **18**.
405 Bouterwek, Karl W., ed. and trans. *Caedmon's des Angelsachsen biblische Dichtungen*. 2 vols. 1849–54. Vol. 1, pt. 1, Gütersloh: Bertelsmann, 1854. Pp. [vi] + ccxxxviii. Vol. 1, pt. 2, Elberfeld: Bädeker, 1849. Pp. [ii] + 353, folded plate. Vol. 2, Elberfeld: Bädeker, 1851. Pp. xxiv + 393. [Vol. 1 was issued as two sequentially paginated pts., the second of which was the first to be pub. Vol. 2 was pub. with the main title, as above, on the series page (facing the title page), and a subtitle, *Ein angelsächsisches Glossar*, on the title page. In addition to the verse of the Junius manuscript, the contents include an ed. and trans. of *Dream of the Rood* ('Das heilige Kreuz [*Seó hálge rôd*],' 1: clxviii–clxxviii, in

intro.), following text in item **404**, as well as other verse and prose.]
Reviews: [Anon.], *Literarisches Zentralblatt* 2 (1851): 739; [Anon.],
Literarisches Zentralblatt 8 (1857): 106–8 [signed by 'Gn']; A. Holtz-
mann, *Germania* (Stuttgart *et alibi*) 1 (1856): 244–7. Repr. Wiesbaden:
Sandig, 1968.

406 Kemble, John M., ed. and trans. 1856. See item **70**. [*Dream of the
Rood*, 2: 83–93, following title in item **404**.]

407 Grein, Christian W.M., ed. 1858. See item **72**. ['Das heilige Kreuz,' 2:
143–7, with corrections at 2: [416].]

408 Stephens, George. *The Ruthwell Cross, Northumbria, from about
A.D. 680, with Its Runic Verses by Cædmon and Cædmon's Com-
plete Cross-Lay, 'The Holy Rood, a Dream,' from a South-English
Transcript of the Tenth Century*. London: J.R. Smith, 1866. Pp. [iv]
+ 46, 2 folded plates. [Pp. 21–30; follows text in **404**; includes trans.]
Rev. reissue in Stephens, *The Old-Northern Runic Monuments of
Scandinavia and England, now First Collected and Deciphered*, ed.
(in vol. 4 only) Sven Otto Magnus Söderberg. 3 vols. in 4. London:
J.R. Smith et al., 1866–1901. Vol. 1, pp. lxxx + 1–404. 1866. Vol. 2,
pp. [vi] + 405–1038. 1866. Vol. 3, pp. viii + 508. 1868. Vol. 4, pp.
[viii] + 108. 1901. [For treatments of *Dream of the Rood*, see, in the
rev. reissue, 1: 405–48; 2: 865; 3: 189; 4: 3.]

409 Pacius, A., ed. and trans. *Das heilige Kreuz. Angelsächsisches Lied,
stabreimend übersetzt und erklärt*. Gera: Rudolph, 1873. Pp. 16.

410 Wülker, Richard P., ed. 1888. See item **74**. ['Traumgesicht vom
Kreuze Christi,' pp. 111–25.]

411 Cook, Albert S., ed. *'The Dream of the Rood,' an Old English Poem
Attributed to Cynewulf*. Oxford: Clarendon Press, 1905. Pp. lx + 66.
Reviews: [Anon.], *Deutsche Literaturzeitung* 27 (1906): 1957; G.
Binz, *Englische Studien* 36 (1906): 255–6; [G.] Herzfeld, *ASNSL* 117
(1906): 187–9; F. Klaeber, *Beiblatt zur 'Anglia'* 17 (1906): 97–102.

412 Hewison, James King, trans. 1911. See item **441**. [Includes OE in
reissue.]

413 Craigie, W.A., ed. 1926. See item **76**. [*Dream of the Rood*, pp. 10–
14.]

414 Ricci, Aldo, ed. and trans. *Cynewulf. 'Il sogno della Croce,' 'Cristo.'
Antichi poemetti anglosassoni riveduti nel testo, con versione a
fronte, introduzione e note*. Biblioteca Sansoniana straniera 57.
Florence: Sansoni, [1926]. Pp. xxxiv + 205. Repr. 1954.

415 Krapp, George Phillip, ed. 1932. See item **77**.

416 Dickins, Bruce, and Alan S.C. Ross, eds. *The Dream of the Rood*.
Methuen's OE Lib. London: Methuen, 1934. Pp xii + 50, illus.

Reviews: H. Bütow, *Beiblatt zur 'Anglia'* 46 *(*1935): 161–5; C.D. Chrétien, *JEGP* 34 (1935): 573–5; W.A.G. Doyle-Davidson, *ES* 18 (1936): 165–72; J.R. Hulbert, *MP* 34 (1936–7): 75–7; A. M[acdonald], *MLR* 30 (1935): 551–2; F. M[ossé], *Revue germanique* 26 (1935): 379; J. Raith, *Beiblatt zur 'Anglia'* 48 (1937): 66–8; F.R. Schröder, *Germanisch-romanische Monatsschrift* 23 (1935): 157; A.E.H. Swaen, *Neophilologus* 21 (1936): 57–8; [Anon.], *TLS* 21 Mar. 1935: 175; C.L. W[renn], *Oxford Mag.* 53 (30 May 1935): 683–4; *idem, RES* 12 (1936): 105–8. 2nd ed. 1945; [3rd ed.] 1951; [4th ed.] 1954. Repr. 1956. Repr. with additions and corrections, 1963. Repr., with further corrections and additions to bibliography, New York: Appleton-Century-Crofts, 1966.

417 Bütow, Hans, ed. *Das altenglische 'Traumgesicht vom Kreuz.' Textkritisches, Literaturgeschichtliches, Kunstgeschichtliches.* Anglistische Forschungen 78. Heidelberg: Winter, 1935. Pp. vii + 185. Reviews: C.D. Chrétien, *JEGP* 34 (1935): 573–5; F. Holthausen, *Literaturblatt für germanische und romanische Philologie* 57 (1936): 100–1; F. Klaeber, *Englische Studien* 71 (1936–7): 84–6; F. M[ossé], *Revue germanique* 28 (1937): 212; F. Norman, *Beiblatt zur 'Anglia'* 47 (1936): 6–10; F.R. Schröder, *Germanisch-romanische Monatsschrift* 23 (1935): 157.

418 Magoun, Francis P., ed. 1960. See item 78. [*Dream of the Rood*, pp. 64–9.]

419 Campbell, Jackson J., and James L. Rosier, eds. 1962. See item 80. [*Dream of the Rood*, pp. 35–40.]

420 Pope, John C., ed. *Seven Old English Poems.* Indianapolis, IN: Bobbs-Merrill, 1966. Pp. x + 213. [*Dream of the Rood*, item 3.] Review: A. Crépin *EA* 22 (1969): 413–14. Repr. New York: Norton, 1981. Reissued and expanded as *Eight Old English Poems.* Rev. R.D. Fulk. New York: Norton, 2001. Pp. xvi + 243.

421 Hamer, Richard, ed. and trans. *A Choice of Anglo-Saxon Verse.* London: Faber, 1970. Pp. 207. [*Dream of the Rood*, pp. 159–71.]

422 Swanton, Michael, ed. *The Dream of the Rood.* Old and Middle Eng. Texts Ser. Manchester: Manchester Univ. Press, 1970. Pp. x + 146. Reviews: G. Clark, *Speculum* 47 (1972): 551–5; H. Pilch, *Anglia* 90 (1972): 518–19; B.C. Raw, *MÆ* 41 (1972): 135–7. Repr. 1978. Rev. ed. Exeter: Univ. of Exeter Press, 1987. Pp. ix + 150. Rev. reissue 1996.

423 Pezzini, Domenico, ed. and trans. *'Il sogno della Croce' e liriche del duecento inglese sulla Passione.* Biblioteca medievale 25. Parma: Pratiche, 1992. Pp. 169. Review: P. Tornaghi, *Aevum* 69 (1995): 431–4.

424 Mitchell, Bruce. 1998. See item **639**. ['Repunctuated' ed.]
425 Kelly, Richard J., and Ciarán L. Quinn, trans. 1999. See item **473**.
[Includes OE, pp. 42–50.]

TRANSLATIONS

–   Kemble, John M. 1843. See item **480**. [Partial trans.]
426 Bouterwek, Karl W., ed. and trans. 1854. See item **405**.
427 Kemble, John M., ed. and trans. 1856. See item **406**.
428 Stephens, George. 1866. See item **408**.
429 Sweet, Henry. 'Sketch of the History of Anglo-Saxon Poetry.' In
Thomas Warton et al., *History of English Poetry from the Twelfth to
the Close of the Sixteenth Century*, ed. William Carew Hazlitt, 2:
3–19. 4 vols. London: Reeves and Turner, 1871. [Abridged trans.,
pp. 18–19; also for *Andreas* and *Fates of the Apostles*.]
430 [Anon.] *Cædmon: The Anglo-Saxon Poet*. London: [n.p.], 1873.
Pp. 64. [Paraphrase, with sporadic metrical trans., of Junius poems,
pp. 13–61, adapted from trans. by B. Thorpe.] Rev. ed. pub. as:
Robert Tate Gaskin, *Cædmon: The First English Poet*. London:
SPCK, 1902. Pp. 75. [Contains additional material including (on
pp. 61–3) a trans. of *Dream of the Rood*, ll. 1–84.] Review: [Anon.],
Academy (London) 62 (1902): 528.
431 Pacius, A., trans. 1873. See item **409**.
432 Hickey, Emily H., trans. '*The Dream of the Rood* (from the English of
Cynewulf).' *Academy* (London) 21 (1882): 248–9. [Trans. of ll. 1–89
only.]
433 — *Verse-Tales, Lyrics, and Translations*. London: Mathews, 1889.
Pp. viii + 120. ['The Dream of the Holy Rood, from the English of
Cynewulf,' pp. 117–20.]
434 Brown, Anna R., trans. '*The Dream of the Holy Rood.*' *Poet-Lore* 2
(1890): 371–4. [Trans. of ll. 1–89 only.]
435 Gollancz, I., trans. In G.F. Browne. *Theodore and Wilfrith: Lectures
Delivered in St. Paul's in December 1896*. London: SPCK, 1897.
[Trans. of *Dream of the Rood* by Gollancz, pp. 248–54]
436 [Anon.] 'The First English Poet: A Cross at Whitby.' *Academy*
(London) 54 (1898): 275–6. [Includes partial trans. of *Dream of
Rood*.]
437 Garnett, James M., trans. 1900. See item **687**, 2nd ed.
438 Cook, Albert S., and Chauncey B. Tinker, trans. 1902. See item **84**.
[Pp. 93–9.]

– Gaskin, Robert Tate. 1902. See item **430**.
439 Postgate, Isabella J., trans. *The Dream of the Rood*. Woodford Green: Maurice, 1904. Pp. 4. Repr. London: Drane's, 1910. Repr. 1924.
440 Kennedy, Charles W., trans. 1910. See item **296**. [*Dream of the Rood*, pp. 306–11; as 'Cynewulfian' verse.]
441 Hewison, James King, trans. '*The Dream of the Rood': A Metrical Translation*. Dumfries: [n.p.], 1911. Pp. 8. [Repr. from *The Dumfries and Galloway Courier and Herald*.] Reissued, with facing text of the OE poem, in his *The Runic Roods of Ruthwell and Bewcastle, with a Short History of the Cross and Crucifix in Scotland*, 154–63. Glasgow: J. Smith, 1914.
442 Roy, J.A, trans. '*The Dream of the Rood': An Old English Poem Done into Modern Verse*. London: Bagster, 1912. Pp. 11.
443 Spaeth, J[ohn] Duncan, trans. *Old English Poetry: Translations into Alliterative Verse with Introductions and Notes*. Princeton, NJ: Princeton Univ. Press, 1921. Pp. xii + 268. ['The Vision of the Cross (Ascribed to Cynewulf),' pp. 123–8.]
444 Gordon, R.K., trans. 1926. See item **87**. [*Dream of the Rood*, pp. 261–4.]
445 Ricci, Aldo, ed. and trans. 1926. See item **414**. [Italian trans.]
446 Malone, Kemp, trans. *Ten Old English Poems Put into Modern English Alliterative Verse*. Baltimore, MD: Johns Hopkins Press, 1941. Pp. 49. [*Dream of the Rood*, pp. 3–7.]
447 Brooks, Harold F., trans. *The Dream of the Rood*. Dublin: Sign of the Three Candles, 1942. Pp. 7. Reviews: [Anon.], *TLS* 18 Apr. 1942: 203; H.A.C. Green, *MLR* 37 (1942): 530.
448 Magoun, F.P., Jr, and J.A. Walker, trans. *An Old-English Anthology: Translations of Old-English Prose and Verse*. Dubuque, IA: William C. Brown, 1950. Pp. x + 108. [Trans. of ll. 1–89, pp. 95–7.]
449 Kennedy, Charles W., trans. 1952. See item **89**. ['A Dream of the Cross,' in ch. 2.]
450 Raffel, Burton, trans. '*The Dream of the Rood*: A New Translation, from the Anglo-Saxon.' *London Mag.* 5 (Sept. 1958): 19–23. Reissued in his *Poems from the Old English*, with a foreword by Robert P. Creed, 21–5. Lincoln: Univ. of Nebraska Press, 1960. [For reviews, see item **53**, p. 35, no. 404.] 2nd ed. 1964. Augmented reissue in item **472**.
451 Kennedy, Charles W., trans. 1960. See item **90**. ['A Dream of the Rood,' pp. 144–8.]
452 Szabó, László C., trans. 'Álom a Keresztről.' *Katolikus szemle* 13 (1961): 15–18. [Hungarian trans.]

453 Bolton, W.F., ed. 1963. See item **370**. [*Dream of the Rood*, pp. 96–101.]

454 Crossley-Holland, Kevin, trans. '*The Battle of Maldon,*' *and Other Old English Poems*. Ed. Bruce Mitchell. London: Macmillan, 1965. Pp. xi + 138. [*Dream of the Rood*, pp. 123–4.]

455 Sanesi, Roberto, trans. *Poemi anglosassoni. Le origini della poesia inglese (vi–x secolo)*. Milan: Lerici, 1966. Pp. 223. ['Il sogno della Croce,' item 8; also for *Elene*.] Reissued, Milan: Guanda, 1975. Pp. 118.

456 Hieatt, Constance B., trans. '*Beowulf*' *and Other Old English Poems*. Intro. by A. Kent Hieatt. New York: Odyssey Press, 1967. Pp. vi + 119. [*Dream of the Rood*, item 6.] 2nd ed. New York: Bantam Books, 1983. Pp. xxxviii + 149. Repr. 1988.

457 Gardner, Helen. '*The Dream of the Rood*: An Exercise in Verse-Translation.' In *Essays and Poems Presented to Lord David Cecil*, [ed. W.W. Robson], 18–36. London: Constable, 1970. [Includes commentary, pp. 24–36.]

458 Hamer, Richard, ed. and trans. 1970. See item **421**.

459 Huppé, Bernard F. 1970. See item **516**.

460 Nist, John, trans. 'Dream of the Cross.' *OEN* 10.2 (1977): 16–18. [Trans. of ll. 1–89.]

461 Kanayama, Atsumu, trans. ['*The Dream of the Rood*: A Japanese Translation.'] *Osaka Gaidai Eng. and Amer. Stud.* 11 (1979): 147–54.

462 Crépin, André, trans. *Poèmes héroïques vieil-anglais. 'Beowulf,' 'Judith,' 'Maldon,' 'Plainte de l'exilée,' 'Exaltation de la Croix.'* Bibliothèque médiévale. Paris: Union générale d'éditions, 1981. Pp. 191.

463 Bradley, S.A.J., trans. 1982. See item **91**. [*Dream of the Rood*, pp. 158–63.]

464 Crossley-Holland, Kevin, trans. *The Anglo-Saxon World*. Woodbridge: Boydell Press, 1982. Pp. x + 275. [*Dream of the Rood*, in sect. 9.] Reissued as *The Anglo-Saxon World: An Anthology*. Oxford: Oxford Univ. Press, 1984. Pp. xii + 308. Repr. 1999. Repr. of original ed. Woodbridge: Boydell Press, 2002.

465 Amano, Koichi, trans. ['A Japanese Translation of an Old English Poem, *The Dream of the Rood*.'] *Treatises and Stud. by the Faculty of Kinio Gakuin Univ.* 119 (1987): 1–20.

466 Dyson, Ketaki Kushari, trans. *Anglo-Saxon Kabita*. Calcutta: Navana, 1987. Pp. 79 [Includes trans. of *Dream of the Rood* into alliterative Bengali half-lines.]

467 DiNapoli, Robert, trans. 'Four Old English Poems in Translation.'
   Scintilla: A Student Jnl for Medievalists (Toronto) 7 (1990): 37–51.
   [Includes trans. of *Dream of the Rood*.]
468 Pezzini, Domenico, ed. and trans. 1992. See item 423.
469 Porter, John, trans. *The Dream of the Rood*. Market Drayton: Tern
   Press, 1992. Pp. 46.
470 Deane, John F., trans. '*The Dream of the Rood*.' In his *Christ, with
   Urban Fox*, 17–22. Dublin: Dedalus Press, 1997.
471 Hillary, David, trans. '*The Dream of the Rood*.' *Epworth Rev.* 24
   (1997): 46–9.
472 Raffel, Burton, trans. *Poems and Prose from the Old English*. Ed.
   Alexandra H. Olsen and Raffel. New Haven, CT: Yale Univ. Press,
   1998. Pp. xxv + 225. [*Dream of the Rood*, pp. 55–60. See further
   item 450.]
473 Kelly, Richard J., and Ciarán L. Quinn, trans. *Stone, Skin, and
   Silver: A Translation of the 'Dream of the Rood.'* Midleton: Litho
   Press, 1999. Pp. xii + 125, 8 plates. Reviews: M.T. Davies, *Speculum*
   77 (2002): 202–4; R. Purdie, *MÆ* 70 (2001): 177; E.G. Stanley, *N&Q*
   n.s. 48 (2001): 1–2.
474 Boenig, Robert, trans. 2000. See item 301. [*Dream of the Rood*,
   pp. 259–63.]
475 Crawford, Robert, trans. 'The Vision of the Cross.' *Stand* (Cambridge
   et alibi) n.s. 2.2 (2000): 143–6.
476 Bradley, S.A.J., trans. '*The Dream of the Rood (ca. 700)*.' In *Christian
   Literature: An Anthology*, ed. Alister E. McGrath, 137–41. Oxford:
   Blackwell, 2001.
477 Schmidt, Charles, trans. '*The Dream of the Rood*.' In Michael
   Schmidt, *The Story of Poetry*, I: *English Poets and Poetry from Cædmon to Caxton*, 149–53. London: Weidenfeld and Nicolson, 2001.
478 Leech, Mark James, trans. *Anglo-Saxon Voices: New Translations of
   the Elegies and Battle Poems into Modern English*. Chippenham:
   Piper's Ash, ca. 2004. Pp. 112. [*Dream of the Rood*, item 15.]
479 Greenblatt, Stephen, and M.H. Abrams, eds. *The Norton Anthology
   of English Literature*. 8th ed. 2 vols. New York: Norton, 2006.
   Pp. xlvi + 2904, xlvi + 2877, illus. [*Dream of the Rood*, in sect. A.]

STUDIES

480 Kemble, John Mitchell. 'Additional Observations on the Runic Obelisk
   at Ruthwell; the Poem of the "Dream of the Holy Rood"; and a Runic

Copper Dish Found at Chertsey.' *Archaeologia* 30 (1843–4): 31–46. [In sect. 1 of the vol., pub. in 1843, at pp. 31–9, Kemble treats ed. in item **404**, including a trans. of some fifty lines. See further Kemble, 'On Anglo-Saxon Runes,' *Archaeologia* 28 (1839–40): 327–72, pub. in 1840, citing Vercelli Book, but not *Dream of the Rood*, at p. 363.]

481 Rieger, Max. 'Über Cynevulf.' *Zeitschrift für deutsche Philologie* 1 (1869): 215–26, 313–34. [*Dream of the Rood*, pp. 313–19; also esp. for *Elene*.]

– Sweet, Henry. 1871. See item **429**. [Sees *Dream of the Rood* as introduction to *Elene*, p. 18.]

482 Ebert, [Karl W.A.] 'Über das angelsächsische Gedicht "Der Traum vom heiligen Kreuze."' *Berichte über die Verhandlungen der königlich sächsischen Gesellschaft der Wissenschaften zu Leipzig*, philologisch-historische Klasse 36 (1884): 81–93.

– Holtbuer, Fritz. 1884–5. See item **101**. [Study of genitives.]

– Wülker, Richard P. 1885. See item **24**. ['Traumgesicht vom Kreuze,' pp. 189–96.]

– Napier, A[rthur S.] 1889. See item **111**. [*Dream of the Rood*, p. 69.]

– Bauer, Hermann. 1890. See item **114**. [Linguistic study.]

– Deering, [Robert] Waller. 1890. See item **358**. [Judgment Day as theme; esp. at pp. 3, 6–9, 13–14, 16, 30, 34, 36, 60–1, 65–6.]

483 Stevens, William O. *The Cross in the Life and Literature of the Anglo-Saxons.* Yale Stud. in Eng. 23. New York: Holt, 1904. Pp. 105. [*Dream of the Rood*, pp. 70–5.] Repr., with a new preface by T.D. Hill, in *The Anglo-Saxon Cross*. Hamden, CT: Archon, 1977. Pp. 7–109. [*Dream of the Rood*, pp. 75–9.]

484 Brandl, Alois. 'Zum ags. Gedichte "Traumgesicht vom Kreuze Christi."' *Sitzungsberichte der königlich preussischen Akademie der Wissenschaften* 1905, 716–23. Trans. and rev. as 'On the Early Northumbrian Poem "A Vision of the Cross of Christ."' *Scottish Hist. Rev.* 9 (1912): 139–47. German version reissued in his *Forschungen und Charakteristiken*, 28–35. Berlin: Walter de Gruyter, 1936.

485 Cook, Albert S. '*Dream of the Rood* 54.' *MLN* 22 (1907): 207.

– Holthausen, Ferdinand. 1907. See item **362**, p. 201. [On line 18.]

– Grau, Gustav. 1908. See item **140**. ['Traumgesicht vom Kreuze,' p. 175.]

– Brandl, Alois. 1912. See item **484**. [Eng. trans. of study pub. in 1905.]

486 Sarrazin, Gregor. *Von Kädmon bis Kynewulf. Eine litterarhistorische Studie.* Berlin: Mayer und Müller, 1913. Pp. iii + 174. [*Dream of the*

Rood, pp. 113–33, and other verse.] Reviews: W.A. Berendsohn, *Literaturblatt für germanische und romanische Philologie* 35 (1914): cols. 386–8; L. Dudley, *JEGP* 15 (1916): 313–17; O. Funke, *Beiblatt zur 'Anglia'* 31 (1920): 121–34; M. Kaluza, *Literarisches Zentralblatt* 66 (1915): 666–8.

487 Patch, Howard R. 'Liturgical Influence in *The Dream of the Rood.*' *PMLA* 34 (1919): 233–57.

488 O'Loughlin, J.L.N. '*The Dream of the Rood.*' *TLS* 27 June 1931, 648. [Also esp. on Ruthwell Cross.]

489 Schlauch, Margaret. 'The *Dream of the Rood* as Prosopopoeia.' In *Essays and Studies in Honor of Carleton Brown*, ed. [Anon.], 23–34. New York: New York Univ. Press, 1940. Reissued in *Essential Articles for the Study of Old English Poetry*, ed. Jess B. Bessinger and Stanley J. Kahrl, 428–41. Hamden, CT: Archon, 1968.

490 Pope, John C. *The Rhythm of 'Beowulf.'* New Haven, CT: Yale Univ. Press, 1942. Pp. x + 386. Rev. ed. 1966. Pp. xxxvi + 409. [Includes notation and analysis of excerpts from *Dream of the Rood*.]

 – Schaar, Claes. 1949. See item **316**. ['Cynewulfian' context, esp. in sect. IV.1.]

491 Utley, Francis Lee. 'The Prose *Salomon and Saturn* and the Tree Called "Chy."' *MS* 19 (1957): 55–78. [*Dream of the Rood*, in sect. IV.]

492 Diamond, Robert E. 'Heroic Diction in *The Dream of the Rood.*' In *Studies in Honor of John Wilcox*, ed. A.D. Wallace and Woodburn O. Ross, 3–7. Detroit: Wayne State Univ. Press, 1958.

493 Woolf, Rosemary. 'Doctrinal Influences on *The Dream of the Rood.*' *MÆ* 27 (1958): 137–53.

494 Burrow, John A. 'An Approach to *The Dream of the Rood.*' *Neophilologus* 43 (1959): 123–33. Reissued in *Old English Literature: Twenty-Two Analytical Essays*, ed. Martin Stevens and Jerome Mandel, 253–67. Lincoln: Univ. of Nebraska Press, 1968.

495 Page, R.I. 'Language and Dating in OE Inscriptions.' *Anglia* 77 (1959): 385–406. [Esp. question of linguistic dating of *Dream of the Rood*.] Augmented reissue in his *Runes and Runic Inscriptions: Collected Essays on Anglo-Saxon and Viking Runes*, ed. David Parsons, 29–46. Woodbridge: Boydell Press, 1995.

496 Bolton, Whitney F. 'Connectives in *The Seafarer* and *The Dream of the Rood.*' *MP* 57 (1959–60): 260–2.

 – Lehmann, Winfred P., and Virginia F. Dailey. 1960. See item **320**. [Alliteration.]

497 Bolton, Whitney F. 'Tatwine's *De Cruce Christi* and *The Dream of the Rood.' ASNSL* 200 (1963–4): 344–6.

498 Fleming, John V. '*The Dream of the Rood* and Anglo-Saxon Monasticism.' *Traditio* 22 (1966): 43–72.

499 Shepherd, Geoffrey. 'Scriptural Poetry.' 1966. In *Continuations and Beginnings*, ed. Eric G. Stanley, 1–36. See item **183**. [Discussion of *Dream of the Rood*, pp. 15–17.]

500 Britton, Geoffrey C. '*Bealuwara weorc* in *The Dream of the Rood.' NM* 68 (1967): 273–6.

501 Farina, Peter. '*Wædum geweorðod* in *The Dream of the Rood.' N&Q* n.s. 14 (1967): 4–6.

502 Kaske, Robert E. 'A Poem of the Cross in the Exeter Book: *Riddle 60* and *The Husband's Message.' Traditio* 23 (1967): 41–71. [Esp. on *Dream of the Rood* 28–31, 46–7, 135–44.]

503 Leiter, Louis H. '*The Dream of the Rood*: Patterns of Transformation.' In *Old English Poetry: Fifteen Essays*, ed. Robert P. Creed, 93–127. Providence, RI: Brown Univ. Press, 1967.

504 Stevick, Robert D. 'The Meter of *The Dream of the Rood.' NM* 68 (1967): 149–68.

505 Bolton, W.F. '*The Dream of the Rood* 9b: *engel* = "*nuntius*?"' *N&Q* n.s. 15 (1968): 165–6.

506 Burlin, Robert B. 'The Ruthwell Cross, *The Dream of the Rood* and the *vita contemplativa.' SP* 65 (1968): 23–43.

507 Isaacs, Neil D. 'Progressive Identifications: The Structural Principle of *The Dream of the Rood.*' 1968. In his *Structural Principles in Old English Poetry*, 3–18. See item **402**.

508 Patten, Faith H. 'Structure and Meaning in *The Dream of the Rood.' ES* 49 (1968): 385–401.

509 Scragg, D.G. '*Hwæt/þæt* in *The Dream of the Rood*, line 2.' *N&Q* n.s. 15 (1968): 166–8.

510 Canuteson, John. 'The Crucifixion and the Second Coming in *The Dream of the Rood.' MP* 66 (1968–9): 293–7.

511 Macrae-Gibson, O.D. 'Christ the Victor-Vanquished in *The Dream of the Rood.' NM* 70 (1969): 667–72.

512 Swanton, Michael J. 'Ambiguity and Anticipation in *The Dream of the Rood.' NM* 70 (1969): 407–25.

513 Hieatt, Constance B. 'A New Theory of Triple Rhythm in the Hypermetric Lines of Old English Verse.' *MP* 67 (1969–70): 1–8. [*Dream of the Rood* 59, 67, p. 4.]

514 Clemoes, Peter. *Rhythm and Cosmic Order in Old English Christian Literature*. Cambridge: Cambridge Univ. Press, 1970. Pp. [ii] + 28. [Inaugural lecture; includes discussion of *Dream of the Rood*, pp. 7–11.]

515 Edwards, Robert R. 'Narrative Technique and Distance in the *Dream of the Rood*.' *Papers on Lang. and Lit.* 6 (1970): 291–301.

– Gardner, Helen. 1970. See item **457**, pp. 24–36.

516 Huppé, Bernard F. *The Web of Words: Structural Analyses of the Old English Poems 'Vainglory,' 'The Wonder of Creation,' 'The Dream of the Rood,' and 'Judith.'* Albany: State Univ. of New York Press, 1970. Pp. xxi + 197. [See pp. 830–9; includes trans.]

517 Raw, Barbara C. '*The Dream of the Rood* and Its Connections with Early Christian Art.' *MÆ* 39 (1970): 239–56.

– Trahern, Joseph B., Jr. 1970. See item **192**. [*Dream of the Rood* 90–4.]

518 Wolf, Carol Jean. 'Christ as Hero in *The Dream of the Rood*.' *NM* 71 (1970): 202–10.

519 Gradon, Pamela O.E. *Form and Style in Early English Literature*. London: Methuen, 1971. Pp. x + 398. [For *Dream of the Rood*, see esp. pp. 308–10.]

520 Hieatt, Constance B. 'Dream Frame and Verbal Echo in the *Dream of the Rood*.' *NM* 72 (1971): 251–63.

521 Tripp, Raymond P., Jr. '*The Dream of the Rood*: 9b and Its Context.' *MP* 69 (1971–2): 136–7.

522 Lee, N.A. 'The Unity of *The Dream of the Rood*.' *Neophilologus* 56 (1972): 469–86.

523 Pezzini, Domenico. 'Teologia e poesia: La sintesi del poema anglosassone "Sogno della Croce."' Istituto Lombardo, Classe di lettere e scienze morali e storiche, *Rendiconti* (Milan) 106 (1972): 268–86.

524 Cherniss, Michael D. 'The Cross as Christ's Weapon: The Influence of Heroic Literary Tradition on *The Dream of the Rood*.' *ASE* 2 (1973): 241–52.

525 Hill, Thomas D. 'Vision and Judgement in the Old English *Christ III*.' *SP* 70 (1973): 233–42. [Includes discussion of *The Dream of the Rood*.]

526 Berkhout, Carl T. 'The Problem of OE *holmwudu*.' *MS* 36 (1974): 429–33. [Esp. for ll. 90–4, 119–21.]

527 Howlett, D.R. 'Three Forms in the Ruthwell Text of *The Dream of the Rood*.' *ES* 55 (1974): 1–5.

528 Kintgen, Eugene R. 'Echoic Repetition in Old English Poetry, Especially *The Dream of the Rood*.' *NM* 75 (1974): 202–23.

529 Taylor, P.B. 'Text and Texture of *The Dream of the Rood*.' *NM* 75 (1974): 193–201.

530 Dubs, Kathleen E. '*Hæleð*: Heroism in *The Dream of the Rood*.' *Neophilologus* 59 (1975): 614–15.

531 Lee, Alvin A. 'Toward a Critique of *The Dream of the Rood*.' 1975. In *Anglo-Saxon Poetry*, ed. Lewis E. Nicholson and Dolores Warwick Frese, 163–91. See item **201**.

532 Smith, James. 'The Garments That Honour the Cross in *The Dream of the Rood*.' *ASE* 4 (1975): 29–35.

533 Whitman, F.H. '*The Dream of the Rood*, 101a.' *Explicator* 33.9 (1975): [3]. [Pub. as item no. 70.]

534 Helder, Willem. 'The *engel dryhtnes* in *The Dream of the Rood*.' *MP* 73 (1975–6): 148–51.

535 Payne, Richard C. 'Convention and Originality in the Vision Framework of *The Dream of the Rood*.' *MP* 73 (1975–6): 329–41.

– Allen, Michael J.B., and Daniel G. Calder, trans. 1976. See item **203**. ['*The Dream of the Rood*,' sect. V; Latin sources in trans.]

536 del Mastro, M.L. '*The Dream of the Rood* and the *militia Christi*: Perspective in Paradox.' *Amer. Benedictine Rev.* 27 (1976): 171–86.

537 Howlett, D.R. 'A Reconstruction of the *Ruthwell Crucifixion Poem*.' *SN* 48 (1976): 54–8.

538 – 'The Structure of *The Dream of the Rood*.' *SN* 48 (1976): 301–6.

539 Ikeda, Tadashi. [*The Dream of the Rood: Mysticism in English Literature*.] Tokyo: Hokuseido Shoten, 1976. Pp. viii + 274. [In Japanese.]

540 Pickford, T.E. 'Another Look at the *engel dryhtnes* in *The Dream of the Rood*.' *NM* 77 (1976): 565–8.

541 – '*Holmwudu* in *The Dream of the Rood*.' *NM* 77 (1976): 561–4. [Line 91.]

542 Renoir, Alain. 'Oral Theme and Written Texts.' *NM* 77 (1976): 337–46. [Formulaic elements in *Dream of the Rood* and questions of written composition.]

543 Niles, John D. 'Hans Christian Andersen's *Grantræct* and the Old English *Dream of the Rood*.' *Anderseniana*, 3rd ser. 2 (1977): 351–60.

544 Hermann, John P. '*The Dream of the Rood* 19a: *earmra ærgewin*.' *ELN* 15 (1977–8): 241–4.

545 Braswell, Bruce Karl. 'The *Dream of the Rood* and Aldhelm on Sacred Prosopopoeia.' *MS* 40 (1978): 461–7.

546 Hill, John M. 'The Good Fields of Grief: Remnants of Christian Conversion.' *Psychocultural Rev.* 2 (1978): 27–43. [Esp. at pp. 32–6; includes caption, 'Attachments and Loss in Early Christian Conversions.']

547 Horgan, A.D. '*The Dream of the Rood* and Christian Tradition.' *NM* 79 (1978): 11–20.

548 Howlett, D.R. 'Two Notes on *The Dream of the Rood*.' *SN* 50 (1978): 167–73.

549 Mahler, Annemarie E. '*Lignum Domini* and the Opening Vision of *The Dream of the Rood*: A Viable Hypothesis?' *Speculum* 53 (1978): 441–59.

550 Napierkowski, Thomas J. 'A Dream of the Cross.' *Concerning Poetry* 11.1 (1978): 3–12.

551 Ó Carragáin, Éamonn. 'Liturgical Innovations Associated with Pope Sergius and the Iconography of the Ruthwell and Bewcastle Crosses.' In *Bede and Anglo-Saxon England: Papers in Honour of the 1300th Anniversary of the Birth of Bede, Given at Cornell University in 1973 and 1974*, ed. R.T. Farrell, 131–47. BAR 46. London: BAR, 1978.

552 Schwab, Ute. 'Das Traumgesicht vom Kreuzesbaum. Ein ikonologischer Interpretationsansatz zu dem ags. *Dream of the Rood*.' In *Philologische Studien. Gedenkschrift für Richard Kienast*, ed. Schwab and Elfriede Stutz, 131–92. Heidelberg: Winter, 1978.

553 Tate, George S. 'Chiasmus as Metaphor: The *figura Crucis* Tradition and *The Dream of the Rood*.' *NM* 79 (1978): 114–25.

554 Bundi, Ada. 'Per la ricostruzione dei passi frammentari dell'iscrizione runica della Croce di Ruthwell.' Istituto universitario orientale, *Annali*, Filologia germanica (Naples) 22 (1979): 21–58.

555 Cleland, John H. 'The Art of *The Dream of the Rood*.' *Faith and Reason* 5.2 (1979): 3–25.

556 Kirby, Ian J. '*The Dream of the Rood*: A Dilemma of Supra-Heroic Dimensions.' *Études de lettres* (Lausanne), 4th ser. 2.1 (1979): 3–7.

– Bolton, W.F. 1980 [pub. 1982]. See item 561.

557 Chase, Christopher L. '*Christ III, The Dream of the Rood*, and Early Christian Passion Piety.' *Viator* 11 (1980): 11–13.

558 Orton, Peter. 'The Technique of Object-Personification in *The Dream of the Rood* and a Comparison with the Old English Riddles.' *Leeds Stud. in Eng.* n.s. 11 (1980): 1–18.

559 Finnegan, Robert Emmett. 'The *lifes weg rihtne* and the *Dream of the Rood*.' *Revue de l'Université d'Ottawa* 51 (1981): 236–46.

560   Ó Carragáin, É. 'How Did the Vercelli Collector Interpret *The Dream of the Rood*?' In *Studies in English Language and Early Literature in Honour of Paul Christophersen*, ed. P.M. Tilling, 63–104. Occasional Papers in Ling. and Lang. Learning 8. Coleraine: New Univ. of Ulster, 1981. [Also esp. for *Soul and Body I*, *Elene*, and *Vercelli Homilies*.]

561   Bolton, W.F. 'The Book of Job in *The Dream of the Rood*.' *Mediaevalia* (Binghamton, NY) 6 (1982 for 1980): 87–103.

562   Faraci, Dora. 'Aspetti eroici nel *Dream of the Rood*.' *Atti dell'Accademia peloritana dei Pericolanti* (Messina), Classe di lettere, filosofia e belle arti 58 (1982): 1–41.

563   Holdsworth, Carolyn. 'Frames: Time Level and Variation in *The Dream of the Rood*.' *Neophilologus* 66 (1982): 622–8.

564   Horgan, Dorothy M. '*The Dream of the Rood* and a Homily for Palm Sunday.' *N&Q* n.s. 29 (1982): 388–91.

565   Klinck, Anne L. 'Christ as Soldier and Servant in *The Dream of the Rood*.' *Florilegium* 4 (1982): 109–16.

566   Magennis, Hugh. '*Beowulf*, 1008a: "swefeð æfter symle."' *N&Q* n.s. 29 (1982): 391–2. [Also on *Dream of the Rood*.]

567   Meyvaert, Paul. 'An Apocalypse Panel on the Ruthwell Cross.' *Med. and Renaissance Stud.* (Durham, NC) 9 (1982): 3–32.

568   Ó Carragáin, Éamonn. 'Crucifixion as Annunciation: The Relation of *The Dream of the Rood* to the Liturgy Reconsidered.' *ES* 63 (1982): 487–505.

569   Ortoleva, Grazia. '*Il sogno della Croce*.' *Glossario*. Quaderni di filologia germanica 1.2. Messina: Sfameni, 1982. Pp. 68.

570   Finnegan, Robert Emmett. 'The Gospel of Nicodemus and *The Dream of the Rood*, 148b–156.' *NM* 84 (1983): 338–43.

571   Ó Carragáin, Éamonn. '"Vidi aquam": The Liturgical Background to *The Dream of the Rood* 20a: "swætan on þa swiðran healfe."' *N&Q* n.s. 30 (1983): 8–15.

572   Graybill, Robert V. '*The Dream of the Rood*: Apotheosis of Anglo-Saxon Paradox.' *Essays in Med. Stud.* (Chicago *et alibi*) 1 (1984): 1–12.

573   Holloway, Julia Bolton. '*The Dream of the Rood* and Liturgical Drama.' *Comparative Drama* 18 (1984): 19–37. Reissued in *Drama in the Middle Ages: Comparative and Critical Essays*, 2nd ser., ed. Clifford Davidson and John H. Stroupe, 24–42. AMS Stud. in the Middle Ages 18. New York: AMS Press, 1990.

574   Pasternack, Carol Braun. 'Stylistic Disjunctions in *The Dream of the Rood*.' *ASE* 13 (1984): 167–86. Reissued in *Old English Literature:*

Critical Essays, ed. R.M. Liuzza, 404–24. New Haven, CT: Yale Univ. Press, 2002.

575 Schwab, Ute. 'Exegetische und homiletische Stilformen in *Dream of the Rood.*' In *Geistliche Denkformen in der Literatur des Mittelalters*, ed. Klaus Grubmüller, Ruth Schmidt-Wiegand, and Klaus Speckenbach, 101–30. Münstersche Mittelalter-Schriften 51. Munich, Fink: 1984.

576 Baird, Joseph L. '*Natura plangens*, the Ruthwell Cross, and *The Dream of the Rood.*' *Stud. in Iconography* 10 (1984–6): 37–51.

577 Bennett, J.A.W. *Poetry of the Passion: Studies in Twelve Centuries of English Verse.* Oxford: Clarendon Press, 1982. Pp. viii + 240. [*Dream of the Rood*, pp. 1–31.]

578 Boenig, Robert. 'The *engel dryhtnes* and Mimesis in *The Dream of the Rood.*' *NM* 86 (1985): 442–6.

579 Fanger, Claire. 'A Suggestion for a Solution to Exeter Book Riddle 55.' *Scintilla: A Student Jnl for Medievalists* (Toronto) 2–3 (1985–6): 19–28. [Includes discussion of *Dream of the Rood.*]

580 Finlay, Alison. 'The Warrior Christ and the Unarmed Hero.' In *Medieval English Religious and Ethical Literature: Essays in Honour of G.H. Russell*, ed. Gregory Kratzmann and James Simpson, 19–29. Cambridge: D.S. Brewer: 1986.

581 Hall, J.R. '"Angels ... and all the holy ones": *The Dream of the Rood* 153b–54a.' *ANQ* 24 (1986): 65–8.

582 Irvine, Martin. 'Anglo-Saxon Literary Theory Exemplified in Old English Poems: Interpreting the Cross in *The Dream of the Rood* and *Elene.*' *Style* 20 (1986): 157–81. Reissued in *Old English Shorter Poems: Basic Readings*, ed. Katherine O'Brien O'Keeffe, 31–63. Basic Readings in AS England 3. New York: Garland, 1994.

583 Irving, Edward B., Jr. 'Crucifixion Witnessed, or Dramatic Interaction in *The Dream of the Rood.*' 1986. In *Modes of Interpretation*, ed. Phyllis Rugg Brown et al., 101–13. See item **226**.

584 McEntire, Sandra. 'The Devotional Context of the Cross before A.D. 1000.' In *Sources of Anglo-Saxon Culture*, ed. Paul E. Szarmach, 345–56. Stud. in Med. Culture 20. Kalamazoo, MI: Medieval Institute Publications, 1986. Reissued in *Old English Literature: Critical Essays*, ed. R.M. Liuzza, 392–403. See item **574**. [Also for *Elene.*]

585 Ó Carragáin, Éamonn. 'Christ over the Beasts and the *agnus Dei*: Two Multivalent Panels on the Ruthwell and Bewcastle Crosses.' 1986. In *Sources of Anglo-Saxon Culture*, ed. Paul E. Szarmach, 377–403. See item **584**.

586 Savage, Anne. 'Mystical and Evangelical in *The Dream of the Rood*: The Private and the Public.' In *Mysticism: Medieval and Modern*, ed. Valerie M. Lagorio, 4–11. Salzburg: Institut für Anglistik und Amerikanistik, Universität Salzburg, 1986.

587 Chappell, Virginia A. '*Reordberendra gesyhthe* and Christian Mystery: Narrative Frames in *The Dream of the Rood*.' *Comitatus* 18 (1987): 1–20.

588 Florey, Kenneth. 'Community and Self in *The Dream of the Rood*.' *Connecticut Rev.* [10].1 (1987): 23–9.

589 Kilpiö, Matti. 'Hrabanus' *De laudibus Sanctae Crucis* and *The Dream of the Rood*.' In *Neophilologica Fennica. Société néophilologique, 100 ans*, ed. Leena Kahlas-Tarkka, 177–91. Mémoires de la Société néophilologique de Helsinki 45. Helsinki: Société néophilologigue de Helsinki, 1987.

590 Le Saux, Françoise. 'Didacticism in the *Dream of the Rood*.' *Études de lettres* (Lausanne) 1987, no. 2–3: 167–77.

591 Rissanen, Paavo. *The Message and the Structure of 'The Dream of the Rood.'* Annals of the Finnish Soc. for Missiology and Ecumenics 52. Helsinki: Finnish Soc. for Missiology and Ecumenics, 1987. Pp. 74. Review: A. Savage, *Mystics Quarterly* 16.1 (1990): 50.

592 Savage, Anne. 'The Place of Old English Poetry in the English Meditative Tradition.' In *The Medieval Mystical Tradition in England: Exeter Symposium IV*, ed. Marion Glasscoe, 91–110. Woodbridge: D.S. Brewer, 1987.

593 Szarmach, Paul E. 'Ælfric, the Prose Vision, and the *Dream of the Rood*.' In *Studies in Honour of René Derolez*, ed. A.M. Simon-Vandenbergen, 592–602. [Ghent]: Seminarie voor engelse en oudgermaanse taalkunde, 1987. Reissued in item 1020, pp. 327–39.

594 Brzezinski, Monica. 'The Harrowing of Hell, the Last Judgment, and *The Dream of the Rood*.' *NM* 89 (1988): 252–65.

 –   Samuels, Peggy. 1988 [pub. 1990]. See item 601.

595 Schwab, Ute. 'Heroische Maximen, homiletische Lehren und gelehrte Reminiszenzen in einigen Stücken christlicher Heldenepik, besonders in England.' In *Heldensage und Heldendichtung im Germanischen*, ed. Heinrich Beck, 213–44. Ergänzungsbände zum *RGA* 2. Berlin: de Gruyter, 1988. [For *Dream of the Rood*, see esp. pp. 215–18, 221–2.]

596 Anderson, Earl R. 'Liturgical Influence in *The Dream of the Rood*.' *Neophilologus* 73 (1989): 293–304.

597 Jones, John Mark. 'The Metaphor That Will Not Perish: *The Dream of the Rood* and the New Hermeneutic.' *Christianity and Lit.* 38.2 (1989): 63–72.

598 McPherson, Clair W. 'Spiritual Combat: *The Dream of the Rood.*' *Anglican Theol. Rev* 71 (1989): 166–75.

599 Holloway, Julia Bolton. 'Crosses and Boxes: Latin and Vernacular.' In *Equally in God's Image: Women in the Middle Ages*, ed. Holloway, Constance S. Wright, and Joan Bechtold, 58–87. New York: Lang, 1990.

600 Pezzini, Domenico. 'La poesia della Passione nella tradizione letteraria inglese. Dal "Sogno della Croce" a R.S. Thomas.' *Rivista di storia e letteratura religiosa* 26 (1990): 460–507.

601 Samuels, Peggy. 'The Audience Written into the Script of *The Dream of the Rood.*' *Mod. Lang. Quarterly* 49 (1990 for 1988): 311–20.

602 Wilcox, Jonathan. 'New Solutions to Old English Riddles 17 and 53.' *PQ* 69 (1990): 393–408. [*Riddle 53* as analogue of *Dream of the Rood*; also on *Homiletic Fragment I.*]

603 Grant, Raymond J.S. '*The Dream of the Rood*, line 63b: A Part-Time Idiom?' *NM* 92 (1991): 289–95.

604 Grasso, Anthony R. 'Theology and Structure in *The Dream of the Rood.*' *Religion and Lit.* 23.2 (1991): 23–38.

605 Lass, Roger. 'Of Data and "Datives": Ruthwell Cross *rodi* Again.' *NM* 92 (1991): 395–403.

606 Raw, Barbara C. 'Biblical Literature: The New Testament.' 1991. In *The Cambridge Companion to Old English Literature*, ed. Malcolm Godden and Michael Lapidge, 227–42. See item **386**. [Includes discussion of *Dream of the Rood.*]

607 Cavill, Paul. '*Engel dryhtnes* in *The Dream of the Rood* 9b Again.' *NM* 93 (1992): 287–92.

608 Pigg, Daniel F. '*The Dream of the Rood* in Its Discursive Context: Apocalypticism as Determinant of Form and Treatment.' *ELN* 29.4 (1992): 13–22.

609 Breeze, Andrew. 'The Virgin Mary and *The Dream of the Rood.*' *Florilegium* 12 (1993): 55–62.

610 Hill, Thomas D. 'The Cross as Symbolic Body: An Anglo-Latin Liturgical Analogue to *The Dream of the Rood.*' *Neophilologus* 77 (1993): 297–301.

611 Stévanovitch, Colette. 'Élevation–abaissement dans l'"Exaltation de la Croix."' *Bulletin des anglicistes médiévistes* 45 (1993): 838–46.

612 Breeze, Andrew. '*Deorc* "bloody" in the *Dream of the Rood*, Old Irish *derg* "red, bloody."' *Éigse* 28 (1994): 165–8.

613 Clemoes, Peter. 'King and Creation at the Crucifixion: The Contribution of Native Tradition to *The Dream of the Rood* 50–6a.' In *Heroes and Heroines in Medieval English Literature: A Festschrift Presented to André Crépin on the Occasion of His Sixty-Fifth Birthday*, ed. Leo Carruthers, 31–43. Cambridge: D.S. Brewer, 1994.

614 Fountain, J. Stephen. 'Ashes to Ashes: Kristeva's *jouissance*, Altizer's Apocalypse, Byatt's Possession and *The Dream of the Rood*.' *Lit. and Theol.* 8 (1994): 193–208.

615 Galloway, Andrew. 'Dream-Theory in *The Dream of the Rood* and *The Wanderer*.' *RES* n.s. 45 (1994): 475–85.

616 Jennings, Margaret. '*Rood* and Ruthwell: The Power of Paradox.' *ELN* 31.3 (1994): 6–12.

617 Johnson, David F. 'Old English Religious Poetry: *Christ and Satan* and *The Dream of the Rood*.' In *Companion to Old English Poetry*, ed. Henk Aertsen and Rolf H. Bremmer, Jr., 159–87. Amsterdam: Vrije Univ. Press, 1994.

618 Murray, Robert. 'Tradition and Originality in the *Dream of the Cross*.' *The Month* 255 (May 1994): 177–81.

619 Schmitt, Jean-Claude. 'Rituels de l'image et récits de vision.' *SettSpol* 41 (1994): 419–62. [Includes discussion of *Dream of the Rood*.]

620 Hawkins, Emma B. 'Gender, Language, and Power in *The Dream of the Rood*.' *Women and Lang.* 18.2 (1995): 33–6.

621 Rodrigues, Louis J. 'The *Dream of the Rood* and Cyn(e)wulf.' In *Papers from the Fourth International Conference of the Spanish Society for Medieval English Language and Literature*, ed. Teresa Fanego Lema, 257–63. Publicacións en lingüística e filoloxía 25 [= Cursos e congresos 74]. Santiago de Compostela: Universidade de Santiago de Compostela, 1995. Reissued in his *'The Dream of the Rood and Cyn(e)wulf' and Other Critical Essays*, 1–12. See item **641**.

–   Page, R.I. 1995. See item **495**. [Problems of dating.]

622 Sola Buil, Ricardo J. 'The Dream Vision as a Literary Convention: A Tradition.' 1995. In *Papers from the Fourth International Conference*, ed. Teresa Fanego Lema, 273–83. See item **621**. [Includes discussion of *Dream of the Rood*.]

623 Hinton, Rebecca. '*The Dream of the Rood*.' *Explicator* 54.2 (1995–6): 77–9. [Comparison with penitential texts.]

624 Glanz, Elaine. '"Standan steame bedrifenne" in *The Dream of the Rood*.' *Mediaevalia* (Binghamton, NY) 21 (1996): 189–208.

625 Harbus, Antonina. 'Dream and Symbol in *The Dream of the Rood*.' *Nottingham Med. Stud.* 40 (1996): 1–15.

626 Head, Pauline. 'Voices of Stone: The Multifaceted Speech of *The Dream of the Rood* and the Ruthwell Cross.' *Assays* (Pittsburgh) 9 (1996): 57–77.

627 Laszlo, Renate, *Das mystische Weinfass: Ein altenglisches Rätsel des Vercellibuches*. Marburg: Tectum, 1996. Pp. 233. [Study of *Dream of the Rood*.]

628 Yoshimi, Akinori. ['On Christianized Germanic Thought in the Old English Poem *The Dream of the Rood*, from the Perspective of Transcending "Exile," and in Comparison with *Beowulf, Elene*, and Other Poems, and also the Ruthwell Cross Inscription.'] *Meiji-Gakuin Rev.: Eng. and Amer. Lit. and Ling.* 96 (1996): 1–58. [In Japanese.]

629 Breeze, Andrew. 'Old English *wann* "dark; pallid": Welsh *gwann* "weak; sad, gloomy."' *ANQ* 10.4 (1997): 10–13.

630 Dockray-Miller, Mary. 'The Feminized Cross of *The Dream of the Rood*.' *PQ* 76 (1997): 1–18.

631 Holderness, Graham. 'The Sign of the Cross: Culture and Belief in *The Dream of the Rood*.' *Lit. and Theol.* 11 (1997): 347–75.

632 Irvine, Susan. 'Adam or Christ? A Pronominal Pun in *The Dream of the Rood*.' *RES* n.s. 48 (1997): 433–47.

633 Stratyner, Leslie. 'The "Battle with the Monster": Transformation of a Traditional Pattern in *The Dream of the Rood*.' *Oral Tradition* 12 (1997): 308–21.

634 Boenig, Robert. 'Pseudo-Dionysius and *The Dream of the Rood*.' *Studia Mystica* 19 (1998): 1–7.

635 Holloway, Julia Bolton. 'The *Dream of the Rood* and Pilgrimage.' In her *Jerusalem: Essays on Pilgrimage and Literature*, 47–66. AMS Stud. in the Middle Ages 24. New York: AMS Press, 1998.

636 Howlett, David. 'Old English *ondgierwan, ongierwan, ungierwan*.' *Anglia* 116 (1998): 223–6. [Esp. on *Dream of the Rood* 33–41.]

637 Kühlwein, Wolfgang. 'Celtic Influence on Old English Rhetoric: A Case Study of the Interface between Diachronic Contrastive Rhetoric and History of Art.' *Studia Anglica Posnaniensia* 33 (1998): 213–43. [Includes discussion of *Dream of the Rood*.]

638 Luiselli Fadda, Anna Maria. 'Osservazioni sulla genesi e sulla struttura del *Dream of the Rood* (Vercelli, Biblioteca capitolare, MS CXVII, ff. 104–106v).' 1998. In *Vercelli tra Oriente ed Occidente*, ed. Vittoria Dolcetti Corazza, 101–15. See item 60.

639 Mitchell, Bruce. 'The *Dream of the Rood* Repunctuated.' In *Words and Works: Studies in Medieval English Language and Literature in Honour of Fred C. Robinson*, ed. Peter S. Baker and Nicholas Howe,

143–57. Toronto OE Ser. 10. Toronto: Univ. of Toronto Press, 1998. [Includes ed.]

640 Ó Carragáin, Éamonn. 'Rome, Ruthwell, Vercelli: *The Dream of the Rood* and the Italian Connection.' 1998. In *Vercelli tra Oriente ed Occidente*, ed. Vittoria Dolcetti Corazza, 59–100, with plates I–V. See item 60.

641 Rodrigues, Louis J. '*The Dream of the Rood and Cyn(e)wulf*' *and Other Critical Essays*. Felinfach: Llanerch, 1998. Pp. vi + 232.

642 Thieme, Adelheid L.J. 'Gift Giving as a Vital Element of Salvation in *The Dream of the Rood*.' *South Atlantic Rev.* 63.2 (1998): 108–23.

643 Bammesberger, Alfred. '*Earmra ærgewin* (*The Dream of the Rood* 19A).' *NM* 100 (1999): 3–5.

644 Flood, John. '*Ar.æred* in *The Dream of the Rood* and the Gospel of St. John.' *ELN* 36.4 (1999): 1–4.

645 Hough, Carole. '*The Dream of the Rood*, line 31.' *ANQ* n.s. 12.2 (1999): 3–4.

646 Yim, Harksoon. 'Dual Perspectives in *The Dream of the Rood*.' *Pub. of the Mississippi Philol. Assoc.* 1999: 1–6.

647 Collins, Janet Duthie. '*Dream of the Rood*: An Internal Analysis.' *LACUS Forum* 26 (2000): 331–42.

648 Ó Carragáin, Éamonn. 'The Annunciation of the Lord and His Passion: A Liturgical Topos from St Peter's on the Vatican in *The Dream of the Rood*, Thomas Cranmer and John Donne.' 2000. In *Essays on Anglo-Saxon and Related Themes*, ed. Jane Roberts and Janet Nelson, 339–81. See item 267.

649 Roberts, Jane. 'Some Relationships between *The Dream of the Rood* and the Cross at Ruthwell.' *Stud. in Med. Eng. Lang. and Lit.* (Tokyo) 15 (2000): 1–25.

650 Sorrell, Paul. 'Word Alchemy: A Window on Anglo-Saxon Culture.' *Parabola* 25.2 (2000): 62–8. [Also on *Riddles*.]

651 Wheelock, Jeremy I. 'The Word Made Flesh: *engel dryhtnes* in *The Dream of the Rood*.' *ELN* 37.3 (2000): 1–11.

652 Conti, Aidan. 'An Anonymous Homily for Palm Sunday, *The Dream of the Rood*, and the Progress of Ælfric's Reform.' *N&Q* n.s. 48 (2001): 377–80.

653 Bammesberger, Alfred. 'A Doubtful Reconstruction in the Old English *Ruthwell Crucifixion Poem*.' *SN* 74 (2002): 143–5.

654 Fell, Christine E. 'Runes and Riddles in Anglo-Saxon England.' In '*Lastworda betst*': *Essays in Memory of Christine E. Fell with Her Unpublished Writings*, ed. Carole Hough and Kathryn A. Lowe, 264–77. Donington: Shaun Tyas, 2002. [Also on *Dream of the Rood*.]

655 Keefer, Sarah Larratt. '"Either/and" as "Style" in Anglo-Saxon Christian Poetry.' 2003. In *Anglo-Saxon Styles*, ed. Catherine E. Karkov and George Hardin Brown, 179–200. See item **275**. [Includes discussion of *Dream of the Rood*.]

656 — '*Ic* and *we* in Eleventh-Century Old English Liturgical Verse.' In *Unlocking the 'wordhord': Anglo-Saxon Studies in Memory of Edward B. Irving, Jr.*, ed. Mark C. Amodio and Katherine O'Brien O'Keeffe, 123–46. Toronto: Univ. of Toronto Press, 2003. [Includes discussion of *Dream of the Rood*.]

657 Bammesberger, Alfred. 'The Half-Line *unforht wesan* in *The Dream of the Rood*.' *NM* 105 (2004): 327–30.

658 Risden, Edward L. 'Old English Heroic Poet-Prophets and Their (Un)Stable Histories.' In *Prophet Margins: The Medieval Vatic Impulse and Social Stability*, ed. Risden, Karen Moranski, and Stephen Yandell, 13–28, 186–9. Stud. in the Humanities: Lit., Politics, Society 67. Frankfurt am Main: Lang, 2004. [*Dream of the Rood* 34–5, 39–41, and other verse.]

659 Robinson, Fred C. 'Old English.' In *Early Germanic Literature and Culture*, ed. Brian Murdoch and Malcolm Read, 205–33. Camden House Hist. of German Lit. 1. Woodbridge: Camden House, 2004. [Pp. 225–6, esp. for *Dream of the Rood* 39–42.]

660 Heckman, Christina M. '*Imitatio* in Early Medieval Spirituality: The *Dream of the Rood*, Anselm, and Militant Christology.' *Essays in Med. Stud.* (Chicago *et alibi*) 22 (2005): 141–53.

661 McGillivray, Murray. '*Dream of the Rood* 9–12 and the Christmas Liturgy.' *N&Q* n.s. 52 (2005): 1–2.

662 Ó Carragáin, Éamonn, *Ritual and the Rood: Liturgical Images and the Old English Poems of the 'Dream of the Rood' Tradition*, Brit. Lib. Stud. in Med. Culture. London and Toronto: British Library and Univ. of Toronto Press, 2005. Pp. xxxii + 427, 16 pp. of colour plates, illus. ['Vision Transfigured into Prayer: The Crucifixion Narrative in *The Dream of the Rood*,' ch. 6.]

663 Duncan, Thomas G. '"Quid Hinieldus cum Christo?": The Secular Expression of the Sacred in Old and Middle English Lyrics.' In *Sacred and Secular in Medieval and Early Modern Cultures*, ed. Lawrence Besserman, 29–46, 187–190. The New Middle Ages. London: Palgrave, 2006. [Includes discussion of *Dream of the Rood*.]

664 Karkov, Catherine E., Sarah Larratt Keefer, and Karen Louise Jolly, eds. *The Place of the Cross in Anglo-Saxon England*. Pub. of Manchester Centre for AS Stud. 4. Woodbridge: Boydell Press, 2006. Pp. xx + 171.

665 Kendall, Calvin B. 'From Sign to Vision: The Ruthwell Cross and *The Dream of the Rood.*' 2006. In item **664**, pp. 129–44.
666 Milfull, Inge B. 'Hymns to the Cross: Contexts for the Reception of *Vexilla regis.*' 2006. In item **664**, pp. 43–57. [Analogues of *Dream of the Rood*.]
667 Ogawa, Hiroshi. ['Alliterating Words and Types in the Old English Poem *The Dream of the Rood.*'] In *The Development of the Anglo-Saxon Language, Series 1: Universals and Variation in Language* I, ed. [Anon.], 39–42. Tokyo: Development and Research Centre. of Socio-Intelligence (Senshu Univ.), 2006. [In Japanese.]
668 Treharne, Elaine M. '"Hiht wæs geniwad": Rebirth in *The Dream of the Rood.*' 2006. In item **664**, pp. 145–57. [Also esp. on context in Vercelli Book.]
 –   Wood, Ian N. 2006. See item **821**. [Northumbrian crosses.]

Elene

EDITIONS

669 [Thorpe, Benjamin, ed.] 'The Invention of the Cross.' 1834. In *Appendices to a Report on Rymer's 'Foedera,'* appendix B, pp. 105–38. See item **18**.
670 Grimm, Jacob, ed. 1840. See item **69**. [Follows text in item **669**; introduces title *Elene*.]
671 Ettmüller, Ludwig, ed. 1850. See item **71**. ['*Elene*, gedihted be Cynevulfe,' pp. 156–63, following text in item **670**.]
672 Kemble, John M., ed. and trans. '*Elene*, or The Recovery of the Cross.' 1856. In *The Poetry of the Codex Vercellensis*, ed. Kemble, 2: 1–78. See item **70**. ['*Elene* and Minor Poems,' internal title in vol. 2.]
673 Grein, Christian W.M., ed. 1858. See item **72**. [*Elene*, 2: 105–37, with corrections at 2: [416].]
674 Zupitza, Julius, ed. *Cynewulfs 'Elene,' mit einem Glossar*. Berlin: Weidmann, 1877. Pp. xii + 100. Reviews: B. ten Brink, *Anzeiger für deutsches Altertum* 5 (1879): 53–70; K. Körner, *Englische Studien* 2 (1879): 252–62; E. Sievers, *Anglia* 1 (1878): 573–81; R.W[ülker], *Literarisches Zentralblatt* 30 (1879): 1462. 2nd ed. 1883. Pp. vi + 80. Reviews: J.M. G[arnett], *Amer. Jnl of Philol.* 5 (1884): 399; F. Kluge, *Literaturblatt für germanische und romanische Philologie* 5 (1884): cols. 138–9; H. Varnhagen, *Deutsche Literaturzeitung* 5 (1884): 426–7. 3rd ed. 1888. Pp. viii + 89. Reviews: O. Brenner, *Englische*

Studien 13 (1889): 480–2; E. Koeppel, *Literaturblatt für germanische und romanische Philologie* 11 (1890): cols. 60–1; E. Löseth, *Le Moyen Âge* 2 (1889): 186–7; K. Luick, *Deutsche Literaturzeitung* 10 (1889): 1835. 4th ed. 1899. Pp. xii + 89. Reviews: G. Binz, *Literaturblatt für germanische und romanische Philologie* 21 (1900): cols. 97–8; K. Bülbring, *Museum. Tijdschrift voor filologie en geschiedenis* 7 (1899): 357; E. Schröder, *Anzeiger für deutsches Altertum* 26 (1900): 170–1; M. Trautmann, *Beiblatt zur 'Anglia'* 10 (1899–1900): 262.

675 Wülker, Richard P., ed. 1888. See item 74. [*Elene*, pp. 126–201.]

676 Kent, Charles William, ed. *'Elene,' an Old English Poem.* Lib. of AS Poetry [6]. Boston: Ginn, 1889. Pp vi + 149. Reviews: [Anon.], *Athenaeum* 1889, pt. 2 (July–Dec.): 595; O.F. Emerson, *MLN* 5 (1890): 20–2; *Nation* 49 (1889): 480; R. W[ülker] *Anglia* 12 (1889): 629–31. Repr. 1891, 1895, 1897, 1902. Repr. New York: AMS Press, 1973.

677 Holthausen, Ferdinand, ed. *Cynewulfs 'Elene' ('Kreuzauffindung') mit Einleitung, Glossar, Anmerkungen und der lateinischen Quelle.* Alt- und Mittelenglische Texte 4. Heidelberg: Winter, 1905. Pp. xvi + 99, folded plate. [Corrections and additions in item 728.] Reviews: A.J. Barnouw, *Museum. Tijdschrift voor filologie en geschiedenis* 14 (1907): 169–70; V. Henry, *Revue critique* 62 (1906): 389; R. Imelmann, *Beiblatt zur 'Anglia'* 17 (1906): 225–6; H. Jantzen, *Literarisches Zentralblatt* 57 (1906): 824–5; H. Jantzen, *Neue philologische Rundschau* (1906): 208–9. 2nd ed. 1910. Pp. xvi + 102, folded plate. Reviews: [A. Brandl], *ASNSL* 125 (1910): 246; F. H[olthausen], *Germanisch-romanische Monatsschrift* 3 (1911): 188; E.A. Kock, *Englische Studien* 44 (1912): 392–5. 3rd ed. 1914. Pp. xvi + 103, folded plate. 4th ed. 1936. Pp. xx + 109, folded plate. Reviews: F. Holthausen, *Germanisch-romanische Monatsschrift* 25 (1937): 229; F. Klaeber, *Beiblatt zur 'Anglia'* 48 (1937): 161–3; G. L[inke], *ASNSL* 171 (1937): 118; F. M[ossé], *Revue germanique* 28 (1937): 214.

678 Cook, Albert S., ed. The *Old English 'Elene,' 'Phoenix,' and 'Physiologus.'* New Haven, CT: Yale Univ. Press, 1919. Pp. lxxxix + 239. Reviews: J.W. B[right], *MLN* 35 (1920): 250–4; E. Ekwall, *Beiblatt zur 'Anglia'* 33 (1922): 61–7; J.H.G. Grattan, *MLR* 15 (1920): 177–8; G. Huet, *Le Moyen Âge* 32 (1921): 91–2; F. Klaeber, *Englische Studien* 55 (1921): 280–5; H.R. Patch, *JEGP* 19 (1920): 418–22; E.E. Wardale, *YWES* 1 (1919–20): 32–3.

679   Craigie, W.A., ed. 1926. See item **76**. [Extracts from *Elene*, pp. 42–59.]
680   Krapp, George Phillip, ed. 1932. See item **77**.
681   Lupi, Sergio, ed. and trans. *Cynewulf, 'Sant'Elena.' Introduzione, versione, note, glossario.* Biblioteca di lingue e letterature straniere, Sezione filologia, vol. 1. Naples: Libreria scientifica editrice, 1951. Pp. xxxvi + 145. [Includes Italian prose trans.] Review: R.M. Lumiansky, *MLN* 69 (1954): 286–8. 2nd ed. Rev. Franco De Vivo. Naples: Liguori, 1993. Pp. xlii + 209.
682   Gradon, Pamela O.E., ed. *Cynewulf's 'Elene.'* Methuen's OE Lib. London: Methuen, 1958. Pp. x + 114, 1 plate. Reviews: P. Bacquet, *EA* 12 (1959): 57–8; K.R. Brooks, *MÆ* 28 (1959): 108–11; J.E. Cross, *JEGP* 58 (1959): 522–3; R.W.V. Elliott, *MLR* 54 (1959): 248; L.A. Muinzer, *MLN* 75 (1960): 154–8; C. Schaar, *SN* 31 (1959): 272–5; C. Sisam, *RES* n.s. 11 (1960): 61–2; G. Storms, *ES* 46 (1965): 52–6; B. von Lindheim, *Anglia* 76 (1958): 544–7. Augmented repr. London: Methuen, New York: Appleton-Century-Crofts, 1966. [Includes additional bibliographical entries.] Corr. repr. Exeter: Exeter Univ. Press, 1977. Pp. x + 115, 1 plate. ['Supplementary Bibliography,' p. 81.] Repr. 1980, 1992. Rev. ed. 1996. Pp. x + 118, 1 plate. [Includes wholly new bibliography, by M.J. Swanton, pp. 77–84.]
683   Magoun, Francis P., ed. 1960. See item **78**. ['*Elene*, or St Helena's Invention of the Cross,' pp. 70–108.]
684   Nelson, Marie, ed. and trans. *Judith, Juliana, and Elene: Three Fighting Saints.* Amer. Univ. Stud., Ser. 4: Eng. Lang. and Lit. 135. New York: Lang, 1991. Pp. ix + 209. [See further item **792**.] Review: E.G. Stanley, *N&Q* n.s. 40 (1993): 427–8.

TRANSLATIONS

685   Kemble, John M., ed. and trans. 1856. See item **672**.
686   Weymouth, Richard Francis, trans. *A Literal Translation of Cynewulf's 'Elene' from Zupitza's Text.* London: [n.p.], 1888. Pp. 38.
687   Garnett, James M., trans. *'Elene'; 'Judith'; 'Aethelstan,' or 'The Fight at Brunanburh'; and 'Byrhtnoth,' or 'The Fight at Maldon.'* Boston: Ginn, 1889. Pp. xvi + 70. Reviews: [Anon.], *Athenaeum* 1889, pt. 2 (July–Dec.): 595; O. Brenner, *Englische Studien* 15 (1889): 116–17; J.W. Bright, *Amer. Jnl of Philol.* 11 (1890): 104–6; F.B. Gummere *MLN* 5 (1890): 83–6. 2nd ed. 1901. Pp. xviii + 77. [Adds *Dream of the Rood*; title varies.] Repr. 1902. 3rd ed. 1911. Pp. xviii + 77.

688 Menzies, Jane, trans. *Cynewulf's 'Elene': A Metrical Translation from Zupitza's Edition*. Edinburgh: Blackwood, 1895. Pp. 82.

689 Steineck, H., trans. *Altenglische Dichtungen in wortgetreuer Über-setzung ('Beowulf,' 'Elene,' 'Cædmons Hymnus,' 'Bedas Sterbeges-ang,' 'Widsith,' 'Waldere')*. Leipzig: Reisland, 1898. Pp. vii + 151. Reviews: G. Binz, *Beiblatt zur 'Anglia'* 9 (1899): 220–2; N. Bøgholm, *Nordisk tidskrift för filologi*, 3rd ser., 7 (1898–9): 193–4; F. Holthausen *ASNSL* 103 (1899): 376-8; E. Nader, *Zeitschrift für deutsches Real-schulwesen* 24 (1899): 548; R. Wülker *Deutsche Literaturzeitung* 22 (1901): 475.

690 Cook, Albert S., and Chauncey B. Tinker, trans. 1902. See item **84**. [Excerpts, pp. 93–9, with *Ruthwell Crucifixion Poem* at pp. 100–2.]

691 Holt, Lucius Hudson, trans. *The 'Elene' of Cynewulf Translated into English Prose*. Yale Stud. in Eng. 21. New York: Holt, 1904. Pp. 42. Reviews: [Anon.], *Deutsche Literaturzeitung* 25 (1904): 1251; V. H[enry], *Revue critique* 57 (1904): 286–7; F. Klaeber, *Beiblatt zur 'Anglia'* 17 (1906): 37–40; [Anon.] *Mod. Lang. Quarterly* (London) 7 (1904): 106.

692 Kennedy, Charles W., trans. 1910. See item **296**. [*Elene*, pp. 87–128.]

693 Spaeth, J[ohn] Duncan, trans. 1921. See item **443**. [*Elene*, pp. 95–107: excerpts.]

694 Gordon, R.K., trans. 1926. See item **87**. [*Elene*, pp. 234–60.]

695 Kennedy, Charles W., trans. 1952. See item **89**. ['St. Helena Finds the True Cross,' in ch. 4.]

696 — 1960. See item **90**. [Excerpts, pp. 26–7, 135–8.]

697 Sanesi, Roberto, trans. 1966. See item **455**. ['Elena,' item 9; excerpts.]

698 Kanayama, Atsumu, trans. ['*Elene*: A Japanese Translation.'] Pub. in 3 pts. Pt. 1: *Osaka Gaidai Eng. and Amer. Stud.* 9 (1975): 151–62. Pt. 2: *Jnl of the Osaka Univ. of Foreign Stud.* 36 (1976): 17–28. Pt. 3: *Jnl of the Osaka Univ. of Foreign Stud.* 39 (1977): 79–100.

699 Suzuki, Shigetake, and Motoko Suzuki, trans. [*Old English Poetry: 'Elene,' 'Beowulf,' and Religious Poetry*.] Tokyo: Guroriya Shuppan, 1978. Pp. 203. [Japanese verse trans.]

700 Bradley, S.A.J., trans. 1982. See item **91**. [*Elene*, pp. 164–98.]

701 Nelson, Marie, ed. and trans. 1991. See item **684**.

702 Raffel, Burton, trans. 1998. See item **472**. [*Elene*, pp. 35–9: excerpt.]

703 Fujiwara, Yasuaki. [*The World of Old English Poetry*.] Tsukuba: School of Modern Languages and Modern Culture, 1999. Pp. 328. [In Japanese; includes trans. of *Elene* and other verse.]

704 Leech, Mark James, trans. 2004. See item **478**. [Excerpt trans. under title 'Constantine's Vision.']

STUDIES

705 Müllenhoff, [Karl]. 'Zeugnisse und Excurse zur deutschen Helden-sage.' *ZDA* 12 (1860–5): 253–386, 413–36. [*Elene*, sect. IV and else-where.]
– Rieger, Max. 1869. See item **481**. [Esp. at pp. 219–26.]
– Sweet, Henry. 1871. See item **429**. [Sees *Dream of the Rood* as intro. to *Elene*, p. 18.]
– Clement, Knut Jungbohn. 1876. See item **94**. [Criticism of Grimm's ed., item **670**, pp. 56–86.]
706 Kern, H. 'Hrêdh en Hrêdhgotan.' *Taalkundige bijdragen* 1 (1877): 29–46.[On ll. 20, 58.]
– – 1877. See item **95**. [On *gehðum, Elene* 531, pp. 208–9.]
– Fritzsche, Arthur. 1879. See item **96**. [Comparison with *Andreas*.]
707 Cosijn, Peter J. 'Anglosaxonica.' *Tijdschrift voor nederlandsche taal- en letterkunde* 1 (1881) 143–50. [Textual notes on *Elene*, pp. 143–8.]
708 Schürmann, Joseph. *Darstellung der Syntax in Cynewulfs 'Elene.'* Münster in Westfalen diss. Paderborn: Schöningh, 1884. Pp. [ii] + 112 + [iii]. Also issued in *Neuphilologische Studien* (Paderborn) 4 (c. 1884): 287–398. Review: R. W[ülker], *Literarisches Zentralblatt* 36 (1885): 979–80.
709 Glöde, Otto. *Cynewulfs 'Elene' und ihre Quelle.* Rostock diss. Rostock: Boldt, 1885. Pp. 61. See further item **711**.
710 Rössger, Richard. *Über den syntaktischen Gebrauch des Genitivs in Cynewulf's 'Crist,' 'Elene' und 'Juliana.'* Leipzig diss. Halle an der Saale: Karras, 1885. Pp. 37. Also pub. in *Anglia* 8 (1885): 338–70.
– Wülker, Richard P. 1885. See item **24**. ['*Elene*,' pp. 174–6.]
711 Glöde, Otto. 'Untersuchung über die Quelle von Cynewulfs *Elene*.' *Anglia* 9 (1886): 271–318. Rev. reissue of item **709**.
712 Frucht, Philipp. *Metrisches und Sprachliches zu Cynewulfs 'Elene,' 'Juliana' und 'Crist' auf Grund der von Sievers Beitr. X 209–314, 451–545, und von Luick Beitr. XI 470–492 veröffentlichten Aufsätze.* Greifswald diss. Greifswald: Abel, 1887. Pp. [iv] + 99.
– Kent, Charles W. 1887. See item **108**. [Place of *Elene* in Germanic tradition.]
– Cremer, Matthias. 1888. See item **109**. [Metrical and linguistic comments on *Elene*.]

713 Leiding, Hermann. *Die Sprache der Cynewulfschen Dichtungen
'Crist,' 'Juliana' und 'Elene.'* Göttingen diss. Marburg: Elwert, 1888.
Pp. 80. Reviews: F. Dieter, *ASNSL* 83 (1889): 351–2; F. Holthausen,
Deutsche Literaturzeitung 9 (1888): 1114–15; [Anon.], *Deutsches
Literaturblatt* (1888): 68 [signed by 'Saalfeld'].

714 Prollius, Max. *Über den syntactischen Gebrauch des Conjunctivs in
den Cynewulfschen Dichtungen 'Elene,' 'Juliana' und 'Crist.'* Marburg
diss. Marburg: [n.p.], 1888. Pp. vi + 60.

– Kail, J. 1889. See item 304. [*Beowulf* and Cynewulfian verse.]

– Deering, [Robert] Waller. 1890. See item 358. [Judgment Day as
theme; esp. at pp. 3, 6–7, 13, 23, 29, 32, 34–5, 38–9, 48–56, 61, 63,
66–7, 69, 74, 76, 79–80.]

715 Erdmann, Axel. 'Bidrag till īni-stammarnes historia i fornnor-
diskan.' *Arkiv för nordisk filologi* 7 [=n.s. 3] (1891): 75–85.
[Contains a note, pp. 77–8, on *feorhlege*, citing *Elene* 458 and other
verse.]

– Holthausen, Ferdinand. 1891. See item 116. [*Elene* 1277, p. 358.]

716 Woodworth, R.B. '*Wendelsæ.*' *MLN* 6 (1891): 135–6. [*Elene* 231.]

717 Cosijn, Peter J. *Aanteekeningen op den 'Béowulf.'* Leiden: Brill,
1892. Pp. 42. [See esp. p. 32, on ll. 942–79, 1132–7.]

718 Tweedie, W.M. 'Kent's Cynewulf's "*Elene.*"' *MLN* 7 (1892): 62.
[On ll. 348–9, 353.]

719 Cook, Albert S. 'The Date of the Old English *Elene.*' *Anglia* 15
(1893): 9–20.

– Wack, Gustav. 1893. See item 124. [Grammatical study.]

720 Swaen, A.E.H. 'Notes on Cynewulf's *Elene.*' *Anglia* 17 (1895):
123–4. [On *Elene* 65–71, 105–8, 140.]

721 Emerson, Oliver Farrar. 'The Legend of Joseph's Bones in Old and
Middle English.' *MLN* 14 (1899): 166–7. [On line 787.]

722 Holthausen, Ferdinand. 'Zu alt- und mittelenglischen Dichtungen.
XIV.' *Anglia* 23 (1901): 516. [On ll. 377–8, 533–5.]

723 — 'Zu alt- und mittelenglischen Denkmälern. XVI.' *Anglia* 25
(1902): 386. [On ll. 30–1.]

724 Strunk, William. 'Notes on Cynewulf.' *MLN* 17 (1902): 186–7.
[*Elene* 581 and other verse.]

725 Brown, Carleton F. 'Cynewulf and Alcuin.' *PMLA* 18 (1903):
308–34. [Esp. for critique of 'Alcuinian' passage in *Elene*.]

726 Holthausen, Ferdinand. 'Zu Cynewulfs *Elene* v. 140.' *Beiblatt zur
'Anglia'* 15 (1904): 73–4.

– Klaeber, Frederick. 1904. See item 361, pp. 147–8. [On *Elene* 140–1,
919–20.]

727 Holthausen, Ferdinand. 'Zur Quelle von Cynewulfs *Elene*.' *Zeitschrift für deutsche Philologie* 37 (1905): 1–19.
728 — 'Zur altenglischen Literatur. II.' *Beiblatt zur 'Anglia'* 17 (1906): 176–8. [Includes extensive corrigenda and addenda to item **677**.]
729 Klaeber, Frederick. 'Notizen zur Cynewulfs *Elene*.' *Anglia* 29 (1906): 271–2. [See further p. 382 for correction of printer's error.]
730 — 'Cynewulf's *Elene* 1262 f.' *JEGP* 6 (1906–7): 197.
731 Holthausen, Ferdinand. 'Zur altenglischen Literatur. III.' *Beiblatt zur 'Anglia'* 18 (1907): 77–8. [*Elene*, ll. 531–5, pp. 77–8, and other verse.]
732 — 'Zur altenglischen Literatur. IV.' *Beiblatt zur 'Anglia'* 18 (1907): 201–8. [*Elene* 532, 1165, 1278, pp. 204–5.]
    – Sarrazin, Gregor. 1907. See item **138**. [Pt. 1, 'Kynewulf,' pp. 145–58.]
    – Trautmann, Moritz. 1907. See item **139**. ['*Elene*,' at pp. 138–9, with appendix 1, 'Zur *Elene*,' pp. 140–2.]
    – Grau, Gustav. 1908. See item **140**. ['*Elene*,' pp. 15–29.]
733 Holthausen, Ferdinand. 'Zur Quelle von Cynewulfs *Elene*.' *ASNSL* 125 (1910): 83–8.
    – — 1910. See item **312**. [*Elene* 293, 607–8, 610, 646–7, p. 174.]
    – Smithson, George A. 1910. See item **142**. [Study of narrative technique.]
    – Trautmann, Moritz. 1910. See item **143**. [*Elene* 1131, pp. 280–2.]
734 Holthausen, Ferdinand. 'Zu altenglischen Denkmälern.' *Englische Studien* 51 (1917–18): 180–8. [*Elene* 533b–35, 1239, pp. 183–4.]
735 Kern, J.H. 'Altenglische *varia*.' *Englische Studien* 51 (1917–18): 1–15. [*Elene*, pp. 8–15; also on *Vercelli Homily* XXIII.]
    – Kock, Ernst A. 1918. See item **146**. [Discusses many lines of *Elene*, pp. 18–24.]
736 Emerson, Oliver Farrar. 'Notes on Old English.' *MLR* 14 (1919): 205–9. ['*Elene*, ll. 899–902,' p. 205.]
    – Kock, Ernst A. 1919. See item **148**. [*Elene* 310–12, p. 302.]
    – — 1920. See item **151**. [Esp. at pp. 105–8, for *Elene* 268–71, 894–6, 1131–5, 1237–40, 1242–4.]
    – — 1920. See item **152**. [*Elene* 19, 1008, pp. 251–2.]
    – Holthausen, Ferdinand. 1921. See item **153**. [On ll. 1238, 1240, p. 136.]
    – Kock, Ernst A. 1921. See item **154**. [On ll. 30–1, 317–18, pp. 124–5.]
    – — 1922. See item **155**. [Line 1157, p. 37.]
    – — 1922. See item **315**. [On ll. 646–7, 767–9, 1238, 1251–2, pp. 5, 18, 26.]
737 — 'Interpretations and Emendations of Early English Texts (cf. *Anglia* XXV–XLVI.): XI.' *Anglia* 47 (1923): 264–73. [See pp. 264–7,

on *Elene*, 15–17, 50–1, 648–50, 814–15, 829–30, 838, 959–61, 1041–2, 1189–90, 1318–20.]

738 Holthausen, Ferdinand. 'Zu altenglischen Dichtungen.' *Beiblatt zur 'Anglia'* 35 (1924): 276–7. [Esp. on *Elene* 17.]

739 Howard, Edwin J. '*Elene* 439.' *MLN* 45 (1930): 22.

740 Johannson, Arwid. '*ÞiaurikR mir hRaiþkutum*.' *Acta Philologica Scandinavica* 7 (1932–3): 97–149. [On onomastic theme *Hrēð*- in *Elene* 20, 58, and in other OE texts, both in verse and in prose; see esp. pp. 119–22, 141–4.]

741 Holthausen, Ferdinand. 'Zur Quelle von Cynewulfs *Elene*.' *Beiblatt zur 'Anglia'* 45 (1934): 93–4.

742 — 'Zur *Elene* (v. 629).' *Beiblatt zur 'Anglia'* 49 (1938): 348–9.

743 Arngart, Olaf. 'Some Notes on Cynewulf's *Elene*.' *ES* 27 (1946): 19–21.

 – Schaar, Claes. 1946–7. See item **169**. [*Elene* 56–61, 924–8.]

744 Gradon, Pamela O.E. 'Constantine and the Barbarians: A Note on the Old English *Elene*.' *MLR* 42 (1947): 161–72.

745 — 'Cynewulf's *Elene* and Old English Prosody.' *Eng. and Germanic Stud.* (Birmingham) 2 (1948–9): 10–19.

 – Brooks, Kenneth R. 1949. See item **170**. [On *wopes hring*, *Elene* 1131.]

 – Schaar, Claes. 1949. See item **316**. [Associations within 'Cynewulf group.']

746 Elliott, Ralph W.V. 'Cynewulf's Runes in *Christ II* and *Elene*.' *ES* 34 (1953): 49–57. Reissued in item **334**, pp. 207–28.

 – Matsunami, Tamotsu. 1953. See item **330**. [Runic signatures.]

747 Klaeber, Frederick. 'Some Notes on OE. Poems.' *ASNSL* 191 (1955): 218–20. ['*Elene*,' sect. 3, on ll. 611–16.]

 – Holthausen, Ferdinand. 1956. See item **175**. [On *Elene* 151, p. 276.]

748 Bonjour, Adrien. '*Beowulf* and the Beasts of Battle.' *PMLA* 72 (1957): 563–73. [*Elene*, pp. 570–2.] Augmented reissue in his *Twelve 'Beowulf' Papers: 1940–1960, with Additional Comments*, 135–49. Neuchatel: Faculté des lettres, 1962.

 – Diamond, Robert E. 1959. See item **319**. [Diction.]

 – Lehmann, Winfred P., and Virginia F. Dailey. 1960. See item **320**. [Alliteration.]

 – Page, R.I. 1964. See item **178**. [Discussion of *rūn* and related terms.]

 – Wolpers, Theodor. 1964. See item **180**. ['Cynewulf's *Elene*,' sect. I.ii.5.]

 – Woolf, Rosemary. 1966. See item **184**, pp. 46–8. [*Elene* and hagiography.]

- Whitbread, L. 1967. See item **372**. [*Elene* 1277–321, p. 472.]
749 Fry, Donald K. 'Themes and Type-Scenes in *Elene*, 1–113.' *Speculum* 44 (1969): 35–45.
750 Stepsis, Robert, and Richard Rand. 'Contrast and Conversion in Cynewulf's *Elene*.' *NM* 70 (1969): 273–82.
751 Watts, Ann Chalmers. *The Lyre and the Harp: A Comparative Reconsideration of Oral Tradition in Homer and Old English Epic Poetry*. Yale Stud. in Eng. 169. New Haven, CT: Yale Univ. Press, 1969. Pp. xii + 279. ['Formulae in *Beowulf* and *Elene*,' appendix B; also esp. in ch. 4.]
752 Gardner, John. 'Cynewulf's *Elene*: Sources and Structure.' *Neophilologus* 54 (1970): 65–76.
- Scragg, D.G. 1970. See item **42**. [Anomalous use of initial *h* in copy of *Elene*, pp. 174, 179.]
753 Sklute, Larry M. '*Freoðuwebbe* in Old English Poetry.' *NM* 71 (1970): 534–41. [Includes discussion of *Elene* 72–5, 88.] Reissued in *New Readings on Women*, ed. Helen Damico and Alexandra Hennessy Olsen, 204–10. Bloomington: Indiana Univ. Press, 1990.
754 Hill, Thomas D. 'Sapiential Structure and Figural Narrative in the Old English *Elene*.' *Traditio* 27 (1971): 159–77. Reissued in item **334**, pp. 159–77.
755 Rogers, H.L. 'Rhymes in the Epilogue to *Elene*: A Reconsideration.' *Leeds Stud. in Eng.* 5 (1971): 47–52.
756 Calder, Daniel G. 'Strife, Revelation, and Conversion: The Thematic Structure of *Elene*.' *ES* 53 (1972): 201–10.
757 Campbell, Jackson J. 'Cynewulf's Multiple Revelations.' *Medievalia et Humanistica* n.s. 3 (1972): 257–77. [Study of *Elene*.]
758 Lehmann, Winfred P. 'Comparative Constructions in Germanic of the OV Type.' In *Studies for Einar Haugen, Presented by Friends and Colleagues*, ed. Evelyn S. Firchow et al., 323–30. Janua Linguarum, Series Maior 59. The Hague: Mouton, 1972. Pp. 573. [Esp. on *Elene* 646–8.]
759 Regan, Catharine A. 'Evangelicalism as the Informing Principle of Cynewulf's *Elene*.' *Traditio* 29 (1973): 27–52. Reissued in item **334**, pp. 251–80.
760 Talentino, Arnold V. '"Causing City Walls to Resound": *Elene* 151b.' *Papers on Lang. and Lit.* 9 (1973): 189–93.
761 Whatley, Gordon. 'Cynewulf and Troy: A Note on *Elene* 642–61.' *N&Q* n.s. 20 (1973): 203–5.
762 Anderson, Earl R. 'Cynewulf's *Elene*: Manuscript Divisions and Structural Symmetry.' *MP* 72 (1974–5): 111–22.

763 Doubleday, James. 'The Speech of Stephen and the Tone of *Elene*.' 1975. In *Anglo-Saxon Poetry*, ed. Lewis E. Nicholson and Dolores Warwick Frese, 116–23. See item 201.

764 Fish, Varda. 'Theme and Pattern in Cynewulf's *Elene*.' *NM* 76 (1975): 1–25.

– Frese, Dolores Warwick. 1975. See item 324. [Runic signature.]

765 Hermann, John P. 'The Theme of Spiritual Warfare in the Old English *Elene*.' *Papers on Lang. and Lit.* 11 (1975): 115–25.

766 Whatley, E. Gordon. 'Bread and Stone: Cynewulf's *Elene* 611–618.' *NM* 76 (1975): 550–60.

767 Wright, Ellen F. 'Cynewulf's *Elene* and the *sinȝal sacu*.' *NM* 76 (1975): 538–49.

768 Whatley, E. Gordon. 'Old English Onomastics and Narrative Art: *Elene* 1062.' *MP* 73 (1975–6): 109–20.

– Allen, Michael J.B., and Daniel G. Calder, trans. 1976. See item 203. ['*Elene*,' sect. VI; Latin sources in trans.]

– Bridges, Margaret. 1979. See item 210. ['*Elene* 1–18a,' pp. 367–70.]

769 Doane, A.N. '*Elene* 610a: *rexgeniðlan*.' *PQ* 58 (1979): 237–40.

770 Hill, Thomas D. 'Bread and Stone, Again: *Elene* 611–18.' *NM* 81 (1980): 252–7.

771 Kretzschmar, William A., Jr. 'Anglo-Saxon Historiography and Saints' Lives: Cynewulf's *Elene*.' *Indiana Social Stud. Quarterly* 33.1 (1980): 49–59.

772 Marino, Cinzia. 'La "Giuliana" e l'"Elena": Una proposta di analisi.' Istituto universitario orientale, *Annali*, Filologia germanica (Naples) 23 (1980): 101–20.

– Ó Carragáin, É. 1981. See item 560. [Context of *Elene* in Vercelli Book.]

773 Whatley, Gordon. 'The Figure of Constantine the Great in Cynewulf's *Elene*.' *Traditio* 37 (1981): 161–202.

– Fell, Christine E. 1981–4. See item 56. [*Elene* and notebook ascribed to Richard Cleasby.]

774 Fujiwara, Yasuaki. ['The Old English Poem *Elene*.'] *Stud. in Eng. Lang. and Lit.* (Kumamoto Univ.) 7 (1982): 21–52. [In Japanese.]

775 Stevick, Robert D. 'A Formal Analog of *Elene*.' *Stud. in Med. and Renaissance Hist.* n.s. 5 (1982): 47–104.

776 van der Wurff, W.A.M. 'Cynewulf's *Elene*: The First Speech to the Jews.' *Neophilologus* 66 (1982): 301–12.

777 Short, Douglas D. 'Another Look at a Point of Old English Grammar: *Elene* 508 and *Psalm* 77:27.' *In Geardagum* 5 (1983): 39–46.

778 Engberg, Norma J. '*Mod–mægen* Balance in *Elene, The Battle of Maldon,* and *The Wanderer.' NM* 85 (1984): 212–26.
–   Olsen, Alexandra Hennessy. 1984. See item **786**. [Cynewulfian context; reissued extracts from 1984 pub.]
779 Biggs, Frederick M. '*Englum gelice: Elene* line 1320 and *Genesis A* line 185.' *NM* 86 (1985): 447–52.
–   Irvine, Martin. 1986. See item **582**. [Cross as theme.]
–   McEntire, Sandra. 1986. See item **584**. [Cross as theme.]
780 Bodden, Mary-Catherine, ed. and trans. *The Old English Finding of the True Cross.* Cambridge: D.S. Brewer, 1987. Pp. xii + 132. ['Relationship between the Latin Version and Auct. F.4.32, CCCC 303, and *Elene*,' ch. VI.]
781 Bosse, Robert Bux, and Jennifer Lee Wyatt. 'Hrothgar and Nebuchadnezzzar: Conversion in Old English Verse.' *Papers on Lang. and Lit.* 23 (1987): 257–71. [*Elene* 417–25, 436–53, 701–8.]
782 Pilch, Herbert. 'The Intonation of Old English Verse.' In *Studies in Honour of René Derolez,* ed. A.M. Simon-Vandenbergen, 427–52. [Ghent]: Seminarie voor engelse en oud-germaanse taalkunde, 1987. [Discussion of *Elene*.]
783 Wheeler, Ron. A Note on *æðele spald: Elene* 297b–300 and John 9:1–7.' *ELN* 25.2 (1987): 7–8.
784 Anderson, Earl R. 'Cynewulf's *Elene* 1115b–24, the Conversion of the Jews: Figurative or Literal?' *ELN* 25.3 (1988): 1–3.
–   Matsunami, Tamotsu. 1988. See item **330**. [Runic signature.]
–   Porter, Nancy A. 1988. See item **233**. [Loan-words.]
–   Renoir, Alain. 1988. See item **234**. [Formulaic elements.]
785 Nelson, Marie. '*Judith*: A Story of a Secular Saint.' *Germanic Notes* 21 (1990): 12–13. [Comparison with *Elene* and other verse.]
786 Olsen, Alexandra Hennessy. 'Cynewulf's Autonomous Women: A Reconsideration of *Elene* and *Juliana.'* In *New Readings on Women in Old English Literature,* ed. Helen Damico and Olsen, 222–32. See item **753**. [Reissue of criticism drawn from Olsen, *Speech, Song, and Poetic Craft: The Artistry of the Cynewulf Canon.* Amer. Univ. Stud., Ser. 4: Eng. Lang. and Lit. 15. Frankfurt am Main: Lang, 1984.]
787 Wright, Charles D. 'The Pledge of the Soul: A Judgment Theme in Old English Homiletic Literature and Cynewulf's *Elene.' NM* 91 (1990): 23–30. [Also for *Vercelli Homily* VIII.]
788 Breeze, Andrew. '*Exodus, Elene,* and *The Rune Poem: milpæð* "army road, highway."' *N&Q* n.s. 38 (1991): 436–8.
–   Donoghue, Daniel. 1991. See item **244**. [Syntax.]

789 Lord, Albert Bates. *Epic Singers and Oral Tradition*. Ithaca, NY:
Cornell Univ. Press, 1991. Pp. xii + 262. ['The Formulaic Structure
of Introductions to Direct Discourse in *Beowulf* and *Elene*,' ch. 9.]

790 Lampugnani, Monica. 'Giochi paronomastici nell'"Elena" di
Cynewulf. Proposta di analisi tipologica.' *Il confronto letterario.*
Quaderni del Dipartimento di lingue e letterature straniere moderne
(Pavia) 10 (1993): 301–17.

791 Harbus, Antonina. 'Text as Revelation: Constantine's Dream in
Elene.' *Neophilologus* 78 (1994): 645–53.

792 Nelson, Marie. 'Judith, Juliana, and Elene: Three Fighting Saints,
or How I Learned That Translators Need Courage Too.' *Med.*
Perspectives (Richmond, KY, *et alibi*) 9 (1994): 85–98. [See further
item **684**.]

793 Alamichel, Marie-Françoise. 'La légende de sainte Hélène de
Cynewulf à Evelyn Waugh.' *EA* 48 (1995): 306–18.

 - Macrae-Gibson, O.D., and J.R. Lishman. 1995. See item **257**.
[Computer-assisted metrical analysis.]

 - Page, R.I. 1995. See item **178**. [Augmented repr.; esp. for term *rūn*.]

 - Rodrigues, Louis J. 1995. See item **333**. ['*Elene*,' sect. I.ii.]

794 Lees, Clare A. 'At a Crossroads: Old English and Feminist
Criticism.' In *Reading Old English Texts*, ed. Katherine O'Brien
O'Keeffe, 146–69. Cambridge: Cambridge Univ. Press: 1997.
[Includes discussion of *Elene*.]

795 Breeze, Andrew. '*Æpplede gold* in *Juliana*, *Elene*, and *The Phoenix*.'
N&Q n.s. 44 (1997): 452–3.

 - Bjork, Robert E. 1998. See item **336**. [Cynewulfian context.]

796 DiNapoli, Robert. 'Poesis and Authority: Traces of an Anglo-Saxon
agon in Cynewulf's *Elene*.' *Neophilologus* 82 (1998): 619–30.

797 Lionarons, Joyce Tally. 'Cultural Syncretism and the Construction
of Gender in Cynewulf's *Elene*.' *Exemplaria* 10 (1998): 51–68.

 - Shippey, T.A., and Andreas Haarder, eds. 1998. See item **264**.
[J. Grimm on *Elene*.]

798 Chuprya, O.G. 'Temporum opinio v drevnem iazyke i soznanii.'
Voprosy iazykoznaniia 1999, no. 5, pp. 87–100. [Concept of time in
Elene, *Beowulf*, and other texts.]

 - Gutiérrez Barco, Maximino. 1999 [pub. 2001]. See item **800**.

 - Roberts, Jane. 1999. See item **337**.[Cynewulfian context.]

 - Schuhmann, Roland. 1999 [pub. 2002]. See item **805**.

799 Bedingfield, M. Bradford. 'Anglo-Saxons on Fire.' *JTS* n.s. 52
(2001): 658–77. [Fire imagery in *Elene* and other verse; also esp. for
Vercelli Homilies.]

390 Paul G. Remley

800 Gutiérrez Barco, Maximino. 'The Boar in *Beowulf* and *Elene*: A Germanic Symbol of Protection.' *SELIM: Jnl of the Spanish Soc. for Med. Eng. Lang. and Lit.* 9 (2001 for 1999): 163–71.

801 Ó Carragáin, Éamonn. 'Cynewulf's Epilogue to *Elene* and the Tastes of the Vercelli Compiler: A Paradigm of Meditative Reading.' In *Lexis and Texts in Early English: Studies Presented to Jane Roberts*, ed. Christian J. Kay and Louise M. Sylvester, 187–201. Costerus 133. Amsterdam: Rodopi, 2001.

802 Olsen, Karin. 'Cynewulf's Elene: From Empress to Saint.' In *Germanic Texts and Latin Models: Medieval Reconstructions*, ed. Olsen, A. Harbus, and T. Hofstra, 141–56. Mediaevalia Groningana 2. Louvain: Peeters, 2001.

– Roberts, Jane. 2001. See item **1023**. [Context of *Elene* and *Vercelli Homily* XXIII in Vercelli Book.]

803 Wedel, Alfred R. 'Alliteration and the Prefix *ge-* in Cynewulf's *Elene*.' *JEGP* 100 (2001): 200–10.

804 Klemina, E.N. 'Obrazy svjatykh v drevneanglijskoj poeme "Elena" (lingvostilisticheskij aspect) [Images of Saints in the Old English *Elene*: Language and Style].' In *Rannesrednevekovyj tekst: Problemy interpretatsii*, ed. N.Yu. Gvozdetskaya and I.V. Krivushin, 219–33. Ivanovo: Ivanovskii gos. universitet, 2002.

805 Schuhmann, Roland. 'Wie "deutsch" ist der erste Merseburger Zauberspruch? Zur Provenienz des ersten Merseburger Zauberspruchs.' *Die Sprache* 41 (2002 for 1999): 206–19. [*Elene* 130–7, in sect. 2.]

806 Zacher, Samantha. 'Cynewulf at the Interface of Literacy and Orality: The Evidence of the Puns in *Elene*.' *Oral Tradition* 17 (2002): 346–87.

807 Conde Silvestre, Juan Camilo. 'Recursos épicos en la caracterización de los demonios en la literatura anglosajona.' *Cuadernos del CEMyR* (La Laguna, Centro de estudios medievales y Renacentistas) 11 (2003): 53–85. [Includes discussion of *Elene*.]

808 Klein, Stacy S. 'Reading Queenship in Cynewulf's *Elene*.' *Jnl of Med. and Early Mod. Stud.* 33 (2003): 47–89.

809 Chance, Jane. 'Hrotsvit's Latin Drama *Gallicanus* and the Old English Epic *Elene*: Intercultural Founding Narratives of a Feminized Church.' In *Hrotsvit of Gandersheim: Contexts, Identities, Affinities, and Performances*, ed. Phyllis R. Brown, Linda A. McMillin, and Katharina M. Wilson, 193–210. Toronto: Univ. of Toronto Press, 2004.

810 Howe, Nicholas. 'Rome: Capital of Anglo-Saxon England.' *Jnl of Med. and Early Mod. Stud.* 34 (2004): 147–72. [Includes discussion of *Elene*.]

811 Scheil, Andrew P. *The Footsteps of Israel: Understanding Jews in Anglo-Saxon England.* Ann Arbor: Univ. of Michigan Press, 2004. Pp. xii + 372. ['Anti-Judaic Rhetoric in the Vercelli and Blickling Manuscripts,' ch. 5, including 'Poetic Variations: *Elene*,' pp. 219–28; also esp. for *Andreas* and *Vercelli Homily* XVI.]

812 Zollinger, Cynthia Wittman. 'Cynewulf's *Elene* and the Patterns of the Past.' *JEGP* 103 (2004): 180–96.

813 Bauer, Renate. 'Opfer "christlicher" Gewalt. Juden in Texten des englischen Mittelalters.' In *Gewalt im Mittelalter: Realität, Imaginationen*, ed. Manuel Braun and Cornelia Herberichs, 181–201. Munich: Fink, 2005. [Esp. at pp. 188–90.]

814 Hill, Thomas D. 'The Failing Torch: The Old English *Elene*, 1256–1259.' *N&Q* n.s. 52 (2005): 155–60.

815 Klein, Stacy S. 'Centralizing Feminism in Anglo-Saxon Literary Studies: *Elene*, Motherhood, and History.' In *Readings in Medieval Texts: Interpreting Old and Middle English Literature*, ed. David F. Johnson and Elaine Treharne, 149–65. Oxford: Oxford Univ. Press, 2005.

816 Vaccaro, Christopher. '*Inbryrded breostsefa*: Compunction in line 841a of Cynewulf's *Elene*.' *N&Q* n.s. 52 (2005): 160–1.

817 Estes, Heide. 'Colonization and Conversion in Cynewulf's *Elene*.' In *Conversion and Colonization in Anglo-Saxon England*, ed. Catherine E. Karkov and Nicholas Howe, 133–51. Med. and Renaissance Texts and Stud. 318 [= Essays in AS Stud. 2]. Tempe, AZ: ACMRS, 2006.

818 Johnson, David F. 'Hagiographical Demon or Liturgical Devil? Demonology and Baptismal Imagery in Cynewulf's *Elene*.' *Leeds Stud. in Eng.* n.s. 37 (2006): 9–29.

819 Kinane, Karolyn. 'The Cross as Interpretive Guide for Ælfric's Homilies and Saints' Lives.' 2006. In item **664**, pp. 96–110. [Esp. on *Elene* and *inventio Crucis* legend.]

820 Orchard, Andy. 'Computing Cynewulf: The *Judith*-Connection.' In *The Text in the Community: Essays on Medieval Works, Manuscripts, Authors, and Readers*, ed. Jill Mann and Maura Nolan, 75–106. Notre Dame, IN: Univ. of Notre Dame Press, 2006. [Verbal parallels.]

– Suzuki, Hironori. 2006. See item **284**. [Alliteration and syntax.]

821 Wood, Ian N. 'Constantinian Crosses in Northumbria.' 2006. In item **664**, pp. 3–13. [*Elene*; also for *Dream of the Rood*.]

– Fulk, R.D. 2007. See item **285**. [Metre and oral tradition.]

Vercelli Homilies

EDITIONS

– Bianchini, Giuseppe Maria. 1748. See item **7**. [Citations of *Vercelli Homilies* VI, XV–XVIII.]
– Blume, Friedrich. 1832. See item **13**. [Citation of *Vercelli Homily* XVII, rev. J. Grimm and W. Grimm.]
– Goodwin, Charles W., ed. and trans. 1848. See item **841**. [Collation of *Vercelli Homily* XXIII (from prose *Guthlac*) on basis of early transcript.]
822 Wülker, Richard P. 1882. See item **23**, pp. 454–65. [Includes ed. of *Vercelli Homily* XIII and beginnings and endings of others.]
823 Gonser, Paul, ed. *Das angelsächsische Prosa-Leben des hl. Guthlac.* Heidelberg: Winter, 1909. Pp. vii + 200, 9 plates. [Includes ed. of *Vercelli Homily* XXIII (adapted from prose *Guthlac*), pp. 117–34; expansion of item **852**.] Reviews: [Anon.], *Athenaeum* 1909, pt. 2 (July–Dec.): 152; C. Bastide, *Revue critique* 67 (1909): 485–8; E. Björkman, *Literaturblatt für germanische und romanische Philologie* 31 (1910): cols. 232–4; A. B[randl], *ASNSL* 122 (1909): 214; K. Brunner, *ASNSL* 136 (1917): 306–7; R. Dittes, *Beiblatt zur 'Anglia'* 21 (1910): 198–207; E. Ekwall, *Englische Studien* 42 (1910): 298–300; [Anon.], *Literarisches Zentralblatt* 60 (1909): 1466–7 [signed by '-tz-'].
824 Förster, Max. 1913. See item **28**. [Includes ed. of *Vercelli Homilies* II, VI, IX, XV, XXII.]
825 Willard, Rudolph. 1927. See item **856**. [Includes ed. of *Vercelli Homily* VIII.]
826 Förster, Max, ed. *Die Vercelli-Homilien zum ersten Male herausgegeben.* [Pt. 1.] Bibliothek der angelsächsischen Prosa 12. Hamburg: Grand, 1932. Pp. viii + 159. [Only pt. issued; includes *Vercelli Homilies* I–VIII; also includes first page of ed. of *Vercelli Homily* IX; typeset sheets for subsequent pt. (or pts.) were destroyed in the Second World War.] Reviews: A. B[randl], *ASNSL* 164 (1933): 130–1; B. Colgrave, *MLR* 28 (1933): 93–5; J. Daniels, *Museum. Tijdschrift voor filologie en geschiedenis* 40 (1933): 151–2; F. Holthausen, *Beiblatt zur 'Anglia'* 44 (1933): 1–2; K. Jost, *Literaturblatt für germanische und romanische Philologie* 54 (1933): 165–7;

H. L[arsen], *PQ* 12 (1933): 92–3; K. Malone, *MLN* 49 (1934): 352; F. Mossé, *Revue germanique* 24 (1933): 53; F.R. Schröder, *Germanisch-romanische Monatsschrift* 21 (1933): 249–50; A.E.H. Swaen, *Neophilologus* 21 (1936): 54–7; W. van der Gaaf, *ES* 18 (1936): 258–61; R. Willard, *Speculum* 9 (1934): 225–31. Repr. (without truncated text of *Vercelli Homily* IX) as *Die Vercelli-Homilien*, I: *I.–VIII. Homilie*. Darmstadt: Wissenschaftliche Buchgesellschaft, 1966. Reviews: D.G. Scragg, *Anglia* 84 (1966): 218–22; E.G. Stanley, *ASNSL* 203 (1967): 298–300.

827 Willard, Rudolph. 1949. See item **865**. [Includes ed. of *Vercelli Homily* XI.]

828 Szarmach, Paul E., ed. '*Vercelli Homily XX*.' *MS* 35 (1973): 1–26. [Corrections in item **829**.]

829 — 'Revisions for *Vercelli Homily XX*.' *MS* 36 (1974): 493–4. [Corrections for item **828**.]

830 Damiani, Martina. 1977. See item **910**. [*Vercelli Homily* XII.]

– Luiselli Fadda, A.M., ed. 1977. See item **911**. [Esp. for *Vercelli Homily* XIX.]

831 Szarmach, Paul E., ed. *Vercelli Homilies IX–XXIII*. Toronto OE Ser. 5. Toronto: Univ. of Toronto Press, 1981. Pp. xxiii + 101. Review: R. Boenig, *JEGP* 82 (1983): 221–2.

832 Stanley, E.G. 1985. See item **947**. [Partial ed. of *Vercelli Homilies* II, XXI.]

833 Pilch, Herbert. 1990. See item **974**. [Includes diplomatic ed. of *Vercelli Homily* XXIII.]

834 Scragg, D.G., ed. *The Vercelli Homilies and Related Texts*. EETS o.s. 300. Oxford: Oxford Univ. Press, 1992. Pp. lxxxii + 478. Reviews: M. Clayton, *RES* n.s. 45 (1994): 615; R. Marsden, *Anglia* 113 (1995): 110–13; H.L. Spencer, *MÆ* 63 (1994): 124–5. [Scragg's apparatus, which primarily makes direct reference to the manuscripts consulted for his ed., may be keyed here to available printed texts which include later copies of individual Vercelli homilies, other reflexes, and the most significant continuous parallels: *Vercelli Homily* I: pp. 7–43 (as E); pp. 35–9 (as M); **930**, 2: 381–90. *Vercelli Homily* II: pp. 1, 61–3 (as O); pp. 53–65 (as N); pp. 58–60 (as L); pp. 351–62 (in *Vercelli Homily* XXI); pp. 395–403 (in appendix); **843**, pp. 182–90 (no. 40), 191–205 (no. 42); **911**, pp. 186–211 (no. 10). See further item **976**, p. 125. *Vercelli Homily* III: **851**, pp. 40–9 (no. 5), 50–9 (no. 6, as analogue). *Vercelli Homily* IV: pp. 90–3 (as R); pp. 395–403 (as appendix); **840**, 2: 394–400 (as parallel text; see item **928**, reissue,

p. 148); **843**, pp. 134–43 (no. 29, as analogue), 143–52 (no. 30), 274–5 (no. 51); **853**, 2: 138. See further item **976**, p. 126. *Vercelli Homily* V: no independently printed text available for either of the two witnesses collated for ed. (as E and F). *Vercelli Homily* VI: no text collated for homily in ed.; no significant OE analogue cited in ed. *Vercelli Homily* VII: no text collated for homily in ed.; no significant OE analogue cited in ed. *Vercelli Homily* VIII: no independently printed text available for either of the two witnesses collated for ed. (as E and F). *Vercelli Homily* IX: pp. 159–83 (as L); pp. 159–60 (as 'm'); pp. 159–61 (as M); pp. 170–8 (as E and O); pp. 395–403 (as appendix); **843**, pp. 143–52 (no. 30), 205–15 (no. 43, as parallel; see item **976**, pp. 126–7), 215–26 (no. 44, as parallel); **845**, pp. 513–15 (no. 14); **896**, pp. 365–71 (as parallel); **911**, pp. 187–8 (with no. 10, as parallels), 186–211 (no. 10); **935**, pp. 57–65 (no. 4, as analogue; see item **928**, reissue, pp. 148–9; **995** (see item **928**, reissue, p. 148). *Vercelli Homily* X: pp. 395–403 (as appendix); **842**, pp. 104–6 (no. 9); **843**, pp. 143–52 (no. 30), 205–15 (no. 43, as parallel), 215–26 (no. 44, as parallel), 250–65 (no. 49); **851**, pp. 124–35 (no. 12); **911**, pp. 186–211 (no. 10); see further item **976**, pp. 126–7. *Vercelli Homily* XI: no text collated for homily in ed.; no significant OE analogue cited in ed. *Vercelli Homily* XII: no text collated for homily in ed.; no significant OE analogue cited in ed. *Vercelli Homily* XIII: **842**, pp. 137–59 (no. 13; see item **934**, p. 27); **851**, pp. 124–35 (no. 12; see item **934**, p. 27). *Vercelli Homily* XIV: pp. 174–84, 240 (as H). *Vercelli Homily* XV: **28**, pp. 128–37; **842**, pp. 83–97 (no. 7; as analogue); **844**, pp. 166–9 (no. 14); **848**; **870** (as analogue); **875** (as analogue); **935**, pp. 40–55 (no. 3; as analogue). *Vercelli Homily* XVI: no text collated for homily in ed.; no significant OE analogue cited in ed. *Vercelli Homily* XVII: no text collated for homily in ed.; no significant OE analogue cited in ed. *Vercelli Homily* XVIII: pp. 297–9 (as B); **842**, pp. 210–27 (no. 18); see further item **849**. *Vercelli Homily* XIX: **38**, p. 402 (no. 332, art. 37; see item **976**, p. 128); **896**, pp. 365–71 (as parallel); **911**, pp. 71–9 (no. 4); **930**, 2: 317–24 (no. I.xviii, as analogue), 2: 381–90 (in appendix); **935**, pp. 6–24 (no. 1); **936** (in prose *Solomon and Saturn*). *Vercelli Homily* XX: pp. 340–2 (as G); **854**, pp. 15–27 (no. 2); **935**, pp. 25–39 (no. 2); and see further items **828**, **976**, pp. 128–9. *Vercelli Homily* XXI: pp. 52–64 (in *Vercelli Homily* II); pp. 395–403 (in appendix); **843**, pp. 143–52 (no. 30), 182–90 (no. 40); **859**, pp. 4–6; **870**, pp. 17–27. *Vercelli Homily* XXII: no text collated for homily in ed.; no significant OE analogue cited in ed. *Vercelli Homily* XXIII (from prose *Guthlac*): **823**, pp. 100–73; **841**.]

TRANSLATIONS

835 Willard, Rudolph. 1927. See item **856**. [*Vercelli Homily* XIII.]
836 — 1949. See item **865**. [*Vercelli Homily* XI.]
– Damiani, Martina. 1977. See item **910**. [Includes Italian trans. of *Vercelli Homily* XII.]
837 Nicholson, Lewis E., ed., James Schoneweise et al., trans. *The Vercelli Book Homilies: Translations from the Anglo-Saxon.* Lanham, MD: Univ. Press of America, 1991. Pp. xiv + 170. [See further item **989**.]
838 Boenig, Robert, trans. 2000. See item **301**. [*Vercelli Homilies* II, VI, XI.]

STUDIES

839 Thorpe, Mary. Transcript of *Vercelli Homilies*. Manuscript. 1835. [For the transcript, following an earlier transcript by C. Maier, and the extant manuscript in London, Lincoln's Inn, Misc. 313, see item **3**, p. 50 n. 1, and item **40**, pp. 168–9; see further item **841**.]
840 Thorpe, Benjamin, ed. and trans. *Ancient Laws and Institutes of England, Comprising Laws Enacted under the Anglo-Saxon Kings from Æthelbirht to Cnut, with an English Translation of the Saxon.* 1 vol. in 2. London: Commissioners of the Public Records, 1840. Pp. x + 548. [Ed. of Ker (see item **28**) 50, art. 2, at pp. 394–400; cited above for *Vercelli Homily* IV with item **834**.]
841 Goodwin, Charles W., ed. and trans. *The Anglo-Saxon Version of the Life of St. Guthlac, Hermit of Crowland, Originally Written in Latin by Felix (Commonly Called) of Crowland, now First Printed from a MS. in the Cottonian Library.* London: J.R. Smith, 1848. Pp. vi + 125. [Includes reference to consultation of transcript of *Vercelli Homily* XXIII, as supplied by B. Thorpe, pp. i–v, with collated readings in notes. On the transcript, possibly the one produced by Mary Thorpe, see item **839**.]
842 Morris, R., ed. *The Blickling Homilies of the Tenth Century, from the Marquis of Lothian's Unique MS. AD 971.* 1 vol. pub. in 3 pts. EETS o.s. 58, 63, 73. London: Trübner, 1874–80. Pp. xviii + 392, folded plate. [Esp. for *Vercelli Homilies* X, XII, XV, XVII. See with item **834**.] Repr. 1967.

– Wülker, Richard P. 1882. See item **23**. [Treatment of *Vercelli Homily XIII*, including ed.]

843 Napier, Arthur, ed. *Wulfstan. Sammlung der ihm zugeschriebenen Homilien, nebst Untersuchungen über ihre Echtheit*, I: *Text und Varianten*. Sammlung englischer Denkmäler in kritischen Ausgaben 4.1. Berlin: Weidmann, 1883. Pp. x + 318. [Includes editions of later copies or other reflexes of *Vercelli Homilies* II, IV, IX–X, XXI, and an additional analogue of *Vercelli Homily* IV. See further the summary in item **834**. Pt. 2 was never pub.] Reviews: [Anon.], *Academy* (London) 23 (1883): 419; J.M. G[arnett], *Amer. Jnl of Philol.* 5 (1884): 398; E. Holthaus, *Anglia* 7 (1884), Anzeiger: 7; F. Kluge, *Englische Studien* 7 (1884): 479–81; H. Varnhagen, *Deutsche Literaturzeitung* 4 (1883): 1431–2; R. Wülker, *Literarisches Zentralblatt* 36 (1885): 314. Repr. with bibliographical suppl. by Klaus Ostheeren. Dublin and Zurich: Weidmann, 1967.

– Wülker, Richard P. 1885. See item **24**. [Sect. III.xiii.2, 'Die Predigten des Vercellibuches und das Leben des Guðlac,' pp. 485–93.]

844 Assmann, Bruno, ed. *Angelsächsische Homilien und Heiligenleben*. Bibliothek der angelsächsischen Prosa 3. Kassel: Wigand, 1889. Pp. viii + 294. [Text ed. here as item no. 14 includes analogue or possible reflex of conclusion of *Vercelli Homily* XV; see with item **834**.] Repr. with suppl. intro. by Peter Clemoes. Darmstadt: Wissenschaftliche Buchgesellschaft, 1964.

845 Logeman, H. '*Anglo-Saxonica minora*.' *Anglia* 12 (1889): 497–518. [Esp. for *Vercelli Homily* IX; see item **834**.]

– Zupitza, Julius. 1893. See item **360**. [Homiletic prose related to *Vercelli Homily* IV.]

846 Priebsch, Robert. 'The Chief Sources of Some Anglo-Saxon Homilies.' *Otia Merseiana: The Pub. of the Arts Faculty of University College, Liverpool* 1 (1899): 129–47. [Esp. for parallels to *Vercelli Homilies* IX–X, as in item **843**, pp. 205–15 (no. 43), 215–26 (no. 44); for these, see further item **834**.]

847 Klaeber, Frederick. 'Notes on Old English Prose Texts.' *MLN* 18 (1903): 241–7. [Esp. for ll. 24–6 of *Vercelli Homily* XXIII (from prose *Guthlac*), as ed. in item **834**, with apparatus.]

848 Hulme, W.H. 'The Old English Gospel of Nicodemus.' *MP* 1 (1903–4): 610–14. [Includes analogue or possible reflex of conclusion of *Vercelli Homily* XV; see item **834**.]

849 Napier, Arthur S. 'Notes on the *Blickling Homilies*.' *MP* 1 (1903–4): 1–6. [Treatment of *Vercelli Homily* XVIII, including collation of Ker (see item **28**) 336, art. 8.]

850 — 'Contributions to Old English Lexicography.' *TPS* 1906: 265–358. [For the lexical entries here, Napier drew on an independently produced transcript of the *Vercelli Homilies* that was used subsequently by M. Förster and R. Willard; see items 3, p. 50 with n. 1, 834, pp. xxi–xxii.]

851 Belfour, A[lgernon] O., ed. and trans. *Twelfth-Century Homilies in MS. Bodley 343,* I: *Text and Translation.* EETS o.s. 137. London: Oxford Univ. Press, 1909. Pp. 141. [See for *Vercelli Homily* III, pp. 40–9 (no. 40); see further item 834.]

— Dudley, Louise. 1909. See item 363. [Parallels to *Vercelli Homily* IV.]

852 Gonser, Paul. *Untersuchungen zum angelsächsischen Prosa-Leben des hl. Guthlac.* Bern diss. Heidelberg: [n.p.], 1909. Pp. [iv] + 97. [Includes treatment of *Vercelli Homily* XXIII (adapted from prose *Guthlac*); see further item 823.]

853 James, M.R. *A Descriptive Catalogue of the Manuscripts in the Library of Corpus Christi College, Cambridge,* 2: 138. 2 vols. Cambridge: Univ. Press, 1912. [Ed. of Ker (see item 28) 63, art. 10; see for *Vercelli Homily* IV, with item 834.]

854 Brotanek, Rudolf. *Texte und Untersuchungen zur altenglischen Literatur und Kirchengeschichte. Zwei Homilien des Aelfric. Synodalbeschlüsse. Ein Briefentwurf. Zur Überlieferung des 'Sterbengesanges Bedas.'* Halle an der Saale: Niemeyer, 1913. Pp. viii + [204]. [See item 834, in bracketed note; for reviews see item 53, p. 303, no. 5290.]

— Förster, Max. 1913. See item 28, pp. 20–148. [Includes texts of *Vercelli Homilies* II, VI, IX, XV, XXII, as well as descriptions and bibliography for all.]

855 Geisel, Ida. *Sprache und Wortschatz der altenglischen Guthlacübersetzung.* Basel diss. Basel: Werner-Riehm, 1915. Pp. 138. [*Vercelli Homily* XXIII (from prose *Guthlac*).]

— Kern, J.H. 1917–18. See item 735. [*Vercelli Homily* XXIII (from prose *Guthlac*), in 'Zum prosa-Guthlac,' pp. 1–8.]

856 Willard, Rudolph. '*Vercelli Homily VIII* and the *Christ.*' *PMLA* 42 (1927): 314–30. [Includes ed.]

857 Schlutter, Otto B. 'Some Remarks on Max Förster's Print of Some OE Homilies Contained in Vercelli Codex CXVII.' *Neophilologus* 15 (1930): 264–70. [Esp. on *Vercelli Homily* XV; addresses item 28.]

858 Willard, Rudolph. 'Gleanings in Old English Lexicography.' *Beiblatt zur 'Anglia'* 54 (1930): 8–24. [Collection of notable words identified in the light of the author's compilation of 'a full glossary of the prose homilies in the Vercelli Book' (p. 8).]

859 — *Two Apocrypha in Old English Homilies.* Beiträge zur englischen Philologie 30. Leipzig: Tauchnitz, 1935. Pp. viii + 149. [Includes ed. Wording of text ed. at pp. 4–6 may reveal brief borrowing from *Vercelli Homily* XXI; see item **976**, p. 129. See further item **834**.] Repr. New York: Johnson, 1967.

– — 1935. See item **367**. [*Vercelli Homilies* IV, VIII, XV.]

860 Heningham, Eleanor K. *An Early Latin Debate of the Body and Soul Preserved in MS Royal 7.A.III. in the British Museum.* 1939. See item **368**. [*Vercelli Homilies* II, IV, pp. 11–13.]

– — 1940. See item **369**. [*Vercelli Homilies* IV, XXII.]

861 Menner, Robert J. *The Poetical Dialogues of Solomon and Saturn.* MLA Monograph 13. New York: Modern Language Association, 1941. Pp. xii + 176. [*Vercelli Homily* IV, pp. 68–9, 143.]

862 Dobbie, Elliott Van Kirk, ed. *The Anglo-Saxon Minor Poems.* ASPR 6. New York: Columbia Univ. Press, 1942. Pp. clxxx + 220. [Verse ed. as *Exhortation to Christian Living*, pp. 67–9, has been viewed as source for (or witness to) *Vercelli Homily* XXI; see item **976**.]

863 Förster, Max. 'Zur Liturgik der angelsächsischen Kirche.' *Anglia* 66 (1942): 1–51. [*Vercelli Homilies* II–III.]

864 Menner, Robert. 'Anglian and Saxon Elements in Wulfstan's Vocabulary.' *MLN* 63 (1948): 1–9. [See esp. pp. 8–9, in discussion of pseudo-Wulfstan XL, XLIX, for possible Anglian elements in *Vercelli Homilies* II, X.]

865 McIntosh, Angus. 'Wulfstan's Prose.' *PBA* 34 (1949): 109–42. Also pub. separately, London: Cumberlege, 1950. Pp. 36. [Esp. for *Vercelli Homily* XXI.]

866 Willard, Rudolph. '*Vercelli Homily XI* and Its Sources.' *Speculum* 24 (1949): 76–87. [Includes ed. and trans.; also for *Vercelli Homilies* X, XII, XXI.]

867 Jost, Karl. *Wulfstanstudien.* Schweizer anglistische Arbeiten 23. Bern: Francke, 1950. Pp. 271. [Esp. for *Vercelli Homily* IV, pp. 208–10; also for *Vercelli Homilies* III, X, and others, in chs. 6–7.]

868 Peterson, Paul W. 'Dialect Grouping in the Unpublished *Vercelli Homilies.*' *SP* 50 (1953): 559–65.

869 Vleeskruyer, Rudolf, ed. *The Life of St Chad: An Old English Homily Edited with Introduction, Notes, Illustrative Texts, and Glossary.* Amsterdam: North-Holland, 1953. Pp. viii + 247. ['The *Vercelli Homilies*,' in intro., sect. II.21, and in sect. II.22 for *Vercelli Homilies* II, XXI; esp. on questions of dialect and origin.]

870 Förster, Max. 'A New Version of the Apocalypse of Thomas in Old English.' *Anglia* 73 (1955): 6–36. [Esp. for discussion of *Vercelli Homily* XV and parallel texts; also for *Vercelli Homily* XXI; see further item **834**; includes ed.]

871 Cross, J.E. '*Ubi sunt* Passages in Old English: Sources and Relationships.' *Vetenskaps-societetens i Lund ärsbok* 1956: 23–44. [Esp. for *Vercelli Homily* X.]

872 Bethurum, Dorothy, ed. *The Homilies of Wulfstan*. Oxford: Clarendon Press, 1957. Pp. xiii + 384. [*Vercelli Homily* II, p. 42; also there esp. on item **843**, pp. 143–52 (no. 30).]

873 Cross, J.E. '"The dry bones speak": A Theme in Some Old English Homilies.' *JEGP* 56 (1957): 434–9. [Esp. on *Vercelli Homily* XIII.]

874 Irving, Edward B., Jr. 'Latin Prose Sources for Old English Verse.' *JEGP* 56 (1957): 588–95. [*Vercelli Homily* VIII.]

875 Bolton, Whitney F. 'The Manuscript Source of the Old English Prose Life of St. Guthlac.' *ASNSL* 197 (1961): 301–3. [Bears on readings of *Vercelli Homily* XXIII (from prose *Guthlac*).]

876 Funke, Otto. 'Studien zur alliterierenden und rhythmisierenden Prosa in der älteren altenglischen Homiletik.' *Anglia* 80 (1962): 9–36. [Esp. on *Vercelli Homilies* IV–V, VII, IX–X, XV, XXI–XXIII, pp. 22–3, 25–36.]

– Bolton, W.F., ed. 1963. See item **370**. [Ed. of *Blickling Homily* VII, analogue of *Vercelli Homily* XV, pp. 102–7.]

877 Turville-Petre, Joan. 'Translations of a Lost Penitential Homily.' *Traditio* 19 (1963): 51–78. [Remarks on *Vercelli Homilies* II–IV, VIII–X, XX–XXI; see further item **939**.]

878 Whitbread, Leslie. '"Wulfstan" Homilies XXIX, XXX, XXXI, and Some Related Texts.' *Anglia* 81 (1963): 347–64. [Esp. for discussion of material related to *Vercelli Homily* XXI.]

879 Cross, J.E. 'The "Coeternal Beam" in the O.E. Advent Poem (*Christ I*), ll. 104–29.' *Neophilologus* 48 (1964): 72–81. [Esp. for *Vercelli Homily* XVI.]

880 Gatch, Milton McC. 'Two Uses of Aprocrypha in Old English Homilies.' *Church Hist.* 33 (1964): 379–91. [Esp. on *Vercelli Homily* XV; also for *Vercelli Homily* IV.] Repr. in his *Eschatology and Christian Nurture*, item VI. 2000. See item **386**.

881 – 'Eschatology in the Anonymous Old English Homilies.' *Traditio* 21 (1965): 117–65. [Sect. II, 'The Vercelli Homilies,' pp. 132–60; esp. on *Vercelli Homily* XV.] Repr. in his *Eschatology and Christian Nurture*, item VII. 2000. See item **386**.

882 Schabram, Hans. *Superbia. Studien zum altenglischen Wortschatz*, I: *Die dialektale und zeitliche Verbreitung des Wortguts*. Munich: Fink, 1965. Pp. 140. [Only pt. issued. 'Die Vercelli-Homilien,' pp. 77–87; esp. on dialect, dating, and localization.]

883 Hallander, Lars-G. *Old English Verbs in '-sian.' A Semantic and Derivational Study*. Acta Universitatis Stockholmiensis, Stockholm Stud. in Eng. 15. Stockholm: Almqvist, 1966. Pp. 619. [Esp. for dating criteria, sect. 2.6.3.]

884 Scragg, D.G. 'Old English *bryt* in the Vercelli Book.' *N&Q* n.s. 13 (1966): 168–9. [*Vercelli Homily* IV.]

885 Tveitane, Mattias. 'Irish Apocrypha in Norse Tradition? On the Sources of Some Medieval Homilies.' *Arv* 22 (1966): 111–35. [Esp. on *Vercelli Homily* VI; also on *Vercelli Homilies* V, VIII, XIV.]

886 Hill, T.D. 'The Seven Joys of Heaven in *Christ III* and Old English Homiletic Texts.' *N&Q* n.s. 16 (1969): 165–6. [*Vercelli Homilies* V, IX.]

887 Schabram, Hans. 'Kritische Bemerkungen zu Angaben über die Verbreitung altenglischer Wörter.' In *Festschrift für Edgar Mertner*, ed. Bernhard Fabian and Ulrich Suerbaum, 89–102. Munich: Fink, 1969. [*Vercelli Homily* XIX, p. 96 with n. 64.]

888 [Anon.], ed. 'Computer Concordances in Progress.' In *Computers and Old English Concordances*, ed. Angus Cameron, Roberta Frank, and John Leyerle, 35–82. Toronto: Univ. of Toronto Press, 1970. [Transcript of conference presentations and discussions; see esp. Richard L. Venezky on concordances to *Vercelli Homilies*, pp. 43–8.]

889 Roberts, Jane. 'Traces of Unhistorical Gender Congruence in a Late Old English Manuscript.' *ES* 51 (1970): 30–7. [See esp. pp. 36–7, for *Vercelli Homily* XXIII (from prose *Guthlac*) and questions of Anglian origin.]

–   Scragg, D.G. 1970. See item **42**. [Anomalous use of initial *h* in prose of Vercelli Book, pp. 174–5, 179.]

890 Szarmach, Paul E. 'Caesarius of Arles and the *Vercelli Homilies*.' *Traditio* 26 (1970): 315–23. [Esp. for *Vercelli Homilies* XIV, XIX–XXI; also for *Vercelli Homily* XI.]

891 Tristram, Hildegard L.C., ed. *Vier altenglische Predigten aus der heterodoxen Tradition, mit Kommentar, Übersetzung und Glossar sowie drei weiteren Texten im Anhang*. [Freiburg im Breisgau]: [n.p.], 1970. Pp. [viii] + 448. [Esp. for *Vercelli Homily* XI, in notes on item 4.]

–   Scragg, D.G. 1971. See item **44**. [Accent marks in texts of *Vercelli Homilies*.]

892 Cross, J.E. '*De ordine creaturarum liber* in Old English Prose.'
Anglia 90 (1972): 132–40. [Esp. for *Vercelli Homily* XIX.]

893 — 'The Literate Anglo-Saxon: On Sources and Disseminations.'
PBA 58 (1972): 67–100. [Esp. on *Vercelli Homilies* V, IX; also for
Vercelli Homilies IV, XXI.]

– Erickson, Jon L. 1972. See item **45**. [Damaged folios containing texts
of *Vercelli Homilies* XIV, XVI.]

894 Goldman, Stephen H. 'The Old English *Vercelli Homilies*: Rhetoric
and Transformational Analysis.' *Jnl of Eng. Ling.* 6 (1972): 20–7.

895 — 'Rhetorical Transformations and the Old English *Vercelli
Homilies*.' In *From Soundstream to Discourse: Papers from the 1971
Mid-America Linguistics Conference*, ed. Daniel G. Hays and
Donald M. Lance, 135–41. Columbia: Linguistics Area Program,
Univ. of Missouri, 1972. [Esp. for *Vercelli Homilies* I, IV–VI, X.]

896 Robinson, Fred C. 'The Devil's Account of the Next World: An
Anecdote from Old English Homiletic Literature.' *NM* 73 (1972):
362–71. [*Vercelli Homily* IX; includes ed. of Ker (see item **28**) 186,
art. 18, pp. 365–71; see item **834** and, further, item **953**.]

897 Szarmach, Paul E. 'Three Versions of the Jonah Story: An Investigation of Narrative Technique in Old English Homilies.' *ASE* 1
(1972): 183–92. [*Vercelli Homily* XIX.]

– Cameron, Angus. 1973. See item **47**. [Citations of manuscripts and
editions for *Vercelli Homilies*.]

898 Cross, J.E. 'Portents and Events at Christ's Birth: Comments on
Vercelli V and *VI* and the *Old English Martyrology*.' *ASE* 2 (1973):
209–20. [Also for *Vercelli Homily* II.]

899 Godden, M.R. 'An Old English Penitential Motif.' *ASE* 2 (1973):
221–39. [Esp. on *Vercelli Homily* VIII; also for *Vercelli Homily* IV.]

– Scragg, D.G. 1973. See item **48**. [Esp. on *Vercelli Homilies* XIX–XX.]

– Szarmach, Paul E., ed. 1973. See item **829**. [*Vercelli Homily* XX; also
for *Vercelli Homily* XI.]

900 Day, Virginia. 'The Influence of the Catechetical *narratio* on Old
English and Some Other Medieval Literature.' *ASE* 3 (1974): 51–61.
[*Vercelli Homily* XIX.]

901 Remly, Lynn L. 'Salome in England: A Note on *Vercelli Homily X*,
165–74 (pseudo-Wulfstan XLIX, 257, 9–18).' *Vetera Christianorum*
11 (1974): 121–3.

902 Tristram, Hildegard L.C. 'Die *leohtfæt*-Metapher in den altenglischen
anonymen Bittagspredigten.' *NM* 75 (1974): 229–49. [*Vercelli
Homilies* XI–XII, XIX–XX.]

903 Godden, M.R. 'Old English Composite Homilies from Winchester.'
     ASE 4 (1975): 57–65. [Esp. for *Vercelli Homily* IV.]
904 Grinda, Klaus R. *'Arbeit' und 'Mühe.'* *Untersuchungen zur
     Bedeutungsgeschichte altenglischen Wörter.* Munich: Fink, 1975.
     Pp. 319. [Non-West Saxon features in *Vercelli Homilies*, p. 184.]
905 Trahern, Joseph B., Jr. 'An Old English Verse Paraphrase of Mat-
     thew 25:41.' *Mediaevalia* (Binghamton, NY) 1.2 (1975): 109–41.
     [Esp. on *Vercelli Homily* X; also for *Vercelli Homilies* II, XXI.]
906 Becker, Wolfgang. 'The Latin Manuscript Sources of the Old Eng-
     lish Translations of the Sermon *Remedia peccatorum.*' *MÆ* 45 (1976):
     145–52. [Esp. for *Vercelli Homily* X; see further item **924**.]
907 Trahern, Joseph B., Jr. 'Caesarius of Arles and Old English Literature:
     Some Contributions and a Recapitulation.' *ASE* 5 (1976): 105–9.
     [*'Vercelli* VIII,' sect. 3; also for *Vercelli Homilies* XI, XIII–XIV,
     XX–XXI.]
908 Gatch, Milton McC. *Preaching and Theology in Anglo-Saxon
     England.* Toronto: Univ. of Toronto Press, 1976. Pp. xiv + 266. [Esp.
     for *Vercelli Homilies* I–II, V, XIV–XV.]
909 Szarmach, Paul E. 'MS Junius 85 f. 2r and Napier 49.' *ELN* 14 (1976–7):
     241–6. [Esp. for *Vercelli Homily* X; includes collation of variants.]
910 Damiani, Martina. 'Un inedito anglosassone. La XII omelia rogazionale
     del Codex Vercellensis.' *Romanobarbarica* 2 (1977): 269–85. [Study
     of *Vercelli Homily* XII, with text and Italian trans. in appendix 1.]
911 Luiselli Fadda, A.M., ed. *Nuove omelie anglosassoni della renascen-
     za benedettina.* Filologia germanica, Testi e studi 1. Florence: Le Mon-
     nier, 1977. Pp. xxv + 248. [Includes ed. of later witness to *Vercelli
     Homily* XIX; also for reflexes and analogues of other *Vercelli Hom-
     ilies*; see item **834** and, further, item **993**.]
912 Roberts, Jane. 'St Bartholomew's Day: A Problem Resolved?' *MÆ*
     46 (1977): 16–19. [*Vercelli Homily* XXIII (from prose *Guthlac*).]
913 Scragg, D.G. 'Napier's "Wulfstan" Homily XXX: Its Sources, Its
     Relationship to the Vercelli Book, and Its Style.' *ASE* 6 (1977):
     197–211. [Esp. for *Vercelli Homilies* IX–X, XIX–XXI; also for
     Vercelli Homily IV.]
914 — 'Old English *forhtleasness, unforhtleasness.*' *N&Q* n.s. 24 (1977):
     399–400. [*Vercelli Homily* I.]
915 Gatch, Milton McC. 'The Achievement of Ælfric and His Col-
     leagues in European Perspective.' 1978. In item **920**, pp. 43–73.
     [Historical context of *Vercelli Homilies*.]

916 Godden, Malcolm. 'Ælfric and the Vernacular Prose Tradition.'
     1978. In item 920, pp. 99–117. [*Vercelli Homily* I, p. 111, and also on
     Vercelli Homily XV, pp. 101–2 with n. 10; see also pp. 107, 109.]
917 Healey, Antonette diPaolo. *The Old English Vision of St. Paul.*
     Speculum Anniversary Monographs 2. Cambridge, MA: Medieval
     Academy of America, 1978. Pp. xi + 98. [Esp. for *Vercelli Homilies*
     II, IV, VI, VIII–IX.]
918 Letson, D.R. 'The Poetic Content of the Revival Homily.' 1978. In
     item 920, pp. 139–56. [*Vercelli Homilies* II, IV, XXI–XXII; also esp.
     on context of *Vercelli Homilies* in Vercelli Book.]
919 Szarmach, Paul E. 'The *Vercelli Homilies*: Style and Structure.' 1978.
     In item 920, pp. 241–67. [Emphasis on *Vercelli Homilies* IX–XXIII.]
920 — and Bernard F. Huppé, eds. *The Old English Homily and Its*
     Backgrounds. Albany: State Univ. of New York Press, 1978. Pp. [vii]
     + 267. [Esp. in sect. 12 (item 921); also in intro.]
921 Remly, Lynn L. '*Ars praedicandi*: Poetic Devices in the Prose Homi-
     ly *Vercelli X.*' *Mid-Hudson Lang. Stud.* 1 (1978): 1–16.
922 Sauer, H. '*Theodulfi capitula*' *in England.* Texte und Untersuch-
     ungen zur englischen Philologie 8. Munich: Fink, 1978. Pp. xv + 521.
     ['Vercelli-Homilie iii.19–37,' pp. 278–81.]
923 Tristram, Hildegard L.C. 'Stock Descriptions of Heaven and Hell in
     Old English Prose and Poetry.' *NM* 79 (1978): 102–13. [Esp. for
     Vercelli Homilies V, IX.]
924 Becker, Wolfgang. 'The Manuscript Source of Ælfric's *Catholic*
     Homily II 7: A Supplementary Note.' *MÆ* 48 (1979): 105–6. [See
     item 906; esp. on *Vercelli Homily* X.]
925 Cummings, Michael J. 'Napier Homily 55 and Belfour Homily 10
     on the Temptations in the Desert.' *NM* 80 (1979): 315–24. [Esp. for
     Vercelli Homily XV.]
926 Roberts, Jane. *The Guthlac Poems of the Exeter Book.* Oxford:
     Clarendon Press, 1979. Pp. x + 232. [*Vercelli Homily* XXIII, esp. at
     pp. 7–9.]
927 — 'An Inventory of Early Guthlac Materials.' *MS* 32 (1979):
     193–233. [*Vercelli Homily* XXIII (from prose *Guthlac*).]
928 Scragg, D.G. 'The Corpus of Vernacular Homilies and Prose Saints'
     Lives before Ælfric.' *ASE* 8 (1979): 223–77. [See further item 999.]
     Reissue in item 1020, pp. 73–150. ['Addenda,' pp. 147–50, esp. for
     Vercelli Homilies II–IV, IX, XIX–XXI.]
 –   Szarmach, Paul E. 1979. See item 52. [*Vercelli Homily* XV.]

929 Wenisch, Franz. *Spezifisch anglisches Wortgut in den nordhum-
brischen Interlinearglossierungen des Lukasevangeliums.* Anglistische Forschungen 132. Heidelberg: Winter, 1979. Pp. 352. [Esp.
on non-West Saxon features in *Vercelli Homilies* I, III, XIX, with
comments on all the other homilies; see pp. 72–8, and, *ad indicem*,
p. 351.]

930 Clemoes, Peter, and Malcolm Godden, eds. *Ælfric's 'Catholic Homilies.'*
3 vols. EETS s.s. 5, 17–18. Oxford: Oxford Univ. Press, 1979–2000.
Vol. 1: *The First Series. Text,* ed. Clemoes. 1997. Pp. xxii + 562, 1 plate.
Vol. 2: *The Second Series. Text,* ed. Godden. 1979. Pp. xcvi + 390,
1 plate. Vol. 3: *Introduction Commentary and Glossary,* ed. Godden.
2000. Pp. lxii + 794. Errata: vol. 3, p. ix. [Esp. for *Vercelli Homily* I,
vol. 2, pp. lv–lvi, with pp. 381–90; see further item **834.**]

931 Sauer, Hans. 'Zwei spätaltenglische Beichtermahnungen aus Hs.
Cotton Tiberius A.III.' *Anglia* 98 (1980): 1–33. [Treatment of
Vercelli Homily IX.]

932 Evans, Ruth. 'An Anonymous Old English Homily for Holy Saturday.' *Leeds Stud. in Eng.* n.s. 12 (1981): 129–53. [Includes ed.; see
for discussion of *Vercelli Homily* IX.]

933 Hill, Joyce. 'The Soldier of Christ in Old English Prose and Poetry.'
Leeds Stud. in Eng. n.s. 12 (1981): 57–80. [*Vercelli Homily* V.]

– Ó Carragáin, É. 1981. See item **560.** [Contexts in Vercelli Book.]

934 Szarmach, Paul E. 'Another Old English Translation of Gregory the
Great's "Dialogues"?' *ES* 62 (1981): 97–109. [Esp. on 'Gregorian'
passages in *Vercelli Homily* XIV; also for *Vercelli Homilies* II–IV,
VI–X, XIX–XXIII.]

935 Bazire, Joyce, and James E. Cross, eds. *Eleven Old English Rogationtide Homilies.* Toronto OE Ser. 7. Toronto: Univ. of Toronto Press,
1982. Pp. xxxii + 143. [Esp. for textual links to *Vercelli Homilies* XV,
XIX–XX, and for analogues of *Vercelli Homilies* III, IX; also esp. on
Vercelli Homilies XI–XII, in intro., pp. xxi–xxii; see further item **834,**
in bracketed note.] Reviews: M. Clayton, *MÆ* 54 (1985): 289–90; M.
McC. Gatch, *Church Hist.* 53 (1984): 432–3; T.H. Leinbaugh, *RES* 36
(1985): 395–7; H. Sauer, *Anglia* 104 (1986): 184–8; C. Sisam, *N&Q* n.s.
32 (1986): 96–7; D. Yerkes, *Speculum* 59 (1984): 368–9. Augmented
repr., King's College London Med. Stud. 4. London: King's College,
1989. [Esp. in 'Preface to the Second Edition,' pp. vii–viii, for *Vercelli
Homilies* III, XIX–XXI.]

936 Cross, James E., and Thomas D. Hill, eds. *The Prose 'Solomon and
Saturn' and 'Adrian and Ritheus.'* McMaster OE Stud. and Texts 1.

Toronto: Univ. of Toronto Press, 1982. Pp. xi + 185. [Esp. for *Vercelli Homily* XIX; see further item **834**, in bracketed note.]

937 Grant, Raymond J.S. *Three Homilies from Cambridge, Corpus Christi College 41: The Assumption, St. Michael, and the Passion.* Ottawa: Tecumseh Press, 1982. Pp. 110. [*Vercelli Homily* IV.]

938 Olsen, Alexandra Hennessey. 'Apotheosis and Doctrinal Purpose in the Vercelli "Guthlac."' *In Geardagum* 4 (1982): 32–40. [*Vercelli Homily* XXIII (from prose *Guthlac*).]

939 Spencer, Helen L. 'Vernacular and Latin Versions of a Sermon for Lent: "A Lost Penitential Homily" Found.' *MS* 44 (1982): 271–305. [Esp. for *Vercelli Homily* III; see further item **877**.]

940 Sauer, Hans. 'Die 72 Völker und Sprachen der Welt: Ein mittelalter-licher Topos in der englischen Literatur.' *Anglia* 101 (1983): 29–48. [*Vercelli Homily* IX, in sect. 7; also in appendix.]

941 Clayton, Mary. 'Homiliaries and Preaching in Anglo-Saxon England.' *Peritia* 4 (1985): 207–42. [Esp. on subgroups within the series of *Vercelli Homilies* VI–XXI, pp. 226–9.] Corr. reissue in item **1020**, pp. 151–98. [For passage cited, see pp. 171–5.]

942 Healey, Antonette diPaolo. 'Anglo-Saxon Use of the Apocryphal Gospels.' In *The Anglo-Saxons: Synthesis and Achievement*, ed. J. Douglas Woods and David A.E. Pelteret, 93–104. Waterloo, ON: Wilfrid Laurier Univ. Press, 1985. [*Vercelli Homily* VI, esp. at pp. 102–3.]

943 Hill, Joyce. 'Ælfric's "Silent Days."' *Leeds Stud. in Eng.* 16 (1985): 118–31. [*Vercelli Homily* I.]

944 Hill, Thomas D. 'When God Blew Satan out of Heaven: The Motif of Exsufflation in "*Vercelli Homily XIX*" and Later English Literature.' *Leeds Stud. in Eng.* n.s. 16 (1985): 132–41.

945 Lees, Clare A. 'The Dissemination of Alcuin's *De virtutibus et vitiis liber* in Old English: A Preliminary Survey.' *Leeds Stud. in Eng.* n.s. 16 (1985): 174–89. [*Vercelli Homily* XX; also for works of Ælfric and other prose.]

946 Scragg, D.G. 'The Homilies of the Blickling Manuscript.' In *Learning and Literature in Anglo-Saxon England: Studies Presented to Peter Clemoes on the Occasion of His Sixty-Fifth Birthday*, ed. Michael Lapidge and Helmut Gneuss, 299–316. Cambridge: Cambridge Univ. Press, 1985. [Esp. for *Vercelli Homilies* X, XVIII, pp. 304–9.] Repr. 1987.

947 Stanley, E.G. '"The Judgement of the Damned" (from Cambridge, Corpus Christi College 201 and Other Manuscripts) and the Defi-nition of Old English Verse.' 1985. In *Learning and Literature*, ed.

Michael Lapidge and Helmut Gneuss, 363–91. See item **946**. [*Vercelli Homilies* II, XXI; includes partial ed.; see further item **834**.]

948 Tristram, Hildegard L.C. *Sex Aetates Mundi. Die Weltzeitalter bei den Angelsachsen und den Iren. Untersuchungen und Texte.* Anglistische Forschungen 165. Heidelberg: Winter, 1985. Pp. 368. [Sect. II.iv.2, esp. for *Vercelli Homily* XI.]

949 Wenisch, Franz. '(*Ge*)*fægnian*: Zur dialektalen Verbreitung eines altenglischen Wortes.' In *Problems of Old English Lexicography: Studies in Memory of Angus Cameron*, ed. Alfred Bammesberger, 393–426. Eichstätter Beiträge zur Sprache und Literatur 15. Regensburg: Pustet, 1985. [*Vercelli Homilies* IV–V, p. 399.]

950 Clayton, Mary 'Delivering the Damned: A Motif in Old English Homiletic Prose.' *MÆ* 55 (1986): 92–102. [Esp. for *Vercelli Homily* XV.]

951 Richards, Mary P. 'The Manuscript Contexts of the Old English Laws: Tradition and Innovation.' In *Studies in Earlier Old English Prose*, ed. Paul E. Szarmach, 171–92. Albany: State Univ. of New York Press, 1986. [*Vercelli Homily* XIX.]

952 Roberts, Jane. 'The Old English Prose Translation of Felix's *Vita Sancti Guthlaci*.' 1986. In *Studies in Earlier Old English Prose*, ed. Paul E. Szarmach, 363–79. See item **951**. [*Vercelli Homily* XXIII (from prose *Guthlac*).]

953 Scragg, D.G. '"The Devil's Account of the Next World" Revisited.' *ANQ* 24 (1986): 107–10. [Esp. on *Vercelli Homily* IX; also for *Vercelli Homily* XIX; see further item **896**.]

954 Sisam, Celia. 1986. See with item **935**. [Review; esp. on *Vercelli Homily* XIX.]

955 Szarmach, Paul E. 'The Earlier Homily: *De Parasceve*.' 1986. In *Studies in Earlier Old English Prose*, ed. Szarmach, 381–99. See item **951**. [*Vercelli Homily* I.]

956 — 'Two Notes on the *Vercelli Homilies*.' *ELN* 24.2 (1986): 3–7. [*Vercelli Homilies* XIV, XXI.]

— — 1986 [pub. 1990]. See item **977**.

957 Cross, James E., ed. *Cambridge Pembroke College MS 25: A Carolingian Sermonary Used by Anglo-Saxon Preachers.* King's College London Med. Stud. 1. London: King's College, 1987. Pp. viii + 252. [*Vercelli Homilies* XIX–XXI, sects. 3–5; also esp. for *Vercelli Homilies* III, V–VI, VIII.]

— Moffat, Douglas, ed. 1987. See item **385**. [Esp. on *Vercelli Homily* IV, pp. 40–1.]

958 Wright, Charles D. 'Apocryphal Lore and Insular Tradition in St Gall, Stiftsbibliothek MS 908.' In *Irland und die Christenheit. Bibelstudien und Mission*, ed. Próinséas Ní Chatháin and Michael Richter, 125–45. Veröffentlichungen des Europa Zentrums, Tübingen: Kulturwissenschaftliche Reihe. Stuttgart: Klett-Cotta, 1987. [Esp. for *Vercelli Homilies* IX, XIX, pp. 136–7.]

959 Cross, James E. 'Hiberno-Latin Commentaries in Salisbury Manuscripts before 1125 A.D.' *Hiberno-Latin Newsletter* (Ottawa) 2 (1988): 8–9. [*Vercelli Homily* XXI.]

960 Lindström, Bengt. 'The Old English Translation of Alcuin's *Liber de virtutibus et vitiis.*' *SN* 60 (1988): 23–35. [*Vercelli Homily* VII, pp. 25–6; also for *Vercelli Homily* XX.]

961 Jeffrey, J. Elizabeth. *Blickling Spirituality and the Old English Vernacular Homily: A Textual Analysis.* Stud. in Med. Lit. 1. Lampeter: Mellen, 1989. Pp. [v] + 196. ['Vercelli Homiliary,' *ad indicem*, p. 196.]

962 Wright, Charles D. 'The Irish "Enumerative Style" in Old English Homiletic Literature, Especially *Vercelli Homily* IX.' *CMCS* 18 (1989): 27–74. [Also for *Vercelli Homily* V.]

963 Hall, Thomas N. 'The Reversal of the Jordan in *Vercelli Homily 16* and in Old English Literature.' *Traditio* 45 (1989–90): 53–86.

964 Bately, Janet. 'Orosius.' In *SASLC* (1990), pp. 141–3. See item **965**. [*Vercelli Homilies* V–VI.]

965 Biggs, Frederick M., Thomas D. Hill, and Paul E. Szarmach, with the assistance of Karen Hammond, eds. *Sources of Anglo-Saxon Literary Culture: A Trial Version.* Med. and Renaissance Texts and Stud. 74. Binghamton, NY: Center for Medieval and Early Renaissance Studies, 1990. Pp. xli + 256. [Cited above and below as *SASLC* (1990).]

966 Clayton, Mary. *The Cult of the Virgin Mary in Anglo-Saxon England.* CSASE 2. Cambridge: Cambridge Univ. Press, 1990. Pp. xiv + 299. [*Vercelli Homilies* VI, XV, XVII, esp. in chs. 7–9.]

967 — 'Apocalypse of the Virgin.' In *SASLC* (1990), pp. 65–6. See item **965**. [*Vercelli Homily* XV.]

968 Cross, J.E. 'A *sermo de misericordia* in Old English Prose.' *Anglia* 108 (1990): 429–40. ['*Vercelli Homily X* and pseudo-Wulfstan Sermon XLIX,' pp. 436–9.]

969 Godden, M.R. 'Ælfric of Eynsham.' In *SASLC* (1990), pp. 17–19. See item **965**. [*Vercelli Homily* XIX, in later witness, p. 18 (with Ælfric, *Catholic Homilies*; as Hom S 34).]

970 Hall, Thomas N. 'Gospel of Ps Matthew.' In *SASLC* (1990), pp. 43–
5. See item **965**. [*Vercelli Homily* VI.]

971 — 'Protevangelium of James.' In *SASLC* (1990), pp. 37–8. See item
965. [*Vercelli Homily* X.]

972 Harbus, Antonina. 'The Use of the Noun *olehtung* in *Vercelli
Homily VII.*' *N&Q* n.s. 37 (1990): 389–91.

973 Healey, Antonette diPaolo. '*Visio Sancti Pauli.*' In *SASLC* (1990),
pp. 66–7. See item **965**. [*Vercelli Homilies* IV, IX.]

974 Pilch, Herbert. 'The Last *Vercelli Homily*: A Sentence-Analytical
Edition.' In *Historical Linguistics and Philology*, ed. Jacek Fisiak,
297–336. Trends in Ling., Stud. and Monographs 46. Berlin: Mouton
de Gruyter, 1990. [*Vercelli Homily* XXIII (from prose *Guthlac*);
includes diplomatic text.]

975 Quinn, Karen J., and Kenneth Quinn. *A Manual of Old English
Prose*. New York: Garland, 1990. Pp. xix + 439. [See p. 71, item
A502, with references.]

976 Scragg, Donald G. 'Homiliaries and Homilies.' In *SASLC* (1990),
pp. 123–30. See item **965**. [Esp. on *Vercelli Homilies* I–II, IV, IX–X,
XV, XIX–XXI, in 'Anonymous Old English Homilies,' pp. 124–9.]

977 Szarmach, Paul E. 'The Latin Tradition of Alcuin's *Liber de virtutibus
et vitiis*, cap. xxvii–xxxv, with Special Reference to *Vercelli Homily
XX.*' *Mediaevalia* (Binghamton, NY) 12 (1990 for 1986): 13–41.

978 — '*Liber de virtutibus et vitiis.*' In *SASLC* (1990), pp. 20–1. See item
965. [On work of Alcuin; see esp. for *Vercelli Homily* XX, and also
for *Vercelli Homily* III.]

979 Whatley, E. Gordon. '*Acta Sanctorum.*' In *SASLC* (1990), pp. 1–15.
See item **965**. [*Vercelli Homily* XXIII (from prose *Guthlac*), in
'*Guthlacus, vita* [Felix.Vit.Guth],' pp. 10–12; now superseded by
entry cited in item **1024**.]

980 Wright, Charles D. 'Apocalypse of Thomas.' In *SASLC* (1990),
pp. 68–9. See item **965**. [*Vercelli Homily* XV.]

981 — '*Catechesis Celtica.*' In *SASLC* (1990), pp. 117–18. See item **965**.
[*Vercelli Homilies* V, IX.]

982 — '*De questione apostoli.*' In *SASLC* (1990), p. 108. See item **965**.
[*Vercelli Homily* IX.]

983 — 'Homilies *in nomine Dei summi.*' In *SASLC* (1990), pp. 120–1.
See item **965**. [*Vercelli Homily* V.]

984 — 'Linz Homily Collection.' In *SASLC* (1990), pp. 119–20. See item
965. [*Vercelli Homily* V.]

985 — '*Pauca problesmata de enigmatibus ex tomis canonicis* (Reference Bible).' In *SASLC* (1990), pp. 90–2. See item **965**. [*Vercelli Homilies* V, IX, XIX.]

986 — '*Prebiarum de multorum exemplaribus*.' In *SASLC* (1990), pp. 115–16. See item **965**. [*Vercelli Homilies* IX, XXI.]

987 — 'Ps Isidore, *Liber de numeris*.' In *SASLC* (1990), pp. 113–14. See item **965**. [*Vercelli Homilies* XIX–XX.]

988 — 'Shepherd of Hermas.' In *SASLC* (1990), pp. 63–5. See item **965**. [*Vercelli Homily* IV.]

– — 1990. See item **787**. [*Vercelli Homily* VIII.]

989 Clough, Francis M. 'Introduction.' 1991. In item **837**, pp. 1–15. [Esp. on *Vercelli Homilies* V–VI, IX.]

990 Vickrey, John F. 'A Source and an Allusion in *Vercelli Homily XIV* (folio 77v, lines 1–17).' *Neophilologus* 75 (1991): 612–18.

991 Wilcox, Jonathan. 'Napier's "Wulfstan" Homilies XL and XLII: Two Anonymous Works from Winchester?' *JEGP* 90 (1991): 1–19. [Esp. for *Vercelli Homily* II.]

992 Frank, Roberta. 'Old English *æræt*: "too much" or "too soon."' In *Words, Texts, and Manuscripts: Studies in Anglo-Saxon Culture Presented to Helmut Gneuss on the Occasion of His Sixty-Fifth Birthday*, ed. Michael Korhammer with the assistance of Karl Reichl and Hans Sauer, 293–303. Cambridge: D.S. Brewer, 1992. [*Vercelli Homilies* XIX–XXI, esp. at pp. 296–8.]

993 Scragg, D.G. 'An Old English Homilist of Archbishop Dunstan's Day.' 1992. In *Words, Texts, and Manuscripts*, ed. Michael Korhammer et al., 181–92. See item **992**. [Esp. on *Vercelli Homilies* XIX–XXI.]

994 Szarmach, Paul E. 'Cotton Tiberius A.iii, arts. 26 and 27.' 1992. In *Words, Texts, and Manuscripts*, ed. Michael Korhammer et al., 29–42. See item **992**. [Esp. for *Vercelli Homily* XX.]

995 Wenisch, Franz '"Nu bidde we eow for Godes lufon": A Hitherto Unpublished Old English Homiletic Text in CCCC 162.' 1992. In *Words, Texts, and Manuscripts*, ed. Michael Korhammer et al., 43–52. See item **992**. [Non-West Saxon features in *Vercelli Homilies* I, III, XIX, pp. 44–5 with n. 11. For links to *Vercelli Homily* IX, and for further discussion of *Vercelli Homily* XIX, see item **1013**, p. 78.]

996 Bately, Janet. *Anonymous Old English Homilies: A Preliminary Bibliography of Source Studies Compiled for 'Fontes Anglo-Saxonici' and 'Sources of Anglo-Saxon Literary Culture.'* Binghamton, NY: Center for Medieval and Early Renaissance Studies, 1993. Pp. vi +

76. ['*Vercelli Homilies*,' sect. A.3, pp. 1–2; and in appendix 2, p. 71, *ad indicem*; also esp. for treatment of **965**, analysed above, items **964, 967, 969–71, 973, 976, 978–88.**]

997 Torkar, Roland. 'Die Ohnmacht der Textkritik, am Beispiel der Ausgaben der dritten Vercelli-Homilie.' In *Anglo-Saxonica. Beiträge zur Vor- und Frühgeschichte der englischen Sprache und zur altenglischen Literatur. Festschrift für Hans Schabram zum 65. Geburtstag*, ed. Klaus R. Grinda and Claus-Dieter Wetzel, 225–50. Munich: Fink, 1993.

998 Wright, Charles D. *The Irish Tradition in Old English Literature.* CSASE 6. Cambridge: Cambridge Univ. Press, 1993. Pp. xiv + 321. ['The Literary Milieu of *Vercelli IX* and the Irish Tradition in Old English Literature,' ch. 5; also esp. on *Vercelli Homily* IX, in chs. 2–3, in appendix and elsewhere.]

999 Scragg, D.G. 'The Corpus of Anonymous Lives and Their Manuscript Context.' In *Holy Men and Holy Women: Old English Prose Saints' Lives and Their Contexts*, ed. Paul E. Szarmach, 209–30. Albany: State Univ. of New York Press, 1994. [See further item **928**.]

1000 — 'Postscript: "Quo vadis editio?"' In *The Editing of Old English: Papers from the 1990 Manchester Conference*, ed. Scragg and Paul E. Szarmach with the assistance of Helene Schock and Holly Holbrook, 299–309. Cambridge: D.S. Brewer, 1994. [Esp. on *Vercelli Homily* I, pp. 305–7.]

1001 — and Elaine Treharne. 'Appendix: The Three Anonymous Lives in Cambridge, Corpus Christi College 303.' 1994. In *Holy Men and Holy Women*, ed. Paul E. Szarmach, pp. 231–4. See item **999**. [Esp. for *Vercelli Homilies* I, XIX–XX.]

1002 DiNapoli, Robert. *An Index of Theme and Image to the Homilies of the Anglo-Saxon Church, Comprising the Homilies of Ælfric, Wulfstan, and the Blicking and Vercelli Codices.* Hockwold-cum-Wilton: Anglo-Saxon Books, 1995. Pp. 122. Review: E.M. Tyler, *EME* 7 (1995): 131–2.

1003 Scragg, Donald. 'The Bible in *Fontes Anglo-Saxonici*.' *Bull. of the John Rylands Lib. of Manchester* 77 (1995): 199–203. [*Vercelli Homily* V as witness to biblical text.]

1004 Tristram, Hildegard L.C. *Early Insular Preaching: Verbal Artistry and Method of Composition.* Österreichische Akademie der Wissenschaften, philosophisch-historische Klasse, Sitzungsberichte 62 [= Veröffentlichungen der Keltischen Kommission 11]. Vienna:

Österreichische Akademie der Wissenschaften, 1995. Pp. [73]. [Esp. on *Vercelli Homilies* II, X, XXI.]

1005 Cross, J.E. 'English Vernacular Saints' Lives before 1000 A.D.' In *Hagiographies. Histoire internationale de la littéraire hagiographique latine et vernaculaire en Occident des origines à 1550*, ed. Guy Philippart, 2: 413–27. Turnhout: Brepols, 1994–. [Vol. 2 pub. in 1996. *Vercelli Homily* XXIII (from prose *Guthlac*), p. 419; also for *Fates of the Apostles* and other Cynewulfian verse.]

1006 Page, R.I. 'An Old English Fragment from Westminster Abbey.' *ASE* 25 (1996): 201–7. [*Vercelli Homily* II.]

1007 Whatley, E.G. 'Late Old English Hagiography, *ca.* 950–1150.' 1996. In *Hagiographies*, ed. Guy Philippart, 2: 429–99. See item 1005. [Vercelli Book and, esp., *Vercelli Homily* XXIII (from prose *Guthlac*), pp. 434–6.]

1008 Scragg, D.G. 'Vercelli Codex, Vercelli-Homilien.' 1997. In *Lexikon des Mittelalters*, 8: col. 1497. 9 vols. + index vol. Munich: Lexma, 1977–99. [Vol. 8 pub. in 1997.]

1009 Wilcox, Jonathan. 'Variant Texts of an Old English Homily: *Vercelli X* and Stylistic Effects.' In *The Preservation and Transmission of Anglo-Saxon Culture: Selected Papers from the 1991 Meeting of the International Society of Anglo-Saxonists*, ed. Paul E. Szarmach and Joel T. Rosenthal, 335–51. Kalamazoo, MI: Medieval Institute Publications, 1997.

1010 Deskis, Susan E. 'Jonah and Genre in *Resignation B*.' *MÆ* 67 (1998): 189–200. [*Vercelli Homily* XIX.]

1011 Guerini, Federica. 'Il periodo ipotetico in inglese antico: Tratti prototipici e neutralizzazioni temporali.' *Linguistica e filologia* (Bergamo) 7 (1998): 221–40. [Includes treatment of *Vercelli Homilies*.]

1012 Scragg, D.G. *Dating and Style in Old English Composite Homilies.* H.M. Chadwick Memorial Lecures 9. Cambridge: Dept. of Anglo-Saxon, Norse, and Celtic, 1998. Pp. 24. [Esp. for *Vercelli Homilies* IV, IX; also for *Vercelli Homily* XXI.]

1013 — 'Cambridge, Corpus Christi College 162.' In *Anglo-Saxon Manuscripts and Their Heritage*, ed. Phillip Pulsiano and Elaine M. Treharne, 71–84. Aldershot: Ashgate, 1998. [Esp. for *Vercelli Homily* III; also for *Vercelli Homilies* IX, XIX.]

1014 — 'Vercelli Homilies.' 1998. In *Medieval England: An Encyclopedia*, ed. Paul E. Szarmach et al., 755–6. See item 62.

1015 Swan, Mary. 'The Apocalypse of Thomas in Old English.' *Leeds Stud. in Eng.* 29 (1998): 333–46. [Esp. for *Vercelli Homily* XV.]

1016 Lees, Clare A. *Tradition and Belief: Religious Writing in Late Anglo-Saxon England*. Med. Cultures 19. Minneapolis: Univ. of Minneapolis Press, 1999. Pp. xviii + 196. [Esp. on *Vercelli Homilies* III, VII, XI–XII, XVI, XIX–XXI.]

1017 Szarmach, Paul E. 'A Return to Cotton Tiberius A.III, art. 24, and Isidore's *Synonyma.*' In *Text and Gloss: Studies in Insular Learning and Literature Presented to Joseph Donovan Pheifer*, ed. Helen Conrad O'Briain, Anne-Marie D'Arcy, and John Scattergood, 166–81. Dublin: Four Courts Press, 1999. [Esp. on *Vercelli Homily* XXII; also esp. for *Vercelli Homily* XX.]

1018 Tripp, Raymond P., Jr. 'No Rest for the Wicked: A New Homiletic Reading of Grendel's Attack.' *Pub. of the Med. Assoc. of the Midwest* 6 (1999): 1–24. [Includes discussion of *Vercelli Homilies*; also for *Blickling Homilies*.]

1019 Roberts, Jane. 'The English Saints Remembered in Old English Anonymous Homilies.' 2000. In item **1020**, pp. 433–61. [*Vercelli Homily* XXIII (from prose *Guthlac*), esp. at pp. 441–3; previously unpub. study.]

1020 Szarmach, Paul E., with Deborah A. Oosterhouse, ed. *Old English Prose: Basic Readings*. Basic Readings in AS England 5. New York: Garland, 2000. Pp. [xvii] + 552.

–   Bedingfield, M. Bradford. 2001. See item **799**. [Fire imagery; esp. on *Vercelli Homilies* II, VIII.]

1021 Hiyama, Susumu. ['Impersonals in the *Vercelli Homilies*: Postscript.'] *Jnl of the Faculty of Foreign Lang.* (Komazawa Univ.) 30 (2001): 127–88; 31 (2002): 111–32. [In Japanese.]

1022 Kabir, Ananya Jahanara. *Paradise, Death, and Doomsday in Anglo-Saxon Literature*. CSASE 32. Cambridge: Cambridge Univ. Press, 2001. Pp. xi + 210. [Esp. on *Vercelli Homily* IX, in ch. 3.]

1023 Roberts, Jane. 'Hagiography and Literature: The Case of Guthlac of Crowland and the Seals of the Cross.' In *Mercia: An Anglo-Saxon Kingdom in Europe*, ed. Michelle P. Brown and Carol A. Farr, 69–86. Stud. in the Early Hist. of Europe. London: Leicester Univ. Press, 2001. [*Vercelli Homily* XXIII (from prose *Guthlac*); also esp. for *Elene*.]

1024 Whatley, E. Gordon, et al. '*Acta Sanctorum.*' In *Sources of Anglo-Saxon Literary Culture*, I: *Abbo of Fleury, Abbo of Saint-Germain-des-Prés, and 'Acta Sanctorum,'* ed. Frederick M. Biggs et al., with the assistance of Deborah A. Oosterhouse, 22–548. Kalamazoo, MI: Medieval Institute Publications, 2001. [*Vercelli Homily* XXIII (from prose *Guthlac*), in '*Guthlacus, vita* [Felix.Vit.Guth],' pp. 244–7.]

1025 Atherton, Mark. 'Saxon or Celt? Cædmon, *The Seafarer*, and the Irish Tradition.' In *Celts and Christians: New Approaches to the Religious Traditions of Britain and Ireland*, ed. Atherton, 79–99. Cardiff: Univ. of Wales Press, 2002. [*Vercelli Homilies* III–IV, IX, XX.]

1026 Biggs, Frederick M. '*Vercelli Homily* 6 and the Apocryphal Gospel of Pseudo-Matthew.' *N&Q* n.s. 49 (2002): 176–8.

1027 Chapman, Don W. 'Poetic Compounding in the *Vercelli, Blickling,* and Wulfstan Homilies.' *NM* 103 (2002): 409–21.

1028 Lendinara, Patrizia. '"Frater non redimit, redimet homo ...": A Homiletic Motif and Its Variants in Old English.' 2002. In item **66**, pp. 67–80. [*Vercelli Homily* IV, pp. 68–71.]

1029 Roberts, Jane. 'The Case of the Miraculous Hand in the Old English Prose Life of Guthlac.' *ANQ* n.s. 15.2 (2002): 17–22. [*Vercelli Homily* XXIII (from prose *Guthlac*).]

1030 — 'Two Readings in the Guthlac Homily.' 2002. In item **66**, pp. 201–10. [*Vercelli Homily* XXIII (from prose *Guthlac*).]

1031 Shimomura, Sachi. 'Visualizing Judgment: Illumination in the Old English *Christ III*.' In *Via Crucis: Essays on Early Medieval Sources and Ideas in Memory of J.E. Cross*, ed. Thomas N. Hall, 27–49. Morgantown: West Virginia Univ. Press, 2002. [Esp. for *Vercelli Homilies* VIII, X, XXI.]

1032 Swan, Mary. 'Holiness Remodelled: Theme and Technique in Old English Composite Homilies.' In *Models of Holiness in Medieval Sermons. Proceedings of the International Symposium (Kalamazoo, 4–7 May 1995)*, ed. Beverly Mayne Kienzle et al., 35–46. Textes et études des Instituts d'études médiévales 5. Louvain-la-Neuve: Fédération internationale des instituts d'études médiévales, 2002. [Esp. for *Vercelli Homily* IX.]

1033 Szarmach, Paul E. 'Pembroke College 25, arts. 93–95.' 2002. In *Via Crucis*, ed. Thomas N. Hall, 295–325. See item **1031**. [Esp. for *Vercelli Homily* XX.]

— Thompson, Nancy M. 2002 [pub. 2004–5]. See item **1047**.

1034 Wright, Charles D. 'More Old English Poetry in *Vercelli Homily XXI*.' 2002. In item **66**, pp. 245–62. [Esp. on distinction of verse and rhythmic prose.]

1035 — 'The Old English Macarius Homily, *Vercelli Homily IV*, and Ephrem Latinus, *De paenitentia*.' 2002. In *Via Crucis*, ed. Thomas N. Hall, pp. 210–34. See item **1031**. [Also for *Vercelli Homily* III.]

1036 — '*Vercelli Homilies* XI–XIII and the Anglo-Saxon Benedictine Reform: Tailored Sources and Implied Audiences.' In *Preacher,*

Sermon, and Audience in the Middle Ages, ed. Carolyn Muessig, 203–27. Leiden: Brill, 2002.

1037 Alamichel, Marie-Françoise. 'Le pouvoir des mots dans la littérature vieil-anglaise.' In *Paroles et silences dans la littérature anglaise au Moyen Âge*, ed. Leo Carruthers and Adrian Paphagi, 73–94. Publications de l'Association des médiévistes anglicistes de l'enseignement supérieur, Hors série 10. Paris: AMAES, 2003. [Esp. for *Vercelli Homily* X.]

1038 Di Sciacca, Claudia. 'Il topos dell'*ubi sunt* nell'omiletica anglo-sassone: Il caso di *Vercelli X*.' In *I germani e gli altri. I parte*, ed. Vittoria Dolcetti Corazza and Renato Gendre, 225–55. Bibliotheca Germanica, Studi e testi 13. Alessandria: Edizioni dell'Orso, 2003.

1039 Hall, Thomas N. 'The Psychedelic Transmogrification of the Soul in *Vercelli Homily IV*.' In *Time and Eternity: The Medieval Discourse*, ed. Gerhard Jaritz and Gerson Moreno-Riaño, 309–22. Turnhout: Brepols, 2003.

1040 Kelly, Richard J. *The Blickling Homilies: Edition and Translation, with General Introduction, Textual Notes, Tables, and Select Bibliography*. London: Continuum, 2003. Pp. lvi + 232, 4 plates. ['Vercelli Book, The,' *ad indicem*, p. 231.]

1041 Salvador, Mercedes. 'The Key to the Body: Unlocking Riddles 42–46.' In *Naked before God: Uncovering the Body in Anglo-Saxon England*, ed. Benjamin C. Withers and Johathan Wilcox, 60–96. Med. European Stud. 3. Morgantown: West Virginia Univ. Press, 2003. [*Vercelli Homily* XV.]

1042 Stanley, Eric G. 'Did the Anglo-Saxons Have a Social Conscience Like Us?' *Anglia* 121 (2003): 238–64. [*Vercelli Homily* IV and other OE texts, in prose and in verse.]

1043 Wright, Charles D. 'The Apocalypse of Thomas: Some New Latin Texts and Their Significance for the Old English Versions.' In *Apocryphal Texts and Traditions in Anglo-Saxon England*, ed. Kathryn Powell and Donald Scragg, 27–64. Cambridge: D.S. Brewer, 2003. [*Vercelli Homily* XV.]

1044 Hiyama, Susumu. 'Old English Verbal-Auxiliary Clusters: Some Notes.' *Neophilologus* 88 (2004): 121–9. [Study of *Vercelli Homilies*.]

– Scheil, Andrew P. 2004. See item **811**. [Esp. for *Vercelli Homily* XVI; also for *Vercelli Homilies* I–II, VII–VIII, XXI.]

1045 Thompson, Nancy M. 'Anglo-Saxon Orthodoxy.' In *Old English Literature in Its Manuscript Context*, ed. Joyce Tally Lionarons,

37–65. Med. European Stud. 5. Morgantown: West Virginia Univ. Press, 2004. [Heterodox elements in Vercelli Homilies.]

1046 Zacher, Samantha. 'Sin, Syntax, and Synonyms: Rhetorical Style and Structure in Vercelli Homily X.' JEGP 103 (2004): 53–76.

1047 Thompson, Nancy M. '"Hit segð in halgum bocum": The Logic of Composite Old English Homilies.' PQ 81 (2004–5 for 2002): 383–419.

1048 Haines, Dorothy. 'Courtroom Drama and the Homiletic Monologues of the Vercelli Book.' In Verbal Encounters: Anglo-Saxon and Norse Studies for Roberta Frank, ed. Antonina Harbus and Russell Poole, 105–23. Toronto OE Ser. 13. Toronto: Univ. of Toronto Press, 2005. [Esp. for Vercelli Homilies IV, VIII, X.]

1049 Hall, Thomas N. 'Old English Religious Prose: Rhetorics of Salvation and Damnation.' 2005. In Readings in Medieval Texts, ed. David F. Johnson and Elaine Treharne, 136–48. See item 815. [Esp. for Vercelli Homilies IV, IX, XXI.]

1050 — 'Preaching at Winchester in the Early Twelfth Century.' JEGP 104 (2005): 189–218. [Includes discussion of Vercelli Homilies.]

1051 Hiyama, Susumu. 'Element Order in the Vercelli Homilies.' Jnl of the Faculty of Foreign Lang. (Tokyo, Komazawa Univ.) 34.2 (2005): 1–288. [See further item 1053.]

1052 Rudolf, Winfried. 'Altenglische Themapredigten als unfeste Texte: Ein elektronisches Textkorpus.' In Englische Sprachwissenschaft und Mediävistik: Standpunkte, Perspektiven, neue Wege, ed. Gabriele Knappe, 295–301. Bamberger Beiträge zur englischen Sprachwissenschaft 48. Frankfurt am Main: Lang, 2005. [Corpus to include texts from Vercelli Homilies.]

1053 Hiyama, Susumu. 'Element Order in the Vercelli Homilies: Postscript.' Jnl of the Faculty of Foreign Lang. (Tokyo, Komazawa Univ.) 35 (2006): 285–317. [See further item 1051.]

1054 Karasawa, Kazutomo. 'OE dream for "Horrible Noise" in the Vercelli Homilies.' SN 78 (2006): 46–58.

1055 Roberts, Jane. 'Guthlac of Crowland and the Seals of the Cross.' 2006. In item 664, pp. 113–28. [Vercelli Homily XXIII (from prose Guthlac)]

1056 Szarmach, Paul E. 'Vercelli Homily XIV and the Homiliary of Paul the Deacon.' Leeds Stud. in Engl. 37 (2006): 75–87. [Includes two plates.]

Index of Manuscripts

COMPILED BY EMILY BUTLER

General Index

COMPILED BY EMILY BUTLER

Toronto Anglo-Saxon Series

General Editor
ANDY ORCHARD

Editorial Board
ROBERTA FRANK
THOMAS N. HALL
ANTONETTE DIPAOLO HEALEY
MICHAEL LAPIDGE

1 *Preaching the Converted: The Style and Rhetoric of the Vercelli Book Homilies*, Samantha Zacher

2 *Say What I Am Called: The Old English Riddles of the Exeter Book and the Anglo-Latin Riddle Tradition*, Dieter Bitterli

3 *The Aesthetics of Nostalgia: Historical Representation in Anglo-Saxon Verse*, Renée Trilling

4 *New Readings in the Vercelli Book*, edited by Samantha Zacher and Andy Orchard

5 *Authors, Audiences, and Old English Verse*, Thomas A. Bredehoft